Public Speaking and Democratic Participation

✦

Public Speaking *and* Democratic Participation

Speech, Deliberation, and Analysis in the Civic Realm

JENNIFER Y. ABBOTT
Wabash College

TODD F. McDORMAN
Wabash College

DAVID M. TIMMERMAN
Monmouth College

L. JILL LAMBERTON
Wabash College

New York   Oxford
OXFORD UNIVERSITY PRESS

Oxford University Press is a department of the University of Oxford.
It furthers the University's objective of excellence in research,
scholarship, and education by publishing worldwide.

Oxford   New York
Auckland   Cape Town   Dar es Salaam   Hong Kong   Karachi
Kuala Lumpur   Madrid   Melbourne   Mexico City   Nairobi
New Delhi   Shanghai   Taipei   Toronto

With offices in
Argentina   Austria   Brazil   Chile   Czech Republic   France   Greece
Guatemala   Hungary   Italy   Japan   Poland   Portugal   Singapore
South Korea   Switzerland   Thailand   Turkey   Ukraine   Vietnam

For titles covered by Section 112 of the US Higher Education
Opportunity Act, please visit www.oup.com/us/he for the
latest information about pricing and alternate formats.

Published by Oxford University Press
198 Madison Avenue, New York, New York 10016
http://www.oup.com

Library of Congress Cataloging-in-Publication Data
Abbott, Jennifer, 1973–
Public speaking and democratic participation : speech, deliberation, and analysis in the civic realm /
Jennifer Abbott, Wabash College, Jill Lamberton, Wabash College, Todd McDorman, Wabash College,
David Timmerman, Monmouth College.
    pages cm
  Includes bibliographical references and index.
  ISBN 978-0-19-933859-7 (acid-free paper)
  1. Public speaking. 2. Public speaking--Political aspects--United States. 3. Rhetoric--Political
aspects--United States. 4. Political participation--United States. 5. Political culture--United States.
  I. Title.
  PN4129.15.L36   2016
  808.5'1--dc23

                                                                              2015013289

Printing number: 9 8 7 6 5 4 3 2 1

Printed in the United States of America
on acid-free paper

BRIEF TABLE OF CONTENTS

TABLE OF CONTENTS

Chapter 6   Organizing Your Public Presentation in a Clear and Compelling Manner   104

Chapter 7   **Writing Effective Preparation and Presentation Outlines   126**

PREFACE

We wrote this textbook to share our powerful experiences teaching undergraduate students public speaking in the context of democratic participation. At its most basic level, democracy needs community members who can both construct messages advocating particular actions and perspectives, and competently understand, analyze, and respond to the messages constructed by others. We designed this textbook to help accomplish these objectives. As students progress through the book, they will study the essentials of public speaking, while also examining the relationship of rhetoric and democracy, considering the state of public discourse today and how to improve it, becoming skilled in leading public deliberations on complex issues, and learning the powerful potential of rhetorical criticism to investigate public communication. Our goal is to help prepare students to join and improve the quality of public dialogue and, in so doing, to contribute to the betterment of society. We have developed a passion for this civically focused public speaking text and are excited to share it with you, our colleagues in the instruction of public speaking. In what follows, we highlight the key features of this textbook, introduce the book to students directly, and provide acknowledgments and information about the authors.

KEY FEATURES OF THIS TEXT

While typical public speaking textbooks frequently focus on students' personal advancement and individual goals in academic and vocational spheres, this book emphasizes public speaking for democratic participation in the civic realm. It cultivates the essential skills necessary to effectively utilize public speaking, public deliberation, and rhetorical analysis for meaningful civic engagement. We will briefly explain each of these key textbook features: speech, deliberation, and analysis in the civic realm.

Speech in the Civic Realm
This text teaches fundamental oral communication skills in the context of democratic participation. In other words, we teach the skills students need to succeed as active community members and as persons. We address the familiar fundamental public

speaking elements: research (chapter 4), audience analysis and adaptation (chapter 5), organization (chapter 6), outlining (chapter 7), style (chapter 8), delivery and memory (chapter 9), reasoning and argumentation (chapter 13), and visuals aids (chapter 14). We also address both informative speaking (chapter 10) and persuasive speaking (chapter 12). However, we approach these skills with an eye toward democratic participation and speaking for the public good. The book lays the groundwork for this context with opening chapters that introduce students to the historical and ongoing relationship between rhetoric—the larger discipline of which public speaking is a part—and democracy (chapter 1), the differences between the unproductive discourse that prevails in the public sphere and more productive ways of talking (chapter 2), and the ethics of speech preparation, performance, and listening (chapter 3).

In addition to the opening three chapters, you will find an emphasis on democratic participation throughout the textbook. The regular use of examples from the civic realm and the recurring *Spotlight on Social Media* features particularly highlight the intersection of civic involvement and public speaking. In each chapter, the *Spotlight on Social Media* box considers how the elements of public speaking might be reconsidered, challenged, or improved in the context of one of the most popular means of public communication today, social media. Every chapter also contains review questions and practical discussion questions that help students identify ways their public speaking skills can improve their communities.

Teaching public speaking skills in the context of civic engagement is quite timely given recent discussions in higher education. Numerous studies and commissions have underscored the importance of speaking skills for students, their potential employers, and for society. The 2006 *Report of the Committee to Review the Teaching of Writing and Speaking in Harvard College* explains:

> Writing and speaking well are both necessary and sophisticated skills. Inseparable from cogent reasoning, clear analysis, and vivid expression, they inform each discipline and belong to every area of intellectual endeavor. Writing and speaking well are not so much bodies of knowledge as life-long practices to be continually improved.[1]

Similarly, as the second component of an "Academic Bill of Rights," the celebrated Boyer Commission identified "training in the skills necessary for oral and written communication at a level that will serve the student both within the university and in postgraduate professional and personal life" as vitally important.[2] By teaching oral communication through a civic lens, this textbook helps students recognize the role that communication skills can play beyond the college classroom and in their postgraduate lives and communities.

We are not blind to the difficulties and frustrations of democratic participation, particularly in a country with over 300 million people and a world with seven billion inhabitants. Neither do we naively believe the United States, nor most other countries and communities, actually practice direct democracy as a system of governance. Even still, we believe that inviting students to adopt the principles of democratic participation on local, national, and global levels—that is, to understand themselves as members of a larger group, to recognize their ability to make a difference for the greater

good, and to use their public voice to tackle difficult civic issues—is in their best interests and that of their communities and nations. We also know from our own experiences that engagement with others through rhetoric can be extremely productive,
enjoyable, and, at times, exhilarating.

Deliberation in the Civic Realm

As part of our mission to train students as public speakers and democratic participants, this textbook teaches students how to prepare and lead their classmates in a
deliberation about a difficult issue. Chapter 10 instructs students how to develop a
deliberative presentation as a form of informative speaking. We give attention to selecting an appropriate topic, discovering a range of perspectives on the issue, framing
it for deliberation, and organizing the information into a presentation. Chapter 11
focuses on effectively leading and productively participating in a deliberative discussion—the group conversation that typically follows a deliberative presentation. The
inclusion of deliberation is fairly unusual for a public speaking textbook but, we believe, essential for exposing students to an additional way their public voice can serve
civic ends. Through deliberation, students learn how to help their fellow classmates
and community members approach a controversial problem in ways that consider
multiple perspectives, develop common ground, and comprehend competing values.

Rhetorical Analysis in the Civic Realm

A unique inclusion, this textbook moves beyond introductory public speaking skills
and teaches students how to make use of rhetorical criticism to describe, interpret,
and evaluate public messages (chapters 15, 16, and 17). From its origins, rhetoric has
focused on both the *construction* of messages (e.g., speeches and presentations) as well
as the *analysis* of such messages. When students become more active democratic participants, their need to analyze messages grows. They will more attentively listen to
television news stories or read news articles and blogs and must understand what they
are hearing or reading. They may find themselves attending a rally, say on lowering
taxes or advocating immigration reform, and listening to speakers on these topics.
This textbook endeavors to teach this ability to critically engage diverse public messages. We introduce rhetorical criticism as a means of civic engagement (chapter 15)
and explain two methods of rhetorical criticism that suit democratic participation
particularly well. Chapter 16 describes public communication analysis, a method that
focuses on the effects of a public message in terms of whether and how it achieved the
rhetor's goal and strengthened or weakened democratic principles. Chapter 17 shifts
to ideological criticism, a method that exposes the expressions of power and control
inherent in public messages with the goal of improving democratic participation.

Together, this textbook's emphasis on speech, deliberation, and analysis in the
civic realm provides a fulsome and enthusiastic guide to the instruction of public
speaking. An instructor's manual with unique activities and exercises to supplement
what most teachers already use is available online at http://oup-arc.com/abbott. We
hope you enjoy teaching public speaking as democratic participation as much as
we do.

TO THE STUDENT

You are part of something bigger than yourself! As a person currently living in the United States, you are an integral part of a democratic society. Democracy requires people like you to discuss the issues and decisions bearing upon your global, national, and local communities. Because democratic participation is difficult and the results are not often immediate or dramatic, we may tend to focus on our personal concerns over which we seem to have more control. Democracy, however, relies on the engagement and participation of societal members. Take that engagement out, replace it with a focus solely on personal success and acquisition, and you will have a society run far more by its experts and officials than residents. While this may seem an audacious beginning for a college textbook on public speaking, it accurately reflects the challenges and opportunities during and after your collegiate experience.

BOX I-1

Top Intellectual and Practical Skills Cited by Employers

- The ability to communicate effectively, orally and in writing (89%)
- Critical thinking and analytical reasoning skills (81%)
- The ability to analyze and solve complex problems (75%)
- Teamwork skills and the ability to collaborate with others in diverse group settings (71%)
- The ability to innovate and be creative (70%)

SOURCE: *Raising the Bar: Employers' Views on College Learning in the Wake of Economic Downturn.* Hart Research Associates on behalf of the AAC&U. January 20, 2010.

This textbook will teach you public speaking skills in the context of democratic participation; although, the skills you develop will also aid your personal life and career. Indeed, numerous studies and commissions have emphasized the importance of communication skills for students, their potential employers, and society. For example, the Association of American Colleges and Universities' (AAC&U) 2007 report *College Learning for the New Global Century* identified "written and oral communication" skills and "civic knowledge and engagement—local and global" as essential learning outcomes to prepare students for "twenty-first-century challenges."[3] In 2010, the AAC&U published a survey of over 300 employers asking what they most looked for and needed in the college graduates they hired. At the top of this list was "the ability to communicate effectively, orally and in writing" with 89% of companies citing this item.[4] In Box I.1, you can see skills most desired by employers, all of which are also important for democratic participation and will be addressed in this text.

To be an effective public speaker in the civic realm, you will need many interconnected skills. This text will teach you the fundamental skills of public speaking from research and reasoning to speech organization and delivery. It will also teach you how to lead and participate in productive community discussions about complex public problems. And it will teach you how to conduct rhetorical criticism to describe, interpret, and evaluate public messages. To be an active democratic participant, you must not only know how to construct your own messages but also how to listen to and analyze the speeches and public statements of your political leaders and fellow residents. With the help of this textbook, then, you will emerge as an effective public speaker and motivated democratic participant, equipped to engage and improve your community.

ACKNOWLEDGMENTS

We are very grateful for the personal and professional support we received while developing this textbook. Wabash College generously facilitated the book's creation and progress through the college's Center of Inquiry in the Liberal Arts (CILA), which awarded three of us Lilly Liberal Arts Fellowships in 2009 and 2010 that supported our initial research on and drafting of portions of the textbook. CILA also helped us organize and fund the Brigance Colloquy on Public Speaking as a Liberal Art in February 2009. We also appreciate the Brigance Forum fund, endowed by the friends and family of W. Norwood Brigance, for financially cosupporting the colloquy. In addition, the college's Faculty Development Committee graciously provided funding to supplement the textbook's art, images, and permissions, and several Wabash College colleagues enhanced the book through their teaching ideas and suggestions. We particularly thank colleagues Sara Drury, Jeff Drury, and Jenny Hamilton, as well as Donovan Bisbee and Kenny Farris, both of whom served as student interns during the development of this book. We also owe a debt to our public speaking students whose reactions and classroom performances helped us refine our ideas for this book and its supporting assignments. Finally, we acknowledge former Dean of Wabash College Gary Phillips for helping to initiate this project by encouraging—and even challenging—us to examine our approach to public speaking and to seek CILA support.

We are also grateful for the professional support we received outside Wabash College. We appreciate the productive discussions we had with the participants of the Brigance Colloquy on Public Speaking as a Liberal Art. We also thank the Charles F. Kettering Foundation and, especially, Alice Diebel (Kettering Program Officer), Martín Carcasson (Director of the CSU Center for Public Deliberation and Associate Professor in Communication Studies), and Betty Knighton (Director of the West Virginia Center for Civic Life) for their expertise, teaching, and inspiration regarding deliberative practices.

In their final stages, many chapters in this textbook benefited from the advice and insight we received from external reviewers who teach public speaking around the country. We extend our thanks to Wendy Atkins-Sayre (University of Southern

Mississippi), Diana Isabel Bowen (University of Houston-Downtown), Dacia Charles-worth (Valdosta State University), Benjamin J. Cline (Western New Mexico University), Suzanne Enck (University of North Texas), Kathleen M. Farrell (Saint Louis University), Lyn J. Freymiller (Penn State University), Lindsey Harness (University of Wisconsin-Milwaukee), Tracey Quigley Holden (University of Delaware), Josh Hoops (William Jewell College), Tressa Kelly (University of West Florida), Bohn David Lattin (University of Portland), Betty Jane Lawrence (Bradley University), Susan Millsap (Otterbein University), Seong Jae Min (Pace University), Mary E. Triece (University of Akron), and Scott Weiss (St. Francis College). We also thank Oxford University Press (OUP) for their enthusiasm for this project, and support and patience during its development. In particular we are grateful to Mark Haynes, formerly the Communication, Journalism, & Media Studies Editor at OUP, the editorial and production staffs of OUP, and Marie La Viña in particular who was of great assistance in working on permissions and keeping us on track as we completed the project.

Finally, we thank our families for their encouragement and patient support throughout this project, especially as our work impinged on vacations and summer and winter breaks. They include Michael and Zoe Abbott; Jeremy, Henry, and Silas Hartnett; Kelly, Lily, Carter McDorman and Dana McDorman-Kolata; and Polly, Matt, and Mark Timmerman.

ABOUT THE AUTHORS

Jennifer Y. Abbott is an Associate Professor and Chair of the Rhetoric Department at Wabash College. Her research focuses on news media rhetoric and mediated depictions of gender. She teaches courses including Public Speaking, Contemporary Rhetorical Theory and Criticism, Gender and Communication, and Rhetoric of the News Media.

Todd F. McDorman is a Professor of Rhetoric and Senior Associate Dean of the College at Wabash College. His research focuses on issues of rhetoric and sport and legal rhetoric. He teaches courses including Public Speaking, Rhetoric Senior Seminar, Rhetoric of Sport, and Reasoning and Advocacy.

David M. Timmerman is Dean of the Faculty and Vice President for Academic Affairs at Monmouth College. His research focuses on the beginnings of rhetoric in ancient Greece, political communication, and religious rhetoric. He has taught courses including Public Speaking, Classical Rhetoric, African American Rhetoric, and Citizenship.

L. Jill Lamberton is an Assistant Professor of English at Wabash College. Her current research focuses on the rhetorical strategies women used to gain access to elite higher education in the United States and United Kingdom at the end of the nineteenth century. She teaches a variety of courses in Composition and Nineteenth-century literature, and frequently cross-lists courses with the Rhetoric Department.

CHAPTER 1

Public Speaking as the Intersection of Rhetoric and Democracy

---

Chapter Objectives

Students will:

- Define rhetoric as a civic art and describe how it functions.
- Describe the origins of rhetoric, its practice, and its study.
- Learn the mutually reinforcing relationship between rhetoric and democracy.
- Understand the contributions rhetoric and rhetorical training can make to democratic practice and civic engagement.

Six people were already dead and 13 others wounded when the shooter stopped to reload. He had just fired a bullet into the head of US Representative Gabrielle Giffords, who at the time represented Arizona's Eighth Congressional District. He would not get another chance to shoot. Attendee Patricia Maisch grabbed the magazine the shooter was seeking to load; another person hit him over the head with a folding chair; and Bill Badger, a 74-year-old retired army colonel wounded by the shooter, nevertheless tackled him to the ground. The crowd had gathered in the Safeway grocery store parking lot in Casas Adobes, Arizona, to ask questions of Representative Giffords.[1] This tragedy took place at an event that is a hallmark of a well-functioning democracy—open, face-to-face exchange between people and their political representatives about their questions, concerns, opinions, and hopes for their city, state, and nation.

The type of public interaction promoted by Rep. Giffords's "Congress on Your Corner" event, and the speaking, listening, and deliberating that take place at multiple levels often over long periods of time, is precisely how democracy functions. The vitality of such public interactions and the production of public discourse are generally dependent on many people and extend beyond those united by citizenship. Throughout this book we define **democratic participants** as all those who participate

Image from the 2008 US presidential campaign. It shows a common way people engage in the democratic process, by attending a public political rally or event.

in public conversations about issues that matter to groups, institutions, and organizations in a democratic society. While it is true that you must be a citizen of the United States to *vote* in local, state, or national elections, citizenship is not a requirement for public communication and community engagement in local, regional, and institutional projects where members of the public work together for social change. On your campus, on the local school board, and at your neighborhood food bank, you probably know community members who are central and invested participants, even though they may be citizens of other countries. For this reason, unless we are talking specifically about voting in political elections or are quoting other authors, in this textbook we generally refer to "democratic participants" and "community members" when we talk about who can help society by practicing productive discourse.

This chapter sets out a definition of rhetoric as a civic art that guides this text and explains the significance of seven features of this definition. The chapter then turns to an explanation of the historical relationship between rhetoric and democracy with a particular emphasis on the beginnings of democracy in ancient Greece. Finally, the chapter offers a consideration of how rhetoric and democracy are mutually reinforcing.

RHETORIC AS A CIVIC ART

Rhetoric is a complex term with a rich heritage. It is one of the seven traditional liberal arts, which included the trivium (i.e., grammar, logic, and rhetoric) and the quadrivium (i.e., arithmetic, geometry, music, and astronomy). While this classification illustrates historical reverence for rhetoric, it also has been subject to serious criticism.

Once associated solely with persuasion, rhetoric has referred both to rich thought and expression as well as empty eloquence. Too often today we hear politicians and those who wish to defeat their opponent refer to the words of their adversaries as rhetoric, by which they mean hollow talk. The student of rhetoric will tell you that there is indeed impoverished and empty rhetoric but also that all discourse, all language—be it rich in meaning and symbolism or nearly devoid of content—is rhetoric. Thus, it is best to think of rhetoric as a master term that refers to all possible communication between people including human language, nonverbal expression, and visual images.

There is no shortage of definitions of rhetoric, ranging from the ancient to the contemporary. However, rather than survey the range of options and possibilities, we set out a positive definition that guides this text: **rhetoric** is a civic art devoted to the ethical study and use of symbols (verbal and nonverbal) in order to address public issues. In selecting this definition we have set a high standard for rhetorical practice in society, a standard that is explored in great detail in this text.

Because rhetoric is such a rich concept, our definition deserves an extended explanation. First, and perhaps most importantly, rhetoric is a *civic art* that is produced and studied for the good of society. We use **civic** in a manner consistent with its Latin origin (*civicus*) to refer to those matters that relate to the city or citizens. In turn, **civic engagement** is participation in organizations, institutions, and societies with the goal of contributing to the public good. Courses that are typically labeled government or social studies in many high schools today were once labeled civics, as in the study of matters relating to public life. We have referred to rhetoric as a civic *art* because it encourages and requires individual expression, interpretation, and style. Rhetoric, and training in it, is crucial for effective public deliberation and democracy, as it is our chief tool for acting in a democracy and expressing our views.[2]

Second, rhetoric entails both the study and use of symbols, which we also refer to as rhetorical theory and practice. That is, rhetoric includes both training in the production, or use, of symbols, such as speech making; and it involves studying the symbols produced by others by means of analysis, interpretation, and criticism. Third, both the study and use of rhetoric are *ethical* practices in that they are grounded in moral principles, based on reason, and attached to rigorous standards of evaluation. This characteristic suggests that rhetoric is actively (or consciously) produced and that the ethical (or unethical) nature of the motives, choices, and effects of a speaker or critic are important. Fourth, while in its most common form rhetoric is discursive or *verbal* (formed in words), it is not necessarily so. Rather, *nonverbal symbols*, particularly visual images, are within the domain of rhetoric and can be powerful in democratic discourse. For example, consider how images of the flag, of war and destruction, of poverty, and so forth can move audiences.

A fifth characteristic of rhetoric is that it is typically used to *address public issues*. Speakers and critics produce rhetoric for public audiences, though the natures and sizes of those audiences may differ significantly. That means that while the producer of a message—the rhetor—is important to the meaning of rhetoric, the listener or reader has a role of equal, if not greater, importance in providing rhetoric with meaning. The listener also possesses the ability to evaluate, respond to, and act on a rhetor's words. Meaning is ultimately negotiated between a rhetor and an audience, often over an extended period of time and in a many different forms.

This relationship between the **rhetor**, one who speaks publicly, and an audience leads to a sixth characteristic of rhetoric: rhetoric is a form of power. One well-known way this has been expressed is by the phrase, "the pen is mightier than the sword." In a most basic example, consider how a parent gets his or her child to do and not do many things, simply through the use of words. Then consider the power of documents such as the Declaration of Independence and the US Constitution. Rhetoric can be a means of control that encourages action or limits an audience's options, sometimes without us even being aware of this effect; and it also has the power to liberate, to achieve freedom from domination. For example, Founding Father Patrick Henry helped launch the American Revolution with his opposition to the Stamp Act of 1765 and his clarion call: "Give me liberty or give me death!" We might also think of Martin Luther King Jr.'s powerful refrain "I have a dream" that captured the vision and essence of the American Civil Rights movement in a speech (of the same name) delivered from the steps of the Lincoln Memorial in August, 1963. Rhetoric has the ability—the power—to put ideas before the eyes and in the minds of audiences and to move audiences through language and imagery. These ideas may be either positive or negative, and history provides plentiful examples of each. At the same time, the audience is able to accept, alter, or resist those efforts.

Seventh, and finally, rhetoric is situational and contingent. Rhetoric operates in specific contexts in order to address and respond to problems that are of a probabilistic nature on which reasonable people are likely to disagree. Rather than dealing with truth claims that are verified through formal logic or scientific demonstration, rhetoric addresses contingent matters that are uncertain, open to multiple possibilities, and dependent on several variables. Consequently, rhetoric itself can have different goals. It is generally intended to persuade, but it is not exclusively so directed. Some rhetoric can attempt to inform an audience, which is valuable and important as community members try to understand an issue through discussion and deliberation absent abrasive efforts to steer one another to a particular position or solution.

BOX 1-1

Seven Characteristics of Rhetoric the Civic Art

1. Rhetoric is studied for the good of society.
2. Rhetoric entails both the study and use of symbols.
3. The study and use of rhetoric are ethical practices grounded in moral principles, based on reason, and attached to rigorous standards of evaluation.
4. Rhetoric includes both verbal and nonverbal symbols.
5. Rhetoric is typically used to address public issues.
6. Rhetoric is a form of power.
7. Rhetoric is both contingent and situational.

This definition places rhetorical practice in a public context as the means of exchange among community members and policymakers. Thus, this is a definition of rhetoric that is specifically oriented to the practice of **public speaking**, which is the process of forming and delivering rhetorical content to an audience in the hopes of persuading, influencing, informing, or entertaining that audience. Public speech is the currency of participation in a democratic society; it provides the means for participation and action, an avenue for civic engagement, and the mechanism with which we can engage in deliberation and dialogue. This civic art of rhetoric finds its origin in the beginnings of democracy in ancient Greece to which we turn in the next segment of this chapter.

THE HISTORICAL RELATIONSHIP
BETWEEN RHETORIC AND DEMOCRACY

From its beginning, democracy was exercised in and through rhetoric. In the West, this relationship first occurred in a particular place and time, in Athens, Greece, in the late sixth century BCE.[3] Imagine an Athenian male during that time. Unlike his ancestors, who lived in a society structured by a noble class, he is an active participant in the governmental functioning of his city-state. He has the ability to speak about the important issues of the day with his fellow citizens, not only informally, but also formally in the Assembly meetings—regular gatherings of Athenian citizens who discussed and voted on the important public issues of the day. During his lifetime, an Athenian citizen was likely to serve in one or more governmental positions as a magistrate of one type or another and to serve regularly as a juror. Historically, it is hard to exaggerate the importance of these advances. As classical scholar Harvey Yunis states:

> *Demokratia* was meant literally: the demos—the adult male citizen body in its entirety—held power (*kratos*), and they did so unconditionally. Traditional social and economic divisions within the citizen body did not disappear; but full and equal political and legal privileges—that is, citizenship—were held by all Athenian men regardless of family background or wealth. The demos delegated no authority or power to any person or group of persons to decide matters independently on their behalf. There was no legislature or parliament. There were no political offices. There were no political parties. The *polis* employed clerks and scribes and possessed slaves for numerous tasks, but there was no professional state bureaucracy. There were no professional politicians, professional lawyers, or professional judges. Neither any religious office nor status of wealth, birth, or education entailed legitimate political authority. Within the citizen body, there was no ruling elite of any kind.[4]

For all its limitations and faults, this expression of democracy in the ancient world was revolutionary and of great significance historically. Successful generals and previously successful politicians did garner ongoing support, but it was nothing like the entrenched politicians in the United States today, where, for example, the reelection rate for congressional incumbents is nearly 90%.[5] Instead, participation in positions of political leadership was widely shared.

Democratic Participation in the Assembly

One of the earliest versions of democratic, deliberative discussions took place in ancient Greece during the sixth and fifth centuries BCE in the form of the Athenian Assembly. This Assembly met 40 times each year on Pnyx Hill (also simply referred to as the Pnyx), with attendance ranging from 3,000 to 6,000 citizens. The Pnyx represented the political center of the city-state, in contrast to the Agora marketplace (the social and legal center) and the Acropolis (the religious center with the Parthenon, Erecthion, and other sacred and ceremonial buildings), which sat adjacent to the Pnyx. These three—Pynx, Agora, Acropolis—formed a physical and visual triangle.

Photograph of the speaker's bench (bema) on Pnyx Hill in Athens as seen from the vantage point of a seated participant. In the late sixth and fifth centuries BCE, the Athenian Assembly met on this hill to deliberate and vote on important matters that faced them as a city-state.

From the speaker's platform, or bema, located on the Pnyx (pictured), the Assembly meetings would begin with the presiding officer offering a sacrifice of a pig and a prayer to the gods. A proposal would then be announced, and the presiding officer would ask, "Who wishes to speak?" Any topic could be raised during the Assembly meetings, but a majority of topics were set out in an agenda that was constructed by a smaller council. Anyone could speak two times on a single issue, and there was no formal time limit on those speeches or comments. There were means for keeping long-winded speakers in check, however, such as heckling and, in more extreme cases, merely shouting the person down. The picture we get of these meetings is that they could sometimes be quite boisterous and contain great emotion. When the moment seemed right, the presiding officer would call for a vote. These votes often took the form of markings made on small pieces of broken pottery (pot shards) with the citizen making a particular mark on it to signify his choice. As such, the participants in this democracy had the opportunity to be fully engaged in listening, speaking, and voting.

These patterns of operation put great responsibility on the shoulders of the average citizen. As scholar and professor of ancient Greece Josiah Ober explains: "The practice of democracy assumed that citizens had a capacity to reason together, in public (as well as in private), via frank speech, and that the results of those deliberations would (in general and over time) conduce to the common good. Deliberating meant listening as well as speaking; accepting good arguments as well as making them."[6]

The result was that the decisions of the Assembly and the decisions of a jury were enhanced. This reveals a very important feature of how democracy can function powerfully and positively as a political system. Through deliberation and debate, the group or nation is able to arrive at sounder and stronger conclusions than an individual or small group of individuals would on their own.

This flourishing of democratic practice through public speaking created the need for educating young men in the practice. This gave rise to the early sophists, like Protagoras, Gorgias, and Isocrates, who taught a range of subjects, including and especially rhetoric, for a fee.[7] This new educational model was integral to the flourishing of democracy and the move further away from a nobility structure. Today, teaching effective public speaking skills, to all persons as a necessary skill for effective democratic participation, is still a core value of liberal arts colleges and universities in this country.

Public Critique in a Democracy

None of this is to say that the ancient Athenian democracy or any other democracy is perfect. Ancient Athenian democracy excluded women and foreign-born males. And, toward the end of its prominence, in the late fifth and early fourth century, major intellectual figures offered extensive critiques of the Athenian democratic experiment. The supposed weaknesses of participants, individually and corporately, are well chronicled in the writings of critics such as Plato, Isocrates, Thucydides, and Aristophanes.[8] Their works paint a consistent picture of an Assembly that at times was easy to manipulate, gullible, distracted, and lacking in motivation for the task of self-governance. Plato feared that those who did not know the truth were leading the Assembly into error. Moreover, the great fear that individual political speakers would seek their own personal gain or other benefits over that of the city-state was also a persistent concern.

Two-and-a-half millennia later, many of these same fears persist. Some people today in the United States are concerned that the majority of participants lack the ability, either intellectually or practically, to stay well-enough informed to engage intellectually and productively in the political process. The enormous size of the United States also poses tremendous difficulties for participation that classical Athens did not face.[9] The presence of in-person, face-to-face rhetorical exchange has receded in the modern context, and the personal nature of democratic exchange that characterized ancient Athenian democracy is rare. Similarly, just as ancient Athenian democracy excluded women and non-Athenian males, today there is concern over whether all members of the public—all races, ethnicities, religions, socioeconomic statuses, and other groups—are fully able to be engaged and have their ideas heard.

Yet, at the same time that Plato and others were offering their critiques of democracy, the works of Isocrates and Aristotle point us to the exciting ways rhetoric continues to enable and improve democratic engagement on local and national levels. Isocrates wrote speeches that addressed many of the important civic issues of his day, from Athens' relationship with Philip of Macedon, to the value of sophistic education, to the need for greater unity among Greek city-states. Scholars who have studied these speeches recognize in them an early example of well-crafted and stylistically rich political speech. In Aristotle, particularly in the *Rhetoric* and *Politics*, we find an early and incredibly insightful description and analysis of Athenian and Greek political practice and the role of rhetoric within it. Aristotle argued, in contrast with his teacher Plato, that rhetoric could aid civic affairs and democratic governance, in part, through its reliance on providing reasons or proofs for a speaker's position or claim. These reasons, as we will discover in later chapters, not only included logical appeals but also appeals to a speaker's character and the audience's emotional state of mind. Audiences, Aristotle believed, were able and willing to judge a speaker's reasons and, consequently, accept or reject a speaker's position.

In addition to studying the principles of rhetoric, both Isocrates and Aristotle taught the art to Athenian students. Isocrates became famous for his school of rhetoric, which emphasized civic participation by training students to focus their rhetorical skills on addressing practical matters of the state. Aristotle similarly designated rhetoric to the realm of public affairs and taught this art, alongside a wide variety of other subjects, at his school that went by the name of the Lyceum. In fact, Aristotle's *Rhetoric* is believed to consist of a collection of his students' notes taken during, or in response to, his lectures. Two of rhetoric's greatest champions from this period, Isocrates and Aristotle, devoted much of their lives to teaching the subject to students, possibly suggesting the difficulty of the skills involved and the importance for democratic participants to receive a rhetorical education.

Much has changed since democracy and rhetoric began in ancient Greece. However, when we turn to the history of our own country, we can see that rhetoric also played a foundational role in the establishment of American democracy. When we examine the debates in the colonial era about how much control the British Crown was to have over the colonists, the debates about taxation during the Continental Congress, and the deliberations that led to the Declaration of Independence and the US Constitution, we see rhetoric functioning as the means by which these issues were reconciled. Today, the relationship between rhetoric and democracy continues to be a logically necessary one in that democracy is impossible without the practice of public discourse and dialogue among democratic participants. Moreover, rhetoric is the tool by which political power and influence are shared.

RHETORIC AND DEMOCRACY
ARE MUTUALLY REINFORCING

Democracy is a political system which locates control and power in the people themselves. Often the most prominent way we think of a democracy is that it is a system in which the people vote for their leaders on a regular basis. While this is certainly an essential element in a democracy, it is not the only significant way that individuals exercise their power. We can see the synergistic manner in which rhetoric and democracy function by noting the ways each encourages the other.

Rhetoric Encourages Democracy

Rhetoric encourages democracy in several ways. First, it does so by being the chief means by which a community of any size is formed. That is, until a group of people— whether it is an organization, a town, a city, a state, or a nation—communicate with one another they do not exist as an entity in any significant way. The fourth-century sophist Isocrates made this point, noting that it was through rhetoric, or the term for it most used in his day, *logos*, that communities came together and formulated the laws and institutions necessary for their corporate existence. While in Isocrates's day this interaction took the form of published speeches and face-to-face conversation, today we know that the means of interaction are much more numerous. Today they include cable and broadcast television, the Internet, cell phones, and many other electronic devices.

Rhetoric also encourages democracy by enabling participants to jointly focus their attention on particular issues at particular times and to act on those issues through political campaigns, public gatherings, debates, and other forms of advocacy. Participants must also employ rhetoric, often in public speaking and public discussion, on matters of public or shared concern. Political scientist Robert McKenzie, in *Public Politics*, states this matter quite eloquently and forcefully:

> In public politics, the public has undelegable responsibilities, things that only the public can do. In the first place, only the public in a democracy can establish the legitimacy of government. Only the public can create and define the public interest. . . . Furthermore, only the public can build common ground on which decisions can be made that provide a steady course for the future. Only the public can generate political will to get anything done with consistency. Only the public can transform private individuals into public citizens. No politicians, however dedicated, and no governments, however effective, can do such things without becoming demagogic and tyrannical. We should ask ourselves who will establish the legitimacy of government, set its direction, and evaluate its actions if the public does not.[10]

McKenzie goes on to explain, as we do here, that the way democratic participants accomplish this influence is through deliberative interaction, that is, rhetoric employed in the civic sphere.

Finally, rhetoric supports democracy by supplying the fundamental skills necessary for effective participation. This includes both the production of the many messages already noted and the analysis of such messages. Democratic participants must be able to understand, assess, and make an evaluation of the messages and advocacy of others in order to function well in a democracy. We fully affirm, along with the late Wabash College speech professor W. Norwood Brigance, that "every educated person ought to know when a thing is proved and when it is not proved, should know how to investigate and to analyze a proposition that confronts him, and how to search for a solution, how to talk about it effectively before others, and how to contribute to a discussion on problems of joint interest."[11] Rhetoric and democracy are related in such a way that they cannot be separated. This is true because rhetoric is both the means by which democratic participation takes place and it is the product which is produced through that participation. When we expand our view from one in which "democracy equals voting" to "democracy is a system in which all the participants, the people, have the power," we see how integral rhetoric is to this process. Therefore we are interested in how participants in a community function when they are surrounded by democratic values—not just in how citizens practice their political rights.

BOX 1-2

Practicing Democracy

American society presents us with multiple and recurring opportunities for civic engagement:

1. Speak up in class to respond to what your professor and your classmates have to say.

2. Ask questions and share your ideas at the rich variety of public events on your campus.

3. Attend the open hearings and meetings of your local school board and city council and ask questions, share your ideas, and advocate for something you care about.

4. Write or call your local representative, mayor, or the governor of your state about an issue or to suggest a new solution to a problem.

5. Send a letter to the editor of your local newspaper, or post a response to a news website, and follow the responses your letter or post receives.

Democracy Encourages Rhetoric

The mutually reinforcing relationship between rhetoric and democracy can also be seen when we consider how democracy encourages rhetoric. It does so in at least three ways. First, elections, the legislative process, and the legal system allow and in many cases require participation by the people. Candidates for office must garner votes and this requires them to speak to, and if they are wise, to listen to, voters. Once elected, those in office must likewise respond to their constituents and listen to them, if for no other reason than to seek reelection. The legislative process often requires a period for the public to provide comment on new laws and regulations, and the judicial process allows and in many instances requires individuals to speak in court. In fact, if you take public communication out of a democratic society, it is impossible to imagine how that democracy can continue.

Second, democracy encourages rhetoric because a fundamental feature of all democratic societies is the right of the people to peacefully gather and to protest. This is because, as Ober contends, "A vibrant democracy depends on the efforts, not only of citizen advocates dedicated to promoting its continued existence, but also of citizen dissidents who advocate its revision or even its replacement."[12] Thus, in this way, rhetoric and democracy, even in the process of challenge and critique, work hand in hand with one another and are mutually reinforcing.[13] We have seen this most dramatically in recent years in the Middle East where democratic movements have formed, gathered extremely large numbers of people for the purpose of protest, and have had significant impact. In these cases, the verbal and nonverbal rhetoric alters the course of decision-making and action of those in leadership positions. We also see this regularly in our own country on issues ranging from the rights of unions to abortion to genetically modified food.

Third, and finally, democracy reinforces rhetoric because, in most cases, victory is achieved by skilled advocacy, and thus democratic participants are encouraged to seek to be so skilled. This does not merely refer to the loudest voices but rather the most persuasive voices. And, while it is possible to identify principles of what makes rhetoric persuasive—it is based on thorough and accurate research, it is constructed in a clear and compelling manner, it is adapted to its audience—the issues, circumstances, goals, and timing of any particular instance of rhetorical action mean that accurately determining what will and will not be persuasive in a given instance is extremely difficult.

Rhetoric and democracy exist in a synergistic relationship; each feeds off of and stimulates the other. Participants in a democratic society engage democratic practice through rhetoric, and they do so in a variety of ways. In the next section we describe a number of examples of how community members like you have engaged at both the local and the global level.

Civic Rhetoric at the Local Level

When citizens are disappointed with representatives or are motivated to act on a community problem that is not addressed through local agencies, they can—and do—initiate the process through bottom-up grassroots movements. Community groups form and can effectively work to address local issues by building coalitions and using the resources and talents of private individuals. Grassroots movements are responsive to local conditions and needs and contribute to the health of a community. These movements often engage in community building by organizing public forums, raising awareness of community issues, rallying the community through petitions and letter-writing campaigns, organizing protests and demonstrations, or forming community organizations that lead fundraising and program development to address a community need.

One example of a citizen-led initiative was an effort in Crawfordsville, Indiana, to build a local skate park. The initiative was led by a local citizens' group that named itself Building a Healthy Future. With a board of local community members, the organization developed a plan for the park and led fundraising efforts. The committee served as the hub of community interest, bringing together businesses and groups to work toward making their vision a reality, all without burdening a tight city budget, as the project was fully funded without taxpayer dollars. One of those involved with this project was Wabash College Professor of Mathematics and Computer Science Chad Westphal. Professor Westphal articulated his motivations for his efforts in a blog posting: "I'm a part of this community, and I want to help these kids feel like their community supports them. When I see these kids, I see myself at their age. And then I see who they can be in five, ten, twenty years."[14]

The work Professor Westphal and others did was rhetorical and varied. They worked closely with the park board and the city attorney on the legal and insurance issues involved, spoke at city council meetings, helped manage the bid process, and were interviewed by the local press. In addition, they set up meetings with representatives of the local businesses that donated funds and advocated for the project with them. Finally, they spoke with local residents who lived near the park to address concerns they had about the proposed skate park.

As a result of the public efforts of Professor Westphal and the committee, local industries such as Alcoa and R.R. Donnelly's contributed to the project, as did the Tony Hawk Foundation, while Nucor Steel donated useful construction materials. Furthermore, the Crawfordsville Kiwanis Club joined the cause by contributing significant financial resources, and Wabash College's Malcolm X Institute of Black Studies held fundraisers, such as a car wash. Upon completing the development plans, raising the necessary funds, and securing construction bids, the ad hoc committee brought the matter to the Crawfordsville Parks and Recreation Department board in June 2010. In unanimously approving the project, board President Dale Petrie told members of Building a Healthy Future, "Congratulations and thanks for handling this project." The park opened in fall 2010.[15]

BOX 1-3

Looking for Civic Engagement

- Name a recent example of a student-organized event intended to help improve your campus or local community.

- Name a recent example of local community members working together to raise awareness of community issues or rally members to public action.

- Name a recent example of people using social media such as Facebook or Twitter to improve the health of the community.

- Go to the website of your local newspaper, and find an example of civic engagement that is highlighted in an article on the front page of the site, such as a fundraising effort for a family that lost their home in a fire or an effort to increase funding for the local school district.

- Go to the website of your city or town, and find a link to an initiative hosted by the city but that engaged community members, such as a tree-planting project or a program to teach entrepreneurship to high school students.

Another example of a grassroots movement, one that exemplifies practices of public deliberation, recently occurred in Philadelphia. In the midst of the economic downturn, Philadelphia Mayor Michael Nutter announced a series of cuts to public services in order to reduce the city's $108 million budget deficit. The cuts included closing 11 public libraries, more than 60 public swimming pools, and eliminating hundreds of city positions. Questioning the value hierarchy of city decision-makers and the cost of the trade-offs in sacrificing public services in order to assist private financial institutions, a community organization called the Coalition to Save the Libraries (CSL) was formed. Concerned citizens attended a series of town hall meetings organized by city leaders and used the deliberative forums to question the values and trade-offs involved. Subsequently, "neighborhood leaders organized impromptu rallies at the eleven branch libraries," garnering significant media attention to the cause. By using legal challenges, the group gained an injunction against the library closures. The point, ultimately, is the power of the people in mobilizing over a cause of community concern to work together in questioning, and ultimately overturning, public policy. These citizens used an array of communication skills—developing media talking points, serving as media spokespersons, writing press releases, developing phone scripts, and more—to influence decision-makers and inform the public about the costs to the community when cutting public services. As Gregory Benjamin, a coalition leader, explained, "The citywide coalition was dynamite. It gave us an opportunity to connect with other people, communities and ethnic groups that really had the same concerns that we had."[16]

SPOTLIGHT ON SOCIAL MEDIA:
Twitter and Public Activism

On July 16, 2013, two days following George Zimmerman's acquittal from murder and manslaughter charges in the death of Trayvon Martin, the juror known as B37 appeared on CNN with television host Anderson Cooper. At the close of an extensive interview in which the juror explained her perspective on the trial and gave insight into the workings of the jury, Cooper disclosed that the juror and her husband planned to write a book about the decision and the experience of being sequestered during the trial.

Viewer Genie Lauren was angry about what she heard in the interview and was outraged over the idea that a juror could profit in the form of a book addressing the trial. Lauren responded by starting a petition at Change.org and going to Twitter, advocating a boycott of the proposed book and seeking information on the literary agent who was pursuing the project. Soon she had information on the agent and tweeted it to her followers. From there, the movement grew quickly. In a matter of hours, Lauren's number of followers grew from 1,600 to more than 9,000, and her petition received more than 1,000 signatures. By the next day, the literary agent and juror B37 issued a statement indicating the book project would not go forward. In the statement, juror B37 said, in part, "Now that I am returned to my family and to society in general [following being sequestered], I have realized that the best direction for me to go is away from writing any sort of book and return instead to my life as it was before I was called to sit on this jury."

This result, and the speed by which it occurred, underscores how social media is changing the nature of public advocacy. In Twitter, Lauren found a powerful tool for public communication, one that allowed her to quickly and persuasively reach a wide audience as her message was retweeted from user to user, and her efforts were picked up by media. Commenting on the experience the next day, Lauren said: "I was shocked because I didn't think the response from other Tweeters would happen so quickly. . . . I thought that even if we got 1,000 signatures that I would hear something like, 'Sorry you feel this way, but we're stilling going ahead with this book.' I really didn't expect for this to happen like this so quickly." In speaking to ABC News, Lauren further explained, "I definitely believe in the power of Twitter. I'm in shock, really, about the whole thing. . . . I'm glad that people didn't brush it off and just say, 'Oh, it's just Twitter, and . . . nothing will come of this.'" As ABC News aptly summarized it: "Genie Lauren proves that the internet can literally change something overnight."[17]

Discussion Questions

- Prior to social media like Twitter and Facebook, how do you imagine Genie Lauren would have gotten her message out, and how effective do you imagine it would have been?

- Do you imagine this use of Twitter and the result it produced will be a rare or a frequent occurrence in the future?

- Can you think of any reason to be concerned about this use of social media in public activism?

Civic Rhetoric at the Global Level

Moving beyond the borders of local communities and causes, what is occuring in the Middle East has allowed the world to witness the fundamental role rhetoric plays in the creation, development, and maintenance of democracies, or at least more democratic governments. The Arab Spring refers to a series of protests and democratic revolutions across the Middle East and northern Africa that began during the spring of 2011, though events and these movements are still unfolding at the time of this writing. In the most dramatic cases thus far, these events have removed dictators in Tunisia, Egypt, and Libya. Large numbers of citizens have protested repeatedly in most of the Arab countries from Morocco to Bahrain and Syria to Yemen. The movement has been led by Arab youth, and the demographics of the region help explain why. The region has the highest percentage of its population, 60%, under the age of 30 of any region in the world. In addition, literacy rates for this group are quite high, above 80% in most of the countries. Sadly, while the percentage of the population with college degrees is rising, the unemployment rates are also quite high, thus leading to the clash between raised expectations and the less than thriving reality.[18]

BOX 1-4

Public Critique in Egypt

Egyptian protesters garnered recognition in the Arab world for creating the most creative antiregime chants during the Arab Spring. They made strategic use of creative one-liners in offering critique of the Mubarak regime. In Arabic the lines had catchy rhythms and rhymed, which are, unfortunately, lost in translation in English. Below are a few of these chants.

Irhal yani imshi, yellee ma batafahmshee.
Get out, walk away, you just don't get it do you. [In reference to Mubarak]

Yaskoot, yaskoot, hookim al askr.
Down, down with the rule of the dictator.

Ya ala, ool abouk, al shab al masriyeen, yakrahook.
Hey son [in reference to Gamal Mubarak], *tell your father: "The Egyptians hate you."*

While the economic, social, and political conditions in the countries involved explain much of the Arab Spring, we can see that it is rhetoric in its multiple forms that is the means by which this movement has functioned. And, particularly as the youth in these countries have demanded greater democratic participation in the governance of their countries, we can see in the movements a current and particularly powerful example of the inextricable connections between democracy and rhetoric. Indeed we would likely have to go back to the founding of our own country to find an example as dramatic.

The proximate cause for the movement is recognized to have been a specific rhetorical act by Tunisian Mohamed Bouazizi. On December 17, 2010, Mohamed Bouazizi, a 26 year old with a college degree in computer science, was selling fruits and vegetables from a street stand in his city of Sidi Bouzid when a female police officer shut down his stand because he did not have a permit. He had been frustrated by government corruption in the permit system, and something of an altercation took place. Bouazizi claims the police officer slapped him, though this claim is denied by the officer. In any case, the next day Bouazizi doused himself in gasoline and set himself on fire in front of the local government building. He clung to life for 18 days before dying, and then his death became a powerful political catalyst. The protests grew and grew in Tunisia into what is now referred to as the Jasmine Revolution after Tunisia's national flower. President Zine el Abidine Ben Ali left in disgrace on January 14, 2011.[19] News of the event spread rapidly across the Arab world, helping incite a wave of protests. Arab youth across the region have made extensive use of social media—principally Facebook, Twitter, and YouTube—to share information and coordinate their efforts.

Bouazizi's act of self-immolation was a rhetorical act and a highly public one.[20] The message it sent to the government of Tunisia as well as to Arab youth inside and outside Tunisia, to leaders in other Arab countries, and to the world community was powerful. Many have come to see that the state of affairs for Tunisia's youth and the rest of its citizens is unacceptable and requires change. While a quite extreme example of rhetoric as a civic art, the case does confirm and reaffirm the role of rhetoric in democracies and in countries where citizens are seeking democracy or a more democratic form of government.

In Sidi Bouzid, Tunisia, people walk past a large poster with Bouazizi's image taken on the first anniversary of Bouazizi's death, December 17, 2011.

This example demonstrates the powerful role of democratic participation. Hundreds of demonstrations, involving hundreds of thousands of people, have taken place throughout the Middle East, and for the most part they have been peaceful. The range of rhetorical acts employed is impressive but not surprising. They include not only the physical act of public demonstration or protest but also the use of websites, blogs, editorials in newspapers, videos posted online, Facebook status updates, and tweets from Twitter accounts. And, what is more, the need for destructive action is lessened to the extent that rhetoric and democracy are functioning productively in a society, which is of course the focus of this book.

These examples of democratic participants taking action on issues of public concern show that avenues for change do exist—and, where they do not already exist, can be created by community-minded individuals with communication skills and an understanding of how civic engagement works. The Occupy Wall Street movement was also an example of this. It began in Zuccotti Park near Wall Street but soon spread to hundreds of cities across the country, including Los Angeles, San Francisco, Chicago, and Boston. With the slogan "We are the 99%" the movement focused attention on the way in which movement members believe the US government and the standard operating procedures of American corporations favor a narrow portion of the population.[21]

It is our hope that through this textbook you will gain an understanding of the relationship between rhetoric and democracy and come to realize the great potential of deliberation for improving public dialogue and the value of practicing productive public discourse in your communication interactions. To assist with this learning, we encourage you to treat your classroom learning environment as a proto-public space.[22] That is, in your classroom speaking, envision yourself as a public actor, not just a student giving graded speeches. You are a democratic participant capable of contributing to the social knowledge of the problems and prospects of our democracy.

The next several chapters give further form to the orientation that has been advanced in this one, providing an explanation of the current state of public discourse; an explanation of ethics that ground public speaking, productive discourse, and deliberation; and more precise instruction in the practices of public discussion and deliberation that allow for thoughtful and nuanced consideration of complex and controversial issues that compete for acceptance by publics.

SUMMARY

This chapter has oriented you toward the necessity of public speaking skills for democratic participation and civic engagement. More specifically you have learned:

- Rhetoric is a civic art devoted to the ethical study and use of symbols (verbal and nonverbal) in order to address public issues.
- Public critique is a natural and important part of a thriving democracy.
- There is a natural and important relationship between rhetorical education and democracy.
- Public speaking is the process of forming and delivering rhetorical content to an audience in the hope of persuading, influencing, informing, or entertaining that audience.

- A rhetor is a person who speaks in public.
- Civic engagement is participation in organizations, institutions, and societies with the goal of contributing to the public good.
- Rhetoric has seven important characteristics: it is a civic art, involves the study and use of symbols, is ethical, makes use of verbal and nonverbal symbols, addresses public issues, is a form of power, and is situational and contingent.
- Democracy is a political system that locates governmental control and power in the citizen body.
- We regularly see examples of people using rhetoric to participate both locally and globally in civic engagement.

KEY TERMS

civic p. 3   democracy p. 8   rhetor p. 4
civic engagement p. 3   public speaking p. 5   rhetoric p. 3
democratic participants p. 1

REVIEW QUESTIONS

1. What is rhetoric?
2. What does it mean to refer to rhetoric as a *civic* art?
3. What are the seven characteristics of rhetoric as a civic art?
4. How do practices from Ancient Greece demonstrate the vital role of rhetoric in democracy?
5. What is the historical relationship between rhetoric and democracy?
6. What did you learn in this chapter about how Plato, Aristotle, and Isocrates contributed to our understanding of rhetoric and democracy?
7. How does the definition of rhetoric used in this textbook challenge the common use of the term?

DISCUSSION QUESTIONS

1. Think of a public speech that made a difference, that is, one that mattered for society. What made the speech a success?
2. Are individuals or groups more likely to make better decisions? Why? When?
3. What are examples of contingent issues? Noncontingent issues? How is rhetoric useful for each?
4. What opportunities exist where you could engage in public projects and initiatives for the common good?
5. How can a better understanding of the role of public speaking as a civic art enhance your ability to contribute to the common good?
6. What kind of speech training is needed to prepare you as a citizen?

CHAPTER 2

The Landscape of Public Discourse and the Politics of Polarization

---

Chapter Objectives

Students will:

- Consider the current state of public discourse in US democracy.
- Identify the qualities of unproductive discourse.
- Explain the contemporary obstacles to productive communication.
- Describe the qualities of productive discourse.
- Articulate the nature of the public sphere and the role of public discourse and "counterpublics" within that sphere.
- Recognize the policing potential in calls for productive discourse and the role of social protest rhetoric in enacting democratic change.

In late summer 2009, the American public was treated—or perhaps "subjected" is a better characterization—to a rash of public statements and outbursts that encapsulate several issues afflicting our public discourse. In August, in the midst of a heated public debate over healthcare, Sarah Palin (the former governor of Alaska and Republican vice presidential candidate) asserted on Facebook that an Obama healthcare proposal contained "death panels" that would put the elderly and infirm at risk of being euthanized. Despite the rejection of this accusation as patently false by liberals and conservatives alike, the sound bite replayed on news programs and discussions for days and echoed for weeks. Not to be outdone, Democrat Alan Grayson, at the time a representative from Florida, asserted—from the House floor no less—"If you get sick, America, the Republicans' healthcare plan is this: Die quickly." Grayson's comments closely followed a trio of surprising public outbursts. First, South Carolina Representative Joe Wilson audibly interjected, "You lie!" in response to a claim about the ineligibility of illegal immigrants to health insurance coverage by President Barack Obama in his speech to a joint session of Congress. Second, four days later

Democratic Representative Alan Grayson engages in unproductive discourse during the 2009 debates over national healthcare.

musician Kanye West commandeered the stage at the 2009 MTV Video Music Awards to interrupt Taylor Swift's acceptance of the award for Best Female Video. West took the microphone away from Swift to protest her award and objected, "I'm sorry, but Beyoncé had one of the best videos of all time." Finally, that same day, tennis star Serena Williams unleashed a profanity-filled tirade at a line judge in protest of a call. Williams allegedly physically threatened the official and was docked a point, which ended the match.[1] In the scope of public discourse these are minor anecdotes, but they are symbolic of deeper issues that plague our public communication.

These deeper issues that plague public communication—and how we might fix them—are our central concerns in this chapter. We begin by highlighting commentary on the problems of public communication, including the qualities of unproductive discourse and some of the obstacles to more productive exchanges. We then explore the characteristics of productive discourse, a form of communication that can be learned and practiced in your public speaking course. Finally we discuss how accusations of unproductive discourse—sometimes labeled "uncivil" discourse—may become a way of policing the rhetoric and the full democratic participation of others. Our goal throughout the chapter is to invite you to reflect on how we, as democratic participants, publicly agree or disagree with each other and what effects these choices have on our democracy and our many public institutions.

THE PROBLEMS WITH PUBLIC COMMUNICATION

It is an unfortunate state of affairs, but our public communication is impoverished. It too often qualifies as what we might call unproductive discourse. **Unproductive discourse** is purposefully sensational public communication designed to promote division and to misrepresent the complexities of public issues. It features poor arguments that appeal to the least common denominator, name-calling that substitutes for nuanced analysis, and an emphasis on points of division rather than points of agreement. Poor arguments are not only frequent, but they also are often encouraged and valorized in the adversarial format that we use to frame our discussions of public issues. For instance, our tendency is to reduce all issues not only to a debate but also to a debate that features two simply distilled sides and can be carried out through empty taglines and personal attacks across a five-minute segment on a news program. This textbook is devoted to addressing such problems in public discourse. We are interested in developing your understanding of, and effectiveness in, various forms of public engagement.

The type of public speech we advance in this textbook can best be termed productive discourse. **Productive discourse** is public communication that is responsible to one's community and manages differences constructively. It requires active engagement in civic life by talking *and* listening; it reflects sound reasoning; it pursues multilateral problem-solving; and it relies on ethical standards of inclusivity, communication, and interaction. It is focused on ideas, not personalities, and it is respectful but not compliant, meaning that it has learning and the public good among its highest ideals.

We are not so bold—or so naive—to suggest a complete sea change in public discourse. Nor do we, as you will see in later chapters of this book, fully reject an adversarial model of persuasion, which we find essential in certain contexts (see the section on social protest that follows, as well as chapter 15 on the necessity of public critique in a functioning democracy). Just as importantly, we are not suggesting that disagreement should be muted. On the contrary, diversity of opinion should be encouraged in order to allow for the best discussion of public policy. But we do hope to encourage you to see richer possibilities for public communication, to help you see behind the accusations and the lack of authentic listening, and to foster your ability to more fully survey the dimensions of an issue before advocating specific conclusions. In order to understand how to reverse the downward spiral in our public discourse, let's begin by examining what type of speech counts as public discourse and what elements in that discourse are increasingly cited as cause for concern by philosophers and public figures alike.

The Public, the Public Sphere, and Public Discourse

First, we will offer some definitions, as "public" is a term with a multiple meanings. For the purpose of this chapter and the textbook as a whole, a **public** refers to a collection or group of people who are joined together in a cause of common concern. Often a public works together to address an issue or question that affects a community. Our definition of a public draws heavily on the concept of the public sphere, as articulated by the sociologist and philosopher Jürgen Habermas. For Habermas, the **public sphere** is the gathering of community members to discuss matters of common concern. The public talks, argues, and reasons together as equals, disregarding social and economic inequalities among participants, ideally arriving at a more fulsome understanding of the issues.[2] In our definition, then, a public is distinctly different from a group of individuals. A group of individuals is composed of people who, while they possibly share a concern, view themselves as separate entities, opposed sides, or factions that are driven by their own particular interests or needs. Such factions usually believe their needs or concerns are in competition with other people's needs and concerns. Those who comprise a public sphere, by contrast, may hold very different views from each other, but they recognize the interdependency of their lives. Thus, a public shares a common group identity. Whereas individuals think in terms of "me" and "them," an ideal public thinks more in terms of "us."

When a public comes together to address matters of shared concern, they participate in public discourse. When we use the term **public discourse**, which we do frequently in this textbook, we are referring to rhetoric that is publicly offered to address an issue, problem, or question of common concern. In our society, public discourse is produced on a range of topics including educational policies, community projects, and political and public policies. On your campus, discourse may be used to discuss national politics, debate curricular change, and engage in dialogue over student services ranging from dining options to relations between the campus and its surrounding community. What makes discourse public, rather than private, are the setting and participants (it is visible and accessible to anyone implicated by the decisions made there); the topics discussed (they impact a whole community); and, ideally, the nature of the communication (it is concerned with the common good rather than the desires of a few individuals). You can see, then, that "public," the "public sphere," and "public discourse" involve many members who may not be united by citizenship but who come together to have a voice and play a vital role in shared arenas of public concern.

When we look at the current state of the public discourse that addresses institutions and issues in our communities, we can see that we've developed a series of bad habits. Oftentimes, we engage in conversational patterns that *prohibit* rather than facilitate the smooth functioning of our community's institutions. In recent years, many scholars and public figures have voiced concern that our contemporary public discourse fails to live up to the ideal standard of prioritizing the public's welfare over individual interests. Their insights may help us understand what, precisely, is wrong with the way we talk to each other.

Growing Concerns about the State of Our Public Communication

The efforts to diagnose and correct our public discourse might be traced back to the work of American philosopher and education advocate John Dewey and his 1927 book *The Public and Its Problems*. Concerned over the problems of the public and obstacles to democracy, Dewey contends that more and better communication is necessary to improve the public and hence democracy. As he explains, "The essential need, in other words, is the improvement of methods of debate, discussion, and persuasion. That is *the* problem of the public." A more recent and more specific diagnosis of the problems of public discourse is offered by communication scholar Deborah Tannen in her 1998 book *Argument Culture*. Tannen critiques the "pervasive warlike atmosphere that makes us approach public dialogue, and just about anything we need to accomplish, as if it were a fight." Tannen suggests that this "is a tendency in Western culture in general, and in the United States in particular, that . . . in recent years has become so exaggerated that it is getting in the way of solving our problems." Communication researchers W. Barnett Pearce and Stephen W. Littlejohn add that "extremism" has become a "winning strategy" as too often it is "the most extreme voices . . . that make news; shrill voices denouncing enemies become identified as the spokespersons of the group." And political theorist Benjamin Barber concurs. He points to broadcast media as symbolic of these problems when he contends, "Talk radio is loudly public without being in the least civil, though it is seductively entertaining. Unfortunately, its divisive rant is a perfect model of everything that civility is *not*: people talking without listening, confirming dogmas, not questioning them, convicting rather than convincing adversaries."[3]

While communication scholars, political scientists, and others have been addressing these problems of public communication for many years, increased public recognition of them might be traced to a rather unlikely source: a comedian. In October 2004 Jon Stewart, host of Comedy Central's *The Daily Show*, appeared on the CNN program *Crossfire*. In his appearance Stewart took the hosts, Paul Begala (a Democratic consultant and commentator) and Tucker Carlson (a conservative commentator), to task for their constant bickering and lack of attention to deeper issues. Accusing them of being "partisan hacks," Stewart contended that shows like *Crossfire* "hurt America" by offering theater rather than substantive discussion and instantiate the idea that debate must be negative and confrontational. The cohosts were clearly taken aback as they were lectured by Stewart on the responsibilities of journalists and political commentators to advance and improve US democracy. Among the many reactions to Stewart's appearance, the late American philosopher Frank Cioffi effectively diagnosed the problematic discourse that is too often promoted in our political media:

> People on shows such as *Crossfire* stake out a position, and they iterate and reiterate that position. They give examples of what they mean, and "defend" themselves by ignoring or deliberately misconstruing vicious attacks from the opposing side. But this is not intellectual discourse; it's discourse packaged as product.[4]

In a victory of sorts, only three months later, CNN president Jonathan Klein announced the cancellation of *Crossfire*. In so doing he explained that he was influenced by Stewart's appearance and that he "agree[d] wholeheartedly with Jon Stewart's overall premise." (The show returned for roughly a year in 2013 and 2014, before it was cancelled a second time. The new version of the show added a closing segment called "Cease Fire," in which participants were asked to look for common ground.)[5]

A second example that demonstrates the problems of our public dialogue is found in the healthcare debates of 2009. In an effort to survey the feelings of their constituents as well as to educate, many representatives of both political parties held town-hall-style meetings to discuss healthcare and legislative proposals. Almost uniformly, ugly scenes broke out, and Americans were treated to video of angry constituents standing next to US senators and representatives while aggressively shouting them down. There were reports of threats and fights, and even evidence that some of the behavior was encouraged by political networks. For example, a banner on the website of talk show host Sean Hannity encouraged readers to "become a part of the mob," while a strategy memo by the Tea Party Patriots provided a list of "Best Practices" for "Rocking the Town Halls." The advice included encouraging attendees to "yell back" at statements they disagreed with in order "to make" the official "uneasy early on and set the tone for the hall as clearly informal and free-wheeling." Such yelling, the strategy memo promised, "will also embolden others." The results included 83-year-old John Dingell, a long-time representative from Michigan, being "shouted down ... by a rowdy crowd," and former Pennsylvania Senator Arlen Specter engaging in a shouting match with an angry attendee.[6]

Unfortunately, too many of the assemblies were a microcosm of how impoverished our discourse has become and our need to devote ourselves to its improvement for the sake of our democracy.

Craig Anthony Miller confronts Senator Arlen Specter at a 2009 town hall meeting on healthcare.

Now that we have firmly established both the problems that plague our public discourse and the many sectors from which we hear calls for reform, we want to outline some of the central features of unproductive discourse. What is it, exactly, that makes such public communication unproductive?

Qualities of Unproductive Discourse

When we look across the multiple examples of what we have identified as unproductive discourse, several qualities repeatedly appear. These qualities include, but are not restricted to, the following: division, dichotomous thinking, combativeness, certainty, lack of listening, winning, distrust, hierarchical communication, and dogmatism. We consider each quality in Box 2-1.

BOX 2-1

Qualities of Unproductive Discourse

- *Division:* Highlights and accentuates differences among participants and their positions.
- *Dichotomous thinking:* Features debate between two (and only two) diametrically opposed and extreme positions instead of exploring additional perspectives or middle ground.

- *Combativeness:* Utilizes aggressive behavior toward other participants and alternative perspectives, such as repeated interrupting, emotionally charged labeling, yelling, and personal attacks. Lacks empathy toward other participants, and views dissenting opinions as the opposition to be defeated.

- *Certainty:* Exhibits sureness about a position without recognizing its weaknesses or drawbacks. Lacks self-reflexivity or room for doubt.

- *Lack of listening:* Only listens to an alternative perspective to find weaknesses in it. Uses questions as veiled arguments ("Isn't it true that . . . ?") or as attempts to humiliate other participants. Instead of truly considering the fellow participants, remarks seem directed at a third-party judge, moderator, or camera audience.

- *Winning:* Fixates on getting one's way, rather than learning or the common good, as the goal. At its worst, this form of communication uses any means necessary to win, such as false or misleading illusions, quoting statements out of context, and misstating or exaggerating the facts. Privileges emotion over logic and proof.

- *Distrust:* Suspects other participants' motives or goals. Presumes they have a hidden agenda, and, thus, lacks faith in the honesty or authenticity of what they say.

- *Hierarchical communication:* Discourages communication among invested community members, and, instead, encourages communication from the "top" decision-makers (officials, leaders, spokespersons, or experts) down, which subjugates ordinary individuals' preferences or insights.

- *Dogmatism:* Features familiar and even predictable talking points as well as entrenched, predetermined positions.[7]

Of course, unproductive discourse does tend to capture our attention and entertain us. The often fast pace of news media coverage relies on "zingers" that require little knowledge or understanding and can be exciting and even fun to watch. And it can bring out important points to consider as it offers two sides to an issue. However, whatever advantages it might have are overwhelmed by the harmful outcomes it produces. Unproductive discourse typically lives up to its name, in that it is, well, unproductive. It produces little new information or real understanding as to why the participants or sides fundamentally disagree. Instead, it can miseducate us since it overly simplifies complex issues, overlooks additional perspectives, and suggests that people on one side all agree with each other. Finally, it discourages us from becoming civically engaged because it emphasizes the divisions among us and turns us into spectators rather than participants. We are reduced to sitting on the sideline and cheering or booing the participants.

This sounds more like reality television than a government by the people and for the people, doesn't it? It's not surprising that many of us opt out of the spectacle altogether, developing cynical attitudes about politics and civic affairs. Scholars J. Michael Hogan, Robert Putnam, and others have chronicled how over the course of decades, as polarized discourse has flourished, voting rates have declined, civic participation has decreased, and newspaper readership and news viewership has dropped.[8] The result is that we are more likely to watch a civic controversy than to actively engage in its resolution.

For those of us who would like to see more active participation in our government and in our communities, what needs to change? The next section suggests that we must become more discerning critics of the news coverage we consume, as well as more attentive to the way politicians' interests may be served by unproductive discourse. Finally, we suggest that we need to examine our own actions and attitudes and to educate ourselves as public speakers who engage in productive discourse.

OBSTACLES TO PRODUCTIVE COMMUNICATION

Examples of incivility in the public eye are not new or novel. Over the course of its history, the United States has seen plenty of political campaigns and public disputes that would fail to satisfy any definition of civility. There was never a golden era of civility to which we can hope to return. But there are aspects of the situation today that exacerbate the problems of the public. We look briefly at four of these to increase our awareness of how we can become more discerning consumers. We conclude this section by discussing how we can become better democratic participants and promoters of productive discourse.

The News Media

What may be most different today is the omnipresent media with the proliferation of cable news. News programs tend to frame, cover, and discuss issues in ways that "favor short, shallow, photogenic messages" rather than those with more depth and nuance.[9] These shows seem geared toward guests who stoke controversy, which not only makes us more aware of breaks in decorum but may also have a way of validating and valorizing such breaches, given the amount of attention they receive. Cable news, in particular, frequently features divisive, adversarial interactions among people with differing views. Consequently, while news programs may draw viewers, they often make the issues they cover appear too distant, too immense, or simply too unattractive to be meaningfully addressed with personal actions.

Incivility as Strategy

A second related, and more disheartening, aspect is one that professor of public policy Susan Herbst calls "incivility as strategy" in which public actors may use ethically suspect tactics to create disruptions or impede meaningful discussions.[10] Purposefully incendiary comments from radio and television personalities come to mind as a broad example, but we think, too, of the so-called Brooks Brothers riot during the 2000 presidential election vote recount. As the country waited weeks to learn the results of the initially inconclusive election—which hinged on the outcome in the state of Florida—some citizens started shouting outside an office in the Miami-Dade county polling headquarters, where a vote recount was underway. These protesters, whom the *Washington Post* later identified as "mostly Republican House Aides from Washington," hoped to stop the recount, and as police tried to disperse the crowd, the protest turned violent. Critics of the protest alleged that some of these staffers were paid for their efforts to stop the recount, and Al Kamen of the *Washington Post* reported that three of the protesters later received positions in the Bush-Cheney administration.[11] When politicians or their employees purposefully employ discourse or actions to impede the democratic process, we may need different approaches to public discourse and democratic participation.

Marketing Ideas Rather Than Working toward Compromise

Third, the political arena has, in many ways, become a "subset of marketing."[12] Politicians (especially candidates) and their ideas are packaged and sold to an American consumer market. Rather than hear our civic leaders productively exchange ideas about particular public concerns, we are more often asked to judge them and their policy proposals through televised debates that reward one-liners (making that person the "winner"); the 30-second television commercials that advertise their family lives and values (with which almost no one disagrees); and memorable sound bites made for the press. Civic engagement becomes reduced to simply choosing which candidate to "buy" with your vote—and later to choosing which prepackaged policy to support when asked by an opinion pollster. As further evidence of this consumer model, note that companies and special interest groups hire lobbyists (akin to marketing firms) and form political action committees to help influence the outcome of elections or legislation. In the process, the public welfare becomes fragmented into the interests of competing groups, and individuals are reduced to passive consumers.

Reluctant Participation in Democratic Processes

Fourth, we have ourselves to blame. Those of us who live in a society that values democratic participation are often too passive; we sit back and watch as decisions are made for us. Many of us believe we are too busy to get involved or do not take the initiative to learn how to become engaged. We readily defer to experts and authorities in discussions of public concern, wrongly assuming their powerful positions or knowledge will somehow enable them to promote the public welfare better than the public itself. Or, as Pearce and Littlejohn note, when we do get involved in civic affairs, we copy some of the more destructive discourse practices we see so frequently. We wrongly assume that participating in a democracy means adopting a boorish persona, thereby replicating unproductive discourse in the public sphere.[13]

There are ways to speak much more productively to bring about the change we wish to see in our institutions and communities. *Education* in the public speaking skills that characterize productive discourse can allow us to correct these shortcomings in ourselves and, more specifically, in our democratic participation. The tools and perspectives you can acquire when studying productive discourse can enhance your knowledge of rhetoric and its relationship to public affairs; your ability to understand, evaluate, and respond to public arguments; and your ability to see through dichotomous thinking in order to seek out additional possibilities. The challenge, of course, is identifying and putting into practice the qualities of productive discourse that will lead to more functional democratic institutions. Many scholars and public thinkers have offered solutions to increase the quality of our public exchanges, and we outline these in the next section.

CHANGING OUR PUBLIC COMMUNICATION:
TOWARD PRODUCTIVE DISCOURSE

How do we, as participants in a communication-based democracy, reform practices of deliberation? We believe the solution starts among small circles of citizens, it starts with our own behavior as communicators, and it starts with our collective education as ethical public speakers. In this section we look more closely at how to implement these solutions.

Rethinking Public Discourse

In critiquing the way we tend to handle disagreements with each other, Deborah Tannen contends that "we, as a society, have to find constructive ways of resolving disputes and differences. Public discourse requires *making* an argument for a point of view, not *having* an argument—as in having a fight."[14] We agree that there is value to debate that thoughtfully and responsibly examines policy issues in ways that assist public deliberation, but we also insist, following Tannen's point, that an approach to public speaking that stresses commonality can help community members find ways to understand and resolve differences. We believe that there are times and places where agonistic, or argumentative, thinking is not only necessary but also productive. For this reason, chapter 13 highlights argumentation and reasoning as tools for discovering the flaws in another's line of argument and offering your audience a compelling alternative. Nevertheless, we believe that debate is neither the only way, nor always the best way, to attend to shared concerns in our government and our communities.

So, how can we speak to understand, work to build relationships, and contribute to problem-solving rather than polarization? To begin with, we can think of public discourse as a space designed *for* respectful explorations of disagreement so that we can understand the reasoning behind different opinions; only then can we make judgments about what is best—most just—for the community as a whole. We advocate ethical rhetorical practice as part of our system of productive discourse in the pursuit of an engaged, civil society. It is a pursuit with deep classical roots, as professor of rhetoric Takis Poulakos explains when he writes that the ancient Greek teacher of rhetoric Isocrates believed "the art of rhetoric was called upon to address and resolve problems of division and unity, fragmentation and consolidation, diversity and cooperation." Isocrates worked to "disassociate rhetoric from its reputation as a tool for individual self-advancement and to associate rhetoric instead with social interactions and civil exchanges among human beings."[15]

We often say that rhetoric and democracy developed together in ancient Greece precisely because democracy *needs* rhetoric to function effectively. When we, with Isocrates, see rhetoric as the central tool for facilitating social interactions and common interest rather than self-advancement and self-aggrandizement, we begin to practice the art of productive discourse. Let's look, then, at the specific qualities that distinguish productive discourse.

Qualities of Productive Discourse

There are many ways we might alter our communication behaviors to engage others rather than automatically argue against them, to be open to new ideas, and to embrace possibilities before advocating solutions. Productive discourse might mean showing a greater understanding of the power of *narrative* in conveying personal experience and in understanding the experiences of others. It might mean approaching public discourse not as an attempt to prove the superiority of your views but as an invitation to consider your ideas—an invitation that, from the perspective of communication scholars Sonja K. Foss and Cindy L. Griffin, is based on principles of equality, value, and self-determination. Or it might mean approaching communication agonistically but with trust, courtesy, and in the service of learning.[16]

In his work on deliberative democracy, political theorist Benjamin R. Barber advances "Nine Characteristics of Civility" to encourage public behaviors that will improve democracy. While Barber adopts the term "civil talk" to describe the communication behaviors he wishes to highlight, we recognize the elements of what we call "productive discourse" in his nine characteristics of civility. For Barber it is important to understand that civility "is not about politeness; it is about *responsibility*."[17] We agree that this emphasis on responsibility in discourse is essential for teaching ethical public speaking. Ethical public speaking is not about avoiding conflict; it is about being responsible in your public discourse, being responsible for the accuracy and impact of your claims, being responsible to your audience, and being responsible to your community.

To demand that we practice productive discourse is an important but tricky proposition in the current rhetorical landscape of our democracy. The emphasis on productive discourse is not intended as a politically correct band-aid or as a way to limit communication, although undoubtedly it can be strategically construed this way (e.g., one might refused to engage a viewpoint or a claim on the grounds that its expression violates the expectations of productive discourse). Instead, as we discussed previously, productive discourse is public speech that is responsible to one's community and manages differences constructively. It requires active democratic participation through talking *and* listening, it reflects sound reasoning, it pursues multilateral problem-solving, and it relies on ethical standards of communication and interaction. It is focused on ideas, not personalities, and it is respectful but not compliant, meaning that it has learning and the public good among its highest ideals. As Barber elaborates on the contours of civility, we can identify behaviors and practices that are at the core of productive discourse, at the core of ethical public speaking: commonality, deliberation, inclusiveness, provisionality, listening, learning, lateral communication, imagination, and empowerment. We briefly paraphrase each of Barber's qualities of civil talk—what we call productive discourse—in Box 2-2, and then we add a tenth quality.

BOX 2-2

Qualities of Productive Discourse

From Benjamin R. Barber

- *Deliberation:* Such discourse does not shut down possibilities but critically engages the arguments and positions rather than the people themselves. It seeks and can accept critique. It can see multiple solutions rather than needing a singular outcome.

- *Inclusiveness:* Productive discourse builds discussions that are multivocal rather than two-sided. It seeks dissenting voices and is aware of the many ways voices are silenced in communities and in conversation. It acknowledges variety within a given opinion or position and offers empathy to other participants.

- *Provisionality:* This approach to communicating among publics recognizes that conclusions are never final because ideas, insights, and possibilities will evolve within the process of public discussion. It remains open to further consideration, reflection, and new ideas.

- *Listening:* Productive discourse recognizes that it is as important to have an *ear* as to have a voice. It therefore attempts to hear and understand alternative perspectives and to incorporate those perspectives into the whole. Participants are reluctant to interrupt each other, and they reference and directly respond to each other's points—which helps conversation build momentum.

- *Learning:* The purpose of this discourse is to better understand the issues, the multiple perspectives, and the people involved. Such speech does more than express fixed opinions or mediate between viewpoints that never alter. Participants may change their minds and approach the rhetorical situation willing to make accommodations based upon what they hear and learn.

- *Lateral communication:* Productive discourse is owned by the community as a whole. It originates and evolves among members of the public who talk to each other in spontaneous, un-orchestrated settings. As opposed to conversation between leaders and those who most closely follow them, this form of communication circulates among community members and is multidirectional rather than one-way.

- *Imagination:* This method of communication depends upon participants who seek creative ways of approaching and rethinking the issues at hand. Imaginative thinking extends to the whole community, not just those most like or most familiar to participants. Discourse is marked by impromptu moments, breakthroughs, and/or fresh ideas as opposed to predictable talking points.

- *Empowerment:* The goal of productive discourse is to enable people to *do* something positive and effective for the community. Productive discourse is not an end in itself. Its results are collaboration, problem-solving, and the achievement of common goals.

SOURCE: Benjamin R. Barber, "Civility and Civilizing Discourse," *A Place for Us: How to Make Society Civil and Democracy Strong* (New York: Hill and Wang, 1998), 114–123.

To Barber's list, we add *trust*. While you might recognize that trust is necessary to sustain any of the nine qualities of productive discourse in Box 2-2, it would probably be irresponsible to leave it as an unstated assumption. Productive discourse exhibits trust by assuming charity toward others. It also assumes general goodwill on the part of participants rather than listening to them with suspicion, assuming they are speaking from a hidden agenda. When we exhibit trust toward others, we are more likely to listen honestly to them, to see things we have in common, and to willingly collaborate with them to reach shared goals.

SPOTLIGHT ON SOCIAL MEDIA:
Keep It to Yourself? Politics on Facebook

Is Facebook a place to engage in political debates? Some users think so. Yet many other users do not. No matter where we fall on this question, social media sites like Twitter or Facebook make it easy to "turn off" voices we don't want to hear by simply unfriending someone or unfollowing someone's feed. Have you ever been tempted to do this?

We may decide to hide or silence people whose views differ from ours in our news feeds for a few different reasons. Maybe we disagree with a friend's politics. Maybe we just don't like to hear so much about politics in a space that is supposed to be more private or personal than sites like Twitter. During the 2012 presidential election cycle, college sophomore Sean Bergan, 19, told reporter Rex W. Huppke, "I've unfriended people on several occasions. . . . Especially if they're so extreme to one side or the other. I like to consider myself moderate. You just don't want to be seeing that stuff three times a day in your own news feed."

Or maybe we unfriend people because we believe sharing similar political opinions is a key component of friendship. Political elections may allow us to discover things about Facebook friends that we didn't know before, and it becomes harder to remain friends once we have made these discoveries. But perhaps hiding the political opinions we disagree with on Facebook lets us avoid one of the real gifts of friendship: the chance to see something from another perspective and to recognize that perspective has a human face. Communication professor Glenn Sparks told Huppke that on Facebook "It's so much easier to say, 'I don't like what you're saying so I'm just going to ignore it.'" The risk in this approach, however, is that it "takes away the need for us to listen to others and the intellectual exercise of reacting to opinions that conflict with our own."[18]

For similar reasons, psychology professor Matthew Lieberman urges readers to refrain from unfriending people over political elections. In an article for *Psychology Today*, he writes:

> When I teach social psychology each fall, I always talk about our inborn tendency to think those who disagree with us have something wrong with them because they fail to see reality for what it is (we call this naïve realism). Comedian George Carlin once pointed out that for most of us, "people driving slower than you are assholes and people driving faster than you are idiots." People who aren't doing what we're doing must be crazy, mean, stupid or biased—one of those almost always applies.[19]

To counteract this inborn tunnel vision, Lieberman argues that we need to engage with people who hold different viewpoints if we want to practice the skill of seeing things—including ourselves—from other people's points of view. In a thriving democracy, we need to think about and reflect on difference—rather than simply unfriending it or unfollowing it.

As you reflect on your engagement with social media, think about friends whose views differ from yours.

Discussion Questions

- Do you work, consciously or unconsciously, to promote a range of opinions on your Facebook page?

- What are potential reasons to be concerned about the use of social media in civic engagement?

- How might we use social media differently if we actively applied some of the qualities of productive discourse outlined in this chapter?

Of course, the exchange of productive discourse is not easy, quick, or even very exciting when compared to interactions marked by unproductive discourse. It requires charity and graciousness toward fellow community members with whom you may severely disagree, and few models of such interactions exist in the media or our everyday lives. If we are willing, however, to devote the time and energy required to learn these skills of democratic participation, then we will find that the benefits are numerous. To begin, we become more truly educated about the important issues that affect our lives by recognizing their complexity and uncertainty and the multiple options available. Such understanding means we can make better, more informed decisions about these pressing issues. In addition, productive discourse helps bring us together as a community. We become more imaginative—able to see past ourselves and those most like us to the lives and concerns of others. We are likely to leave an exchange with a more sympathetic understanding of where someone else is coming from and with a stronger sense of what we hold in common. Finally, productive discourse inspires and enables ordinary individuals not only to make better decisions but also to act on them. Rather than sit on the sidelines and watch other people fight it out or make our policies for us, we are more likely to get directly involved to solve the issues that concern the public and improve our communities. Consequently, because of its numerous positive outcomes, we consider productive discourse a much more responsible, and promising, form of communication than unproductive discourse.

UNPRODUCTIVE DISCOURSE
AND THE ROLE OF SOCIAL PROTEST

Before we leave the topic of productive and unproductive discourse, however, we would be remiss not to acknowledge the relationship between unproductive discourse and the rhetoric of social protest. It is important to note that a frequent critique of those who speak out against established and powerful institutions is that their speech or actions are "uncivil." In other words, their symbolic action (verbal or nonverbal) resembles what we have called "unproductive discourse" throughout this chapter. Those who challenge the established order may use speech that displays such characteristics as distrust, lack of listening, combativeness, and a focus on winning. And they may do so because it is one of their only routes to protest and social change.

How can we distinguish, then, between the speech that challenges and confronts but leads to significant social change and the unproductive discourse that stalls democracy? One answer may be whether such discourse aims to include or exclude members of the public from democratic participation. We might ask *who* is labeled as a practitioner of uncivil discourse. Does this speaker represent a section of the public that holds power or is denied power in the civic arena?

Although in a democratic society community members are supposed to gather as equals, many scholars have pointed to the ways in which reality often fails to meet that ideal. Not all members of a democracy have equal access to the public sphere. In response to Habermas's notion of the public sphere, for instance, philosopher Nancy Fraser has argued that such gatherings of citizens have historically been created through the exclusion of some members of society, such as the poor, women, and children. Exclusions from the public sphere continue to exist, even if they are subtler than the open discrimination of America's past. Given the many ways communities can express disapproval, discomfort, or simply fail to consider full inclusion, it is more difficult to participate in civic affairs if you are poorly educated, undocumented, transgendered, or a minor. Getting involved means drawing public attention to yourself and—just as importantly—knowing the codes and norms of participation. Some people are excluded because they do not speak the language or know the grammar that marks one as a participant and a member of the public. To account for these and other concerns of exclusion from the public sphere, Fraser recognized the existence of what she called subaltern **counterpublics**, gatherings of people excluded or dissuaded from the public sphere who raise and discuss issues ignored or trivialized by the broader public and form responses to discourse produced in the public sphere.[20] While members of counterpublics find affirmation and a sense of belonging among other members of a counterpublic, these groups also have important political potential. They may learn and teach methods of challenging their exclusion. The problem, of course, is that such methods of challenge and resistance may include actions and discourse that those in power label as "uncivil."

Social Hierarchy and Policing Discourse

Scholars and activists have noted that those in positions of power or privilege have historically used accusations of incivility as a policing discourse. **Policing discourse** aims to censor the speech or actions of others, and this censorship is frequently

Audre Lorde (1934–1992), the daughter of Caribbean American immigrants, was a writer, teacher, and activist. She often described herself as "a black feminist lesbian mother poet."

accomplished by calling another's words inappropriate—whether misinformed, too angry, poorly timed, or aimed at the wrong audience. Contemporary professors of communication Anna M. Young, Adria Battaglia, and Dana L. Cloud succinctly explain this tactic: "With the invocation of civility, calls for change are muted in favor of the status quo."[21]

Those who call for changes to the status quo are often labeled as radicals and criticized for their angry speech. In an effort to defend the productivity of some angry speech—and to give voice to subaltern counterpublics—the twentieth-century poet, professor, and activist Audre Lorde gave an address to the National Women's Studies Association Conference in 1981 that she titled "The Uses of Anger." Lorde noted that our culture has frequently branded public expressions of anger— particularly when those public expressions come from women—as inappropriate, but she argued, "We cannot allow our fear of anger to deflect us into settling for anything less than the hard work of excavating honesty." Lorde challenged her audience to listen to the content behind anger because, she said, the object of such expressions of anger is change. In this case, Lorde suggests that some speech may be both angry and productive. It is angry because it originates from women whose voices and experiences have been excluded from the public realm, not because it seeks to exclude or stall the political process. While Lorde's speech certainly made some audience members uncomfortable, we should recognize that it is itself a call for productive discourse, specifically, for meaningful dialogue among women about racism. She told her audience:

> The angers between women will not kill us if we can articulate them with precision, if we listen to the content of what is said with at least as much intensity as we defend ourselves against the manner of saying. When we turn from anger we turn from insight, saying we will accept only the designs already known, deadly and safely familiar. I have tried to learn my anger's usefulness to me, as well as its limitations.[22]

"When we turn from anger we turn from insight," Lorde writes. Are those who label speech as "uncivil" actually trying to silence expressions that expose something uncomfortable or unjust in the current public realm? Do they turn from learning when they dismiss angry discourse as uncivil or unproductive? In Lorde's speech, productive discourse and uncivil speech are not incompatible; rather, she suggests the speech we typically label "uncivil" may actually be a catalyst for positive change. Lorde challenges her audience to set aside their impulses to police this rhetoric until they have examined whether its content has social value.

Social Protest as Political Strategy

Audre Lorde's speeches contain echoes of other transformative twentieth-century leaders who publicly spoke out against injustice and made many uncomfortable in the process; for challenging the status quo, their speech and actions were called uncivil— and worse. For example, in 1963, Martin Luther King Jr. went to Birmingham, Alabama, to support local organizations that were protesting racial segregation and the Alabama leadership that perpetuated it. King was jailed for his role in the protest, and eight white clergymen wrote an open letter published in the local newspaper which criticized King for leadership that disturbed the peace. Because King was a resident of Atlanta, Georgia, the clergymen accused him of being an outside agitator, coming in to cause civil unrest. King's response to these critics is known as the "Letter from Birmingham Jail," and it is a model of productive discourse and a masterpiece of ethical rhetorical persuasion. The letter, however, offers a defense of the words and actions that may be labeled uncivil when a counterpublic is engaged in social protest. King, in fact, defends the creation of tension and carefully orchestrated misunderstanding in order to prompt social change. We might say the letter—like Lorde's speech—employs productive discourse to defend unproductive discourse. Consider King's argument in the following passage:

> I have earnestly opposed violent tension, but there is a type of constructive, nonviolent tension which is necessary for growth. Just as Socrates felt that it was necessary to create a tension in the mind so that individuals could rise from the bondage of myths and half truths to the unfettered realm of creative analysis and objective appraisal, so must we see the need for nonviolent gadflies to create the kind of tension in society that will help men rise from the dark depths of prejudice and racism to the majestic heights of understanding and brotherhood. The purpose of our direct action program is to create a situation so crisis packed that it will inevitably open the door to negotiation. I therefore concur with you in your call for negotiation. Too long has our beloved Southland been bogged down in a tragic effort to live in monologue rather than dialogue.[23]

The "monologue" King refers to in this final line is the monologue of the powerful. It is the absence of dialogue between those who hold power and those who are excluded from democratic participation. There is no way for the oppressed to ask for inclusion through the productive discourse used by those in power; the oppressed have not been taught to speak this language, nor are they invited to the public sphere where discussions of shared concern take place. In this case, King argues, social protest and what some may see as uncivil discourse are the necessary routes to social change.

Reaching similar conclusions, professors of communication Nina M. Lozano-Reich and Dana L. Cloud have noted that while ethical, productive discourse is certainly valuable, those who promote this type of civic engagement frequently *assume* that all participants are equal in economic, political, and social status. There is a problem with this assumption because "the powerful rarely are willing to invite those less powerful into dialogue; the oppressed are hard pressed to convince oppressors who benefit materially from oppression to be open to dialogue, let alone radical change. Many discussions are by 'invitation only,' a phrase suggesting that invitation belongs to those who set the rules for exclusion."[24]

When we examine the arguments of scholars like Dana Cloud and Nina Lozano-Reich, together with the work of social critics like Nancy Fraser, Audre Lorde, and Martin Luther King Jr., we are cautioned not to uncritically promote productive discourse and denounce unproductive discourse. In doing so, we might fail to consider whether we eliminate participants by assuming the equality of all persons, believing in the access of all persons to public conversation, or demanding that each speak in a manner we find acceptable. People with high levels of education or powerful connections (or both) can often leverage language in a way that makes people with less education or less power appear ignorant, misinformed, or unreliable. Such moves shut down participation and serve the interests of the status quo by making protestors feel un-welcome, uncomfortable, or inarticulate. True inclusion does not leave one group to set the terms and name the participants of debate; sometimes it takes social protest to force us to remember this fact.

As you continue to study the qualities of productive discourse and to develop your skills in deliberation, do not overlook the silent and the vocal ways the discourse of others can be policed. Ask yourself, do calls for productive discourse include those who are often left out of this decision-making process? Do the methods of deliberation assist those included in, but also marginalized by, the public? These are questions we hope you will debate with your classmates, as well as questions we hope you will keep in mind as you're working to promote civic engagement in your many public relationships.

SUMMARY

This chapter has outlined the contemporary state of our public discourse and has distinguished between the qualities of unproductive and productive discourse. It addressed both the obstacles to effective public discourse and the potential for reviving our democracy that we access when we change the way we speak with one another and are attentive to whom we include and exclude in such conversations. In this chapter you have learned:

- Public discourse today is largely problematic. It frequently features qualities we associate with unproductive discourse, partly due to the obstacles that prevent speakers from engaging in more productive forms of communication.
- While unproductive discourse can be sensational and entertaining, its growth has resulted in lower participation in democratic institutions and organizations at all levels of society (local, regional, and national).
- Unproductive public discourse is characterized by the following features: division, dichotomous thinking, combativeness, certainty, lack of listening, winning, distrust, hierarchical communication, and dogmatism.
- Obstacles to productive discourse abound. They include the news media's pressure to entertain and constantly generate new content; the need of elected officials to keep themselves and their ideas in the spotlight; and the inertia or disillusionment of many everyday people who choose not to become involved and change our public conversations.
- Productive discourse is public speech that is responsible to one's community and manages differences constructively. It requires talking *and* listening, it reflects sound reasoning, it pursues multilateral problem-solving, and it relies on ethical standards of communication and interaction.
- The demand for productive discourse is about making arguments but not about picking fights. Such speech results when we commit to the values of commonality, deliberation, inclusiveness, provisionality, listening, learning, lateral communication, imagination, and empowerment. All of these values are more readily enacted when we approach participants with trust.
- While productive discourse is the goal and ideal, it is important to recognize that we often assume that all people living in a democracy have equal access to

civil talk; this is not the case. Key conversations are often by invitation only or effectively silence those who do not speak according to the rules (whatever those often unstated rules may be).

- Uncivil discourse can play a key role in social movements. Those who speak out against the status quo are frequently accused of uncivil speech, but this accusation can be an effort to police—that is, silence—the efforts of the disempowered to work for the common good. We must, then, be willing to listen to and evaluate the *content* of the speech labeled uncivil to determine whether it is working to include or exclude individuals in the democratic process.

KEY TERMS

counterpublics p. 32

policing discourse p. 32

public discourse p. 21

productive
   discourse p. 20

public p. 20

public sphere p. 20

unproductive
   discourse p. 19

REVIEW QUESTIONS

1. What are some reasons unproductive discourse is a popular means of public conversation?
2. What is the public sphere, and how is it related to public discourse?
3. What are the central qualities of unproductive discourse?
4. What are the qualities of productive discourse?
5. What is policing rhetoric? At whom is it usually directed?

DISCUSSION QUESTIONS

1. Who are examples of public figures that practice productive discourse? Can you think of examples of public figures or public discussions that reflect unproductive discourse?
2. Do you agree that in our contemporary culture we seem to rarely see and use productive discourse? Why do you think this is?
3. How do the speech by Audre Lorde and the letter from Martin Luther King Jr. support or contradict the goals of productive public discourse outlined in the rest of this chapter?
4. What are the positive and negative impacts of productive discourse? What is gained or lost with its use?
5. Can you think of a contemporary counterpublic? Is this counterpublic a source of empowerment or isolation? How is the counterpublic included or excluded from public discourse? Explain.

CHAPTER 3

The Ethics of Public Speaking

Chapter Objectives

Students will:

- Explore the meaning of ethics and ethical codes.
- Understand the ethical responsibilities of preparing to speak in public.
- Practice the ethical communication behaviors expected of public discourse.
- Enact the obligations of ethical listening.

Every spring thousands of schools—high schools, colleges, universities, and others—have graduation exercises that feature commencement speeches. To be invited to deliver such an address is an honor, an opportunity, and a responsibility. The speaker is asked to enter a community to provide future inspiration or to give voice to a relevant civic challenge. Even more daunting is to be selected as a representative of a community, to be the voice of your classmates, reflecting on where you have been and where you might yet go, separately and collectively. Understandably, a prospective speaker might look into the vast ocean of previous commencement addresses for guidance and inspiration. Examples litter the Internet, from those delivered by the well-known and stately to scores of YouTube postings of the anonymous, curious, and cringe-inducing. Certainly there is no harm in examining how others have approached this familiar yet challenging rhetorical situation. In fact, it makes sense to investigate the genre before embarking on a speech outline. One might discover an ingenious theme, locate a clever reference, or learn "what not to do." Take a few notes from this speech, "copy and paste" a paragraph from that speech, and before you know it, you have a page or two of promising ideas. However, what is the distance between cultivating a promising idea based on your study of other speeches and plagiarizing their content?

In March 2010, prominent Filipino businessman Manuel V. Pangilinan, the chairman of the board of trustees at Ateneo de Manila University (ADMU), delivered a commencement address to the university's School of Social Sciences and School of Humanities that seemingly crossed the line, although he may have been caught unaware. Within days of delivering his address celebrating ADMU's 150th graduating class and receiving an honorary doctorate, it was discovered that sections of Pangilinan's speech closely matched commencement addresses delivered by the likes of J. K. Rowling, Oprah Winfrey, and Conan O'Brien. After studying the similarities between his speech and others, Pangilinan offered a public apology for presenting a speech that "had been borrowed from certain other graduation speeches." Pangilinan said, "I am truly regretful" and, in a letter to the university that offered his retirement, admitted that the episode "has been a source of deep personal embarrassment."[1] A year later, graduating law school student Preston Mitchum delivered the student body commencement address at North Carolina Central University's School of Law. Mitchum offered a well-received reflection on "the triumphs of being average, not exceptional." Unfortunately, the address used segments of Anthony Corvino's humorous and introspective commencement speech from Binghamton University the previous year. The act produced a harsh rebuke from the law school dean, who expressed his "disgust" and "shock." Mitchum, who had intended to acknowledge Corvino's speech—and had even shared his speech in advance with Corvino through Facebook—apologized and said, "I feel terrible and I know this is going to have a horrific backlash."[2] Only a few weeks later the University of Alberta's medical school dean Philip Baker delivered a speech to his institution's medical graduates that mimicked portions of an address given by Dr. Atul Gawande to Stanford University's medical degree recipients, which was reprinted in the *New Yorker*. When students brought forward the similarities between the speeches, Dr. Baker admitted he was inspired by Dr. Gawande's speech, said he had intended to acknowledge Dr. Gawande's address, and offered his "sincere and heartfelt apology" for what he called a "lapse in judgment." The controversy did not end with the apology; a few days later Dr. Baker resigned as dean of the medical school.[3]

These examples illustrate that ethical lapses in public address do occur and that such lapses can have significant consequences. With so much information readily available at our fingertips, it is only too easy to commit significant acts of academic dishonesty, whether it is the result of less than precise note taking, a failure to attribute critical information, or willful deception. The prospect of such transgressions—and their consequences—explains why ethics is a topic of central concern and much confusion in the realm of public speaking. We admit ethical questions and dilemmas are not always easy to evaluate, but we also hold that there are recognized practices that should govern our speaking and listening behaviors and that provide ethical expectations for public speaking. In this chapter, we consider ethics from three dimensions: the ethics of speech preparation, the ethics of speech performance, and the ethics of listening. However, first, we consider the meaning of ethics and, in particular, the rhetorical ethics of public speaking.

ETHICS AND RHETORICAL ETHICS

The term **ethics** is generally associated with the field of philosophy and can be defined as a set of moral principles governing human action or conduct as it pertains to motives,

ends, and the quality of one's actions. The ethical quality of an action or conduct is generally evaluated based on how it reflects what is deemed "good" or "bad" or "right" or
"wrong" in a culture. We frequently use criteria such as honesty, morality, equality, and
justice that are derived from influences including culture, religion, upbringing, and
community and institutional contexts to judge the ethics of a practice or behavior.[4]

Ethical Codes

A more specific articulation of ethics is an **ethical code**, a set of rules or guidelines
agreed to by a culture or group in order to regulate behavior. For instance, the
American Medical Association (AMA) has a "Code of Medical Ethics" that sets out
values and principles for the medical profession and is deemed to be the "authoritative
ethics guide for practicing physicians." To be sure, the code is debated. For instance
the ethical code prohibits euthanasia and physician-assisted suicide, both of which
are the subject of professional and public dispute. Regardless, the code provides a set
of principles physicians are expected to adhere to in their professional conduct and
can be the basis for sanctioning members who violate those principles.[5]

Similarly, many college communities operate under their own code of ethics. The
Virginia Military Institute (VMI) has one of the most historic ethical codes in higher
education in the form of its honor system. As the VMI website explains:

> The heart of VMI's student government is the honor system. Although honor, like
> many idealistic concepts, defies exact definition, it clearly refers to relationships
> which govern society and which yield to the members of that society immediate and
> tangible benefits. The honor system at VMI is not so much a set of rules—although
> rules are published and distributed to every cadet—as it is a way of living. Lying,
> cheating, stealing, or tolerating those who do are considered violations of the Honor
> Code. A cadet's statement in any controversy is accepted without question as truth-
> ful; examinations are not proctored; the word "certified" on a paper means that the
> work is the cadet's own and that the cadet has neither given nor received help.[6]

While such codes provide guidance to communities, inevitably there is the need to
clarify their meaning and, often, debates over their interpretation and enforcement.
VMI has contributed to the discussion of ethical codes and ethical living with an
annual Leadership Conference dedicated to discussing topics such as how to build
and strengthen honor codes in high schools, colleges, and universities.[7]

As a college community engages in public discussion of the merits of various acts
committed on a campus and their relationship to their accepted code—the ethics of
underage drinking and the expectations of good spectator behavior are but two possible examples—it is deliberating over the character of the institution. Such discussion is valuable, even necessary, for a community as it sets the expectations for both
personal conduct and public discourse, and does so in a communal fashion. Yes, there
are sources of authority who influence the outcome of discussions (medical review
boards, the dean of students), but the conversations themselves prompt reflection on
the wisdom and virtue—*on the ethics*—of our actions.

The difficulty in identifying a singular, universal ethical code is that as individuals and communities we have different worldviews, experiences, and values; behavior
that is accepted and expected in one community may be out of bounds in another.

And actions that we would readily dismiss as unethical in the abstract—lying for instance—might be more complicated when put into specific contexts. The point is that ethical standards are community standards and, thus, we can expect disagreements about their meaning. That does not mean that all actions are acceptable or defensible, only that ethical evaluations are based on many factors.

Rhetorical Ethics

While no single, widely known code of rhetorical ethics exists on the level of the AMA's "Code of Medical Ethics" or a school's code of conduct, we can identify communication behaviors that are deemed acceptable and unacceptable. **Rhetorical ethics**, or the ethics of public speaking, refers to the behavioral expectations we have for communication exchanges that bond speaker and audience in the shared consideration of a topic that affects the public good. Examining the history of rhetoric, scholar James Herrick identifies a set of ethical goods inherent to rhetorical practice: "(1) discovering truths and arguments relevant to decision-making on contingent issues, (2) advocating, interpreting and propagating ideas before publics, and (3) testing propositions in debate." Thus, the virtuous—or ethical—rhetor "exhibits regard for people as givers and hearers of reasons, respect for the argumentative context, and attending virtues such as rhetorical persistence."[8] Adherence to these practices enriches our public discourse. Moreover, it reflects the principles of productive discourse discussed in chapter 2. Specifically, we contend that rhetorical ethics involve the preparation of public speakers, the actions of speakers in presenting information, and the listening behaviors of audiences.

THE ETHICS OF SPEECH PREPARATION

The consideration of rhetorical ethics begins far before a speaker stands in front of an audience. That is, it is not measured only on the basis of what a public official says to a constituent or what a school administrator says to a student; instead, the chain of events that brings forth an ethical evaluation begins with the speech preparation process. This includes the commitment a speaker shows to an audience through preparation as well as the ethical choices made in the selection of information. While the next section discusses the latter topic, here we consider the ethics of speech preparation.

The Deceptively Hard Work of Speech Preparation

One of the challenges to understanding the complexities of public discourse is that when done well, public speaking looks deceptively easy—it is "just talking" after all. Apart from the person who develops the speech, few people have true appreciation for how difficult it is to craft a successful presentation—the time it takes to develop the main idea, do the research, choose the language and tone, practice the delivery, and so forth. In fact, one might say we are trained to *not* notice these efforts. Few football coaches give the sort of refined inspirational speech offered by Denzel Washington's Coach Boone on the field of Gettysburg in *Remember the Titans*, and few debate coaches are as precise and lyrical in their speech as Washington's Professor Tolson in *The Great Debaters*. In a different context, we have noted that when our students have the opportunity to watch a real legal proceeding, one of their consistent reactions (generally voiced as criticism) is that the attorneys are not flawless; they do not sound like the prosecutor from *Law & Order*. These polished images make the task of speakers we witness in person all the more challenging. When attending public lectures on your college campus, you probably have noticed that many speakers rely extensively on notes or even use a full manuscript. You are justified in desiring more eye contact and interaction from such speakers. But that a likely expert on a topic relies so much on his or her text is also a reflection of just how difficult a public speaking situation can be, particularly one in which specific terminology is important.

The point is that preparing a speech is hard work. Denzel Washington is an effective actor because he has honed his craft over many years. A politician gives an effective "stump speech" on the campaign trail because it is often a variation of a speech that she or he has given time and time again. A classic example is "The Speech" given by Ronald Reagan between 1964 and 1966 as he rose to national prominence as a conservative political voice. Over the course of 15 months, Reagan gave a variation of his standard speech more than 150 times; it developed into the basis of his California gubernatorial candidacy.[9] With such practice Reagan came across as a master presenter. We are not suggesting that the accolades were unwarranted, only that they were achieved after a significant investment of time and effort.

Ronald Reagan campaigning in 1966.

Before concluding that such effort, and success, is reserved for actors or politicians, consider the speech preparation process of the late Steve Jobs, cofounder and chief executive officer of Apple. Before his death, Jobs was a highly anticipated and captivating business speaker and his "tech-talks" were "must-see TV" for computer geeks and investors alike as he introduced new products and updates. Watching Jobs, one might note his easy extemporaneous style, his eye contact, the engaging gestures, and the integration of his content with his visual aids. And while he had a tendency to pace, it fit the persona he developed.[10] In his appearances at the Macworld Expo, for example, Jobs appeared casual and relaxed, perhaps giving the impression that he had not prepared very much or was not trying very hard. On the contrary, this was part of the appearance Jobs worked diligently to cultivate. Mike Evangelist, a former associate of Jobs at Apple, explains that Jobs started preparing for his keynote addresses *weeks* in advance, not just developing his speech but also reviewing all the products and technologies that might be relevant. Evangelist says that Jobs would go through multiple dress rehearsals that focused on every conceivable element. Evangelist explains his personal experience of watching this process before one of Jobs's speeches.

> "It was fascinating to watch. No detail was overlooked: for example, while rehearsing the iDVD demo, Steve found that the DVD player's remote control didn't work from where he wanted to stand on the stage. The crew had to make a special repeater system to make it work."

Then, once all the details were in place, Jobs would do one to two full-dress-rehearsals that gave the presentation his complete focus.[11]

Speech Preparation as an Ethical Demand

What Washington, Reagan, and Jobs have in common is that they take their development of public discourse, their speeches, *their work*, very seriously. They are responsible to their audience; they are *ethical* in their preparation. The idea that speech preparation is not only important but also truly an ethical demand for speakers was well explained by professor W. Norwood Brigance in a public speaking textbook chapter entitled "Four Fundamentals for Speakers."[12] In his direct and challenging style, Brigance set out high expectations for speakers, making it clear how much work is required and why the work is necessarily an ethical concern: "Effective public speaking is a technique, as definitely as are the techniques of designing airplanes and removing appendixes, except that it is older and more complex than either."[13] How can Brigance make such a claim—that public speaking is more complex than the precise calculations required for keeping an aircraft in flight or the delicate movements necessary in surgery? His point is that there is not a single, rote method for speechmaking, nor is there an equation available to insure success. With so many human factors and variables, public speaking requires constant revision and adaptation.[14] To be sure, natural ability is an asset, but you must also have training; no pocket guide or YouTube video claiming you can master public speaking in "Ten Easy Lessons" can teach you the range of speaking situations and ethical concerns one might face in the public sphere. Instead, as Brigance counsels, "Public speaking . . . requires an expert method of procedure. Do not look for short cuts."[15]

BOX 3-1

Ethical Preparation

Elements of ethical preparation are addressed across this book, including instruction on research, reasoning, outlining, and delivery. However some of the practices that demonstrate ethical speech preparation and that will prepare you for a public presentation include:

- Advance planning: Begin working on your speech well in advance of its due date, at least one week, longer for lengthier and more significant presentations.

- Information selection: Research your ideas, and select your supporting material carefully.

- Note taking: Take careful notes while researching in order to keep track of sources, catalogue Internet URLs, and to be sure to properly attribute information.

- Revise and refine: Engage in revision, and refine your ideas as you develop the presentation.

- Practice: It is essential that you practice your presentation multiple times before giving it to a public audience.

- Earn the right to speak: Give your best effort in preparing the speech.

- Responsible and respectful: Make your message meaningful to your audience out of respect for their time.

Another Brigance maxim to which we subscribe is his belief that a speaker "must earn the right to give every speech." The point is that while many people "like to talk" or "like to debate," they overlook the responsibility that comes with the opportunity. Cutting right to the point, the cantankerous but insightful Professor Brigance gives a dose of indispensable advice:

> A good part of every college speech course is wasted by students who try to speak without earning the right. Their technique is feeble, their discipline of ideas is flaccid—the stuff is simply not there—not because they are beginners and not because they cannot learn or have no talent, but because they do not put forth the effort. Months go by, and a large part of the course is gone, and yet they have not learned one simple fundamental—that a speaker must earn the right to give every speech.[16]

Brigance's point, which we hope you will take to heart, is that when you are given an opportunity to speak, it comes with a concomitant *responsibility*, an ethical responsibility, to take the occasion seriously, to treat your audience respectfully, and to come prepared to offer your audience something important and meaningful. See Box 3-1 for advice on practices important to ethical speech preparation.

THE ETHICS OF SPEECH PERFORMANCE

We began this chapter with three instances of ethically suspect choices by public speakers. These real examples troubled their audiences because each speaker gave the impression that the ideas and words being presented were his own. Occurring as they did during commencement exercises, the speeches came with perhaps even higher expectations for ethical conduct, conduct fitting for a learned audience and in an educational setting. But why does it matter if the speech used was not invented by the speaker? And does it really change the message or how an audience should understand and respond to the rhetoric? Yes, it very well might.

The Ethics of Public Influence

Perhaps *the* central reason rhetorical ethics are important is that audiences make decisions based on the public discourse they experience. We form judgments based on listening to commencement speakers, watching the nightly news, reading a trusted information source on the Internet, even when making travel decisions after seeing a forecast from the local meteorologist. In each case rhetors communicate information to the public that is used in decision-making: How can I give back to society? Which candidate should I vote for? What can I do about environmental problems in my community? Is it safe to travel today? Public rhetoric—*your rhetoric*—has consequences for which you are responsible, and, thus, you have an ethical duty to your audience.

While it is less well-known than the AMA and less familiar to you personally than your college's ethical code, the National Communication Association (NCA) has adopted a Credo for Ethical Communication (see Box 3-2). With a membership of more than 8,000 communication scholars and practitioners, NCA is the most influential communication organization in the United States. While the credo extends beyond the confines of public speaking, it provides a useful perspective on ethical communication behaviors.

BOX 3-2

NCA Credo for Ethical Communication

(Approved by the NCA Legislative Council in 1999)

Questions of right and wrong arise whenever people communicate. Ethical communication is fundamental to responsible thinking, decision making, and the development of relationships and communities within and across contexts, cultures, channels, and media. Moreover, ethical communication enhances human worth and dignity by fostering truthfulness, fairness, responsibility, personal integrity, and respect for self and others. We believe that unethical communication threatens the quality of all communication and consequently the well-being of individuals and the society in which we live. Therefore we, the members of the National Communication Association, endorse and are committed to practicing the following principles of ethical communication:

We advocate truthfulness, accuracy, honesty, and reason as essential to the integrity of communication.

We endorse freedom of expression, diversity of perspective, and tolerance of dissent to achieve the informed and responsible decision making fundamental to a civil society.

We strive to understand and respect other communicators before evaluating and responding to their messages.

We promote access to communication resources and opportunities as necessary to fulfill human potential and contribute to the well-being of families, communities, and society.

We promote communication climates of caring and mutual understanding that respect the unique needs and characteristics of individual communicators.

We condemn communication that degrades individuals and humanity through distortion, intimidation, coercion, and violence, and through the expression of intolerance and hatred.

We are committed to the courageous expression of personal convictions in pursuit of fairness and justice.

We advocate sharing information, opinions, and feelings when facing significant choices while also respecting privacy and confidentiality.

We accept responsibility for the short- and long-term consequences for our own communication and expect the same of others.

SOURCE: National Communication Association. Credo for Ethical Communication. 1999. http://www.natcom.org/uploadedFiles/About_NCA/Leadership_and_Governance/Public_Policy_Platform/PDF-PolicyPlatform-NCA_Credo_for_Ethical_Communication.pdf

You should quickly recognize that the qualities endorsed in the NCA credo have been promoted in the opening chapters of this book. And if you review the practices of productive discourse from the previous chapter, you will see a close connection between those practices and the expectations set out for ethical communication by the NCA. Before moving on, however, let's more closely consider the meaning of ethical conduct in public speaking contexts.

Ethos and Five Ethical Practices of Public Communication

When focused exclusively on the act of public speaking, be it to your classroom audience or another community, there are five ethical practices that deserve additional attention: plagiarism, ethical research, sound reasoning, respectful language, and taking responsibility for consequences. In each case, a violation results in a loss of ethos. **Ethos** is one of the three modes of proof, used in the service of invention, identified by Aristotle. It refers to the state of one's public character or persona—what we commonly call credibility. In the context of public speaking, ethos involves a listening audience's perceptions of a speaker's goodwill, trustworthiness, competence, and dynamism.[17] As listeners, one of the ways we determine how much merit to place on a speaker's message is by assessing credibility: Does the speaker seem honest and of high integrity? Does she—by reputation and performance—demonstrate herself capable? Does she demonstrate care and concern for the audience? Is her performance engaging? All of these components have ethical implications; although, understandably, it is the expectation of trustworthiness that is most often invoked in ethical evaluations.

Avoiding Plagiarism

Certainly the most commonly recognized ethical responsibility of a speaker—or a writer, or a student—is to refrain from plagiarism. **Plagiarism** is the unacknowledged use of another's words and ideas as one's own. As a college student you should understand the importance of original work that is free of plagiarism as well as the broader meaning of academic dishonesty, which includes various forms of cheating. Original, ethical work is expected from you because it is fundamental to learning (you cannot learn if you only reproduce the work of others) and it is a core component of honesty. In codifying such expectations, your school has likely adopted a "rule of conduct" or policy on plagiarism and academic dishonesty.

In a public speaking class, it constitutes plagiarism if you submit as your own a speech, outline, or paper prepared by someone else. Plagiarism also includes using language and ideas developed by another source without appropriate citation. Submission of such work is contrary to academic principles because it thwarts the process of education and is dishonest. Even if you develop delivery skills through the performance of someone else's work, you cannot learn about the speech-making process and all of its complexities, ranging from topic selection to thesis development to research to argumentation, nor can you engage in the internal dialogue necessary to prepare for public deliberation.

Plagiarism is not only a concern in the classroom but in society as well. As the chapter introduction suggests, a number of public figures, from politicians to academics, have been accused of plagiarism. That such instances occur underscores that it is incumbent upon speakers and writers to carefully document their sources and to not use the work of others as their own. Failing to do so can have devastating consequences and creates the need for public explanations and apologies. In July 2014, the *New York Times* reported that Senator John Walsh (D-MT), an Iraq war veteran who was seeking election to a full Senate term, had plagiarized significant portions of his final project for a master's degree from the Army War College. Analysis conducted by the *Times* revealed that between a quarter and a third of Walsh's paper was plagiarized. Walsh relied on sources without attribution and used other sources verbatim but without supplying quotation marks to indicate such use. Within weeks of the report, Walsh ended his Senate campaign and shortly thereafter the War College rescinded his master's degree. In response, Walsh issued a statement indicating, "I apologize to all Montanans for the plagiarism in my 2007 paper, and I am prepared to live with its consequences."[18] Another widely publicized example of plagiarism involved *Time* columnist and host of CNN's "Global Public Square," Fareed Zakaria. In 2012, in a column he wrote for *Time*, Zakaria inadvertently plagiarized a segment of material from a piece Jill Lepore wrote for the *New Yorker*. Zakaria explained that he had confused notes he had taken on Lepore's article with notes he had taken from an original source used in Lepore's story. Zakaria subsequently apologized and called his actions "a terrible mistake" that were "a serious lapse and one that is entirely my fault." *Time* responded by accepting the apology while restating its ethical expectations: "TIME accepts Fareed's apology, but what he did violates our own standards for our columnists, which is that their work must not only be factual but original; their views must not only be their own but their words as well. As a result, we are suspending Fareed's column for a month."[19] These examples demonstrate the importance of taking care during the research process in order to prevent plagiarism and also the consequences of such acts.

Ethical Research
The plagiarism examples in this chapter also illustrate failings of ethical research and, most specifically, proper practices for using supporting materials. While these ideas

are addressed with additional depth and from another angle in our discussions of research (chapter 4) and reasoning (chapter 13), here we are interested in how source use involves important ethical considerations. So while ethical research implicates issues of plagiarism—for instance not citing sources or giving the impression that the ideas or words of others are your own—it also extends to the larger realm of academic dishonesty based on how research is gathered and credited.

One of the most common issues faced by speakers is how to give proper credit to sources. In written work there is the expectation that we use formal modes of documentation ranging from in-text acknowledgement of a source to endnotes to bibliographies. Given that an oral presentation is a different format, there is sometimes confusion over how to approach such issues. However, the basic expectation is that materials that merit citation in written form also merit citation in an oral form. Chapter 4 specifically addresses how to orally cite research and more thoroughly addresses its importance. Keep in mind that all sources, in a complete form, should appear on any outline you have prepared, and you should be able to supply source information to audience members on request. Ultimately, a good rule of thumb is that when you are uncertain if material needs to be cited, err on the side of inclusion and provide a verbal acknowledgement.

Beyond citation there are three additional ethical issues related to the interpretation and use of sources: do not overstate or manipulate evidence, do not fabricate evidence, and do not suppress counterarguments. As a speaker you must represent evidence accurately rather than manipulate it to fit your desired conclusion. This is part of establishing public or audience trust as the information conveyed can influence decision-making. Moreover, even if you are confident evidence exists, you must not take a shortcut by inventing what you know—or *think* you know. Instead, you must locate credible evidence for the idea and use it. If you cannot locate the evidence, then the legitimacy of your assumed conclusion is also in doubt. Finally, it is to your advantage to acknowledge counterarguments and opposing evidence rather than ignore them. This is important because it allows a community to thoroughly consider policy options, particularly since some in your audience are likely aware of such evidence. You will be unable to persuade a knowledgeable audience without addressing these competing ideas, and your credibility will suffer. It is through addressing counterevidence that you can supply important analysis and refutation that can ultimately strengthen your case.

Practicing Ethical and Sound Reasoning

A third ethical responsibility for speech performance is that we make reasonable claims supported by evidence. It is important that we supply the basis of our argumentation rather than rely on assertion. An **assertion** is a claim that lacks an evidentiary basis and is offered without reason, support, or data. Relatedly, we must balance appeals to **pathos**, more commonly called emotional appeals, with the use of reason. Pathos refers to the psychological state of the audience and rests upon a speaker's effective, ethical appeals to its emotions and motivations. However, to rely exclusively on pathos in ways that deter critical thinking is unethical. For instance, to ignore the facts of a situation in favor of preying on audience fear is considered unethical because it encourages audiences to forgo reasoned analysis.

Ethical Language Use

Fourth, as a speaker it is your responsibility to respect your audience through your language use. Keep in mind that words are crucial to our understanding of the world and help construct identities. Through our words we can bring a community together to pursue improvements or our rhetoric can be divisive and hinder such progress. Think about competing ways to discuss substance addiction, transgender persons, or national identity and ethnicity. Our language can be constructive and inclusive in advancing dialogue, or it can severely undermine it. Therefore, it is important to avoid rude, vulgar, sexist, and racist language as we treat audience members humanely.

Ethical language is accurate and reflects the preferred identity of those included in the discussion. Using oppositional, charged, or derogatory language contributes to the creation of damaging perspectives on the world and of individuals. Sexist language excludes a portion of your audience and does so in a way that creates negative perceptions based on sex, but it is easily avoided. Similarly, to use racist language is to deny the importance and value of members of our community. The labels, metaphors, and euphemisms that are used to characterize groups of people make it easier to dismiss them, and sometimes to even forget their humanity. Certainly we might inflict such impacts unintentionally but to do so willfully is to deny and damage identity, can reinforce stereotypes, and is purposefully disrespectful. The ethical speaker thinks about the context within which he or she is communicating, attempts to avoid charged language, and discusses people and objects in appropriate and neutral terms.

Being Responsible for the Consequences of Your Rhetoric

Finally, the ethical speaker considers and accepts the consequences of his or her rhetoric and rhetorical choices. Remember, people base decisions on what you say. Therefore, you must consider the consequences of your message for them and their lives. Just as we expect that investment advisors have training and act ethically in their dealings, we expect public speakers who advocate actions and policies to behave similarly. A spectacular example of an "investment advisor" who acted fraudulently is Bernie Madoff. Thousands of investors lost billions of dollars when they gave Madoff control of their assets. While they assumed the monies were being invested, Madoff was actually keeping many of the assets. There were devastating consequences for investors with many losing a good portion or all of their life savings. A public speaker may not stand to eliminate an audience member's retirement nest egg, but the point is the same: there are consequences to what we say, and we must consider those consequences in forming our message.

There are, no doubt, other ways a speaker can fail to satisfy his or her ethical obligations, but these five ideas are at the core of ethical speaking behavior. A speaker must not plagiarize. A speaker must be careful to engage in ethical research. A speaker must rely on sound reasoning in advancing conclusions. A speaker should use respectful language. And a speaker must own the consequences of his message. As a checklist, prior to giving a presentation, review your speech preparation and message to see that it reflects these practices of ethical communication.

====================== **BOX 3-3** ======================

Practicing Ethical Communication

- Respect the audience by *preparing thoroughly* for your presentation.
- Recognize the *responsibility* of public speaking—decisions are made based on what you say—by accepting the consequences of your claims.
- Be *truthful* and *honest* in your communication.
- Be *accurate* and *careful* with your claims and evidence.
- Do not *fabricate* or *misrepresent* evidence to bolster your claims.
- Practice sound *reasoning*.
- Do not *degrade*, *disrespect*, or *intimidate* the audience through your language choices.
- Do not use irrelevant *character attacks*.
- Do not use irrelevant or excessive *emotional appeals*, particularly emotional appeals that lack evidence or overwhelm reason.
- Do not conceal your self-interest or a conflict of interest.
- Do not take credit for the ideas of others; instead, acknowledge your sources.
- Do not submit the work of others as your own.

SOURCES: Several concepts drawn from the NCA Credo for Ethical Communication; and Richard Johannesen, *Ethics in Human Communication*, 4th ed. (Prospect Heights, IL: Waveland Press, 1996).

THE ETHICS OF LISTENING

The third key component of public speaking ethics is listening. At first glance you might question how a listener can be ethical—it is the speaker, after all, who prepares the speech, not the listener. However, speech-making is a transactional act *between a speaker and an audience*. Thus, by listening to a speech you are participating in it. You do that through your feedback to the speaker, but also through how the information impacts your communication. That is, if we listen actively, if we interpret and respond to information, we as listeners also participate in the speech act. We might do this by participating in a discussion that follows a speech. Or perhaps we do this by using the knowledge we gain from the presentation to enrich our education and abilities to participate in public dialogue.[20] For this reason, listening is also an ethical enterprise. Just as there are ethical responsibilities for the speaker, because he or she is conveying information that influences audience decision-making, an **ethical listener** demonstrates responsibility to the speaker and to the society in which we live through *how* he or she listens. Here we consider the ethics of listening by considering active listening, listening to improve as a speaker, and the qualities of ethical listening.

Active Listening

Communication scholars sometimes lament that listening is a "lost art." Perhaps this is related to changes in public communication and public dialogue. You might recall from the previous chapter the notion that citizens have been transformed from participants into spectators of the public dialogue. Thus, if we are to reinvigorate democratic practices, if we as individuals are to meaningfully participate in the political and civic world, we need to avoid the tendency to be passive recipients of information. Instead we must strive to always practice active, engaged listening.[21] When we say that an ethical listener practices **active listening**, we mean she participates in the speech act by listening closely, critically, and constructively. That is, an active listener concentrates on what the speaker is saying, thinks about and reflects on the meaning of the speaker's content, and focuses on the potential of the message rather than on merely tearing it down.

Listening to Improve as a Speaker

As a developing speaker it makes sense to focus your listening on your improvement as a speaker. By listening to *how* others present speeches, you can improve your speech technique. Concentrate on the speaker's structure, development of the argument, and use of quality sources. However, also reflect on speaking techniques; that is, think about common strategies used to introduce and frame the topic, how the speaker modulates his voice for emphasis, and how she engages her audience.[22] By listening attentively we can analyze the speech technique in ways that provide us understanding of the speech *and* can improve our abilities as speakers. We can do this regardless of the topic of the speech or its occasion. We can always listen to improve our own speaking performance.

Qualities of Ethical Listening

There are several characteristics and qualities of good, ethical listening. In suggesting a set of such qualities we are indicating a broad skill-set that should be employed by listeners. Situational factors—such as the goals of the message and the occasion—determine which qualities are most important in a given case, but all the characteristics have a role to play in virtually any setting. Listening qualities or postures that encompass the ethical demands of listening include possessing an ethical listening attitude, providing appropriate attention, and practicing message evaluation.[23]

Ethical Listening Attitude

A key ethical demand in listening is to approach a speaking occasion with an appropriate attitude. An **ethical listening attitude** consists of a positive disposition in which you approach discourse with an open mind and without fixed opinions. Doing so allows you to undertake appreciative listening, makes you available for empathetic listening, and orients you toward listening that is learning focused. **Appreciative listening** is an attitude that allows us to enjoy a presentation and its aesthetics. We can and should appreciate, even be inspired by, a well-crafted speech when its style and the spirit of its message are pleasant to the ear.[24] This is only one element of an ethical attitude toward listening, and by itself appreciative listening is not ethical listening; equally important is the practice of empathetic listening.

BOX 3-4

Practicing Ethical Listening

As a listener there are several behaviors and actions you can undertake to be more ethical. These include:

- Listen to learn: Approach the speech as a learning opportunity.
- Provide feedback: Respond to the speech with positive nonverbal feedback to show your engagement.
- Listen actively: Stay mentally alert and engaged with the message.
- Listen to improve: Think about how the speaker can assist you in improving your speaking technique.
- Listen with appreciation: Enjoy the speaker and her message.
- Listen with an open mind: Be receptive to the message.
- Listen empathetically: Try to see the message and point from the speaker's perspective.
- Take notes: Stay engaged by writing down key ideas from the presentation.
- Create a speech outline: Chart the speaker's structure, including noting key sources and supporting material.
- Compose questions: Be prepared to engage the speaker in discussion.

Empathetic listening is ideally suited to deliberative practices as it considers "the humane aspects of public issues." As communication scholars Michael Osborne and Suzanne Osborne explain, this listening quality encourages a "closeness" between the listener and speaker and a concern "for others in the immediate or larger cultural audience, who might be affected by his or her words."[25] This characteristic of listening reflects that we are open to change, that we respect and value the speaker, and that we have a sense of social responsibility that extends beyond self-interest.[26] Think for a moment about a situation you have experienced in which the speaker or members of the audience were radically different than you. For instance, perhaps you are from an urban area, and you are listening to a speaker advocate rights for wildlife enthusiasts to hunt and fish in certain areas and using means that you lack experience with and are inclined to reject. You lack a personal connection to the topic, but empathetic listening allows you to see the issue from the speaker's view. Or imagine being a burgeoning small-business owner engaged in a community discussion about zoning, one that could potentially adversely affect your ability to place your business in a particular location. Empathetic listening means working to understand the issue from the perspective of those who support zoning regulations, despite your personal interest. Practicing empathetic listening means, as best we can, seeing the world through the eyes of another and feeling as they do.

Listening to Comprehend and Retain Information

When we say ethical listening requires attention, we are underscoring the practice of active listening but doing so in the context of listening that seeks to comprehend and retain. Thus, attention in listening enables learning and prepares us for the deliberative process by providing us with relevant resources for discussion. It is only by comprehending an issue—be it the presentation by the wildlife enthusiast or the discussion of zoning—that we will be able to intelligently participate in its discussion in the public sphere. Similarly, through retention we are able to carry the issue forward into later discussions and to deftly incorporate new information with our existing knowledge of a public issue.

As listeners we can adopt habits and exercise techniques that will test and improve our attention. Being prepared to listen, being appropriately focused on the speaker and his or her message, is a starting point. We also aid attention and retention by taking notes—outlining a speech and its key ideas, identifying key sources worth remembering or consulting later, and even composing questions. Subsequently, we can check our listening during discussion through paraphrase ("Did I understand you to mean . . ." or "Is it your contention that . . .") and through questioning.

One of the challenges for speakers and audiences today concerns the effective, ethical use of electronic devices. Tablets and laptops can allow for effective and efficient listening in the form of note taking and interacting with supporting materials. However, these same electronic devices—as well as smartphones—create listening challenges too. A room full of laptops creates obstacles to speaker-audience intimacy as listeners can hide behind screens and type on keyboards. Likewise, they create temptations, as do smartphones, to surf the web and frequent social media sites. Speakers and listeners must increasingly work together in navigating the potential and problems of such electronics. As Table 3.1 suggests, the ethics of using these devices is often situational and governed by the conventions of the speaking environment and

Table 3.1 Electronic Devices and Listening: What Are the Ethics?

Should you use a tablet or laptop while listening to a presentation? Is it ever okay to access your smartphone while listening to a speaker?

POTENTIALLY PRODUCTIVE USES OF ELECTRONIC DEVICES IN A SPEAKING SITUATION	UNPRODUCTIVE USES OF ELECTRONIC DEVICES IN A SPEAKING SITUATION
• Note taking • Fact checking • Interacting with supporting materials • Looking up the meaning of terms used in the talk • Tweeting feedback—increasingly conventions and workshops assign official hashtags to inspire participant communication and some even project Twitter feeds during talks or in common spaces	• Web surfing • Checking and composing personal e-mails • Checking and posting status updates on social media sites • Gaming • Smartphones that beep or ring during presentations—even loud vibrations from hard surfaces can be disruptive

We should be mindful that use of electronic devices, even use that we think is discreet (such as looking at a cell phone under the table) can often be seen by the speaker and can disrupt audience members. Give speakers your attention out of ethical responsibility and respect, and also so you can effectively retain and evaluate information.

purposes of use. Remember, when speaking and listening in an educational setting such as a classroom that you want others to listen to your speech—and you should extend equal respect by listening to their speech. It is an ethical responsibility that you listen rather than engage in superfluous use of electronic devices.

Listening for Message Evaluation

A final component of ethical listening is message evaluation. **Evaluative listening**, also called critical listening, means thinking critically about a speech's content and testing its claims in order to form judgments about its ideas. In this type of listening, we practice critical thinking by evaluating the argument and evidence; we assess source credibility; analyze reasoning patterns and consider logical fallacies; and begin to form our own perspectives on the issues that have been presented.

You should recognize that these three core ethical listening qualities correspond with elements of productive discourse discussed in chapter 2. That is, it is important that a participant be receptive to the possibility of change by having an open mind in first considering a question of public concern (e.g., an ethical listening attitude). The weighing of options and the full consideration of an issue requires that one supply fixed attention in order to understand the issue. Finally, once one has considered the public benefits and costs of an idea and sufficiently studied the issue, one is ready to reach a critical judgment and one is prepared to offer evaluation.

SPOTLIGHT ON SOCIAL MEDIA:
Ethical Listening in the Electronic Age

We've all seen it—the well-intentioned electronic discussion board that erupts into a vicious free-for-all that focuses on personalities rather than issues. What obligation should online discussion participants have to be respectful and civil? And what challenges to listening are posed by these instant, distant, and often anonymous reactions on message boards? Author Jonah Lehrer's February 2013 appearance at the Knight Foundation's "Media Learning Seminar" provides an excellent entry point into the consideration of such issues.[27]

In 2012 questions arose about some of the work produced by Lehrer, a prominent blogger and writer who frequently addressed subjects at the intersection of science and culture. Lehrer faced accusations including plagiarism, fabrication of quotations, and recycling past work (what some also call self-plagiarism). Investigations verified many of the charges with the result being that Lehrer lost his staff positions and a publisher recalled unsold copies of two of his books.[28]

Speaking at the Knight Foundation's "Media Learning Seminar," Lehrer addressed a live audience while the event also streamed over the Internet and was open for comment from viewers around the world. The subject of Lehrer's talk was the neuroscience of decision-making, with much of it focusing on his own situation. Included in the presentation was a list of rules—standard operating procedures—that Lehrer said he needed to follow in his writing, while he also admitted that these rules are considered common journalistic practice for many.

While Lehrer serves as another example of a public figure who violated ethical expectations for public communication and was left to deal with the consequences, what makes his example interesting is the unique elements of the setting. While he spoke on the Knight Foundation stage, Lehrer was flanked by two large projection screens, one of which continually scrolled tweets that reacted to his speech in real time. Most of the comments were critical of Lehrer.[29]

Brooke Borel @brookeborel · 12 Feb 2013
Don't understand why Lehrer needs a set of special rules. Just follow one simple rule of journalism: tell the truth. #infoneeds

🔁 4   ⭐ 2   •••

Mario Christodoulou @Mariocracy · 12 Feb 2013
@jonahlehrer's public display is definitely a good deterrent for plagiarism/fabrication #infoneeds

🔁   ⭐   •••

Sara Morrison @SaraMorrison · 12 Feb 2013
It's weird. I don't need to put a list of rules in place in order to not plagiarize or make stuff up in my writing. #infoneeds

🔁 1   ⭐ 2   •••

Paul Goldsmith @PaulJGoldsmith · 12 Feb 2013
Twitter's new era of awkward: People tweeting insults on big screen behind author @jonahlehrer while he apologizes for lying. #infoneeds

🔁 17   ⭐ 4   •••

Heather SouvaineHorn @heathershom · 12 Feb 2013
so unseemly #infoneeds MT @DKThomp: Lehrer is apologizing next to a live Twitter feed of people mocking him - a town square flogging

🔁   ⭐   •••

Lehrer's experience underscores some of the ways public communication and the act of listening are changing in the age of social media. Lehrer was simultaneously speaking to a live audience and being subjected to instantaneous responses from viewers watching his talk live online. Further, the archival of Lehrer's talk as a perpetually available reminder of his ethical lapse and the real-time responses of scores of online viewers underscore how notions of audience, listening, and feedback are also undergoing serious transformation. Not only does one no longer need to be present to watch a speech in real time—which, of course, hasn't been a requirement since the creation of radio and television—but now one can provide instant feedback. This both has the ability to expand opportunities for listeners to participate in the public dialogue and creates questions about the role and responsibilities of the listener in the media age.

Discussion Questions

- How do real-time tweeted responses to Lehrer's message change the nature of communication interaction or help us understand it differently?
- Did Lehrer's online listeners behave ethically?

These and other questions are ones that speakers and listeners will grapple with as communication channels and the means of instant feedback multiply.

SUMMARY

This chapter has explored the importance of rhetorical ethics in maintaining the reputation of rhetorical practice and making public deliberation possible. Public speaking ethics include the ethics of speech preparation, the ethics of speech performance, and the ethics of listening. Specifically, in this chapter we have observed:

- Ethics and ethical codes are used to evaluate our actions and behaviors.
- Rhetorical ethics provide guidelines for the practice of public communication.
- A casual attitude about ethics has profound implications of a personal and public nature. Ethical faults lead to negative personal evaluations and a loss of ethos, thereby damaging one's personal and professional opportunities.
- There are significant public implications to unethical behavior including poisoning public discussion, making reasoned decision-making more difficult, and leading publics toward unwarranted conclusions.
- Sound rhetorical ethics begin with the speech preparation process as we earn the right to address audiences by being prepared, well informed, and practiced.
- Ethical speaking behavior also means being mindful of our conduct as a speaker and, in particular, avoiding plagiarism, practicing ethical research, bringing forward reasonable claims that are supported by evidence, treating audiences with respect, and taking responsibility for the consequences of our rhetoric.
- Rhetorical ethics demand ethical listening. As audiences of public discourse, it is our dual responsibility to respect the speaker and to openly, carefully, and critically consider his or her message.

KEY TERMS

active listening p. 50
appreciative listening p. 50
assertion p. 47
empathetic listening p. 51
ethical code p. 39

ethical listener p. 49
ethical listening
   attitude p. 50
ethics p. 38
ethos p. 45

evaluative listening p. 53
pathos p. 47
plagiarism p. 45
rhetorical ethics p. 40

REVIEW QUESTIONS

1. What are ethics? What is rhetorical ethics?
2. What is ethical speech preparation?
3. What are your primary ethical concerns in speech preparation?
4. What is plagiarism?
5. What is ethos, and its component elements?
6. What are qualities of ethical listening?

DISCUSSION QUESTIONS

1. What is your school's code of ethics? What obligations and responsibilities does it create for community members?
2. What is your school's plagiarism or academic honesty policy? How is your work in public speaking related to that policy?
3. What can you do to be a more ethical speaker?
4. How can you be an ethical listener? What practices can become commonplace in your listening efforts?
5. Why can ethical, active listening be difficult? What are obstacles to ethical listening?
6. How common is unethical communication? Where is it most prominent or frequent?
7. How is ethos developed, and what might we do to repair or improve our ethos if it has been damaged in the eyes of an audience?

CHAPTER 4

Conducting Credible
and Effective Research

Chapter Objectives

Students will:

- Understand the importance of sound research for civic engagement and communal problem solving.
- Distinguish between researching as a mode of inquiry versus researching as a strategy.
- Explore a wide range of sources for their research.
- Conduct an interview effectively.
- Improve efficiency when searching the Internet for sources.
- Assess the value and reliability of sources.
- Accurately document sources in their speeches and bibliographies.

When Adam Phipps, a college senior theater major enrolled in a public speaking class, watched his friend throw away another water bottle, he knew he had to do something. He was tired of witnessing his friends, classmates, and teachers regularly trash empty plastic bottles and used paper rather than recycle them. As president of his fraternity, Adam had tried to convince his brothers to recycle their paper, bottles, and plastics, but with little success. Why didn't his peers and the college faculty recycle more? How did his school compare to other colleges when it came to recycling? Adam thought there were recycling options on campus for many of the items being thrown away, but he wasn't entirely sure. Where were the recycling bins, anyway? he wondered. He decided to give a speech advocating recycling, but knew he needed to find some answers first.

Perhaps you are in a situation somewhat like Adam's. You need to develop a speech and have a few ideas about what to say. But you don't know enough about your topic to speak for more than a minute or two. And why should an audience accept

Adam Phipps Delivers His Speech, "Recycling at Wabash" for the Baldwin Oratorical Contest at Wabash College, 2011.

your opinions or observations as valid? This situation calls for **research**, the process of learning about a topic by discovering what credible sources have said or written about it. The best speakers find, incorporate, and cite trustworthy information and arguments by outside sources. They use these sources to help form and ultimately support their opinions and observations. Strong research sets apart powerfully compelling speeches from merely interesting or entertaining ones.

Good research also improves civic engagement and aids productive discourse. At a minimum, it enables you to speak accurately; you avoid basing presentations on unproven assumptions, guesses, hearsay, or stereotypes. At most, research helps you to better understand complex topics. You discover multiple perspectives, including several you may not have previously considered or appreciated. Consequently, you can help your community more fully comprehend the complexity of the issues facing it. Finally, good research gives you an appropriate way to critically examine, and even refute, alternative positions. Whether you are speaking or listening, research focuses your attention on ideas rather than on the people advocating positions. Such effort enables you to interrogate the credibility and validity of opinions and information as you construct a speech or thoughtfully respond to someone else's address. For all these reasons, this textbook assumes effective civic engagement requires community members like you to locate, evaluate, and cite strong sources.

To help you conduct credible and effective research, this chapter will teach you how to utilize a wide variety of sources, schedule and conduct interviews, access online sources efficiently, evaluate sources using four criteria, and accurately document your sources. As this long list of topics and the length of this chapter suggest, adequate research involves multiple tasks and skills. We recommend you familiarize yourself with the chapter's content so you can return to it, as needed, as a resource to guide your research. We will begin by distinguishing between approaching research as inquiry versus approaching research as strategy.

RESEARCH AS INQUIRY VERSUS STRATEGY

To some of us, research means gathering several sources or Internet "hits" simply to fill a required bibliography. Or maybe it means strengthening your position by finding data and testimony to back it. Both of these ideas are overly simplified. Research means educating yourself. Recall we defined research as *learning* about your topic by discovering what credible sources have said or written about it. Notice the goal here is discovery, even if you have already determined the solution you like best. By approaching **research as inquiry**—that is, the process of studying a topic with the desire to learn—you leave yourself open to discovering perspectives and arguments you had not considered before.[1] Such new information will broaden and deepen your knowledge of the topic. It will also help you locate and advocate the most suitable way forward for your community. If you primarily approach **research as strategy**—that is, the process of studying the topic only to find sources and evidence that support your preferred solution—you close yourself off from potentially compelling reasons to reject or rethink your desired option. Remember your goal is to seek the best outcome for your community, not simply to win the debate.

When Adam decided to give a speech advocating recycling at his college, he needed to research why the current attempts fell short. Why did his classmates and teachers consistently throw away recyclable items? Why hadn't his recent attempts to engage his fraternity in recycling gone as well as he had hoped? He assumed his college community simply didn't care enough about the environment and waste management to recycle. Because Adam researched with a spirit of inquiry, however, he discovered widespread misunderstanding about what could be recycled, an underfunded campus program, and a sometimes poorly executed system rather than willful inaction. Had he only sought sources that proved the benefits of recycling, Adam would not have uncovered the complicated reasons why it wasn't happening regularly. He would have missed out on a much-needed opportunity to educate his audience instead of simply admonishing them about their lack of interest in recycling. We recommend you follow Adam's example of approaching research as inquiry as you look for sources related to your topic. In the next section, we provide an overview of the numerous, diverse types of sources available to you. Perhaps you will discover one or two you had not before considered exploring.

TYPES OF SOURCES

A far wider variety of sources exist than many students realize. We all know the familiar options: news outlets, books, blogs, and generalized knowledge bases. But have you considered also finding relevant scholarship, governmental texts, or legal documents? Finding public opinion polls related to your topic? Conducting interviews? We urge you to discover a diverse group of sources for your speech. Doing so will help you gain a deeper understanding of your topic and allow you to speak with more confidence. With a variety of sources, your audience will more likely perceive you as credible, improving the likelihood they will accept the validity of your observations and arguments. You will also make your speech more inclusive to diverse audience members. Different people in your community are likely to find some sources more credible and convincing than others. Long-time residents may perceive interviews with community leaders as most persuasive; teachers might prefer scholarly publications; and college students might favor firsthand accounts found in blogs. By utilizing multiple types of sources, you will do a better job of drawing in and educating audience members about the issue you are addressing.

So how do you find and access a diverse group of sources? If you haven't already, acquaint yourself with your college library and possibly with your local public library as well. Most libraries make recent, hard copy editions of newspapers, news magazines, and scholarly journals readily available for browsing. And accessing the library's vast print collections is typically as simple as learning the online catalog system. Perhaps your library's greatest asset, however, is its reference librarian—a specialist in library resources who can quickly guide you to credible sources on the Internet and in print. Whether you draw on the expertise of a reference librarian or not, we can help get your research started by considering below the benefits of discovering, and some ideas for accessing, generalized knowledge bases, news, scholarship and trade journals, books, government documents, legal texts, corporate materials, and people's experiences and opinions. We will begin, however, by encouraging you to think of yourself as a resource.

You as a Resource

When you start your research, your first instinct might be to dive into Google searches and news outlets—What does the *New York Times* say about recycling?—but instead you should begin with your own mind. You may already be aware of the topic in ways that can focus and guide your research. Sit down and type or write in single words or phrases what you already know and have experienced about the topic, and then list the sources you imagine will be most helpful in researching it.

If we consider Adam Phipps's recycling speech again, we can picture Adam writing down his observations of waste management on his campus; a reference to landfills in a textbook for a class; a recollection of a documentary he watched about the process of recycling; and then perhaps a list of sources to consult, such as the Sierra Club's website and *Newsweek*. Maybe Adam had heard about an organization that assesses campus sustainability efforts. Or perhaps Adam had a memory of a professor on campus who made art with discarded objects. Getting these thoughts down will help Adam avoid being overly influenced by the first handful of web links he happens to see in an Internet search. In other words, Adam's speech may not be about recent Sierra Club lobbying in Washington, DC (something a major newspaper or search engine may feature first) but about funding for a recycling program on his college campus.

General Knowledge

If, after writing down your thoughts about a topic, you find you know very little about it, then you should read generally about the issue using an encyclopedia or even an online source like *Wikipedia*. Obviously, for college-level writing and speaking, these general sources will not factor significantly in your research. Your audience will likely not see these sources as highly reliable. We will discuss concerns with credibility, particularly for *Wikipedia*, later in the chapter when considering criteria used to evaluate sources. Still, these general sources can help teach you the basics about your topic and point you to more credible and detailed sources through the citations and endnotes associated with an entry. The point is to not end your research with general sources. If you do, your listeners may dismiss your message because it is based on simplistic or superficial research. Popular general sources include Wikipedia.org and Britannica.com.

News

The news media provide excellent up-to-date information about various topics. News media sources include local, national, and international newspapers, news magazines, and television and radio broadcasts. News articles and broadcasts are typically written for a common audience with little to no previous knowledge about the topic. That makes them easy to read and incorporate into a speech.

Though most news outlets strive to present the news objectively, some are known to have a political bias (such as the conservative bent of FOX news and the liberal slant of MSNBC). Other news organizations report and analyze the news from an explicitly stated point of view, such as religious news periodicals (like *Christianity Today*) or political opinion magazines (like *New Republic* and *The American Spectator*). As we will discuss later in the chapter when we consider how to evaluate sources, bias does not disqualify a source from being used. Rather, when integrated with a diverse range of sources, biased sources can suggest that you are open-minded and inclusive—but only when you openly acknowledge the sources *as* biased. Therefore, you should know and tell your audience if you are using a news outlet that gathers and reports news from a particular perspective or else they may believe you are trying to manipulate or deceive them.

To locate a relevant news article or broadcast, search for news on the database LexisNexis or on the specialized sites Bing News, Google News, or Yahoo News, all of which are discussed later in the chapter. If you are seeking local news, go directly to the websites of your town or regional newspaper(s) and college paper, or look for print copies on campus or at your local grocery or convenience store.

SPOTLIGHT ON SOCIAL MEDIA:
Social Media Deliver and Shape the News

Social media sites are playing an increasingly significant role in how news is delivered and developed. According to the Pew Research Center's *The State of the News Media 2013* annual report, more Americans, especially young adults, are turning to social media for news. In 2012, the percentage of Americans aged 18 to 24 who reported seeing news on a social networking site "yesterday" nearly tripled (from 12% in 2010 to 34% in 2012).[2]

And news consumers aren't the only ones turning to social media. Journalists are progressively using social networking sites such as Facebook and Twitter to learn about breaking news—and to write their own stories.[3] Social media can help journalists find leads, sources, and reader-provided information.

Indeed, social media can turn anyone into a budding journalist. Network sites typically allow any user to post an update, comment, or picture without being filtered by an editor or reviewer. Such direct participation has enabled ordinary people to break news or aid developing stories. In 2011, when protests broke out in the Middle East in what has been named Arab Spring—a movement we discussed briefly in chapter 1—social network media sites functioned as a primary means of spreading information about the movement. According to researcher Ekaterina Stepanova, "Facebook reportedly outmatched Al Jazeera in at least the speed of news dissemination."[4]

The increased reliance on social media for news can be dangerous, however. Rumors and hearsay spread quickly, and even traditional news companies get fooled into reporting false information as true. After the 2013 bombings of the Boston Marathon, CNN and the Associated Press (AP) initially claimed both bombing suspects were in custody when one was still on the run.[5] And the social networking news site Reddit mistakenly misidentified a Brown University student as a suspect.[6] Similarly, after the 2012 Newtown, Connecticut, elementary school shootings, CNN and FOX News both incorrectly reported the suspect's brother as the shooter.[7]

Such misinformation not only misleads the public but can also devastate the victims who are wrongly accused. Sensational posts get reposted millions of times, quickly creating a witch hunt for the mistaken suspects. The Brown University student wrongly accused of the Boston Marathon bombings committed suicide four days afterward, possibly due to the anguish he experienced during that time.[8]

Discussion Questions

- How might social media sites aid your research?
- How can you prevent being duped by a false or misleading social media report?

Scholarship and Trade Journals

Scholarship consists of specialized publications (books or journals) produced by professional academics or researchers. Every scholarly field publishes multiple books and journals. For instance, the academic discipline of communication has over 100 journals devoted to its study, including *Quarterly Journal of Speech, Rhetoric & Public Affairs*, and *Argumentation and Advocacy*, to name just a few. Sources like these are highly credible because they are typically peer reviewed or edited, meaning knowledgeable people within the academic field have scrutinized the work before allowing it to be printed. Scholarly sources also tend to provide terrific depth on very specific topics. Consequently, however, they can be difficult to read. They often use highly technical or jargon-filled language, assuming readers possess previous knowledge about the field.

Trade journals are publications written by industry professionals about their business. For instance, trade journals for the news media business include publications such as *Columbia Journalism Review, Nieman Reports*, and *Broadcasting & Cable*. Such sources tend to be highly credible and up to date, and their output can vary from short news updates to longer, in-depth analyses. Because trade journals are typically written for industry insiders, however, they may assume readers have previous knowledge about the business and use technical jargon.

To locate a scholarly or trade journal or book, search your library's catalog or journal index. You might also use one of the databases or the specialized Google search called Google Scholar (scholar.google.com) discussed later in the chapter.

Books

Books cover a wide variety of topics and styles, ranging from fiction to nonfiction, persuasive to informational, and those authored by highly regarded individuals or groups to those produced by self-proclaimed experts. Many of the source types already listed can be published as books, such as generalized knowledge, news, and scholarship.

The length offered by books allows authors to provide extended treatments of their topics. A book, for instance, is more likely to include in-depth background information as well as consideration of many specific aspects of a topic. And the footnotes, endnotes, or bibliography provided in most books can guide you toward an additional set of sources. Finally, more reputable books—those printed by a credible publisher, such as a university press, that is very selective in what and how many books they publish—have typically undergone an intensive editing and/or peer review process, similar to journals. Such scrutiny makes their information and arguments more reliable.

We all know that many books are available in your academic library and local public library. Simply use the library's catalog system (typically online) to search for books on your topic. Then follow the classification numbers to locate them on a bookshelf. What you may not know is that once you have found a few relevant books near each other on bookshelves, you should look at the other nearby books. Library classification systems group books on the same subject together, so you can quickly find several useful sources that you may not have discovered otherwise.

Library Bookshelf with Books about US Immigration Grouped Together.

Whatever kind of book you want to include in your research, you may find it available online as an electronic book, or e-book. The full texts of many e-books are searchable online, making them a much easier and faster means for you to find relevant information. Most e-books require payment for you to download them to an electronic device. However, if you'd prefer to save money, you're in luck. Several sites offer free access to e-books, and they continually add to their collections. First, an increasing number of libraries (public and academic) lend e-books. Check the website of, or ask a librarian at, the local libraries where you have a library card to see if they lend electronic books. Second, Project Gutenberg (gutenberg.org) provides tens of thousands of free e-books that are searchable from its website. Third, Google has a specialized search feature called Google Books (books.google.com) that allows you to peruse many e-books for free. Fourth, several sites that sell e-books also offer some selections for free, such as Google Play (play.google.com) and the Kindle store on Amazon (amazon.com). Finally, all the databases mentioned later in this chapter include some e-books.

Government Documents

The government provides valuable, up-to-date information about a broad range of topics. Government sources are typically deemed authoritative because they include officials and agencies with the power to access, collect, and disseminate information. And so many government sources are available to you. Just think about how many governmental bodies exist. First, each state government and the federal government includes three branches—executive, legislative, and judicial. And the functions of each branch are often recorded and retrievable. For instance, you can read the laws passed by legislative bodies, and you can often study the debates over those bills and laws. Second, governments also function at the local level, from counties to townships or municipalities. These governmental bodies often include some type of elected board, counsel, or commission; mayor or other executive official; and other types of officials (such as treasurers, etc.). Each state handles its local government somewhat differently, but all local governments create documents you might find useful, particularly for local topics. Third, both state and the national governments have many departments and agencies that focus on particular topics, about which they produce a wealth of specialized and in-depth information. The US Department of Health and Human Services, for instance, concentrates on the health needs of Americans. It provides news, facts, and advice on health topics ranging from Medicare and health insurance to vaccinations and nutrition.

One of the best ways of searching all government sites—local, state, and national governments and agencies—is the US government's official portal: USA.gov. Among the helpful information this site provides is (1) a list of all government agencies, bureaus, and departments; (2) national (federal) government sites, including those devoted to each of the three branches of the federal government; and (3) state, local, and tribal government sites. The USA.gov site is exhaustive; spending just a few minutes on it will open your eyes to the plethora of governmental sources available.

Legal Documents

Legal documents include any written materials formally recognized as enforceable by a court of law. Such documents can include anything from a contract or deed to a marriage license or legal decision. Indeed, you may find the documents associated with a court case to be particularly useful when researching a topic. Levels and types of courts vary, but a single court case can produce many documents to process or try the case, such as materials produced by the prosecution and defense, amicus briefs (supporting testimony, opinions, etc. provided by a third party to the case), and the final judgment, to name a few. Two of the best ways to find legal documents are by using LexisNexis, a database discussed later in the chapter, and by searching the official Supreme Court website at supremecourt.gov. Alternatively, you can find expert legal analysis of Supreme Court cases and rulings, along with a few legal documents related to the cases analyzed, at SCOTUS blog (scotusblog.com). SCOTUS refers to the Supreme Court of the United States.

Corporate Materials

Most major companies publicize information about themselves, often in the form of public relations materials broadly (commercials, press releases, basic information) or those targeted at investors (investors relations information, annual reports). In addition, the United States Securities and Exchange Commission (SEC) requires public companies—those that make their securities (stocks, shares) available to the general public—to publicize information about their financial performance, company history, and organizational structure, such as in an annual (10-k) report. Finally, sometimes people associated with a company publish memoirs or autobiographies that reflect on their work with the company. You might find corporate materials helpful when researching how a company has aided or harmed a topic that concerns the community, such as the community's economic health, working conditions and compensation, local politics, and the environment.

You can often find corporate materials on a company's official web page. If the company is public, its website will likely include a link specifically for investors, or you can search the SEC's database called EDGAR at sec.gov/edgar/searchedgar/companysearch.html. According to the SEC, its database "allows you to research a company's activities, registration statements, prospectuses, and periodic reports, which include financial statements."[9] Alternatively, you can try using one of the databases or specialized searches available through Google (google.com/finance) or Yahoo (finance.yahoo.com), discussed later in the chapter.

People's Opinions and Experiences

Whatever your topic, you can find people who have already devoted considerable time thinking about it. A governmental official, a community activist, or the person down the street might have suffered the consequences of, or been working to improve, the issue you're addressing. They can contribute their experiences, stories, and opinions. In the process, you will gain additional perspectives, a feel for public sentiment, and personalized accounts of the topic. Interviewing is an excellent way to ascertain other people's opinions, and it will be discussed at length in the next section. In addition, several other kinds of sources convey people's experiences and opinions, including the following:

- Public opinion polls: Several companies and organizations survey large groups of people about various topics and then report the results. To locate a public opinion poll, try searching gallup.com or pewresearch.org.
- Social media: Many technologies qualify as social media, but some of the most popular are social networking sites such as Twitter and Facebook and weblogs, or blogs. A blog is a website that typically consists of a series of entries by a single author and is written in the first-person. Social media have exploded in number in recent years. As of 2012, Facebook claimed to have 845 million users, and Twitter claimed to have 140 million active tweeters.[10] The number of blogs worldwide reached 181 million by the end of 2011.[11] Social media can be used for multiple purposes, but many participants use the technologies to broadcast their opinions and experiences. To locate a relevant blog, find a specialized blog search engine such as blogsearchengine.org. To find helpful Facebook profiles, use any search engine to search for your topic and the word "Facebook." Keep in mind, though, that you sometimes have to be "friends" with someone to read their Facebook page, though that's less true of pages

created by organizations and companies. In contrast, Tweets are public. To search Tweets, go to twitter.com/search and use the search box provided.

- Other opinion sources: Most newspapers and news magazines include opinion sections where you can find opinion editorials (also called an "op-ed") and letters to the editor. There are also periodicals and websites largely devoted to expressing opinions and perspectives. To locate many of these sources, use the LexisNexis news search option discussed later in the chapter.

Hopefully this section has introduced you to, or reminded you of, numerous kinds of sources available for your research. We have included suggestions for where to find each source type on the Internet, and we will soon focus more specifically on how to search the Internet efficiently for appropriate sources. Before we do, however, we will more fully consider one of the best, but often overlooked, methods of obtaining information: the interview.

INTERVIEWS

One of the best ways to ascertain people's opinions and experiences is to interview them. Choosing a relevant person for your topic and interacting with him or her face to face or by phone or e-mail can provide excellent insights into your issue. You can solicit the precise kinds of information most useful to crafting your speech and form a new community relationship in the process.

Setting up and conducting an interview may seem like a daunting task. Who should you contact? What might you ask? Fortunately, by following a few simple guidelines, interviewing can be a relatively easy, fun, and effective way to research your topic.

Making a Contact

Consider your interviewing options broadly. Given your topic, would it be most helpful to talk with someone from another country? Another state? Or someone locally? We stress the value of initiating a local interview. Certainly interviewing someone internationally or nationally can provide very useful information and input. But part of becoming involved in your community involves learning who are the local experts. Whether you live in a small town or urban setting, you can find people nearby to contribute wisdom regarding your topic. Indeed, if you are addressing an issue impacting your community, then some people have likely already invested considerable time toward studying and improving it. They can often help convey the local impact of the issue, no matter how global its scope, and provide possible solutions your community might adopt to improve it. In the case of Adam's recycling speech, he discovered there was a local college group that had been trying to improve the campus-recycling program, a group called Students for Sustainability. He scheduled interviews with its president and faculty sponsor. In addition to learning about this group's initiatives, Adam found he could inform his audience about their work when he gave his speech.

To find a local person to interview, research your area. You might ask local community members (nonprofit organization participants, professors, coaches, religious leaders, etc.) for suggestions, or you can search the Internet for relevant groups and organizations by looking through the local Yellow Pages (yellowpages.com) or visiting your local visitors' bureau (possibly online, where you might find a list of local organizations). Alternatively, you might use Yahoo's specialized Local search tool, which you can find from Yahoo's home page by clicking on "More" and then on "Local." Once there, type in the name or zip code of your city and your search term. Finally, you can even use Google Maps to search for your town and then use the "Search nearby" hyperlink for the kind of organization or company you'd like to find. Once you've identified an appropriate group or organization, you might search its web page (if one exists) to discover the exact individual to contact, or you can simply call or e-mail the organization and ask (whoever answers the phone, for example) who they recommend you speak to.

Once you have chosen a person to interview, make an initial connection. Introduce yourself by stating who you are (a student, for instance) and what you are doing (conducting research for an assignment in your public speaking class, for example) and tell him or her why you chose to talk to them. For instance, explain you would like input to help develop your speech, and be clear and specific about the subject matter you want to discuss. This allows the interviewee to reflect on the topic in advance and if appropriate, to review and collect relevant information to share with you. Likewise, you might offer to share your questions in advance, particularly if the questions involve specific information or require the respondent to recall particular details. Finally, ask to set up a time to conduct the interview and clarify his or her preferred means of communication (via phone, e-mail, in person, etc.). Don't assume an interviewee has time at that moment or when it is most convenient for you.

Preparing for the Interview

Prepare for the interview by carefully crafting your questions. Keep your questions specific, but open-ended and neutral. Be prepared to ask follow-up questions to gain the information you're seeking. End the interview by allowing the respondent to offer additional thoughts. You might ask, for instance, if there is anything else he or she wants to add or whether there is a question he or she wishes you had asked.

When writing your questions, consider the kind of information you'd like to learn.[12] For instance, *if you want factual information* about your chosen issue, ask for the exact data and facts you need. You might also tactfully request how the person knows these facts or from whom or where the information comes. If the interviewee references a report or study, for instance, ask where you might find a copy. *If you want information about the person's experiences*, ask how he or she has been affected by the topic or what a typical day at work or at the organization they belong to looks like. Or you might request the interviewee to relate his or her most vivid memories associated with your topic. *If you want to learn the person's opinions or feelings*, explicitly invite a perspective on or response to an opinion you've read or heard. *If you want the person's ideas for local actions community members can take to help improve the issue you're researching*, simply ask what local people, including college students, can do to help address or solve the problem. If the person is part of an organization devoted to the issue you're exploring, you might ask how local community members can aid their organization—what needs or opportunities it currently has—and get all the necessary details to relay to your peers if you choose to advocate one of these options.

Conducting the Interview

Having made a contact and prepared your questions, you are ready to conduct the interview. Follow a few simple guidelines to help ensure an enjoyable and productive exchange:

- For phone and in-person interviews, make sure you are **punctual** for your scheduled time.
- **Reintroduce** yourself and remind the respondent why you asked for the interview.
- **Ask** your questions one at a time.
- For phone and in-person interviews, either **take great notes** during the interview or **ask permission to record the interview**. Don't count on your memory to recall their answers. But recognize that some people may feel uncomfortable being recorded. If you rely on notes and want to directly quote something the person said, ask him or her to repeat it to ensure you quote them accurately.
- **Make clear to the interviewee how you will use the information** provided and **verify you have permission** to use their input and quote them. Sometimes people will share information with you off the record or will not want some ideas attributed to them. You need to respect their wishes.
- **Thank** the person for taking time to talk with you.
- **Keep an eye on the time**. For in-person and phone interviews, stick to the amount of time you agreed to when scheduling the interview. If you come to the end of that time and wish to continue, ask if the person can answer one or two more questions. Provide the option of ending the interview in case he or she cannot linger.
- When you leave, **spend time immediately going over your notes**. Make sure you have the date of the interview and the name and title of the person you interviewed.
- Give the person the option to **review any quotations** you plan to use from the interview for accuracy.

By following the guidance we have provided for making a contact and preparing for and conducting an interview, you should enjoy a very positive interviewing experience. Your exchange will likely provide helpful information and opinions for your speech. And you will probably feel more closely joined to your community afterward because you connected with another member. Of course, you will likely pair your interview(s) with research you conduct on the Internet. We will now turn to considering how to conduct that research efficiently.

ONLINE ACCESS TO SOURCES

One of the first places students typically turn to research their topics is the Internet, and for good reason. Millions of websites offer an array of diverse information, opinions, arguments, images, and videos. But such immensity can quickly overwhelm us. You likely know the feeling of searching for a word associated with your topic—say "college recycling" or "immigration reform"—and drowning in the many, disparate returns the search engine provides. You may then fall victim to relying on the top search returns, forgetting that companies and websites can pay for the right to have their sites appear at the top of some search lists.[13] On the other hand, you may become frustrated by how little *helpful,* truly relevant information appears. Either way, don't fret. There are smarter ways to search. To make your Internet research more efficient, you can educate yourself about the kinds of websites available and the smartest ways to search them. In what follows, we discuss research databases, specialized search engines, domain name labels, site-specific searches, field searches, Boolean searches, searches using punctuation marks, and how to gather your Internet findings into one convenient location.

Research Databases

A **database** is an organized online storehouse of information that can easily be searched to retrieve desired materials. Fortunately for our purposes, there are many research databases online that store hundreds of sources electronically, often in full-text versions. Their collections range from including scholarly articles and e-books to news media broadcast transcripts and legal documents. Many of the best research databases require payment or a subscription to access them. However, college libraries typically subscribe to several databases, allowing students to access them for free as long as you enter through the library's portal. So check your library home page or talk with a reference librarian about the databases available and how to access them.

Most of the popular research databases are actually databases *of* databases. That is, each includes multiple collections of sources. Here are four popular research databases:

- EBSCO: Offers dozens of databases focusing on a wide range of topics. Each college and university library chooses the databases to make available to students. Possible topics covered by databases within EBSCO include, but are not limited to, business, the environment, medicine, news, gender studies, home improvement, music, psychology, education, political science, philosophy, the military and government, religion, art and architecture, and communication and media. The types of sources available include general interest materials, scholarship, trade journals, books, and other types of documents. One of the most popular databases is Academic Search Premier, which provides full-text access to more than 4,600 popular and news magazines, trade journals, and scholarly publications. You might also look for Communication & Mass Media Complete, which includes more than 770 titles related to the field of communication.
- JSTOR: Focuses exclusively on scholarly journals and books, but from a broad range of academic fields and subjects. These subjects include, but are not limited to, area studies (such as African American studies and Jewish studies), arts, business and economics, history, humanities, law, medicine and allied health, science and mathematics, and social sciences.
- LexisNexis: Includes databases devoted to the topics of news, legal cases, company information, and people. You can also search using a combination of these topics. This is a great resource for finding the most up-to-date news from around the world, legal decisions, biographies of public figures, and corporate

information. The "news" database includes wire services (like the Associated Press) and broadcast transcripts (for news shows such as ABC News and National Public Radio) along with access to newspapers and news magazines.

- ProQuest: Offers multiple products, each containing one to many different research databases. Among the most popular products is ProQuest Central, which offers databases covering subject areas including, but not limited to, business, science and technology, health and medicine, social sciences, arts and humanities, and news.

When using any large research database, first take a moment to find a list of all the source collections included. That list will typically allow you to choose one or more specific collections to search and ignore the rest. Such selectivity will enhance the likelihood of retrieving fewer, but more helpful, results. Otherwise, some database systems automatically default to searching just one of its collections or every collection available. Neither default mode may be helpful.

Specialized Search Engines

Google is the most heavily used Internet search engine, with 70% of the search engine market share across the United States, followed by Bing and Yahoo with just over or under 8% each.[14] But you may not realize that all three major search engines offer several specialized search options. For instance, all of them provide a news search. Additional specialized searches you may find useful include Yahoo's Finance, Health, and Sports searches; Bing's Business News and Local News options; and Google's Finance, Scholarship, and Trends searches. You can find these specialized search options through links on the companies' home pages (bing.com, yahoo.com) or by searching for the option (such as by searching for "Google scholar"). Indeed, you should occasionally visit each company's website or Google's list of specialized searches (available at http://www.google.com/about/products/) to discover new tools they may have developed. Once you have chosen your specialized search engine (say, Google Scholar or Yahoo Finance), type in your search terms knowing you will only retrieve sources directly relevant to the type of specialized search you selected.

BOX 4-1

Sources and the Internet at a Glance

If you want to find . . .	Then try using or searching . . .
General knowledge	Wikipedia.org; Britannica.com
News	LexisNexis News; Bing News; Google News; Yahoo News; Specific collections within EBSCO and ProQuest
Scholarship	JSTOR; Specific collections within EBSCO and ProQuest; Google Scholar
Trade Journals	Specific collections within EBSCO and ProQuest

E-Books	Guttenberg.org; Play.google.com; Amazon.com; Specific collections within EBSCO, JSTOR, LexisNexis, ProQuest; Local libraries' home pages
Government documents	USA.gov; Specific collections within EBSCO
Legal documents	LexisNexis Legal Cases; Supremecourt.gov; Scotusblog.com
Corporate materials	LexisNexis Company Information; Sec.gov/edgar/searchedgar/companysearch .html; Google Finance; Yahoo Finance; Specific collections within EBSCO and ProQuest
Public opinion polls	Gallup.com; Pewresearch.org
Blogs	Blogsearchengine.org; LexisNexis News
Tweets	Twitter.com/twittersearch
Facebook	Google (include "Facebook" with your search terms)
Other opinion sources	LexisNexis News

Domain Name Labels

When you receive search results or go directly to a website, notice its web address. Each web address ends with a top-level domain name after the dot. Some of the most widely used top-level domain names are

.com   Commercial organization. Examples: exxonmobil.com, facebook.com.

.edu   US postsecondary educational institution. Examples: willamette.edu, usc.edu.

.gov   US government entity. Examples: whitehouse.gov, senate.gov.

.mil   US military organization. Examples: army.mil, usa4militaryfamilies. dod.mil.

.org   Noncommercial organization, such as an interest group, nonprofit or activist organization. Examples: habitat.org, teapartypatriots.org.

These examples are for US websites. But other countries issue domain names as well and, when they do, they include a country code at the end of the website address. For instance, all website addresses that end with uk, such as parliament.uk, refer to domain names issued by the United Kingdom. Additional country codes include .ca (Canada), .de (Germany), .nl (Netherlands), and .ru (Russia). Country codes typically indicate that the website caters to members of that country in terms of the language, focus, and so forth.

Thinking about top-level domain names can expand your awareness of the types of websites available. Rather than relying mostly on .com and .org pages, you can target alternative domain names, possibly from other countries, to gather additional perspectives and information. Doing so will enhance your understanding of the topic and the stakeholders involved.

Site-Specific Searches

Another way you can smartly use an Internet search engine is by conducting a site-specific search. This type of search limits your research results to matches found only on one particular website. For instance, you might want recent analyses of stem cell research, but only those published on the National Institutes of Health (NIH) pages. You would simply type your search terms "stem cell research," then add the word "site:" with the colon, and then type the web address of the website you want to target. So our search would read: "stem cell research site: nih.gov." Every result listed would include nih.gov in its web address. A site-specific search is, therefore, a helpful way to focus your Internet searches. It also enables you to harness the power of a major search engine, such as Google's, which searches every word of millions of web pages, rather than rely on the search box occasionally provided on the front page of a website. The latter might only search the key words or tags of material on its pages and, thus, overlook useful information.

Simple and Advanced Field Searches

Most online databases and some search engines default to the most basic type of search: a single word or short phrase found anywhere in a document. To make your searches more efficient, look for an "advanced" search option, which typically results in a field search. A **field search** looks for the search terms you provide within a specific section, or field, of the documents in its collection. Sample fields include the author's name, publication title, article title, publication date, abstract, keywords, and so on. Very often, in an advanced search, you can conduct more than one field search simultaneously, such as by searching both the abstracts and author names.

We recommend you begin an advanced field search by selecting the article title field to search for your topic. That field is best equipped to quickly identify sources that directly address your subject. After that, you might try searching the abstract field. An abstract is a brief summary of an article, so it is longer than an article's title, enabling you to receive more results. But an abstract is also much shorter than the entire document, preventing you from being overwhelmed with the results produced by a full-text search. At least three additional options can help you further find or narrow your search results. First, try specifying a range of publication dates, for example, by limiting results to pieces printed within the last two years to ensure recency. Second, you might consider focusing your search results on peer-reviewed publications only (which typically means scholarship), often by checking a box that indicates peer review. Third, reduce your search results either by adding an additional search term or field or by finding a "search within the results" option to which you can add a key term.

Boolean Searches

Most Internet search engines use what is called Natural Language searches. You simply type in words like you would naturally speak them, such as "college recycling programs." The search engine automatically adds AND between each of the terms to find sources that include all the terms ("college" AND "recycling" AND "sources") somewhat near each other, but not necessarily in the order you typed them.

Online databases and some search engines benefit from using a Boolean search. A **Boolean search** is a method to retrieve relevant research by using specific operating terms to improve search results. For a Boolean search, you exercise more control over the kinds of results you achieve by providing more explicit instructions. You add specific terms, such as OR, AND, and NOT, to combine key words in more helpful ways:

- Use <u>OR</u> to *expand* your search by asking that either term be present in a source. Example: army OR navy.
- Use <u>AND</u> to *limit* your search by requiring that both terms be present for a source to qualify. Example: poverty AND unemployment.
- Use <u>NOT</u> to *limit* your search by requesting sources that include the first term or phrase without the second term or phrase. Example: Franklin Delano Roosevelt NOT Theodore Roosevelt.

You can combine Boolean terms into more complex, and likely more useful, searches. And you can use parentheses to clarify the relationship of terms, though you don't have to. For instance, you might type "obesity AND (children OR toddler)" or "(women OR female) AND athletics NOT cheerleaders." You do not have to capitalize your Boolean terms, though you may find it easier to read your search terms when you do. Most databases and advanced searches will recognize the terms whether capitalized or not.

Searches Using Punctuation Marks

Punctuation marks are helpful when conducting a Natural Language or Boolean search. Three of the most convenient punctuation marks are quotation marks, asterisks, and question marks.

- <u>Quotation marks</u> around two or more words indicate you want to search for the exact phrase. Examples: "prison recidivism" or "I Have a Dream."
- An <u>asterisk</u> at the end of a word tells the search engine to search for any possible endings to the root term. Example: America* will find sources with any version of that word, such as America, American, Americans, and Americanism.
- A <u>question mark</u> within a single term instructs the search engine to find any variant of that term. This can be helpful if you're unsure of the spelling of a key term. Example: Bo?lean would retrieve Boolean, Boalean, and Boulean.

You can combine different types of punctuation marks when searching, such as "prison re?idivism" (notice the use of quotation marks and a question mark); and you can use punctuation marks with a Boolean search, such as by adding "AND substance abuse" to the previous example.

Saving Sources from the Internet

When you search the Internet efficiently, you should find many helpful sources. You may wonder how best to save them. Internet "bookmarks" are one way, but several other free and more flexible options exist as well. Think of each like a virtual junk drawer you can throw useful electronic sources in until you're ready to sort through them later.

- Wikipedia Book: This feature of *Wikipedia* allows you to combine several *Wikipedia* articles into a single "book" about your topic for free. You can save the book and convert it into a variety of formats. Just search for "*Wikipedia* book creator" to learn more.
- Zotero and Evernote: Both of these tools work similarly. Each allows you to collect research from a wide variety of online sources and saves the website address, date accessed, and actual content of the pages. Both tools place the saved Internet sources in one virtual place, which enables you to easily sort and search through the full text of those sources. You can also share the sources collected with other people. Simply go to zotero.org or evernote.com to download the program for free.
- RefWorks: This program requires a subscription, but many academic libraries subscribe to it (or something like it) for their students. RefWorks specializes in scholarly research, so it limits you to collecting sources only from research databases (including EBSCO and ProQuest) and scholarly search engines (including Google Scholar) rather than other types of websites. Once collected, RefWorks helps you organize, search through, and share the research with other subscribers. Search your academic library's home page, or ask your reference librarian if you have access to RefWorks or a similar program.

We have tried to demonstrate that multiple tools exist to assist your Internet research. Few people utilize all the tools. We recommend you experiment with several and then opt for those you find easiest and most helpful. Remember that research is hard work. It requires time, patience, and diligence. But if you persevere and practice effective source-retrieval techniques, researching will become a bit easier and faster. And you may even discover you enjoy the research "hunt" as you experience the pleasure of finding strong sources for your topic. We turn next to the four criteria you should consider when evaluating the strength of a source.

FOUR CRITERIA TO CONSIDER
WHEN CHOOSING SOURCES

As you find, collect, and sift through sources, do so thoughtfully. You will be able to read only a fraction of the relevant information available about your topic. Being thoughtful about the fraction you choose will better enable you to construct a competent and convincing speech. Consider the following four issues for all sources: their relevancy to your topic, their recency, their credibility, and their position on or potential bias regarding the topic.

Relevance
Not every source that mentions your topic is as relevant as another. **Relevance** refers to the degree of association between the source, a speaker's topic, and his or her audience. Highly relevant sources offer information that directly addresses your particular angle on your topic and resonate with your specific audience. No matter how interesting the information or ideas presented by a source, it won't help your speech if it doesn't relate directly to your topic or your audience.

Consider Adam Phipps's recycling speech. He wanted to motivate his college community to recycle, and so he needed to find sources relevant to that topic and group. While he could certainly find sources on college recycling using LexisNexis, the information would not be as relevant to his audience or particular angle as local evidence. Instead, Adam found several articles in his college newspaper about problems with recycling on campus. In addition, he discovered *The College Sustainability Report Card,* an annual survey conducted by the Sustainable Endowments Institute, that grades each college and university's efforts at sustainable living. Adam thought the fact that his college's chief rival consistently scored a much higher grade than did his campus would get his audience's attention and perhaps bring out its competitive spirit! Finally, in addition to interviewing people on campus who were involved with recycling efforts, he chose to educate his audience on what materials could be recycled locally. He learned the name of the local recycling agency and found a list of acceptable recycling items on its website. He also discovered that a student involved with his campus' sustainability group had already created a poster showing these items. All these sources—the college newspaper articles, annual survey, local recycling website, and campus poster—were highly relevant to Adam's locally focused topic and well adapted to his specific audience, a concern that is addressed in more detail in the following chapter. The sources would have had much less significance if he had approached the topic of recycling from a broader state or national perspective. The point, then, is that with each speech, you must consider which sources work for your particular topic angle and audience.

Recency

The **recency**, or timeliness, of your sources is also important. If the source is old, then the information it provides is probably outdated and, thus, not terribly useful to you or your audience. Imagine if Adam had begun his speech by telling his audience the recycling grade his college received four years earlier. "What about now?" they would immediately wonder. "Have we improved in four years?" "What does the most recent report say?" Using dated material will make an audience question your information as well as your research skills and credibility. Instead, seek sources published fairly recently. This advice holds especially true when addressing the topic of technology or any ongoing community issue. Fields of technology—from the speed of microprocessors to the latest smartphones and their features—change so quickly that what was once new quickly can become old. And nearly any persistent community issue can change at any moment. If Adam's college president had announced a new recycling program the day before he delivered his speech, Adam would need to incorporate that announcement and revise his speech accordingly. Otherwise, his audience would likely dismiss his speech as obsolete. The bottom line is that you must seek the most recent information about your topic up to the very day of your assignment deadline.

Not every topic requires the use of recent sources, however. For example, historical facts seldom change and thus can be supported by older sources. Landmark works that have received acclaim and awards might maintain a timeless character. On the other hand, our understanding of history can alter with new archival research, the release of private papers, and new interpretations of historical documents. Thus, a more recent treatment of a traditional topic may, depending on its credibility, prove to be a superior source.

Credibility

Credibility relates to the authority, expertise, or reputation a source has concerning a topic. A movie star may have a popular reputation as an actor, but that doesn't mean her opinion on healthcare necessarily holds any authority. It is important for you to assess credibility to determine how much you can trust a source to help you understand the topic. As a speaker, you are also responsible for assessing credibility on behalf of your audience as part of your obligation to ethical speech preparation, discussed in chapter 3.

While the Internet puts an incredible amount of information at our fingertips, it also presents special concerns with credibility. There is no gatekeeper for the vast majority of Internet sites to verify the content. While some people argue the Internet itself, and websites like *Wikipedia* in particular, are in fact checked by users, this checking is uneven at best. In fact, while speaking at a conference at the University of Pennsylvania, *Wikipedia* founder Jimmy Wales discouraged use of the site for serious research. Although he defended *Wikipedia* as "good enough, depending on what your purpose is," he also said he has "no sympathy" for students who are penalized by professors for citing information on *Wikipedia* that turned out to be incorrect.[15] Wales was speaking specifically of *Wikipedia*, but his point has broader relevance: we must be wise and responsible for evaluating the Internet sites we use.

BOX 4-2

Issues to Consider When Evaluating a Source's Credibility

Publisher or Sponsor

- Who are the publishers or sponsors of the source? What can you learn about them?
- What type of publication or website is the source you're interested in? For a website, consider the top-level domain name. For a print source, you may need to research the publishers if you're unfamiliar with them.

Author

- Who is the author? Is an author listed?
- Is the author an authority on the topic?
- What can you learn about the author's reliability?

Material

- Has the material been vetted by an editor or reviewers? Or is it self-published?
- Can you find reviews or responses to the material?
- What is the purpose of the document (academic, personal, commercial)?
- Is there evidence of bias?
- What makes the information trustworthy?
- What is the date of publication or the date the material was last updated? Is it recent?

Of course, credibility might best be considered on a continuum, varying from sources known for having high credibility, such as *The Economist*, to explicitly partisan sources, such as Drudgereport.com. Reference librarians are great resources and can answer questions you may have about finding credible material. Don't be afraid to approach one of them at your university or college library to ask for help.

Bias

Bias is a predetermined commitment to a particular ideological or political perspective. A biased source is one that openly professes such a commitment or is commonly recognized as doing so. Biased sources can range from sources that see the world through a predetermined set of presumptions, beliefs, and/or philosophies, such as the liberal magazine *Mother Jones* and the conservative magazine *National Review*, to sources that express particular judgments because they stand to gain personally by what they are saying. For example, a political campaign manager has a lot to win or lose from how her candidate is perceived by the public. If asked how well she thought her candidate handled a particular debate, for instance, the campaign manager would surely respond positively, as the success of the candidate is directly tied to the manager's success at her job!

The point of this is not that you should never make use of biased sources. Rather, you should do so knowingly. To return to Adam's recycling speech again, by choosing to interview the president of the sustainability group on his campus, he was certain to get information on why recycling was important and should be improved. Similarly, a student who seeks news or analysis from *The Rachel Maddow Show* on MSNBC or *The O'Reilly Factor* on FOX should anticipate the news stories will reflect the hosts' strong political beliefs (liberal and conservative, respectively). Instead of avoiding biased sources like these, you should incorporate them into a broad range of sources, including those that aren't inherently biased. And when you use a biased source in your presentation, you must acknowledge it as such. This shows the audience you are an honest speaker because you make your sources fully known rather than deceptively using biased sources to manipulate your listeners. They will also recognize you as a fair-minded advocate who is willing to look at all sides of an issue when coming to your conclusions.

If you find the inevitable bias of sources frustrating or discouraging, realize you are in good company. There really are only two basic reactions to the presence of biased and manipulative rhetoric in human society: censorship or encouragement of multiple perspectives; that is, less rhetoric or more rhetoric. If we choose the former, the inevitable question is who gets to decide what rhetoric to silence? Or in this example, which news sources to silence and which to air? Do we consider Fox News the only legitimate news source? Should we shut down all the others? Interestingly, when a person watches only Fox News or only reads the *New York Times*, they are effectively doing just that. Second, notice that, while difficult, there is a clear strategy for overcoming this reality on the research side—more research, from more and varied sources. This is your task.

Together, the four criteria discussed—relevance, recency, credibility, and bias—can help you decide which sources to use to develop your speech and which to dismiss. Even when you search for sources in print and online efficiently, you may find more results than you can use. Don't assume the first five or so Internet hits or books on the library bookshelf are best. Instead, opt for sources that best meet the criteria outlined and reflect the types of sources listed earlier in this chapter. When in doubt, you can also always ask a reference librarian for help.

SOURCE DOCUMENTATION

Once you have located strong sources for your topic, how do you properly and effectively use them in your speech? Before concluding, we answer this question by considering how to document your sources during a speech and in an associated bibliography.

Oral Citations

As noted in the previous chapter's discussion of ethics, you must give credit to sources as you present research in a speech. To do that, provide an oral **citation**, or basic identifying information, for your sources. What you include in an oral citation depends on the type of source you are identifying:

- Interview: Name the person you interviewed and his or her title, if relevant, as well as the date you conducted the interview. Example from Adam's speech: "During our interview on February 23rd, Professor Doug Calisch of the Faculty Environmental Concerns Committee explained, quote, 'Students For Sustainability was charged with enlisting student workers to pick up recycle bags from each living unit on a scheduled basis last year,' unquote."
- Printed source: Name the author and their title, if relevant; the title of the publication; and the date the source was published (such as a copyright date). Example: "In his 2005 book, *Why Video Games are Good for Your Soul*, linguist and literacy studies scholar James Gee argues that good video games nourish players' souls by providing a sense of control and meaningfulness."
- Website: Citations for many websites can follow the guidelines for printed sources. For an article from the *New York Times* online, for instance, you would name the article's author, the publication (*New York Times*), and date the article was published. For other kinds of websites, state the individual, group, or company who authored, edited, or compiled the page; the title of the website; and the date the page was last updated (if available). Example from Adam's speech: "Our local recycling company, Walden Transport and Recycling, has a web page called 'Recycling Items Accepted' that lists more than twenty different objects they can recycle." Whatever website you cite, do not state the web address.

Notice that in all the examples just given, the speaker provided the citation *prior* to giving the information or quotation. Announcing the source first alerts the audience that they are about to hear something from an outside source, and it allows them to scrutinize the credibility of the information in light of that source. Moreover, providing a citation allows interested listeners to jot a note and find the material if they would like to read more about the topic after hearing your speech. Notice also in the first example (Adam's citation of his interview) that Adam made clear he was providing a direct quote from his source by verbally noting where the quote began and ended. It is important you indicate direct quotes, either by noting it as such or by changes in your vocal inflection.

Contrast the previous examples to the following alternative: "Good video games nourish players' souls by providing a sense of control and meaningfulness." The omission of an oral citation for this statement is very damaging to your speech. Now this statement rests solely upon *your* authority of literacy studies, video games, and sociolinguistics; and it obscures the fact that you needed the source to draw this conclusion. The bottom line is, give credit to the source for the information it provided. In the process, you will give yourself credit for finding and using the source. The audience will recognize your careful research and be much more inclined to view your presentation in a favorable light.

Bibliographies

When writing a speech, your instructor may require you to submit a written bibliography of your sources, perhaps as the last page of a speech outline or manuscript. Or you may choose to provide a copy of your bibliography to a community group you are addressing about a civic concern so they can further pursue the topic. There are several existing **style guides**, or instructions for writing, formatting, and referencing sources, that include guidelines for writing a bibliography. Style guide authors include, but are not limited to, the Modern Language Association (MLA) and the American Psychological Association (APA). Ask your instructor what style guide she or he prefers, or you might resort to the style guide frequently used by your major area of study. Humanities scholars, for example, tend to use MLA, while social scientists often prefer APA.

When writing your bibliography, follow the style guide instructions precisely, including the placement of punctuation. Both the APA and MLA publish style guides with detailed instructions on how to correctly list any kind of source. Your college or university library likely has copies of both guides. There are shortcuts to physically accessing these hard copies. But beware of the dangers of such shortcuts:

- Automated bibliography generators: Several companies offer software that will create a bibliography for you. They typically allow you to specify the style guide you'd like to use. However, we have found these generators frequently produce inaccurate and even confusing bibliographies. So if you use one, check the results against the style guide requirements.
- Online style guide instructions: Many websites provide detailed information about style guides, but none are officially sponsored by the MLA or APA. Therefore, you should ensure the website you follow is offering accurate instructions.

When you document your sources, both orally and in a bibliography, you follow the best practices of excellent speakers. And you can feel pleased by how well you discovered, learned from, and utilized strong and diverse sources for your speech.

SUMMARY

This chapter has introduced you to the resources, techniques, and evaluative criteria needed to conduct and document credible and effective research. Good research produces more effective speeches and aids productive discourse.

- By emphasizing learning, research helps a community better understand and scrutinize an issue rather than base decisions on unproven assumptions or speakers' personalities.
- We recommend you approach research as inquiry to leave yourself open to discovering perspectives and arguments you had not before considered. If you approach research as strategy, you close yourself off from potentially compelling reasons to reject or rethink your desired option.
- A wide range of sources exist for your research, including your knowledge and experiences, general knowledge bases, news, scholarship and trade journals, books, government documents, legal texts, corporate materials, and people's experiences and opinions.
- Conducting an interview is an excellent way to ascertain people's opinions and experiences related to your topic. To ensure an interview is effective, you should follow basic instructions on how to make a contact, prepare for the interview, and conduct the interview.
- Many tools can help you locate useful sources on the Internet efficiently. These tools include research databases, specialized search engines, domain name labels, site-specific searches, field searches, Boolean searches, searches using punctuation marks, and programs to save the sources you find on the Internet.
- To narrow your selection of sources, evaluate the strength of each according to its relevancy, recency, credibility, and bias.
- Ethical speakers give credit to their sources through oral citations during their speech and in a typed bibliography.

KEY TERMS

bias p. 77	field search p. 72	research as inquiry
Boolean search p. 73	recency p. 75	p. 59
citation p. 78	relevance p. 74	research as
credibility p. 76	research p. 58	strategy p. 59
database p. 69		style guide p. 79

REVIEW QUESTIONS

1. What role does research play in civic engagement? How does research aid communal decision-making?
2. What is the difference between researching as a mode of inquiry and researching as a strategy?
3. What are five different types of sources you might use to research a speech or paper? And where might you find them on the Internet?

4. When conducting an interview, what should you make sure to do or not do?
5. What are the differences between a specialized Google search, Boolean search, site-specific search, and a field search on the Internet?
6. What are four criteria you should consider when choosing sources? What does each refer to?
7. What should you include in an oral citation for a print source? For an interview? For a website?

DISCUSSION QUESTIONS

1. Is it ever appropriate to approach research as a strategy? When? Why?
2. Which of the sources discussed in this chapter is the strongest in your opinion? Why?
3. How might social media aid or harm your research? How have you used them for a class assignment, or how have you heard other people using them for research? Which networks?
4. Who might you interview for an upcoming assignment? How could you research your local area to find a group or individual relevant to your topic? What questions might you ask?
5. Try searching for a topic using Natural Language on a basic Google search. Then try searching for the same topic on a specialized Google search or an online database and use some of the search techniques discussed in this chapter (Boolean terms, site-specific search, field search). How do the results compare? What did you learn in the process?
6. Which databases do you have access to through your library? How have you used databases in the past? What tips have you discovered to search databases more efficiently?

CHAPTER 5

Knowing and Adapting
to Your Audience

Chapter Objectives

Students will:

- Learn the importance of audience to public presentation.
- Apply common elements of audience analysis.
- Practice the process of audience adaptation.
- Demonstrate how to work with their audience in imagining a productive future.

On April 4, 1968, New York Senator Robert F. Kennedy, a presidential hopeful, spent the day campaigning in the state of Indiana. He began his day by visiting the University of Notre Dame before proceeding to Ball State University. As Kennedy boarded a plane for Indianapolis, where he was scheduled to hold an evening event in a deeply impoverished area of the city, he was informed that Martin Luther King Jr. had been shot in Memphis. During the course of the flight, Kennedy contemplated the shooting and took notes for what he might say that evening. Upon arriving in Indianapolis, Kennedy learned that King was dead. Would it be appropriate to go on with the event as initially planned? Could Kennedy acknowledge King's death and incorporate it into his message? Would it be better to cancel altogether? The rhetorical situation Kennedy anticipated had changed substantially, and it was incumbent on Kennedy to adapt to the new reality.

Against the advice of the Indianapolis chief of police, Kennedy insisted on proceeding to the event, but in analyzing the situation he transformed it into something much different than a campaign stop. Despite the chilly evening, Kennedy arrived at a jubilant political rally decorated with campaign banners and signs. The assembled crowd of approximately 1,000 people, 70% of whom were African American, had not yet heard of Dr. King's death. Without formal introduction, Kennedy mounted the back of a flatbed truck to address the onlookers. As he prepared to break the news, a

US Senator Robert F. Kennedy greets supporters during his 1968 presidential campaign.

somber Kennedy asked supporters to lower their campaign signs. He then began: "I have bad news for you, for all of our fellow citizens, and people who love peace all over the world, and that is that Martin Luther King was shot and killed tonight." Kennedy's announcement was met by gasps of shock and disbelief. As he continued to speak he did not talk about the 1968 election, his political opponents, or make campaign promises. Instead, Kennedy expressed his personal grief, sought to identify with the people in attendance—many of whom were mourning the loss of both a civil rights and spiritual leader—and made a plea for racial reconciliation and national unity.

A key element of Kennedy's speech was to acknowledge the anger of the crowd while relating to them through his own personal experience:

> For those of you who are black and are tempted to be filled with hatred and distrust at the injustice of such an act [as King's assassination], against all white people, I can only say that I feel in my own heart the same kind of feeling. I had a member of my family killed, but he was killed by a white man. But we have to make an effort in the United States, we have to make an effort to understand, to go beyond these rather difficult times.

Kennedy continued by calling his audience to turn away from division, hatred, and violence and, instead, to turn toward love, wisdom, and compassion in seeking justice. In doing so Kennedy imagined the future community that he, the audience, and the country could yet become. Near his conclusion he asked his audience to "say a prayer for the family of Martin Luther King" and to "say a prayer for our own country."

The impact of Kennedy's speech was magnified because of his known support for society's disadvantaged and disenfranchised members. It was also the first time he spoke publically about his own experience of having lost a brother—President John F. Kennedy—to an assassin's bullet.[1] Americans were understandably angry that evening, and rioting occurred across the nation resulting in deaths, injuries, and destruction—but not in Indianapolis.[2]

The recognition of the significance of a speaking situation and the effort both to understand the needs of an audience and adjust to them accordingly—embodied in Robert Kennedy's speech in Indianapolis—are the center of this chapter. We discuss how we engage public audiences through the practices of audience analysis and adaptation. We undertake such efforts not just to be more successful—not just to persuade or influence others—but also to come together as a community in the mutually beneficial consideration of our communal life.

In this chapter we begin with a consideration of audience and its importance to the public speaking situation. Second, we explore the concept of audience analysis, its potential uses, and its limitations in public speaking. Third, we consider the practice of audience adaptation, how we can better connect with and engage our audience. Finally, we address how rhetoric allows us, as speakers, to work with our audience in imagining a more productive future together.

THE IMPORTANCE OF AUDIENCE

It is natural that when we think about public speaking our first thought is of the speaker. However, the audience is at least as important. In a reflection of this central role, audience is a focus of attention throughout this book. For example, in chapter 3 we addressed the ethical obligations of public speaking and of earning the right to speak—that is the responsibilities we have to our audience. In later chapters, such as those on style and delivery, we consider how those two canons of rhetoric engage and affect the audience. In the chapters on deliberation and discussion, we consider the importance of localizing presentations and of incorporating audiences into discussions. And in the chapter on persuasion, we address how you must present your audience a problem worthy of their attention and demonstrate that they have the means and power to act to lessen the problem. In each example audience is central to the rhetoric.

This consistent attention to audience underscores that discourse is not the sole creation or property of a speaker. Public speech only has meaning in its relationship to an audience that listens and responds to it. It is not unlike the quasi-philosophical (or perhaps just nonsensical) riddle, "If a tree falls in the forest, and no one is around to hear it, does it make a sound?" That is: If a speech is given, but no one is there to listen to it—or pays attention to it—is it actually a speech? The point is an important one: without an attentive audience a speech lacks purpose, meaning, relevance, and impact. For this reason public discourse must not only have an audience, but productive public discourse is also developed for the specific audience that will receive it and has the potential to act on the problem or issue under discussion.

A seminal essay that captures many components of our point is communication scholar Lloyd Bitzer's "The Rhetorical Situation."[3] Professor Bitzer offers important insight on the production of rhetoric, how the context shapes that rhetoric, and the role of the audience in addressing and resolving a situation. A **rhetorical situation** is an occasion or situation in which speech, while taking into account the constraints or limitations of the immediate context, can be used to call an audience of listeners and decision-makers into action in order to address a rhetorical exigence. According to Bitzer, a **rhetorical exigence** is an urgent need that can be improved or changed through communication. In other words, any pressing public problem that rhetoric might help fix (by drawing public attention to the problem, assuaging fears, offering a solution, etc.) is a rhetorical exigence. The audience constitutes the second component of Bitzer's theory. Individuals who experience the artifact (i.e., hear or watch it), are open to being influenced by it, *and* are capable of facilitating the change(s) called for by the rhetor (to improve the rhetorical exigence) qualify as the **rhetorical audience**. People who deny the existence of a problem and/or are immovably entrenched against the rhetor's message are not part of the rhetorical audience, nor are people who are unable to make the rhetor's desired changes. Identifying the likely rhetorical audience for your speech can help you think about who you should target with your message. Constraints make up the final aspect of Bitzer's rhetorical situation. Those things that can restrain, influence, or even dictate the "decision and actions needed" to improve the exigence count as **constraints**. Consequently, they can influence the form and content of the message a rhetor develops to improve the situation. Considering the constraints posed by a rhetorical situation prepares you to better understand how to effectively develop your rhetoric.

Our assessment of the rhetorical situation provides a sort of situational diagnostic, one that calls on us to clearly identify the pressing issue or problem, to think about the limitations or constraints on action, and to develop a response that reflects the capabilities of our audience to address that problem. The point is that we encounter a variety of rhetorical situations, and our task in public speaking is to develop the most effective speech for our audience given the circumstances of the occasion. How do we craft a speech that is most fitting to our audience? What sorts of appeals will be most effective in stimulating audience interest and bringing about community change? To help answer such questions, we employ audience analysis.

AUDIENCE ANALYSIS

Audience analysis is the practice of assessing audience factors and characteristics that are likely to influence an audience's reception of a message. In turn, **audience adaptation**, which is addressed in the next section, is how you make use of audience-analysis cues to explain, frame, and support ideas in order to increase your chances of achieving the desired audience response. Here we explore the concept of audience analysis by considering its relationship to advertising, its historical roots in the ancient world, and its contemporary practice in public speaking.

Audience Analysis and Advertising

You experience the principles of audience analysis and adaptation in your daily life, although perhaps not always with full awareness. For instance, if you read *ESPN The Magazine*, you are regularly exposed to ads for automobiles (often sports cars), athletic gear, action films, men's clothing and grooming products, and alcohol and tobacco. The product pitches reflect the presumed interests of the magazine's targeted audience—generally younger, upwardly mobile, adult men. These products are substantially different from what you find in *Better Homes and Gardens* where ads for household goods, food, and female beauty products are commonly featured. We don't find this surprising, because even if you have never named it specifically, audience-targeted advertising (audience analysis and adaptation) makes intuitive sense. It makes sense for companies to use targeted advertising to reach the consumers who are most likely to be interested in purchasing their specific products and services. In addition, targeted advertising makes our lives easier as we don't have to endure (as many) advertisements for products we are not interested in.

We are often targeted even more specifically by Internet advertising. Through the use of cookies that store information about our page access at particular websites and other techniques, online ads are often adapted to our individual interests in an effort to better target ideal consumers. If you have recently looked at the Kia Soul on the Internet, then you might suddenly find it advertised on another website you visit. Have you been to the Disney World website recently? If so, chances are you are now seeing banner ads for Disney on various websites you visit. Likewise if you search for a hotel for an upcoming trip, or you look for a product on Amazon, you can expect to see ads tailored to the interests you expressed via product searches. As Yahoo explains in "AdChoices," a link which appears beneath some advertising on its website, ads are selected for you based on your previous web activity and search history, activity that signaled an interest in a product.[4] In these ways your activity has been analyzed and advertising is adapted to you. There are, of course, potential concerns as your behaviors are to an extent being monitored. Take for instance the case in 2009 when Google placed a "Stardate" box on the Google Calendar of any user who had noted the premiere of the *Star Trek* reboot.[5] The action raised questions about the use of private information to target potential consumers. On balance, however, consumers indicate, in a Zogby Analytics poll, that they prefer targeted ads by a ratio of more than 2 to 1.[6]

Our purpose in offering these examples is to identify some of the similarities between these marketing practices and public speaking—both are interested in critically assessing their audience and adapting to (or targeting) that audience in the most effective way possible. However, we add a significant note of caution as well: capitalist-consumerism and civic engagement begin from different premises and can often be at odds with one another. A speech is more than selling a product; ideally it is about contributing to the public good. We also remind you that just because something is effective, be it a marketing ploy or a persuasive message in a speech, does not guarantee that it is ethical.

Audience Analysis and the Ancients

The practice of audience analysis and adaptation is not recent or tied exclusively to marketing. Not surprisingly, its roots are found in ancient Greece. The first explicit references to it are found in the dialogues of Plato. In his *Phaedrus*, Plato defines the function of oratory as the attempt to "influence men's souls" and says that as a result the orator must know the different types of soul. He explains this is necessary because "a certain type of hearer will be easy to persuade by a certain type of speech," while another will not.[7] Plato expresses concern, however, that orators may abuse audience analysis and adaptation through persuasion that simply tells their audiences what these groups want to hear or tells them what the orators *think* they know, rather than the truth.[8] Plato's exploration of the possible uses and abuses of audience makeup, then, is the beginning of the explicit discussion of audience analysis and adaptation in the classical period. We add, however, that rhetorical theorists and scholars generally assume an obligation on the part of the speaker to be honest, as we explained in chapter 3. It is imperative that your rhetoric not cater only to what is likely to be persuasive or popular but to speak with the public good in mind.

Plato's *Phaedrus* was written in the mid-third century BCE, and several decades later his student Aristotle gave the first description of various types of audience members, including tendencies they have and their likely beliefs, values, and motivations. These categorizations were based largely on age (and emotion), dividing the audience according to the young, the old, and those in the prime of life. While today we consider a greater diversity of audience characteristics, Aristotle's point is that effective speakers analyze their listeners and select appeals that will best speak to their experiences, knowledge, and desires.

The evaluations provided by Plato and Aristotle are significant as they are the intellectual and conceptual beginning of our contemporary understanding of audience. Both philosophers encourage us to think deeply about the values and motivations of the people who make up our audiences and to speak to them accordingly. However, as targeted marketing indicates, those understandings have also developed over time.

Contemporary Audience Analysis

If a student planned to give a speech on a prominent campus issue, the issue of choice would likely differ at Denison University in Granville, Ohio, from Willamette University in Salem, Oregon. Why? Because those campuses—and their audiences—probably have different concerns. Similarly, a presidential candidate is likely to emphasize somewhat different issues, use different examples, and even offer different points of personal connection (in expressing interests and sometimes even in the use of accents and pronunciation) in a campaign speech given in Florida than one given in Michigan, because the pressing issues related to employment, environment, and quality of life will be both similar and different in those locations. So if audiences differ in their nature—who they are, what they know, what they are interested in—how do we as speakers determine our best path forward? Moreover, since these audiences cannot be considered monolithic—within an individual audience you may encounter broad diversity—what do we do? Much like advertisers, we employ audience analysis. As we discuss more directly momentarily, there are limits to the conclusions that can be drawn from audience analysis—after all, very rarely do we know exactly who our audience will actually be or can we predict their interests and concerns precisely—but it is a valuable tool nonetheless. Good speakers take the characteristics of their specific audience into consideration at every stage of the speech process, including research, organization, outlining, and delivery. Audience analysis often begins with basic demographic features but should take into account psychological and environmental factors as well.

Demographic Factors

Audience demographics are personal characteristics of the audience that are likely to shape their views and perspectives on a topic. We consider audience demographics in thinking about how we explain, frame, and support our speech, which is discussed more fully in the section on audience adaptation.

BOX 5-1

Audience Demographics

As a speaker, it is valuable to consider the demographic characteristics of your audience as you plan your message. Relevant demographic factors may include:

- Age
- Gender
- Race and ethnicity
- Socioeconomic status
- Culture—values and customs
- Geography—where the audience is from and where you are speaking
- Education
- Occupation
- Group memberships—religious and political affiliations, civic clubs, and so on

In using such information ask yourself, how does the particular factor potentially affect

- the relevance of the topic to my audience;
- my audience's interest in the topic;
- my audience's knowledge of or exposure to the topic;
- my audience's likely perspective on and reaction to the topic.

Audience demographics are useful in providing a sort of shorthand for audience interests and beliefs. It is important, however, to keep in mind that when making demographic assessments, we are generalizing about tendencies that are only associated with audience characteristics. Particular individuals, and thus particular audiences, differ from the generalized conclusions that might be drawn from audience demographics. Common demographic factors to consider in evaluating an audience include age, gender, race and ethnicity, socioeconomic status, culture, geography, education, occupation, and group memberships. The age of an audience, for example, is a proxy for their experiences and likely stage in life. If you attend a residential liberal arts college, the typical age of your classroom audience will in itself suggest that few in your class have children or own their own home. This knowledge may influence how you address topics ranging from concerns over the potential health consequences of childhood vaccinations to why the tax system should be overhauled. For instance, if you wanted to address the economic impacts of existing or potential tax deductions, focusing on the child tax credit or mortgage deduction would probably be less relevant to this audience than examining deductions available for college tuition and school expenses. Likewise, a traditional college audience (ages 18–23) has a different range of experiences with the social world than more mature audiences. Most traditional college students today haven't known a time without cell phones or the Internet, and, thus, using pay phones or having to go to the local library to access research sources is probably foreign to them. On the other hand, those in their 60s are less likely to be familiar with Pinterest, Taylor Swift's "Shake It Off," or the Harlem Shake. The point is that age is often a demographic signifier for a range of information about an audience, including experiences, personal concerns and interests, and cultural knowledge or awareness.

In a similar fashion, considering other demographic characteristics can be useful in thinking about how to approach a speech. The gender composition of an audience might influence your use of examples and metaphors or encourage a certain diversity of examples and metaphors. The socioeconomic status or class of an audience might influence their life experiences, access to certain consumer goods, and their ability to contribute to a cause financially. Geographic location often dictates local customs, language patterns and terminology, and concerns of a given area. Markers such as education and occupation likewise speak to the sorts of knowledge and familiarity we might expect the audience to have on a particular topic. For example, if you were to give a speech on the results of a study you conducted on narcissism, you would approach it differently if the audience was a classroom of public speaking students as opposed to a room full of psychology professors at a national conference. Your topic—a study conducted on narcissism—would be the same in each case but how you approached it—details on methodology and explanations of p values (a measure of effect size), how you talk about the limitations of the study's sample, the way you talk about the supporting literature, and the examples used to explain narcissism itself—would likely differ. In each case you would think about how knowledge of these demographic factors could be used to improve your speech—how you could make the speech relevant, how you could speak in a language and with examples that the audience would connect with, and how you could be most productive in achieving your purpose in speaking with the particular audience listening to the presentation.

BOX 5-2

Who Is My Audience?

Sometimes you will know a great deal about and be very familiar with your audience. When you are not, there are a number of ways you can learn about the demographics and attitudes of your audience. Some of the most useful techniques are addressed in chapter 4 on research.

- Internet research: Do advance online research on the location, membership, or event in order to gain more understanding of your likely audience.
- Interviews: Do advance interviews of group leaders or members in order to gain a perspective of the likely audience.

- Ask questions: If you are giving an invited talk, ask questions of whoever extended the invitation to learn more about the speaking situation and audience.
- Observe: If you will be speaking to a particular group or at a particular location, try to observe a meeting or speaker at the location prior to your presentation.

Regardless of your topic, however, the questions you want to ask about your audience remain remarkably similar: What are the likely demographics of my audience? How might those demographic factors be important to their awareness, interest, and predispositions on my topic? How can I use this demographic information to better relate to my audience, make my presentation more relevant to them, and encourage them to understand my perspective?

Limitations to Using Demographic Factors

There are, however, some limitations in demographics-based audience analysis. Notably, there are questions about how well you can know your audience, how accurately demographic factors will predict their predispositions, and what audience analysis means for audience members that fall outside the majority or are part of an unintended audience.

When an attorney argues before the US Supreme Court, he or she knows exactly who the immediate audience is—the nine justices sitting on the Court. As a result, the attorney can prepare based on what is known about those justices—their previous opinions and writings, available information about their disposition on the issue, and even their habits during oral arguments. Rarely, however, will you know your audience so specifically. And even when you have a reasonable idea about your likely audience, it will not be as easy to gain insight into their perspectives as we often can about Supreme Court justices.

Because of this reality, you will often be forced to generalize about the composition and beliefs of your audience. However, a key concern is how much you can reasonably generalize before you reach a point where you are creating stereotypes about the audience. A **stereotype** is a generic categorization of individuals and groups based on the inaccurate conclusion that people sharing a particular characteristic will automatically possess like qualities and beliefs. Remember that people—regardless of similarities such as age, gender, and race—are individuals. Thus, while there is some evidence that allows us to generalize possible views based on these sorts of demographic factors, any individual can defy that generalized pattern. You must be careful not to create a caricature of your actual audience or to construct a stereotype of them. To presume too much about your audience can not only lead to faulty conclusions but can also harm your relationship with them as you fail to think about the audience as full people but, instead, as a collection of tendencies. Barring a survey or other measure of your actual audience, audience analysis is only an educated guess that provides another useful piece of contextual information in crafting a speech.

Finally, in assessing demographics you are generally concentrating on the majority views of your immediate and intended audience for reasons that can be pragmatic but also limiting. This means you are at risk of overlooking or marginalizing audience members who are exceptions to the predominant factors found in the audience. Occasionally you might purposefully and rationally decide that your message will not be directly targeted at audience outliers, but it is often beneficial to include appeals that allow you to connect with those in the audience beyond the demographic norm. Similarly, our ability to account for audience demographics is complicated when our message is reproduced in different contexts—if it is preserved on YouTube, for instance, and available for future audiences. In such a case, with changing contexts, circumstances, and listeners, our ability to analyze our audience effectively is necessarily limited.

BOX 5-3

Sizing Up Your Classroom Audience

As you consider the prospect of delivering a speech in your present course, consider your specific classroom audience, their psychology, and the environment.

- How would you characterize your class's demographic elements such as age, ethnicity, geographic background, religious affiliation, political affiliation, and socioeconomic status? How might such factors shape your choices as a speaker?
- What have you learned about your classmates' knowledge, beliefs, and convictions so far during the course? How might such knowledge influence your approach to the topic?
- What are the specific aspects of the communication environment that will have an impact on the audience? For example, will your speech take place early in the morning or right before lunch? Will your speech take place on a Friday afternoon or just before an important event?

These are questions of audience analysis that, for a thoughtful speaker, provide the basis for audience adaptation.

Psychological Factors

Audience analysis extends beyond demographic characteristics to factors related to audience psychology. Like audience demographics, you want to consider how **psychological factors**—audience predispositions related to their mental state, attitude, interest in and experience with the topic, occasion, and speaker—may influence reception of your message.

Psychological factors such as audience interest in and experience with the topic, their relationship with the speaker, and the occasion or purpose of a speech can influence how an audience reacts to a message. For example, one measure of audience interest is the extent to which members attend a presentation on a voluntary basis or are what is called a captive audience. We generally assume that audience members who attend voluntarily have more genuine interest in a topic and are inclined to show more goodwill toward the speaker. In contrast, when you address a largely captive audience—an audience that is required to be in attendance—it becomes even more important that you make additional efforts to engage them and work to make the presentation individually relevant. Another psychological factor subject to audience analysis is the familiarity of the audience with the speaker. This element, which is intimately related to chapter 3's discussion of ethos, concerns the amount of experience the audience has with the speaker and the speaker's reputation. When a speaker has a past relationship with the audience, he or she can draw on that familiarity to more easily adapt a speech to the audience's needs and interests. Familiarity is often a source of goodwill between speaker and audience, and the speaker can capitalize on that positive rapport. In contrast, a speaker with whom the audience is unfamiliar will often need to work to build a positive relationship. Finally, it is important that the speaker consider the occasion or purpose of the speech when shaping it for a particular audience. This includes factors such as the expected formality of the event, its tone or mood, and its importance. As a speaker you want your presentation to reflect the demands of the situation, and you should adapt accordingly.

Environmental Factors

Finally, as a speaker you should also consider environmental factors and how they can impact your message. **Environmental factors** refer to elements of the speaking situation such as time of day, location, size of audience, and configuration of the speaking venue that can influence how the audience receives the message. For instance, the time of day a speech is given—early, late, near mealtime—can influence audience attitudes and reactions. Anyone who has taken an 8:00 a.m. class understands audience alertness and geniality is often lower at that time of morning! Likewise, speaking immediately prior to a meal or at the end of a long day of events—particularly when an event runs long or falls behind schedule—can produce different audience reactions. In each case, you want to reflect on how it might be beneficial to change your speaking plans or approach due to such factors—how long you speak, the sorts of supporting media you use, your use of humor, and so on. In a similar fashion, you want to analyze the place of address—whether it is indoors or outdoors (are participants standing in the cold or in the hot sun?), if there is sound equipment, the acoustics of the venue—and adjust accordingly. To assist in doing so, try to learn as much as possible about your speaking environment, visiting it in advance in order to stand in the speaking space, test equipment, and so forth. You will want to account for many of these environmental factors by modulating your delivery. Being flexible and adjusting to the environmentally influenced needs of the audience will allow you to be more effective.

Brief remarks made by Boston Red Sox star David Ortiz at Fenway Park on April 20, 2013, served to bring together many elements related to audience, including assessing the rhetorical situation and audience analysis. That day's game, the Red Sox's first home game since the terrorist attack near the finish line of the Boston Marathon on April 15, brought to a close an emotional week for the city of Boston and the nation. In the days following the attack, the national audience participated in charity benefits and embraced the symbol and phrase "Boston Strong"; members of the running community, interpreting the act of terrorism as in part directed at them, donned clothing featuring "I run for Boston"; and Major League Baseball responded with teams across the country wearing special uniforms and uniform patches in an act of solidarity, and all stadiums repeated the Fenway Park ritual of playing "Sweet Caroline" (even the arch-rival New York Yankees).

David Ortiz addresses the crowd at Fenway Park before the Boston Red Sox game on April 20, 2013.

Prior to the April 20 game, there was an on-field ceremony featuring public leaders who had coordinated the city's response to the attack, as well as stories from people present at the bombing and acts to honor marathon volunteers and rescue workers. The ceremony also included as its backdrop a giant American flag that spanned Fenway Park's famed "Green Monster" wall in left field, a respectful crowd holding signs of thanks and many American flags, and Boston police officers. The ceremony closed with brief remarks from Ortiz, a native of the Dominican Republic who is affectionately known as "Big Papi." After taking the microphone, Ortiz noted that rather than saying "Red Sox" the front of the team's uniforms said "Boston," making the team a symbol for the entire city. He also thanked those who spoke at the ceremony and who were directly involved in the situation—first responders, law enforcement, and community leaders. Finally, he spoke to the crowd in a frank manner that reflected the emotions of the city when he said: "This is our fucking city. And nobody is going to dictate our freedom. Stay strong."[9] Ortiz's statement was met with enthusiastic applause.

Public profanity over open airwaves would generally be condemned, and potentially subject to fines for violating Federal Communications Commission (FCC) rules. But instead of condemning this act in front of a packed stadium that no doubt included children, Major League Baseball Commissioner Bud Selig gave the statement his endorsement. Noting that he found the entire ceremony "really emotional" and that it brought him to tears, Selig said, "I thought David Ortiz's choice of words was outstanding given what he was trying to say. I mean that sincerely."[10] FCC Chairman Julius Genachowski, charged with enforcing standards for communication decency, agreed with Ortiz and Selig and tweeted from the FCC's official account:

 **The FCC** ⊘
@FCC

 Follow

David Ortiz spoke from the heart at today's Red Sox game. I stand with Big Papi and the people of Boston - Julius

4:55 PM - 20 Apr 2013

6,481 RETWEETS **2,225** FAVORITES

On a different day—one not immediately following the emotional capture of a terrorist suspect and connected to the return of baseball to Boston—and in a different place (a city where the bombing did not occur), Ortiz's remarks would have been considered inappropriate. But in this case his comments matched the rhetorical situation as well as the emotion, interests, and geography of his audience. His speech underscores that understanding the rhetorical situation and one's audience is much like most elements of public speaking—it is about understanding the moment, the context of one's remarks, and connecting with the audience.

AUDIENCE ADAPTATION

Lisa was preparing to give a speech in class on the benefits of community supported agriculture (CSA) as a valuable source of local, organic food. In analyzing her audience she realized that most were of a traditional college age (18–23 years old), lived in campus housing and were on a school dining plan, had minimal disposable income, and were from urban areas and unfamiliar with either growing their own food or CSAs. Given this information Lisa began thinking about how she might best develop her speech while recognizing her audience's experiences, opportunities, and constraints. Doing so led her to focus on the environmental, health, and economic benefits of local, organic food because she knew that these three values were generally held in esteem by her classmates. Lisa also conducted an interview with her campus's food services manager to learn how they were using local products. That meeting alerted her to a local farmers market and the array of products available there. Collectively, these efforts allowed Lisa to focus on three important values held by her audience, gave her a means to localize the issue in a community familiar to the audience, provided her with local sources and examples that would have more credibility with her audience, and led her to a plan that was feasible. In her speech she encouraged class members who belonged to a fraternity or sorority to work with their house managers to make purchases from a local CSA to supplement their existing food service; she urged students from residence halls to join her during a meeting with the director of campus food services to encourage better utilization of local products; and she asked all students to visit the local farmers market for fresh fruits and other area bounty. In short, after considering the composition and means of her audience, Lisa transformed a topic that sounded good in principle but was distantly abstract into one that was relevant and suited to her peers. She practiced audience adaptation.

When we adapt to an audience, we use knowledge gained from audience analysis to optimize our speech. By necessity the previous section indirectly addressed audience adaptation as each example of audience analysis was accompanied by implicit suggestions about what particular demographic, psychological, and environmental factors might mean for a speech. Here we bring together some key principles and techniques in the use of audience adaptation.

It's Still Your Message

A key principle at the center of audience adaptation is that you, as the speaker, must continue to own the message. That is, your efforts at audience adaptation must not compromise your voice and vision. Your intent is not to tell the audience merely what they want to hear or talk about what would be popular. Instead, use audience adaptation to build a stronger relationship with the audience while seeking to improve the clarity and effectiveness of your message in ways that advance the public good. This means there are necessary limits to how you will use audience adaptation. Your ideal is to search for relationships and common ground from which to build your message—ways to connect with the audience and make your message relevant to them while maintaining your authenticity. Here we identify six methods or techniques for adapting your message to your audience. As with audience in general, many of these techniques resurface in other sections of this book.

Finding Common Ground

At the center of audience adaptation is the effort to find common ground—a mental space in which you and the audience can effectively relate to one another and join when considering your shared interest in and concern for a topic. This common ground is the basis for other elements of adaptation because it is how you connect with the audience, stimulate mutual interest, and demonstrate the relevance of your message.

The forging of common ground is expressed through the concept of identification. **Identification** is the degree to which individuals or groups find their interests joined or linked. For literary critic Kenneth Burke identification is the primary means of persuasion; it is in essence the center of rhetoric. As Burke explains, "You persuade a man only insofar as you can talk his language by speech, gesture, tonality, order, image, attitude, idea, *identifying* your ways with his."[11] For Burke, an audience will be persuaded by a speaker only to the degree that they feel a connection with him or her. When we identify with someone, when we have a sense of commonality, we also can share a view of life, demonstrate similar values, or develop a sense of trust. In terms of audience adaptation, the speaker attempts to cultivate identification with the audience and between the audience and the topic.

You have undoubtedly experienced identification in your everyday life. You can probably think of a time when you were on a trip or vacation and felt a sense of camaraderie with someone you came across who shared the same hometown as you, or a time you engaged in conversation with a stranger you saw wearing the hat of your favorite sports team. The connection you felt in these situations and the sudden comfort you felt in sharing came from identification. Similarly, think about a time when you first met a group of people—maybe eating for the first time with a group from your campus residence or at a camp you attended. The conversation may have been difficult until something was shared that you could relate to and then, in turn, you shared your similar story. Conversely, it is on those occasions when we can't find a point of identification that we are likely to sit out the conversation and perhaps conclude that these are people with whom we do not want to be "stuck with" in the future. What is at work in these examples is identification—our ability (or inability) to locate common ground with others. As a speaker you hope to apply information gleaned from audience analysis to adapt to your audience in ways that foster identification, that create a connection which will allow the audience to connect with what you are saying.

Using Appropriate Language

Another way to adapt to your audience is to use appropriate language. Think for a moment about our common expectation that our teachers, doctors, lawyers, and religious leaders will adjust what they have to teach or say to our level and our specific needs and interests. We would be very frustrated with a professor who spoke to a college class with the same vocabulary and expectation of knowledge with which he or she writes a journal article for specialists in their academic field. If we meet a lawyer who speaks in the highly technical language of the law, including the use of Latin terms and phrases, we fairly quickly ask, "Could you please explain that idea in a way I can understand?" In other words, if a speaker does not analyze and adjust to his or her audience, the audience is likely to ask them to do so. If you don't comply, the audience is likely to tune you out.

In speaking situations you should adjust your language based on audience characteristics such as age, education, and knowledge. This means you should adjust the complexity of your language—the amount of technical language you use and even the possible use of popular slang terms—depending on the audience and situation.

Adjusting Depth and Complexity of Content

Audience adaptation also means adjusting the depth of information presented on a topic and its complexity. You will want to consider your audience's familiarity with or knowledge of a topic as you assess how much background is needed on it. Likewise, you need to adjust the depth and complexity of your content based on situational factors such as the time available to speak and the purpose of the occasion.

It is frustrating for an audience when a speaker spends a significant amount of time explaining an idea or event with which they already have high familiarity. When a speaker uses much of his or her allotted time rehashing common knowledge rather than addressing present issues that have drawn the audience to a presentation, it is a speaking opportunity squandered. Adapting to the needs and knowledge of the audience ensures your presentation will be relevant and timely.

Appealing to Deeply Held Values

A fourth way to adapt to your audience is through appeal to values that they identify as important. Demonstrating in a speech how a problem violates or jeopardizes a deeply held value motivates an audience. Similarly, explaining how a particular action or a particular decision will advance an important value makes an audience more likely to lend their support to a cause. Common values that work in such a fashion in the American context are those such as freedom, justice, and equality. Value appeals are discussed in more depth in chapter 10's discussion of deliberation and chapter 12's exploration of persuasion.

Using Compelling Supporting Appeals

One of the most effective ways to employ audience adaptation is through supporting appeals. As a speaker you should select examples, analogies, metaphors, and narratives that reverberate with your audience. You benefit from selecting points of explanation and comparison that will be more familiar to them and thus easier to relate to. An example is an illustration that serves to support a broader point or conclusion. However, if a selected example is unfamiliar to the audience or too obscure, it is unlikely to be effective. Metaphors and analogies seek to compare two items or situations, one of which is familiar to an audience and the other one less so. Popular sources for metaphors include sports, the home, and corporate culture, among many possibilities. For example, sports metaphors that are used to quantify the quality of an effort include characterizing a heroic effort as "swinging for the fences," a successful effort as a "touchdown," an intense effort as a "full-court press," and a desperate effort as a "Hail Mary." Such metaphors can be very effective for some audiences, but in adapting you should think about the interest and relevance they have for your particular audience and, by all means, use a variety of such appeals rather than constantly returning to the same subject area. Finally, you can adapt to the audience through the use of narratives and familiar stories, stories featuring common themes and values or individuals that are respected by the audience. The stories draw an audience into the speech while, if they are properly adapted, also link your topic with interests held by the audience.

Selecting Credible and Familiar Sources

Finally, even your sources should be influenced by audience factors and can be adapted to your audience. As discussed in chapter 4, there are a variety of standards for evaluating research materials. However, you can also select sources likely held in high esteem by a particular audience; doing so helps build your ethos and the strength of your argument. It is one thing if you make a claim, it is another if a source supports your claim, and it is quite another (and very helpful) if a source known to and respected by the audience supports your claim.

Adaptation, Not Manipulation

Before closing we return to a point alluded to at the outset of this section and a concern that implicates ethical communication—adaptation does not mean saying merely what the audience wants to hear or what is popular. Nor does it mean ignoring ethical concerns and manipulating the audience to achieve your desired response. One adapts to connect with the audience, to clarify content, and to assist with decision-making that benefits the public good, not to mislead or prey upon one's audience, whether that be by magnifying fears or promising the fulfillment of personal desires. Returning to marketing practices, consumer groups and the federal government have voiced concerns over how some appeals have been manipulatively adapted to audiences who are vulnerable or at risk. In particular there is concern over how advertising targets children, tempts illegal behavior, or exploits groups such as the elderly. For instance, in recognition of concerns that sugary drinks are contributing to rising obesity rates, in 2013 Coca-Cola announced that it would change its advertising practices in ways that would reduce children's exposure to advertisements for their products.[12] Similarly, voluntary efforts and government regulations are aimed at limiting the amount and type of advertising used during children's television programs, the use of animation to sell some products (e.g., Joe Camel), and how some advertising is targeted. The point is that speakers, like advertisers, need to examine the ethics and implications of targeted messages and be mindful that adaptation and manipulation are not the same nor are they equally acceptable. Just as the motion picture, recording, and gaming industries have begun to examine the ethics of advertising practices that market violent content to minors, the ethical speaker is mindful that manipulation of the audience is not included in the practice of audience adaptation.[13]

The means by which we can adapt to our audience are numerous while sharing a common denominator: each is designed to enhance our connection to the audience while capitalizing on the audience's unique characteristics and qualities. In adapting to the audience, we seek to cultivate their interest, demonstrate the relevance of our message, and forge a bond with them.

SPOTLIGHT ON SOCIAL MEDIA:
Mitt Romney and the Challenges of the Unintended Audience

Every political candidate has challenges. For 2012 Republican presidential nominee Mitt Romney, the former governor of Massachusetts, one of his challenges was to successfully define himself by more than his considerable net worth. On one hand, that net worth demonstrated his success in the world and, thus, was an asset. On the other hand, his wealth made him unlike most Americans and created questions about his ability to relate to the concerns of the common person and family. In order to broaden his appeal, Romney made a number of efforts—as do almost all political candidates—to connect more with the proverbial "common man." His efforts at adaptation included public appearances and photo-ops in casual dress, visiting a Little Caesar's pizza outlet, running on a beach, eating hotdogs at sporting events, and the like.

At a small May 17, 2012, private fundraising event in Boca Raton, Florida, for which it reportedly cost $50,000 a plate to attend, Governor Romney was speaking to a different and decidedly more upscale audience. In his remarks, which were secretly recorded by a member of the catering staff, Romney said:

There are 47 percent of the people [in the United States] who will vote for the [current] president [Barack Obama] no matter what. All right, there are 47 percent who are with him, who are dependent upon government, who believe that they are victims, who believe the government has a responsibility to care for them, who believe that they are entitled to health care, to food, to housing, to you-name-it. That that's an entitlement. And the government should give it to them. And they will vote for this president no matter what. . . . These are people who pay no income tax. . . . My job is not to worry about those people. I'll never convince them they should take personal responsibility and care for their lives.[14]

Governor Romney's message at the fundraiser, regardless of what one might think of its content or accuracy (which has been both defended and challenged), can be seen as fitting the presumed interests of many in attendance. Thus, based on individual wealth, personal interests, and political beliefs, the message may have been resonant to the immediate audience, speaking of issues and reflecting perceptions that were relatable.

Protestor outside a Romney fundraiser in September 2012.

Soon, however, snippets of Romney's remarks began appearing on YouTube, and references to what he said at the dinner were made on the message boards of a variety of online news outlets. By the fall, the entire video was in the hands of the liberal political magazine *Mother Jones*, and the reporting of it created something of a firestorm.[15] The remarks were no longer only being made to Romney's immediate and intended audience—they were available to everyone. Writing in the Huffington Post, Marty Kaplan, director of the Norman Lear Center and professor at the USC Annenberg School, summarized reaction to the comments and why they were so damaging to Romney: "It's plausible that footage cost Romney the presidency. It validated his biggest perceived weakness—his image as a cartoon plutocrat, Mr. Moneybags, the Bain guy who fired workers and saddled companies with debt, the country club Republican who . . . didn't have a clue about how ordinary Americans were hurting."[16]

Months after the conclusion of the presidential campaign and more than a year after the fundraiser, Romney reflected on the experience of the campaign and the

47% comment: "One of the interesting things about campaigns today, unlike probably 25 or 30 years ago, is that everything you say is being recorded. And you know now and then things don't come out exactly the way you want them to come out. They don't sound the way you thought they sounded. And now with a good opposition campaign they grab it, they blow it up, maybe they take it a bit out of context, maybe they don't. But obviously it's paraded in a way that you hadn't intended."[17]

The problem—and the lesson—is that today messages and audiences are fluid in nature. Our message may be effectively adapted to our immediate audience, and yet that message may ultimately be ineffective and even damaging when viewed by a wider public. A comment at a speech may be covered in the newspaper, but it is also quickly tweeted or included in a Facebook status update. The example demonstrates that even if you know most of your audience is in agreement on a particular issue, it's always risky to speak as if there is not another side to or perspective on the argument. Moreover, your immediate audience may not be your only audience, and that changes the nature of public speaking and how you should think about your audience.

Discussion Questions

- What is the best explanation in support of Mitt Romney's application of audience analysis and adaptation at the Florida fundraiser?
- Did Mr. Romney stereotype his intended and unintended audiences with his comments? What image of his unintended audience did Romney create?

IMAGINING THE FUTURE TOGETHER

Thus far we have concentrated on the process of gaining an understanding of who your audience is and how you can adapt to them in public speaking. Before closing, however, there is another dimension of audience to consider, one that is particularly important in efforts at civic engagement and occasions for public discussion—who your audience wants to be and how you can all work together to accomplish that. That is, in considering your audience, you are not restricted to who they are now; but, rather, you can engage in brainstorming, problem-solving, and even dreaming as you work with your audience to imagine a better future together.

As a speaker, you are often working with an audience in an effort to improve some aspect of society—to address a rhetorical exigence. Bobby Kennedy did that when he spoke in urban areas about improving quality of life and advocating for equal justice; Martin Luther King Jr. did that when pursuing his dream of equality; and Barack Obama did that when promoting hope and change during his first presidential campaign. These public figures didn't take audiences just as they were but presented a vision where, by working together, it was possible to imagine what they and the nation could become.

In his essay "In Search of 'the People': A Rhetorical Alternative," Michael Calvin McGee theorized a rhetorical conception of "the people" that speaks to how we, as rhetors, might work with our public audiences in shaping the future.[18] As a rhetor you have the potential to lead your audience by offering a collective vision of their existence and future potential, and working to transform them from a mass of individuals into a collectivity with a defined purpose. The point is that through public speech we can bring a people—a community—together in the service of a cause. It is a process which recognizes that as a speaker you can be a force for change but rarely can you create change alone. You need a community audience that you can work with and who can inspire others.

McGee approaches "the people" as a rhetorical construct that is called in to being by an advocate. In this way a community is activated through rhetoric. To be sure a community always exists to some extent, but "the people" are drawn into a collective in particular moments. As McGee explains, the people "are conjured into objective reality, remain so long as the rhetoric which defined them has force, and in the end wilt away, becoming once again merely a collection of individuals."[19] In thinking about how to improve your community by confronting its problems, you are seeking to bring people together to address issues like teen pregnancy, urban blight, lack of adequate healthcare, and other problems. While your local community always exists, it is through rhetorical advocacy that it might be actively brought together for a cause.

People are typically activated in times of crisis and change: in responding to a natural disaster, during a political campaign and, of course, in times when a community comes together to consider a civic challenge. Imagine, for instance, that your community is considering a ballot referendum that would increase property taxes to fund the building of a new school. If you were to advocate that cause, you would, of course, be interested in appealing to parents of school children. However, when activating the political community and offering a vision for what new school facilities could provide the community, your vision for the future is likely broader than those parents and children. You would be interested in appealing to lifelong residents of the city, grandparents of school children, small-business owners, and others by imagining what improved educational opportunities might mean for the future; it could attract people to the town, help produce citizens and workers, and so on. If effectively drawn together during the course of the campaign, volunteers would form a people, a collective working on behalf of their common cause through phone calls, placement of yard signs, development of campaign literature, door-to-door canvassing of neighborhoods, and other activities. Once the referendum was complete, this collective would disperse as the rhetoric that drew this diverse set of individuals together would cease to be a unifying force.

As a speaker working with public audiences, you too have the opportunity to work with them in imagining a better future. By analyzing your audience and adapting to them, you can work together in not only imagining but in constructing a better future together.

SUMMARY

This chapter has demonstrated that understanding your audience is critically important to public speaking. Without an attentive audience that has the means and will to act on the rhetoric they hear, public speech will be ineffective. It is in our understanding of and relationship to our audience that we, as speakers, can maximize our effectiveness and best contribute to public life.

- Effective public speaking is dependent upon understanding and responding to the rhetorical situation. A speaker must assess a rhetorical exigence that invites action; consider the constraints on acting; and seek to identify, persuade, and influence a public audience who is capable of contributing to positive change in the situation.

- Audience analysis, the practice of assessing audience factors and characteristics that are likely to influence an audience's reception of a message, is a valuable resource for public speakers when developing their message. Audience analysis functions by considering demographic factors, psychological factors, and environmental factors.
- Audience demographics are personal characteristics of the audience that are likely to shape their views and perspectives on a topic. Common demographic factors include age, gender, race and ethnicity, socioeconomic status, culture, geography, education, occupation, and group memberships.
- Psychological factors to consider in audience analysis include the audience's mental state, attitude, and interest in the topic, occasion, and speaker.
- Environmental factors that can affect audience reception of a message include elements of the speaking situation such as time of day, location, size of audience, and configuration of the speaking venue.
- Despite its utility, audience analysis is also subject to important limitations including how well we can know our audience, how accurately demographic factors will predict predispositions, and what audience analysis means for audience members who fall outside the audience majority. To generalize about an audience too broadly risks stereotyping individuals and groups based on inaccurate conclusions about the meaning of particular audience characteristics.
- Audience adaptation is how you make use of audience-analysis cues to shape your approach to a topic. Your goal in using audience adaptation is to build a stronger relationship with the audience while seeking to improve the clarity and effectiveness of your message in ways that advance the public good. Common means to practice audience adaptation include promoting identification, using appropriate language, adjusting the depth and complexity of material, appealing to deeply held values, using compelling supporting appeals, and selecting credible and familiar sources.
- When working with an audience, you are not restricted to who they are in the present. Rather, by engaging in brainstorming, problem-solving, and dreaming you can work with an audience to imagine a better future together. Through rhetoric a speaker can bring a people—a community—together in the service of a cause.

KEY TERMS

REVIEW QUESTIONS

1. What is a rhetorical situation? Why is understanding the rhetorical situation essential for effective public speaking?
2. Why is audience analysis a useful tool in public speaking?
3. How can a speaker employ information derived from audience analysis to adapt to an audience?
4. What are the risks and limitations of audience analysis?
5. As a speaker, how might you learn more about the demographics and attitudes of your audience in advance of a public speech?
6. What is identification? What is its relationship to audience adaptation?

DISCUSSION QUESTIONS

1. Recall a recent speaker on your campus who did a particularly good or poor job of adapting to their audience. What audience and environmental factors did he or she account for or overlook?
2. How does one adapt to an audience without losing one's voice, without selling out one's message, even when doing so will be popular with the audience?
3. To what degree should you adapt your sources to your audience? How might you choose different sources if preparing a speech on global warming for a group of scientists versus a group of elected governmental officials? Are there any ethical concerns involved in differently selecting sources?
4. Are Plato's and Aristotle's assessments of audience and audience character relevant today? Have they been reinforced, complicated, or rejected in contemporary times?
5. How can you use audience analysis in your present classroom when preparing for your next speech? What demographic, psychological, and environmental factors are likely to be relevant to your planning?
6. How is social media changing our understanding of audience? What might social media's continued growth mean for audience analysis and adaptation?

CHAPTER 6

Organizing Your Public Presentation in a Clear and Compelling Manner

---

Chapter Objectives

Students will:

- Consider the purpose of organization.
- Recognize the characteristics of a strong thesis statement.
- Learn the common patterns of arrangement for the presentation of main ideas.
- Evaluate the strengths and weaknesses of different arrangement patterns for a given rhetorical purpose.
- Analyze the functions of effective introductions and conclusions.
- Craft preview statements, signposts, and transitions, and understand their function in oral presentations.

When Aristotle outlined the five canons (laws or principles) of rhetoric in the fourth century BCE, he called the second canon "arrangement." Today, we more frequently use the term "organization" to understand what Aristotle included in the canon of arrangement. **Organization** refers to how you order your points in a speech and how you verbally connect those elements so your audience can follow. Aristotle, one of the earliest known scholars of rhetoric, recognized that speakers who wish to capture *and hold* an audience's attention must think about how to arrange and connect their content so that the audience is best prepared to receive it. But even before Aristotle's teaching notes on rhetoric were compiled and widely circulated, many ancient rhetors were practicing and perfecting the art of organization in public speaking.

For example, one of the earliest surviving speeches from antiquity was written by the sophist Gorgias, who came to Athens from Sicily in 427 BCE. His speech titled Encomium of Helen is one he presented repeatedly to advertise his teaching ability in the art of rhetoric. (An "encomium" is a speech of enthusiastic praise, and a translation of part of the speech appears in Box 6-1). Gorgias's purpose in the Encomium of Helen

Organized Hard Drives. One interpretation of this photograph by Uwe Hermann is that with the proliferation of information in the twenty-first century, organization is vital so that we can access and share that information with others.

is to redeem the reputation of an infamous woman in mythology, Helen of Troy, whom many blamed for the Trojan War. Helen was taken from her husband, King Menelaus of Sparta, by Paris of Troy. The question of whether Helen was abducted, seduced, or simply used as a pawn in the gods' eternal struggles was a common theme in ancient Greek poetry. All agreed, however, that the desire to right the wrong of her capture (or seduction) sparked the Trojan War.

Gorgias's speech asks whether Helen could be blamed for the abduction and war, and he argues that she is blameless. He ends the introduction to his speech by stating, "I wish, by giving some logic to language, to free the accused of blame and to show that her critics are lying and to demonstrate the truth and to put an end to ignorance."[1] This is his thesis: Helen is not at fault and those who think otherwise are ignorant. The speech is admired for many reasons, including the creativity of its arguments, its style—it is filled with elements such as rhyming word endings and parallel structures—and its organization. In this chapter, however, we will focus on the speech's organization.

Gorgias structures his speech with a lyrical introduction and a clear preview of the four main points he will offer to support his thesis. His preview reads: "For [either] by fate's will and gods' wishes and necessity's decrees she did what she did or by force reduced or by words seduced or by love induced."[2] Following this preview of arguments, each of the sections in the body of the speech addresses one of these topics outlined: Helen was either a pawn of fate and warring gods; taken by force and raped; wooed by an insincere speech (in which case the speaker bears the blame); or she fell in love, and everyone knows love is not a sin, but rather a spell that clouds the mind. When Gorgias has laid out all four of these arguments, he concludes by restating them, in reverse order: "How, then, can blame be thought just? Whether she did what she did by falling in love or persuaded by speech or seized by violence or forced by divine necessity, she is completely acquitted. By speech I have removed disgrace from a woman."³ In each case, he argues, Helen is absolved of guilt.

One of many lessons students of ancient rhetoric continue to draw from this very early speech is the importance of clear organization. Gorgias begins with an introduction, posits an argumentative thesis, provides a clear preview of the speech's main arguments, offers clear transitions and connectives between main points, and concludes decisively after reviewing the content he has covered.

While Gorgias makes these organizational elements of his speech seem straightforward, even natural, *we know they are the result of careful thought and hard work*. His skill is one of the reasons he was a sought-after teacher in the fifth century BCE. Since ancient times, scholars and practitioners of public speaking have classified, studied, and practiced methods of organization; and this chapter provides an overview of some of their collected wisdom so that you, too, may implement it as you write your speeches.

BOX 6-1

Gorgias's Encomium of Helen

The Encomium of Helen, by the Sicilian rhetorician Gorgias, has been studied as a model of organization for centuries. Here we present a translated selection from the introduction and preview.

[Prooemion] 1. Fairest ornament [*kosmos*] to a city is a goodly army and to a body beauty and to a soul wisdom and to an action virtue and to speech truth, but their opposites are unbefitting. Man and woman and speech and deed and city and object should be honored with praise if praiseworthy, but on the unworthy blame should be laid; for it is equal error and ignorance to blame the praiseworthy. 2. It is the function of a single speaker both to prove the needful rightly and to disprove the wrongly spoken. Thus, I shall refute those who rebuke Helen, a woman about whom there is univocal and unanimous testimony among those who have believed the poets and whose ill-omened name has become a memorial of disasters. I wish, by giving some logic to language, to free the accused of blame and to show that her critics are lying and to demonstrate the truth and to put an end to ignorance.
[Narration] 3. Now that by nature and birth the woman who is the subject of this speech was preeminent among preeminent men and women, this is not unclear, not even to a few. . . . On many did she work the greatest passions of love, and by her one body she brought together many bodies of men greatly minded for great deeds. Some had the greatness of wealth, some the glory of ancient noblesse, some the vigor of personal prowess, some the power of acquired knowledge. And all came because of a passion that loved conquest and a love of honor that was unconquered. 5. Who he was and why and how he sailed away taking Helen as his love, I shall not say; for to tell the knowing what they know is believable but not enjoyable. Having now exceeded to my time allotted for my introduction [*logos*], I shall proceed to my intended speech [*logos*] and shall propose the causes for which Helen's voyage to Troy is likely [*eikos*] to have taken place.
[Proposition] 6. For [either] by fate's will and gods' wishes and necessity's decrees she did what she did or by force reduced or by words seduced or by love induced.⁴

We will return to the elements of thesis statements, logical arrangement of main points, strong introductions and conclusions, and transitional elements later in the chapter, but first we want to discuss the purpose of organization for the speeches you compose in contemporary times. Many inexperienced or ineffective public speakers may believe that once the speech topic has been selected and researched, the speech-writing process will flow naturally. On the contrary! Skilled speakers know that selecting and organizing the material for a speech requires time and critical thinking.

THE PURPOSE OF ORGANIZATION

We begin this chapter with the *purpose* of organization, rather than jumping directly into the steps for writing an outline, which is to foreground the critical thinking that is at the heart of strong organization. On occasions where you speak to build civic engagement in your community, you will probably find that by paying close attention to organization, you facilitate productive discussion and fuller participation. When you present and distill complex issues clearly, you better prepare your audience to think through pressing issues and to deal fairly with the people and values implicated in your decisions.

You must also think about the complexity of your information and imagine what it might be like to be *unfamiliar* with that material (as you likely were when you first began your research). How can you make your message comprehensible and compelling to people who have spent much less time with the material than you have? How can you best prepare your audience to tackle an intricate issue of shared concern? You ask a lot, even too much, of your audience when you give them a poorly organized speech. Your decisions about organization should therefore be motivated by the desire to make your ideas as clear and as logical as possible for those who are giving you their time and attention.

Four Benefits of a Well-Organized Speech

There are at least four benefits of a well-organized speech, yet they are all rooted in the principle that an organized speech is both easier to deliver and follow. The first benefit is that you increase the likelihood of your audience's active engagement. Have you ever listened to a speaker and thought, "She is certainly very smart and knows a lot, but I couldn't follow what she was saying"? Or perhaps you've attended a presentation and thought, "He has a lot of passion for the topic, but I don't see how his concerns are relevant to me." When a presentation is disorganized, listeners have two options. They may labor to make sense of the presentation, in effect, constructing a coherent outline for the material in their minds. (As you might guess, this takes a great deal of mental energy and discipline on the part of listeners, and most will not do it for very long.) The second and more likely response is that listeners check out, let their minds wander, or discretely turn their attention to their cell phones. Thus, a jumbled speech tends to elicit passive listening from an audience, whereas a clearly structured speech enables active listening.

Second, an organized speech is easier to remember. A member of your audience may report after listening to your speech, "He made three main points." Or, "She first explained the problem, then the causes of the problem, and offered three solutions for us to consider."

Third, a well-organized speech is easier for the speaker to deliver. A disorganized presentation is very difficult to deliver because you have to work to make sense of your own material as you are presenting it. On the other hand, when your speech is well organized, it gives you confidence; you can more easily remember the main points because they are structured in a logical fashion. Thus you can focus your energy on *delivering* the ideas, and this allows you to give a more fluent and compelling presentation.

Finally, careful organization can make you more persuasive. When you present an organized speech, you implicitly show your audience how much thought and care went into preparing the speech. In this way, organization builds credibility. If listeners can easily see the connections between ideas, they may find your line of reasoning more convincing. They may even see connections among ideas or outcomes in a way they had not previously considered. When your audience makes connections *with* you, they more readily grant or even anticipate your conclusions.

BOX 6-2

Four Benefits of a Well-Organized Speech

1. It is easier for your audience to follow.
2. It is easier to remember and summarize.
3. It is easier for you to deliver.
4. It is potentially more persuasive because you appear more credible to your audience.

The Recursive Nature of Organization

As we present the next section on the steps of the organization process, keep in mind that your true organizing process may not be as linear as we make it seem here. Composing a speech is in reality much more recursive—that is, the process moves forward and backward; it circles on itself. You may write a thesis statement and then craft an introduction that leads up to it. You then turn to your main points, but as you organize the body of your speech, your purpose may evolve and you will find you need to go back and revise your thesis. Then again, some speakers may find they can more easily start with main points and allow the thesis to emerge from the body of the speech. Whatever process works best for you, expect this recursivity as you draft your speech. The best speakers find themselves honing or tightening all the elements of the speech throughout the process. The bottom line, however, is that speeches that lack a clear purpose and central claim (thesis) will never be very successful. For this reason, we begin with the strategic choices that will help ensure that your thesis is a strong foundation for the rest of your speech.

THESIS STATEMENTS: FRAMING A CLEAR PURPOSE

The **thesis statement** is the central statement of the speech for which the speaker seeks adherence or acceptance from the audience. Another way to explain the thesis is as the focal point of the entire presentation. It is the idea that the audience must understand and contemplate in order to receive your overall message. In argumentation, the thesis is often referred to as the proposition or claim. Recall the thesis from the Encomium of Helen: "I wish, by giving some logic to language, to free the accused of blame and to show that her critics are lying and to demonstrate the truth and to put an end to ignorance."[5] After hearing this line, listeners know where the speaker will focus his persuasive efforts.

It is important that all speeches center on one key idea or proposition, ideally captured in a single sentence. This keeps the focus of your speech straightforward, simple, and clear—for you *and* your audience. The rest of the speech should employ proper illustrations and arguments to support this theme.

Fashioning a clear and concise thesis statement requires you to focus the presentation in a particular way. It necessarily excludes other methods of argumentation or presentation of evidence that you might have taken in the speech. As you craft your thesis, consider the following questions:

- Is my purpose to inform my audience about relevant perspectives on a topic before they engage in a public deliberation or begin to consider solutions?
- Do I want my audience to consider more than one approach to address an established need?
- Am I writing a speech to advocate for a specific plan of action on a matter of shared importance to my audience?

The answer you give to these questions will lead you to different decisions about what material you will include in your thesis and what you will leave out. As we discussed in chapter 4, not everything that is interesting or related belongs in your speech; letting go some of your hard work may be painful, but you must focus on what makes your purpose and ideas most clear and relevant to your audience. Let's look now at a few speakers' attempts to come up with effective, appropriate thesis statements.

A Thesis to Inform an Audience as They Prepare for Deliberation

Damien was a member of a high school football team, and at the recent homecoming game, the star quarterback, one of his good friends, got a severe concussion. This was the fourth concussion of the season for Damien's team, and it seemed that, following homecoming, every community member he talked to—parents, teachers, friends, his family physician—went on and on about the dangers of football or had a way to "solve" this problem. On top of that, Damien frequently saw stories on the news about NFL players who were suing the league due to severe brain injuries. Some suspected recent suicides by former NFL players might also be linked to concussions. Damien was scared about concussions, but he also felt the game of football was under attack, and this upset him.

He noticed that members of his community had a tendency to advocate for one particular point of view and overlook several important, often competing, perspectives.

Damien's first instinct was to shut down or to ask everyone to shut up. He wasn't sure his community members could ever *really* talk to each other about football and concussions. At the same time, he felt that if he and several trusted mentors could sit down and discuss a variety of perspectives, they might stop making such close-minded statements and might be in a better position to advocate for new rules or policies. He decided to write a speech that informed community members about the potential solutions to the problem of concussions in high school football. His purpose was to ask his audience to weigh the benefits and drawbacks of several approaches.

Damien's Draft Thesis

Damien began with this thesis statement:

> We need to stop judging one another and listen better. We need to hear what other people in the community think because this is a way to show respect.

Damien's draft thesis offers a clear claim: we need to listen to and respect one another. But the thesis statement is also rather imprecise. He could say the same thing about any number of topics. The focus of his speech is not really about the importance of listening to one another, but about *the question he wanted his audience to consider more fully.* After more thought, Damien rewrote his thesis so that it better aligned with his goals.

Damien's Revised Thesis

> The first thing we in Columbus need is a fuller understanding of the problem, as well as of multiple perspectives on addressing concussions in high school football, before we are ready to advocate and implement specific changes. <u>With this goal in mind, the question that guides my speech this morning is: How can we best address the issue of concussions in high school football?</u>

This revised thesis, you will notice, is not a clearly stated argument, but remember, advocacy is not Damien's goal in this speech. His purpose is to inform his audience about a problem and possible solutions and to invite them to weigh options. (This is a necessary step before they move toward action in the future.) To this end, Damien's thesis statement does offer a directly stated focal point for his presentation. It is still the foundation upon which the rest of his speech will be built. Not all thesis statements, then, are decisive arguments or claims. This is important to remember because, as discussed in chapter 2, many participants in public debates make the point of arguing without acknowledging the complexity of the problem or the competing interests of those they need to involve in addressing the problem. Often, productive civic engagement must begin by weighing trade-offs before advocating a solution.

Let's turn now to a different type of speech, and, therefore, a different type of thesis statement.

A Thesis for Persuasion: Advocating Community Involvement in Animal Welfare

Ryan was passionate about the problem of animal abuse and neglect, and he wanted to give a speech on how to address this problem in his local county. Some approaches he considered included (1) allowing private or government agencies to more easily intervene when abusive or neglectful pet owners were identified; (2) organizing adoption days for his local animal shelter; (3) providing pet food for needy but loving pet owners; and (4) using Facebook and Twitter to raise awareness about local animal welfare issues. Ryan decided that the first of these four options, changing local law, was too time consuming. In fact, local activists had recently tried to pass legislation that would increase penalties for abusive pet owners, and they had not been successful. But he realized that the other three solutions were all ways that local community members could have an immediate impact on the lives of animals in his county, either by volunteering time, donating resources, or raising awareness. He decided to write a speech that discouraged audience members from putting more time into legal reform but that urged them to act in other tangible ways to improve the lives of local pets.

Ryan's Draft Thesis
Ryan's first thesis read:

> We should strengthen local animal control agencies that care for abused pets in our county.

The strengths of this thesis are that it states the solution Ryan prefers, it is simple and direct, and it offers a narrow focus for the action he advocates. This thesis does not, however, indicate exactly what Ryan means by "strengthen" or how the audience might make that happen. (Presumably, Ryan would identify and explain those actions in the speech.) Ryan may have been drawn to this approach because it provides a clear claim and focus, yet the thesis does not give everything away. But there is a risk here. The thesis might not provide enough information, and, consequently, Ryan might lose some audience members until he names specific actions within the speech.

Ryan's Revised Thesis
Ryan decided to experiment with a more detailed thesis:

> There are several ways to strengthen our local animal control agency's power to remove and care for abused animals in Montgomery County, but the most important thing you can do for neglected pets is to volunteer time and resources at your local animal shelter.

This thesis is more specific than the first thesis because it names the ways audience members can "support" local agencies. They can volunteer various resources at the local animal shelter. Here, audience members know exactly what Ryan means by "support"—unlike before. With this revised thesis, the purpose and direction of the speech are very clear.

   The advantage of this type of thesis is that it prepares the audience to hear Ryan's request in a specific way; they will probably listen to the entire speech with an ear for *how* they can volunteer time and resources.

   Once you have crafted your thesis statement, you need to determine the best way to develop and support your thesis for a given audience. It is time to turn to your main points.

BOX 6-3

Questions to Ask Yourself When Crafting Your Thesis Statement

1. What do I want to convey to my audience? Or, what is the position I am advocating?

2. How can my thesis statement appropriately limit my topic and make the boundaries of my argument clear?

3. Will those unfamiliar with my topic or my research be able to follow my thesis?

MAIN POINTS: THE BODY OF YOUR SPEECH

As you work to identify the main sections of your speech, turn to the parts of your research that seem most pertinent to your thesis statement. What relationships can you identify among these parts? In selecting main points, you are seeking the best way to present, develop, and support your thesis for the audience. Anything that does not speak directly, simply, and concisely to your thesis should be eliminated.

Gorgias's Main Ideas

What should main points look like? It depends upon your thesis and the type of speech you're giving. Recall that Gorgias had four main points for why Helen should not bear the blame for the Trojan War. Either she was:

1. used by the gods in their own game;
2. abducted and forced to leave;
3. persuaded by insincere words; or
4. blinded by love.

Each of these points is considered in turn—that is, further developed and supported—in the Encomium of Helen. For instance, as support for the fourth point, Gorgias argues that even if she fell in love, Helen should not be disparaged or hated because love is more powerful than human reason. As evidence, he reminds his audience that love makes both humans and gods act stupidly or against their best interests.

Ryan's Main Ideas

As a second example of how the main points might follow the thesis, we can return to Ryan's speech from the previous section. When Ryan thought about the variety of ways to improve animal welfare, he noted:

- Some people are not aware of the current laws governing animal abuse and neglect in the county; if they were, many would be more involved in rescuing pets.
- Stiffening penalties for pet owners is a good idea, but it takes too long. There are more effective ways to help pets.
- Community members can volunteer at shelters by cleaning pet cages and interviewing potential owners.
- Concerned community members can also raise awareness about pet issues through a variety of media.

Ryan decided his speech would begin by exploring a recent attempt in his community to address pet abuse and neglect. Then he would explain why people should explore solutions beyond legal reform. Finally, he would advocate two ways to immediately improve the lives of local pets: volunteer and raise awareness through many media outlets.

Ryan's main ideas:

1. First, concerned citizens must know animal welfare laws but also recognize what these laws fail to do.
2. A frequently proposed solution in our county is that we support legislation to stiffen penalties against abusers, but this solution is inadequate.
3. Instead we can and should take a much more immediately effective, two-pronged approach: volunteering in local shelters and increasing awareness in our county and more broadly.

Your Main Ideas

As you turn to your own evidence, begin grouping information into one-sentence points as best as you can, and then evaluate what you have. How do they fit together— or what does not fit with the others? Once you have a good sense of your main ideas, you can turn to a common pattern of arrangement to help you order the material in your speech. We noted earlier that scholars and practitioners of public speaking have studied, crafted, and experimented with methods of organizing speeches since ancient times. Over time, they have collected the most common patterns of arrangement as tools for identifying and constructing the type of speech you want to give and adapting that message to what you know about your audience. In the next section, we outline the most common patterns of arrangement in public speaking.

SPOTLIGHT ON SOCIAL MEDIA:
Twitter and Conference Presentations

One of the key organizing features of Twitter is the hashtag, the # symbol that allows Twitter users to search and follow a particular conversation. Many professional conferences now create hashtags for their events and display tweets on a conference blog, on screens in convention center hallways, or even on the screen as the presenter speaks.

Those who tweet about public presentations are often picking up on the internal *organization* of the speaker's message. Audience members may also use Twitter to take notes during a presentation; their tweets highlight central ideas and key relationships between main points. Such Twitter "notes" are also permanent and searchable. You might think of such a twitter feed as a collaboratively created outline and Q&A session.

For speakers, there are many ways Twitter works to expand audience engagement and to discover and share how the audience follows your speech. If a speaker cites a source, audience members may tweet links to that resource so that listeners may more easily locate the article, image, or video clip. Sometimes those who are reluctant to speak in a discussion are very active tweeters—the silent are not uninterested; they may simply prefer a different mode of participation.

Ryan Trauman, creator of the New Media Scholar blog, writes about how speakers themselves may play to Twitter's strengths—for instance, incorporating tweets about their presentation into the speech as a way of visually representing audience response. As he writes in his post "Twitter as Digital Scholarship: Why You Might Want to Sign Up":

> A backchannel occurs when several people attending the same small event (like a lecture, a class, or presentation) tweet about what the lecturer/teacher/presenter is saying. Those tweets can get picked up by other people in the room, if they're following that hashtag. They begin to respond to each other with a sort of "meta conversation" or "underlife" related to the common event/experience. In some cases, especially savvy speakers are able to project or display the backchannel and respond to it in real time. It's a pretty amazing way to increase opportunity of audience engagement and interaction (and, admittedly, distraction). When it works, it's pretty amazing. When it doesn't, it generally doesn't do much harm.[6]

As you organize your speech, especially if you tweet, it might be useful to think about how other tweeters may *use* your organization, transitional phases, and other signposts to locate, follow, and spread your main points through their tweets. In an appropriate time and place, you might even consider using a screen and inviting your audience to tweet to a designated hashtag during your presentation.

Keep in mind, however, that not all members of your audience may have equal access to the technology that drives social media. Before you incorporate Twitter into your presentation and invite your audience to join, ask yourself whom you are including and excluding by this decision.

Discussion Questions

- Have you ever been part of what Ryan Trauman describes as a "backchannel" Twitter conversation during a speech or public event? Do you agree with his assessment that "When it works, it's pretty amazing. When it doesn't, it generally doesn't do much harm"? Discuss your experience with classmates.

- You might try an in-class experiment if your instructor and classmates are willing: *Designate one or a few class days where the class has a live Twitter feed on a classroom screen, and have classmates tweet questions, summaries of important points, or resources to a common class hashtag.* When the experiment is over, discuss how Twitter changed the classroom experience. How did it help and/or hinder your engagement with the material? Did live tweets change classroom engagement? Were there other advantages or drawbacks? Explain.

PATTERNS OF ARRANGEMENT

A **pattern of arrangement** is a specific guide, or template, for choosing and organizing the main points of a speech. The arrangement helps determine both the content of the main points and their order. As you consider how to arrange the body of your speech, spend some time thinking about the type of claim you are making, the type of evidence you are presenting, and the type of response you are asking of your audience. Knowing what you want your audience to get out of the speech (or what an assignment asks you to demonstrate) will help you consider how best to arrange your material.

Interestingly, each of these patterns is not only reflective of a clear speech structure but is also representative of the most common ways we tend to think. So while you might be tempted to see them as simple organizational devices, recognize that by using them you are tapping into human logic at a deeper level. It is important to keep in mind that there is not a single, correct pattern for arrangement. You may decide on a different organizational structure depending upon subject, specific purpose, thesis, or audience.

Categorical Arrangement

A categorical or topical approach uses elements such as parts, forms, functions, methods, characteristics, perspectives, or qualities of a topic as its organizing principle. For example, Gorgias used this pattern of arrangement, organizing his speech according to the *explanations* for why Helen left for Troy and then demonstrating why each explanation did not place the blame on Helen herself.

A word of caution about categorical arrangement: Novice speakers too quickly resort to this pattern of organization without considering other options more carefully. For this reason, we suggest you use it as a last resort. Without clear connectives and transition words (discussed later) that clearly define the relationships between your categories, this pattern runs the highest risk of seeming random or disorganized.

Chronological Arrangement

A chronological structure uses time as its organizing principle. Thus a chronological speech often takes a past-present-future approach, organizes its main points by historical era, or addresses issues as they unfolded through time. If you are giving a speech requesting more funding for your community charity, you might persuade your audience to donate based on a chronological pattern that shows the positive impact your agency has had over time. You might end by stressing what the agency could do in coming months and years with more support.

Spatial Arrangement

A spatial structure is linear or sequential, moving through a progression of elements. The pattern essentially demonstrates how we get from point A to point B or what is similar and different as we move from point A to point B. Often overlooked by speakers, this pattern can be a powerful tool if you want to show, for example, how different regions of the country are affected by a particular policy or how different sites in a city appeared before and after a historical event.

Cause-Effect Arrangement

In the cause-effect arrangement, a speaker offers two main points—one on "cause" and the other on "effect." The pattern describes a situation or condition as it exists and then looks at or predicts its effects, often as a step in a process that will ask audience members to respond. Cesar Chavez, an influential twentieth-century civil rights activist and first president of the United Farm Workers, used this pattern when he called for the ban of pesticides closely associated with birth defects and cancer among farm workers and their children in California's San Joaquin Valley.[7]

Cause-effect arrangement is a particularly useful approach in showing the relationship between ideas or actions. For example, you might use this pattern if you wish to show how a local organization has been positively affected by a grant you seek to renew.

A word of caution about this pattern: when talking about cause and effect, a speaker needs to be careful of oversimplifying a situation. Before you use this pattern, ask yourself whether there are multiple causes that should be considered in order to do justice to a problem. Will your ethos and strength of reasoning be undermined if you address only one of those causes?

Three Problem-Based Arrangements

The next three patterns of arrangement are variations on a theme. They all begin with a statement of a problem in need of a solution. What follows after the problem is established can vary by the main points, evidence, and purpose you believe your audience needs to consider in order to be persuaded to address the problem.

Problem-Solution Arrangement

The problem-solution pattern is frequently used in persuasive speeches and proceeds by first documenting the nature, extent, and source of the problem before advocating a solution. Like the cause-effect arrangement, this type of speech typically has two main points that are succinctly divided between aspects of the "problem" and the "solution" advocated by the speaker. Examples might include explaining a particular solution to the deteriorating middle school in your community or a plan for improving air quality in your city.

Problem-Alternatives-Solution Arrangement

An attractive alternative to the problem-solution arrangement, the problem-alternatives-solution arrangement includes a middle main point that names and counters one or more alternative solutions before advocating for the solution the speaker sees as most promising. This approach allows the speaker to address popular counterarguments and policies in the alternatives section of the speech. Recall Ryan's speech on animal welfare in the thesis statement section. He ultimately chose the problem-alternatives-solution arrangement for his speech. The body of his presentation examined a recent initiative to raise fines for pet abuse and discussed why it was a less effective solution than multifaceted volunteer work at the local shelter.

Problem-Cause-Solution-Solvency Arrangement

A second alternative to the problem-solution structure, the problem-cause-solution-solvency pattern typically includes four main points. After identifying the nature and extent of the problem in the first point, the speaker addresses the cause, or source, of the problem in the second main point. The third step emphasizes how the proposed solution directly targets the cause of the problem, and, finally, the fourth step discusses the practicality, or costs and benefits, of implementing the solution. You might use this arrangement if you wanted to start a Backpack Food Program for hungry families in your local community. As you crafted the "solvency" section of your speech, you might cite the many other successful Backpack Food Programs around the country.

Refutative Arrangement

The refutative arrangement, sometimes called negative method of arrangement, is best suited to a hostile or apathetic audience because it allows the speaker to focus on the counterarguments the audience brings to the rhetorical occasion before making his or her appeal. This speech usually consists of three or four main points. In the first two to three points, the speaker acknowledges and refutes the strongest opposing arguments or most common solutions to the topic at hand. Each opposing argument constitutes one main point in the body of the speech. In the final main point, the speaker identifies his or her preferred solution and argues for its ascendancy. You might use this arrangement when you expect your audience's resistance to your proposal will be strong. For example, a speech that calls for an investment in downtown recycling bins in a city that has shown little commitment to recycling might be well served by this pattern of arrangement.

Monroe's Motivated Sequence

Monroe's motivated sequence was developed by Alan H. Monroe, a twentieth-century professor of communication. It is based on the idea that when one feels psychological discomfort, one is motivated to resolve that discomfort through some sort of action. The speaker who employs this sequence begins by getting the audience's attention, then convinces the audience of a need that exists, explains how that need can be satisfied, and allows the audience to visualize the solution. Finally, the speaker provides the audience with a means to act or respond. Barack Obama's 2013 "Address on Comprehensive Immigration Reform" is a real-world example largely patterned on Monroe's motivated sequence.[8]

1. **Attention step (introduction):** Catch the audience's interest.
2. **Need step:** Convince the audience that something is presently wrong that needs their attention.
3. **Satisfaction step:** Provide the audience with a solution that is within their power to correct the need.
4. **Visualization step:** Let the audience see how the satisfaction step will really change things in the future and/or see how bad things will get if they fail to adopt your method of satisfying the need.
5. **Action step (conclusion):** Ask the audience to participate and do something specific to satisfy the need.

Table 6.1 summarizes the primary patterns of arrangement addressed in this section. It lists the primary strengths of each pattern of arrangement, and then offers an example of a speech topic that *could be* a potential candidate for this pattern of arrangement. It is important to note that in the case of some example topics, there are additional approaches or patterns of arrangement you might choose. The table is designed to help you imagine possibilities for a given topic rather than dictate a pattern of arrangement. Ultimately, the pattern of arrangement you choose should be determined by your primary arguments and your purpose for the speech, rather than by our chart.

Whatever pattern of arrangement you choose to follow in your speech, your goal should be to select the most logical progression for your main points. As you select an arrangement to help you organize the material, think about which one will be easiest for the audience to follow and which one makes your desired response most clear. The arrangement is a tool that assists your audience in thinking through your claim and evidence. It also helps them know what type of action you hope they will take at the

Table 6.1 Primary Patterns of Arrangement

PATTERN OF ARRANGEMENT	PRIMARY STRENGTHS	EXAMPLE TOPICS
Categorical	• Straightforward way to divide a topic into parts, aspects, characteristics, or perspectives.	• Ways to get involved with youth mentorship in the community. • Multiple benefits of buying locally sourced food.
Chronological	• Demonstrates a process across time. • Shows historical relationship or connections between past, present, and future. • Speaker chooses to move forward or backward from a chosen point in time.	• Call for environmental intervention that focuses on how a habitat has changed over time. • How a brief history of civil rights in the US helps illuminate civil rights issues in the contemporary era.
Spatial	• Enables speaker to organize topic geographically. • Can illustrate spatial connection or relationship.	• How various sites in the community have improved in relation to one another, thanks to a grant you want to renew. • Ways different regions of the country have been affected by manufacturing outsourcing.
Cause-effect	• Shows a direct relationship between one condition or situation and another.	• How child obesity in the local school district rose after the introduction of soda vending machines and the reduction of required physical education courses in schools. • Ways new tax laws have curtailed downtown revitalization.
Problem-solution	• Invites audience to consider the nature, extent, and source of a shared problem. • Advocates a viable solution to a shared problem.	• Appeal to shut down local manufacturing plant to improve air quality and decrease high rates of asthma. • Introduction of a transition-to-college mentoring program to improve the success of first-generation college students at top schools.
Problem-alternatives-solution	• Acknowledges the inherent complexity of many issues by noting several possible solutions. • Allows the speaker to address counterarguments before advocating a preferred solution.	• Call for fuller integration of international students into campus life after declining enrollment. Alternatives consider the role of clubs, living units, tutoring centers, and campus employment. • Why green cards for illegal immigrants who have completed eight years of schooling in the US is a better first approach to immigration reform than other popular proposals.

Table 6.1 Primary Patterns of Arrangement (*continued*)

PATTERN OF ARRANGEMENT	PRIMARY STRENGTHS	EXAMPLE TOPICS
Problem-cause-solution-solvency	• More complex, balanced approach than the two previous problem-solution models. • Emphasizes how the problem came about and considers the viability of the proposed solution. • Speaker may move audience to act more quickly than in other arrangements because the speech has answered questions about the solvency of the solution.	• Appeal to start summer and weekend food backpack program for hungry children. • Request to fund local boys' and girls' club in an effort to reduce after-school truancy in community—based on a similar, successful program in a neighboring community.
Refutative	• Allows speaker to acknowledge and refute prominent opposing arguments. • Well-suited for a hostile or apathetic audience who brings counterarguments to the rhetorical occasion.	• Appeal to build a treatment center for juvenile delinquents in the county. Residents oppose the move, fearing it will raise crime and truancy. • Proposal to fix traffic gridlock by a major, multiyear investment in a light-rail system.
Monroe's motivated sequence	• Creates or amplifies psychological discomfort in the audience by elaborating on a significant problem. • Satisfies audience's sense of need by visualizing a solution. • Provides a clear and specific call to action.	• Plan to destigmatize mental health treatment and provide psychological services for military personnel and their families. Speech begins with recent tragic news about families on the local base and ends with well-researched steps for audience to implement solution. • Appeal to increase funding for coach training, assessment, and oversight in treating concussions. Speech offers comparison to data from a successful, similar program in a nearby school district and ends with a community action plan for fundraising.

conclusion of your speech. Finally, using one of these patterns of arrangement helps you emphasize the most relevant material and eliminate the evidence which detracts from your rhetorical purpose.

Once the body of your speech is organized, you are ready to take on the introduction and conclusion. You might wonder why we are discussing introductions now, near the end of this chapter, since they come first in a speech. That is because it is hard to introduce something when you don't yet know what you're introducing. For this reason, it is a good idea to have a working outline of your main ideas before you write the frame—that is, the introduction and conclusion—for your speech.

FRAMING WITH EFFECTIVE
INTRODUCTIONS AND CONCLUSIONS

Most listeners make an initial decision about how seriously to take your speech or how much to pay attention based on what they hear in the introduction. While there is no easy formula, there are principles that help us understand the way in which introductions and conclusions work for different rhetorical occasions. Of course, because each speech is unique, the approach that is well suited for one speech may be ill suited for another. It can be useful, then, to have a series of tools in your rhetorical toolbox as you craft the introduction and conclusion.

The Functions of Introductions

In order to write a strong introduction, you must understand what you want your introduction to *do*. Most introductions try to accomplish five functions, in the following order:

- Get attention
- Raise a need
- Establish credibility and goodwill
- State thesis or focal point
- Preview the body of the speech

We address each of these functions in turn.

Get Attention

Your audience members have many things on their minds when you stand before them. As a speaker, you must find a way to get their attention that is appropriate to the occasion, your topic, and the audience. Avoid starting with "Uh, thanks, for, uh, coming" or "My topic today is. . . ." These are too bland. Instead, have a clear plan for how to grab their attention with your first words. Several specific strategies for attention-getting introductions appear in Box 6-4.

Raise a Need

You are much more likely to hold your audience's attention if you articulate something they need (broadly defined). You must convince them that they want to listen to your speech because they will find it interesting, will learn something important from it, or will benefit from it in some way.

Establish Credibility and Goodwill

Assure the audience that you are a credible source on the topic. This does not necessarily mean that you are the foremost expert on the topic, but your introduction should give them a sense that you have done your research and that you know and care about the issue. You can also build credibility by making your relationship to the topic clear. When the audience understands your investment in the issue at hand, they are often willing to listen to what you have to say. You should express your interest or investment in the topic *while also* communicating research and/or knowledge. Your audience may grow wary, for instance, if they sense you want to sway their emotions without providing solid reasons for why they should assent to your viewpoint.

State Your Thesis or Focal Point

The thesis of your speech should be clearly stated in the introduction. (There are exceptions to this, for example, when using the refutative pattern of arrangement, but those cases are not the norm.) As you craft your introduction, make sure the thesis you constructed in the early stages of planning still accurately expresses your central idea or claim. It is possible that the speech has progressed in a different direction as you arranged and wrote the body of your outline. If this is the case, rewrite the thesis to reflect the current speech.

Preview the Body of the Speech

A **preview statement** elaborates on your thesis by announcing the main points of your speech. It is a clear indication of how the speech will proceed. In many ways, it tells the audience what to listen for. Here are two examples of preview statements from sample speeches we examined earlier in this chapter.

> **Gorgias's thesis statement:** I wish, by giving some logic to language, to free the accused of blame and to show that her critics are lying and to demonstrate the truth and to put an end to ignorance.
>
> **Gorgias's preview statement:** For [either] by fate's will and gods' wishes and necessity's decrees she did what she did or by force reduced or by words seduced or by love induced.
>
> **Ryan's thesis statement:** There are several ways to strengthen our local animal control agency's power to remove and care for abused animals in Montgomery County, but the most important thing you can do is to volunteer time and resources at your local animal shelter.
>
> **Ryan's preview statement:** In my speech, I will first outline the laws that govern local animal control and explain why they are inadequate. Next, I will examine a frequently proposed solution and tell you why it will not make an immediate difference in the lives of our animal friends. Then I will conclude by telling you how and where you can make a difference in pets' lives starting right now.

As you can see, the goal of a preview statement is to allow audience members to anticipate the progression of your speech. When they know where you are going, they begin to listen for how to support your points, and you have a much better chance of holding their attention throughout your presentation.

The Functions of Conclusions

Because conclusions, like introductions, are part of the frame for your speech, they share many characteristics with introductions; however, they tend to be shorter.

There are four primary functions of conclusions. They should:

- Summarize your main points
- Restate your thesis or focal point

- Articulate implications or give call to action
- End decisively

Again, we look more closely at each of these functions.

Summarize Your Main Points

Your audience hears your speech only once, but with the benefit of a summary (and of a preview), they can hear your central points three times. This increases the possibility that they will remember your message. When you summarize your main points, you encourage your audience to hold onto what you have said. Also, in the event that someone was distracted during a part of your speech, a summary of your points is an occasion for him or her to review the whole progression of your argument.

Restate Your Thesis or Focal Point

Because your thesis statement captures the main point of the entire speech concisely and compellingly, state it again in the conclusion. This is another way to reinforce your ideas with the audience before you finish speaking.

Articulate Implications or Give Call to Action

At the end of your speech, help your audience understand the implications of your presentation. Particularly when you speak on a matter of civic concern, you are often asking your audience to make a particular response. The conclusion, then, is where you reiterate your desire that they change a particular belief or take a specific action on the issue at hand.

End Decisively

Conclusions should also be decisive. They should make it clear to the audience that you are at the end of your presentation. Speakers commonly end by saying "thank you" or "thank you for your time," and while it is nearly always a good thing to express gratitude, be careful not to rely on "thank you" as a signal that you have finished. Try to craft something that is unique to the speech and is decisive enough that audiences automatically know to begin their applause without needing to hear you say "thank you" or "that's it."

Now that you see what your introduction and conclusion can accomplish, refer to Box 6-4 for ideas that help you get audience attention in introductions and end decisively in conclusions. Your goal in any approach is to find a way to relate the topic to the audience and command their attention.

BOX 6-4

Strategies for Getting Attention and Ending Decisively

- Use a quotation from a well-qualified or well-known individual.
- Make a joke—using tasteful and relevant humor, of course.
- Ask a rhetorical question or a series of questions to engage your audience.

- Tell a brief story or anecdote that introduces the topic of your speech in a compelling manner. This narrative should be connected to your topic in some way.

- Share your personal experience as it relates to some aspect of your speech.

- Make a brief (possibly ceremonial) reference to the occasion. "Mr. president, members of the board of trustees, family and friends of the graduates, and members of the graduating class of 2035. . . ."

- Use a surprising statistic discovered in your research to awaken the audience's curiosity.

CONNECTING SPEECH ELEMENTS

After writing your introduction and conclusion, and developing and arranging your main points, it is tempting to think you are done crafting your speech. However, you can significantly improve the flow of your speech by turning your attention to transitional words and phrases. **Transitions** connect ideas and move from one point to the next. They help readers navigate your presentation, often summarizing a central idea they have just heard or providing a clue of where they are along their journey.

Think about the way a GPS operates. As the computerized voice gives you driving directions, it says something like, "In two miles, take a left onto Park Place," or "Continue 4.6 miles to exit 14 for Roosevelt Street." Then as you get closer to your exit or turn you might get a reminder, "In half a mile, turn left onto. . . . " If the GPS were to wait until you were at the exit, and then say, "Get off here!" you would very likely miss the exit. You were not prepared for the change in direction.

The same concept applies to public speaking. We call the verbal hints or signals that new information is coming **signposts.** They indicate the beginning of a new element of your speech. You can signpost your speech by offering internal summaries and internal previews between the sections of the presentation. (Note that the terms "transition" and "signpost" are used similarly or sometimes interchangeably. Ask your instructor how he or she would like you to distinguish between a signpost and a transition.)

Ryan wrote the following signpost after the section of his speech that explained why legal reform was not the best approach to helping pets in his county: "I have now outlined a popular solution for decreasing pet abuse and neglect in Montgomery County, and I have told you why—though I support the measure—I do not think it is the best way to approach this problem. Next, I will turn to my preferred solution." Here he quickly summarizes what he has just covered and highlights where he will go next. After the section on his preferred solution, he will again quickly summarize what he's covered and signal his turn to his conclusion.

Rhetorical questions can also be employed as creative signposts and transitions. For example, Ryan could have written the following transition: "You may ask, 'If stiffening penalties for pet owners is not the right approach, how can we help?' and in the next section I address this question."

One reason transitions and signposts are so important is that listening to a speech is unlike reading text. When you read an article or book, you can always go back a few paragraphs if you find your attention wandering, if you are interrupted by a text message, or if you did not catch the relationship between ideas the first time through. We do not have this luxury when we listen to a speech. We hear the words only once, and if we miss something, we cannot go back and hear it again. When you as a speaker understand this obstacle for listeners, you also understand how to help them keep track of your progress or catch something they did not hear the first time: you can summarize, transition, preview, and signpost as you go.

BOX 6-5

Ideas for Writing Transitions and Signposts

- Try numerical sequencing: First . . . , Second . . . , Third . . . , In conclusion . . . , or Next . . . , In addition. . . .
- Stress relationships between elements: Just as we have . . . so we also have . . . , To the left . . . To the right. . . .
- Summarize what you have covered: In short . . . , To summarize . . . , To clarify . . . , That is . . . , Keep in mind . . . , Before I move on to the next point, take note of. . . .
- Ask a rhetorical question: "You may ask 'What does this have to do with me?'" "You may wonder what caused this situation in which we find ourselves," or "How do we work through these conflicts?"

When it comes to connectives like transitions and signposts, the bottom line is that your audience will thank you for using them. They are ways of giving your listeners handles or holds to grab onto as they travel through your speech with you.

Now that you have examined the purpose of organization and the various elements of planning and arranging a speech, in the next chapter we turn to the concrete principles of composing an outline.

SUMMARY

This chapter has covered three overarching aspects of organization. First, we discussed the purpose of organization. Second, we turned to the building blocks of any outline: the thesis and main arguments. Third, we looked at other elements of organization. These included the common patterns of arrangement, the functions of introductions and conclusions, and the importance of clear transitional elements. More specifically, this chapter covered:

- Organization as a focus and practice of speakers since ancient times.
- Organization as a tool that helps both speakers and audience members. Speakers, in the process of delivery, more easily remember a well-organized speech. Audience members more easily remember a well-organized speech once it is over.

- Strong thesis statements are the first step in good organization, and they succinctly and directly state the argument or central focus of the speech.
- Once speakers have a working thesis, they can draft the main ideas of their speech.
- Main ideas can be organized according to several common patterns of arrangement.
- The patterns of arrangement are not equally appropriate for every rhetorical occasion; each has its strengths.
- After the main body of the speech has been arranged, speakers should turn attention to introductions and conclusions as a frame for the speech.
- Introductions should include a preview statement that outlines what the speech covers.
- Conclusions should review the main points before ending decisively. Speakers should not rely on "thank you" to signal the audience that they have finished.
- Connectives like transitions and signposts improve the flow of a speech and, just as importantly, help audience members navigate material they hear.

KEY TERMS

organization p. 104
pattern of arrangement
    p. 114

preview statement p. 121
signpost p. 123

thesis statement p. 109
transition p. 123

REVIEW QUESTIONS

1. Why is organization important to a speech?
2. What questions are most important to consider in crafting your thesis statement?
3. How does a preview statement differ from a thesis statement?
4. What are two good strategies for introductions?
5. What are the functions of signposts and transitions in public speaking?

DISCUSSION QUESTIONS

1. Think of a particularly well-organized public presentation you attended. What did the speaker do that made the speech easy to follow?
2. Can you recall a poorly organized public presentation you attended? What specifically were the organizational flaws? How did the lack of organization affect you as a listener?
3. What does it mean to say the process of organization is recursive? How should you use this concept in crafting a speech?
4. In terms of writing an outline for a speech, what similarities and differences do you notice from other outlining assignments you've had in the past? Is there a difference between how you outline a speech and a written essay?

CHAPTER 7

Writing Effective Preparation and Presentation Outlines

Chapter Objectives

Students will:

- Understand the purpose and the benefits of outlining.
- Employ the principles of outlining to visualize arguments and clarify thinking.
- Distinguish between a preparation outline and a presentation outline.
- Craft an effective outline for various speaking purposes.

Jon Favreau, who famously became director of speech writing for the US president at just 27 years of age, was profiled in the *Washington Post* in 2008 as he worked on Barack Obama's first inaugural address. The profile stresses the long hours and intense focus that go in to preparing a presidential speech. Reporter Eli Saslow wrote of Favreau, "He moves while he writes to avoid becoming stale—from the Starbucks, to his windowless transition office, to his new, one-bedroom condo. . . . He sometimes writes until 2 or 3 A.M., fueled by double espresso shots and Red Bull. When a deadline nears, a speech consumes him until he works 16-hour days and forgets to call home, do his laundry or pay his bills. He calls it 'crashing.'"[1] While the preparation you put into your first speeches will not be nearly so consuming, writing powerful speeches *is* hard, concentration-demanding, time-intensive work. The payoff is the tremendous opportunity you have through public speaking to build commitment among audiences for the issues you care about, and it is worth it.

When Obama first interviewed Favreau for the speech-writing job, Obama asked about Favreau's theory of speech writing. After a pause, Favreau gave the answer that got him the job: "A speech can broaden the circle of people who care about this stuff. . . . How do you say to the average person that's been hurting: 'I hear you. I'm there. Even though you've been so disappointed and cynical about politics in the past, and with good reason, we can move in the right direction.'"[2] As you do the hard work

White House Chief Speechwriter Jon Favreau (seated) works with Senior Advisor David Axelrod (left) and speechwriter Cody Keenan (center) on President Obama's remarks in response to the shooting of Arizona Rep. Gabrielle Giffords and 18 others.

of outlining your speech, stay focused on the overall purpose and significance of what you are doing. A well-constructed speech can broaden the circle of people who are willing to work together for a common goal.

In this chapter, we will talk about the basics of speech writing, or outlining. We begin by looking at the importance of outlining, then we turn to the principles of crafting an outline, and we conclude with the differences between a preparation outline and a presentation outline. At the end of the chapter, we present models of speech outlines for your reference.

THE IMPORTANCE OF OUTLINING

The speech outline is an important part of the speech-writing process because it helps the speaker think through her material and provides her with guidance. An **outline** is a sketch or condensed version of your speech, including its arguments, supports, transitions, and references. There is a difference between the **preparation outline**, that is, the draft you write as you plan and organize your speech, and the presentation outline. The **presentation outline** is a much briefer sketch of the speech, designed to help you deliver your speech as free from your notes as possible—so you can make maximum interpersonal connection with your audience. Sometimes called a "key word" outline, the presentation outline allows you to remember the structure and main points of your speech, but it should also compel you to speak extemporaneously.

It should be condensed enough that you cannot actually read your speech, yet detailed enough to help you get back on track if you lose your place.

While outlining can be onerous and time-consuming, there are several benefits for you as a speaker when you take time to write a well-crafted outline. First, it provides a visual representation of the speech, which helps you *learn* the speech. Second, an outline helps you arrange your ideas and supporting evidence in the most logical manner for your given purpose. Third, the outline helps you diagnose and address potential problem areas in your speech because it allows you to locate points of repetition, gaps in reasoning, or extraneous information.

When a speech is organized sloppily and awkwardly, you can lose your way, and then very quickly your audience is also lost. The results can be disappointing, if not disastrous, both for your ethos as a speaker and for the community issue your speech seeks to ameliorate. Time spent constructing, arranging, and outlining your speech now can be very rewarding later when the audience members who wish to join your cause have a clear sense of how to proceed.

The presidential speechwriter Peggy Noonan said of speech preparation, "If you find yourself doing draft after draft, this is good. As you write and rewrite you are unconsciously absorbing, picking up your own rhythm and phrasing. This will show itself in a greater ease, a greater engagement when you stand up and give the speech. People will know that you know your text."[3] Outlining is the work you do to learn your speech, to know it well, and to communicate that deep knowledge to your audience. If you put the time in, it will show.

There are several specific guidelines that will help you write your preparation outline. Many instructors have strict requirements about how preparation outlines should look and what elements should be included, so be certain to check with your professor about his or her preferred format before you turn in your document. In the following section, we look at the general principles of outlining.

THE PRINCIPLES OF OUTLINING

You have probably written an outline before, so you are familiar with some of the basic steps. At the same time, you may be unclear about how to order your ideas or how much to include with each element. The system we present here is widely employed in public speaking courses because its symbols and indentation provide a *visual* representation of the logical structure of your speech. One of the ways you learn your speech is to outline and study the relationship among your ideas, and you can work out these relationships through the outlining process.

Consistent Indentation and Symbolization

First, make sure that your outline is structured with a consistent pattern of symbols and indentations. Main points should be identified by Roman numerals, subpoints by capital letters, and sub-subpoints by Arabic numerals.

    I. First main point
      A. First subpoint
      B. Second subpoint

II. Second main point
    A. First subpoint
        1. First sub-subpoint
        2. Second sub-subpoint
    B. Second subpoint
III. Third main point, and so on. . . .

The system of indentation and symbolization does two things for you as a speaker. First, it helps you see the flow of your speech. Second, it helps you decipher the relationship among your ideas. (These are the three main points. That idea is not really a main point, but it does *support* a main point, etc.) This visual relationship among ideas is built on the principle of subordination.

Subordination

Subordination is the practice of making material that is less important or primarily supportive secondary to more central ideas. Material in your outline should descend in order of importance. That is, supporting ideas or evidence should be listed under main points. Move from the most general idea to the most specific as you order material. As Damien worked on his deliberation speech, he knew he wanted to list the benefits and drawbacks of each potential solution after he explained each approach. He created an element after each explanation that acknowledged there were "benefits" and "drawbacks" to the solution. These points he labeled "B" (benefits) and "C" (drawbacks). *Underneath* each of these points, he gave more detail about what the benefits and what the drawbacks were. This portion of his outline reads as follows:

    B. This approach foregrounds two benefits.
        1. It tries to address the unhealthy aspects of hypermasculinity within football culture, like ignoring pain and ignoring the recovery protocols that may slow the chances of repeated concussion.
        2. The education extends beyond players and coaches to include parents, fans, and community members who often perpetuate attitudes that celebrate players for sacrificing their bodies for the game.
    C. But there are also drawbacks to this approach.

Here we see that points 1 and 2 are each listed under *and support* the claim "there are benefits to this approach." Similarly, the drawbacks will follow as points 1 and 2 under C. The individual examples of benefits (1 and 2) are subordinate to the claim that benefits exist (B). Subordination is closely related to the next principle of outlining, coordination.

Coordination

Coordination is a visual representation of the proper relationship among ideas. It is related to subordination because it stresses that ideas of similar importance should be on the same level of the outline. Here is an example from Ryan's speech, discussing how members of the community can support animal welfare on a local level:

        2. The agency has a great website, with many volunteer roles that need to be filled.

    a. Volunteers can interview potential pet owners to expedite pets for adoption.

    b. Volunteers can set up community adoption events at festivals and local pet stores.

    c. They can care for pets currently in shelters by cleaning facilities and playing with animals.

    d. Those who are allergic to pets or cannot afford the time to volunteer can donate pet food for loving pet owners who cannot afford the expense.

Here we see coordination in that the four ways for community members to volunteer at the local animal shelter are listed on the same level of the outline. Each has a lower case letter, each refers to sub-subpoint 2, and each has identical indentation.

After you have sketched the subordination and coordination in your outline, you can turn to another important outlining principle: parallelism.

Parallelism

The **parallelism** principle dictates that you balance your points and subpoints as you divide them. Just as you cannot balance two ends of a scale with only one object, each level of your outline needs at least two points to be in balance or to justify the subdivision. To explain this concept another way, we often say when it comes to outlining, "every little one has a little two." In other words, there must be at least two relevant and worthy subordinate ideas in order to make the subdivision, otherwise the division is not warranted. Compare the two examples from Ryan's speech below.

  Not Parallel:

  II. Concerned citizens must know animal welfare laws but also recognize what these laws fail to do.

    A. There are laws and penalties in place for owners who abuse their pets.

  III. A frequently proposed solution is that we support legislation to stiffen penalties against abusers.

  Parallel:

  II. Concerned citizens must know animal welfare laws but also recognize what these laws fail to do.

    A. There are laws and penalties in place for owners who abuse their pets.

    B. While tough laws are important in the lives of innocent animals, there are five ways these laws are inadequate.

  III. A frequently proposed solution is that we support legislation to stiffen penalties against abusers.

Note that in Ryan's sample outline at the end of this chapter, both subpoint A and B are supported with sub-subpoints. Once you have established parallelism in your outline, the final outlining principle to consider is balance.

Balance

Balance in speech outlining dictates each main idea receives roughly the same amount of time and attention in the speech. If the first main point of your speech lasts three minutes, the second main point lasts thirty-seven seconds, and the final main point is four minutes—then the audience suspects that your second "main" point really isn't important. If you find yourself in this situation, consider whether you can add or subtract material so that the main ideas are in balance.

Now that we have explained the guiding principles that will help you construct a coherent outline, we turn to the specific tasks of writing the preparation outline.

THE PREPARATION OUTLINE

As we said, the preparation outline is designed to help you think through and learn your speech. In a public speaking course, it is generally the version of a speech that you submit to your instructor for review and comments before you give the speech. Your preparation outline will be too detailed to serve as the notes you use in delivering your final speech, but writing a preparation outline is essential to the thinking and planning process. Unless your professor tells you otherwise, preparation outlines should include the following elements.

Begin with the Speech Title

You may not be required to state a speech title in a classroom-based speech. Coming up with one, however, may help you claim ownership of your speech and say something about it that will pique your audience's interest. In the real world, of course, many public speakers are asked to provide titles well in advance of their speech date, and these titles are published on websites, in newsletters, in church bulletins, and so forth. Whether or not you share your title with your audience, practice coming up with an attention-getting title for your speech as a first step in speech writing.

State Your Specific Purpose

The purpose statement is related to, but not the same as, your thesis statement. Another way to think of it is as the goal or the objective for your speech. Clearly label your purpose statement at the top of your outline. Here is Damien's purpose statement:

> **Specific purpose:** To inform community members about the problem of concussions and high school football and about a range of approaches to solving the problem they should consider before they deliberate on the problem.

Knowing and succinctly stating your purpose can help you write a good speech. *You will not read or state the purpose statement in delivery*, but including one in your outlining process adds focus. If you do not know what you want your speech to accomplish, there is a good chance the rest of your speech will betray that lack of purpose.

Label and State Your Thesis

We discussed the characteristics of strong thesis statements at length in chapter 6. Refer to that chapter if you would like to review those guidelines. In your outline, stating your thesis clearly will help you diagnose whether your central idea is well-developed and is fully addressed by the main points and subpoints that follow.

Label and Offer a Preview of the Speech

Before you move to your main ideas, preview the material or ideas your speech will cover. Tell the audience what will come first in your speech, what will come second, and so on. This will help your audience know what to listen for as you progress through the speech. Here is Ryan's preview:

> **Preview:** I will first outline the laws that govern local animal control and explain why they are inadequate. Next, I will examine a frequently proposed solution and tell you why it will not make an immediate difference in the lives of our animal friends. Then I will conclude by telling you how and where you can make a difference in pets' lives starting right now.

The preview is one way that readers can orient themselves to your content as your speech unfolds. (Note—There is one exception to the preview requirement: if you are using the Monroe's Motivated Sequence pattern of arrangement, you withhold the preview as you want to raise a sense of urgency in your audience without revealing the resolution upfront.)

Label Your Introduction and Conclusion

In addition to illustrating their place in your outline with Roman numerals, you should clearly label these parts of the outline as "Introduction" and "Conclusion."

Write Main Points and Subpoints in Complete Sentences

Writing full sentences is a way to discipline yourself to complete your thought. If you offer only a key word or a label for each element of your outline, there is no way to ensure you have done the thinking necessary to really plan what you will say in your speech. It's much better to complete the thought in the planning stages than to find yourself in front of your audience wondering what you were going to say about the vague label or term in your notes.

Label Transitions and Internal Summaries or Internal Previews as Signposts

Signposts are the internal summaries and internal previews that frame each section, and they are crucial to how an audience makes sense of and follows your speech as you progress. The primary reason we ask you to clearly label your transitional elements in a preparation outline is to ensure that you include them.

The signposts should also refer to the preview or overview you give at the beginning of the speech. The main difference between the preview that appears at the beginning of the speech (immediately after your thesis) and the internal summaries and previews is that the internal summaries and previews refer only to their own section and not to the speech as a whole. They say, in essence, "Here's what we have covered, and here is where we are going next." They are the transitional elements that get you from one point to the next.

Include a Bibliography

Providing full citations for all your sources is a sign of ethical and responsible speech writing. Be sure to include texts or websites where you gleaned *ideas* as well as those that you specifically quote or paraphrase. Too often speakers believe they only need to cite those sources they specifically quote, but this has led more than one speaker into trouble, not to mention questionable ethical territory.

Be sure to check with your instructor about his or her preferred format for the bibliography (Modern Language Association, American Psychological Association, Chicago Manual of Style, etc.)

Now that we have explained each element of the preparation outline, let's look at how they come together in a full outline. At the end of this chapter, we included a second presentation outline for your reference. The second speech's purpose is to advocate a particular solution to a problem. This first speech, however, has a different purpose. It is to inform an audience about the multiple solutions to a shared problem as they prepare to deliberate together. This first sample outline is for a type of informative speech for deliberation you will learn more about in chapter 10. Damien's speech states a problem followed by different perspectives or "categories" of solution, but it does not advocate for one particular resolution; therefore, our students have sometimes found it helpful to think of the speech as having a problem-alternatives-solution arrangement *without the solution.*

SAMPLE PREPARATION OUTLINE

Damien's Speech to Inform Community Members about Multiple Perspectives on High School Football and Concussions Before They Engage in Deliberation

Pattern of Arrangement: Problem-Alternatives-Solution (without the solution)

Title: Putting Our Heads in the Game: Deliberating Concussions and High School Football

Practice writing a title that is descriptive and grabs interest

Specific Purpose: To inform community members about the problem of concussions and high school football and about a range of approaches to solving the problem they should consider before they deliberate on the problem.

The purpose statement is not spoken in delivery, but it can add focus in the outlining process—it reminds you what your speech will do.

I. Introduction

    A. Three weeks ago, after our favorite local quarterback, Brian Ramos, suffered a severe concussion during the homecoming football game—the fourth football player on our team to suffer a concussion this season—it seemed everyone in Columbus was an expert on concussions.

Begin decisively and get attention. Damien chooses the strategy of naming a well-known local figure and reminding his audience of an important event in their recent past. This helps him connect with his audience.

        1. Parents blamed coaches for not protecting "our" kids.

        2. Coaches claimed school districts did not provide adequate funding for athletic trainers and on-the-field

Notice that each element in this outline is phrased as a full sentence. This helps ensure (and illustrate to your professor) that you have outlined a complete thought.

medical care—something college and NFL coaches can count on for expert advice.

3. Parents and coaches both blamed players who downplayed their injuries so they wouldn't be cut from games.

4. If you turned on the TV, it seemed Americans across the country were blaming "football culture" for glorifying violence and aggression at the expense of players' health.

5. Some of us wondered, is this the last generation of high school students who will know the warmth of *Friday Night Lights*?

B. As "the great concussion debate" came to our town, we all agreed that Columbus needed fewer concussions and less blame but, at the same time, many of us feared the beloved game of football might suffer under a cloud of reactionism and misunderstanding.

Damien compels his audience to listen by appealing to their desire and to a common need.

C. As a member of the football team and as a concerned friend, I would also like to see fewer concussions on the field. But while changes in high school football programs and culture may be needed, we know that looking at a problem from only one angle is a poor way to make community decisions.

Establish credibility. By stating his own investment in the problem and his desire to see a full consideration of the issue, Damien builds his own ethos and increases his audience's trust that he will approach the topic thoughtfully.

D. (Thesis) So, the *first thing* we in Columbus need is a fuller understanding of the problem as well as multiple perspectives on addressing concussions in high school football before we are ready to advocate and implement specific changes. With this goal in mind, *the question that guides my speech this morning is: How can we best address the issue of concussions in high school football?*

State and clearly mark the thesis. In an outline to inform your audience in advance of deliberation, the thesis is a focusing or guiding question. See Ryan's outline at the end of the chapter for a thesis that makes a claim rather than asks a question.

E. (Preview) I will first outline the problem of concussions and youth sports and then turn to three different perspectives on how to solve this problem. The first solution advocates an end to the football program and suggests that we redirect resources to sports and activities that high schools students can pursue for a lifetime. The second solution calls for a change in the culture of football, specifically the model of masculinity that encourages players to downplay the gravity of their injuries. The third solution calls for better funding for medical expertise to increase player safety on the field. Each potential solution foregrounds an important value in our community that we need to weigh together as we proceed, and I will discuss these values as I present each solution. As I conclude, I will turn the guiding question over to you as concerned community members.

The preview is an element that also signals the end of the introduction. It tells the audience where the speech is going and helps them know what to listen for next.

*Transition: First, however, I will begin by out-lining the problem we face as a community.

Transitions are clearly marked.

II. There is no denying that concussions are a real danger in football and youth sports in general.

    A. According to the Centers for Disease Control and Prevention (CDC), emergency rooms in the United States treat over 1.7 million cases of traumatic brain injury, including concussions, each year.

        1. This number is up over 60% in the last decade.

        2. The two sports most likely to see concussed athletes are football and girls' soccer. (CDC, "Concussions in Sports and Play.")

    B. Several studies on repeated head injuries (or multiple concussions) document an enduring negative impact on cognitive function, according to a 2013 report on *Sports-Related Concussions in Youth* by the Institute of Medicine and National Research Council.

        1. Multiple concussions can permanently affect memory and processing speed.

        2. Once an athlete has had a concussion, subsequent concussions may be more severe with longer recovery time.

        3. Retired professional football players seem to show some correlation between multiple head injuries and risk for depression (Graham et al. 8–10).

    C. While many are hopeful that helmet technology will advance and help prevent future concussions, the CDC reminds parents and players that "there is no 'concussion-proof' helmet." Therefore, players must continue to avoid hits to the head (CDC, "Heads Up . . . Fact Sheet for Parents").

    D. Despite these serious medical concerns, experts worry that many head injuries in high schools sports go unreported (Breslow).

*Transition: Now that I have covered the growing problem of concussions and the long-term medical risks that come with them, I will move to the first perspective on how to solve this problem.

III. The first solution that is gaining proponents in Columbus is to end the high school football program.

    A. This solution argues that the growing medical research on lifelong cognitive effects of concussions requires adults who can make tough—even painful—decisions for kids' safety. They note the many parents are already effectively making this decision for kids by encouraging them to pursue sports like soccer and basketball. You now hear parents say, "My son can play any sport but football."

        1. One suggestion for eliminating football suggests the school district reallocate funds currently dedicated to football to developing other athletic activities and club sports that students can participate in *for a lifetime.*

The principle of subordination is illustrated here and throughout the outline. The items listed as 1, 2, and 3 all refer to and support A.

            a. Football—which has high rates of injury—is a sport players tend to outgrow with age and often leaves them with lingering ailments.

    b. Clubs and teams that create skills and enthusiasm for hiking, golf, and canoeing teach students to love a physical activity they can participate in for years to come.

  2. Another suggestion for implementation—recognizing the loss of community spirit if we were to end our football program—would explore moving fall soccer matches to Friday nights.

  3. The value prioritized in this first solution is *lifelong health*. The approach embraces the necessity of sport and physical activity in the lives of young people, and it recognizes the role football plays in building community spirit, but it places more value on those sports that have a better track record of long participation and a pain-free lifestyle into adulthood.

> *Parallelism is also at work in this outline. Notice that under point a there are three subpoints, and under point 1 there are two sub-subpoints (a and b). This is what we mean by "every little one has a little two."*

B. The benefits of this approach are many, but I will name two of the most salient:

  1. First, we would see a reduction in head injuries and the high-profile pressure to return to play quickly after a concussion.

  2. Second, we would invest as a community in students' lifetime involvement in low-impact sports. This turns schools back into educational institutions that put their resources into teaching and modeling lifetime physical fitness. It downplays what can sometimes feel like an obsession with varsity athletics, which provide a community pastime but can compete with the curriculum.

C. As with any approach, there are drawbacks to this one, and I will outline two of the most central.

  1. First, football teaches many important lessons that are not easily replicated in another team sport and are certainly not taught in more individualized physical activities like hiking and canoeing.

  2. Second, many argue that football doesn't feed or promote aggression, but rather—and especially in high school—it may provide a suitable channel for boys to express innate aggression. This outlet for aggression is not the same in other team sports like diving or golf. If you would like more information about this particular drawback to eliminating football (a perspective that has not received as much media attention as other aspects of the debate), I recommend two 2014 articles: "In Defense of Male Aggression: What Liberals Get Wrong about Football," by Jonathan Chait, from *New York Magazine*, and "The Beautiful, Awful Game of Football," by Timothy Michael Law, from the *Los Angeles Review of Books.*

D. To summarize, the first approach prioritizes lifelong health over a sport that is increasingly dangerous, even deadly, for young men. It advocates an end to the football program in Columbus, but offers a vision that involves more students in sports they can play for a lifetime. Drawbacks include a loss of the lessons unique to football, and the loss of a sport that provides a ritualized place for young men to express innate aggression.

*Transition: Now that I have covered the first solution to the problem of concussions and youth sports in Columbus, I will move to the second solution.

Transitions continue throughout the speech. They refer only to the two sections of the speech they connect.

IV. The second solution to the problem of concussions in high school football argues that we need to change the culture of toughness that dominates football, for this culture is a major contributing factor in concussions. Players, parents, and fans can work together to change this culture.

A. The widely cited and NFL-funded study titled *Sports-Related Concussions in Youth* that I mentioned in the introduction calls for a change in culture as one of its official recommendations. It reports that athletes are still likely to view the game and the team as more important than their own health (Graham et al., 289). Just as players are reluctant to report concussions, they also tend to be lax about following treatment plans when they have been diagnosed (Graham et al., 7). It may not be "manly" to follow the doctor's orders.

1. One suggestion for implementing a change in football culture is to emphasize the ways that team health depends on individual health among players.

2. Another approach encourages parents and fans to help by creating new mottos and catch phrases about safety. These would counter mottos like "There is no 'I' in 'team'" or "No pain, no gain." One example of a new motto is prominently placed on the CDC's *Heads Up* educational materials. It reads: "It's better to miss one game than the whole season." (CDC, "Fact Sheet for Coaches," and "Fact Sheet for Parents").

3. This call to change football culture prioritizes the value of *education*. It believes that fans, parents, coaches, and teammates need to buy into a change in football culture, so that players recognize that the game and the team can go on without the individual player.

Notice that each solution requires Damien to articulate a common value that the solution prioritizes. We will say much more about the specifics of this type of speech in chapter 10.

B. This approach foregrounds two benefits.

1. It tries to address the unhealthy aspects of hypermasculinity within football culture, like ignoring pain and ignoring the recovery protocols that may slow the chances of repeated concussions.

2. The education extends beyond players and coaches to include parents, fans, and community members who often perpetuate attitudes that celebrate players who sacrifice their bodies for the game.

C. But there are also drawbacks to this approach.

1. Many question whether the emphasis on the team and the game over the individual is so thoroughly ingrained in football culture that it cannot be extricated. Would doing so change the game beyond recognition or eliminate heroism in the game?

Notice that as each solution is presented, Damien outlines the benefits and drawbacks of each solution. This will help his audience focus on the impact of a given solution in deliberation.

2. The second drawback is time. Changing culture is a long project, and given the growing concern about football and concussions, it seems we need a quicker, more decisive solution.

D. In summary, the second approach seeks to change the culture of football by prioritizing education. It advocates the importance of changing or thinking differently about mottos like "No pain, no gain." Major cautions about this approach include the feasibility of changing an entrenched culture and the time it takes to do so.

*Transition: Having looked at a second solution to the problem of concussions and youth sports in Columbus, I will move to the third and final solution.

V. The third solution is to increase player safety on the field by helping coaches get better, more consistent medical care for high school players.

A. Advocates for this solution point out the vast advantage in medical expertise that college players and coaches have over high school players and coaches. *ClearedToPlay.org* notes that "Only 42% of high schools have access to athletic training services" and "47% of schools nationally fall short of the federally recommended nurse-to-student ratio" (*ClearedToPlay*).

1. The first suggestion stresses that coaches may need parents and community members to advocate for more and higher quality student-athlete healthcare from school boards and community partners.

> *Internal signpost words like "first" and "second" remind the audience of the speaker's well thought-out organization.*

2. A second suggestion mandates that schools should require football programs themselves to fund athletic-training services and on-the-sidelines medical expertise. For a football budget to be approved, a certified athletic trainer must be available to supervise and follow-up with injured students both during the game and in the weeks after the injury.

3. This approach prioritizes the value of *safety* and insists that easy access to skilled medical care must be evenly distributed among players; it should not be a luxury.

B. I would like to highlight two of the benefits of this approach.

1. First, it ensures safety and good medical care for our kids and takes some of the burden off high school coaches. Knowing what we know about the likelihood of repeat concussions when players are not properly diagnosed or rehabilitated, this approach goes a long way toward faster, healthier recovery.

2. Second, it is a more fair system. The risks of football are the same whether a student plays for a school with access to good medical care or not; we would end a two-tiered system of care for those who play by making sure every football program or school district offered skilled care to players.

C. There are also drawbacks to this approach.

1. The first is cost. Skilled personnel are costly, and many school districts might have to take money away from other programs if they were forced to provide skilled trainers or more medical staff for athletics.

2. The second drawback, as with any policy change, is time. While most parents and coaches would support more consistent medical care, they recognize that many teams and injured players need better medical intervention now.

D. To review, this final solution calls for better medical expertise both on the field and in the recovery period following a high school student's injury. It prioritizes safety and promises to more evenly distribute the quality of care that high school football players receive. Drawbacks to this approach are money and time.

*Transition: Now that we have examined a third solution to the problem of concussions and high school football, I will conclude by reviewing what my speech has covered and turning this topic over to you—the concerned community members—for deliberation.

VI. Conclusion

A. When Brian Ramos was injured during the homecoming game, it was clear our community was ready to *do* something about high school football and concussions. But *how* can we best address concussions in high school football? My speech today has used this focus question to explore three different solutions.

> *In his conclusion, Damien reminds the audience of the problem that leads to the need for deliberation. He restates the focus question that appears as part of his thesis.*

B. The first solution we explored was to end the high school football program and invest our resources in clubs and sports that kids can pursue for a lifetime. The second solution was to rally parents, coaches, players, and fans to change the culture of football, specifically the aspect of the culture that encourages players to downplay or ignore their injuries for the game and for the team. The final solution stressed the necessity of better-trained medical care to support coaches and players both on the field and in the weeks after an injury.

> *Next, he summarizes the three solutions he's covered.*

C. Each of these approaches has advantages and disadvantages. As you consider these solutions and weigh the values they prioritize, what do *you* think is the best way for Columbus to address our shared concern for our football players?

> *He closes by turning the question for deliberation over to his audience.*

Works Cited

> *A bibliography is an absolute must in ethical speech preparation. Ask your instructor about which citation style you should use. (This one follows MLA style.)*

Breslow, Jason M. "High School Football Players Face Bigger Concussion Risk." *FRONTLINE PBS.org.* WGBH Educational Foundation, 31 Oct. 2013. Web. 27 Dec. 2014.

Centers for Disease Control and Prevention. "Concussion in Sports and Play: Get the Facts." *Injury Prevention and Control: Traumatic Brain Injury. CDC.gov.* Centers for Disease Control and Prevention, 6 Oct. 2011. Web. 27 Dec. 2014.

———. "Heads Up: Concussion in High School Sports." *Injury Prevention and Control: Traumatic Brain Injury. CDC.gov.* Centers for Disease Control and Prevention, 9 Jul. 2013. Web. 27 Dec. 2014.

———. "Heads Up: Concussion in Youth Sports: A Fact Sheet for Coaches." *CDC.gov.* Centers for Disease Control and Prevention, April 2013. Web. 27 Dec. 2014.

———. "Heads Up: Concussion in Youth Sports: A Fact Sheet for Parents." *CDC.gov.* Centers for Disease Control and Prevention, April 2013. Web. 27 Dec. 2014.

Chait, Jonathan. "In Defense of Male Aggression: What Liberals Get Wrong About Football." *New York Magazine.* New York Media LLC, 7 Oct. 2014. Web. 28 Dec. 2014.

Graham, Robert, Frederick P. Rivara, Morgan A. Ford, and Carol Mason Spicer, eds. *Sports-Related Concussions in Youth: Improving the Science, Changing the Culture*. Report of the Committee on Sports-Related Concussions in Youth, Board on Children, Youth, and Families. Institute of Medicine and National Research Council. Washington: National Academies P, 2014.

Law, Timothy Michael. "The Beautiful, Awful Game of Football." *Los Angeles Review of Books*. Los Angeles Review of Books, 27 Oct. 2014. Web. 29 May 2015.

"Statistics on Youth Sports Safety." *ClearedToPlay.org*. Swarm Interactive, 2013. Web. 27 Dec. 2014.

THE PRESENTATION OUTLINE

Once you have had a chance to do the thinking and learning that comes with the preparation outline, it is time to work on a much thinner version of the outline to use as you present your speech. The goal of the presentation outline is to provide you with speaking notes while limiting your ability to read the speech. You want to speak extemporaneously and to know your speech well enough so that you can make eye contact with your audience as you speak; at the same time, you want enough of an outline available to you that—if you need it—you can remind yourself of where you are going next.

A presentation outline is sometimes called a "key word" outline. The idea is that you go from full sentences in the preparation outline to the descriptive words that will jog your memory about your complete thoughts. Even in a presentation outline, you still want to write out fully the most important elements of the speech: the quotations you need to offer word for word, and perhaps parts of your introduction or conclusion.

Strive for Brevity

A presentation outline should be as pared down as possible, allowing you maximum freedom from your notes. You want to avoid the temptation to have your head buried, and if you know there are only a few details there, you may be inclined to look at them less frequently. At the same time, do not try to remember quotations, statistics, or other precise information. Write that information down exactly as you want to say it.

Maintain Indentation and Other Visual Guides

In chapter 9, we discuss at much greater length tips and strategies for delivering your speech. Here, we simply want to preview a few of the ideas for how to mark up your presentation outline for delivery. Part of the value of the system of indentation and symbols that we presented earlier in this chapter is that it allows you to visually skim the page and easily locate the information you need. You must be sure you can read your notes—this is one reason many people prefer to type them and to print them in a large font—but you also want to maintain the space and indentation from the preparation outline so that you are not forced to read through dense text or a full paragraph to find the section you are looking for.

Include Delivery Notes

As you practice your speech, you may receive feedback that you consistently mumble a phrase or that you tend to read quotations too quickly for an audience to follow. You may find that you have trouble pronouncing a word or that you tend to leave out one subpoint repeatedly. All of this information is useful as you write your presentation outline. You can include delivery notes to help yourself through problem spots. Highlight the point you tend to skip. Write out the difficult word phonetically. Remind yourself to "slow down here!" or "pause" in places where those elements of delivery will help your audience absorb the full impact of your words. Box 7-1 includes some delivery notes you might add to your presentation outline.

BOX 7-1

Delivery Notes for Your Presentation Outline

- Pause
- Go slowly here
- Make eye contact
- Repeat

Format Presentation Outline for the Rhetorical Situation

"Back in the day" public speaking instructors placed a high value on the 3x5 note card. These cards fit easily in the hand, so they are discrete. They are thicker than notebook or typewriter paper, so they do not make noise as the wind blows or as the speaker moves from card to card. And their small size helps speakers keep notes brief. With the evolution of technology, however, it is harder to recommend one preferred format for speaking notes. Some prefer a sheet of paper (especially tucked inside a professional-looking folder), others may use a digital tablet or other handheld device. As you prepare your speaking notes, try to learn as much about the speaking situation as possible. Will you have a podium? If so, printer paper can rest easily and rather noiselessly there. Will you speak in a windy, outdoor setting? If so, perhaps a tablet or note cards are better. Make your final choices for the format of your presentation outline based upon what will be, first, most reliable and comfortable for you, and second, least distracting to your audience.

So that you can see an example of how presentation and preparation outlines differ, we have included Damien's presentation outline below.

SAMPLE PRESENTATION (KEY WORD) OUTLINE

Damien's Speech to Inform Community Members about Multiple Perspectives on High School Football and Concussions Before They Engage in Deliberation

Title: Putting Our Heads in the Game: Deliberating Concussions and High School Football

    I. Introduction
        A. Brian Ramos's injury made everyone in Columbus an expert on concussions.

Notice there is no longer a purpose statement. Purpose statements are important for thinking and planning, but are not part of the oral presentation itself.

1. Parents blamed coaches.

2. Coaches blamed school districts.

3. Both blamed players for down-playing injuries.

4. Media and whole country blamed "football culture."

5. Was this the last generation of players who would know warmth of *Friday Night Lights?*

The introduction is now summarized. Not writing it out word for word will encourage Damien to look up and connect with his audience at the start of his speech.

Complete sentences are condensed now. There is just enough to recall thought.

B. Columbus needed fewer concussions and less blame, but many feared football's benefits were buried and misunderstood in our conversations.

C. As a member of the team and a friend, I agree we may need changes, but looking at a problem from one angle is a poor way to make decisions.

D. **(Thesis)** So, the *first thing* we in Columbus need is a fuller understanding of the problem as well as multiple perspectives on addressing concussions in high school football before we are ready to advocate and implement specific changes. With this goal in mind, *the question that guides my speech this morning is: How can we best address the issue of concussions in high school football?*

The thesis is not condensed because it's important to get it right.

E. **(Preview)** First: outline the problem; then, turn to three solutions: The **first** calls for dissolution of the football program and a reallocation of resources to activities students can do for a lifetime. The **second** solution calls for a change in the culture of football. The **third** calls for better funding for medical expertise to increase player safety on the field. **Each prioritizes a different value**.

The preview is condensed. Notice that Damien put the different elements of his preview in bold so that he can easily spot them in delivery. The bold print will help him see the parts of a longer point and find his way if he glances down at his notes partway through.

*Transition: First, however, I will begin by outlining the problem we face as a community.

II. Concussions are a real danger in football and youth sports.

A. According to the Centers for Disease Control and Prevention (CDC), emergency rooms in the united states treat over 1.7 Million cases of traumatic brain injury, including concussions, each year.

The key word outline includes oral citation information. You must have citation signal phrases—ones that name the source orally—when you introduce a new source, whether your use of the source is a quote or a paraphrase. It is not sufficient to have citations in parentheses for a speech; the audience must hear you name your sources.

1. Up over 60% in the last decade.

2. Football and girls' soccer highest rates of concussion (CDC, "Concussions in Sports and Play").

B. Repeated head injuries show negative impact on cognitive function, according to a 2013 report on *Sports-Related Concussions in Youth* by the Institute of Medicine and National Research Council.

      1. Affect memory and processing speed.

      2. After first, subsequent concussions may be more severe with longer recovery.

The coordination and parallelism of the outline remain. If Damien loses his place within point b, subpoint 1, he can more easily locate subpoints 2 and 3 to find his way again.

      3. Correlation between multiple head injuries and risk for depression in pros. (Graham et al., 8–10).

    C. The CDC reminds parents and players, "There is no 'concussion-proof' helmet" (CDC "Heads Up . . . Fact Sheet for Parents").

    D. Many head injuries in high schools sports go unreported (Breslow).

*Transition: Now that I have covered the growing problem of concussions and the long-term medical risks that come with them, I will move to the first perspective on how to solve this problem.

III. First solution: end the high school football program.

    A. Explanation: Research requires adults to make tough decisions for kids' sakes. Many parents already make this decision: "My son can play any sport but football."

      1. Suggestion #1 for implementation: reallocate funds to sports students can play for longer time.

        a. Players outgrow football but live with lingering ailments.

        b. Hiking, golf, and canoeing students can pursue for a lifetime.

      2. Suggestion #2 for implementation: Move soccer to Friday nights to avoid loss of important community events.

      3. Prioritizing value: lifelong health.

    B. Benefits:

      1. Reduction in concussions and pressure to minimize injury to return to play sooner.

      2. Investment in lifetime fitness. Schools refocused as educational institutions.

    C. Drawbacks:

      1. Lessons of football not easily replicated.

      2. Football offers an important outlet for ritualized aggression. Less popular perspective. Can read more in:

Though these titles are part of subpoint 2, Damien used spacing to single them out so they could be easily spotted in delivery.

        "In Defense of Male Aggression: What Liberals Get Wrong about Football" by Jonathan Chait from *New York Magazine*.

        "The Beautiful, Awful Game of Football" by Timothy Michael Law from the *Los Angeles Review of Books*.

    D. Summarize solution: First approach advocates end to football and a reallocation of resources to lifelong sports and activities. It prioritizes the value of lifelong health, but drawbacks are the loss of football's unique life lessons and an acceptable space where some can channel aggression.

*Transition: Now that I have covered the first solution to the problem of concussions and youth sports in Columbus, I will move to the second solution.

IV. Second solution: Change the culture of toughness that dominates football.

    A. Explanation: This approach recommended by the study titled *Sports-Related Concussions in Youth*. Athletes still view the game and the team as more important than their own health. Are reluctant to follow doctor's orders after injury because it's not manly.

        1. Suggestion #1 for implementation: Emphasize how team health depends on healthy individuals.

        2. Suggestion #2 for implementation: Players and fans can create new catch phrases "There is no 'I' in 'team'" or "No pain, no gain" might

Material that includes direct quotations is still written out word for word. Damien will read this information.

be joined by a new motto in the CDC's *Heads Up* educational materials: "It's better to miss one game than the whole season" (CDC, "Fact Sheet for Coaches," and "Fact Sheet for Parents").

        3. Prioritizing value: education.

    B. Benefits:

        1. Addresses unhealthy aspects of hypermasculinity within football culture.

        2. Education extends to parents, fans, and community members who often perpetuate attitudes that celebrate self-sacrifice.

    C. Drawbacks:

        1. Is this possible? Would this change the game beyond recognition?

        2. Time. It takes a long time to change culture when we need a much quicker solution.

    D. Summarize solution: Second approach seeks to change the culture of football by prioritizing education. Advocates changing or thinking differently about mottos like "No pain, no gain." Major cautions include the feasibility of the change and the time it takes to do so.

*Transition: Having looked at a second solution to the problem of concussions and youth sports in Columbus, I will move to the third and final solution.

Transitions can still be written out word for word in a key word outline. These will help orient Damien during delivery.

V. Third solution: Increase player safety through access to better, more consistent medical care.

    A. Explanation: College players and coaches have much more access to medical expertise than high school players and coaches. *ClearedToPlay.org*: "Only 42% of high schools have access to athletic training services" and "47% of schools nationally fall short of the federally recommended nurse-to-student ratio" (*ClearedToPlay*).

        1. Suggestion #1 for implementation: Parents and community members must advocate for better medical care with school boards and community partners.

        2. Suggestion #2 for implementation: Schools should require football programs to fund a certified athletic trainer to assist during the game and in weeks after the injury.

        3. Prioritizing value: Safety.

B. Benefits:

    1. Ensures good medical care and concussion rehab for our kids, takes some burden off coaches.

    2. More fair. Would end a two-tiered system of care based upon the district or the school the student plays for.

C. Drawbacks:

    1. Cost. Personnel are costly, and many school districts are already strapped.

    2. Time. While many support this idea, we need better medical intervention immediately.

D. Summarize solution: Calls for better medical expertise on the field and in recovery following concussion. Prioritizes safety. Promises to more evenly distribute the quality of care that high school football players receive. Drawbacks to this approach are money and time.

*__Transition:__ Now that we have examined a third solution to the problem of concussions and high school football, I will conclude by reviewing what my speech has covered, and turning this topic over to you—the concerned community members—for deliberation.

VI. Conclusion

    A. Brian Ramos's injury was the final straw. We had to do something. *But how can we best address concussions in high school football?* This has been my focus question.

> *In his conclusion, Damien returns to the problem that brings the group to the deliberation. Then he summarizes the three solutions he has offered.*

    B. The first solution: End the high school football.

    The second solution: Change the culture of football, specifically as it encourages players to downplay injuries.

    The third solution: Advocate for better trained medical care to support coaches and players on the field and in the weeks after injury.

    C. Each of these approaches has advantages and disadvantages.

What do *you* think is the best way for Columbus to address our shared concern for our football players?

> *He concludes by turning his guiding question over to his audience for deliberation.*

Works Cited

> *Don't leave citations off of the presentation outline. Someone may ask you for a specific title or other citation information during a question period or after the speech. Having it readily available increases your credibility.*

Breslow, Jason M. "High School Football Players Face Bigger Concussion Risk." *FRONTLINE PBS.org.* WGBH Educational Foundation, 31 Oct. 2013. Web. 27 Dec. 2014.

Centers for Disease Control and Prevention. "Concussion in Sports and Play: Get the Facts." *Injury Prevention and Control: Traumatic Brain Injury. CDC.gov.* Centers for Disease Control and Prevention, 6 Oct. 2011. Web. 27 Dec. 2014.

———. "Heads Up: Concussion in High School Sports." *CDC.gov.* Centers for Disease Control and Prevention, 9 Jul. 2013. Web. 27 Dec. 2014.

———. "Heads Up: Concussion in Youth Sports: A Fact Sheet for Coaches." *CDC.gov.* Centers for Disease Control and Prevention, April 2013. Web. 27 Dec. 2014.

———. "Heads Up: Concussion in Youth Sports: A Fact Sheet for Parents." *CDC.gov.* Centers for Disease Control and Prevention, April 2013. Web. 27 Dec. 2014.

Chait, Jonathan. "In Defense of Male Aggression: What Liberals Get Wrong About Football." *New York Magazine.* New York Media LLC, 7 Oct. 2014. Web. 28 Dec. 2014.

Graham, Robert, Frederick P. Rivara, Morgan A. Ford, and Carol Mason Spicer, eds. *Sports-Related Concussions in Youth: Improving the Science, Changing the Culture.* Report of the Committee on Sports-Related Concussions in Youth, Board on Children, Youth, and Families. Institute of Medicine and National Research Council. Washington: National Academies P, 2014.

Law, Timothy Michael. "The Beautiful, Awful Game of Football." *Los Angeles Review of Books.* Los Angeles Review of Books, 27 Oct. 2014. Web. 29 May 2015.

"Statistics on Youth Sports Safety." *ClearedToPlay.org.* Swarm Interactive, 2013. Web. 27 Dec. 2014.

Now that you have had a chance to study and to compare Damien's preparation and presentation outlines, we want to close the chapter with a final outline example. Ryan's preparation outline, presented below, is an advocacy speech. It contains all of the same building blocks or outline elements as Damien's preparation outline, but it differs in that the thesis statement is a more direct argument or claim. It also differs by ending with a clear call to action. Throughout your public speaking course and, we hope, throughout your life as an active democratic participant, you will have an opportunity to write and deliver many different types of speeches for civic engagement.

ANOTHER PREPARATION OUTLINE

Ryan's Advocacy Speech for Animal Welfare Activism

Pattern of Arrangement: Problem-Alternatives-Solution

Title: Advocating for Our Animal Friends:
Time for Compassion and Action

Purpose Statement: To urge audience members to become animal welfare volunteers in our county.

The purpose statement is an important focusing step in the speech-writing process, but will be eliminated in delivery.

I. Introduction

    A. In 2007, Atlantic Falcons quarterback Michael Vick dominated the national headlines—but not for his achievements on the field.

        1. Fans, teammates, and many other Americans were horrified to learn that Vick and friends ran a dog fighting operation at a home he owned in Virginia.

The introduction should get attention. Ryan chooses the strategy of telling a brief news story that some of his audience members may recall.

            a. According to the Newport News, Virginia *Daily Press,* investigators "seized 66 dogs, mostly pit bulls, some with scars and injuries. They also seized equipment commonly used in dogfighting, including treadmills used for conditioning dogs, a stick to pry fighting dogs apart, and a . . . device used to hold down aggressive females for breeding" (Wittmeyer).

            b. Vick was eventually sentenced to 23 months in prison.

        2. As he apologized to the court and his family at the sentencing, Judge Henry E. Hudson captured the feelings of many when admonished, "I think you need to apologize also to the millions of young people who look up to you" (Gorley Chufo).

B. While the Michael Vick story is, we hope, an extreme example of animal cruelty, for a few months, the case did bring issues of pet rescue and the ethical treatment of animals to the forefront of our national consciousness. How many young football fans now had the impression that it was no big deal, or even cool, to terrorize animals?

C. Today I want to talk about this issue that is of great importance to me, and I know to many of you. I'm an animal lover, and I became aware of pet abuse in our county through my volunteer work at the animal shelter. I was horrified by Michael Vick's story and was motivated to do something about it.

Raise a need. Establish credibility. By turning from the national stage to the local county, Ryan raises a need for his community to think about these issues. Stating his own investment in the issue and acknowledging that some of his audience members care about animal rights helps Ryan build credibility and audience engagement.

   1. Pet abuse is not only an issue in Virginia or among high-profile celebrities; we see it right here in Montgomery County.

   2. But the good news is, there are ways we can quickly and tangibly change the lives of local pets.

D. (Thesis) There are several ways to strengthen our local animal control agency's power to remove and care for abused animals in Montgomery County, but the most important thing you can do is to volunteer time and resources at your local animal shelter.

Thesis is clearly marked and stated.

E. (Preview) In my speech, I will first outline the laws that govern local animal control and explain why they are inadequate. Next, I will examine a frequently proposed solution and tell you why it will not make an immediate difference in the lives of our animal friends. Then I will conclude by telling you how and where you can make a difference in pets' lives starting right now.

The preview is an important signpost. It tells the audience where you are going and helps them know what to listen for.

II. First, concerned citizens must know animal welfare laws but also recognize what these laws fail to do.

A. There are laws and penalties in place for owners who abuse their pets.

   1. According to the Animal Services Divisions page on the Montgomery County government website, any pet owner or pet caretaker who "inflicts unnecessary suffering or pain upon the animal, or unnecessarily fails to provide the animal with nutritious feed in sufficient quantity, necessary veterinary care, proper drink, air, space shelter or protection from the weather" is subject to a $500 fine (Dept. of Police).

   Here we see the required verbal citation of the source for the quotation Ryan includes.

   2. Owners who physically mutilate their pets or allow their pets to be used for dogfights are subject to the same fine (Dept. of Police).

   Notice that each element is phrased as a full sentence. This helps ensure that each point has a complete thought.

   3. Criminal charges may also be filed with a penalty of $1,000 or a three-year jail sentence or both (Dept. of Police).

B. While tough laws are important in the lives of innocent animals, there are five ways these laws are inadequate.

The principle of subordination is at work here and throughout the outline. Those items listed as 1, 2, 3, 4, and 5 are all in support of item b. Ryan uses internal signposts (first, second, third, etc.) To help his audience follow the progression of his argument.

   1. First, local animal control and welfare agencies must have the knowledge of pet mistreatment in order to intervene.

   2. Second, most pet abuse takes place on private property, where animal welfare personnel are unlikely to see or hear it.

   3. Third, unlike state police departments with highway patrol divisions, animal welfare agencies lack personnel to look for and ticket those breaking the law.

   4. Fourth, a $500 fine is not a significant deterrent for many people.

   5. Finally, the laws are designed to punish the worst, most egregious abusers, but they do not reach the pets who are simply neglected or whose owners lack resources to give them adequate care.

      a. As of this morning, the Animal Services & Adoption Center website lists 38 dogs available for adoption in our county (Dept. of Police).

      b. The same website lists 95 cats available for adoption (Dept. of Police).

*Transition: Having addressed the problem, that is, inadequate laws that govern animal abuse in our county, I will now turn to a potential solution to this problem.

This transition contains a mini-summary and mini-preview

III. A frequently proposed solution is that we support legislation to stiffen penalties against abusers.
   A. There are clear benefits to this approach.
   1. First, through these laws, pet owners and local citizens show that we take animal welfare seriously.
      a. We have seen a ballot measure to stiffen penalties in the last two elections, and this keeps the issue in the public eye.
      b. Though the measure was defeated both times, the publicity for pet care surrounding the elections did much to raise awareness and put concerned citizens in touch with one another.
   2. Second, local shelters report more calls from concerned citizens and more pets rescued from neglectful homes. This suggests that increased awareness leads to more rescued pets.
   B. While I actually support tougher penalties, and I love to hear about the increased awareness and number of rescued pets in Montgomery County, I do not think tougher fines are the best solution for increasing the quality of life for pets in our county.
   1. As I mentioned, the last two ballot measures were defeated. Our current local government, despite the fact that we have many excellent elected officials, will not support increases in pet fines for two reasons.
      a. First, they are unsure of the law's necessity in relation to other, more immediate needs of the citizens who elected them.

   b. Second, they do not have the personnel in local government to en-force animal welfare as it is and fear they cannot put "teeth" in the new fines, so even if the law passed, there is a question about the degree to which it would be enforced.

   2. The other reason I do not think tougher penalties are the best solution for abused and neglected pets in our county is that tougher penalties, if ever viable in Montgomery County, will take years to come to pass.

   a. As the last two elections have shown, building support for this measure is painfully slow, if not impossible.

   b. Pets will suffer years of continued neglect while we wait for penalty increases to gain support.

   c. Furthermore, the reports from local activists and shelters suggest that we do not need a ballot measure to improve the lives of neglected pets.

*Transition: I have now outlined a popular solution for decreasing pet abuse and neglect in Montgomery County, and I have told you why—though I support the measure—I do not think it is the best way to approach this problem. Next, I will turn to my preferred solution.

IV. Instead of focusing more time and energy on changing laws, I recommend we take a much more immediately effective, two-pronged approach. These two prongs are volunteering at local shelters and increasing awareness in our county and more broadly.

   A. First, I will address the ways volunteering can make a difference in the lives of local animals. Our local animal shelters need many volunteers with a range of skills and pet interests.

   1. The Montgomery County Humane Society serves dogs and cats, birds, fish, and some mammals such as hamsters and rabbits (Montgomery County Humane Society).

   2. The agency has a great website, with many volunteer roles that need to be filled.

   a. Volunteers can interview potential pet owners to expedite pets for adoption.

   b. Volunteers can set up community adoption events at festivals and local pet stores.

   c. They can care for pets currently in shelters by cleaning facilities and playing with animals.

   d. Those who are allergic to pets or cannot afford the time to volunteer can donate pet food for loving pet owners who cannot afford the expense.

   B. In addition to volunteering (or, if you can't volunteer but would still like to help), the second prong of this approach is to raise awareness. There are also several ways you can participate in raising awareness.

   1. Use social media to broadcast pet news in our county and across the country.

    a. Spread news about pet abuse and neglect to broaden awareness of this issue.

    b. Spread news about attempts to improve laws protecting pets.

    c. "Like" your favorite pet protection agencies on Facebook.

    d. Follow your favorite pet advocates on Twitter, and retweet often.

  2. Make up, update, and circulate posters and fact sheets about pet care, pet resources, and phone numbers concerned citizens can call if they are concerned about the life of a local pet.

C. Volunteering and spreading awareness can have an effective, more immediate impact on the lives of neglected pets than waiting for the laws to change.

  1. When citizens are frequently reminded about the needs of pets, they become more watchful of the pets in their neighborhoods.

  2. When they know shelters need help, they are more likely to volunteer.

  3. When young children and adolescents hear and see adults in their community engaged in ethical pet care, they are more likely to see how unacceptable and unworthy of admiration pet owners like Michael Vick are.

D. If you are ready to join me in volunteering and spreading social awareness, here are two ways to get started:

  1. Go to the Montgomery County Humane Society Website at www.mchumane.org and click the "Ways to Help" link.

Notice how Ryan ends his speech with a clear call to action and one that encourages civic engagement in his audience. A call that empowers the audience to act on the problem is an integral element of an advocacy speech.

  2. Follow the Montgomery County Human Society on Twitter and "like" them on Facebook. Then put your own social media accounts to good use by posting frequently and thoughtfully.

*Transition: I have explained what I believe to be the most viable and immediate solution to the problem of pet abuse and neglect, and so I turn to my conclusion.

Signaling the conclusion often makes the audience more attentive—but don't abuse this verbal device by using it more than once or by using it too early in the speech.

V. Conclusion

A. In my speech today, I have argued that we should volunteer at our local animal shelter and spread awareness about issues regarding ethical pet care.

Ryan restates his thesis and mentions his main points.

B. As I explained, doing so will tackle the problem of pet abuse and neglect *much* more effectively than spending more time and energy on laws that stiffen penalties for animal neglect.

C. We can make a big difference in the lives of many animals and doing so is good for us. As the famous medical

He closes decisively with a memorable quotation.

missionary Albert Schweitzer said, "Until he extends the circle of his compassion to all living things, man"—I will add *and women*—"will not himself find peace" (Global Animal).

Works Cited

Animal Welfare League of Montgomery County. Animal Welfare League of Montgomery County, 2009. Web. 21 July 2013.

Department of Police, Animal Services Divisions. "Animal Control and Anti-Cruelty Laws." Montgomery County Government. 2014. Web. 31 Dec. 2014.

Global Animal. "Best Ever Quotes about Animals & Activism." *GlobalAnimal.org.* Global Animal, 22 Apr. 2015. Web. 29 May 2015.

Gorley Chufo, Veronica. "An 'Inhumane Activity': A 23-month Sentence Could End Vick's NFL Career." *DailyPress.com.* Daily Press, Newport News, VA, 11 Dec. 2007. Web. 31 Dec. 2014.

Montgomery County Humane Society. Montgomery County Humane Society, 3 Mar. 2015. Web. 29 May 2015.

Wittmeyer, Alicia P.Q. "Michael Vick Indicted, Faces Fines and Up to Six Years in Prison" *DailyPress. com.* Daily Press, Newport News, VA, 17 Jul. 2007. Web. 21 Jul. 2013.

> *Be sure you include bibliographic entries for all sources, whether directly quoted or just consulted. Your instructor may ask you to use a specific citation style. (This one follows MLA style).*

SUMMARY

This chapter stressed the importance of outlining and presented the principles of writing a strong preparation outline. It also discussed the difference between preparation and presentation outlines.

- Outlines have several benefits for you as the speaker: They help you learn your speech, they help you arrange ideas in the best order for your purpose, and they allow you to see where potential problems in evidence or logic emerge.
- Outlines should be written by following the principles of subordination, coordination, parallelism, and balance.
- Preparation outlines are full sketches of your speech, with ideas written in complete sentences, to ensure complete thoughts. They contain signposts and transitions. A bibliography is a must.
- Presentation (key word) outlines are much briefer. They avoid paragraphs and full sentences, except for directly quoted material, so you are forced to speak extemporaneously from your outline. They still maintain the visual coordination and subordination of the preparation outline so that you may find your way if you lose your place. They also include signposts, transitions, and a bibliography.
- It is a good idea to include delivery notes in your presentation outline.

KEY TERMS

balance p. 130
coordination p. 129
outline p. 127

parallelism p. 130
preparation
  outline p. 127

presentation
  outline p. 127
subordination p. 129

REVIEW QUESTIONS

1. What is the purpose of an outline?
2. Why is it so important to write the elements of your presentation outline in full sentences?
3. What is the difference between a preparation outline and a presentation outline?
4. How do the principles of coordination and subordination help you deliver a speech?

DISCUSSION QUESTIONS

1. What are the benefits and drawbacks of delivering a speech from a written transcript versus an outline?
2. What parts of the outlining advice in the chapter seem the most daunting? The most useful? Explain your answers.
3. Can you think of a speaker who uses transitions and signposts well? What do you notice about his or her speeches when you listen to them?
4. Discuss with your classmates the best format/technology for delivery notes in a presentation: Note cards? A printed page? A digital tablet or smartphone? Explain your answers, and take into account the space where the speech will occur.

CHAPTER 8

Using Style to Harness the Power of Language

┌───┐

Chapter Objectives

Students will:

- Define style.
- Recognize stylistic devices.
- Effectively use stylistic devices in a presentation.
- Discover the concept of framing.
- Demonstrate how to make use of framing in a presentation.

└───┘

Hillary Clinton is a major US political figure. First nationally recognized as the First Lady during Bill Clinton's presidency, she later became a US Senator from New York, a Democratic presidential candidate in 2008, secretary of state from 2009 to 2013, and again a Democratic presidential candidate for the 2016 election. Through most of her political career, Clinton has adopted a lawyerly style of speaking, consisting of a somewhat impersonal tone, deductive structure, and a lack of personal examples or emotion.[1] In 2008, however, while campaigning for the Democratic presidential nomination at a New Hampshire coffee shop with a small group of undecided female voters, Clinton broke from her typical way of speaking to use a much softer and more intimate style. In response to a voter's question about how she, as a woman, gets out of the door every day, Clinton made a few jokes about getting help with her hair and then more quietly stated: "I have so many opportunities from this country. I just don't want to see us fall backwards. You know, this is very personal for me. It's not just political. It's not just public. I see what's happening. We have to reverse it."[2]

Her response made headlines, partly because Clinton spoke with tearful eyes, but also because it marked such a departure in her style of speaking. She chose a means of expression that employed an emotional tone, simple vocabulary and grammar, and a

Photo taken Monday, January 7, 2008, in New Hampshire. The previous week Hillary Clinton lost to Barack Obama in the Iowa caucuses and was polling behind him in New Hampshire. She won the primary the next day, and in exit polls many female voters cited this event, where Clinton revealed her deep feelings about the importance of the election, as the most significant influence on their vote.

personalized emphasis on "I" and "me." After winning the Democratic primary election in New Hampshire one day later, Clinton declared, "Over the last week, I have listened to you, and in the process I found my own voice."

The voice Clinton referred to is what we who study public speaking refer to as style. And she—along with many media outlets at the time—concluded that her more intimate and vulnerable speaking style more effectively communicated her message. In an interview with *Newsweek* a few days after winning the New Hampshire primary, Clinton stated, "What I realized is that the reason I do this, why I get up every day, why I believe in our country and the importance of leadership, was not getting across the way that I wanted it to."[3] To enhance the impact of her message, she did not change its content so much as the manner or way in which she expressed it. She changed her style. And, while it is also the case that this shift included elements of delivery and even her patterns of reasoning, it was primarily a shift in style.

Style is the language or expression you use—the words you choose. It refers to all those aspects of a speech that constitute the manner or way in which ideas are verbally expressed or stated. As one of the five canons, or fundamental principles, of rhetoric, style holds an important place in speech construction as it can significantly influence the reception of your message. We believe that your understanding of style—your ability to find and adapt your own voice—is critical to becoming an effective speaker. Interestingly, to be effective in a particular community, we must have a presentational style that fits the community. Imagine how different the style expectations are between someone speaking to voters in the rural Midwest in contrast to someone speaking to voters in lower Manhattan.

At the same time, as a presenter you need to develop your own style that can be adapted to different situations and audiences. Too often those new to public speaking seek to copy the style of other speakers they have seen. This is rarely effective and more typically detrimental. Below we discuss the many uses of style, a few of the most common and helpful stylistic devices for speakers, and the impact that framing can have on public discussions.

THE USES OF STYLE IN PRESENTATIONS

When you hear the term style, perhaps you first think of the manner in which a person dresses, the way someone walks, or the car a person chooses to drive. This common use of the term "style" may cause you to imagine that the use of style in public speaking is the way a speaker adds flash and pizzazz to their presentation. This understanding misses most of what style actually accomplishes. Our selection of particular words and phrases is critical to making ideas engaging, memorable, and persuasive. When the language we use falls flat, so do our ideas. In this section we discuss four of the chief uses and outcomes of style: to create clarity, to maintain audience attention, to construct an appropriate mood or emotional state for the speech, and to generate a perspective on a topic or idea for the audience. Our language can accomplish all of these purposes and more.

Clarity

In discussing style, Aristotle identified clarity as the single most important characteristic our language choices should contain and in fact referred to clarity as "the virtue of style."[4] By this he meant that making ideas clear to the listener was the proper goal and result of all our stylistic choices. Language must be clear in order to perform its proper function. If an audience is confused by the language of a speech—if the speech is composed primarily of technical language, puzzling language, or language that is not fitting for the situation—then they will not be able to understand nor to act upon the information presented. They are also not likely to listen for very long. Standing up in front of a group of people and speaking about a substantive matter requires great effort, thought, and preparation, including the selection of specific stylistic devices.

Attention

Similarly, through our language we can capture the attention of the audience and hold it. You have probably experienced speakers whom we would characterize as "boring" or "dry." To be sure, this can be a product of delivery, but it is also an element of style insofar as a speaker must create interesting, engaging images in our minds through words. Through the use of interesting anecdotes, statistics, quotations, and rhetorical questions speakers can gain and maintain the attention of audience members.

Emotion

There is an emotional element in all communication. We may not always recognize it or attend to it or be able to name it, but it is present. Stylistic choices shape this emotional element in significant ways. Language has the power to bring us together by emphasizing communal values and using inclusive language. Stylistic language also can be used to overcome apathy by creating a feeling of intensity in the audience through word choice and artistry. When a public presentation goes well there is a powerful bond created between the speaker and the audience. By extension this bond unites the listeners with one another in the shared experience they have had and this can increase the persuasiveness of it. Speakers must be ethical and reflective about the creation and use of these emotional bonds.

Perspective Creation

Finally, language shapes perspectives on the world, an idea that was alluded to in chapter 3 in the discussion of ethical language use. Language is flexible and offers an infinite number of ways to describe events, people, and ideas. The particular words we use create our world of understanding and perception, influencing how we see and react to that which is around us. Word selection has incredible power. Imagine, for instance, a man sleeping on a bench in a park. A court judge walks by, sees this publicly intoxicated man, and thinks, "Criminal." A priest walks by, sees the same man, and thinks, "Sinner." A medical doctor passes by next and thinks, "Sufferer." Finally, a business owner walks by and thinks, "Loafer."

Four different words are used to label the same person in the same situation, and each of these words is likely accompanied by a whole vocabulary. For example, along with sinner, the priest might utilize words like repentance, forgiveness, God, weakness, spirit, and flesh. The doctor, on the other hand, might adopt words like blood alcohol level, addiction, healing, patient, and withdrawal.

Each label—and the vocabularies that accompany them—evokes a different set of attitudes and, likely, encourages a different set of actions toward the drunkard. The judge might fine or even incarcerate the man; the priest might attempt to bring the man to repentance to experience forgiveness and spiritual renewal; the doctor may want to examine him to help him physically recover and possibly overcome an alcohol addiction; and the business owner may simply walk past the man, determining to never hire him.

This example underscores the power of language. The words you choose to label or characterize your subject matter (and the people involved with it) invite your audience to adopt a perspective on that subject matter. In fact, most of what we know has been learned through words rather than firsthand experience. These words may have been read in books, magazines, or on the Internet. The words may have been spoken by teachers, family members, or friends. True, we also know a great deal from our own personal experience but that is a much smaller share of what we know. For example, many people know a good bit about the country of China, including specific features of the topography such as the Yangtze River and the Great Wall, the population size, and the dramatic economic development it has experienced over the last several decades. However, relatively few Americans have traveled to China and seen any of this firsthand. Rather, we have learned about it through words chosen by the media, from teachers, and from friends and acquaintances.

We must also recognize that because words evoke a set of accompanying words, or what we will later in this chapter call a frame; they can help or hamper efforts to advocate a particular position or to lead a productive discussion. Your style, then, is critical to forming your community's attitudes, identity, thinking, and even the power to act. The language choices you make and the stylistic devices you use enable clarity in the communication of your ideas, help you capture the attention of your audience, appeal to the emotions of listeners, and generate new perspectives for them. The next section examines specific devices in more detail.

STYLISTIC DEVICES

Good speakers take great care with their words and the manner in which they present their ideas. **Stylistic devices** are language techniques and literary tools that clarify meaning, express ideas in a compelling manner, and appeal emotionally to an audience. Such devices can be used to create a sense of rhythm, provide visualization, enhance argumentation, or develop a sense of community. As we examine each of these devices, we also use examples to discuss how they function.

Rhythm

One effective function of stylistic language is to create a sense of rhythm in a speech. **Rhythm** draws an audience into a speech and helps maintain attention. Through rhythm, which can be created through style as well as delivery, we create a sense of familiarity with the audience, a pattern or a cadence that keeps the audience engaged while also heightening emotion. There are several ways in which rhythm might be developed, but here we briefly comment on four: parallelism, repetition, antithesis, and alliteration.

Parallelism

Parallelism is a series of ideas that are constructed in a similar way. This can occur in a single sentence or across successive sentences. For example, at the end of a 1992 campaign video Bill Clinton states: "I still believe these things are possible. I still believe in the promise of America. And I still believe in a place called Hope."[5] In these three sentences, the sentence stem "I still believe" is employed in a parallel fashion and thus encourages listeners to join in the rhythm created and the meaning attached. That is, the parallelism encourages them to believe as Bill Clinton did in the promise of America and in hope.

On the fortieth anniversary of the D-Day invasion of Normandy by American and allied forces, President Ronald Reagan spoke at Pointe-du-Hoc, where American Rangers climbed the 100-foot cliffs under heavy fire to take the strategic location during the invasion. Some of the surviving Army Rangers were seated before him as he spoke. Reagan began the speech with a description of the battle and the incredible bravery of the men. Two hundred and twenty-five Rangers had started the battle, and when it was done only 90 of them remained alive. He closed this section by stating: "These are the boys of Pointe-du-Hoc. These are the men who took the cliffs. These are the champions who helped free a continent. These are the heroes who helped end a war."[6] The four parallel phrases build emphasis and powerfully recognize the sacrifice and effort of both those Rangers who died and those who were there that day.

Repetition

When using repetition a speaker repeats a sentence, idea, or theme. In using repetition a speaker can bring great emphasis to a point and also improve retention. Nine days after nearly 3,000 died in the attacks on the World Trade Center towers on September 11, 2001, President George W. Bush gave a speech to a joint session of Congress. He used a rhetorical question, "Why do they hate us?" and answered it in part: "They hate our freedoms: our freedom of religion, our freedom of speech, our freedom to vote and assemble and disagree with each other." The repetition of the word freedom places emphasis on this American value and the threat that the president believes the attacks have made on freedom. He then uses repetition when describing the response of the country: "We will direct every resource at our command—every means of diplomacy, every tool of intelligence, every instrument of law enforcement, every financial influence, and every necessary weapon of war—to the destruction and to the defeat of the global terror network."[7] The repetition of the word every makes the point that the president intends the country to respond to the terrorist attacks in absolutely every way possible. Interestingly, this use of the word every is both repetition and parallelism due to the way President Bush begins several consecutive phrases the same way, and it demonstrates how stylistic devices can work in tandem.

Antithesis

Antithesis is the juxtaposition of contrasting ideas, typically in the same sentence. For example, in his inaugural address, former President John F. Kennedy famously stated: "Ask not what your country can do for you; Ask what you can do for your country."[8] The positioning of the sentence is catchy to the ear and encourages the audience to reorient themselves to the situation. It is an invitation to rethink a familiar idea. Civil Rights activist and Nation of Islam leader Malcolm X's famous speech, "The Ballot or the Bullet," contains a powerful antithesis wherein he uses this device to encourage his listeners to consider that while he is an American, he really is not as we commonly understand the term.

> No, I'm not an American. I'm one of the 22 million black people who are the victims of Americanism. One of the 22 million black people who are the victims of democracy, nothing but disguised hypocrisy. So, I'm not standing here speaking to you as an American, or a patriot, or a flag-saluter, or a flag-waver—no, not I. I'm speaking as a victim of this American system. And I see America through the eyes of the victim. I don't see any American dream; I see an American nightmare.[9]

This section climaxes with this antithesis between the American dream, with which his audience is well familiar, and the American nightmare, which he argues African Americans experience.

Alliteration

Alliteration is the repetition of a single consonant in a sentence or series of sentences. One reason we like alliteration is that it is poetic or melodic. It is a frequent feature in songs and poetry. Alliteration causes us to want to repeat a phrase over and over in our minds. For example, in his famous "I Have a Dream" speech given during the March on Washington on August 28, 1963, Martin Luther King Jr. made use of many stylistic devices, including alliteration. In one instance, in describing how the full promise of the Emancipation Proclamation of 1863 had not yet been realized in 1963, he gives force to his point by use of alliteration with a consonant: "But we refuse to believe that the bank of justice is bankrupt." Later in the speech he famously stated: "I have a dream that my four little children will one day live in a nation where they will not be judged by the color of their skin but by the content of their character."[10] The use of several words beginning with the letter *b* in the first example and the letter *c* in the second helps make these statements melodic and memorable, thus augmenting their persuasiveness.

Visualization

A second use of stylistic language is to provide visualization for audiences through the use of vivid imagery. Such language heightens audience interest and also helps with audience understanding and retention. Many stylistic devices can be used for visualization; here we highlight the use of five such figures of language: concrete language, visual imagery, simile, metaphor, and personification.

Concrete Language

Concrete language focuses on the value of grounding ideas in actual examples from the physical world. Good speakers move up and down the ladder of abstraction as they discuss their ideas. We can take the concept of transportation as an example. We can imagine a speaker discussing transportation and as they do, also discussing automobiles, then American-made cars, and finally, Ralph's beat up '75 metallic blue Ford Maverick. In this way the speaker will make the concept of transportation concrete and easier for the audience to understand. We find a gripping example of the use of this device in President Reagan's speech at Pointe-du-Hoc referred to earlier. Reagan first describes the events abstractly as when "the Allies stood and fought against tyranny," and the particular battle as when the Rangers "began to seize back the continent of Europe." But then he turns to very concrete language to describe this battle:

> We stand on a lonely, windswept point on the northern shore of France. The air is soft, but 40 years ago at this moment, the air was dense with smoke and the cries of men, and the air was filled with the crack of rifle fire and the roar of cannon. At dawn, on the morning of the 6th of June, 1944, 225 Rangers jumped off the British landing craft and ran to the bottom of these cliffs. Their mission was one of the most difficult and daring of the invasion: to climb these sheer and desolate cliffs and take out the enemy guns. The Allies had been told that some of the mightiest of these guns were here and they would be trained on the beaches to stop the Allied advance.

> The Rangers looked up and saw the enemy soldiers at the edge of the cliffs shooting down at them with machine guns and throwing grenades. And the American

Rangers began to climb. They shot rope ladders over the face of these cliffs and began to pull themselves up. When one Ranger fell, another would take his place. When one rope was cut, a Ranger would grab another and begin his climb again. They climbed, they shot back, and held their footing. Soon, one by one, the Rangers pulled themselves over the top, and in seizing the firm land at the top of these cliffs, they began to seize back the continent of Europe. Two hundred and twenty-five came here. After 2 days of fighting, only 90 could still bear arms.[11]

This extremely powerful passage helps us see how a concrete description of events and acts can help clarify and drive home a much more abstract point such as the battle of freedom over tyranny as seen in the specific actions of the soldiers in battle.

Visual Imagery

The use of visual imagery is a way for speakers to describe their ideas with word pictures so that the audience can see in their mind's eye what a double-decker bus looks like traveling through downtown London or a seagull flying in the sky above the beach in Santa Monica, California. The idea is to help the audience see, hear, and even smell and taste what is described. In his speech to Congress on the terrorist attacks of September 11, 2001, President George W. Bush began the speech with powerful visual imagery to help Americans see the state of the union, nine days after the attacks.

> Mr. Speaker, Mr. President Pro Tempore, members of Congress, and fellow Americans, in the normal course of events, presidents come to this chamber to report on the state of the union. Tonight, no such report is needed; it has already been delivered by the American people.
>
> We have seen it in the courage of passengers who rushed terrorists to save others on the ground. Passengers like an exceptional man named Todd Beamer. And would you please help me welcome his wife Lisa Beamer here tonight?
>
> We have seen the state of our union in the endurance of rescuers working past exhaustion.
>
> We've seen the unfurling of flags, the lighting of candles, the giving of blood, the saying of prayers in English, Hebrew, and Arabic.
>
> We have seen the decency of a loving and giving people who have made the grief of strangers their own.
>
> My fellow citizens, for the last nine days, the entire world has seen for itself the state of union, and it is strong.[12]

Here President Bush used visual imagery and descriptions of actions his listeners could actually see in their minds to capture an abstract idea—that the state of union of the United States was strong.

Simile

Similes are explicit comparisons (i.e., like or as) between things that are essentially different yet have something in common. For example, the great boxer Muhammad Ali described his boxing style in this way, "I float like a butterfly and sting like a bee." Their value is in how they invite listeners to think about something in a new and interesting way. In the New Testament we read of Jesus trying to help his followers understand his teaching and the nature of what he sought to accomplish. He referred to his work as bringing the kingdom of God to earth and used similes to describe it such as:

> The kingdom of heaven is like a mustard seed that someone took and sowed in his field; it is the smallest of all the seeds, but when it has grown it is the greatest of shrubs and becomes a tree, so that the birds of the air come and make nests in its branches.

> The kingdom of heaven is like treasure hidden in a field, which someone found and hid; then in his joy he goes and sells all that he has and buys that field.

> The kingdom of heaven is like a merchant in search of fine pearls; on finding one pearl of great value, he went and sold all that he had and bought it.[13]

In each case the simile makes the point that though the item is small and perhaps hard to see, it is of incredible value and will grow or produce something remarkably grand.

Metaphor

Metaphors are implicit comparisons between things that are essentially different yet have something in common. For example, students may wish to describe a college in terms we associate with a business. They might say that when taking classes, they are buying a product and believe they should get their money's worth. This would conveniently put them in the position of being the customers, and since in business the customer is always right, they might find the metaphor helpful. Frederick Douglass, an African American and former slave, was asked to speak in celebration of Independence Day in Rochester, New York, on July 5, 1852. His speech, "What to the Slave is the 4th of July?" is recognized as one of the greatest speeches in American history. After praising the courage, determination, and ideals held by the Founding Fathers, he forthrightly critiques the nation for failing to live up to the Declaration of Independence, the Constitution, and its commitment to Christian ideals. He uses a physical object—the ring-bolt which American slaves knew well as an integral part of the chains that kept them bound—to describe the Declaration of Independence as a document so tied to the destiny of the nation that it cannot be separated from it. And, because within the Declaration resides the very principles that demand full freedom for the African American slaves, Douglass celebrates it.

> Pride and patriotism, not less than gratitude, prompt you to celebrate and to hold it in perpetual remembrance. I have said that the Declaration of Independence is the RING-BOLT to the chain of your nation's destiny; so, indeed, I regard it. The principles contained in that instrument are saving principles. Stand by those principles, be true to them on all occasions, in all places, against all foes, and at whatever the cost.[14]

Personification

Personification involves making reference to an inanimate object or an abstract concept as if it were alive. For example, "Tradition richly rewards those who stick to the path she has set." At a basic level personification works on the basis of giving human characteristics or abilities to something that is not human. We might say that someone is a slave to money or that they are driven by a desire for success. In these cases money and success are given human abilities.

In his speech to the Joint Session of Congress, President George W. Bush personified both freedom and fear in stating that the two were at war with each other. He stated: "Freedom and fear are at war. The advance of human freedom, the great achievement of our time and the great hope of every time, now depends on us."[15] Freedom is a held American value. Fear is a human emotion. But war is something human beings engage in. In personifying both qualities, Bush seeks to shape the understanding his listeners have about the reason for the terrorist attacks.

Strengthening Argument

A third function of stylistic language is to enhance *argumentation* and to develop the content of a speech. Ideally *all* stylistic language contributes to this end, but some devices can be seen as extending beyond language itself to directly contributing to the development of an idea. The element of style that has received the most attention in this regard is one that was previously introduced: metaphor. Metaphor is the subject of a wealth of scholarship and discussion dating back to Aristotle and the fourth century BCE. At the center of such discussion, is an investigation about the extent to which metaphor is primarily a tool of language or an essential element of human thought. Beyond metaphor, other elements of style that can be seen to directly advance the content or argumentation of a speech include irony, satire, and reference to the unusual.

Irony

Irony is the use of words in a sense that is opposite of their intended or normal use (an effort that we also might term sarcasm). For example, when someone says to you "nice shot" in a basketball game when the ball entirely misses the rim and backboard, they have employed irony. This technique has content insofar as it expresses an unexpected or surprising perspective on and attitude about the underlying idea or thought.

While irony can occur within a single sentence, more extended forms are more common. The famous Frederick Douglass speech "What to the Slave is the 4th of July?" is just such an example of the extended use of irony. Douglass answers the question of the title of his speech by noting that, ironically, it is a day that points out more than any other day of the year "the gross injustice and cruelty to which he is the constant victim." That is, the day highlights for him not only the lack of independence and freedom that African American slaves enjoy but also the oppression and brutalization they experience.

> But, such is the state of the case. I say it with a sad sense of the disparity between us. I am not included within the pale of this glorious anniversary! Your high independence only reveals the immeasurable distance between us. The blessings in which you, this day, rejoice, are not enjoyed in common. The rich inheritance of justice, liberty, prosperity and independence, bequeathed by your fathers, is shared by you, not by me. The sunlight that brought life and healing to you, has brought stripes and death to me. This Fourth of July is yours, not mine. You may rejoice, I must mourn. To drag a man in fetters into the grand illuminated temple of liberty, and

call upon him to join you in joyous anthems, were inhuman mockery and sacrilegious irony. Do you mean, citizens, to mock me, by asking me to speak today?[16]

And so, Douglass even asks his audience to consider the fact that in asking him to speak, which they might view as extending him a privilege, is for him, ironically, a form of mocking. While they may celebrate and rejoice the Fourth of July, he wants them to understand that, ironically, he must mourn. Thus he uses the device of irony to powerfully drive this point home to his audience. He speaks of the holiday in the opposite manner of their expectations.

Satire

Satire is a particular form of ridicule that is usually used to attack persons or ideas or to hold up and place focus upon human vices and failings. Rather than referring to a specific device or speech element, satire is a device that often characterizes the entirety of a piece of discourse. Malcolm X was well-known for using satire to chide and provoke his listeners, particularly his African American listeners. For example, in his speech "The Ballot or the Bullet," Malcolm X uses satire to both chide the African Americans in his audience for believing the empty promises of white politicians during campaign season and white politicians for pretending to befriend African Americans simply to garner votes and for their manipulation of voting by redrawing voting districts to minimize the influence of African Americans and to maximize the influence of white Americans, a process called gerrymandering.

> They have a system that's known as gerrymandering, whatever that means. It means when Negroes become too heavily concentrated in a certain area, and begin to gain too much political power, the white man comes along and changes the district lines. You may say, "Why do you keep saying white man?" Because it's the white man who does it. I haven't ever seen any Negro changing any lines. They don't let him get near the line. It's the white man who does this. And usually, it's the white man who grins at you the most, and pats you on the back, and is supposed to be your friend. He may be friendly, but he's not your friend.[17]

Malcolm X's words here are sharp and pointed, and no doubt they stung many of his listeners. This is the way satire functions, by putting a spotlight on what the speaker believes are the weaknesses of individuals or groups, often in an exaggerated and humorous manner. He or she intends to startle listeners into reconsidering their beliefs and actions.

Reference to the Unusual

In making use of a reference to the unusual, a speaker includes an unbelievable story or even a startling statistic or fact to catch people's attention and interest. The uniqueness and often surprising nature of such references grabs the attention of audience members as they process and reflect on the reference. In his "The Ballot or the Bullet" speech, Malcolm X uses this device to point out the ridiculous logic of racism in America. He tells the story of an African American who dressed as an African and in so doing received extremely different treatment than he would have had he been viewed as an African American.

> Right now, in this country, if you and I, 22 million African-Americans—that's
> what we are—Africans who are in America. You're nothing but Africans. Nothing
> but Africans. In fact, you'd get farther calling yourself African instead of Negro.
> Africans don't catch hell. You're the only one catching hell. They don't have to pass
> civil-rights bills for Africans. An African can go anywhere he wants right now. All
> you've got to do is tie your head up. That's right, go anywhere you want. Just stop
> being a Negro. Change your name to Hoogagagooba. That'll show you how silly the
> white man is. You're dealing with a silly man. A friend of mine who's very dark put
> a turban on his head and went into a restaurant in Atlanta before they called them-
> selves desegregated. He went into a white restaurant, he sat down, they served him,
> and he said, "What would happen if a Negro came in here?" And there he's sitting,
> black as night, but because he had his head wrapped up the waitress looked back at
> him and says, "Why, there wouldn't no nigger dare come in here."[18]

This is an unusual story, and the response of the waitress both in serving the person
and then in what she says is surprising and perhaps shocking, even if it meets our
expectation of how racism functioned in the United States at that time. But the unusual nature of the story startles us and is memorable and thus more persuasive and
powerful.

Community

Finally, speakers can utilize stylistic devices to create or reinforce the idea of *community*. Such devices are used to bring an audience together for a common cause or concern, or to create separation between one audience ("us") and "others" or an
oppositional group ("them"). Language tools that accomplish such ends include the
use of inclusive pronouns, gender neutral language, maxims, and ideographs.

Inclusive Pronouns

Inclusive pronouns are those pronouns that create community and unity between the
speaker and audience. Most prominently they include the terms "we," "us," and "our."
The terms are used to create identity and put the speaker in league with the audience,
expressing shared purpose and concern, which can be particularly useful when a
community experiences fracturing and division. President Ronald Reagan closed his
speech at Pointe-du-Hoc by looking forward and committing the United States to an
ongoing partnership with the democracies of Europe even as he described his hope
that the Soviet Union would also become democratic. In doing so he made use of inclusive pronouns throughout the section.

> We are bound today by what bound us 40 years ago, the same loyalties, traditions,
> and beliefs. We're bound by reality. The strength of America's allies is vital to the
> United States, and the American security guarantee is essential to the continued
> freedom of Europe's democracies. We were with you then; we are with you now.
> Your hopes are our hopes, and your destiny is our destiny.[19]

In making use of the inclusive pronouns "our" and "we," President Reagan sought to
affirm and reestablish the bond between the United States and her European allies for
the future.

Gender Neutral Language

Gender neutral language refers to language choices that do not explicitly or implicitly favor one gender over another. This can happen, for example, when a speaker refers to all humans as "man" or in speaking in the third person about individuals of both genders but only using "he." It can also happen when a speaker uses terms like "policeman" instead of "police officer" or assumes all nurses are female or all doctors are male.

Maxim

A maxim is a statement of a general truth or rule of conduct believed by a culture, such as "the best defense is a good offense." When a maxim is used to reinforce or to help make a main point of a speech, the audience has an accessible and memorable way to recall the point. However, speakers must be careful not to overuse this device because it can also cause a speech to seem trite. Yet when used well, maxims can enable a speaker to make unfamiliar topics seem familiar such as when female politicians and advocates state "A woman's place is in the house . . . and the Senate." President Reagan used a maxim in noting to the survivors of the D-Day battle at Pointe-du-Hoc that "some things are worth dying for."

> You all knew some things are worthy dying for. One's country is worth dying for, and democracy is worth dying for, because it's the most deeply honorable form of government ever devised by man. All of you loved liberty. All of you were willing to fight tyranny, and you knew the people of your countries were behind you.[20]

Here the use of the maxim captures the nobleness and heroic nature of the actions of the Rangers and other soldiers on D-Day. They were willing to sacrifice their lives for others and for something—the ideals of freedom and liberty—bigger than themselves.

Ideograph

An ideograph is a culturally specific term that has great emotive power in that it represents a deeply held value or vice within a culture.[21] Core positive ideographs in American culture include equality, freedom, liberty, and property. Core negative ideographs include terrorism, communism, and slavery. Appeals to such values and vices generally need little elaboration and are accepted easily as rallying points for what is *right* or *wrong*. Toward the end of his "I Have a Dream" speech Martin Luther King Jr. builds toward the ideograph of freedom that all Americans must possess and experience fully if the country is to live out the promise of its founding documents and ideals.

> This will be the day, this will be the day when all of God's children (Yes) will be able to sing with new meaning:
>
> My country, 'tis of thee (Yes), sweet land of liberty, of thee I sing
>
> Land where my fathers died, land of the pilgrim's pride (Yes),
>
> From every mountainside, let freedom ring!

And if America is to be a great nation, this must become true.

And so let freedom ring (Yes) from the prodigious hilltops of New Hampshire.

Let freedom ring from the mighty mountains of New York.

Let freedom ring from the heightening Alleghenies of Pennsylvania.

Let freedom ring from the snowcapped Rockies of Colorado.

Let freedom ring from the curvaceous slopes of California.

But not only that: Let freedom ring from Stone Mountain of Georgia.

Let freedom ring from Lookout Mountain of Tennessee.

Let freedom ring from every hill and molehill of Mississippi.

From every mountainside let freedom ring.[22]

King here drives the point and goal of his speech home by calling for freedom to spread to all Americans across the country. The use and effect of stylistic devices can be observed by examining the style of nearly any speech, from that which is well known to the everyday sermon or lecture. If you take the time to consider a piece of discourse, you will probably be surprised at the number and range of purposefully created stylistic appeals you can locate.

SPOTLIGHT ON SOCIAL MEDIA:
DePaul University Social Media Guidelines

As new means of communication open up and develop new understandings and uses of style a new format inevitably follows. Companies, universities like DePaul University in Chicago, and other organizations have an interest in having those who represent them prepared to utilize social media effectively to advance their goals.

DePaul has an online policy for social media use that covers items such as rules to follow when an employee posts something online as a representative of the university and when and how it is appropriate to use the DePaul University name and logo. It also gives guidance on how to handle negative social media posts against the university.

The guidelines include the now fairly widely known list of abbreviations utilized on Twitter. Twitter is a medium that by design limits users to 140 characters for each message sent. This limiting parameter has had a dramatic impact on stylistic choices as the requirement to be concise limits choices dramatically.

Commonly Used Social Media Abbreviations

LOL: Laugh out loud

LMFAO: Laugh my f****** a** off

LMAO: Laugh my a** off

NSFW: Not safe for work (something that may not be appropriate to open on a work computer)

ROFL: Roll on the floor laughing

FML: F*** my life (something is going wrong)

TTFN: Ta-ta for now

IDK: I don't know

SMH: Shaking my head

Fail: Something goes wrong, isn't working, is failing

"Fail whale": When Twitter is down, an image of a cartoon whale pops up, coined by Twitter users as this

@TEOTD: At the end of the day

IMO: In my opinion

IMHO: In my humble option

H/T: Hat-tip (giving credit to someone)

CC: On a tweet, you would use this just like you'd use it in e-mail

PRT: Partial retweet (you retweeted most of the original) or please retweet

OH: Overheard

BTW: By the way

FTW: For the win (excited about something)

SM: Social media

FB: Facebook

FWIW: For what it's worth

IRL: In real life

FTF: Face to face

IOW: In other words

LMK: Let me know

Re: Reply (just as in e-mail)

STFU: Shut the f*** up

YW: You're welcome

Discussion Questions

- In what ways does the 140-character limit for a tweet encourage stylistic innovation?
- In what ways does the 140-character limit hamper stylistic innovation?
- If the medium doubled or tripled the possible number of characters how would this change style on Twitter and how would it change Twitter overall as a medium?

The document on the use of social media at DePaul can be found at http://brandre sources.depaul.edu/vendor_guidelines/g_socialmedia.aspx.
The specific list of abbreviations for use on Twitter is found at http://brandresources .depaul.edu/vendor_guidelines/EMM_Social_Media_Guidebook_Final%2010_10 .pdf.

FRAMING

The stylistic devices described in the previous section hold great potential and power for speakers and writers. They do more than make a particular sentence memorable or engaging; they work to shape how audience members think about the topic the speaker is addressing. In this section we discuss framing, which is a way of talking about this larger goal toward which particular language choices and stylistic devices work.

Framing refers to the use of language to order and make sense of the world; that is, framing is how we employ language to help shape perceptions of reality.[23] Frames provide perspectives on, or ways of seeing, much like we discovered earlier with how different labels for a man sleeping on a bench offered very different ways of perceiving, judging, and acting toward him. Indeed, frames are created and expressed by the words we use. For another example, think about the fervor created in September 2010 when the Obama administration renamed the Iraq War from "Operation Iraqi Freedom" to "Operation New Dawn." The new name was intended to suggest the war had essentially ended and that remaining US forces were operating under a new mission— a much more positive and hopeful mission. The use of dawn, in this case, implied that the brightness of morning had replaced the darkness of night (war) that preceded it. Critics took umbrage with the word because they thought it diverted attention from what they felt was really happening: the continuation of an expensive and violent war. They offered alternative names such as "A New Way of Forgetting This Ever Happened" and "This is All a Scam to Get Your F***ing Oil."[24] Clearly, the latter titles provide a very different, albeit somewhat sarcastic, perspective on the nature and goals of the war than the title offered by the White House.

To better understand the power of language, we might pause a moment to consider how we typically use the words frame and framing. You might think about the border around a picture or piece of artwork. If you have chosen a frame for a picture at a frame shop, then you know the wealth of options offered to you and, more importantly, how much the size, color, and pattern of the frame can influence what you see or notice in the picture itself. You may also have had the experience of needing to downsize or crop your picture. Choosing what parts of the picture to include inside the frame and what parts to exclude significantly affects what viewers ultimately see and notice in the resulting framed image.

We might think of the frames on a pair of glasses or sunglasses working somewhat similarly. Based on how thick or thin the frames are and how narrowly or widely they fit your face, the glasses will slightly alter what you can or cannot see—either because the frame literally blocks your view or because looking outside of the frame means looking without your prescription lenses or looking into the bright sun, both of which obscure your view. This also works the other way around. The glasses or sunglasses you choose to frame your face influences how your face looks to other people. Wearing large aviator-like frames can make the shape and size of your face appear quite differently than when wearing, say, the small, round spectacles John Lennon made popular. Anyone who has spent time picking out a pair of glasses or sunglasses from a vast array of options has experienced this difference.

Somewhat similarly to picture frames and the frames on glasses, discursive frames (i.e., frames created and expressed by language) influence what we see, notice, or highlight about a situation or issue. The words "illegal aliens" or, more simply, "illegals," for instance, conjure images, characterizations, and moral evaluations somewhat different from those suggested by the words "undocumented workers." That is among the reasons why you should be conscious of the language you employ when discussing public issues. For any complex and controversial social issue, the words we use can influence what the audience notices, highlights, or magnifies when shaping meaningful observations or conclusions, as well as what they overlook, ignore, or downplay. Speakers aid their cause when they choose words that offer their desired presentation, or framing, of the issue.

Frames *help* people absorb and make sense of facts and information. Another more typical use of the words frame or framing may help to clarify this point. Think of the wood frame constructed to build a house. That frame is built directly on top of the foundation and it creates the solid structure upon which the rest of the housing materials (drywall, roofing tiles, window panes, etc.) will stand.

That is similar to how frames help us think and understand. They form the basis or context on which we hang or make sense of truth or facts. Truth or facts alone are meaningless to us without a frame or context to give them significance, somewhat like drywall is useless without a wood frame on which to hang it. According to Linguist George Lakoff, "Facts can be assimilated into the brain only if there is a frame to make sense out of them."[25] So by using language to either reinforce existing frames or pose a new alternative frame, speakers enable other citizens to make sense of otherwise meaningless facts or to make order out of otherwise incoherent information.

Of course, different people will choose to frame the same issue differently. We talked earlier in this chapter about how different people might see the same drunk person but label, or frame, him differently. Many of our disagreements with each other result from conflicting frames for the same issue. For instance, Citizen A might frame the issue of unlawful immigration as illegal aliens while Citizen B might frame it as undocumented workers. Citizen A might frame the United States' involvement in Iraq from 2003 to 2011 as a war on terror, whereas Citizen B might frame it as a foreign occupation.

We can notice at least two things in these examples of conflicting frames. First, every issue-specific frame includes and typically even promotes a definition of the problem, its cause (i.e., who's to blame), and the best solutions.[26] Framing unlawful immigration in terms of illegal aliens, for example, points to immigration as the problem, blames the immigrants for entering the country unlawfully, and typically promotes the solutions of deportation and securing our borders. Framing the same issue in terms of undocumented workers, in contrast, identifies the lack of proper documentation (such as a certificate of citizenship) as the problem, blames the long delays and significant costs immigrants face when applying for legal US citizenship, and typically promotes the solution of legislative reform to the citizenship process. Notice how the problem, cause, and solutions identified in both cases correspond with each other; they compose an internal logic or coherent point of view.

Second, when advocating a particular frame, speakers should adopt language that reflects or offers that frame. If you want to introduce or promote an option that is lesser known, you will need to find new language to express it. Beware of simply negating a popular or well-known position because you will likely re-enforce its framing while doing so. As Lakoff notes: "When former president Richard Nixon spoke his famous line, 'I am not a crook,' *everyone thought of him as a crook*."[27] If you try to argue on behalf of undocumented workers while calling them illegal aliens or illegals, it will be difficult for your audience to think of them as anything other than violators of the law who deserve to be punished or to see you as their genuine advocate. It is an old truism that once you adopt the words or terms of an alternative perspective, you are arguing at a disadvantage.

When leading a deliberative discussion, it is important that you frame the conversation as neutrally and fairly as possible or, better yet, that you identify the framing of each of the options you present. Political scientist Will Friedman calls this "nonpartisan framing-for-deliberation," and we will discuss it in more depth in chapter 10. Alternatively, it is possible to frame an issue or topic in a partisan fashion. Such efforts can vary from honest attempts to advocate or counter positions to dishonest efforts to simply manipulate the discussion.[28] Lakoff distinguishes between the two by calling honest efforts framing and the dishonest efforts either spin or propaganda.

Dishonest efforts to frame occur when one attempts to win the debate (or election or vote) by intentionally confusing the audience's understanding of the issue, such as through words that suggest the exact opposite of what you mean or that hide the truth. For instance, some critics contend that the "Clear Skies Initiative" proposed in 2003 would actually have allowed *more* pollution into the air than enforcing the existing Clean Air Act.[29] The title of the initiative, in this case, suggested the opposite of what it may have been intended to achieve. Obviously, such framing efforts should be avoided as they are unethical and, therefore, lead to divisiveness, confusion, and cynicism rather than fair and open discussions and debates about shared concerns.

Another dishonest means of framing occurs when a speaker unfairly maligns the opposition. That is, they may take a person's words or actions out of their original context and recontextualize them—that is, reframe them—to make the person appear despicable. An egregious example occurred in fall 2010 when Democrat Alan Grayson, campaigning to represent Florida in the US House of Representatives, ran a television advertisement that presented his opponent, Republican Daniel Webster, as a sexist religious fanatic who desired the complete subjugation of women. The ad referred to Webster as "Taliban Dan" and repeatedly played a clip of Webster saying, "Submit to me now." The clip was stripped from its original context (at a Christian conference) in which Webster actually told husbands *not* to demand submission from their wives.[30]

Framing the opposition in a way that damages them can also occur by adopting charged labels for them. Taliban Dan is obviously a charged label but so are many of the terms some people use for their opposition. When someone identifies those who support the Tea Party and its ideas as tea baggers, they are functioning in a similar way. As discussed in chapter 3, speakers should be careful with the labels, metaphors, and euphemisms they use to characterize groups of people. Harmful terminology makes it easier to dismiss alternative perspectives before truly considering or understanding them or the people who disagree with you, and it sometimes causes us to even forget their humanity.

But, as a reminder, framing in and of itself is not unethical; it's simply the way our minds and human language work. Facts are very important in our speeches and conversations about public issues, but framing is critical to enable those facts to make sense so we can better understand the issues facing us and the merits and drawbacks of the solutions—and perspectives—we may adopt.

SUMMARY

In this chapter we have addressed the canon of style, or *how* one conveys information to the audience. Through style one attends to the words that are used to communicate with an audience. Reflection on those choices, ranging from word choice to particular literary devices to framing, can help speakers engage their audience while clarifying their content and reinforcing their perspective. More specifically, this chapter has made clear that:

- Style is the language or expression you use—the words you choose.
- The stylistic use of language serves the important goals of creating clarity, interest, emotion, and perspective.
- Stylistic devices are language techniques and literary tools that clarify meaning, express ideas in a compelling manner, and appeal emotionally to an audience.
- Stylistic devices can be used to create a sense of rhythm (e.g., parallelism, repetition, antithesis, alliteration).
- Stylistic devices can provide for visualization (e.g., concrete language, visual imagery, simile, metaphor, personification).
- Stylistic devices can enhance argumentation (e.g., metaphor, irony, satire, reference to the unusual).
- Stylistic devices can develop a sense of community (e.g., inclusive pronouns, maxims, ideographs).
- Framing refers to the use of language to order, make sense of, and shape perceptions of the world.

KEY TERMS

framing p. 168   style p. 154
rhythm p. 157   stylistic devices p. 157

REVIEW QUESTIONS

1. How is style defined in this chapter?
2. What are the four devices for generating rhythm discussed in this chapter?
3. What are the five ways of fostering visualization?
4. What are the three devices mentioned to aid argument?
5. What are the four ways for building community through language choices?
6. What is framing and how is it accomplished?

DISCUSSION QUESTIONS

1. Think of a public presentation that had particularly good "style." What sort of devices did the speaker use? What was their impact on the message and audience?
2. What kind of voice or style have you developed for presentations in the past? What kind of language did you use? Imagine an occasion that might call for an alternative style. How might you adapt your language to better suit it?
3. How does—or should—style change based on the audience, setting, and occasion?
4. Think of a public issue and identify several different ways of framing it. For each frame, name its definition of the problem, who is to blame for that problem, and some likely solutions.
5. This chapter warned against using charged labels when talking about your opposition, yet it also warned against evoking a counter-frame. Very often, groups name themselves in a way that resonates with their framing of an issue (think of "pro-life" and "pro-choice," for example). Should you use the title that a group chooses for itself even when it evokes a counter-frame? Or should you create your own label for them? How might you refer to an alternative group without evoking a counter-frame AND without maligning them?

CHAPTER 9

Engaging Your Audience through Delivery and Memory

Chapter Objectives

Students will:

- Learn about delivery as a fluid and constantly developing skill.

- Understand communication apprehension and strategies for overcoming it.

- Examine the most important elements of vocal and nonverbal delivery and their influence on a presentation.

- Use memory to effectively implement any of the four common modes of delivery.

Following his 2004 Democratic National Convention Keynote Address in Boston, Barack Obama, then a Senate candidate from Illinois, was showered with praise for his performance. In describing the scene, Katherine Seelye of the *New York Times* wrote that the address drew "rousing applause" and prompted "tears" from the assembled onlookers. Delegates were equally enthusiastic, with one presciently predicting Obama "is going to be a star in the Democratic Party," and another saying that "based on that speech, he personifies this party's future."[1] While Obama's future success in twice winning the presidency was due to much more than his speaking skills, he is unquestionably an effective speaker, perhaps even one who, in the words of Mark Bowden in the *Philadelphia Inquirer*, "is rehabilitating rhetoric itself." In particular, observers have noted Obama's skill in using his oratorical abilities to forge a connection with his audience. This includes his engaging nonverbal cues, vocal tones that create melodic refrains, and even his excellent comic timing that can put an audience at ease. In short, Barack Obama knows how to deliver a speech.[2]

However, an interesting competing narrative regarding Obama's oratorical prowess has emerged. After he won the presidency, a number of commentators began to criticize Obama's public speaking due to what they perceive as an overreliance on the

173

President Barack Obama addresses an audience while using a teleprompter.

teleprompter. Columnist Raymond J. de Souza remarked on the changing perceptions of Obama the speechmaker, writing, "A year ago, one skirted sacrilege to" criticize the president. Then, de Souza explained, "he was the orator whose very words would shape history. [But] . . . his greatest asset has apparently lost its power. . . . The teleprompters are trivial. But they stand for something serious, namely that Obama appears to be heavy on presentation, and light on substance. . . . The words don't last, disappearing from memory soon after they scroll past on those screens.[3] Obama's frequent use of a teleprompter prompted stingingly humorous jokes about TOTUS— Teleprompter of the United States—and occasional embarrassment when a teleprompter malfunctioned or the wrong remarks were incorrectly loaded. In turn, during his 2012 re-election campaign it was announced that Obama was "scaling back his teleprompter use" and would use notes on paper more often in order to "help him connect with voters."[4]

These assessments of Obama's speaking—that he has outstanding delivery skills and that his delivery skills are overly dependent on the use of a teleprompter—are central to this chapter: the role of delivery and memory in engaging public audiences. By **delivery** we mean how you as a speaker physically convey words and ideas, vocally and nonverbally, to the audience. **Memory** refers to how you store and recall the information that is shared in a speech. Teachers and theorists of rhetoric traditionally addressed delivery and memory with a degree of reluctance or hesitancy, for reasons that foretell reactions to President Obama's speechmaking. They feared that too much attention to them might reinforce critics' fears—and accusations—that rhetoric is nothing more than the use of those components to manipulate the audience. We can sense the ambivalence even Aristotle felt in taking up the topic when he wrote, "one should pay attention to delivery, not because it is right but because it is necessary."[5] Ultimately rhetorical theorists, including Aristotle, worked past this reluctance to develop principles and practices on delivery and memory that are ethical and yet effective in enhancing the speaker-listener relationship.

These principles and practices for cultivating delivery and memory remain highly relevant today. Nearly everyone must speak in public. Your future occupation, be it as a teacher, salesperson, civil servant, healthcare professional, attorney, or some other vocation, will likely make use of public speaking. And beyond your profession, nearly all efforts at civic engagement—and certainly all public discussions—involve public speaking, whether it consists of city council work, school board service, or public forums on important community issues. To do your job effectively and to participate in your community, you will need to speak in public. To assist with that task, this chapter provides an introduction to delivery and memory. We begin with four principles of delivery, move to the particular vocal and nonverbal elements of delivery, and conclude with a discussion of memory.

DELIVERY

The goal of speech delivery is to effectively and clearly communicate with the audience. To that end, delivery is a means of conveying, enhancing, and reinforcing your ideas in public presentation. Ethical, engaged delivery clarifies speech content for the audience without becoming the focus of attention in a presentation. However, as the most visible element of speechmaking, we also understand that delivery often commands the most immediate attention from speakers and audiences. With this level of focus, one can easily get caught up in delivery, whether it is the student speaker who equates success with entertaining the audience or the listener who comments only on delivery when offering peer feedback. Our placement of delivery in this book—in the middle—underscores its role as one of many elements of public speaking and not a singular focus of attention. We begin consideration of the topic with four conclusions about delivery: (1) it is normal to feel anxiety about speaking in public; (2) no one manner of delivery is right for all speakers; (3) delivery is situational; and (4) your skill in delivery will develop over time.

Speech Anxiety Is Normal

Don't panic. It sounds easy, but we know it can be a challenge. If you experience **communication apprehension**, a heightened fear or anxiety that arises when you anticipate public speaking and that interferes with your ability to do so effectively, telling you not to panic probably doesn't sound very helpful. If relaxing was that simple, you wouldn't need the reminder or the encouragement! Feelings of anxiety arise for many reasons, including a general nervousness about being in front of public audiences, poor preparation, the stress or importance of the situation, unease about the subject matter, worry over audience evaluation and reaction, and fear of failure. We understand that no matter what we say here, ultimately you will have to navigate a variety of feelings to give a speech. We don't say that to diminish the usefulness of our advice but to acknowledge that written words may not calm all of your fears. That said, the practices promoted in this book will benefit you if given a chance. We have years of experience teaching, and we've seen a variety of reactions to the stresses of the speaking situation—an inability to look at the audience; the podium death grip; hands deep in pockets; chewing on the ends of one's hair; and even leaving the room—but we've never lost a student! Public speaking is a survivable experience with a mortality rate of zero! Does that alleviate some of your concerns? It should because no matter what happens in your speech, life will go on and so will you. Remember also that your audience will want you to succeed; your classroom audience, and often other audiences too, will be "rooting" for you because seeing a speaker struggle with anxiety makes the audience uncomfortable too. Let's start with some of what we know about communication apprehension before considering strategies for controlling it.

BOX 9-1

Common Symptoms of Communication Apprehension

- Nervousness when anticipating speaking
- Feeling that your heart is "racing"
- Perspiration
- Shaking or trembling
- Dry mouth
- Feeling a "knot" in stomach
- Slight sense of nausea
- Going "blank" while speaking
- Swaying
- Pacing
- Avoidance of eye contact
- Reading speech
- Gripping lectern
- Hands in pockets
- Folding arms and "hugging" oneself
- Speaking too quickly
- Fidgeting
- Frequent touching of face and hair
- Communication avoidance

These symptoms may be manifestations of speech anxiety and also reflect delivery behaviors that can be perceived by the audience as signs of anxiety, regardless of how you actually feel.

A review of speech anxiety research is located in Graham D. Bodie, "A Racing Heart, Rattling Knees, and Ruminative Thoughts: Defining, Explaining, and Treating Public Speaking Anxiety," *Communication Education* 59 (2010): 70–105.

Nervousness before, and even during, the act of public speaking is normal. Researchers have found that communication apprehension—or speech anxiety—is among the most common fears we have and often one of the most intense. One recent study, by communication scholars Karen Kangas Dwyer and Marlina M. Davidson, found that 61.7% of participants identified being fearful of speaking in front of a group, a higher number than the 43.2% of respondents who indicated a fear of death. However, when asked to rank their top fear, slightly more (20%) indicated death than did public speaking (18.4%).[6] In putting such apprehensions in perspective, comedian Jerry Seinfeld has joked, "According to most studies, people's number one fear is public speaking. Number two is death. Death is number two. Does that seem right? That means to the average person, if you have to go to a funeral, you're better off in the casket than doing the eulogy."[7] Of course Seinfeld is not serious, but his observation is helpful because it reminds us that anxiety about speaking in public is quite common.

The best way to manage communication apprehension is to focus on the skills and preparation techniques described in this textbook, including preparing well, rehearsing your speech, and having realistic expectations about your speech performance. Experience is also an antidote; your level of speech anxiety will likely decrease naturally over time. Still, you are unlikely to completely eliminate speech anxiety—and that can even work to your advantage. A speaker who seems uninspired and unmotivated to speak is deflating to the audience; an absolute lack of anxiety can actually cause a speaker to sound bored or flat. In contrast, the energy and passion conveyed by the slightly anxious speaker can encourage the audience to collectively think, "The speaker is excited about this topic, so it must be something worth getting excited about!"

Strategies to Use Prior to a Speech

Some of the most effective techniques for responding to communication apprehension are practices of ethical speech preparation discussed in earlier chapters of this book. This preparation includes researching your topic thoroughly, thinking about your likely audience, understanding the expectations and constraints of the speaking situation, and familiarizing yourself with the location of the speech. By preparing thoroughly, including developing a clear outline and practicing your speech several times, you are reassured that you are more likely to have a positive speaking experience. You can further reduce anxiety by learning your introduction particularly well, helping to make sure the speech starts smoothly. Also, practicing the speech in front of a friend both builds confidence in your preparation and helps you visualize successfully giving your speech. Finally, relax or unwind in advance of the speech. Rather than enter the speaking situation tense and on edge, take a little time for yourself, be that by practicing meditation, engaging in light exercise, working a logic game, or undertaking another activity which you enjoy and that releases tension.

- Research and learn your topic well.
- Construct a clear and easy-to-follow outline.
- Learn your introduction well.
- Rehearse your speech several times.
- Ask a friend to listen to you practice.

- Think about your likely audience.
- Familiarize yourself with the location of the speech.
- Visualize yourself giving a successful speech.
- Relax prior to the speech.

BOX 9-2

Managing Speech Anxiety during Civic Engagement

Settings of civic engagement are often more flexible and hence less predictable than some other public speaking opportunities. They also more often involve informal, impromptu remarks. Nonetheless, there are several steps you can take to lessen your anxiety when speaking before a civic group or at a public forum.

- Try to meet the organization's leaders or forum organizers in advance.
- Visit the location of the meeting in advance to learn about the speaking environment.
- If it is a recurring meeting, attend a gathering in advance of your speech to gain an understanding of its normal operation.
- If you are giving a formal presentation, discuss the expectations and constraints with the organizers.
- Learn about common patterns of interaction between speaker and audience in this setting.
- Think about the likely audience for the meeting.
- Speak with people who will attend the meeting or have attended the meeting in the past to gain their insights.
- Plan your remarks in advance, forming a speech outline and notes if it is a formal presentation.
- For less formal situations, fill out note cards identifying key points on the topics you are most interested in and most anticipate raising in discussion.

Strategies to Use During a Speech

You also can employ strategies during the course of your speech that will help you control your anxiety and limit its visual manifestation. As you will discover in the final section of this chapter, which addresses memory, using notes rather than a manuscript will improve your engagement with the audience and reduce the temptation to break eye contact for extended periods. This is a much better strategy than sophomoric advice about managing anxiety by imagining your audience in their undergarments or looking slightly above their heads in attempting faux eye contact (all you manage to do is look like you are gazing above their heads!). You can also position yourself in the speaking situation so as to not grip or lean on the podium (if one is present). Remind yourself to breathe in order to calm your nerves, perhaps even making notations on your speaking notes to assist with this. You might also consider working with a speaker's lab, speech tutor, or friend to identify any distracting physical mannerisms or signs of anxiety and practice to limit them. However, if during the course of the speech you make a verbal stumble or notice yourself falling into a physical pitfall, do not draw the audience's attention to the behavior ("Gosh, I'm really nervous," or "I guess I'm pacing a lot"). Doing so typically exaggerates, rather than lessens, the impact of the behavior by highlighting it—and often what feel like obvious signs of speech anxiety to the speaker are barely noticeable to the audience. So, instead, offer a subtle correction and keep going. Finally, don't expect to deliver a perfect speech—this is an impossible expectation, one that will only heighten your communication apprehension.

- Speak extemporaneously with a few notes rather than memorize the speech word for word or use a manuscript.
- Stand back from the podium and do not grip the sides.
- Use pauses to catch your breath and calm your nerves.
- Include helpful reminders and notations on your speaking notes.
- Don't draw attention to verbal and nonverbal stumbles.
- Trust yourself and remember the perfect speech will never be given.

Strategies to Use after a Speech

Just because the speech is over doesn't mean you should stop working to address speech anxiety. Postspeech reflective exercises and techniques are also productive and will help reduce future anxiety. Take time to think about—and even take notes on— how the speech went. Reflect on the positive elements of the speech while also taking note of areas you can improve. You will also benefit from getting reactions from your peers and carefully considering instructor feedback. We often find we are our own harshest critics, while the feedback of others lends reassuring perspective and provides confidence when thinking about future speaking occasions. Following these few steps will help you continue to improve your delivery—and reduce your anxiety— each time you speak.

- Reflect on how it went, and focus on the positives.
- Make notes, or journal about the experience.
- Ask a few people for their reactions.
- Carefully consider instructor feedback.

Find a Manner of Delivery That Works for You

You can undoubtedly think of a number of speakers with great delivery. However, just because they have great delivery in public presentations doesn't mean you should emulate them. You must find a style of delivery that works for you as an individual. What works for Stephen Colbert will not necessarily work for you. What worked for John F. Kennedy and Barbara Jordan probably is not right for you either. We learn many things from watching great speakers—how to employ vocal variety, the strategic use of volume modulation, the impact of physical engagement, and so on—but that doesn't mean you should try to sound and look just like them. To be effective as a speaker you must develop a delivery that is consistent with who you are as a person. You will figure this out with practice and experience. Over time you will learn the ideal amount of notes for you, effective and natural gestures, and if you can tell a joke and when to tell it. Through these efforts you will start to become *you* and not an imitation of Colbert, Kennedy, Jordan, or another speaker.

Delivery Is Situational

It might sound logical to think that a speaker should always be "engaging"; that a speaker should always speak with energy and passion, incorporate physical movement and gestures, and smile. While that is often good advice, in practice it isn't always appropriate and doesn't always work. Instead, vary your delivery based on the dictates of the situation. For instance, Bill Clinton's delivery of his "map room" speech in 1998, in which he explained his relationship with former White House intern Monica Lewinsky, was substantially different than his delivery when speaking before the Democratic National Conventions in 2008 and 2012. One situation was solemn and serious, while the other was raucous and celebratory. Bill Clinton's delivery reflected these differences.

You want to vary your delivery based on situational factors that include occasion, purpose, audience composition, and audience size. Likewise, conditions and constraints such as your distance from the audience, the arrangement of the speaking platform or lectern, and the degree of formality of the occasion dictate adjustments to your tone, rate, and volume (all discussed later in the chapter), as well as determine how you dress. "I Have a Dream" is a remarkable speech, but its delivery is suited to a large audience and significant occasion, not to a boardroom presentation or for a speech honoring the accomplishments of a departing coworker. The situations are different and so too will be the delivery.

Your Delivery Will Develop over Time

Finally, realize that your delivery will develop over time. As you gain more experience, you will learn what works for you in delivery—the way you can modulate your voice, if and how humor works, what gestures are natural—and what does not. When you finish your present class, your delivery will be different than it is now. And you will be somewhere else in the months and years ahead because while any one course will improve your speaking abilities, it will not "finish" you as a speaker.

The finer points of delivery are limitless, and there is always room to improve, even for the best speaker. The target is constantly moving because the subject matter, occasion, audience, and the historical moment change. This is what makes public speaking more art than science. However, as you work on your delivery, the next section offers a few basic elements, divided between vocal and nonverbal delivery, to keep in mind as you assess a situation and prepare to speak.

ELEMENTS OF DELIVERY

People often use the word delivery to capture a number of quite different components. In individually exploring elements of delivery, we consider their meaning and how they can be used to engage public audiences. The first distinction to make concerns the difference between vocal (or verbal) and nonverbal elements.

Vocal Delivery

Vocal delivery refers to how the voice and mouth are used to deliver words. Certainly this involves the delivery of content to the audience, but it is also important for how we connect with—or engage—our audience. Effective vocal delivery establishes a speaking voice that is inviting, easy to listen to, and clear. Different vocal techniques can draw the audience into a speech, including how we vary our volume, our tone, and our rate. Likewise, different adjustments to those vocal features can open space for and encourage audience participation and discussion. Key elements of vocal delivery include volume, tone, rate, pauses, articulation, pronunciation, and avoidance of vocal fillers.

Volume

Volume, or vocal amplification, refers to the loudness of your voice. If you fail to be heard while speaking, nothing else you do will matter. Of course, your volume can also be used strategically. Speaking particularly loudly can reinforce the importance of your subject matter and signal passion for the topic. You can also underscore the importance of information or suggest its sensitivity and confidentiality by using a whisper or drop in voice. In determining vocal amplification, remember to balance the need to be heard with the risk of overpowering the audience and creating the sense you are yelling at them.

Further volume modification is required based on factors such as the setting and audience size. Speaking outdoors, which is common for rallies and many civic events, requires more vocal projection to overcome background noise, particularly when a microphone or other amplification is unavailable. Similarly, the size of the audience and your distance from them requires adjustments to your volume. Finally, when using a microphone or other sound equipment you will want to monitor your volume. In such cases testing the equipment in advance, when possible, is an asset. When you are uncertain about your volume, you might ask the audience for feedback on the ease with which you can be heard, but if you are provided with a microphone use it. While you might feel self-conscious about using a microphone, it is made available both to help you as a speaker *and* to assist differently abled hearers. And even if you speak loudly enough at the outset of a speech, your voice may begin to falter over the course of the speech, with the result being that you become increasingly difficult to hear.

Tone

Vocal tone refers to the sound of your voice and how you vary it during a presentation. This vocal element is also referred to as pitch, vocal emphasis, vocal variety, and vocal range. Increased vocal variety, efforts at strategic emphasis, and a broader vocal range are more engaging to listeners over the course of a longer speech. This element of vocal delivery, combined with volume, is most often associated with perceptions of speaker enthusiasm. On the other hand, when a speaker talks monotonously (marked by a lack of change in intonation), you can almost feel the energy drain from the room as the audience becomes bored and is eventually lulled to sleep by the dullness of the speaker's voice.

Your tone affects how easy you are to listen to, how engaging you are to the audience, and potentially even how the audience perceives you. One particular way to express this concept is the term pitch, the placement of your voice—its highness or lowness—on the musical scale. A speaker with a consistently high pitch can be grating and difficult to focus on (for instance Melissa Rauch's portrayal of Bernadette on *The Big Bang Theory* or the public persona adopted by comic and voice actor Gilbert Godfrey). Likewise, a speaker with a consistently low voice can sound "gravelly" and risks the audience not being able to pick up or hear his voice. Finding the right tone— one we might call inviting, open, and soothing—is particularly important when leading a public discussion. In a discussion, one's vocal tone or pitch can be used to frame topics in a vocally neutral fashion that welcomes participant contributions.

An example of a speaker who purposefully changed her tone or pitch in order to engage public audiences differently was British Prime Minister Margaret Thatcher. Early in her public life, Thatcher had what was described as a higher pitched or shrill voice. As she rose to political prominence in the 1970s and 1980s, she worked with a political advisor on how to change her tone. In particular Thatcher worked to lower her pitch to project a calmer, more authoritative voice. The change in tone better conveyed the sense of power and command associated with a political leader and was accompanied by other changes in her speaking style, such as speaking more slowly and lessening her accent. Such changes became part of the persona of "The Iron Lady" and were features of Thatcher's public speaking and political presence.[8]

Rate
Rate is the speed at which you speak. Again, you should vary your rate based on the material in your speech, the occasion, and the audience. Your goal need not be to speak at a particular word count—although generally a speaker can reasonably deliver the equivalent of a double-spaced typed page of standard-sized text in about two minutes—but to speak at a pace that is comfortable for you and the audience. In seeking that comfortable rate, be mindful of adopting a speed that is either too fast or too slow. If you speak too quickly the audience will struggle to comprehend the information, particularly complex material. You also risk, much as you do with excessive volume, overpowering the audience and becoming too difficult to listen to. On the other hand, if you speak too slowly you risk losing the audience's attention, particularly since consistently slow speaking is often monotonous.

You might selectively increase your rate of delivery when covering less important material. Rate can also be adjusted to add verbal emphasis (slowing down for instance) or to provide a sense of energy or enthusiasm (increasing your rate at a particular point in a speech). Changes in rate can be particularly effective in situations urging civic action—using your rate to establish urgency and to convey excitement commensurate with your content in rallying support for a cause.

Pauses
Pauses refer to those places where you strategically choose not to speak as a means to fix the attention of the audience on what you have just said or are about to say. A pause also allows the audience to catch up with the speaker or to ponder an idea for a

moment. A pause is best used between significant points in a speech, often in con
tion with a verbal transition. However you should also be mindful about pausir
frequently or at awkward moments. Doing so can make the presentation choppy,
result in unintended divisions in content, and create perceptions of nervousness.

You should also learn to use pauses as a means of incorporating audience feedback and reaction. For instance, if the audience laughs in response to something you
say, pause or else your next thought will be lost in the laughter. You should make similar allowances for audience applause and the occasional "aha" moment when you have
made a significant point. In each case, a strategic pause will maintain your clarity.
Your ability to incorporate such audience feedback will also encourage their participation while talking over their reactions will do the opposite. You can often practice
your presentation with such pauses in mind by working to identify moments in your
speech that are likely to provoke laughter and places where applause—in recognition
of a person or accomplishment for instance—are likely.

Articulation

Articulation refers to speaking each word with clarity. A speaker with poor articulation—
a "mumbler"—undermines the clarity of his or her speech. If you know you speak
with an accent that is unfamiliar to many in your audience, you can help ensure they
follow your message by concentrating on your articulation. Moreover, if you struggle
with articulation, you must also monitor your speaking rate. When you speak too
quickly you risk running words together, thereby decreasing your clarity. Similarly,
articulation—or what is more precisely called enunciation—is a factor in properly
forming words. For instance, you may have a habit of dropping the endings from
words, such as words ending with "ing" ("runnin" instead of "running," for example)
or mashing words together ("gonna" instead of "going to"). Such constructions not
only decrease clarity, but informality can also damage perceptions of speaker competence and education. Finally, articulation is an issue to monitor in settings or venues
with poor acoustics. In such situations clear articulation, a slow rate, and purposeful
volume will increase your clarity.

Pronunciation

Pronunciation is the manner in which particular words are spoken or given sound.
Proper pronunciation shows command of vocabulary while mispronouncing terms
(particularly when done multiple times) may cause an audience to question your
understanding of the word, term, or concept. This can also be an issue of respect and
cultural awareness when we consistently mispronounce a person's name or a cultural
custom.

Vocal Fillers

Vocal fillers, also called nonfluencies, are sounds ("um" and "er" most prominently)
and words (e.g., "like," "you know," and even "and") used on a repetitive basis that do
not add content to a speech. They are often used out of habit, in which case they can
become distracting to the audience. In fact, in extreme cases when a filler is repeatedly
used, an audience may begin to anticipate the filler rather than listen to the speech

itself. This can become a significant impediment to offering an effective message while harming your credibility. A few "ums" and "uhs" are natural, but if you have more than a few, your audience will begin to notice them and can find them distracting. As you practice your speech, try to get comfortable with brief silences by learning to pause instead of using a vocal filler. A small space of silence is much more effective and useful than a nonfluency.

The conclusions to draw regarding vocal delivery have already been addressed— find a delivery that suits you, remember that delivery is situational, and recognize that your delivery will develop over time. Your ultimate goal is to use your voice to enhance and clarify your content while encouraging audience attention. Through practice you will be able to refine your vocal delivery in ways that allow you to best achieve your goals. Practicing in front of a peer or tutor will also help as they can provide feedback on issues such as pronunciation, rate, and vocal fillers. Another strategy is to record your speech or a segment of your speech, something you can do on most smartphones. You can then playback the presentation, taking note of your clarity, tone, rate, vocal fillers, and other qualities. Warning: you will sound different on the recording because we generally only hear our voice from inside our head, which changes its sound. Don't be alarmed by this difference.

Nonverbal Delivery

In contrast to vocal delivery, **nonverbal delivery** refers to how the body is used to communicate. The audience reads or interprets nonverbal cues just as they do a speaker's vocal delivery. Consequently, nonverbal delivery can add to or detract from a speech, underscoring or undermining the message, and affect the speaker's effectiveness. Important nonverbal cues include eye contact, facial expressions, gestures and movement, and appearance.

Eye Contact

It is difficult to overemphasize the importance of establishing eye contact with audience members. In fact, eye contact may be of such importance as to qualify as another principle of good delivery. Culturally, we associate eye contact with truthfulness and sincerity, regardless of whether these perceptions are grounded in reality. As you speak, try to look at specific people in the audience, establishing and holding eye contact with them for several seconds at a time, and then move to someone else.[9] This works to better establish a connection with individual audience members, a connection that both draws them in and makes it more difficult to not listen. In making eye contact with the audience you want to include people throughout the space rather than concentrating on a particular location where you find one or two familiar, friendly, or interested faces. You also want to do more than bob your head up and down while constantly accessing your notes. Finally, do not direct too much of your eye contact toward a visual aid—keep most of your focus on your audience.

We understand that maintaining eye contact can be a challenge for reasons ranging from nervousness to note dependence to differences in culture and status. However, we also encourage you to think about the issue from the audience's point of view. Think back to a time when you were an audience member and a speaker had very little eye contact. How did that make you feel? How did you perceive the speaker and react to his or her message?

Finally, establishing eye contact provides you with an excellent way to gain audience feedback. By making eye contact with your audience you will often pick up on signs of encouragement and agreement from audience members, signs that will likely lessen your anxiety. Other times you will be able to determine that you can move on or that you need to slow down and offer a deeper explanation of a point based on how the audience is responding. Eye contact provides direct feedback—take advantage of it.

Facial Expressions

One of your most expressive physical attributes is your face. A smile can establish goodwill and create warmth. Or you can encourage a discussion participant to contribute or to continue talking with a warm facial expression, by making eye contact, or with a nod of the head. You also can indicate disagreement and even anger with how you change your expression. And you can express disbelief, either with or without humor. Taken together with tone, your facial expressions help establish the meaning of the message. Think for a moment how difficult it can be to interpret an e-mail, text, or tweet, and how we are sometimes left to wonder if the message is serious or sarcastic. The uncertainty is because of the lack of vocal tone and facial expressions that give messages meaning—and we've even developed symbols—emoticons or emojis—that we can include in our written messages to try to clarify that meaning. Learning to be nonverbally expressive is an asset to your public speaking.

Of course we can also send unintended messages through our facial expressions. As a speaker, you need to think about what message you might send if you never smile during a speech (or if you smile all the time). And in a civic context, be mindful of how you interact with other participants through your expressions. Remember that a flash of anger, a dismissive look (like rolling your eyes), or an expression of frustration can and will be seen by the audience or participants and it stands to impact a discussion.

Gestures and Movement

Gestures refer to the movement of your hands and body while you speak. Well-placed gestures draw emphasis to points in your speech, provide another form of audience engagement, and can even assist with transitions and internal summaries (gestures that indicate number, for example). Gestures can also accentuate words by almost physically drawing objects and by illustrating actions. For instance, if you are discussing a meeting at which the committee chair pounded her gavel on the table, you can represent that action through gesture. On the other hand, repetitive gestures that are not strategically designed should be avoided as they are distracting for the audience. The challenge, then, is to strike an effective balance between random or repetitive gestures on the one hand and overly rehearsed (and, thus, artificial) gestures on the other.

When offering gestures think about their visibility and purpose. If you are standing behind a lectern, your gestures must be high enough to be seen by the audience.

Gestures are frequently offered by extending the arms with one's palms upward or by raising a hand with the thumb and forefinger in a closed position. The latter is a gesture meant to engage the audience without pointing at them, which can be interpreted as aggressive. Avoid excessive waving of the arms and leave your arms relaxed at your sides when not gesturing.

Along with gestures, a speaker can strategically use movement to aid the message. When speaking, you can reposition yourself to mark major transitions and to give the audience an opportunity to reset their attention. Such strategic movement can also help you engage different segments of the audience, while releasing nervous energy, and is much preferred to random pacing. Another element of movement to consider is body positioning in the speaking setting. As a speaker you should be cognizant of where you stand and the distance between you and the audience. While you do not want to crowd the audience and make them anxious by violating their space, standing too far back from the audience, at the back of a platform or in a classroom with your back near a chalkboard, can increase a sense of separation and make you appear uncomfortable or disengaged. Similarly, to stand to the side of the room or speaking platform—rather than in a central position—weakens your presence and can redirect the audience's focus. In civic and discussion settings you will often be most effective in moving among and sitting with other participants. This helps strengthen your connection with them and lessens the sense of a barrier between you and others, who you hope will become involved in the issue and the discussion.

Appearance

Appearance is an interesting aspect of nonverbal delivery in that there are some factors that we can control more than others. An element of physical appearance in your control is dress. The way you dress should be fitted to the occasion, the audience, your topic, and you as a person. Dress conveys the formality of the situation and is seen as a sign of speaker competence. It also can identify you as part of a group or apart from it. Think for a moment about the idea of "looking presidential" and how we expect the president or presidential candidates to appear in official settings. Then contrast that with how the president generally appears when surveying a disaster site or on the campaign trail—finely tailored suit with tie versus rolled-up sleeves and casual dress. In each case the attire communicates to the audience the role the president or presidential candidate is assuming in the situation.

The same principle applies to your speaking experiences, be they in the classroom, leading a public rally, or at a job interview. And while your classroom speeches are generally more casual, you might think about the perceptions you risk creating if you roll out of bed for an early morning speech and arrive with hair standing on end and still wearing pajama bottoms. Your dress can communicate to your audience that you take the occasion seriously, that you have put forethought into your preparation, and that you want to make a good impression, all of which contribute to your ethos.

Conclusions about Vocal and Nonverbal Delivery

A now classic *Saturday Night Live* parody of the first presidential debate from the 2000 election brings together many of the concepts addressed in this section. The skit also provides an interesting perspective on how delivery can potentially undermine the content of a message. Much of the humor of this particular skit was created by magnifying elements of Al Gore and George W. Bush's vocal and nonverbal deliveries. Cast member Darrell Hammond, portraying Al Gore, spoke at an exaggeratedly slow rate and constant tone while magnifying his sighs and using facial expressions that mingled exasperation and a sense of superiority. Cast member Will Ferrell's portrayal of George W. Bush mixed facial expressions depicting confusion, disinterest, and smugness while making light of Bush's inability to pronounce the names of foreign leaders and words in general. The parody had enough impact that Gore's aides had him watch it in advance of their second debate. When responding to a question by the media about how he would act differently in their second encounter, Gore jokingly but purposefully said, "I think I'll sigh a little bit less."[10] The lesson, in part, is that our vocal and nonverbal delivery can make a significant impact on the audience, even sending unintended and damaging messages that create perceptions regarding our attitude toward the audience and others. The example also provides a near inventory of nonverbal behaviors and distracting mannerisms you want to avoid as a speaker.

Elizabeth Dole speaks from the floor of the Republican National Convention on August 14, 1996.

A second example that illustrates the range of concepts we have discussed in this section, and to much greater positive effect, is Elizabeth Dole's address at the Republican National Convention on August 14, 1996. Dole, later a Senator from North Carolina, spoke from the convention floor in support of her husband, Republican presidential nominee Bob Dole. Her speech, which was widely praised, consisted of a series of personal reminiscences of life with Bob Dole while emphasizing his character, humanity, and humor.[11] Watching Dole's address illustrates how one can use vocal and nonverbal delivery to clarify and accentuate a speech. In the speech Dole varies her tone and uses vocal emphasis to express a range of meanings from enthusiasm to humor to sincerity. Dole's nonverbal delivery is even more noteworthy. Dole created an intimate setting for the speech by leaving the platform and moving into the crowd. Circulating among state delegations as she spoke, Dole created a conversation with convention attendees and home viewers while she physically connected with six audience members whom she featured at various points in her speech. It is interesting to watch parts of the speech without sound to see, for example, how Dole interacts with the audience as she moves among them, uses facial expressions to signal a friendly and joyous environment—she smiles throughout the speech—and how her gestures provide emphasis for her words and engage and acknowledge the audience.

This listing of vocal and nonverbal delivery cues provides a range of considerations for you to make as a speaker. However it is important to again recognize that all speaking situations and all speakers are different. In the end, good delivery does not call undue attention to itself. It helps the audience understand, remember, and act on the speech, and it appropriately suits the situation. Finally, recall that public speaking is as much art as science. The perfect speech has never been given, and no public speaker ever stops learning. The best speakers learn the principles while finding a delivery that matches their personality and in so doing move beyond the principles themselves. View each speaking opportunity you have like a painter with a blank canvas; it is your opportunity to create something that no one else ever would or could create.

MEMORY AND MODES OF DELIVERY

At the outset of this chapter we defined memory as how one stores and recalls the information that is shared in a speech. As you likely see, that means delivery and memory go hand in hand. Indeed, beginning speakers often find that they most effectively improve their delivery when they improve memory of their material through the use of mnemonic devices, visual images, and brief, key words that capture sections of their speech. As with many aspects of public speaking, how we use our memory is dependent on the expectations and constraints of the speaking situation.

Public speaking scholars commonly recognize four **modes of delivery**, methods by which a speaker delivers his or her information. While we advocate one of the four modes—extemporaneous delivery—as the most preferred across the largest range of speaking contexts, each approach has its merits in particular situations. We begin discussion of modes of delivery by considering extemporaneous delivery before briefly addressing impromptu, memorized, and manuscript delivery in turn.

Extemporaneous Delivery

In **extemporaneous delivery**, the speaker devotes significant time to preparing and practicing a polished speech but uses limited notes during presentation. For extemporaneous delivery, you need to effectively research your topic, carefully plan your speech, develop an outline, move from that outline to a set of key word notes, and practice the speech several times. Over the course of your practice, you should commit the structure, key ideas, and important examples to memory. At this point, speakers commonly make the error of trying to learn the speech word for word. Instead, capture sections of the speech with key words and then commit only these key words to memory. Often referred to as remembering "ideas not words," this practice forms a central tenet of extemporaneous speaking. It will, however, benefit you to learn some ideas with more precision such as the introduction (including thesis and preview) and conclusion. You may also want to memorize a few specific details that you want to recall with exactness. This will help ensure you begin the speech smoothly, have clarity of purpose, and have a good design for closing the speech.

We advocate the regular use of extemporaneous delivery because this form best enables speakers to maintain a natural and energetic delivery while connecting with audience members. By concentrating on ideas rather than specific words, you can keep the speech fresh during the course of its practice and delivery. In fact, each time you practice or give the speech it will be a little different in terms of the language you use and how you deliver it. In this way you will remain conversational. Also, by being fully present in the moment, you can retain a sense of spontaneity and react to the situation as appropriate. The fourth-century BCE rhetorician Alcidamas, a student of Gorgias, advocated this style, noting that with an extemporaneous delivery small errors can be easily covered by the speaker. He went on to note that with an extemporaneous delivery the speaker can most easily adjust to the reactions of the audience and that this manner of delivery best enables the speaker to bring the speech to life.[12] Indeed, the flexibility offered by extemporaneous speaking allows you to react to audience feedback, be that an unexpected audience reaction, a question posed during the speech, or when you detect the need to add or remove material based on audience feedback.

Extemporaneous delivery particularly suits public settings that discuss issues of community importance. In such situations, elements like setting, audience, and the time available for presentation can change. For instance, when using an extemporaneous delivery you will be more able to adjust your remarks based on what others have said at a public forum or to respond to interjections by another participant or an audience member. If another speaker has already addressed the problem in detail, using an extemporaneous delivery will allow you to modify your remarks when it is your turn to speak. Or perhaps after hearing another speaker present an alternative solution to the one you planned to present, you would adapt your speech by incorporating some responses or offering some comparisons between your perspective and one the audience has just heard. In these ways and others, extemporaneous speaking offers a valuable and flexible approach, one that capitalizes on your advanced preparation while allowing you to respond to the needs of a given situation as they arise.

Impromptu Delivery

You have probably heard of the mode of delivery frequently called impromptu speaking. In an **impromptu delivery** you must rely on instant recall as it refers to a situation in which you speak publically without advance preparation or warning. In such an instance your delivery is integrally linked to what you can recall about a topic and articulate on the spot.

This form of speaking comes with a rush of adrenaline as you are either thrust unexpectedly into a speaking situation or feel compelled to suddenly, voluntarily enter a discussion of an issue. As such, it is a reactionary form of speaking, often characterized by high energy and spontaneity while featuring less polish and being more prone to vocal fillers. Due to the lack of preparation, you may feel more anxiety and pressure with impromptu speaking, and almost inevitably when looking back later, you will think of other things you might have said. As these difficulties suggest, impromptu speaking challenges even seasoned speakers.

While impromptu speaking does not lend itself to formal preparation, you can adopt strategies to help you be more effective. First, take a breath! While you will not have time to develop a speech, you can take a brief moment to collect your thoughts. If your comment has been requested, you might clarify what the question was or the point to which you have been asked to respond. In those moments you can also write down two or three key words, each of which might represent a central point or example you want to mention. Second, remember the organizational principles you have learned because they are helpful even in impromptu speaking. Begin your remarks by stating your central point, perspective, or position. Follow that with a short series of brief supporting ideas, probably no more than two or three. You might number the ideas or offset them with transitions to keep the points distinct. Where possible, offer detail in support of your claim in the form of specific examples or illustrations. When you conclude, offer a brief summary of what you have said. Third, be succinct with impromptu remarks. It is to your benefit to be short and to the point rather than to talk excessively and in a circuitous fashion. Fourth, be prepared. That undoubtedly sounds paradoxical but there are ways you can mentally prepare for the prospect of impromptu speaking. This starts with following the principles of ethical listening discussed in chapter 3. By being present and engaged in a communication setting, listening actively, and being mentally alert, you will be better prepared to speak if called on. Also, whenever you know the topic of a meeting or forum in advance, take some time to think about it. By doing so, you will have already started to informally collect your thoughts and ideas—ideas that will prove valuable if you are suddenly drawn into the conversation. Lastly, take pen and paper with you, so you can jot down ideas during the course of the discussion. This too will spark your thinking and allow you to formulate a response or question to contribute to the ongoing dialogue.

Memorized Delivery

As its title suggests, in **memorized delivery** you memorize the speech word for word with the intent of precisely recalling and delivering its content without the aid of notes or a manuscript. This mode of delivery emphasizes and stresses your memory, requiring extensive practice to not only recall ideas but the exact words prepared for the presentation.

As you can no doubt imagine, effective memorized speaking is difficult, particularly for lengthy presentations. It also comes with substantial risks, including "blanking" on what you plan to say, needing to rebound from a lapse in memory, and finding the flexibility necessary to adapt to a challenging situation or adverse audience feedback. One veteran presenter we know, one who has recited a particular poem hundreds of times for public audiences, shared his infrequent but serious struggles when memory fails. He says that when he lost his place during a recitation, he occasionally had to start the poem over rather than resume it in the same spot. Similarly, when the audience supplied the wrong cue in response to a line in the poem, he found himself unable to continue smoothly. A final concern for memorized speaking is the adoption of a mechanical delivery and a vacant or distant look—one that lessens engagement with the audience—that can be the result of either the strain or monotony of recalling the words. This sort of "canned" presentation, one that is fully prepared in advance, can result in the speaker losing touch with the moment during the presentation.

Ultimately, memorized speaking should be used sparingly, limited to short speeches on special occasions, although even then extemporaneous speaking is generally preferred. More likely, you will find good reasons to memorize segments of speeches where precise wording is important, such as a quotation, thesis statement, or the specific wording of a policy proposal. If you must give a memorized speech, allow plenty of time to commit the speech to memory and attempt to do at least one full rehearsal with a listener who can provide feedback on your vocal and nonverbal delivery.

Manuscript Delivery

Finally, in **manuscript delivery** the speaker writes the entire address—including prompts for vocal and nonverbal delivery—in advance and utilizes the text in delivering the speech. Recalling the example of President Obama that opened this chapter, a skilled manuscript speaker maintains significant eye contact with the audience, and, depending on the technology available (e.g., a teleprompter), the use of a manuscript may not be readily apparent.

Manuscript speaking is best suited to formal situations with a large audience. This includes platform speaking and occasions where the speaker and audience are physically separated, such as occurs in many presidential addresses and commencement ceremonies. Manuscript speaking also aids occasions where precise wording matters and you have given particular attention to the artistry and style of the speech. Manuscript speeches are more common for lengthy addresses and have the advantage of letting you know more precisely how long your speech will take to deliver. As we note, however, it takes real skill and practice to effectively deliver a manuscript speech, and it should not be envisioned as simply reading to the audience.

When preparing the manuscript, double-space the typed text and use a larger font (14, 16, or 18 point). Also include prompts or reminders in the manuscript regarding pronunciation, eye contact, tone, volume adjustments, and, potentially, gestures. These prompts, often signaled through underlining and bolding key words, will remind you of ways to enhance your vocal and nonverbal delivery. Such cues also can be used to encourage eye contact while reducing the risk that you will lose your place. Finally, secure and number the pages so you are confident the manuscript will remain intact.

In preparing for manuscript speaking you will want to practice multiple times with the completed text. During your practice work on making eye contact with the audience, maintaining a conversational tone, and incorporating gestures as appropriate. As with other modes of speaking, you will benefit from practicing the speech in front of a listener to gain feedback and, when possible, in the same or similar venue of the actual speech so you can gain an understanding of your position in relation to the audience, test any sound equipment, effectively position your manuscript for use, and evaluate the effectiveness of your projection and nonverbal delivery.

Returning to Elizabeth Dole's unique 1996 Republican National Convention speech provides the opportunity to reflect holistically on the modes of delivery. Dole took an unconventional approach to her address, abandoning the speaking platform and the typical practice of delivering such speeches with a manuscript or teleprompter. Instead, Dole gave an address that had the precision of a memorized speech, the flexibility of an extemporaneous speech, and the spontaneity of impromptu speaking. In her speech Dole is purposeful and careful with her vocabulary and even recites quotations from memory. And yet she demonstrates an extemporaneous sensibility in how she adapts to and incorporates her live audience, interacting with them. Finally, there are impromptu elements in her remarks, including when she incorporates Bob Dole's sudden "surprise" appearance on a large video screen. Likewise Dole masterfully handled an unexpected technical difficulty when her microphone started buzzing. Accepting this as a hazard of her nontraditional approach to delivering the speech, Dole quickly switched to a handheld microphone and continued unfazed. In her speech Dole illustrates the nuances of modes of delivery while expertly speaking with her audience.

SPOTLIGHT ON SOCIAL MEDIA:
Phil Davison Wants Your Support

When Phil Davison stood before members of the Stark County Ohio Republican Party on September 8, 2010, he didn't expect to become nationally known for giving a speech that would go viral and be viewed literally millions of times. Davison, a councilman for the village of Minerva, Ohio, for more than a decade (population approximately 4,000), is a common man who wants to be a valuable public servant; a citizen who has sought to do his part to improve public life.

Davison's speech, given when he was seeking the county's Republican nomination for treasurer, was recorded by Martin Olson, a citizen journalist for the Huffington Post.[13] In the speech Davison spoke with great passion and emotion while explaining his political vision and commitment to the public. Davison was, though, also overcome by his passion and emotion and his speech was marked by aggressive gestures, intense facial expressions, overpowering vocal projection, and a tendency to stalk around the lectern while frequently referring to his notes.

Davison did not win the party's nomination and, never having heard of YouTube, went to bed not expecting to hear much about the speech. However, social networks and the Internet assure that Davison's talk will have a long life, which is instructive and potentially problematic. It reminds us that our public speech—particularly speech linked to civic participation—is unpredictable, and it may long be available for anyone to see. It also reminds us, though, that a speech doesn't have to define us. Davison's grace and humor in dealing with what happened, his willingness to talk about it, and his desire "to help people who don't have much," demonstrate that he is a reflective and well-meaning participant in public life.[14] Davison moved on from the experience and talked openly about it with journalists, as well as appearing in a humorously crass "web redemption" on the Comedy Central program *tosh.0* and in an online 2013 Super Bowl "teaser ad" from Volkswagen.

We can, however, also learn from Davison. We can model his passion for and interest in improving society. And there are also lessons about how delivery impacts the reception of a presentation. For one, Davison presents a case study in the importance of controlling one's emotions in a public speech.

Discussion Questions

- What other lessons related to delivery can be drawn from Davison's experience?
- What might Davison have done to refine his delivery?
- What does the example say about the role of memory in speechmaking?

SUMMARY

This chapter addressed the importance of delivery and memory to public speaking. While aiding content (or invention) in important ways, these two speech concepts are more attuned to issues of form, or *how* one conveys information to the audience. Specifically, we have observed:

- Delivery is a fluid and constantly developing skill that changes over time and according to the situation. With experience you will find a form of delivery that is most natural and comfortable for you.
- Delivery is a means of conveying, enhancing, and reinforcing your ideas in public presentation. Ethical, engaged delivery clarifies speech content for the audience without becoming the focus of attention in a presentation.
- Communication apprehension, or speech anxiety, is common but can be effectively managed with preparation, practice, and other strategies employed before, during, and after a speech.
- Vocal delivery, how a speaker uses his or her voice and mouth to deliver words, is important in connecting with—or engaging—an audience. Effective vocal delivery establishes a speaking voice that is inviting, easy to listen to, and clear. Key elements of vocal delivery include volume, tone, rate, pauses, articulation, pronunciation, and avoidance of vocal fillers.
- Nonverbal delivery, how the body is used to communicate, can add to or detract from a speech, underscoring or undermining the message, and affect the speaker's effectiveness. Important nonverbal cues include eye contact, facial expressions, gestures and movement, and appearance.
- While each of the four common modes of delivery—extemporaneous, impromptu, memorized, and manuscript—have their benefits and limitations, extemporaneous delivery is the most versatile and widely appropriate approach.

KEY TERMS

communication
  apprehension p. 175
delivery p. 174
extemporaneous delivery
  p. 188

impromptu delivery
  p. 189
manuscript delivery
  p. 191
memorized delivery p. 190

memory p. 174
modes of delivery p. 188
nonverbal delivery p. 184
vocal delivery p. 181

REVIEW QUESTIONS

1. What is delivery? What is its relationship to memory and style?
2. What is communication apprehension, or speech anxiety? What are some common strategies for reducing anxiety?
3. What are important features of vocal delivery that impact the effectiveness of a presentation? How can you adjust these features to benefit your speeches?
4. What are important features of nonverbal delivery that impact the effectiveness of a presentation? How can you adjust your nonverbal delivery to increase your connection with the audience?
5. What is memory?
6. What are the four common modes of delivery? What are the advantages and disadvantages of each type of speaking?

DISCUSSION QUESTIONS

1. Why do we commonly focus on delivery in contemporary evaluations of public speakers?
2. Name three speakers who you think are good or excellent. What makes their delivery good? How do these speakers differ from one another in terms of their delivery?
3. Think about a time you were an audience member in a public presentation that featured very little eye contact from the speaker. How did that make you feel? How did the rest of the audience react?
4. What about public speaking makes you apprehensive or anxious? What strategies have you used to lessen your anxiety when preparing to speak before an audience?
5. Think of a situation in which manuscript delivery would be appropriate. How about a situation when impromptu delivery would be appropriate?
6. Imagine that you have been asked to speak at a local civic organization like the Kiwanis Club or at a League of Women Voters meeting. What questions would you ask, and what information would you seek, to effectively prepare and deliver your speech?

CHAPTER 10

Speaking Informatively
through Deliberative Presentations

Chapter Objectives

Students will:

- Define informative speaking.
- Understand the need for informative speaking in civic affairs.
- Name different types of informative speaking.
- Explain the role of deliberative presentations in engaging public controversies.
- Describe and demonstrate the process of forming a deliberative presentation.
- Assess the limitations of informative speaking.

When asked by his public speaking teacher to identify a difficult issue, Arizona native Zeno Joyce thought about the dispute over Arizona Snowbowl, a ski resort north of Flagstaff, Arizona. The resort enjoyed one of its most successful ski seasons during the winter of 2012–2013. For the first time by any ski resort in the world, Arizona Snowbowl blanketed a portion of its slopes with snow it produced using 100% reclaimed wastewater. By enabling a longer and more predictable ski season, the artificial snow helped the resort draw over 57,000 additional visitors than average and increased sales of Flagstaff hotel stays, dining, and alcohol by 15% over the previous season.[1] Snowbowl owners and supporters celebrated the economic boon the artificial snowmaking created. As the Snowbowl general manager said, "Everyone does well when the ski area does well."[2] But not all Arizonans agreed.

Numerous local American Indian tribes protested the resort's use of treated wastewater. The mountain range on which Snowbowl sits is public, leased to the ski resort by the US Forest Service. Native Americans have long believed the land to be sacred, regularly praying and holding ceremonies there. Consequently, they have

In 2005, several American Indian tribes sued the US Forest Service because it allowed the Arizona Snowbowl ski resort to make artificial snow using treated wastewater. In this picture, Navajo Nation President Joe Shirley Jr. addresses the news media after testifying in court in support of the lawsuit.

fought expansions of Arizona Snowbowl and viewed its use of reclaimed wastewater as a further desecration of the mountains and as an additional impingement on their cultural traditions. Several environmental groups also protested the use of wastewater. They worried the artificial snow might damage the mountain's alpine tundra and the health of skiers who fall and ingest the snow. They highlighted a study that found endocrine-disrupting chemicals, or EDCs, in the treated wastewater.[3] They implored the government to halt Snowbowl's plans until scientists learned the impact these chemicals might have on the soil and rocks, as well as the fresh water the mountain ultimately yields to the community.

The conflicting perspectives about the mountains and artificial snow resulted in years of protests, arrests, and legal battles. In 2005, after the US Forest Service approved Snowbowl's use of artificial snow, 13 American Indian tribes, backed by environmentalist groups, sued the Forest Service but ultimately lost in 2009. Soon after that loss, another suit to stop the artificial snow was launched by a group called Save the Peaks Coalition. They lost their suit in February 2012, finally clearing the way for Arizona Snowbowl to spray the reclaimed wastewater on its slopes, which it did for the first time on December 24, 2012.

So which group's position and whose concerns are most important: the financial welfare of Snowbowl employees and Flagstaff businesses, the spiritual and cultural interests of Native Americans, or the health of the alpine tundra and the public who recreate on the mountain or utilize its water? Difficult cases like this rarely offer one right answer or one universally satisfying way forward. Instead, they raise the need for communities to learn about the problem, possible options, and opposing perspectives before making a decision. In this chapter, we turn to a form of speech that effectively meets that need: informative speaking.

In what follows, we first provide a broad outline of the major features and types of informative speaking. We will focus most of the remainder of the chapter on one particular version of informative speaking, the deliberative presentation. We will define and explain the deliberative presentation as an especially useful way to address public controversies similar to the Arizona Snowbowl conflict. The chapter will end with a consideration of the limitations and benefits of informative speaking in all its forms.

INFORMATIVE SPEAKING

Informative speaking is a form of rhetoric through which the speaker strives to educate an audience about a topic without leading them toward a particular position, conclusion, or outcome. In this type of speaking, you set your personal preferences or beliefs aside and present a neutral, fair, and inclusive understanding of the topic as possible. Of course, none of us are capable of remaining completely impartial, and one can argue that even the selection of a topic is an act of persuasion by upholding the topic as worthy of attention. Most rhetorical scholars would agree, however, that some presentations are fairer or more neutral than others. The goal, then, is to do your best to keep your opinions in check to allow audience members to arrive at their own conclusions. Before describing several types of informative speeches, we will pause to argue the importance of such speech in civic affairs.

The Need for Informative Speaking in Civic Affairs

The need for informative speaking in civic affairs may not be self-evident. After all, information has never been easier to obtain. Anyone with access to the Internet can learn tremendous amounts of information about nearly any topic. However, as we discussed in chapter 4 on research, the material provided by the Internet can quickly become overwhelming, and not all of it is reliable. Unless required or especially motivated, few of us have the time—or, at least, take the time—to thoughtfully discover, evaluate, read, and process information provided by a variety of sources about a topic. Instead, we may glance at a couple of quickly found sources or, worse yet, simply rely on our assumptions or well-known opinions. Sometimes, of course, our first instinct or quick decision is the best one. But other times we close ourselves off to equally valid, if not better, options. Alternatively, we might abandon the effort to become informed altogether and leave civic affairs to the experts (e.g., public officials and specialists), thus removing ourselves from decision-making that may directly impact our quality of life.

Informative speaking, then, is critical to civic engagement and democracy. Informative speaking helps empower ordinary community members to understand often complex or difficult topics so they are more able and likely to participate in civic life effectively and thoughtfully. An informative speech serves the public by drawing attention to public concerns, presenting relevant and reliable information from credible sources, and helping a community make sense of that information. We can find examples of informative speeches accomplishing these goals at every level of society. At the college-campus level, you have likely listened to informative speeches by librarians, registrars, advisors, financial aid officers, or student affairs representatives to learn about resources available to you and how to access them. Your local community likely has a chapter of the League of Women Voters, a nonpartisan, nonprofit organization that makes information about local topics and governance available, such as directories of local government officials. Nationally, we might point to the informative programming occasionally offered by *This American Life,* a popular radio show that airs regularly on National Public Radio. In recent years it has dedicated some episodes to explaining the causes and components of national crises, such as the housing crisis,[4] the associated banking crisis in 2008 and 2009,[5] as well as exploring the dangers of acetaminophen (which is in Tylenol).[6] An example of a group that offers informative speaking about global issues is the World Affairs Councils of America, a nonprofit and nonpartisan US grassroots organization that has chapters in over 40 states. Most chapters meet regularly to educate their members and the larger public about global issues, often by hearing from an invited speaker on a specific topic. Individuals from each of these groups—from the college campus to the World Affairs Council—have educated the public about civic affairs through some form of informative communication—be it in person, on the radio, in print, or on the Internet.

SPOTLIGHT ON SOCIAL MEDIA:
Mediated Learning Communities Expand Our Understanding of Informative Speaking

Informative speaking traditionally presumes a speaker, who possesses knowledge or expertise, communicating information to an audience who lacks such knowledge. And we have typically considered that communication occurring in real time, often face to face. Social media applications, however, such as Digital Commons, Twitter, Flickr, and Pinterest, have expanded our understanding of informative speaking because they have enabled learning communities to develop online. A learning community typically consists of members who share a common interest or educational pursuit. Of course, learning communities have always existed. You might think of the members of any college campus as constituting a learning community, for instance. But social media have dramatically altered such communities by expanding their reach, enabling them to be more egalitarian between "speakers" and "audience members," and utilizing large numbers of people to improve the accuracy or relevance of information and resources.

First, social media have enabled learning communities to dramatically expand their geographic reach and to escape time constraints, allowing asynchronous communication. Consequently, people around the world can form connections and even friendships much more easily, improving their ability to teach and learn from a broader segment of the population. For example, the Kettering Foundation, a nonprofit organization devoted to improving democracy, established "The Commons"—an open access digital commons space—in order "to stay connected with the network of people working on issues that involve problems of democracy." That network includes nearly 400 people from several countries who use the site to "post comments and share links, documents and videos."[7]

Second, social media have enabled informative speaking to be more egalitarian because members of learning communities function as co-teachers *and* co-learners. Members function collaboratively as users offer each other ideas, insights, personal experiences, knowledge, and links to relevant resources. Consequently, people who are not naturally connected to a traditional learning community (i.e., not enrolled in a class) can find a community to which they can contribute. And one's standing in the community—that is, the authority and credibility a single user develops within a group, often determined by the number of "followers" one has—depends more heavily on the accuracy and relevance of the information and ideas they share than on their title, position, or class. For example, A Mighty Girl, a resource site "for parents, teachers, and others dedicated to raising smart, confident, and courageous girls" has a Facebook page with over 1 million "likes," a Pinterest site with over 23,000 followers, and a Twitter handle with 14,000 followers.[8]

Third, the large numbers of people involved in social media learning communities, as the previous example attests, can improve the accuracy or relevance of information through crowdsourcing. Crowdsourcing is "the practice of obtaining needed services, ideas, or content by soliciting contributions from a large group of people and especially from the online community rather than from traditional employees or suppliers."[9] This practice presumes that a preponderance of opinions—as large numbers of individuals recommend, rate, follow, or like a resource—will accurately reflect the quality or correctness of the information or resource. Through such large numbers, the learning community highlights the most relevant, useful, and accurate resources, which may range from the best restaurants in town or most dependable backpack to buy to the most popular social protest groups or social commentators.

Discussion Questions

- How have social media influenced how you gather information from and offer information to others?

- What might be the dangers of relying on crowdsourcing for determining the quality of information?

- What are the merits or demerits of determining a user's authority and leadership from the number of followers they have?

Types of Informative Speeches in a Civic Engagement Context

Different kinds of informative speeches enable civic engagement in varying ways. In this section we briefly describe three types of informative speeches that aid democratic participation: instructional speeches, problem-focused speeches, and deliberative presentations.

Instructional Speeches

An instructional speech explains or teaches an audience about a process, concept, or entity to enable community members to more easily and confidently participate in civic affairs. For instance, an instructional speech related to the Arizona Snowbowl controversy might describe how Flagstaff treats its wastewater for reuse, spending time explaining the legal standards required by the Environmental Protection Agency (EPA). As another example, a person might educate new members of an organization about the rules used to run meetings. Several of this textbook's authors, for instance, have delivered an informative speech to new faculty members at their college about the parliamentary procedures used at faculty meetings. Their goal was to educate new members so they could understand what was happening during a meeting and more easily participate. Somewhat similarly, a student might deliver a speech about the history, membership, and local community service of a charitable organization, such as the collegiate fraternity Alpha Phi Omega and sorority Epsilon Sigma Alpha or the noncollegiate fraternity Freemasons or sorority Beta Sigma Phi. In all the examples provided, the speaker's emphasis is on providing information to enable audience members to better understand and participate in the affairs of their community. The instructional speech stops short of actively promoting involvement or prescribing particular types of behavior or actions. The speakers mentioned here would not explicitly advocate support for Snowbowl's use of wastewater or participation in faculty meetings or charitable organizations. Instead, they would simply lay the groundwork for involvement should an audience member choose to do so.

Problem-Focused Speeches

Problem-focused speeches identify, describe, and explain a civic problem so as to aid the community's understanding of the issue and possibly prepare the public to address it. Most typically, a problem-focused informative speech will explain the problem's history, impact on those affected by it, probable cause(s), and major components. Such a speech avoids naming or advocating a solution, though it might explain previous efforts made to address the problem as part of the historical background.

The problem you address might be something you noticed but has largely been ignored or overlooked by others. For instance, you may be aware of a dangerous intersection in town because you commute to campus while most of your peers live on-site. In this case, your speech would seek to raise the audience's awareness of the problem as you inform them about it. You might, instead, focus on a problem you perceive as very significant while your audience sees it as a minor issue. Perhaps you view your city's slackening enforcement of housing standards as a major concern. Or maybe the overpopulation of animals at your community's animal shelter has you much more worried than your classmates. In these instances, you would attempt to establish the seriousness of the problem as you explained the problem itself. Alternatively, you may educate your audience about a well-known problem that is already widely perceived as an issue. Examples of such topics include the rising cost of college tuition or the growing "digital divide" between underprivileged people who cannot easily access the Internet and wealthier people who can. Though issues like these are broadly recognized as concerns, some community members may actually know rather little about them. An informative speech that addressed these problems would need to verify, possibly correct, and supplement popular beliefs about them.

Deliberative Presentations

A **deliberative presentation** fairly and even-handedly describes a civic problem and multiple approaches to solving the problem with emphasis on the benefits and drawbacks of each approach. Notice the emphasis here on finding, explaining, and contrasting specific *solutions* to the problem, unlike a problem-focused speech. A deliberative presentation functions as the setup or preparation for a **deliberative discussion,** which is a group conversation through which a community, guided by one or more moderators, thoughtfully and thoroughly examines a complex public problem as well as a range of available solutions to ultimately arrive at a choice, decision, or conclusion. Together, the deliberative presentation and subsequent discussion form the **deliberative process** or, what some people refer to simply as, deliberation. The deliberative process involves both a presentation of the problem and multiple options and the subsequent moderated discussion of those options (though the format and timing of both can vary).

The nature and emphasis of both the deliberative presentation and discussion are educational; we want to better understand the problem and ascertain the advantages, disadvantages, tensions, and motivations of each option or solution in the most open and fair manner possible. The ultimate end goal—and a key distinguishing feature of the deliberative process—is that the participating community chooses the option it wants to pursue or the next step required to continue making progress. Ideally, the process results in consensus on a way forward, but that may not always be the case. Eventually, traditional persuasive efforts and voting may be appropriate.

The deliberative process is ideally suited to address a **public controversy**; that is, a matter that concerns the community and is difficult to resolve as it involves diverse perspectives and more than one possible option or answer. A public controversy is already widely acknowledged as a problem and draws broad concern. The size and scope of the community affected is typically defined by the people who perceive the controversy as impacting their lives. Thus, that community may be local, national, or even international in scope. Public controversies may be persistent, such as the issues of abortion, capital punishment, and immigration; or they may become prominent at certain moments and then die down, such as controversies over oil spills and nuclear power. In your college community, you may find that controversies occasionally pop up over concerns such as race relations on campus, administrative oversight of student behavior, or rising tuition costs and student fees.

All public controversies are marked by **contingency**, a condition in which events and circumstances are dependent on a number of variables that change in unpredictable ways. Contingent matters typically consist of many variables, so the effects and consequences of any decision made about such matters cannot be fully anticipated. Will allowing Arizona Snowbowl to use treated wastewater help the resort continue to draw large crowds? Would such success lead to a higher employment rate and more successful businesses in Flagstaff? Or will use of the wastewater create more sympathy for the Native Americans as more visitors experience the grandeur of the mountains? Might the American Indians' protests ultimately gain enough support to drive visitors away from the ski resort? Would ending the use of wastewater financially ruin Snowbowl or ensure protection of the alpine tundra on the mountain? We cannot know the answers to these questions with absolute certainty because too many unpredictable variables influence the outcomes. If we knew the answers with certainty, disagreements and discussion would be unnecessary because the best decision would be evident. As Aristotle observed, "We debate about things that seem to be capable of admitting two [or more] possibilities; for no one debates things incapable of being different either in past or future or present."[10] Most people, for example, unless they are being facetious, do not argue about whether a cement sidewalk is hard or the sky is blue. Rather, we deliberate and debate those many things that are, well, debatable or contingent. One of the stunning things to realize about the human condition is just how little there is that falls into the category of certainty.

Because the thrust of informative speaking is educational, this form of communication takes place *before* we select or advocate any particular solution, conclusion, or belief. Communities need to know and understand before they can select and decide. Whatever the type of speech, informative speaking should result in an improved and ideally shared understanding of a process, concept, entity, problem, or issue. In the case of deliberative speaking, audience members should also have a thorough review of several possible solutions. Because of the importance of deliberative presentations, we will focus the remainder of this chapter on the steps involved in producing and delivering such an address.

PREPARING A DELIBERATIVE PRESENTATION

For community members to productively tackle a public controversy, they must be presented with a clear, thorough, and even-handed presentation of the problem and a range of perspectives on the issue. A deliberative speech, therefore, needs to be as neutral and objective as possible and offer a thorough yet concise presentation of the facts and perspectives on the issue. Such a presentation best prepares a community to participate in a deliberative discussion that follows. We now turn to the specific steps involved in preparing a deliberative presentation. These include selecting a public controversy, discovering a range of perspectives, framing for deliberation, and organizing and delivering the presentation.

Selecting a Public Controversy

The process of forming a deliberative presentation begins with identifying a public controversy. You may start this task by listing all the communities of which you are a part. These could include groups related to your residence, college, hometown, college town, church, clubs, state, and so on. Now think about the problems each of these groups is facing. Which of these meets the definition of a public controversy, that is, an issue that is difficult to resolve, affects a range of people, causes concern throughout that community, and elicits more than one possible answer or solution? Using this approach helped Zeno Joyce, the aforementioned public speaking student, choose the controversy over the Snowbowl resort for his deliberative presentation. You might also approach the task of identifying a public controversy by asking, "What's important to me? Which issues really matter to me?" Your answers will likely point you in the direction of a significant controversy, presuming other members of a community share the concern.

As you engage in this process of finding a public controversy, your instinct may be to shy away from difficult issues, particularly those about which you know little. This is a natural instinct, but also a very unfortunate one for several reasons. First, effective democracies rely on informed participants who continue to learn about civic matters in order to productively engage in decision-making about them. Second, particularly as a college student, you are enrolled in classes for this very purpose, the pursuit of knowledge. Discovering how to learn about complex issues now will make this task easier later in life when you will likely have even more responsibilities. Third, democracy thrives on diverse views and on reasoned, thoughtful discussion among people holding them. Several scholars have argued that we should approach competing perspectives and ideologies as valued viewpoints that assist society rather than threaten it.[11] As a student of public communication, you must learn to embrace productive conflict as a natural element of a healthy, pluralistic democracy. You cannot avoid conflict without also avoiding discussion of the most important issues and thus decreasing your participation in democratic discourse.

Once you have selected a public controversy, use the advice provided in chapter 4 to research and learn about the issue. This will help you begin to form the part of your presentation that focuses on the problem itself. Consider researching the history or background of the controversy, the impacts on people affected by the problem, possible causes of the problem, and various concerns related to the problem itself. And try to identify key facts related to the problem.[12] A **key fact** is a piece of information that can be measured or tested, often by an expert, *and* is critical to understanding the problem. Not all facts are key. For instance, in his deliberative presentation about Arizona Snowbowl, Zeno did *not* need to spend time establishing the number of ski resorts in Arizona, the size of Snowbowl in comparison to other ski resorts, or the amount of wastewater available in Flagstaff. That information may have been interesting, but its absence would not critically alter an audience's understanding of the controversy. Zeno *did* need to tell his audience key facts related to the wastewater (how much was used by the ski resort, when, and where), the known environmental impact of the wastewater (EPA standards for the wastewater; scientific studies that have been conducted on the wastewater, by whom, and their findings), and Native Americans (how often they hold activities on the mountains and on which part of the mountains in relation to the wastewater). Such key facts would help ensure the audience would base their considerations on a more accurate knowledge of the problem than on presumptions or guesses. Ultimately, however, it is important to remember that facts alone will not resolve a public controversy because such controversies are composed of multiple variables.

Discovering a Range of Perspectives

Once you have selected a public controversy, you need to identify a range of perspectives on the issue. As discussed in chapter 2, we tend to divide issues into two sides. The abortion debate, for example, becomes pro-choice versus pro-life. This approach is popular, because it offers a simplistic symmetry with only two options that promote debate. Indeed, our political system is largely premised on this method of organization. We have two major parties, Republican and Democratic, and we generally talk about ideological views as being either conservative or liberal. Of course, additional parties and perspectives exist—Independents, libertarians, and the Green Party among them—but somehow these viewpoints frequently get lost in broad discussions of the big issues. This is an unfortunate practice that reduces complicated issues to tidy, oppositional dichotomies as if everyone on each side is in complete agreement and no one from opposing sides agrees on anything. It creates the perception of either-or decisions by depicting issues as black and white, right and wrong, or left and right.

A public controversy representative of these tendencies is gun regulation. This complex matter is often characterized in the simplest of terms: people are identified as being either for or against gun regulation, assumed to mean advocacy for either unrestricted gun access or for total prohibition. In the arena of informed public discourse, very few people hold such extreme views. Generally speaking, those in favor of gun regulation do not propose that all guns be removed or banned from law-abiding citizens. And those against gun regulation are not in support of all persons having unlimited access to all types of weapons. When we oversimplify positions as one extreme or another, we lose sight of the overriding or common problem, such as "How do we best protect the public's safety?" We also overlook more moderate options, such as legislation based on factors like age, criminal record, and mental capacity; safety measures including waiting periods, registration, and permits; and limitations on types of weapons and locations where they may be carried.

Reducing possible viewpoints to either unqualified support for or opposition to gun ownership creates a **false dilemma**, a type of reasoning fallacy that presents only two possibilities or outcomes for an issue. Inaccurately presenting one's opponent as holding to one set of these extreme beliefs produces a **straw man** reasoning fallacy. This unethical argumentative strategy depicts an illusory opponent and oppositional perspective, one so extreme, patently flawed, and lacking nuance or qualification that it is easily countered. Linguist Deborah Tannen contends that such practices encourage "us to believe that every issue has two sides—no more, no less" when, in fact, most public issues are like "a crystal of many sides."[13]

Perhaps unsurprisingly, one of the initial difficulties students typically experience with a deliberative presentation is discovering a third perspective, and they are often tempted to make that option a halfway measure or compromise between two extremes. The challenge of discovering at least three sides can be overcome by brainstorming, thoroughly researching the issue, and identifying the multiple stakeholders in the issue.

A good first step to discover multiple perspectives on your public controversy is simply to brainstorm. Try writing down all the pertinent beliefs, opinions, and specific public actions that come to mind. Refrain at this stage from evaluating their merit; just try to generate as many ideas as possible. Recall positions with which you are familiar, but also imagine additional perspectives or possible actions even if you believe you may be the first to consider them. The sole criterion is that all perspectives listed are reasonable. Options that no one in his or her right mind would choose are not useful.

Next, you should research your topic broadly. Use the types of sources discussed in chapter 4, such as news, books, and government documents, to name a few. But especially avail yourself of sources that express public opinions and perspectives related to your topic. These include, but are not limited to, letters to the editor or opinion editorials, news interviews, pamphlets, websites devoted to advocating a group's perspective, opinion polls, and interviews you conduct with community members and leaders (using the guidelines provided in chapter 4). These sources provide an especially good way of identifying specific and varying concerns people have about the problem.

Finally, take a moment to identify the major stakeholders in this controversy. You may have already discovered them during your research. But consider whom you might have missed. Who stands to personally lose or gain something? Who may have needs or concerns related to the controversy? Every public issue impacts many different groups. Discovering them can help you see the issue from multiple angles. For instance, when Zeno decided to explore the controversy around Arizona Snowbowl, he was initially only aware of two perspectives—the ski resort and Native Americans. He struggled to see more until he imagined who else might have a stake in whether the ski resort used treated wastewater: residents of nearby Flagstaff who benefit from tax income and the business generated by the ski resort; those who enjoy hiking in the unspoiled mountains; those who appreciate the revenue from tourists who enjoy hiking and picnicking there; those who have concerns about the environment and how artificial snow might impact the unique vegetation on the mountain top; and finally, stakeholders for whom some of the above concerns may overlap. Having identified several stakeholders, you might return to your research to learn more about perspectives you may have initially overlooked, and you may wish to interview stakeholders to learn about their views firsthand.

In important respects, the ability to understand, evaluate, and accurately communicate multiple perspectives reflects a tradition with roots in the classical period, when the formal study of rhetoric first emerged. In particular, the practice resembles *dissoi logoi,* an exercise first illustrated in an anonymous text (referred to as the *Dissoi Logoi*) from approximately 400 BCE. The phrase **dissoi logoi** means contrasting arguments or twofold arguments,[14] drawing from the Greek words *dissoi,* which means twofold, double, or contrasting; and *logoi,* which forms the plural of *logos,* meaning word, speech, reason, or even rationality.

As philosopher David Roochnik explains, the *Dissoi Logoi* "contains a series of arguments offered on both sides of a variety of questions."[15] For instance, in *Dissoi Logoi 1.3,* the author claims "sickness, moreover, is bad for the sick but good for doctors." In *1.4,* the author acknowledges, "It is bad for the ship-owner if his merchant-ships are involved in a collision or get smashed up, but good for the shipbuilders." In both examples, the author recognizes the opposing impact one situation can have on two different stakeholders. What may be beneficial to one group of people may be simultaneously deleterious to another group. But the practice of *dissoi logoi* is not limited to seeing just two sides of an issue. Communication scholar Stephen Gencarella Olbrys explains that *dissoi logoi* reflects "a rhetorical and pedagogical strategy of arguing *many* sides of an issue that advances a particular relativism as constitutive of ethical action and a democratic polity."[16] (Emphasis in original.) In other words, the practice of *dissoi logoi* encourages students to recognize and consider the existence of multiple points of view and the differences among them concerning a particular public issue. Such inclusion is vital to maintaining a vibrant democracy and making good decisions as a community.

BOX 10-1

Dissoi Logoi: An Ancient Resource for Deliberation

The text known as *Dissoi Logoi* was constructed circa 400 BCE. The text is believed to be a compilation of arguments influenced by the Greek sophists (teachers) Protagoras and Hippias. Scholars have made sense of this fascinating rhetorical writing in different ways. Some see it as an early form of philosophical relativism. Others see it as instruction on argumentation. Still others see it as an innovative version of teaching using thought experiments. Finally, some view the text as a tool used by sophists to teach students how to engage in civic discussions. In any case, it is a valuable model from ancient times for understanding how various events and issues differently affect members of a community. Have you considered how an event or issue can help or hurt different people in your community? What can you learn from such an exercise?

Recognizing, critiquing, and even empathizing with multiple perspectives on an issue will enhance your comprehension of a public controversy, which was clearly the goal of the *Dissoi Logoi* text. As Olbrys explains, "The aim of practice in *dissoi logoi* is not simply *awareness* of other ideas . . . but rather the ability to reproduce them, to understand them, and to critique them all" (emphasis in the original)—including one's own perspective.[17] The goal is to move beyond the simple articulation of the prominent talking points of multiple perspectives toward a deeper appreciation of and reflection on them. Interestingly, all through the *Dissoi Logoi* the author seems to labor to fully and faithfully present two perspectives on a given issue. Both sides are presented with vigor and in a convincing manner. Indeed, the technique of *dissoi logoi* encourages empathy and an "ethical appreciation of other positions."[18] Using similar practices, you can help your audience understand and, even value, positions opposed to their own and the people who champion them. Presentations and exchanges characterized by *dissoi logoi* have the potential to create "civic friendships" between those of differing views as they work together as community members on issues of the common good.[19]

Ultimately, your efforts to discover a third side to your public controversy—through brainstorming, researching, and considering stakeholders—should result in a long list of individuals and groups and their opinions, concerns, and solution proposals related to the controversy. Sort through this list, looking for repetition or similarities, to choose the three perspectives to present to your audience. Each perspective you ultimately identify should represent a broad category of similar opinions, typically gathered around a shared general solution or value. People who fall within the pro-choice perspective on abortion, for instance, generally agree that pregnant women should have some degree of power over the decision to bring their pregnancy to term. That action (to give women power over their pregnancies) and value (freedom to choose) draw proponents of this perspective together. But notice how general and inexact both of these gathering points are. Consequently, pro-choice supporters may strongly disagree with each other about specific policy proposals that could fall within the pro-choice perspective, such as the point in the pregnancy at which a woman might lose the right to choose, what regulations should be required for an abortion clinic to operate, and whether a minor should be required to get her parent's permission. As this example demonstrates, a single perspective, as we use the term, is not synonymous with a specific policy proposal or actor. Each perspective should capture a shared general approach to solving the problem. But there should be room within a single perspective for several, and possibly conflicting, policy options by multiple actors.

Rest assured that there is no one right set of three perspectives for any public controversy. Your goal, then, is simply to provide a set of divergent approaches that account for most, if not all, of the concerns and opinions you discovered about the public controversy. Everyone in the community who hears your deliberative presentation should be able to find or see their own outlook somewhere in the perspectives you provide.

Framing for Deliberation

Having chosen a public controversy and discovered a range of perspectives that address it, you are ready to frame the topic for your audience. Recall from chapter 8 that framing is the process by which people use language to order and make sense of the world. For a deliberative discussion, you use language to help the audience make sense of a public controversy. That means presenting the controversy in a way that encourages thoughtful and direct comparison of the approaches you discovered.[20] This can be tricky, for at least two reasons. First, each of the perspectives you explore will likely include its own strategic framing of the topic that promotes a particular way of understanding and resolving the issue.[21] For instance, a strategic framing might try to gain adherents by defining the problem to lead the audience to a particular solution, overlooking the drawbacks of a favored solution, and/or ignoring underlying disagreements. Second, public discussions of controversies rarely invite the public to consider more than one way of solving the problem (or often invite only for-and-against arguments over a single solution). According to Kettering Foundation President and CEO David Mathews, "Typically, an issue is framed around some plan or solution and the public sees opposing arguments rather than all the available options."[22] So your framing of the issue needs to differ from the advocacy and excessively narrowed presentations we most often hear and read.

In contrast to strategic framing, framing for deliberation helps community members make decisions by recognizing multiple perspectives in a controversy. As Mathews explained, "In order for our decisions to be sound, issues must be presented so that we see all our options—as well as where various approaches to a problem conflict."[23] In other words, framing for deliberation involves laying out multiple perspectives on the controversy and revealing the tensions between them as well as the strengths and weaknesses of each as fairly as possible. By doing so, you will enhance the audience's ability to understand, compare, and contrast the options and, ultimately, to make progress toward a group decision or conclusion.

Framing for deliberation, then, involves presenting the issue in a way that clarifies the problem and enables participants to directly compare and contrast multiple solutions. The goal is to help the group make progress toward a thoughtfully and thoroughly discussed—and, ideally, consensual—choice for how to move forward.

We now turn to the work required to successfully frame a public controversy for deliberation: define the problem fairly, identify the trade-offs of each approach, and specify the value(s) that seem to motivate each option.

Defining the Problem Fairly

People with differing viewpoints will often disagree about the nature of a problem. In the abortion debate, for instance, some may argue the problem is the current legal status of abortion, while others identify the lack of resources for impoverished pregnant women, and still others point to the relative scarcity of abortion clinics. Finding a common definition of the problem—one that identifies the core issue all the approaches are trying to solve—can better prepare the audience to directly compare and contrast the options. Otherwise, participants who identify the key issue differently will likely talk past each other, making it difficult to weigh the advantages and disadvantages of each perspective. Thus, you need to find a definition of the problem that all interested parties can agree on. To do so, you want to define the problem somewhat abstractly, that is, phrase it as a question using the words "how" or "what," and avoid using language that favors one of the solutions.

First, express the problem at a greater level of abstraction or generality than the definition offered by any one of the groups involved. That means presenting the problem as bigger than any specific actor (person, group, organization, or institution) or action. We might define the abortion controversy as unwanted pregnancies because most involved in the debate would agree that this is the central issue that each group is attempting to resolve in its own way. Another example is in higher education, where there have been ongoing debates over the merits of single-sex student bodies, particularly for the three remaining colleges in the United States for men only (Hampden-Sydney, Morehouse College, and Wabash College). Most typically in these debates, the problem is stated as whether one (or all) of these colleges should admit women. But that articulation narrows the conversation to a single policy proposal (i.e., admit women) and to two sides (for and against). Instead, we might define the problem as how to provide the highest quality education for the student body or how to best serve the needs of the community. Such statements capture the ultimate goal of all interested parties, invite a variety of perspectives to be expressed, and enable a community to more easily compare them. For either expression of the problem, for example, imagine a speaker identifying the three perspectives of keeping the student body exclusively male, conducting research about the effects of student body makeup on learning, and incorporating gender more conscientiously into the college, such as by requiring students to take a gender studies course, admitting women, or pairing with a sister school if they had not already.

Second, phrase the problem as a "how" or "what" question: For instance, "How can we best reduce the number of unwanted pregnancies?" or "What should we do to decrease unwanted pregnancies?" Notice how these questions invite multiple answers. Avoid using "should" or "is" to begin your question. "Should abortion be made illegal?" or "Is it acceptable for a woman to choose to have an abortion?" are questions that permit only one of two solutions and recognize only two sides (for and against, or yes and no).

Third, avoid language or phrasing that favors one of the solutions. "How can we avoid killing babies through abortions?" is a question that unfairly favors a pro-life perspective. It presumes the number of abortions should be lowered, it utilizes the particularly provocative verb "killing," and it refers to fetuses as "babies." Similarly, "How can we improve women's choices when they have an unwanted pregnancy?" unfairly favors a pro-choice perspective. In this case, the word "choices" evokes that point of view, and the question presumes women should have multiple options. Both examples, then, pay too little attention to style as discussed in chapter 8.

Identifying Trade-offs

In addition to finding a common definition of the problem, framing for deliberation requires that you identify the trade-offs in every solution. Once we comprehend that every public controversy has multiple sides, we realize no magic solution exists—one choice that stands out as the most obvious, that defeats the opposing views, or that will result in 100% agreement. Indeed, any approach involves **trade-offs**, the relative advantages and disadvantages that accompany every solution to a public controversy.[24] Each solution offers certain benefits and drawbacks, prioritizes some people's needs and neglects or diminishes others, and poses challenges for implementation. Making wise choices requires understanding the drawbacks to each approach as well as the benefits. To discover trade-offs, ask:

1. What are the benefits of this approach? For instance, what advantages are gained? Who benefits from this approach, or whose needs are prioritized by this approach?
2. What are the drawbacks of this approach? For instance, what disadvantages are incurred? Whose needs are neglected or devalued?
3. What challenges might arise when implementing this approach?

You may find the answers to these questions in several ways. Check your research first. Often, proponents of one perspective point out flaws in the others. Alternatively, simply think about possible benefits and drawbacks. For example, you can use the model of *dissoi logoi*, discussed previously, to discern how each solution helps or hurts different stakeholders. Returning to the example of the Arizona ski resort, we can predict that allowing the resort to use treated wastewater to extend its season would likely draw more skiers, which would create more jobs and revenue for the resort and nearby Flagstaff. But it would simultaneously violate the religious beliefs and hamper the cultural practices of Native Americans, who believe the land is sacred, as well as possibly damage vegetation that grows there. The practice of recognizing how a single perspective can simultaneously benefit one stakeholder while hurting another can help you identify trade-offs associated with the approach.

You will have discovered a trade-off when you can fill in the blanks of this sentence: "Some people favor the ideas in approach #1, *even if* _____ *because* _____."[25] For example, in the abortion issue you might learn, "Some people favor the idea of not allowing abortions in any circumstance, *even if* that could mean allowing a mother's health to be compromised *because* they believe abortion is murder." The "even if" part of the sentence recognizes a sacrifice or loss if the option were chosen. For example, "Some people favor the idea of allowing an abortion at any point during pregnancy, *even if* that could mean aborting a baby later in the pregnancy *because* they believe the woman's life is more important than the fetus's life."

These are rather extreme examples, of course, but they illustrate that people may support a solution despite its drawbacks and challenges because its benefits are valued so highly or because the drawbacks of alternative approaches are disliked so greatly.

Weighing Competing Values

After determining the trade-offs inherent in multiple perspectives, you will need to further frame your topic for deliberation by identifying the value or set of values that motivate each perspective. A **value** refers to a principle or quality that human beings are committed to and upon which they base their thinking and decisions for important issues. Central to our self-identity and our beliefs about how life should be lived, values are believed to be our deepest motivations for choosing a course of action.[26] To understand more clearly how values function in public controversies, we need to establish several principles.

First, "when considered abstractly and one at a time, values are universally supported."[27] In general, society agrees on our basic values, such as family, security, freedom, and equality. In public disputes, however, advocates too often suggest that their adherence to or promotion of a value (freedom, for instance) stands in contrast to that of an opponent. This is rarely the case. As linguist and cognitive scientist George Lakoff explained, "For all our political differences, we share far more ideals in common as Americans than one would think from all the harsh rhetoric of Sunday morning talk shows."[28]

Second, though we agree on most values, we rank them differently, even when speaking abstractly—that is, in relation to no particular issue. A **value hierarchy** is a list of values ranked from the most to the least important.[29] If you and another person were to create a value hierarchy for equality, responsibility, freedom, family, cooperation, and creativity, you might each , for your own reasons, designate distinct orders. And if that occurs with a group of just six values, imagine how much you would diverge when ranking a significantly larger number of the hundreds of values that exist!

When you and another person prioritize different values, a value dilemma emerges. A **value dilemma** represents a difficult choice among competing values, especially those associated with policy options.[30] Consider, for example, the debate sparked in June 2013 over PRISM, the US National Security Agency's (NSA) mass surveillance program of private communication by users of Google, Microsoft, Facebook, and several other companies. Defenders of the program argued that the threat of terrorism called for these measures, and some of these defenders labeled Edward Snowden, the NSA contractor who leaked the program to the news media, a traitor. Opponents of the PRISM program argued in favor of personal freedom, and some of them called Snowden a hero. However, defenders of the program were not against freedom, and opponents of the program were not against security. The problem was the value dilemma created by the two groups' arrival at different value hierarchies in relation to PRISM. To what extent does one prioritize security at the expense of freedom? Or might there be a third value, such as equality, that both sides could agree upon or that was championed by a third group? This value dilemma is an ongoing issue as we address a range of questions from the requirement of mandatory government-issued identification to be allowed to vote to methods and subjects of airline screening.

BOX 10-2

The Value Dilemma Over the NSA's PRISM Program

On June 18, 2013, NSA Director General Keith Alexander (pictured) defended the PRISM program to the House Select Intelligence Committee. He argued the program was necessary to protect the United States from terrorist attacks. On June 19, 2013, a demonstrator (pictured) protested against the program in Berlin, citing freedom as too important to sacrifice to gain security. What do you think? How would you resolve this value dilemma? What current public controversies are creating tension between freedom and security?

Political scientists Kenneth Janda et al. identify two enduring value dilemmas that continually challenge American governance. The first, the dilemma between freedom and order (the latter includes security), remains a fundamental tension for policy-making as illustrated in the previous examples. The second, the dilemma between freedom and social equality, arose more recently as our government added social equality as one of its objectives. The more a particular policy prioritizes order or equality, the more it deprioritizes freedom. As Janda and his coauthors explain, "Both order and equality are important social values, but government cannot pursue either without sacrificing a third important value: individual freedom." People's political ideologies tend to indicate which of these three values—equality, order, and freedom—they are most likely to prioritize. Libertarians, for instance, typically prioritize personal freedom above all else. Liberals tend to favor social equality over order and freedom, and conservatives tend to value order more than social equality or freedom.[31]

Third, our value hierarchies typically shift when applied to a specific issue. In fact, our value hierarchies often change from issue to issue and sometimes even from case to case. A person who prioritizes "life" in the abortion controversy (and thus opposes most or all abortions) might prioritize justice over life in the case of capital punishment (and thus favor the death penalty even though it means terminating a life). Or someone who generally favors capital punishment might oppose it when the criminal is mentally retarded or underage, thereby placing fairness (in that these criminals cannot be held fully responsible for their actions) over justice. Janda et al. suggest that most Americans' value hierarchies change from issue to issue or policy to policy, categorizing them as liberal on some issues and conservative on others.[32] Changing your value hierarchy does not mean you lack principles or that you flip-flop; it simply means you recognize the contingent nature of public controversies and relevant values.

When forming a value hierarchy for a particular issue, an individual can experience their own internal value dilemma as they feel the "pulls and tugs among [their] deepest motivations."[33] Even the most committed pro-life supporter, for instance, is likely concerned for the woman who became pregnant through rape (feeling the pull and tug between the sanctity of the life of the unborn child and compassion for the woman), and even the most committed pro-choice supporter is probably ill at ease with abortions late in pregnancy (feeling the pull and tug between the woman's choice and compassion for the unborn child). A deliberative presentation—and the deliberative discussion that follows—can help identify these dilemmas within ourselves. That internal conflict may draw us together through the recognition of our shared struggles.

In many ways, value dilemmas—whether within ourselves or between democratic participants—represent a type of trade-off, and prioritizing these concerns becomes one of many factors we weigh when choosing a policy option. Yet values are not *just* another factor, equal in importance to other kinds of trade-offs. As noted previously, differing values are typically at the root of our disagreements. Values represent something of great significance to a community: a stake in the climate or overall direction of their group. Over time, a community's values help shape the place where they live, develop their collective identity, and direct their leaders on public policy. A community might define itself as a place that values personal freedom and creativity (consider, for example, Greenwich Village or SoHo in New York City), while another group might choose security and conformity as its most resonant values. (Consider, for example, gated communities with homeowners' associations that enforce residential rules.) Imagine how much living in these environments would differ! Still, shared values help both these groups bond and make decisions on matters that affect all their members. Opting out of your community's decision-making by not voicing your interests and values lessens your ability to shape the character of that community. As interdisciplinary social sciences professor Robert McKenzie claims, "When citizens realize that decisions on issues affect the overall climate of the community or organization in which they live by developing accumulated value preferences for that group, they have greater reason to be sure that what they value is considered in deciding public issues."[34]

Fourth, even when we agree to prioritize the same value for a specific case, we may define or apply the value differently. Regarding unwanted pregnancies, we might prioritize life yet answer related questions differently, such as "Whose life should be considered primary?" and "Should we consider the child's life in terms of its mere existence or its quality?" Regarding illegal drug abuse, many people argue that public safety is most important. But how can we best ensure the public's safety? By locking up drug abusers for longer amounts of time? Providing alternative treatment options, such as wellness programs and employment training? Or putting more programs in place to prevent drug abuse in the first place? Safety could arguably be named as the motivating value for all three suggestions, though applied quite differently. As these examples demonstrate, a speaker should not merely name the value prioritized by a perspective but explain how it is defined and applied to the problem.

Part of framing for deliberation—that is, part of preparing the audience to participate in a productive deliberative discussion about the controversy—is helping the audience recognize the value dilemmas that undergird their disagreements about an appropriate solution. Too often, rhetors speak of values in simplistic ways that obscure or hide value conflicts rather than expose them. Only by acknowledging value dilemmas can we reflect on their implications and critically assess our choices. The Center for Public Deliberation at Colorado State University explains the benefits gained from recognizing and discussing value dilemmas:

> One of the key consequences of deliberation is that participants uncover the underlying values (and value dilemmas) inherent to public issues, and thus often learn more about the issue, themselves, and, in particular, people that think differently than them. Once people realize that the people that think differently than they do have reasons for doing so, such as focusing on an opposing value, then the conversation changes. It isn't whether or not someone values security or individual freedom, but rather how a community can best decide to balance the important values. Such a conversation is much more difficult, but also much more rewarding and realistic.[35]

Deliberative presentations that prepare an audience to have conversations about balancing important values provide the foundation for a community to understand their conflicts and find creative ways to move forward together.

Organizing and Delivering the Deliberative Presentation

We have established that a deliberative presentation prepares an audience for a subsequent deliberative discussion by clarifying the problem and a range of perspectives, emphasizing the trade-offs and value dilemmas inherent in making a choice. In order for your presentation to serve its purpose, however, it must be clearly organized. Refer to chapter 6 to recall the importance of clear organization and the steps for accomplishing that. In particular, recall chapter 6's instructions for developing the introduction of a deliberative presentation. It should include a thesis that expresses the focus of the presentation as an overarching problem or question. It should also include a preview statement that indicates the main points or sections. You will likely structure your main points using the problem-alternatives-solution pattern of arrangement discussed in chapter 6 *without the solution step included*. That means the body of a deliberative presentation would include four main points: one main point that explains the problem, and a main point devoted to each of the three perspectives explained. The points devoted to the perspectives should explain what that approach is, its benefits and drawbacks, and the value(s) it prioritizes and how. You should conclude by restating the problem and three perspectives, and inviting the audience to engage the information you provided through a deliberative discussion.

A deliberative presentation can take at least three different forms. First, it may be a speech delivered by an individual or group of people. Often the same person or people who deliver the speech then function as moderators of the deliberative discussion (discussed in the next chapter). Second, a deliberative presentation may be delivered as a short film or video. A video can more easily humanize the issue by including video clips of people affected by the problem and/or people voicing support for each of the perspectives. Third, a deliberative presentation can be offered in the form of a written booklet. The National Issues Forum has made what it (and now others) call "issue books" popular. Such booklets are typically concise, yet dense, explanations of a public controversy and three perspectives, though their precise format varies. Of course, a deliberative presentation can be delivered with two or more of the forms listed. Some deliberation practitioners, for instance, opt to provide an issue book to the public in advance of a deliberative discussion and then show a short video right before the discussion to remind them of the options and to educate anyone who did not read the booklet.

Ultimately, creating a deliberative presentation using the steps outlined will help you prepare an audience for a deliberative discussion. A successful deliberative presentation—in any form—helps create a safe and trusting climate in which participants willingly examine beliefs, including their own.[36]

LIMITATIONS AND BENEFITS OF INFORMATIVE SPEAKING

Informative speaking can empower ordinary people to more knowledgably and actively participate in public concerns. But it can also harm civic engagement if it is poorly or dishonestly used. We will briefly consider some of the limitations of informative speaking before summarizing its benefits.

If done poorly, informative speaking can leave an audience confused, overwhelmed, and even less likely to become active in civic affairs. You might think of a speech you heard that simply regurgitated piles of information. Maybe the speaker stated statistic after statistic, or maybe she simply compiled a list of facts or quotations. Though the information offered may have been accurate and unbiased, the audience probably did not leave with a significantly better or clearer understanding of the topic. The speaker needed to help the audience make sense of the information. For instance, she could have provided a clear organizational structure for the speech, more effectively explained how the information provided related to each other, and more selectively offered evidence. Offering and then explaining the significance of two or three statistics can be more helpful than simply stating 10, for instance. Without such efforts, informative speeches may actually confuse or overwhelm the audience, making it less likely they will engage the issues.

Informative speaking can also manipulate or constrain an audience. When dishonestly developed, a speech can disguise itself as educational when it actually promotes a particular viewpoint, solution, or action. We might think of the example of infomercials, so called for presenting themselves as informative programs but actually functioning as commercials to sell particular products. Audiences must always be wary of informative speeches that rely on biased sources, fail to provide more than one perspective, present alternative viewpoints as straw men, or identify only the positive points of a perspective. Of course, as mentioned previously, even when developed and presented honestly and ethically, an informative speech will have persuasive, even constraining, functions. A problem-focused speech, for example, tries to provide a fair and balanced understanding of the issue, but no speech can provide a comprehensive account. The speaker will have to make choices about what to exclude. Somewhat similarly, deliberative presentations name three or four perspectives the audience will consider during the deliberative discussion to the exclusion of additional options. So we should remember that the distinction between informative and persuasive speaking is probably more like points along a continuum than a sharp demarcation.

Third, even the best informative speech cannot guarantee the audience will become involved. Because an informative speech stops short of promoting or prescribing an action, attitude, or belief, audience members may not feel sufficiently motivated to get involved. Or, since the type of informative speaking we encourage avoids the adversarial drama of unproductive discourse described in chapter 2, an audience may deem the speech insufficiently exciting to get involved.

Finally, we have encouraged the use of deliberative presentations to tackle public controversies, but they incur drawbacks in addition to the limitations already stated. From chapter 2, for instance, you may recall philosopher Nancy Fraser's critique of the public sphere—a theory developed by sociologist and philosopher Jürgen Habermas.[37] While the public sphere is meant to be a gathering of community members to discuss public issues as equal participants, it can actually privilege those members with higher social status and increased knowledge of the participation norms—such as how the group expects you to talk and behave during a deliberative presentation and discussion.

Though these limitations are concerning and even disappointing, the benefits of informative speaking far outreach the dangers. Well-researched, fair, and balanced informative speeches have the capacity to equip ordinary community members to take an active and influential role in civic affairs. They supply the public with the information they need to overcome unfamiliarity with rules, concepts, and entities or with problems and possible ways to tackle them. In the process, informative speaking encourages productive discourse and an interest in community and the public good. If done well, informative speech should demonstrate the productive discourse qualities, discussed in chapter 2, of emphasizing *learning* and offering *empowerment* to your audience to participate in civic affairs. Deliberative presentations, in particular, also encourage *inclusiveness* of alternative viewpoints, demonstrate the *provisionality* of viewpoints, and encourage the *imagination* necessary to find options that improve public welfare.[38]

SUMMARY

Sound understanding and thoughtful reflection, based on credible information, are necessary precursors to productive public exchanges and decision-making. Informative speaking seeks to provide these ends by educating an audience about a topic without biasing them toward a particular position, conclusion, or outcome. Deliberative presentations, a particular type of informative speaking, involves preparing an audience to talk about a public controversy in a way that helps them move toward a decision or solution. The hard work lies in coming to a fair and accurate understanding of the multiple, competing perspectives on any public problem.

- By providing an audience with reliable and balanced information from credible sources on topics related to public affairs, informative speaking enables community members to more confidently and actively participate in civic concerns.
- Three common types of informative speeches include instructional speeches, which explain or teach an audience about a process, concept, or entity; problem-focused speeches that identify, describe, and explain a civic problem; and deliberative presentations that fairly and even-handedly describe a civic problem and multiple approaches to solving the problem with emphasis on the benefits and drawbacks of each approach.
- A deliberative presentation is ideally suited to address a public controversy, which is a matter that concerns the community and is difficult to resolve as it involves diverse perspectives and more than one possible option or answer.
- The process of forming a deliberative presentation involves selecting a public controversy, finding a range of perspectives, framing the topic for deliberation, and organizing and choosing a method of delivery for the presentation.
- Framing a topic for deliberation requires a speaker to fairly define the problem so that all parties would agree with its characterization, identify trade-offs for every perspective, and weigh the competing values among the perspectives.
- If done poorly, informative speaking can endanger civic engagement by overwhelming or confusing an audience or failing to excite an audience to get

involved in civic affairs. If a speech is presented dishonestly, it advocates a particular solution or perspective. Deliberative presentations, in particular, can also exclude some community members because they may not know the expected norms of participation.

KEY TERMS

contingency p. 201
deliberative discussion
  p. 201
deliberative presentation
  p. 200
deliberative process
  p. 201

dissoi logoi p. 205
false dilemma p. 204
informative speaking
  p. 197
key fact p. 203
public controversy
  p. 201

straw man p. 204
trade-off p. 209
value p. 210
value dilemma p. 210
value hierarchy p. 210

REVIEW QUESTIONS

1. What is informative speaking, and what role can it serve in civic affairs?
2. What are three different types of informative speeches, and how do they differ?
3. What does it mean that public controversies are marked by contingency?
4. What are the steps for developing a deliberative presentation?
5. What is framing for deliberation, and what does it entail?
6. What are the limitations of informative speaking?

DISCUSSION QUESTIONS

1. Where can you identify an example of each of the three types of informative speaking discussed in this chapter? Which have you seen or experienced? What did you learn?
2. Think about the communities of which you are a part. What might be suitable topics for an instructional speech, problem-focused speech, or deliberative presentation for one of those communities? What topics or problems need clarification and understanding?
3. Choose a recent public controversy and find or name conflicting perspectives on how to solve it. How does each perspective define the problem and argue for a particular solution? What do you learn or notice by contrasting the viewpoints?
4. How might you identify the differences between a presentation framed for deliberation and one strategically framed to persuade? What might be the differences in their goals and in the speaker's means of achieving those goals?
5. Where or when might informative speaking not be the best option? When might persuasion be preferable?

CHAPTER 11

Helping Communities Make Difficult Decisions through Deliberative Discussions

---

Chapter Objectives

Students will:

- Accurately describe the nature and goals of a deliberative discussion.

- Name several historical movements that compose the United States' lineage of deliberative discussions.

- Identify the five stages of a deliberative discussion, and describe the goals for each stage.

- Explain what it means for a deliberative discussion group to talk through an issue as opposed to talking about an issue.

- Exhibit the qualities and tasks of an effective deliberative discussion leader.

- Adopt the virtues and abilities necessary to productively participate in deliberative discussions.

- Elucidate the benefits of leading and participating in deliberative discussions.

Like so many towns, cities, and municipalities across the United States, central Indiana's Montgomery County has struggled with how to reduce substance abuse among its residents. In 2012, the Indiana State Epidemiology and Outcomes Workgroup gave Montgomery County a "Top 25%" overall priority drug rating. That meant that in comparison to other Indiana counties, Montgomery County was among the quarter of counties most severely affected by alcohol and drug problems. Specifically, Montgomery County rated in the top 25% of counties for marijuana, heroin, and cocaine use and arrests; and it ranked in the top 50% for methamphetamine, prescription drugs, and alcohol.[1] Those statistics are particularly concerning because Indiana as a whole has registered higher substance abuse than many other states.[2]

To help address this problem, over 100 community members of Montgomery County gathered on November 6, 2013, to discuss how to reduce and prevent

Wabash College freshman Anthony Douglas leads a small group of Montgomery County, Indiana, residents in a deliberative discussion about ameliorating substance abuse in their community.

substance abuse among its residents. Participants watched a short video and read a four-page document that, together, functioned as a deliberative presentation about substance abuse in the community.[3] Recall from the previous chapter that a deliberative presentation provides a fair and even-handed description of a civic problem and multiple approaches to solving the problem with emphasis on the benefits and drawbacks of each approach. In this case, the document and video featured the three approaches of increasing law enforcement activities, improving prevention efforts, and developing better treatment options. This presentation provided the basic framework for the deliberative discussion that followed.

This chapter focuses on deliberative discussions by defining and distinguishing them from other types of interactions and introducing you to the history of deliberative discussions in America. The chapter will then identify the basic structure of deliberative discussions and the major goal of talking through a difficult issue, followed by instructions in the principles for effectively leading and participating in productive deliberative discussions. The chapter ends with a consideration of the general benefits and drawbacks of these engagements.

DISTINCTIVE QUALITIES OF DELIBERATIVE DISCUSSIONS

In chapter 10 we defined a deliberative discussion as a group conversation through which a community, guided by one or more moderators, thoughtfully and thoroughly examines a complex public problem and a range of available solutions to ultimately arrive at a choice, decision, or conclusion. We explained that the deliberative discussion nearly always follows some type of deliberative presentation (though both may vary in format and timing). Together, the deliberative presentation and subsequent discussion form the deliberative process, or what some people refer to simply as deliberation.

A deliberative discussion is distinct from other types of interactions that may follow a presentation. For instance, you have probably seen a speaker answer questions from the audience after delivering a speech. Such question-and-answer sessions provide valuable opportunities for audience members to interact directly and immediately with the speaker. They rarely allow audience members to exchange ideas directly with each other, however. The speaker remains the hub of conversation. The interaction typically jumps sporadically from one idea to the next as each audience member offers a new question. Consequently, it is difficult to sustain attention on a single idea or to gain much momentum in talking through a line of thought.

Alternatively, debates allow for a direct exchange between the participants as they voice clashing arguments in favor of, or against, the topic or resolution being discussed. Consequently, debates typically ensure that the audience gains a fuller and more balanced comprehension of a topic, and participants frequently sustain and develop several lines of thought as the debate progresses. However, debates tend to divide issues into only two sides and emphasize the disagreements between them. Because debates are inherently competitive, they imply that one position is a winner and the other is a loser. Debates typically discourage participants or audiences from exploring additional perspectives or recognizing or finding common ground between the sides.

Discussions compose a more collaborative type of interaction between speaker(s) and audience members. There are several different forms of discussions. In *brainstorming discussions* members are encouraged to speak freely, offering ideas and perspectives they may not ultimately favor after all the ideas have been expressed. When an idea is shared, discussion members initially reserve judgment so the focus remains on seeing the idea's potential and generating more ideas. In *intellectual discussions* participants work primarily with the nature of a particular idea, text, or question; its implications; and its connections to other ideas, texts, and issues. A good college class discussion about a text or artwork can illustrate this category. *Strategy discussions* are pragmatically focused on how to best accomplish previously agreed upon goals or on how to best implement a plan previously passed rather than engaging in discussion of the broader principles that led to the options. These discussions have a practical and pragmatic focus on what will work best for each step or element of an implementation plan. A *dialogic discussion*, or simply a dialogue, encourages participants to share their personal experiences and insights related to a public controversy. The goal is to better understand alternative perspectives and to find common ground or empathy with opposing viewpoints.

A deliberative discussion shares many characteristics with the aforementioned types. It is most similar to a dialogic discussion in that both seek to explore, understand, and appreciate multiple perspectives as participants discover common ground. And both types require a community—a public of some kind—to occur. Whereas an individual can engage in some degree of brainstorming, strategizing, and thinking intellectually by him- or herself alone, deliberation and dialogue necessitate interaction with others. Rhetoric scholar William Keith argued regarding deliberation, "Individual citizens can't be deliberative in isolation; a person who didn't converse with her neighbors wouldn't count as deliberative unless she read widely and thoughtfully, putting her in contact with a larger community."[4]

Discussions like deliberation and dialogue that require interacting with others produce **public knowledge**, which refers to participants' shared and improved understanding of the problem and possible solutions as they offer and hear multiple points of view.[5] As participants in the Montgomery County, Indiana, discussion shared how substance abuse had directly or indirectly affected them, and as they offered—and even clashed with others'—opinions about how to solve the problem, their knowledge of the issue and its trade-offs expanded. Indeed, through such interactions, discussants tend to better recognize the complexity of the problem, the merits of alternative views, and the demerits of their originally preferred solution. Such recognition and understanding is produced and gained together as a group. Consequently, public knowledge requires a public to produce it.

Yet, a deliberative discussion differentiates itself from dialogue in that deliberation also produces **public judgment**, community wisdom about a problem and possible solutions, accrued through the discussion, that aids a group's ability to make a thoughtful choice and take collective responsibility for the outcome.[6] Such judgment "rests on what we think the second time—*after* we have talked with others, considered the consequences of our options, and worked through the conflicts that arise."[7] (Emphasis in the original.) Indeed, unlike dialogue, a deliberative discussion uniquely seeks to move participants through sharing and exploring to *choice-making*. The goal of a deliberative discussion is for participants to choose the next best step(s) to solve the problem and ease the controversy, having considered the trade-offs of at least three broad approaches. An example of a deliberative discussion that ends in choice-making is jury deliberation, the time after the completion of a legal proceeding in which the jury contemplates the case. Given the stakes often involved, we have high expectations of the efficacy of jury deliberations. We hope juries think carefully and comprehensively about matters before them based on the presented information and the relevant criteria for legal decision-making. Indeed, all deliberative discussions require participants to thoughtfully consider issues with other community members to better understand the key considerations and points of division and to arrive at a recommendation for moving forward.

When we engage in a deliberative discussion, we assume the choice made by several minds—and their interaction—is better than the decision reached by one individual alone. Of course, the assumption that groups tend to make better choices than individuals has been challenged, perhaps beginning with Plato in the fourth century BCE who feared that group decision-making enabled uneducated people and those pursuing personal gain to unduly influence the masses to make harmful choices. Modern psychology scholars have established **groupthink** as a phenomenon that occurs when members' desire for harmony outweighs their willingness to critically examine alternative perspectives.[8] However, other people have championed the power of group decision-making. Aristotle, for example, while recognizing the dangers in the process, contended that, on balance, groups arrive at better decisions than individuals. He argued that "each individual, left to himself, forms an imperfect judgment," and that when many meet together they arrive at conclusions "better than the few."[9] More recently, Kettering Foundation President and CEO David Matthews argued that deliberative discussion "increases the likelihood that our decision will be sound by helping us determine whether we are willing to accept the consequences of the action we are about to take."[10] A public can only make such choices together through group decision-making.

BOX 11-1

Distinctive Qualities of Deliberative Discussions

- Produce public judgment.
- End with choice-making.

Of course, the type of action a deliberative discussion group chooses can vary greatly. The participants may decide to adopt one of the three approaches discussed during the discussion, some combination of the presented approaches, or a new, fourth option they construct. They may decide to pursue an underlying cause of the problem rather than the problem they focused on during the discussion. Alternatively, they may choose to find answers to questions raised during the discussion. Participants at the Montgomery County, Indiana, deliberative discussion decided they needed to learn more about what was happening in their community to address substance abuse before pursuing additional actions. Consequently, they organized public educational meetings with county leaders involved with law enforcement and treatment centers, and those who work with the youth.[11] Naturally, participants in a deliberative discussion, despite their best efforts, will not always come to an agreement about the next step(s) to take. But because they have thoughtfully considered the options together and arrived at a greater understanding of the issue, each will be prepared to advance a thoughtful proposal. Everyone may not fully embrace the final choices, but at least the competing interests have been considered in their formation. Such faith in the benefits of deliberative discussions has helped motivate their use historically.

DELIBERATIVE DISCUSSIONS IN HISTORICAL CONTEXT

Since the birth of rhetoric, people in the Western political tradition have turned to deliberative discussions to enact and improve democratic practices. In chapter 1, we located the birth of rhetoric in ancient Greece during the sixth and fifth centuries BCE to accompany the beginnings of democratic governance. One of the earliest venues for such governance was the Athenian Assembly, during which Greek citizens raised, discussed, and made decisions about public issues. Perhaps because of the strengths of such deliberative exchanges, we find a number of movements in the United States that show strong resemblance to the Athenian precursor, albeit undertaken on a smaller scale.[12] We will briefly highlight several of these American movements to reveal the continued belief in deliberative discussions as successful venues for meaningful civic engagement and vibrant democratic exchanges.

You have probably heard of a "town hall meeting." Today, that phrase typically refers to a public meeting where audience members speak directly to public officials

Boston's historic Faneuil Hall continues to host meetings and speeches. Here Senator John Kerry addresses the crowd on January 31, 2013, the day before he became secretary of state.

about their concerns. It derives from the New England town hall meeting begun by colonists in the seventeenth century that lasted through the Revolutionary period. These meetings had an informal structure, met on an ad hoc basis, and included citizens, town officials, and magistrates, who discussed significant issues. As colonists grew dissatisfied with British rule, town hall meetings became a place to discuss their situation and to deliberate possible actions. In Boston in 1772 in Faneuil Hall, for example, several Patriot leaders organized a town hall meeting to garner support to oppose Britain. Their efforts were successful and helped lead the way toward the Revolutionary War.[13]

After the United States gained independence, new efforts to promote public discussions arose, often as part of adult education to "transform an entire people from subjects to citizens."[14] The Lyceum Movement, for instance, emerged in the 1820s near the end of the Industrial Revolution and during the era of Jacksonian Democracy and lasted until just after the Civil War. Teacher and scientist Josiah Holbrook began the movement to help adult participants "improve *each other* in useful knowledge, and to advance the interests of their schools." (Emphasis in the original.) Taking its name from Aristotle's school, the movement provided adult education in America, spreading the advances taking place in science. But lyceums also functioned as places to discuss public issues. Holbrook encouraged participants to "hold weekly or other stated meetings, for reading, conversation, discussion, illustrating the sciences, or other exercises designed for their mutual benefit."[15] Holbrook established the first town lyceum in Millbury, Massachusetts, in 1826, and others soon followed; but by the 1850s they had dissolved "from associations of local townsfolk for the mutual study and discussion of educational matters and public affairs, to . . . [a] system of booking lectures and entertainments."[16]

The Chautauqua Movement began on the heels of the Lyceum Movement in 1874 at Lake Chautauqua, New York, at the Chautauqua Lake Sunday School Assembly as a kind of instructive summer camp. The focus was on adult education, originally restricted to religious topics but quickly expanded to include "virtually the entire field of general education and the discussion of public affairs that [were] in the foreground of public thinking."[17] Additional Chautauquas soon formed near lakes and in tree groves across the country, creating the Chautauqua Movement. "By 1880 the Chautauqua platform had established itself as a national forum for open discussion of public issues, international relations, literature and science."[18] The movement hit a high in 1907 with over 100 Chautauqua assemblies meeting across the country.[19] Most of the groups ended by the 1930s; however, many Chautauquas are again thriving due to renewed interest in their offerings.[20]

Despite the Chautauqua Movement's decline after its 1907 heyday, the 1920s and 1930s marked additional periods of attention to public discussions in both American academic and public contexts. This time period corresponds with the aftermath of World War I; the Progressive Era, when many social reformers attempted to strengthen national democratic practices; and the Great Depression. Some collegiate speech teachers responded to societal concerns by teaching students how to engage in discussions to better prepare them for democratic duties.[21] Speech professor J. Jeffery Auer, in a 1939 article published in the flagship journal for the speech communication discipline, explained:

> While demonstrative oratory and formal debate were the accepted patterns of public discussion in the nineteenth century, the social and political scene has so changed within the past fifty years that these alone are no longer the most effective bases for determining collective action. . . . We see, then, as observers of the social scene, that the conference method and the discussion technique have become the accepted patterns for public discussion and determination of collective action.[22]

Beginning around 1922, interest in teaching discussions increased and extended through the mid-1950s, largely fading out of university curriculums by the 1960s.[23]

Also during the 1920s and 1930s, the Open Forum Movement utilized community discussions to educate and engage adult citizens in social and political topics.[24] The open forums typically paired an expert lecturer with a subsequent question-and-discussion period with the audience, therein combining "the best features of the old New England town meeting and the modern lecture course."[25] The movement identified its forebears as previously established open forums, including the Cooper Union in 1859 in New York City and the Ford Hall Forum in 1908 in Boston.[26] Open forums gained popularity across the country during the 1930s, resulting in at least 450 local forums by 1937 and 19 federally funded public forums as part of the Federal Forum Project from 1936–1941.[27]

Collectively, these movements demonstrate that deliberative discussions have played an important role in American democratic governance, and efforts to encourage them have persisted over time. As Keith proclaimed in 2007, "Almost a hundred years ago, Americans were struggling to find new modes of participation in a seemingly moribund democratic process, and they are again today."[28] We see enthusiasm for deliberative discussions currently across the nation through collegiate efforts to promote and enable such conversations as well as through the efforts of a variety of nonprofit organizations and networks.[29] The Kettering Foundation and National Issues Forum, for example, teach, research, and promote deliberative discussions with the goal of improving democracy, while the National Coalition for Dialogue & Deliberation serves as a meeting place for practitioners. Numerous nonprofit organizations have utilized the Internet to update and adapt deliberative discussions for the twenty-first century.

SPOTLIGHT ON SOCIAL MEDIA:
The Advantages and Challenges of Online Deliberative Discussions

When we talk about deliberative discussions, we typically assume they involve face-to-face conversations among small groups of participants. Several efforts have been made, however, to hold deliberative discussions partially or wholly online:

- During the 2012 presidential election season, the non-profit, non-partisan organizations America*Speaks* and Face the Facts USA organized several online interactions, including the use of Google Hangouts web-chat function. Participants in the Hangouts engaged in a deliberative discussion about the economy with an America*Speaks* facilitator and three to seven other participants. Pennsylvania State University researchers discovered that the Hangouts produced in participants a greater sense of understanding the issue than people participating in other formats, and Hangouts participants developed an appreciation for deliberation.[30]

Second Life users participate in the June 26, 2010, deliberation on the national economy.

- Several organizations have used the online virtual world *Second Life* to hold real-time deliberative discussions among users through avatars. One group, Deliberative IDEAS, even created the virtual "Commonwealth Islands" within *Second Life* to "encourage and support deliberative conversations in SL [*Second Life*] and RL [Real Life]. . . ."[31] In June 2010, several non-profit groups, led by America*Speaks*, partnered to co-sponsor a deliberative discussion on the national economy.[32]

- The digital company Intellitics produces technological tools to help organizations run online deliberations and dialogues. In June 2014, the company produced a 5-day asynchronous online deliberation about mental health, involving 100 college students from across the United States.[33]
- Emerson College has developed the Engagement Lab, an applied research lab that builds "engagement games." Such games "bring play and serious real-world processes together, so that real action occurs while playing the game." One such process facilitated by the games is the deliberative discussion.[34]

Deliberative discussions through digital media can help gather a more diverse set of participants than face-to-face events as they free people from the costs of traveling to a particular site. For asynchronous online deliberations, participants can also join the conversation at more convenient times for their schedule. Consequently, the resulting conversations may be richer and capture more variant viewpoints. Participants can also frequently multitask, simultaneously attending to the conversation while also researching information online. They may accompany their comments with links to sources that support and develop their claims. The additional information may improve a group's discussion and decision-making. Finally, digital media hold the possibility of allowing participants to interact without revealing their true identities. This option can liberate participants to speak more openly and force a group to judge others' comments based on their merits rather than on who said them.

Of course, social media and the Internet pose drawbacks for deliberative discussions as well. Laura Black accounted for several of these challenges in her report, "The Promise and Problems of Online Deliberation." Multitasking online can quickly become a distraction for participants who try to simultaneously attend to their e-mail and social media feeds, causing them to lose focus on the conversation. Asynchronous communication may ultimately discourage participation because discussants are more likely to write longer comments (that others don't take the time to read), and participants tend to lose interest in the conversation over time and dropout. In addition, anonymity may encourage unproductive discourse since participants are not held to the same level of accountability for their comments. However, anonymity may be difficult to achieve, even if desired, because online accounts are more frequently tied to real identities. Black concluded her report, "The internet provides new and exciting ways to name and frame information, engage people in conversation, visualize options and trade-offs, and make choices to act together. Yet, there does not seem to be a magic bullet for engaging everyday citizens in deliberative discussion."[35]

Discussion Questions

- When would you prefer an online deliberative discussion rather than a face-to-face encounter?
- Which features of an online discussion most intrigue you?
- How might you differently approach an online deliberative discussion as a participant? As a discussion leader?

Despite such efforts, with the population of the United States above 300 million, many would argue that today few Americans have been trained in, experienced, or even witnessed a deliberative discussion. Instead, unproductive discourse dominates, as we established in chapter 2, and few Americans know how to engage in a deliberative discussion. This provides the motivation and context for the remainder of this chapter: instructions in leading and participating in a productive deliberative discussion.

DELIBERATIVE DISCUSSION STRUCTURE

Over time scholars and practitioners have developed several best practices for convening a deliberative discussion. Based on their work, we know a deliberative discussion typically works best with a small group of seven to ten people.[36] Fewer people can quickly jump to a consensus or make the conversation difficult to keep going. Including more than 10 people limits how much any one person can contribute and makes the process cumbersome. Consequently, conveners of large public gatherings usually divide attendants into smaller groups, each with its own facilitator(s).

BOX 11-2

National Issues Forums Five Stages of a Deliberative Discussion

1. Personal stakes
2. Approach one
3. Approach two
4. Approach three
5. Reflection period

Once a small discussion group is established, the facilitator(s) can use a template or structure for guiding participants through a deliberative discussion. We will adopt the structure produced by the National Issues Forums (NIF), which includes five major stages: personal stakes, approach one, approach two, approach three, and reflection period.[37] Before briefly explaining the goals and content of each stage, we mention two things. First, keep in mind that this structure can and should be adapted to suit a specific community's problems and needs, and the structure itself evolves as NIF and related scholars and practitioners develop adaptations. Second, the deliberative presentation and discussion work hand in hand. Recall from the previous chapter that in setting up the discussion, the deliberative presentation identifies and explains the problem and each of the approaches participants will consider during the discussion. The organizer of the Montgomery County, Indiana, deliberative discussion, for example, focused the deliberative presentation (by means of an opening video and framing document) on illegal substance abuse and the three approaches of increasing law enforcement activity, improving prevention efforts, and expanding treatment options. So the focus of the deliberative discussion—that is, the major approaches to solving the problem—are preselected by the convener(s) of the deliberation event based on their research and efforts to capture the range of public beliefs about the issue. With these reminders in mind, we now explain each of the five stages of deliberative discussions.

Deliberative discussions often begin with personal stakes by inviting participants to state their connection to the issue. Rather than ask participants to self-disclose personal information, however, this stage allows discussants to share broadly why they chose to attend the forum or how they became concerned with the problem. This opening encourages participants to express their observations, experiences, feelings, and stories, which can help them empathize with each other and draw together around shared concerns and interests. It helps to immediately move the discussion from an abstract consideration of the topic to something more tangible and personal.[38] This type of opening also helps equalize the participants as it avoids formal introductions that could emphasize differing degrees of societal power.

After the personal stakes stage, a deliberative discussion group typically explores each of three approaches, one at a time. The goals for the discussion of each approach are to help participants understand the general spirit of the approach, consider and possibly generate specific actions that fall within that approach, and evaluate the benefits *and* drawbacks of the approach. For example, when facilitators focused participants at the Montgomery County, Indiana, deliberative discussion on the first approach—improving law enforcement activity—they asked participants to summarize the perspective and consider specific actions that fell within it, such as conducting drug tests at the local high school more frequently and creating neighborhood watch groups, and share what they liked and disliked about it. Because examining each of the approaches constitutes the bulk of a deliberative discussion, we will more fully consider strategies for navigating this part of the discussion later in the chapter.

A deliberative discussion usually ends with a reflection period. This stage allows discussants to reflect on the conversation they just had. The goal is to identify, together, which approaches and actions they prefer and the next steps to address the issue. In doing so, the group attempts to name actions appropriate for a wide range of actors, making sure to include ideas for community members in addition to elected or appointed officials or experts. This is the stage in which participants begin to form public judgment, defined earlier as the accrued community wisdom that aids a group's ability to make a thoughtful choice and take collective responsibility for the outcome. During the reflection period, a group may find it useful to highlight common ground and key tensions that arose during the discussion. While the group may not achieve consensus about the actions it prefers, the members should be able to decide the next steps to take to forward their momentum.

Talking through all five stages of a deliberative discussion can be time-consuming and tiresome, and participants may end feeling frustrated by the difficulty and complexity of the problem. However, they are also likely to emerge with an improved understanding of the issue and each other as well. They might think of themselves as a public rather than a collection of individuals and feel an increased sense of ownership and empowerment when tackling the problem.

THE HEART OF A DELIBERATIVE DISCUSSION:
WORKING THROUGH THE ISSUE

We have already established that a deliberative discussion ends in public judgment when participants, together, make choices about how to ameliorate the problem after working through multiple perspectives and options. Here we briefly explore the "working through" process as the heart of the deliberative discussion.[39]

Working through issues is one of the distinguishing features of deliberative discussions. It entails participants *exploring* their value dilemmas, disagreements, and desired trade-offs rather than just naming them. As you recall from chapter 10, a value dilemma occurs when two people's preferred values conflict, and a trade-off is the relative advantages and disadvantages of a solution. Group decision-making tends to begin with participants sharing their varied perspectives and preferred options and values. Decision-making consultant and researcher Sam Kaner and associates call this "divergent thinking," during which discussants offer or discover a wide range of diverse perspectives on the issue.

When divergent thinking has been successfully achieved, groups typically encounter what Kaner and associates have labeled the **groan zone**, a stage of confusion and frustration that results from the broad representation of viewpoints, opinions, and ideas shared. "Group members have to struggle in order to integrate new and different ways of thinking with their own" and "build a shared framework of understanding."[40] Effectively dealing with this zone "requires a very different form of communication than" divergent thinking, according to deliberation scholar and practitioner Martín Carcasson. "People need to interact and listen to each other. . . . Most importantly, they need to engage the tensions, and struggle with the best way to address them."[41] Such engagement and struggle constitutes working through the issue. It requires participants to probe more deeply into why they prefer positions in order to understand the deeper motivations or values at play and to bring conflicting perspectives into conversation with one another.[42] The goal is to discover and reflect upon the real underlying sources of conflict and to ultimately move through the groan zone into what Kaner and associates have determined as the third stage of group decision-making: "convergent thinking." According to Carcasson, this stage "requires people to prioritize, work toward a decision, and move to action."[43]

Due to the discomfort of the groan zone, deliberative discussion participants may try to avoid it by deciding they need more facts, creating a false polarization, or too quickly agreeing with each other. First, groups may claim they need more facts to engage in a productive deliberative discussion. Of course, there is some truth to this. In the previous chapter, we discussed the importance of identifying and supplying key facts when preparing a deliberative presentation. Recall that such facts can be measured or tested, often by an expert, *and* are critical to understanding the problem. During the actual discussion, a facilitator may need to intervene if an egregiously incorrect "fact" is asserted by a discussant; the untenable alternative is to allow the deliberation potentially to be swayed or misled by faulty information. However, sometimes participants can become mired in questions about facts rather than focus on the heart of the topic. Rarely is a dearth of facts the reason a public controversy exists. Instead, public controversies result from deep disagreements over underlying values. Thus, if questions about facts emerge during a discussion for which the discussion leader does not have answers, then the leader should encourage discussants to temporarily set these questions aside and focus their conversation, instead, on the larger issues involved. For example, rather than quibble over the number of substance abuse treatment centers available in Montgomery County, participants at the deliberative discussion needed to grapple with whether they wanted to prioritize helping people in recovery to rejoin the community, more severely punish them with stronger legal penalties, or prevent others from becoming addicted to drugs. Wasting time on missing facts would have distracted them from the more important conversation.

Second, groups may try to avoid the groan zone by claiming a "false polarization."[44] When participants encounter a vast array of diverse viewpoints, they may fall into discord, emphasizing their differences from one another, similar to the practices of unproductive discourse in chapter 2. One way of countering this tendency is for participants to identify their **common ground** in a controversy. Common ground refers to any perspectives, interests, values, or concerns shared by some or all members of the discussion.[45] Common ground is often obscured because of misconceptions that opposing sides hold about one another. Yet opposing sides are actually likely to agree on important core values, fundamental aspects of the problem, or particular needs, and these serve as a basis for common ground. For example, the Montgomery County, Indiana, deliberative discussion on substance abuse revealed that participants shared common ground regarding the need to decrease abuse, though they disagreed about the values they prioritized in doing so and the trade-offs they were willing to accept. Questions a discussion leader can use to help the group identify common ground are listed in Box 11-5 "Questions to Advance Deliberative Discussions" later in the chapter.

Alternatively, a third way groups may try to avoid the discomfort of the groan zone is by regressing to familiar positions and too quickly claiming common ground or agreement on the best solution to the issue under discussion. Essentially, these groups never explore divergent thinking to even arrive at the groan zone.[46] They may be reluctant to engage in consideration of the trade-offs and value dilemmas implicated by the issue, or they may simply state preferences without offering the reasoning behind them. Several participants at the Montgomery County substance abuse deliberative discussion, for instance, quickly agreed that building strong families was essential to curbing abuse. However, they didn't define what they meant by "strong families," explain why families were important, or consider the best ways to build them. In cases like this, a discussion leader should probe the participants for the reasons, motivations, values, and personal experiences that inform their conclusions.[47] A discussion leader may also ask the group to consider the costs, challenges, and trade-offs of their preferred option to encourage the discovery and exploration of possible disagreements.[48] Suggested questions a discussion leader may ask to prevent a group from agreeing too quickly are listed in Box 11-5 "Questions to Advance Deliberative Discussions" later in the chapter.

Ideally, as the discussion progresses through the groan zone using the strategies summarized in Table 11.1, participant investment increases. Discussants begin explaining the reasons behind their preferences; listening to the views of others; and showing a willingness to compare, contrast, and weigh multiple options. Participants move past speaking from their individual perspective ("I") and begin speaking in

TABLE 11.1 Working through the Groan Zone

WAYS PARTICIPANTS AVOID THE GROAN ZONE	STRATEGIES TO HELP PARTICIPANTS ENTER AND WORK THROUGH THE GROAN ZONE
Participants claim they need more facts.	Encourage participants to temporarily set fact questions aside and focus on the trade-offs and value dilemmas.
Participants claim a false polarization by emphasizing differences.	Help participants identify their common ground.
Participants regress to familiar positions and quickly claim agreement on the best solution.	Probe participants for the reasoning, motivations, values, and personal experiences that inform their conclusions. Ask the group to consider the implications, consequences, and trade-offs of their preferred option.

more collective terms that reflect the needs of the community ("we"). References to group action ("should we" or "we can") help distinguish deliberative activities from alternative approaches to politics.[49] Encouraging a group of participants to talk through the groan zone and affirm their shared community identity requires significant discussion leading skills, which we turn to next.

DISCUSSION LEADING

Leading a discussion is an important task. The facilitator sets the ground rules and tone, and guides participants through the five stages of a deliberative discussion, from personal stakes through the reflection period, with an eye toward helping the group work through the groan zone toward decision-making. We explore how the leader can create a comfortable environment for a deliberative discussion and then describe the many tasks a leader must undertake to enable a productive discussion, including asking good questions.

Creating a Comfortable Environment

At a fundamental level, much of the discussion leader's task is about setting the proper tone and establishing mutual respect between discussants. One image that may prove helpful is to think of a good discussion leader as something of a referee at a football game or soccer match. The leader is not focused on who wins or loses but rather on how the game is played. He or she refrains from dominating the discussion or taking sides. Instead, this person seeks to have all participants, no matter their ideological, political, or personal perspectives, fully engaged in a productive manner. The participants will naturally look to the leader for cues, so if you are prepared and take the initiative, you can succeed at guiding the discussion into a productive and healthy conversation. To begin, take note of the list of strategies to try and behaviors to avoid in Box 11-3, and then consider the tasks a facilitator should fulfill.

Specific Leadership Tasks

The tasks of a deliberative discussion leader can be thought of as the many jobs a single facilitator must accomplish or as tasks that can be shared among a group of

═══════════ **BOX 11-3** ═══════════

Creating a Comfortable Environment for Deliberative Discussions

Strategies to Try

- Create an atmosphere in which members can participate without being personally attacked or ridiculed or having their ideas quickly dismissed.
- Allow for silence after you ask a question, as that is normal. Discussants need time to consider their response to a question. If, after a period of silence, no one responds, try rephrasing the question or directing it toward a specific person.
- Redirect the conversation if it turns into a fight or competitive debate.
- Express enthusiasm since the manner in which you ask a question can significantly influence the participants' willingness to respond.
- Use effective nonverbal behavior. Maintain direct eye contact with group members and be conscious of your facial expressions, posture, and so forth because your body may communicate messages you don't intend to send (disgust, disinterest, anger, etc.).

Behaviors to Avoid

- Stop anyone from dominating the conversation, including yourself or participants who are—or present themselves as—experts on the issue.
- Prevent participants from completely withdrawing or failing to join the discussion by remaining silent.
- Withhold your opinions about the topic.
- Don't let the group turn the conversation into a question-and-answer session with you giving the answers.
- Avoid sticking too strictly to your prepared list of questions if the conversation flows differently than you anticipated.

Some of the suggestions, and the general format of behaviors to adopt and to avoid, were inspired by National Issues Forums and appear in W. Barnett Pearce and Stephen W. Littlejohn, *Moral Conflict: When Social Worlds Collide* (Thousand Oaks, CA: Sage, 1997), 177.

facilitators. Typically, at least two facilitators lead a deliberative discussion: a moderator, who sits with the group and guides them through the five stages of a discussion, and the recorder, who takes notes of the group's conversation. It is very difficult to guide a group's discussion and take notes simultaneously. Splitting the tasks between two people lessens the burden on each, yet it still requires the moderator to juggle multiple tasks at once. Further dividing these tasks among a small group of discussion leaders enables each person to focus on just one or two jobs, yet it also necessitates a greater degree of cooperation among group members. Either way, the tasks listed in Box 11-4 should be accomplished during a deliberative discussion to help ensure its success.

BOX 11-4

Facilitation Tasks for Deliberative Discussions

Initiate questions—Asks questions to get a chain of conversation started. See the next section on asking good questions for guidance.

Play devil's advocate—Helps respondents dig deeper into the issues and avoid rushing to consensus. Invites discussants to share or consider a differing viewpoint, or require the group to address and work through trade-offs of a desired approach. ("How might someone disagree with you?")

Clarify/summarize—At appropriate times, helps the group uncover common ground *or* points of disagreement by identifying and summarizing the discussion and relevant points being made ("It sounds to me as if we have been talking about a few major themes. . . . " "I hear several of you agreeing on. . . . " "It seems that there is a split here . . ."). Requires attentive listening to make connections between respondents' comments.

Record—Captures the *key* points of common ground, tensions, and conclusions made during the discussion. Notes may be written where participants can see them as the deliberative discussion occurs or on an individual notepad. This task works well with the job of clarifying/summarizing.

Observe—Observes the process of the discussion with the goal of making it as inclusive and productive as possible. Attempts to get everyone engaged without allowing a few participants to dominate. ("Jane, you look like you're about to say something." "Mike, can you hold that thought for a moment while a few others respond?") Responsibilities include noticing when a participant wants to talk but hasn't (such as by raising a hand, making a facial expression in reaction to another respondent, or taking a breath to talk), and prompting people who have withdrawn to rejoin the discussion.

Manage time/shift focus—Ensures that participants address and compare/contrast all the approaches within the discussion's time limits. Requires an eye on the clock and, when needed, encouraging the group to shift focus to an aspect not yet addressed. ("We've been focusing on approaches one and two, but what about three?") Alternatively, this job involves prompting a group to return to the issue should the conversation stray too far off topic. This task can work well with the job of observing.

Manage conflict—Helps conflict and disagreement among members be productive by keeping the conflict focused on the issues, rather than on personalities; helps participants explore their differences; and defuses "heated" conflicts when needed. ("What seems to be at the heart of this issue?" "What do others think?" "We seem to be stuck. What can we do to move forward?") This task works well with the task of observing, since defusing conflict often requires bringing other participants into the conversation.

Developing Discussion Questions

Asking good questions is crucial to many of the tasks previously listed. Questions drive discussions. When the questions posed are too specific, the discussion can become mired in details and lose the interest of those participants who don't know enough to meaningfully contribute. For instance, if a discussion leader at the Montgomery County, Indiana, deliberative discussion opened by asking, "Do we need an in-patient treatment facility in our community?" only those who understand the differences in types of care could meaningfully participate, and the conversation would become a debate over this specific proposal. On the other hand, if the questions are too broad or unclear, the discussion will suffer from multiple and varied understandings of what the group is in fact discussing. If a discussion leader in Montgomery County asked, "What should we do?" or "What do you think?" the respondents would not know where to start. Poor questions will produce a poor discussion. Formulating good questions, knowing when and how to ask them, and recognizing when a group is ready to move on are skills a discussion leader must learn over time. Teachers at all levels of the education system spend their careers developing these skills.

Discussion leaders who utilize questions should, at the broadest level, reflect on both the form and direction of questions. There are two major forms of questions: open and closed. The **open question** calls for more than a one-word response, making possible a range of answers. Examples include, "What are your reactions to . . . ?"; "For what reasons do you believe that . . . ?"; and "How do you feel about . . . ?" Open questions are usually the best type of questions to generate discussion because they allow a wide variety of responses. The **closed question** prompts a single, one-word answer— usually yes or no. Examples include, "Which option is the best choice?"; "Would you agree that . . . ?"; and "Can we conclude, then, that . . . ?". Closed questions can be helpful for shifting the focus of discussion, for stopping someone from going on a tangent, or for preventing someone from dominating the discussion. However, closed questions should be used sparingly because they tend to shut down conversation. You should almost always avoid "Don't you think . . .?" questions, because they are actually veiled arguments.

A question can take at least four directions. **Direct questions** target one individual and are especially useful for drawing out timid group members ("Tim, how do you respond to what Joan just said?"). **Indirect questions** target the entire group and tend to stimulate thought ("What might be the consequences of choosing this solution?"). **Reverse questions** reflect a question back to the group and are especially helpful in preventing the discussion from turning into a question-and-answer session (After Tim has asked which approach you personally like best, you could respond by asking the whole group, "Well, how would you all answer Tim's question?"). **Relay questions** encourage group members to share experiences ("Molly, could you tell us about your experience with . . .?").

You can see a list of largely open-ended, indirect questions in Box 11-5. Early in a discussion relatively broader questions tend to be helpful. As the discussion progresses, more specific questions work well to guide participants through the approaches. For each approach, a discussion leader might ask questions that reveal what the participants believe to be the benefits, consequences, trade-offs and value dilemmas of the approach, as well as the common ground being established during the discussion. Finally, the reflection period can be a time to return to broader questions as the discussion leader invites participants to think about the entire issue and begin to think ahead to the next steps.

BOX 11-5

Questions to Advance Deliberative Discussions

Concerning Participants' Personal Stakes

- Why are you concerned about this issue?
- How have you witnessed or experienced the problem in our community?
- How has this issue impacted you?

Concerning the Benefits of a Solution or Action

- What are the benefits of that option for our community?
- How might someone argue on behalf of that idea?
- Why do you find that option attractive?

Concerning the Costs or Challenges of a Solution or Action

- What are the drawbacks to that solution?
- What might be an argument against that suggestion?
- What will the consequences of that action likely be for our community?

Concerning the Value Dilemmas and Trade-offs

- What is the central trade-off involved between these two actions or options?
- What values conflict among these approaches?
- Who are the major stakeholders, and what do they stand to lose or gain in each option under consideration?

Concerning Common Ground

- What can we all agree on X (the problem, a particular solution, etc.)?
- What trade-offs are we all willing to accept? What trade-offs do we agree are unacceptable?
- What way might we proceed that would address everyone's most serious concerns?

Concerning Participants' Reflections

- Having discussed several approaches to solving the problem, which do you prefer? Why?
- What actions would you prioritize? Who should do them? What might ordinary community members do to address this problem?
- What are the next best steps to keeping momentum moving forward on this topic?

SOURCES: Colorado State University Center for Public Deliberation, *CSU Center for Public Deliberation: Student Associate Training Workbook* (Fall 2011); National Issues Forums lists appear in W. Barnett Pearce and Stephen W. Littlejohn, *Moral Conflict: When Social Worlds Collide* (Thousand Oaks, CA: Sage, 1997), 178, 79; and Elizabeth M. Smith and National Issues Forum Institute, *National Issues Forums in the Classroom: A High School Program on Deliberative Democracy* (Dayton, OH: Kettering Foundation, 2001).

Ultimately, keep in mind that good discussion leading is both an art and a science. That means, in part, that a good leader prepares for a discussion as much as possible. For example, develop a list of questions for each of the five stages of the discussion; anticipate how the discussion is likely to unfold given the topic and specific participants; and think through how you might respond to potential difficulties, such as members who dominate, withdraw, or try to debate. At the same time, the art of discussion leading lies in the following abilities: remaining present during the actual discussion, listening closely to the participants' comments, observing nonverbal communication, and guiding the discussion accordingly. The discussion may take a totally different direction than anticipated and unforeseen challenges may arise. A good discussion leader adapts to the situation as it develops.

PARTICIPATING IN A DELIBERATIVE DISCUSSION

All participants in a discussion play a role in the outcome. Those who engage in behaviors such as seeking to dominate the discussion, blocking the ideas of others, seeking attention for themselves, or engaging in excessive sarcasm obviously harm the discussion. Those who participate in the discussion with an open mind, frankness, and sensitivity to others help the discussion thrive. Box 11-6 highlights six intellectual virtues utilized by good participants in a deliberative discussion, which we will now discuss.

BOX 11-6

Intellectual Virtues of Good Discussion Participants

- Active listening
- Intellectual humility and doubt
- Inclusiveness
- Imagination
- Reflectiveness
- Responsibility for the quality of the discussion

The first of these virtues is the ability to be an active listener. *Active listening*, as we explained in chapter 3, is a behavior that seeks to understand the comments made by others. When ideas are not clear, an active listener will ask questions. ("Anne, could you help me understand what you mean by that?") If the ideas are clear, then an active listener will check the accuracy of their understanding by briefly paraphrasing what a speaker has said. ("So it sounds like you're saying . . . "). *Intellectual humility and doubt* are virtues wherein those who exercise them make clear the limitations of their knowledge and their perspective. They come to a discussion with this recognition and an open-mindedness that seeks out new knowledge, understanding, and a broader perspective. ("From what I understand . . . but I could be wrong.") *Inclusiveness* is a virtue that seeks to ensure that all perspectives on an issue and all participants in a discussion are heard fully and fairly. ("I'm interested in hearing from Marcus." Or "I think we're missing teachers here. I wonder what they'd think about this issue.") *Imagination* is a virtue that aids discussions by entertaining and developing ideas that might not be realistic when first presented but can be made more practical with a little creative thinking. ("What if . . . " or "Maybe we could try. . . . ") *Reflectiveness* is the intellectual virtue wherein a person is eager to think in new and constructive ways and is willing to challenge even long-held beliefs or ideas. ("I never realized that before.")

One final master concept for leading and participating in productive deliberative discussions is that the *responsibility for the quality of the discussion* rests on everyone involved. When discussants place complete responsibility for the discussion on the leader(s), the very nature of discussion is changed in harmful ways, and the leader is likely to play too strong a role, shutting down and shutting off many good ideas and points. Yet, most of us are not used to accepting responsibility for a discussion when we are not leading it. Thus, Box 11-7 offers the following practical responses to very concrete situations you are likely to face in deliberative discussions.

BOX 11-7
Sharing Responsibility for Our Process

1. If you feel cut off, say so or override the interruption. ("I'd like to finish.")
2. If you feel misunderstood, clarify what you mean. ("Let me put this another way.")
3. If you feel misheard, ask the listener to repeat what he or she heard you say and affirm or correct the statement.
4. If you feel hurt or disrespected, say so. If possible, describe exactly what you heard or saw that evoked those feelings. ("When you said X, I felt Y.")
5. If you feel angry, express the anger directly, rather than expressing it or acting it out indirectly. ("I felt angry when I heard you say X.")
6. If you feel confused, frame a question that seeks clarification or more information, and/or paraphrase what you have heard. ("Are you saying that . . . ?")
7. If you feel uncomfortable with the process, find a way to comment that will move things forward, or state your discomfort with or without a suggestion of what might work better for you. ("I think we have been talking past each other for the last five minutes. Does anyone else have a similar perception?")
8. If you feel the conversation is going off track, make a process observation or refocus the conversation. ("We seem to have moved away from the topic at hand; I suggest we refocus the conversation on. . . . ")

Source: "Self-Help Tools for Participants," in *Fostering Dialogue across Divides: A Nuts and Bolts Guide from the Public Conversations Project*, ed. Margaret Herzig and Laura Chasin (Watertown, MA: Public Conversations Project, 2006), 153.

BENEFITS OF DELIBERATIVE DISCUSSIONS

The importance of deliberative discussions can hardly be exaggerated. First, public deliberation provides us the invaluable opportunity to engage in discussion with those whose opinions differ. When discussing a problem of mutual concern and exploring the basis of our disagreements, we realize those who disagree with us are reasonable, engaged individuals. We may even learn that how we characterize such people is untenable. The "lazy druggie," for example, may turn out to be a woman— say, Amanda—who is seeking help from a bad addiction but cannot find the community support she needs. The "heartless narc" may be a man—say, Dan—who wants to do something about the increased number of drugs he sees in his community so his kids will stay safe and healthy. When the opposition is given a name, a face, and a voice to explain the reasons for his or her position, we find that our previous modes of communication were poorly chosen, be they incensed public diatribes or fiery e-mail messages composed in private. Deliberative discussions offer the means for illuminating, productive conversations to connect with the people around us.

Second, while deliberative discussions are hard work, if done well, they result in better decisions than when experts or officials make decisions without public input, or when private citizens form opinions without encountering diverse viewpoints. When community members come together to participate in a deliberation, they typically avoid the pitfalls of groupthink and emerge with a wiser set of choices. The wisdom results from the public knowledge and public judgment formed while sharing opinions and experiences as well as from systematically considering the benefits and drawbacks of every approach.

Of course, it would be naive to believe that participants in a deliberative discussion will always have the best intentions. Some—perhaps all of us in the right (or wrong) circumstance—might work to subvert others or the deliberative process itself. Yet despite these risks and the realization that a deliberative discussion will not always succeed, the potential for productivity is always there. A public meeting whose objective is more deliberation than competition allows us to better understand our assumptions, values, and objectives.

Finally, deliberative discussions model and teach the civic skills people need to productively contribute to their communities. When moderated well, participating in a discussion teaches participants to listen as much as they talk; to ask questions that explore the issue as well as eloquently advocate ideas; to identify the challenges posed by their preferences as much as the benefits; and to consider the consequences of any choice upon a wider range of community members than themselves. Such abilities constructively carry over into a community's broader civic life as members develop the inclinations and habits that unite rather than divide them.

SUMMARY

The ability to discuss civic concerns productively with your fellow resident is an integral aspect of public speaking. This chapter has offered you an explanation of the nature, benefits, and American lineage of deliberative discussions as well as guidance on how to effectively lead and participate in such discussions—with the goal of preparing you to undertake this endeavor.

- A deliberative discussion is a group conversation through which a community, guided by one or more moderators, thoughtfully and thoroughly examines a complex public problem as well as the range of available solutions to ultimately arrive at a decision or conclusion.
- The traditional importance of citizen-centered discussions about public affairs is demonstrated through several historical American movements and organizations dedicated to public discussion and adult education.
- For our purposes, a deliberative discussion consists of five stages: Personal stakes, during which participants share why they attended the discussion and what concerns they have about the problem; a discussion of each of three approaches to solving the problem, one at a time, during which participants consider the benefits, challenges, and trade-offs of each approach and specific actions within them; and a reflection period, during which participants reflect on the problem and approaches, naming the preferred actions and next steps.
- Ideally, participants in a deliberative discussion enter the groan zone during which they may feel overwhelmed and uncomfortable as they work through multiple viewpoints and options.
- An effective deliberative discussion leader creates a comfortable communication environment for participants by enabling everyone to speak and to focus on the issues rather than attack each other. He or she also accomplishes a large number of specific facilitation tasks, which can be shared by two or more discussion leaders. The discussion leader develops questions by considering possible directions, forms, and the stage of the discussion.
- Productively participating in a deliberative discussion requires exhibiting several intellectual virtues, including active listening, intellectual humility and doubt, inclusiveness, imagination, reflectiveness, and responsibility for the quality of the discussion.
- Leading or participating in a deliberative discussion can result in better decision-making, potentially help you connect with people whose opinions differ from your own, and teach civic skills that people need to productively contribute to their communities.

KEY TERMS

closed question p. 234
common ground p. 230
direct question p. 234
groan zone p. 229

groupthink p. 221
indirect question p. 234
open question p. 234
public judgment p. 221

public knowledge p. 221
relay question p. 234
reverse question, p. 234

REVIEW QUESTIONS

1. What is a deliberative discussion, and how is it different from other types of discussions?
2. With what historical American movements are deliberative discussions associated?
3. What are the five stages of a deliberative discussion, and what are the goals of each?
4. What is the groan zone, and what does it mean to work through it? Why is it important to do so?
5. What are three ways groups tend to avoid the groan zone, and how can a discussion leader guide them back to the zone?
6. What are some of the major tasks of a deliberative discussion leader?
7. What virtues does an effective participant in a deliberative discussion exhibit?
8. What are three benefits of a deliberative discussion?

DISCUSSION QUESTIONS

1. How might you prepare for or solve the following common pitfalls in leading a deliberative discussion?
   - You ask a question but are met with silence from the discussion participants.
   - You interpret the tone and nonverbal messages of the participants to communicate a lack of enthusiasm for the discussion.
   - One person is dominating the discussion (or one person is completely quiet).
   - The discussion erupts into an unproductive debate.
   - The conversation moves to a distant tangent.
2. Who is a good discussion leader you know? What makes his or her discussions effective? How might you adopt some of his or her strategies?
3. In which of your communities could you start practicing deliberative discussions? What problems might such discussions help your group to solve or, at least, to make progress on? What challenges might you encounter when introducing deliberation?
4. How do public knowledge and public judgment differ from individual knowledge and judgment? How do they overlap?

CHAPTER 12

Persuading an Audience to Modify Their Beliefs, Values, or Actions

---

Chapter Objectives

Students will:

- Understand the elements of invention.
- Learn the steps of the persuasive process.
- Distinguish between different types of persuasive goals.
- See how to frame advocacy regarding an issue that requires persuasion.
- Discover and advocate a means of enacting a solution.

On November 5, 2013, Sy Stokes, then a junior at UCLA, posted a video on You-Tube which he titled "The Black Bruins."[1] The video features Stokes speaking to the camera with fellow African American male students standing behind him, each dressed in a UCLA sweatshirt. The video highlights the experience of black students at the school. Stokes argues that the diversity the university claims to promote is on the surface only and that the voices of black males are not heard or appreciated. The video ends with the visually dramatic action of each student taking off his sweatshirt and standing dressed in a black T-shirt and black jeans. The persuasive video went viral and sparked vigorous debate on campus.[2]

The form of communication most closely associated with rhetoric—and the form of communication we most often hear—is persuasion. **Persuasion** is the strategic use of verbal and nonverbal symbols in an attempt to influence the beliefs, values, and/or actions of an audience. Recall from chapter 1 that rhetoric (and, thus, persuasion as a subcategory of rhetoric) includes both written words (verbal symbols) and visual imagery (nonverbal symbols) since speakers can use both types of signs to address public issues.

Persuasion is a necessary and important aspect of civic engagement for at least three reasons. First, in many cases, diverse audiences will not arrive at a consensual decision after reviewing the facts, trade-offs, and value dilemmas of a complex and

This screenshot is from a video created and posted on YouTube by UCLA student Sy Stokes.

difficult issue. Advocacy is necessary to move audiences toward a position or conclusion. Eventually the audience must decide how a city might best address sanitation challenges, how a judge or jury resolves a legal dispute, or whether to confirm a nominee for the Supreme Court. Second, the course of advocacy often helps us see the greatest advantages—and disadvantages—of an idea as it is advanced by a committed advocate and critically examined by a listening audience. Third, as citizens, our own convictions and beliefs, tested and shaped by the deliberative process, may compel us to advocacy for the common good.

Persuasion, however, can be negatively perceived as a form of manipulation—a perception that has plagued persuasion, and rhetoric more generally, since at least the Classical Period. In the *Gorgias*, Plato demeaned rhetoric as a knack akin to cooking and a form of flattery devoid of substance and, by implication, ethical value.[3] Ironically he did so even as he skillfully utilized rhetorical technique to make his own arguments persuasive. This included the unique use of the dialogue form itself. In contrast, Aristotle defined rhetoric more fundamentally as the ability in each particular case to see the available means of persuasion.[4] This placed rhetoric in an ethically neutral place. That is, it can be used in an ethical or unethical manner. He taught that rhetoric was about developing the ability to discover or see the elements of persuasion in specific situations. As scholars of the rhetorical tradition will tell you, even if one simplifies rhetoric to persuasion there has been a set of ethical expectations inherent in its practice from its beginnings. These expectations range from Plato's depiction of a true rhetoric in the *Phaedrus* to Isocrates's vision of rhetoric as a civic art that improves the community to Cicero's and Quintilian's vision of rhetoric as the joining of wisdom and eloquence by the good person speaking well.

Given the goal of persuasion—attempting to influence others—it is easy to understand why it has been subject to special scrutiny. We contend, however, that ethical persuasion is essential for the public good, that it advances public discourse, and is often necessary for communities to resolve complex public questions once an issue has been adequately vetted through deliberation. In this chapter we first explain how speakers and writers can use principles and practices of invention to generate arguments for advocacy. Second, we describe the persuasive process. As we will see, taking particular note of your audience members and being thoughtful about what you hope to accomplish in a persuasive interaction takes great care on the part of speakers.

INVENTION: THE SUBSTANCE OF PERSUASION

Invention is a term that might strike you as odd. Yet, it does emphasize the reality that when we speak and, to put the matter more formally, when we advance arguments intended to persuade, we do so by making them up in our minds. **Invention** is the process of investigation and thought that produces the content of your speech. This designation and definition of invention originated in rhetoric's ancient past. There are two items of importance to note about this definition. First, notice that *you* come up with what you say in your speech, which, as noted in chapter 3, means being careful you are not using the words or arguments of others without attribution. Second, when done properly—and ethically—your words and arguments will be based on thorough research that makes use of balanced sources or the thoughtful and acknowledged use of biased sources as described in chapter 4.

But how is it that individual, innovative thinking can be stimulated? If you have ever sat in front of your computer screen stumped about what to write, you have experienced precisely what the canon of invention is designed to overcome. The principles of invention suggest paths for research, help overcome dreaded writer's block, and enable the consideration of a number of ways to construct a speech. Let us begin, first, by considering available strategies, or heuristics, of invention and how they can be translated into speech construction. Second, we will consider the central proofs or means of invention that are used to develop the substance of persuasion in typical situations and for typical topics.

Heuristics

Imagine a legal pad with page after page of information and quotations you have collected or, perhaps more likely, an electronic document into which you have captured the best of your research. What to do with all of this information and what you have learned? How to generate a thesis statement? How best to develop and explain your thesis? To resolve such questions, thinkers and speakers in the past turned to **heuristics,** specific strategies for generating new ideas. Also referred to as topics, loci, and lines of argument, the term heuristic comes from the Greek word *heuriskein* which means "to discover." The Greek term *topos* means "place" and seems to have referred to the spot or place on a scroll wherein a particular common pattern of argument was written. The first formal presentation of these devices occurs in Aristotle's *Rhetoric,* book 2, under the heading of topics. There he outlines 28 heuristic devices for constructing arguments. These devices stimulate intellectual discovery as a person is struggling to make sense of an issue, formulate a thesis statement, consider patterns of arrangement, and solve difficult tensions. Another way of explaining what heuristics make possible is that they encourage novel observations and inferences about an issue or topic. When successful they generate new perspectives, new knowledge, and a more productive construction of a presentation or speech than would occur otherwise. Box 12-1 contains a selection of the most commonly used strategies of rhetorical invention, or heuristics.

BOX 12-1

Selected Heuristic Devices

1. Definition: What is it?
2. What are the parts and how are they related?
3. How the subject and object can be reversed, or how the order of ideas can be reversed.
4. How an idea or physical entity compares with another.
5. How an idea or physical entity contrasts with another.
6. Has something happened or not happened? Will something happen or will it not happen?
7. Is one item greater or is it smaller than another item?
8. Is something possible or is it not possible?
9. What is and what is not?
10. How big is something and how far does it reach?
11. In the past what was something like?
12. In the future what will something be like?

SOURCE: Numbers 6–12 based on Sharon Crowley and Debra Hawhee, *Ancient Rhetorics for Contemporary Students* (Boston: Allyn and Bacon, 1999), 82–83.

So, how do heuristic devices work in developing a speech? In many ways, it is comparable to the stunningly successful, and always enjoyable, original Play-Doh machine. The device took a blob of Play-Doh and turned it into a circular spaghetti type noodle, a star noodle, a lightning bolt, or an L-shaped noodle. In the end there were perhaps 20 or 30 different shapes you could mold the Play-Doh into, depending on which shape you lined up with the hole coming out of the maker. Put the Play-Doh in the slot, line up the shape, and squeeze the Play-Doh through. Easy!

Heuristic devices make use of your research in much the same way; they show you various ways to shape that information and those ideas for your audience into a thesis statement, supporting arguments, or even organizational structures. The best thing to do is to try several, see how they work and what they generate, and then make a selection from your creations taking into account your audience, goals, and context.

Imagine you are preparing a speech on gun regulation and have information explaining various positions that have been taken on the subject, various court cases

that have made rulings on it in specific instances, statistics on gun violence in the United States as well as the use of guns for hunting, and testimonials from people who own guns and keep them for safety. Taking *compare* as a heuristic device, you might consider the idea of comparing various views on the subject, or comparing rural versus urban views on the possession and uses of guns. Perhaps the comparison can be used to argue the strengths of certain views and the weaknesses of others.

Alternatively, also taken from the list in Box 12-1, the heuristic phrase *how things used to be* could be employed to consider how laws and public perceptions about gun ownership have evolved in the United States to argue the worthiness or unworthiness of the trend. We know that owning a gun when one lived on the prairie in the nineteenth century was quite different than owning a gun and living in the suburbs today, for example. Finally, taking up the device of *definition*, you might consider what both pro- and antigun regulation advocates tend to mean when they use the phrase gun control, that is, how they define it. In all likelihood the phrase has very different meanings to the two groups, and you might argue for a particular definition.

In the example cited at the beginning of this chapter, we can see the powerful use of the heuristic device of *contrast*. Sy Stokes uses this in stating:

> When most of us are dropping out for lack of financial aid, while Judy Olian, dean of the Anderson School of Management, just spent $647,000 on first-class flights and hotel stays.
>
> When we have more national championships than we do black male freshmen, it's evident that our only purpose here is to improve your winning percentage. [The text on the screen lists the 109 national championships and the 48 African American male freshmen.]

These contrasts are startling and seek to support the message of the video—that the number of African American male freshman at the school is low and that the support they receive in comparison to other expenses incurred at the college is out of balance.

Once you have employed a number of these heuristic devices, you can lay out the results before you (like Post-It-Notes on a wall) and then consider which ones to use and how. The time you take in this step of imaginative rhetorical invention, drawing from your research, is always well spent. At this point, envision that you have three or more possible arguments for your presentation. Now consider your audience, the occasion, and your specific purpose to select the one that will work best. This task can lead to a wonderfully freeing and empowering realization: for any given topic, audience, and purpose there are many good ways to form a thesis and build a case, and reflecting on which one will be best is an enjoyable task.

Modes of Proof

Aristotle identified three artistic modes of proof as central to invention and critical for advancing persuasive efforts. By modes, he simply meant the ways people are persuaded or what they find persuasive. In differentiating the modes, Aristotle explains that ethos is found "in the character of the speaker," pathos relies on "disposing the listener in some way," and logos depends on "the argument itself, by showing or seeming to show something."[5] In each case the proof is the substance, the information, the persuasive appeal you share with your audience. And depending on the goal, audience, subject matter, and context, you will vary the proof you use.

Sound persuasion is based on evidence and valid reasoning. In Aristotle's words this is the work of logos. **Logos** is the logical or reasoned basis of an appeal. Thus, for our purposes logos refers to the argumentative substance of the presentation. This aspect of public presentations is fundamental and is the focus of chapter 13. However, argumentation is only one element of persuasion. Persuasion is a broader subject containing argument but not consisting solely of it; persuasion is more than good and proper reasoning, no matter how important this is to a message.

Persuasion is also a matter of credibility or ethos. You can, no doubt, recall several points at which we discussed ethos in this book, most notably the discussion of ethics in chapter 3 but also in relation to source credibility. Ethos, as described in chapter 3, is drawn from the audience's perception of the credibility of the speaker or source. When an audience perceives you as credible, or "worthy of confidence," they are more likely persuaded by you. Your credibility functions as further proof of the truth or validity of your argument. Notice, however, that your ethos exists only to the degree that your audience *perceives* you as credible, and their perception is based on how you present yourself in and through your speech. You may have established a public reputation that precedes your speech, but you must further develop, reinforce, and/or improve your ethos in and through each presentation you make. According to Aristotle, speakers can develop their ethos by demonstrating one or more of the following four qualities through their speech: (1) competence (expertise, preparation, intelligence); (2) trustworthiness (moral standing, integrity); (3) goodwill (having the audience's best interests at heart); and (4) dynamism (charisma).[6] We are persuaded by advocates and sources that best display these qualities. And, in fact, Aristotle went so far to suggest that moral character (ethos) "constitutes the most effective means of proof."[7] You might consider why that might be and whether you agree with him.

Finally, there is the role of emotion or pathos. Recall from chapter 3 that pathos is concerned with the psychological state of the audience and rests upon effective, ethical appeals to their emotions and motivations. Practically speaking, pathos is a measure and reflection of the extent to which we are moved by and feel invested in a topic and a message. Such feelings may be appealed to or cultivated in a multitude of ways. Aristotle makes the intuitive argument that we desire emotions that result in pleasure and want to avoid emotions that result in pain. A speaker can use this observation when crafting his or her message. In his formulation Aristotle offered an array of emotions to which speakers might appeal, including anger, patience, friendship, enmity, fear, confidence, shame, shamelessness, emulation, contempt, kindness, pity, indignation, and envy. Realize that these are only a sampling of possible appeals to emotion, and you should be able to readily imagine other possible uses of emotion or pathos in a speech.

The effective use of pathos can be seen in President George W. Bush's 2002 ceremonial address commemorating the one-year anniversary of the 9/11 terrorist attacks. He sought to remember and honor the victims of the attacks, while rededicating the efforts to capture the perpetrators and fight terror generally. To do so, President Bush began his speech by calling on the *sadness* and *outrage* the American people felt toward the attacks on the United States before relating more positively by projecting *confidence* that those responsible would be apprehended. The opening of the speech recounts the attacks and how, "We've seen the images so many times they are seared on our souls, and remembering the horror, reliving the anguish, re-imagining the terror, is hard—and painful." However, the sadness gives way to confidence as the president claims that the response to the challenging events showed the positive character of America "that will deliver us":

> We have seen the greatness of America in airline passengers who defied their hijackers and ran a plane into the ground to spare the lives of others. We've seen the greatness of America in rescuers who rushed up flights of stairs toward peril. And we continue to see the greatness of America in the care and compassion our citizens show to each other.[8]

The combined use of sadness over the events and confidence in the American spirit was followed by another combination of emotions by President Bush—that of *love* and *shame*. The president appealed to our "love for our families, love for our neighbors, and love for our country" by suggesting it would be shameful to not deliver what we owe to those who sacrificed their lives in the attacks. And what we owed, according to President Bush, was to continue the fight against terrorism and to seek retribution for the perpetrators of the 9/11 attacks in particular. There are other emotional appeals found in the address as well, with a mix of positive emotions offered to allies (friendship, kindness, love, and hope) and negative emotions directed at enemies (contempt and indignation). On balance the speech is a good example of the range of emotional appeals available to a rhetor when identifying with an audience.

Similarly, an example of the power of pathos is found in "The Black Bruins" video. Stokes makes use of the emotion of shame in a repeated refrain, slightly altered each time, delivered with growing passion, and in the last instance turning what has been a statement into a question and phrasing it even more strongly:

> First instance: "Now you tell me I should be proud to be at UCLA."
> Second instance: "But you tell me I should be proud to be a Bruin."

Third instance: "And you tell me I should be proud to be a Bruin."

Final instance: "How the hell am I supposed to be proud to call myself a Bruin?"

Each time Stokes puts the greatest emphasis on the word proud and his emotion and insistence rises with each use. This tied to the visual image of the students removing their UCLA sweatshirts is emotionally stirring. It demonstrates the persuasive power of pathos.

While appeals to pathos are potentially very powerful and useful, excessive use of pathos can distract from the reasoning process and can be considered unethical, particularly when used to the exclusion of reason. It is this dimension of rhetoric—emotional appeal—that has caused some scholars of public deliberation and deliberative democracy to distrust rhetoric. The concern is that rhetoric, providing space as it does for emotion, can obstruct good decision-making by displacing reason. We have certainly seen examples of this through speakers who rely excessively on emotional appeals and frequently on the emotion of fear. For instance, whenever alterations to Social Security or Medicare are proposed (by either political party), opponents often use proposed changes to frighten seniors to vote against the changes or politicians supporting the changes rather than deliberate over the actual policy options. This strategic use of fear has become identified with the shorthand "scaring seniors in the voting booth." We can see similar scare tactics in the accusations about President Obama's alleged Muslim allegiances, or claims made in 2010 that the Muslim imam who proposed a mosque near Ground Zero implicitly threatened to attack New York if construction was blocked.[9] Appeals to fear have become so common that comedian Stephen Colbert was driven to respond with an ironic protest, "March to Keep Fear Alive" on October 30, 2010, in Washington, DC. This event sought to critique the use of fear-appeals through humorous satire. On the same day and location, fellow comedian Jon Stewart also staged an event, a "Rally to Restore Sanity." Both events help us see the interesting ways that humor can be used to make serious political and social points in an engaging manner. Although emotion can be overused, as Colbert and Stewart pointed out, it is also valuable to observe that some scholars, from both rhetoric and political science, see rhetoric, including its propensity for emotional appeals, as a valuable part of deliberation and as a corrective to an idealized, coldly rational perspective. These scholars point to the use of rhetoric and pathos in promoting trust and friendship through expressions of civil passions that can be beneficial to productive deliberation.[10]

THE PERSUASIVE PROCESS

Once you have developed the content of your speech (using the principles of invention), you are ready to take the next steps in the persuasive process, a process that moves from audience analysis to calls for action. Taking an idea and developing it into a compelling persuasive appeal can be envisioned as a six-part progression that begins with adjusting your approach to your audience and ends with the audience taking actions in the world based on your persuasive efforts and their changed perspective. Along the way, a speaker must analyze the audience and adapt his or her message accordingly, choose a persuasive goal, frame the speech, demonstrate a subject worthy of attention, and present an appropriate response to it.

BOX 12-2

The Persuasive Process

1. Consider audience analysis and adaptation
2. Select a persuasive goal
3. Frame your persuasive efforts
4. Identify an issue worthy of attention
5. Offer a superior response
6. Empower your audience and provide a means to act

Audience Analysis and Adaptation

The persuasive process begins with studying your audience and tailoring your speech to them and the environment where the speech will occur. This topic is addressed in a comprehensive manner in chapter 5. And so, as in every type of presentation, the character of your audience is central to the development of a persuasive presentation. In fact, if you were to deliver the same ideas to two different audiences, then you would best prepare two different speeches. The more the two groups diverge, the more distinct your speeches would need to be, because what is likely to persuade one audience in a particular environment may not be effective for another group in a different setting.

Persuasive Goal

A speaker must keep her goals clearly in mind when crafting a speech. Such goals exist on at least two levels. First, she must keep in mind her ultimate goal, which will range from personal gain to the public good. If we imagine these ambitions as existing on two ends of a continuum, then we can envision extreme versions of each. On one hand, a speaker entirely motivated by personal gain may say anything to persuade her listeners, and her presentation will seek to directly benefit herself. Think of a stereotypical used car salesperson who is deceptive in order to make a commission on a car she knows is a lemon. On the other hand, a speaker motivated by the public good will speak truthfully even when that may not help her individually. She will aim for outcomes that will benefit the whole group, even when that means making personal sacrifices. Think of a whistleblower who exposes her company's wrongdoings in order to protect victims of that wrongdoing even though she risks damaging her company and being fired as a result. Of course, most presentations fall somewhere in the middle of this continuum. You should keep this tension in mind by continually asking for whom or what you are speaking. It is easy to begin with the best of intentions and then get caught up in winning as you develop and deliver your speech. When that happens, we reinforce the qualities of unproductive discourse discussed in chapter 2 and the outcomes this discourse generates including divisiveness, apathy and cynicism, and indifference or disdain for those not like us.

Second, in addition to an ultimate or broader goal, you must identify your initial, or more specific, persuasive goal. This goal will—and should—change depending on your audience, context, and topic. In this regard, you might best view persuasion as existing along another continuum—one that moves from thought to action. At one end of the continuum is a relatively subtle approach to persuasion that brings the problem to the attention of the public; that is, a **conscious-raising speech** is designed to create audience awareness of a problem or issue. This is perhaps the most basic, yet potentially most inspiring, form of persuasion in that it seeks to inform, motivate, and persuade an audience all at once. A deliberative presentation is a form of consciousness-raising in that it stimulates audience thought on a public problem in new ways. It does not seek to convince the audience that one particular approach to the problem is correct, nor does it ask for specific audience action, but, instead, it offers a balanced presentation that raises awareness of multiple approaches to the issue and the implications of each choice.

Taking another step along the continuum, there are **speeches to convince**. While a deliberative presentation attempts to highlight a new concern or increase understanding of a current topic, a speech to convince seeks to challenge the audience more directly by influencing values or beliefs. An example would be a speaker attempting to convince an audience to agree that more resources should be invested in developing alternative energy sources. While the speech might not contain a specific plan or request audience action, it could build the case that fossil fuel use is damaging the environment and alternatives should be sought.

Finally, we would note that often the most powerful presentations offer listeners a specific way to proceed; that is, they are **speeches that offer means to action**. In this way the rhetor does more than encourage agreement on an issue—he or she actually requests that the audience act on the issue. As a result, the speaker's strategy is complicated by the need to provide real and tangible ways for audience members to contribute to the solution of the problem. Often this means presenting a plan or policy and then asking the audience to enact or implement the plan; although, it can alternatively mean asking the audience to learn more about the issue so they can overcome any remaining resistance and ultimately join your plan. Either sort of persuasive effort requires (1) the presentation of a solution that can be implemented and (2) that the speaker includes ways that the audience can realistically participate or learn more about the issue. This call-and-response models civic engagement as its success depends on citizen or audience participation subsequent to the speech. The importance of this move to action should not be underestimated, because it is where we go from what sounds good in theory to actually carrying it out. As a result, a persuasive speech that includes a call to action requires more thought, research, and planning than other types of persuasive speeches.

Framing Persuasive Efforts

Once you have chosen the goals of your persuasive speech, you are ready to frame its content. Recall from chapter 10 that framing is the process by which people use language to present and make sense of their world. In chapter 10, we discussed how to use nonpartisan framing to set up a deliberative presentation. We concluded that since such presentations are largely educational, a speaker must frame the problem and possible solutions as clearly and fairly as possible. You will now be involved with advocacy, however, whereby you try to influence the beliefs, values, and/or actions of audience members.

A good example of persuasive framing can be found in the initial testimony that University of Oklahoma professor of law Anita Hill gave to the Senate Judiciary Committee during the confirmation hearings for Supreme Court Justice Clarence Thomas in 1991. Hill sought to prevent Thomas's confirmation by providing evidence against his character and judgment due to numerous unwelcomed sexually explicit statements he made to her while she worked for him. In her opening statement, prior to taking questions from the Senate Judiciary Committee, Hill sought to present herself as a good and credible woman. She also sought to frame her experiences with Justice Thomas in terms of how these sexual innuendos and brash statements caused her to feel and not in terms of his intentions or motives. It is a persuasive speech in that Hill seeks to convince the senators to conclude that Clarence Thomas engaged in behavior that should disqualify him to serve on the Supreme Court.

Hill sets the frame of her testimony against Thomas with appeals to her own character. She describes for the senators how she was raised on a farm and in a Baptist church in Okmulgee County, Oklahoma. She indicates that this church continues to have special meaning for her up to the present moment. She then states that she completed an undergraduate degree at Oklahoma State and her law degree at Yale University Law School. She was first hired by Judge Thomas after he had been appointed assistant secretary of education for the Department of Education's Office of Civil

On October 11, 1991, Anita Hill, professor of law at the University of Oklahoma, gave testimony concerning her interactions with then Supreme Court nominee Clarence Thomas when she worked for him first in the Department of Education and later at the Equal Employment Opportunity Commission. While this was not the first time the phrase sexual harassment was used in American society, many scholars credit these hearings with helping make the phrase and, more importantly, the concept and the experience of those who are sexually harassed widely understood.

Rights, and then she moved with him when he was later appointed chairman of the Equal Employment Opportunity Commission. She is a highly educated and accomplished lawyer. She indicates that giving this testimony is possible "only after a great deal of agonizing consideration."

Having established her good character, Hill then paints a contrasting image of Thomas. She describes several incidents where "Judge Thomas began to use work situations to discuss sex." These occurred over several years and despite her requests that he not do so.

> On these occasions he would call me into his office for reports on education issues and projects, or he might suggest that because of the time pressures of his schedule we go to lunch to a government cafeteria. After brief discussions of work, he would turn the conversation to a discussion of sexual matters. His conversations were very vivid. He spoke about acts that he had seen in pornographic films involving such matters as women having sex with animals and films showing group sex or rape scenes. He talked about pornographic materials depicting individuals with large penises or large breasts involving various sex acts. On several occasions, Thomas told me graphically of his own sexual prowess. Because I was extremely uncomfortable talking about sex with him at all, and particularly in such a graphic way, I told him that I did not want to talk about this subject. I would also try to change the subject to education matters or to non-sexual personal matters, such as his background and his beliefs. My efforts to change the subject were rarely successful.[11]

Hill's description of Thomas's character is all the more damning given the contrast, which she set up, to her own character. This powerful contrast was produced through Hill's use of framing. She framed her description of Thomas's deficient character with a description of her own good character.

In this case Hill's efforts to convince her audience were not fully successful. Interestingly, while many credit her testimony with dramatically raising awareness of sexual harassment in the United States, Thomas was still confirmed by the Senate Judiciary Committee. Thomas gave a vigorous self-defense, denying the claims of Anita Hill. Several senators on the all-male committee also vigorously challenged Hill and, in the end, Hill's characterization of herself as good and Thomas as bad was flipped. Thomas serves as a justice on the Supreme Court to this day. Anita Hill is currently a professor of law and women studies at Brandeis University. The hearings remain a significant event in rhetorical studies because many feel Hill was more credible witness than she was made out to be by Thomas and the senators on the committee.

As you can see from the Thomas-Hill example, framing is a significant feature of the persuasive process. At this point it is useful to borrow Will Friedman's broad distinction between honest and dishonest ways of "framing-to-persuade." Friedman defines *honest* framing efforts as "sincere rhetorical advocacy" in which the speaker says, "'I believe this because' and . . . means it." Such framing efforts attempt to persuade the audience in an ethical, open, and trustworthy manner with the public good in mind. In so doing, honest framing-to-persuade is a necessary component of presentations and communication intended to stimulate public debate on an issue. In contrast, *dishonest* framing efforts are damaging to public deliberation and the public good, fostering instead the vices of unproductive public discourse. We have all seen how attack ads during election season can take an opponent's statements out of context, feature unflattering pictures, and publicize rumor as if it's truth. Motivated almost solely by the desire to win the argument by any means necessary, this dishonest framing-to-persuade prioritizes personal gain and can "more or less destroy" public debate.[12] We invite and strongly encourage you, then, to advocate a position as skillfully and passionately as possible, using strategic framing to make your solution look attractive, but to do so with honesty and integrity for the benefit of the public good.

Identify an Issue Worthy of Attention

The next step is to demonstrate that the issue you have chosen to address is worthy of the audience's attention. Unless you can demonstrate a worthy problem, the audience won't have reason to consider the issue, let alone to change their beliefs, values, or actions.

Persuasive speaking requires you to take on the same issues you would for a deliberative presentation, but requires a different and more directed focus. First, deliberative presentations describe the issue in a way that encourages a subsequent nonpartisan deliberative discussion. Persuasive speaking requires convincing the audience the issue you have selected is significant. It also requires presenting the problem in a way that is logical with, and prepares the audience for, the desired solution, response, or resolution you have identified. Somewhat like the relationship between a question and an answer, you must present the issue in a way that demonstrates your solution to be superior.

Consider the example of how a student might treat the topic of new housing regulations first for a public deliberation and second for a persuasive speaking presentation. A deliberative presentation on the topic addressed the difficulties created by dilapidated housing in a small town in the rural Midwest. As the residents and city government sought to rejuvenate the town after an economic downturn, many believed the sight of rundown homes was holding the town back. The student presented three approaches to the problem: focus on organizing volunteer groups to work with low-income homeowners to repair and paint the homes, provide incentives to the homeowners themselves to do repairs and upkeep, or use financial penalties to enforce the existing city ordinances on property within the town limits, including the use of fines. After the presentation and the discussion that followed in a persuasive speech the student might decide to advocate for a mixture of two of the approaches by focusing on the development and enforcement of locally generated codes and regulations while including a sustained effort to mobilize volunteers to help needy homeowners.[13]

Persuasive speeches differ from deliberative presentations in that a persuasive speech will likely target a smaller piece of the larger issue than a deliberative presentation on the matter. Because public controversies are so thorny and difficult, and because the length of a persuasive presentation is typically brief, it is very challenging to successfully advocate one position in contrast to other positions. For instance, it would be a tall order to convince your audience in 10 minutes that all abortions should be banned. It would be more realistic to whittle the problem of unwanted pregnancies down to something narrower. For example, a student who led a discussion on the issue of unwanted pregnancies might choose to focus his persuasive speech on the difficulties and costs associated with domestic infant adoption or on the lack of services available to young mothers who want to pursue their education.

When focusing on an issue worthy of attention, there are three strategies, or pointers, to keep in mind when giving persuasive presentations: First, be sure to offer high-quality, tangible evidence of the problem or community concern, whether that be through a reliance on logos that demonstrates the scope of a problem; pathos that appeals to the emotional and human toll of an issue and highlights specific examples; or ethos generated when a subject is explained through credible sources and credible testimony. Ideally, a combination of all three types of appeals forms the strongest presentation. Second, make the issue real through vivid detail, examples, and narrative. Whenever possible, relate the issue directly to your audience by showing how and where it is evident in their lives and communities. Such an approach will not only create audience understanding but will also heighten audience identification with the issue. Finally, beware of making an issue seem so immense or difficult that you paralyze your audience; don't inadvertently give the audience the impression or feeling that nothing can be done.

Offer a Superior Response

A fifth element of the persuasive process is to present a good way to respond to the problem. It isn't enough to demonstrate for your audience that an issue is well-worthy of their attention or that their present belief is incorrect—you have to persuade an audience what the proper belief, value, or action should be in response. Here you ask for a commitment from your audience, be that a change in behavior, thought, or attitude. There are four considerations to take into account:

- You should *explain how* the desired value, belief, or behavior would address the problem. What will it improve, solve, or help? How might recognizing the reality of Internet addiction enable sufferers to get help? How would eating locally grown produce improve the city's economy and possibly the health of its residents?
- You should *support* your explanation of how the desired outcome will improve the problem with evidence derived from examples, statistics, and testimony.
- Recall that there is more than one viable way to approach most problems. Therefore, it is important to *account for alternatives* that you have dismissed as less attractive. Explain the benefits of your selected approach compared to the less preferred side effects or failures of other possibilities. This will likely require you to explain your decision calculus and how you resolved the competing values and trade-offs that may have been identified in a deliberative presentation or discussion.
- Finally, *consider counter-arguments* the audience will likely raise. This is particularly important and requires additional elaboration.

By its very nature, a persuasive presentation will encounter resistance. You are attempting to persuade people to think or act in a way that is counter to what they are presently doing; you want them to change their beliefs, actions, or perspectives.

Listeners generally have reasons they disagree with your perspective—some good, some bad. However, in order to persuade an audience to change its mind, you have to address their reasons. If you ignore common counter-arguments, the audience is more apt to ignore you, will feel like you haven't challenged their perspective, and may think you are uninformed about the topic. As a result, an important component of nearly every persuasive speech is attention to counter-arguments.

One option available is to explicitly acknowledge a counter-argument in the context of your own argument by stating it and then refuting it; that is, giving the reasons why you think it is invalid. A second organizational option is to devote a main point of your speech to refuting several counter-arguments. This often occurs when you discuss alternative solutions to a problem, such as in the problem-alternatives-solution or the refutative patterns of organization discussed in chapter 6.

The benefits of acknowledging counter-arguments are many: it makes your argument more persuasive to those with opposing views, it shows you are prepared and thoughtful, and it demonstrates you are willing to confront difficult choices. In terms of addressing counter-arguments, one caveat is in order: While you have a responsibility to refute a prominent counter-argument, don't feel obliged to *make* the counter-argument. That is, don't provide evidence that proves the opposing position. Too often this reinforces the opposing view held by those in your audience. This is an additional way persuasion differs from deliberation.

Empower Your Audience—Provide a Means to Act

Finally, whenever possible you should empower your audience by giving them a means to act. Your audience should not just be passive receptacles of your information. Instead, you should turn them into advocates for your cause. This means offering listeners legitimate ways they can contribute to solving the problem identified in your speech. Provide clear options they can enact to change their behaviors, values, or beliefs. This is not always appropriate, given the issue or topic, but when it is, identifying means for action is the most ethical choice.

The type of action you advocate depends on your persuasive goal. If your objective is to change your audience's *beliefs or attitudes*, then you might ask the audience to participate in an activity that will help accomplish that goal. Very often that activity will be educational in nature. For instance, a student who wants his audience to approve of gay marriage may ask them to attend an upcoming lecture or documentary on the topic or even to attend a meeting of a relevant campus organization. Each of these activities would further expose audience members to a supportive point of view without yet requiring them to actively support a change in law or policy. If your goal is to influence the audience's *behavior*, then ask them to help you enact your policy or plan. Returning to the gay marriage topic, a student who wants his audience to work on legalizing gay marriage in their state might ask them to participate in an upcoming protest against a gay marriage ban or to volunteer their efforts with an interest group devoted to the topic. A student pursuing a large policy change such as the legalization of gay marriage might break that goal into a number of smaller steps and ask the audience simply to take the first step. The audience's predisposition toward the desired policy will determine the first step. If the audience is initially resistant to the new policy, then the first step toward enacting it is to ask the audience to attend an educational activity. If the audience is largely receptive, however, then the first step can be a move toward actually laying the groundwork to begin the work of enacting the policy.

Whatever your goal, keep in mind that most actions are of two types. First, there are *already existing opportunities* that you need to discover and then encourage or enable your audience to participate in. For instance, if you are concerned with the high school dropout rate, you might ask the audience to volunteer to mentor local youth. With a little searching, you will likely discover several such mentoring programs already existing at your school and the surrounding area (Boys and Girls Club, tutoring programs, community centers, etc.). You simply need to contact the organization to assess their needs and discuss the details about how to get involved. Second, there are *opportunities that you create*. Sometimes you need to use your imagination and creativity to offer your audience a chance to get involved. For example, you might want the audience to improve social services for mothers-to-be in financial need. Find a local organization devoted to these women that has a list of items it would like to have donated. You could ask your audience to help organize and execute a donation drive on campus or, at a minimum, to donate an item to the drive. Creating opportunities just takes a little imagination.

Whenever possible, find or create an opportunity close at hand for the audience. Your audience will be more likely to take advantage of the opportunity, and doing so will help them notice ways to directly improve their local community. Of course, finding or creating local opportunities can seem challenging at first. Often we have never noticed or participated in such chances and/or have come to believe there is little we can do locally to improve really tough issues. To overcome these challenges, we recommend that you become familiar with the nearby community by talking to local citizens about opportunities and by searching for your issue in the city's Yellow Pages or on the local visitors' bureau webpage. Such searches are likely to identify organizations or other groups devoted to the issue. Also watch for announcements of upcoming events in the local news and on campus. When you find a local connection, research the program or organization and consider interviewing someone associated with it. People regularly involved with the issue usually offer great insight, and they often provide ideas about ways citizens can get involved to alleviate the problem.

Once you have chosen an action to advocate, give the audience the specific information they need to participate. Provide them with ideas for how to encourage others to become involved in the cause. For example, imagine a speech that encouraged the audience to donate their time mentoring youth as a means of lowering the high school dropout rate. The action step of this hypothetical speech includes three appeals:

III. You, too, can change a child's life by becoming a mentor.
   A. Please donate your time.
   B. Contact local schools to see how you can help.
   C. Call the local Boys and Girls Club or Big Brothers/Big Sisters.

The ideas here are a good start, but they lack the sort of development and detail needed to drive home a persuasive speech. Rather than giving the audience the means to act, the speaker is relying upon the audience to finish doing the work. How likely are they to do that? Not very likely at all! Instead, the speech might fill in the blanks with pertinent information, such as the following revised example provides:

III. You, too, can change a child's life by volunteering at the local Boys and Girls Club and becoming a mentor.
  A. You can visit the club at _____ [provide the address]. Their facilities include a gymnasium, pool tables, playground equipment, computer lab, and soccer fields. Or contact the director via phone at (333) 333-3333 or e-mail ourtownbgc@hotmail.com to see how you can help.
    1. _____ [name of person] is responsible for the mentoring program and would be happy to speak with you.
    2. [Include specific testimony from the person about the value and need for mentors. Now you have provided the exact person your audience would talk to—you are making this person real to them.]
    3. [Include testimony from a volunteer or from a child or other person who has benefited from the program.]
  B. So please visit, call, or e-mail _____ [name] to find out more information about the available opportunities.
    1. This fall there will be youth soccer leagues that could use your assistance.
    2. There is also a valuable after-school program that would benefit from college-aged mentors and role models.
      a. The program meets from 2:30 to 5:30pm Monday through Friday.
      b. I volunteer on Tuesday afternoons and could provide a ride if you'd like to go with me.

The key is to reduce the burden on your audience in pursuing your persuasive alternative while simultaneously proving that they can truly make a difference. If you give them a simple means to act, they are much more likely to act than if you give them the idea of acting without the details. Not all persuasive speeches are the same, so the preceding is by no means a comprehensive template, but it does cover the basics of the persuasive process as you move from identifying your listeners to putting a plan into action.

SPOTLIGHT ON SOCIAL MEDIA:
Persuasive Advocacy Using Facebook and Twitter

One of the more interesting ways that participants in the democratic process engage in the persuasive process today is through sharing and commenting on articles produced and posted on websites. The ease and pace at which such persuasive attempts can now take place over the Internet is astounding. As an example, in September 2013 a Facebook (FB) friend of one the authors of this book shared an article on the results of a US Department of Education study on the effectiveness of the Teach for America program. The article was published on the online magazine Slate website on September 10, 2013.[14]

The article positively portrayed Teach for America. In posting the article to his Facebook page, the individual was making a statement in favor of the current policy of the federal government to support the Teach for America program. However, this program continues to receive criticism from undergraduate and even graduate programs in teacher education and certification because it places teachers in schools without the extended, formal training these programs provide.

This FB friend shared it on his FB page on the same day it was published on Slate. If his FB friends clicked the link, it would take them to the article; and they could read the article, read the comments, and then have the choice to comment on it, share it on Facebook, like it on Facebook, tweet it, bookmark it on their My Slate page, have it automatically updated in RSS form, print it, or e-mail it. From the FB page itself, they could share it with their friends to comment on it and to like it.

In part what is happening is that social media is being used in the service of public discussion and attempts at persuasion. In this case, within a week, there were nearly 200 comments on the article on the Slate website. The comments ranged from questioning the data used in the article to questioning the interpretation of the data and all that was not included in the data. Others commented on the Teach for America program, some speaking positively about the goals and results of the program, some negatively. Some of the comments were a paragraph in length or longer while others were quite brief.

Below are three examples of comments made, each person replying to the previous person.

Nylund   *6 Days Ago* from *slate.com*

Should it really come as much of a surprise that a smart person with a degree from a good school can be an effective teacher even without any rigorous training or certification program? It's the norm for university professors. They don't get training or enter into any certification programs. I don't think I've ever heard anyone suggest that our universities are totally screwed up for not requiring professors to go through some teaching certification program.

It seems odd to me to think that people assume this whole training/certification thing is super important for someone teaching a high school senior, but utter unimportant when that same student goes off to college the next year.

Reply   👍 *mpart likes this.*

The Hegemon   *6 Days Ago* from *slate.com*

"Should it really come as much of a surprise that a smart person with a degree from a good school can be an effective teacher even without any rigorous training or certification program? "

yes. many of my fellow TAs in grad school were simply *awful* at teaching (and this is teaching college students who want to be there, not low-income kids who don't) without any training and while you're correct that professors aren't required to be certified, they certainly get quite a bit of training and experience. *NO* hire on my campus happens without looking at teaching reviews, or in the case of beginning professors, a teaching demonstration

Reply   👍 *nyer11 likes this.*

jamesbeaz   *6 Days Ago* from *slate.com*

Yes, it should be a surprise. A lot of university professors are absolutely horrible teachers.

Reply   👍 *nyer11 likes this.*

Figure 12.1

One of the interesting features of this form of policy advocacy is that it involves those using it to affiliate themselves, in one way or another, with a particular source such as *The New York Times, Slate,* or the *Huffington Post.* They may do this by sending an article from these sources that they are in agreement with or that they are directly opposed to.

Discussion Questions

- This use of social media enables the person who posted the article to engage with others in discussion about an important education policy. In this case the person was able to call attention to a study of Teach for America that highlighted its effectiveness. Identify similar advocacy you have seen on social media recently.

- Social media also has limitations. What are the most significant of these limitations in your opinion?

- Would you be inclined to join such a discussion online? Why or why not?

SUMMARY

This chapter explained persuasion as the strategic use of verbal and nonverbal symbols in an attempt to influence the beliefs, values, and actions of an audience. It has contrasted the manner in which a presentation used to begin deliberation differs from a presentation designed to persuade audience members toward a particular position. Specifically, we have seen:

- Persuasion is a necessary and important aspect of civic engagement as democratic participants move from deliberation to advocacy.
- The important role that invention plays in the process as a rhetor seeks to identify the strongest arguments in favor of his or her approach and respond to the arguments of others.
- The value of using heuristic devices to generate ideas and specific arguments from the research and study that speakers conduct in order to engage in advocacy.
- The three primary modes of proof—logos, pathos, and ethos—employed in the construction of persuasive presentations.
- The six steps in the persuasive process to move audience members to change their thinking, convictions, and their actions (consider audience analysis and adaptation, select a persuasive goal, frame your persuasive efforts, identify an issue worthy of attention, offer a superior solution, and empower your audience and provide a means to act).
- Framing an issue for an audience for a persuasive presentation differs from framing an issue for a deliberative discussion.

KEY TERMS

consciousness-raising
  speech p. 250
heuristics p. 243
invention p. 243
logos p. 246

persuasion p. 241
speeches that offer
  means to action
  p. 250

speeches to convince
  p. 250

REVIEW QUESTIONS

1. What is invention?
2. How do heuristic devices help speakers and writers form their ideas?
3. What are the three modes of proof for proving an idea or claim as identified by Aristotle?
4. What are the three different persuasive goals that can be pursued in a speech?
5. What are the six steps in the persuasive process?

DISCUSSION QUESTIONS

1. Aristotle asserts that ethos is the most important of the proofs. Do you agree with this assessment?
2. For Aristotle, the modes of proof were to be used in combination but with the special instruction that pathos *not* be used as the sole means of persuasion. Why do you think Aristotle objected to basing persuasion solely on pathos? Do you agree with that instruction? Why or why not?
3. How can we distinguish between personal gain and the public good in relation to persuasion? How might these motivations or goals differ? Overlap?
4. Do the means of persuasion ever justify the ends? That is, as long as the behavior, value, or belief that you convince an audience to accept is in their best interest, does it really matter how you convince them to do it? What about when a political candidate uses dishonest framing in order to win an election—but then ultimately governs well?

CHAPTER 13

Practicing Good Reasoning through Quality Arguments

Chapter Objectives

Students will:

- Construct sound arguments.
- Analyze arguments for their strengths and weaknesses.
- Evaluate common types of evidence to assess their quality.
- Learn patterns of reasoning.
- Identify common reasoning fallacies.

On June 14, 1993, in the White House Rose Garden, President Bill Clinton introduced Ruth Bader Ginsburg as his choice to fill a vacancy on the US Supreme Court. The Supreme Court serves a vital civic function and public service as the ultimate interpreter of the Constitution and maintaining the rule of law. Supreme Court justices regularly make arguments that justify their decisions in cases ranging from voting rights to employment discrimination to the meaning of the First Amendment. These decisions are informed by the Constitution, federal and state statutes, prior legal precedents, wisdom of past justices, and other sources.

Although not a legal opinion, future Justice Ginsburg's brief address accepting her nomination also reflected principles of argumentation. In her remarks of appreciation, Ginsburg advanced arguments regarding the significance of her nomination and her perspective on the work of a Supreme Court justice. Ginsburg's first claim was a personal one, offering that her nomination to the Supreme Court, where she would join Justice Sandra Day O'Connor as only the second female ever to sit on the Court, "contributes to the end of the days when women, at least one-half the talent pool in our society, appear in high places only as one-at-a-time performers." In support of her claim, she provided examples and statistics that demonstrated the expanding presence of women in the federal judiciary, starting with Shirley Hufstedler's status as the

Judge Ruth Bader Ginsburg in the Rose Garden of the White House on Monday, June 14, 1993, after President Bill Clinton announced her nomination to the Supreme Court.

only woman federal judge in 1976 to the nearly 25 women who served on federal courts in 1993. Moreover, Ginsburg pointed to changes in law school enrollments as further evidence of the growth in equal opportunity in the legal sphere. Drawing from her own experience, Ginsburg noted that she was one of fewer than 10 women in her law school class of more than 500, while "today few law schools have female enrollment under 40 percent, and several have reached or passed the 50 percent mark." Ginsburg thus used these examples and statistics as evidence of a trend that signaled growing equality of opportunity.

For her second argument, Ginsburg reasoned from two pieces of testimony that provided preliminary evidence for her "views of the work of a good judge on a high court bench." Her evidence drew on the authority and credibility of then Supreme Court Chief Justice William Rehnquist and his view that each case demands a fair decision divorced from what might be seen as popular. Further, she quoted law professor Burt Neuborne's assessment of the lessons of judicial etiquette provided by the former Justice Oliver Wendell Holmes, and the necessity of "intellectual honesty," "disciplined self-restraint," and "defense of individual autonomy."[1] In this way, on a ceremonial occasion, Justice Ginsburg used examples, statistics, and testimony—common forms of evidence—to advance important arguments about the growing opportunities for women in the law and the obligations of a Supreme Court justice in deciding difficult cases.

While you are not in the position of a Supreme Court justice evaluating and issuing arguments on significant legal matters, every day you encounter and make a variety of arguments. You might advance an argument in your living unit encouraging members to organize a charity walk or to form a study group in hopes of strengthening your academic standing. Alternatively, you might present a series of arguments to your parents about why they should purchase you a car for school or send (more) spending money to you while at college. Then, later that night, while watching ESPN's

Sports Center, you might watch an argument that makes a case for Clayton Kershaw as the best pitcher in baseball or why Jamaal Charles is a better option than Aaron Rodgers for the number one pick in a fantasy football draft.

Of course, as the chapter's opening example demonstrates, we also routinely experience arguments about important civic matters. We might read a letter in the local paper by a school board member arguing why a local property tax increase is necessary to improve area schools. At a League of Women Voters candidate forum, a city council candidate might make an argument about why the city should annex county lands to raise revenues. And on news programs and in public speeches, we daily hear politicians and political operatives advance competing arguments over the best way to run the country: whether health insurance should be mandatory; if National Security Agency (NSA) telephone surveillance programs are necessary; or the best approach for addressing a nation in possession of chemical weapons.

With so many different arguments competing for our adherence, how do we make decisions about personal matters, about what is best for our local community, and about what direction the nation should pursue regarding the vital issues of the day? Throughout this textbook we have encouraged you to think carefully and critically about public issues. By learning more specifically about reasoning, about argumentation, you will improve your ability to make sound decisions and critically analyze public options. You will also learn about the substance of speechmaking as most speeches are formed from of a series of arguments. This chapter examines reasoning in public speaking by considering three fundamental issues: the meaning of argument and its structure, the evaluation of evidence, and patterns of reasoning and reasoning fallacies.

ARGUMENT AND THE TOULMIN MODEL

An **argument** is the advocacy of an idea, position, or course of action that is supported by evidence. An argument (or series of arguments) gives reasons why a listener or reader should agree with a perspective being advocated. We begin by considering the study of argument and the development of what is known as the Toulmin model as well as some limitations to the practice of good reasoning.

Classical Reasoning

Aristotle advocated the syllogism as the proper form of argument.[2] A **syllogism** is a three-step proposition that consists of two premises and a conclusion; if the premises are valid, then the conclusion must be true. This is also what is known as **deductive reasoning**, or reasoning that moves from valid premises to a specific conclusion. The classic example of a syllogism is:

> All men are mortal. (major premise)
> Socrates is a man. (minor premise)
> Therefore Socrates is mortal. (conclusion)

If the two premises can be proven true, then it follows that the conclusion *must* also be true. This is also the process of formal logic, which relies upon the certainty of the offered premises in reaching what is considered an unquestioned, or true, conclusion.[3] The effective use of a syllogism is demonstrated in an argument advanced by Hogwarts Headmaster Albus Dumbledore in J. K. Rowling's *Harry Potter and the Order of the Phoenix*, Rowling's fifth entry in her best-selling series. At a hearing held to consider Harry's unauthorized use of magic to repel a dementor (creatures that guard Azkaban, the wizard prison) attack, Dumbledore argued: "If it is true that the dementors are taking orders only from the Ministry of Magic, and it is also true that two dementors attacked Harry and his cousin a week ago, then it follows logically that somebody at the Ministry might have ordered the attacks."[4] Dumbledore employed deductive reasoning in making his argument and expressed his case in the form of a syllogism:

> Dementors take orders only from the Ministry of Magic. (major premise)
> Harry and his cousin were attacked by two dementors. (minor premise)
> Therefore, somebody at the Ministry ordered the attacks. (conclusion)

If his two premises are established as accurate, then under the conventions of deductive reasoning Dumbledore has made a logical—and indisputable—argument.

While the syllogism is a useful, valid argumentative form—as is deductive reasoning generally—it is overly restrictive given the nature of public communication. In argumentative situations and general conversation, we rarely have premises and conclusions that are accepted as absolutely true, and just as often some premises are omitted from an argument. Reflecting such tendencies of rhetoric, Aristotle identified the enthymeme as a rhetorical syllogism. An **enthymeme** is an informal, incomplete syllogism in which a speaker, rather than stating all premises, relies on the audience to use its knowledge and experience to supply missing information or alternative explanations that complete the argument. For example, in the underdeveloped argument, "NSA surveillance is justified because it is crucial to the nation's antiterrorism efforts," a central, unstated premise is "the government should vigorously pursue terrorists." The enthymeme relies on, even expects, listeners to supply the missing reasoning that completes the argument.

But notice that these premises can also be debated or argued. Even if, as an audience member, we are able to supply a missing premise, we might still choose to reject the argument, in this case that "NSA surveillance is justified."[5] This is because the probabilistic and contingent nature of enthymematic premises allows reasonable people to disagree on uncertain public matters that are open to multiple possibilities and perspectives.[6] We typically see shades of gray—exceptions and possible objections or counter-arguments—in premises and conclusions, with the accompanying result that we frequently offer complex arguments that defy categorization in classical syllogistic form.

Using the Toulmin Model

Because of concerns over the application of syllogistic reasoning, in the late 1950s Stephen Toulmin developed an alternative approach that is now accepted as the standard in argument studies.[7] This approach, popularly known as the **Toulmin model**, provides a way to conceptualize, verify, and critique arguments. In its full form, the model consists of as many as seven parts (see Box 13-1); however, we primarily focus on its three most central components: claim, data, and warrant.

The **claim** of an argument is what you are attempting to prove and want an audience to accept. Examples of claims include "I should study chemistry this evening." "I attend an outstanding school." "My public speaking professor is the best ☺." In public speaking, we use claims in multiple ways. First, a thesis statement is itself a claim—in fact it is the most important claim you make in a speech. For instance, in a persuasive speech you might offer the thesis: "Procedures for Greek rush should be revised." While this thesis will guide your speech, it is not the only claim you will make. Each main point—each reason for changing how Greek rush is handled—is itself a claim that supports your thesis. These are what we call *subclaims* because they are subordinate to the larger argument.

BOX 13-1

The Toulmin Model

Born in London, Stephen Toulmin (1922–2009) originally studied mathematics and physics before turning to philosophy after World War II.[8] The primary focus of his work was on ethics, logic, and reasoning. While Toulmin authored several books and taught at a number of institutions in the United States, he is best known for the model of argument that came to be identified with his name. In his 1958 book *The Uses of Argument*, Toulmin originally posited the model as consisting of six parts, but following the work of argumentation scholars Richard D. Rieke, Malcolm O. Sillars, and Tarla Rai Peterson, we offer the full model as containing seven elements:

- **Claim**: The idea one is trying to prove and desires an audience to accept.
- **Data**: Material that supports the acceptance of the claim. It answers the question, "Why?" or "What have you got to go on?"
- **Warrant**: Bridge-like statement that justifies the connection between data and claim. The warrant is often implied and answers the question, "How do you get there?"
- **Backing**: More specific evidence that reinforces data or warrant. It explains data or warrant as being, "On account of."
- **Qualifier**: A term that modifies the strength or force of the claim such as "might," "usually," or "always."
- **Reservation**: A condition of exception in which the claim would not be advanced or advocated. A reservation might be noted by terms like "except" or "unless."
- **Rebuttal**: A basis for challenging the validity of the claim.

A claim alone, however, does not complete an argument. When a claim is offered without reason, support, or what we call data it is merely an assertion, a term previously introduced in chapter 3. An assertion fails to qualify as an argument because no reason is given as to why it should be accepted. This is why **data**, material and reasons that support the acceptance of the claim, are essential in forming a valid argument.

Data are typically found throughout a speech and take on a variety of forms, which we address momentarily. Data fill in the "why" or "because" for the thesis. Taking the earlier thesis statement on Greek rush as our example, one might ask, "Why should Greek rush be changed?" Your answer—"Rush should be altered *because* . . ."—would reveal useful data supporting the claim. Data could consist of statistics on recent (de)pledging, testimony about unfair rush practices, testimony from prospective pledges about their perceptions of the process, examples of problems with the rush system, and so on. Each piece of information allows you to better support the claim and, thus, to more convincingly persuade an audience to accept your argument.

Finally, a valid argument rests upon an acceptable warrant. The **warrant** provides justification for using the data to support the claim. In essence the warrant is a bridge, often in the form of a value statement, that connects the data with the claim, reinforcing their relationship. Because of this, the warrant, according to Toulmin, answers the question, "How do you get there?" Warrants are typically implied rather than stated; however, at times it is important to state your warrant as well. Consider the following example to understand how a warrant functions:

Claim: I should replace my old truck with a new hybrid vehicle.
Data: because hybrid vehicles produce significantly less environmental pollution.

Now, the question the warrant wants to answer is how we get from the data to the claim—or what makes this data a justifiable reason to accept the claim.

Warrant: Reducing automotive emissions is environmentally responsible.

It is likely that this warrant would be implied, in essence relying on enthymematic reasons from an audience. Presumably, the positive contribution to the environment is a strong enough incentive to cause the person making this argument to take action. However, keep in mind that there could be counter-arguments or rebuttals that might cause this person to decide not to enact this action (the cost of a new vehicle for example). A more developed argument would consider these possibilities by providing *backing* for the warrant and/or data in quantifying the environmental benefits.

Finally, we can visualize this argument in the form of a Toulmin model:

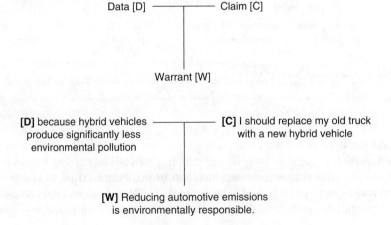

The Toulmin model is more than a way of diagramming arguments—it is a way of improving how you *think* about arguments. It allows you to conceptualize and diagnose your own arguments and those produced by others. You can put an argument into the Toulmin form to see what the claim is and if it is reasonable; to consider what the data are, if there is enough, and the data's quality; and if there is a reasonable warrant, or one can be inferred, that connects the data and the claim. Because the model promotes clearer thinking about how we reason together, it is a way of enriching our civic engagement and the messages we send and receive about democratic participation. That is, analyzing an argument in the form of a Toulmin model lets us see exactly what it is we are asking others to accept, how we are supporting our view, and what we are taking for granted and assuming others will accept at face value. In reexamining such assumptions, we can strengthen our argument by clarifying and limiting our claims and by providing data and warrants that might not be taken for granted or easily accepted by our listeners.

Arguments and Their Limits

Rhetorical arguments are powerful but inexact. Due to the nature of audiences and their views (see chapter 5), arguments that are formally accurate and complete sometimes fail to gain adherence, while other arguments that seem deficient, to some listeners at least, can prove successful. Such a possibility is realized in how respected and knowledgeable public servants, including judges, legislatures, and city councils, can advance and weigh arguments on public issues and yet still come to different conclusions about their merit. As an example, think about this abbreviated (and asserted) causal argument: "People should not smoke because scores of scientific studies have proven that smoking has significant adverse health effects, including death." In a Toulmin form the argument would appear:

[D] because scores of scientific studies —————— [C] People should not smoke
have proven that smoking has
significant adverse health effects,
including death

[W] [Implied] We should not harm our bodies.
Staying alive is important.

While the specific evidence has not been provided, a wealth of valid backing is available from the Centers for Disease Control and Prevention and other sources.[9] What is important for the point being made, however, is that according to the American Cancer Society, as of 2012 approximately 42 million adults in the United States (18% of the adult population) smoked.[10] This suggests that despite strong evidence supporting the argument, millions of people fail to give it adherence. The reasons are no doubt varied, including value hierarchies that justify the decision to smoke, challenges to the evidence concerning the impacts of smoking, and the difficulty of kicking the habit. The example, however, demonstrates that sometimes people refuse to reason; that some appeals, urges, and habits overcome reason; and that not all decision-makers will weigh competing arguments, values, and concerns the same way. The point, which is an important one, also underscores that public speaking is a holistic enterprise not only consisting of sound arguments but how those arguments are presented to and received by particular audiences. Public speakers must utilize a range of rhetorical and persuasive techniques, and they must be presented in a clear and organized manner to be effective.

EVIDENCE AND ITS EVALUATION

Evidence is data and backing in the form of examples, statistics, and testimony that is used to support a claim. As examined in chapter 4 on research, evidence can be obtained from a variety of sources including books, newspapers, popular magazines, scholarly journals, interviews, official documents, common knowledge, direct observation, and, of course, the Internet. However, as that earlier chapter demonstrates, the key is finding not just any evidence, but the *best* evidence to support your argument. Consequently, you need to learn to not only locate relevant evidence but also to *evaluate* it. Strong evidence justifies your claim. When you use weak evidence, your data will generally be insufficient to convince an audience of the validity of your argument. The following sections discuss types of evidence that you will encounter and provide instructions for selecting quality evidence and evaluating its strength.

BOX 13-2

Four Criteria to Consider When Choosing Sources and Evidence

1. Relevance: The evidence must be relevant to your claim.
2. Recency: The evidence should be timely or considered current for the situation and topic.
3. Credibility: The source of the evidence should be of appropriate authority, expertise, or reputation.
4. Bias: The evidence should have a low degree of bias, and any bias should be acknowledged.

For more information see chapter 4, pp. 74–78.

Examples

An **example** is evidence that supports a claim by providing a concrete instance in the form of a fact or occurrence. An example seeks to make a claim tangible or verifiable to the audience. For this reason, the most valuable type of example is known as a *specific example* or *specific instance*. A specific example is one that is factual, one that has actually happened or is being experienced. A specific example prompts the audience to recognize that the claim (or a similar claim) has been demonstrated or proven true on a prior occasion. In a December 2012 speech following the school shootings in Newtown, Connecticut, National Rifle Association Executive Vice President Wayne LaPierre advanced the argument that the media and media producers bore responsibility for some of the violence plaguing American culture. In support of the claim that "there exists in this country, sadly, a callous, corrupt, and corrupting shadow industry that sells and stows violence against its own people," LaPierre named a series of media products as supporting examples. Specifically, he identified "vicious, violent video games . . . like 'Bullet Storm,' 'Grand Theft Auto,' 'Mortal Combat,' and 'Splatterhouse,'" as well as "blood-soaked films . . . like 'American Psycho,' [and] 'Natural Born Killers.'"[11] The power of the examples is in their succinct expression and concrete existence as media messages containing large amounts of violent content.

In selecting examples, speakers should favor examples that are believable and detailed over those that have lost their effectiveness because of overuse. However, combining a familiar, commonly accepted example with a second example that is unique, memorable, and recent can solidify a point by demonstrating both the historic and contemporary relevance of the argument.

A less powerful, but still useful, type of example is a *hypothetical example.* A hypothetical example is based on an event or circumstance that is plausible but does not represent an actual event. This sort of example is helpful by allowing the audience to visualize the claim, but it does not provide the concrete data that a specific example does. For instance, in 2009 when President Obama signed an executive order lifting the prohibition on federal funding for embryonic stem cell research, he pointed to the possible future benefits of such research "to regenerate a severed spinal cord and lift someone from a wheelchair. To spur insulin production and spare a child from a lifetime of needles. To treat Parkinson's, cancer, heart disease and others that affect millions of Americans and the people who love them."[12] President Obama could not use specific examples as support because the potential benefits of embryonic stem cell research have not yet been realized. However, by referring to potential uses of the research in the form of hypothetical examples, he allowed his audience to visualize his message and, in turn, understand his decision for signing the order.

Finally, *anecdotes, extended examples,* or *illustrations* are more elaborate examples that include additional detail. Often presented in the form of personal narratives, these examples attempt a deeper, more extended connection with the audience, and rather than rely on the power of the audience's memory or their knowledge, as specific examples frequently do, these examples create a sense of visualization or identification. While powerful, these take more time for a speaker to develop and present. An example of a speaker who effectively used an illustration, or personal narrative, is Mitt Romney in his August 30, 2012, speech accepting the Republican presidential nomination. In that speech Romney claimed that he possessed a quality that Barack Obama lacked—successful experience working in business. As evidence of his success, Romney offered an extended example:

> I learned the real lessons about how America works from experience. When I was 37, I helped start a small company . . . called Bain Capital. The only problem was, while we believed in ourselves, nobody else did. We were young and had never done this before and we almost didn't get off the ground. In those days, sometimes I wondered if I'd made a really big mistake. . . . That business we started with 10 people has now grown into a great American success story. Some of the companies we helped start are names you know. An office supply company called

Staples. . . . The Sports Authority, which of course became a favorite of my sons. We helped start an early childhood learning center called Bright Horizons. . . . [And] at a time when nobody thought we'd ever see a new steel mill built in America, we took a chance and built one in a corn field in Indiana. Today, Steel Dynamics is one of the largest steel producers in the United States.[13]

Here Mitt Romney offers an illustration of his business success, one that is much richer than referring to Bain Capital alone or simply stating his net worth. The illustration works by naming specifics of the situation and tangible outcomes, but also by providing insight into the effort and life of Romney.

Not all examples are equal, and thus you must take time in the selection and evaluation of examples. If you select a poor example—an example that upon closer inspection does not justify your claim—you risk damaging your credibility and failing to achieve your argumentative objective. Similarly, if as a listener you uncritically accept examples offered by a speaker, you may be duped by an unscrupulous or uninformed orator. It is your responsibility to critically examine the worth of an example.

Selecting and Evaluating Examples:

1. Is the example *representative* of the broader situation or experience? That is, is it typical?
2. Are there a sufficient number of examples to prove the claim? If only a single example has been provided, it is unlikely to prove persuasive to the audience.
3. Have negative examples (counter-examples) been addressed? Why are they insufficient to disprove or refute the claim?
4. Is the example compelling in its detail, clarity, and vividness? Does it work to verify the claim and make it tangible?

An example may not meet all of these standards and still be satisfactory, but these are the sorts of questions a skilled speaker and listener should consider when evaluating the worth of an example.

Statistics

Statistics, a second common form of evidence, represent information in numeric form according to the size, quantity, or frequency of an idea, outcome, or occurrence. In public speaking, statistics are most commonly used to demonstrate public opinion and efficiently express the distribution and allocation of resources. Speakers love statistics—and with a little searching it seems we can find a statistic for just about anything, be it the number of pieces of mail delivered annually by the US Postal Service (160 billion), the percentage of people who believe in extraterrestrials (about 50% of Americans), or the average night's sleep in America (six-and-a-half hours on workdays).[14]

Because statistics have an air of tangibility, appear to be exact, and seem authoritative, we too often accept that if there is a number for it, then it must be true. In reality, statistics should be carefully scrutinized. As American author and satirist Mark Twain is purported to have once said: there are lies, damned lies, and statistics.

In his July 18, 2012, appearance before the House Committee on Financial Services, Ben Bernanke's report on the state of the US economy relied heavily on statistics.

Nonetheless, statistics are an important, useful, and frequent basis of proof in many speeches. For instance, in his July 18, 2012, remarks before the US House of Representatives' Committee on Financial Services, former Federal Reserve Board Chairman Ben Bernanke relied heavily on statistics in advancing his case for the nation's economic outlook. Bernanke began by explaining that growth in gross domestic product (GDP), a measure of the nation's economic health, had slowed from an annual rate of increase of 2.5% in the second half of 2011 to only a 2% increase in the first quarter of 2012. Similarly, Bernanke pointed to improvements in the labor market in late 2011 with unemployment falling about a percentage point and around 200,000 jobs being added per month. However, those gains had slowed to only 75,000 new jobs added monthly in the second quarter of 2012. Due to such changes, the Federal Open Market Committee predicted only moderate economic growth in the near term with the committee members' projections "for growth in real GDP" having "a central tendency of 1.9 percent to 2.4 percent for" 2012 and "2.2 percent to 2.8 percent for 2013." These statistics, which reflect the use of raw numbers, trends, and averages, three of the types of statistics explained next, were only a few of the many numbers offered by Bernanke as he proceeded to address the performance of the Personal Consumption Expenditures price index, inflation projections, housing market statistics, and more.[15]

Four of the most common forms of statistics called upon by public speakers are averages, raw numbers, trends, and polls. An *average* is a common and seemingly benign statistic that is quite frequently used and is of value to a speaker. In principle it represents what is typical—what is average—and we see Federal Reserve Board Chair Bernanke making use of the average projected GDP growth predicted by members of the Federal Open Market Committee. In this way an average can allow a speaker to communicate to the audience a typical experience, be it the average income in a profession or community, the average number of sick days taken by workers in a particular industry, or another useful number.

However, an average may be more complicated than it initially appears because there are at least three methods for determining an average—through mean, median, or mode. The most common method for representing an average is the mean. A *mean* is derived by taking all the data and dividing it by the total number of data points. The median, by way of contrast, is the data point that appears in the exact middle of a sample, and the mode is the number that appears most frequently. Suppose, for instance, you were leading a discussion about the low working wages available for college students seeking summer employment. A statistic you might find valuable is the amount earned by the average student worker in your class during the previous summer (this would be a small sample, but a relevant one to your audience). If you had access to all the financial data, you could determine the mean income by adding together the total dollars earned by your classmates and then dividing it by the number of student workers. If 25 students had combined wages of $120,000, the *mean* student income was $4,800. Seems clear enough, right? However, what if you found that this included $40,000 earned by a single student in an astoundingly successful entrepreneurial venture? How does this change the average, and what does it do to the value, meaning, and accuracy of this statistic for your speech?[16]

A second common statistic is a *raw number*. In the previous example, the raw number is $120,000—the total wages earned—while we also saw Ben Bernanke make use of two raw numbers—200,000 jobs added per month to the economy in late 2011, and 75,000 jobs per month added in the first quarter of 2012. We use raw numbers when we want to draw on the power of the magnitude of a number. An average may make a number seem small or insignificant, but by giving the entire scope of the data through the use of raw numbers, the audience may gain a better grasp of the situation. However, the opposite may also be true: a raw number can make a problem look much worse than it actually is because it combines all the data into a single representation. For instance, if you were to learn that the United States reduced its 2014 defense budget by $25 billion (a raw number), you might be concerned about the seemingly large amount cut. However, if you also were provided with a trend statistic that clarified this represented a budget cut of only about 4.8% and that defense spending grew from $287 billion to $530 billion between 2001 and 2013, you would probably reevaluate the meaning of the $25 billion cut.[17]

When a speaker wants to demonstrate a change that has occurred over a period of time, the statistic that is most often used is called a *trend*. By using a trend statistic, you can emphasize change in a clearer and more meaningful way because it gives two points of comparison. The defense budget example shows the percent decrease in the budget but also a 12-year trend in budget growth. And, as the Bernanke example demonstrates, trend statistics are common for economic measures as economists and investors watch trends in such areas as GDP, unemployment, interest rates, inflation, and housing starts. Trend statistics can provide a more focused and efficient evaluation of the immediate economic climate.

Finally, perhaps the most popular type of statistic is polling data. A valid, scientific *poll* attempts to measure the opinions or beliefs of a large group of people by collecting data from what is known as a representative random sample—a sample that is similar in its demographics to the rest of the population—and then generalizes the results. Polling data is collected on a variety of topics, ranging from whom one intends to vote for in a presidential election to what is the best movie ever made. One of the oldest and most recognized polling researchers is Gallup, which bills itself as knowing "more about the attitudes and behaviors of employees, customers, students and citizens than any other organization in the world." Gallup regularly tracks opinions on various topics, such as consumer confidence, presidential approval, and even happiness.[18]

While polling data must be carefully analyzed, it also can be very valuable in giving your specific audience an indication of what a larger public thinks. That is, while the majority may not always be right, their opinion can be very influential. Thus, in attempting to persuade an audience to act in a certain way, it is common for a speaker to call on public opinion to demonstrate that people support or believe in a proposed change, course of action, or decision. For example, in *Speaking with the People's Voice: How Presidents Invoke Public Opinion*, rhetoric scholar Jeffrey P. Mehltretter Drury provides a series of examples and case studies that consider how presidents invoke and lead public opinion in order to justify and promote their own policy positions. By examining how presidents use public opinion on specific issues, ranging from war and foreign policy to the need for a balanced budget amendment, Drury demonstrates the rhetorical force of public opinion as data for claims advanced by presidents.[19]

Not all polls, however, are equally valid, and in selecting polling data there are several items you should consider. In particular, you should verify that the poll is based on a representative random sample. This can be determined by examining how the poll was conducted—who was polled, how they were polled, how many people were polled, when they were polled—and what the margin of error is. You also must be careful how you use nonscientific Internet polling that asks website visitors their opinion on an issue. Such polls have a selection bias in terms of who chooses to take the poll. For example, ESPN's SportsNation gives fans the opportunity to express their opinion on various issues, including who should be elected to the Baseball Hall of Fame, who will win the Super Bowl, and who is the National Football League MVP. Such polls are interesting to sports fans, and do show something of popular opinion, but be mindful that the results are not statistically valid.[20]

BOX 13-3

The American Freshman

The Cooperative Institutional Research Program (CIRP) Freshman Survey, administered by the Higher Education Research Institute (HERI) at UCLA, is taken by tens of thousands of first-time full-time college students each fall. In 2012, 192,219 new students from 283 four-year schools participated in the survey. Among the results:

- 87.9% of respondents indicated that getting a better job was a "very important" reason they decided to attend college.

- 74.6% of respondents indicated making more money was a "very important" reason they decided to attend college.

- 81% of respondents indicated a personal goal of being well-off financially.

- 47.5% of respondents perceived themselves as "middle-of-the-road" politically.

The survey also measures new students' opinion on social and political issues of the day:

ISSUE	2012 RESPONDENTS INDICATING AGREE STRONGLY OR AGREE SOMEWHAT	2008 RESPONDENTS INDICATING AGREE STRONGLY OR AGREE SOMEWHAT
A national healthcare plan is needed to cover everybody's medical costs	62.7%	70.3%
Abortion should be legal	61.1%	58.2%
Students from disadvantaged social backgrounds should be given preferential treatment in college admissions	41.9%	39.5%
Racial discrimination is no longer a major problem in America	23%	20.1%
Same-sex couples should have the right to legal marital status	75%	66.2%

- What other information would you want to know about the data before deciding whether to use it?
- How useful might this information be to a speaker planning a presentation on a related topic?
- How might the information be misused or overgeneralized?
- What information do these results leave out?

SOURCE: *The American Freshman: National Norms Fall 2012*, Higher Education Research Institute Research Brief, Jan. 2013, http://heri.ucla.edu/briefs/TheAmericanFreshman2012-Brief.pdf. The American Freshman Survey Publications, Higher Education Research Institute, http://heri.ucla.edu/tfsPublications.php.

In sum, it is crucial that you carefully scrutinize statistics. You should learn and understand as much as possible about how a statistic was derived so that you have a good grasp of its validity. It is ethically suspect to simply report a number without some understanding of what it means and how it was calculated. Similarly, as a listener, be skeptical of statistics presented without enough information to evaluate their credibility. A statistical conclusion is only as good as the method by which it was derived. For that reason, here are a few questions you should ask when *selecting and evaluating statistics*:

1. If the number is an average, how was it determined? Is it the mean, the median, or the mode? Is it representative of the data, or is it skewed by a data point that is unique because it was either extremely large or small?
2. What was the sample size? How many people were used to determine the average represented in the number? How many people were polled to determine the final polling results?

3. If using polling data, what is the margin of error or reliability? Polls that have a margin of error greater than a few percentage points are suspect, particularly if the final polling numbers are very close.
4. What do you know about the sample? Was it randomly selected? Where were the data collected? Are there factors about the sample population that make the data suspect?
5. When was the data collected? Perhaps more than any other type of evidence, the validity of a statistic is dependent on its date of origin. Public opinion can change quickly. Similarly, averages and raw numbers collected even a year or two prior may no longer reflect contemporary conditions.

Testimony

Testimony is a third common form of evidence that serves as data and backing for arguments. **Testimony** is facts or opinions derived from the words, experiences, and expertise of another individual. Speakers use testimony to supplement their own opinions and experiences. Testimony should come from experts and people with firsthand experience on an issue. Suppose you decide to give a speech on US foreign policy in the Middle East. You may have some very clever and sensible ideas, but since it is improbable that you possess foreign policy expertise, the audience is unlikely to accept your position based on your opinions alone. For that reason you would do well to build your credibility by supplying well-informed testimony as data for your claims. Perhaps you would draw on testimony from Secretary of State John Kerry or from former Secretary of State Condoleezza Rice. Testimony from these figures about the wisdom of your proposal would significantly aid the power of your argument.

In a 2011 speech at the Lyndon Baines Johnson Presidential Library on the subject of voter registration and rights, then Attorney General Eric Holder used testimony to support his contentions that voting rights are important and in need of attention. Near the start of his address, to underscore the importance of his topic, Holder quoted former President Johnson as saying "the right to vote is the basic right, without which all others are meaningless." Moreover, in urging his audience to action in defending voting rights, the last evidence used in the speech was also testimony from President Johnson, this time appealing to the concept of justice: "America was the first nation in the history of the world to be founded with a purpose—to right wrong, [and] to do justice." In these passages Holder drew from Johnson's authority as president, the president who in 1965 signed the Voting Rights Act into law, and his credibility as the namesake of the library in which this speech was given. In turn, to establish that there was a threat to this essential right, Holder called on US Congressman John Lewis, a civil rights leader from the 1960s with firsthand knowledge and experience of the struggles over voter registration and voting rights. Holder quoted Lewis as evidence that voting rights are "under attack . . . [by] a deliberate and systematic attempt to prevent millions of elderly voters, young voters, students, [and] minority and low-income voters from exercising their constitutional right to engage in the democratic pro[cess]."[21] In this way Attorney General Holder, himself a credible source based on his title and position, enhanced his argument through the use of testimony.

As with the other forms of evidence, there are some considerations to make when *selecting and evaluating testimony*:

1. The individual providing testimony should be a qualified authority on the topic being discussed. The testimony will strengthen your speech only if the person can truly add insight; just because you find a source on a topic doesn't mean that the source's testimony is worth using.

2. Testimony is best when the source has clear expertise and firsthand knowledge of the issue. Ideally, the testimony is based on experience rather than opinion, and the source has had close dealings with the issues you are addressing. In demonstrating this expertise, you should clearly identify the person as an authority by giving their qualifications *prior* to presenting the evidence.

3. The source of the testimony should not have excessive personal interest in the issue, which we established earlier as a form of bias.

4. Finally, be sure to understand the *assumptions* of the testimony. You should not pull testimony from a source and place it in a different context. You must consider what the speaker assumed when he or she made the comments and consider whether those assumptions fit with your own assumptions and argument.

Examples, statistics, and testimony are necessary components of arguments as they provide the substance used to verify claims. While these forms of evidence have been introduced separately, they are best used together. That is, strong arguments combine examples, statistics, and testimony in appealing to audiences in complex, multifaceted ways. In fact, it is not uncommon for a piece of testimony to include an example or statistic or for a statistic to be conveyed in an example. Moreover, effective speakers frequently use all three types of evidence in building their credibility (primarily testimony), making their points concrete (primarily examples), and providing evidence of the scope of an issue (primarily statistics). For example, in addition to using testimony in his previously mentioned speech on voting rights and registration, Attorney General Holder also used examples of redistricting plans that would impact minority voters and "misinformation campaigns" that sought to convince citizens that they lacked the right to vote. Likewise, Holder used Census Bureau data—statistics related to population growth and voter registration numbers—to make claims about the allocation of congressional seats and the need to ease the voter registration process. Holder's address thus reflects the principle that a speech that relies exclusively on any one form of evidence will likely be found lacking by an audience. Table 13.1 summarizes useful guidelines for selecting and evaluating examples, statistics, and testimony as you build and listen to speeches and arguments, there are two additional questions you can ask about evidence, regardless of what form it takes:

- Does the evidence provide explanation and analysis? Short examples that don't demonstrate a connection to your situation or testimony that is declarative often won't further your argument. For example, a piece of testimony from an economic analyst that says simply, "the current economic recovery will not continue," really *doesn't say much*. The testimony fails to provide explanation or analysis for *why* the perspective is justified.

Table 13.1 Guidelines for Selecting and Evaluating Evidence

UNIVERSAL CRITERIA	USING EXAMPLES	USING STATISTICS	USING TESTIMONY
• Is the evidence relevant?	• Is the example representative?	• How was the average arrived at?	• Is the source a qualified authority?
• Is the evidence recent?	• Are there a sufficient number of examples?	• What is the sample size?	• Does the source have firsthand knowledge?
• Is the evidence credible?	• Have negative examples been addressed?	• What is the margin of error or reliability of the poll?	• Does the source have excessive personal interest
• Does the evidence contain bias?	• Are the examples compelling in their detail and clarity?	• What is known about the sample?	or bias?
• Does the evidence provide explanation and analysis?		• When was the data collected?	• Have assumptions in the testimony been accounted for?
• What is the certainty of the evidence?			

- What is the certainty of the material? Examine the evidence for qualifiers. A *qualifier*, which is a component of the Toulmin model, is a term that impacts the strength of the evidence. Qualifiers such as "could," "might," and "should" weaken the strength of the argument by reducing the level of certainty. In contrast, qualifiers such as "will" and "must" can strengthen an argument.

PATTERNS OF REASONING AND REASONING FALLACIES

When you develop arguments in a speech you have a variety of different approaches available. These options are located in what we call **patterns of reasoning**. A reasoning pattern is derived from *what kind* of data or evidence is selected and *how* that data or evidence is used to prove a claim. A typical speech uses a variety of types of reasoning to demonstrate that the thesis should be accepted. And while no one pattern is necessarily superior to any other, some patterns naturally lend themselves to certain types and locations of arguments. For example, arguments dealing with religion are more likely to use reasoning from authority. In contrast, arguments that rely heavily upon statistics often utilize reasoning from sign.

Generally, these patterns of reasoning reflect the practice of **inductive reasoning**, a form of reasoning in which a speaker uses a series of examples, instances, or cases to support the likelihood or probability of a conclusion. While inductive reasoning is less formal than deductive reasoning, it can be effectively used to build quality arguments. Inductive arguments are judged based on their quality more than their logical validity; they are evaluated based on the strengths (or weaknesses) of the observational data offered in support of a claim. For example, an inductive argument might be based on a series of examples (the most common form for inductive reasoning), analogies, or even signs that collectively suggest the likelihood of a particular conclusion that can be generalized from the data.

Working in concert with reasoning patterns is a concern for reasoning fallacies. A reasoning **fallacy** refers to a flaw or a defect in reasoning that undermines the validity of an argument. A fallacy doesn't exist simply because we disagree with an argument; instead, it occurs when a reasoning pattern is used incorrectly or ineffectively. This incorrect use is generally due to poor evidence or an implied warrant that is found faulty upon closer inspection. The remainder of this chapter focuses on five patterns of reasoning and how these patterns are sometimes used ineffectively, resulting in reasoning fallacies.

Reasoning from Example

The first type of evidence we discussed was examples. The effort to prove a claim through examples is called, rather obviously, reasoning from example (this type of argument is also called a generalization). If you return to the earlier discussion of examples as evidence, you will find several ways to evaluate reasoning from example. If an example passes those tests and there are a sufficient number to prove the claim, then you can reasonably conclude that you have presented a valid argument (or at least that *this portion* of your argument is valid). If, however, the example(s) violates those conditions, isn't representative of the larger situation, or a sufficient number of examples aren't presented, then a reasoning fallacy has been committed. This reasoning fallacy is known as a **hasty generalization**.

> *Example 1:* President Barack Obama's broken promise that no one would be forced to change their healthcare plan under the Affordable Care Act proves that all presidents mislead the public.[22]

Analysis: Is this example representative? Are there a sufficient number of examples to prove the claim that all presidents mislead the public? Is there enough detail to make this example believable or to prove the president made misleading statements? While one can always ask a variety of questions about an argument, it would appear that this singular, brief example is insufficient to prove that *all* presidents mislead the public.

> *Example 2:* President Obama's broken promise that people could maintain their existing healthcare plans under the Affordable Care Act, President George W. Bush's inaccurate claims about Iraq possessing weapons of mass destruction, President Clinton's denial of a relationship with White House intern Monica Lewinsky, and President George H. W. Bush's violation of his "no new taxes" pledge prove that all recent presidents have misled the country during their public statements.

Analysis: While certainly one could challenge the veracity of the examples, overall this argument is much stronger. Rather than presenting only one example, *four* are offered, which would seem to be a sufficient number. And by limiting or qualifying the claim to "recent" presidents instead of making a claim about all presidents, this argument is initially of sufficient strength to avoid being considered a fallacy.

Reasoning from Analogy

A second common form of argument is to reason from analogy. When you use **analogical reasoning**, you attempt to prove a claim by comparing two situations or cases. For example, when the United States becomes embroiled in a protracted military conflict—or simply risks doing so—it is not uncommon to hear references to "another

Vietnam." This phrase is used as a shorthand argumentative analogy to express reservations about again sending US soldiers abroad for unclear reasons. While the power of this analogy temporarily lessened with the rapid conclusion of the high-tech military intervention in Iraq in 1991, it had a resurgence during the course of the US military involvements in Iraq and Afghanistan beginning in 2003. For example, in a column written for the *Washington Post* in 2009 former South Dakota Senator and one-time Democratic Party nominee for President George McGovern offered reasoning from analogy in comparing US military engagement in Afghanistan with that earlier war:

> As a U.S. senator during the 1960s, I agonized over the badly mistaken war in Vietnam. After doing all I could to save our troops and the Vietnamese people from a senseless conflict, I finally took my case to the public in my presidential campaign in 1972. Speaking across the nation, I told audiences that the only upside of the tragedy in Vietnam was that its enormous cost in lives and dollars would keep any future administration from going down that road again.
>
> I was wrong. Today, I am astounded at the Obama administration's decision to escalate the equally mistaken war in Afghanistan, and as I listen to our talented young president explain why he is adding 30,000 troops—beyond the 21,000 he had already added—I can only think one thing: another Vietnam. I hope I am incorrect, but history tells me otherwise.[23]

In his statement McGovern demonstrates the principle of analogical reasoning—comparing a new situation (a more recent conflict in Afghanistan) with one known by the audience (Vietnam).

In testing analogies speakers and listeners need to examine the similarities and differences between the implicated circumstances. In doing so you might ask:

- Are the situations reasonably comparable?
- Do the situations possess more similarities than differences?

If you answer "yes" to these questions, then you should feel comfortable with the analogy. If, however, you find that the answer to both is "no," then you have encountered or created a fallacy known as a **faulty analogy** (also known as a faulty comparison).

> *Example:* To control rising healthcare costs and protect the poor and uninsured, the United States should adopt a policy of socialized medicine. Socialized medicine has been a success in Canada, so surely it will work in the United States.

Analysis: The first sentence of the example provides the claim and the initial motivation for the claim. The second sentence provides the data intended to explain why the policy will be successful. What your analysis is attempting to do is decide if the link between the claim and data—that is the warrant—is valid. What would the warrant be? The United States and Canada are similar enough that what works in Canada will work in the United States ("so surely it will work in the United States"). Is this warrant, and hence this analogy, valid?

Reasoning from Cause
Another popular pattern of reasoning is causal reasoning. **Causal reasoning** occurs when a speaker claims that an event is caused by a particular circumstance or action.

When a direct link between an action and a consequence is exhibited, then a causal argument can be very effective. A civic issue that produces a range of causal arguments is that of substance abuse. As we demonstrated in the chapter on deliberative discussions, communities have pursued a variety of actions in the hopes of reducing substance abuse, including increasing law enforcement and drug penalties, expanding treatment and recovery options, and providing youth increased education about drugs. In each case an action is adopted in hopes of producing a particular effect on the community. Consider the following causal argument related to the relationship between drug regulation and its production.

> *Example:* By placing new restrictions on the retail availability of products (such as cold medicines) containing pseudoephedrine, 11 states saw their methamphetamine (meth) incidents drop between 2004 and 2010. In Iowa, for example, after adopting regulations requiring pseudoephedrine to be kept behind pharmacy counters and implementing electronic tracking of purchases, the number of meth lab incidents dropped from approximately 1,500 in 2004 to only 200 in 2008.[24]

Analysis: This is a cause-effect argument that offers data related to meth lab incidents to support the claim that regulation has resulted in a particular effect. The argument may need additional development to withstand heavy scrutiny, but in this form it appears a reasonable argument concerning a cause-effect relationship.

In determining whether a causal argument is valid consider the following criteria:

- Does the fact that the effect has occurred after the cause reasonably signify a relationship between the two events?
- Are there important alternative reasons or causes that have been ignored?

When a speaker is guilty of attributing a cause-effect relationship between two items that are not connected, they have created what is known as a **faulty cause** fallacy. Further, when the faulty attribution of cause occurs only after the conclusion of an event (e.g. in hindsight) the reasoning error is more specifically known as a post hoc ("after the fact") fallacy. Take the following example heard from a discouraged New York Mets fan: "I never watch the Mets on television because they always lose when I do." If we return to the Toulmin model we can pinpoint the reasoning flaw in this causal argument:

Claim:	I never watch the Mets on television
Data:	because they always lose when I do.
Warrant [implied]:	What I do determines whether the Mets win or lose.

Does whether or not the person watches the Mets actually determine their performance? There might be a miraculous coincidence between this fan's viewing habits and his favorite team's performance, but in reality we know there is no causal connection between the two. Hence, this beleaguered fan has (knowingly, no doubt) created a faulty cause fallacy of the post hoc variety.

Relatedly, speakers sometimes attempt to use causal reasoning to argue that a single event or action will lead to a chain reaction of cause-and-effect events, typically ending with a catastrophic final effect. To effectively make such an argument, the speaker would need a significant amount of evidence to suggest that one cause-and-effect sequence will lead to another, to another, and to another. However, when speakers advance such arguments without providing the necessary support they commit a reasoning fallacy known as a **slippery slope**, by which they suggest that if a first step is taken, then we will slide all the way down the slope to the very bottom. Consider this response by Steve Jenner, spokesperson for the Plain English Society, after Britain's Mid Devon district council voted to "abolish the apostrophe" from community signs (e.g., "Becks Square" as opposed to "Beck's Square"):

> *Example:* "It's nonsense. . . . Where's it going to stop? Are we going to declare war on commas, outlaw full stops?"

Analysis: This argument advocates the reconsideration of Mid Devon's decision on the grounds that a range of grammatical changes would be expected to follow. What is provided, however, are only asserted assumptions about what a ban of a single type of punctuation might lead to—changing other writing practices. Although that outcome is possible, there is nothing to suggest that it is likely or imminent. Consequently, as Geoffrey Pullum points out in the *Chronicle of Higher Education*, Jenner's response reflects the fallacy of a slippery slope.[25]

Reasoning from Sign

A fourth form of reasoning is called reasoning from sign. **Reasoning from sign** relies on circumstantial evidence, or signs, to demonstrate a claim. For instance, when in response to a dashboard warning light indicator a driver says, "There must be something wrong with my car. The check engine light is on," they have created (and are reacting to) a sign argument. They are basing their claim—"There must be something wrong with my car"—on sign data—"The check engine light is on." The implied warrant to the argument—"vehicle warning lights signal a possible problem"—demonstrates how the sign creates the connection between data and claim. The warning light indicates to the driver that the car should be checked by a mechanic. Note, however, that the engine light is not the cause of the problem, nor is it the problem itself; it is only a sign, or indicator, of it.

Another way to understand sign arguments is to again call upon the economic indicators discussed earlier in Fed Chair Bernanke's testimony. His congressional report relied upon several signs of economic health, such as GDP growth, unemployment figures, and inflation. In his testimony, Bernanke was reporting and using economic signs to diagnose the performance of the economy. As this example suggests, when statistical data is used as evidence, we are often using sign reasoning.

It is important to note, however, that it is possible to commit the mistake of misreading a sign. This happens when one assumes that a certain sign is a reliable indicator of something else, when it is not. The use of economic indicators is again a potential example. The overall operation of the economy is so complex that it can be difficult to interpret an economic sign with certainty, as some of the volatilities of the stock market, set off in reaction to various perceived signs of growth or recession, indicate. Similarly, in the wake of the 2012 shooting death of Trayvon Martin, there was a national debate over the meaning of his clothing—a hoodie—and if it could be reasonably interpreted by George Zimmerman as a sign of Martin being a threat or a gang member. The hoodie became a prominent part of national discussion, an exhibit in the criminal trial, and might even end up as part of a Smithsonian exhibit that reflects on its cultural meaning.[26]

Making faulty associations between circumstances and an outcome, or erroneous interpretation of actions (or appearance of actions), is what we mean by "misreading signs." Thus, in considering a sign argument, you should inquire about the connection that is being made between the claim and the data. If the sign evidence is an accurate referent or indicator, if you can expect that the events reasonably occur together (but one does not cause the other), then you have a valid basis for a sign argument.

Reasoning from Authority

A final pattern of reasoning is reasoning from authority. **Reasoning from authority** occurs when a speaker supports a claim with the testimony or credibility of a qualified source. In the earlier discussions of testimony and source credibility, we considered several ways to evaluate reasoning from authority. If the use of authority passes those tests—the source is a qualified authority that has expertise and firsthand experience without undue bias—then this part of the argument would seem valid.

The use of authority is common in argumentation. For example, after a proposal was made to increase the minimum wage to $10.10 an hour, the Congressional Budget Office (CBO), which provides Congress with nonpartisan analysis of budget and economic issues, said that such a change could reduce employment by 500,000 jobs but also raise 900,000 families above the poverty line. In reaction, political actors seized upon the CBO's authority, due to its standing as a credible source, to support their preferred claims.[27]

If, however, the source of authority is removed from its area of expertise or is perceived as biased, then basing a conclusion on evidence from that source can produce an **appeal to authority** fallacy. For example, when Dr. Robert Jarvik promoted the popular cholesterol drug Lipitor in a national television campaign, parent company Pfizer was questioned over its use of Jarvik's authority. In the commercial Jarvik is accurately credited as the inventor of the artificial heart and is ostensibly shown rowing across a body of water. Jarvik goes on to speak about the wonder of the heart and the risks associated with excess cholesterol while verbally and visually offering an argument from authority:

> *Claim:* "When diet and exercise aren't enough, adding Lipitor significantly lowers cholesterol."
> *Data:* Jarvik's endorsement of the drug, and his performance of the physical activity of rowing.
> *Warrant:* [Implied] If Dr. Jarvik, a heart expert, trusts the drug, I should too.

The argument would seem to be a reasonable one at the surface—a nationally renowned doctor who has studied the heart endorses a drug as improving health. However, Dr. Jarvik is a medical researcher rather than a cardiologist, and he is neither licensed to practice medicine nor prescribe medication. Furthermore, it turns out Jarvik doesn't row, and the commercial featured a body double to simulate his physical activity. On the whole, the commercial reflects an appeal to authority fallacy for how it used Jarvik, something that eventually caught the attention of Congress and resulted in Pfizer ending the campaign.[28]

Additional Common Fallacies

The list of potential reasoning fallacies is long, and you can find more examples in argumentation and logic courses.[29] We limit our additional consideration of the topic to five other common fallacies.

Appeal to popularity: Do you remember your mother asking, "If everyone else jumped off a bridge, would you do it too?" This was her way of introducing you to the **appeal to popularity** fallacy, even if she didn't identify it as such. The basic idea is that popularity alone doesn't make for a good argument.

> *Example:* The success of the AMC's *The Walking Dead*, the highest rated television show since 2007–2008, proves that it is the best show on television.[30]

Analysis: The only basis this argument offers for being "best" is popularity. While that might be one relevant piece of data, in itself it would be a fallacy to contend that popularity and being the best are synonymous.

Appeal to common practice: This fallacy is also called an "is/ought" fallacy because the speaker suggests that just because something *is* a certain way, then it *ought* to be that way. Whereas an appeal to popularity relies on people's positive feelings about, or approval of, a statement or activity, an **appeal to common practice** relies on the commonality or tradition of the belief or activity as justification for its continuance or validity.

> *Example:* I know many professors look down on using *Wikipedia* as a source in research papers, but most students use it so it must be okay.[31]

Analysis: The only justification offered is that the action (use of a questionable source) is reasonable because it is a common habit on the part of students. However, as explored in chapter 4's discussion of research and this chapter's exploration of evidence, research quality is an important element of constructing a strong speech. A more specific example that reflects this appeal emerged in some of the public responses to a 2013 incident involving charges of racism and bullying in the Miami Dolphins' locker room. After football player Jonathan Martin relayed his experiences of being threatened, demeaned, and called racial epithets, some sports figures sought to defend the general tenor of such practices while rejecting the specific elements of this particular situation. For example, well-known basketball personality Charles Barkley explained, "The language we use in the locker room, sometimes it's sexist, sometimes it's homophobic, and a lot of times it's racist. We do that when we're joking with our teammates, and it's nothing personal."[32] Barkley's statement, not dissimilar from a member of a Greek organization justifying questionable pledging practices because he or she was previously subjected to them too, reflects an appeal to common practice.

Begging the question: This fallacy is also known as circular reasoning. When **begging the question**, the speaker fails to provide evidence for their claim and, instead, restates the claim in place of additional data.

Example: My argument is better than yours because it is superior.

Analysis: In this example the beleaguered advocate has offered an argument in which claim and data are nearly identical, with no offer of proof beyond a slight restatement of the claim (substituting superior for better). If the argument truly is better, the advocate must supply a substantive explanation as to why!

Ad hominem attack: An **ad hominem** fallacy occurs when the person, rather than the argument, is attacked. Certainly, on occasion, character is an issue in an argument, and in those cases questioning a person's character is not a basis for deeming an argument fallacious. However, when the substance of a disagreement is ignored in favor of a blatant attack, an ad hominem fallacy has been committed.

> *Example:* "I have obviously failed to galvanize and prod, if not shame, enough Americans to be ever vigilant not to let a Chicago communist-raised, communist-educated, communist-nurtured subhuman mongrel like the ACORN community organizer gangster Barack Hussein Obama to weasel his way into the top office of authority in the United States of America."—Ted Nugent in an interview with Guns.com on January 18, 2014.[33]

Analysis: In the example Nugent throws insults and makes negative comments about personal character, including utilizing language with suspect racial overtones, in attacking President Obama rather than discussing his policies. Moreover, inflammatory statements such as this one bring media attention that deflect from pertinent issues such as Mr. Nugent's defense of gun rights and his advocacy for Texas Attorney General Greg Abbott in his campaign to be governor of Texas. In the resulting tumult, Nugent apologized for his remarks, saying he "did cross the line" with his language.[34]

False dilemma: You have probably heard a variation of the phrase, "You're either with us or against us" (it was particularly prevalent in the aftermath of the September 11 terrorist attacks). This familiar ultimatum, like all false dilemmas, eliminates alternative options by suggesting there are only two conclusions available when additional possibilities exist. Perhaps you side "with us," but you're "against" some of our particular ideas or tactics. While campaigning for the presidency in 2008, Hillary Clinton invoked a false dilemma in calling for Congress to suspend the gasoline tax to offset high gas prices during a trying economic time. In making her point in a campaign stop in Indiana, Clinton asked: "Do they [Congress] stand with the hard-pressed Americans who are trying to pay their gas bills at the gas station or do they once again stand with the oil companies?" She further said, "I want to know where people stand and I want them to tell us, are they with us or against us when it comes to taking on the oil companies?"[35] Clinton offered a false dilemma in which opposition to suspending the gas tax was an endorsement of "big oil" and a rejection of common citizens.

A sharp understanding of reasoning patterns and reasoning fallacies provides an effective means to exercise democratic participation and civic engagement through the ability to evaluate the strength of your arguments and the arguments of others. By reflecting on the reasoning patterns you employ in your public communication, you can more critically examine the foundation(s) you used to request adherence from community members to support your cause. Suppose upon completing your preparation for a public speech you discover that the entire speech is based on sign argument.

That means you have relied extensively on circumstantial evidence, and it is likely that there is a lot of statistical data throughout the speech. How might that affect the audience's reaction to your argument? In this case you might find it helpful to balance the speech by including reasoning from authority through the use of testimony—to add a human dimension and gain source credibility—as well as an example or two to which the audience can relate (reasoning from example or reasoning from analogy). Such balancing can create a stronger argument by broadening the speech's overall appeal to your community.

Similarly, understanding reasoning fallacies will make you a more skilled student of argument and a more effective participant in public discussions. If you are able to identify faulty reasoning, you should also be able to avoid it. This skill will allow you to build stronger arguments and avoid the embarrassment of having an opposition speaker or an audience member expose a flaw in your reasoning. Likewise, it provides you with critical-thinking skills that can be vital in discussing public matters because you will be better versed in how to not just name but explain reasoning flaws in addressing public issues.

SPOTLIGHT ON SOCIAL MEDIA:
Taking Academic Debate Online

Debate has a long history as part of public speaking education. Debating societies began emerging at American colleges and universities in the middle of the nineteenth century, and they were an integral source of public speaking instruction in the early twentieth century. Specialized organizations and societies soon emerged to govern intercollegiate tournaments and scores of colleges have fielded debate teams. Among the most prominent debating organizations are the American Forensic Association's National Debate Tournament, the Cross Examination Debate Association, and the National Parliamentary Debate Association. A range of benefits to debate have been identified, including developing skills in communication, critical thinking, argumentation, listening, organization, and leadership.

However, challenges of organized academic debate include the costs involved in fielding a team and the specialization of the activity. In response to these and other concerns, some members of the debate community are experimenting with alternative formats that open up the activity while reducing entry barriers. One such effort is that of Joe Leeson-Schatz, director of Speech and Debate at Binghamton University. Since 2013, Binghamton has organized free online debate tournaments. Individuals from any school are permitted to participate in the tournaments, which feature one-on-one debates that are recorded, uploaded to YouTube, and evaluated by judges.[36]

The video format provides ease of participation at a low cost while also allowing for the long-term documentation of the debates. As Leeson-Schatz explains, the effort was motivated "in hopes of making debate accessible to individuals without programs, programs with little funding, and other populations that may not [otherwise] have the access to compete with students from across the nation (or world)."[37]

In this online incarnation, debates consist of five speeches—three by the proposition (the side advocating the resolution or question) and two by the opposition. Participants must submit a speech every 24 hours, and, upon the completion of a debate, judges have two days to offer a decision. The online format not only creates ease of access but also provides enhanced opportunities for participants to improve the quality of their contributions in that they can undertake research; plan what they desire to say; and even record, watch, and rerecord their speeches before submitting them. As Leeson-Schatz notes, "This enables students to workshop their videos and speaking," unlike in other debate formats. There is even the ability to more critically consider sources by following evidence links that participants are encouraged to supply during the debates. Ultimately, it is a novel public forum that provides for the possibility of expanding access to debate while giving participants a new means to practice and refine their speaking and argumentation. And at that, offered in a new form—prerecorded video—it allows speakers to think more about the nature of mediated communication and how that format shapes the way we present, understand, and respond to arguments. Looking for ways to further your argumentation skills and public speaking experience while engaging in discussion with people from across the country, perhaps even around the world? Try an online debate tournament!

Discussion Questions

- What advantages does the online debate format offer for improving argumentation and public speaking skills?
- How does participation in mediated formats change the act of public speaking and the considerations speakers need to think about when communicating with audiences?

SUMMARY

Arguments form the basis of decisions we make daily, thus, the ability to produce and evaluate arguments is of vital concern to public speaking and civic participation. In this chapter you have learned fundamental qualities of reasoning that will improve your ability to make quality arguments and sound decisions, and your ability to critically analyze public discourse.

- An argument is the advocacy of an idea, position, or course of action that is supported by evidence. An argument (or series of arguments) gives listeners reasons for adopting or agreeing with the perspective advocated.
- Deductive reasoning is reasoning that moves from valid premises to a specific conclusion. Generally offered in the form of a syllogism, a three-step proposition that consists of two premises and a conclusion, deductive reasoning relies on the accuracy of the premises in drawing a true or logical conclusion.
- In inductive reasoning a series of examples or instances are used to support the likelihood or probability of a generalized conclusion. Inductive arguments, less formal than deductive arguments, are expressed in a variety of forms and are judged based on quality more than logical validity through examination of the strength of the observational data offered in support of a claim.
- The Toulmin model of argument is a seven-part model that provides a way to conceptualize, verify, and critique arguments so that one can more effectively understand and evaluate public arguments.
- The central elements of the Toulmin model are claim, data, and warrant. The claim of an argument is what the speaker is attempting to prove and wants an audience to accept. Data are material and reasons that support the acceptance of the claim. The warrant provides the justification for using the data to support the claim, acting as a bridge between the two concepts.

- Evidence is data and backing in the form of examples, statistics, and testimony that is used to support a claim. Evidence is vital in providing support, and without evidence or data a speaker is left only with assertion.
- An example is evidence that supports a claim by providing a concrete instance in the form of a fact or occurrence. The principle forms of examples are specific examples or specific instances, hypothetical examples, and anecdotes, extended examples, or illustrations. When selecting and evaluating examples, one should judge if the example is representative, if a sufficient number of examples have been provided to prove the argument, if negative examples have been accounted for, and if the examples have been expressed with sufficient detail and clarity.
- Statistics represent information in numeric form according to the size, quantity, or frequency of an idea, outcome, or occurrence. Four common forms of statistics are averages, raw numbers, trends, and polls. When selecting and evaluating statistics one should pay attention to how an average was derived, observe the selection and size of a sample population, review margin of error or reliability for polling data, and consider the source and date of the statistics.
- Testimony is facts or opinions derived from the words, experiences, and expertise of another individual. When selecting and evaluating testimony, one should use a qualified authority who has clear expertise, firsthand knowledge of the topic, and a minimum of personal interest or bias. It is also important to understand the assumptions of testimony in order to be confident it is utilized in a fair and accurate manner.
- A pattern of reasoning is located in what kind of data or evidence is used in an argument and how that data or evidence is used to prove a claim. The prominent patterns of reasoning are reasoning from example, reasoning from analogy, reasoning from cause, reasoning from sign, and reasoning from authority. A typical speech uses a variety of reasoning patterns in urging acceptance of the thesis.
- A reasoning fallacy is a flaw or defect in reasoning that undermines the validity of an argument. There are many different reasoning fallacies, some of which are identified with the faulty use of particular reasoning patterns. Among the most common reasoning fallacies are hasty generalization, faulty analogy, faulty cause or post hoc fallacy, slippery slope, appeal to authority, appeal to popularity, appeal to common practice, begging the question, ad hominem attack, and false dilemma.

KEY TERMS

REVIEW QUESTIONS

1. What is an argument?
2. What is a syllogism? Why is it no longer the standard for argument evaluation?
3. What are the primary parts of an argument according to the Toulmin model? What function does each element of argument serve?
4. What are the primary forms of evidence? What tests should you perform in evaluating the quality of each type?
5. What is the difference between deductive reasoning and inductive reasoning?
6. What are the five common reasoning patterns?
7. What is a reasoning fallacy?

DISCUSSION QUESTIONS

1. What is required to make a "good" or "quality" argument? Why do people sometimes reject "good" arguments?
2. What is the value of the Toulmin model?
3. Test your ability to identify arguments by analyzing an editorial from *USA Today* or the *New York Times*. First identify the thesis, the subclaims, the data, and the warrants. Second, identify what types of data (i.e., examples, statistics, testimony) are used and what types of reasoning patterns are employed. Third, analyze the reasoning—are there fallacies? Finally, create an overall assessment of the editorial—is it a good argument?
4. As you watch television or read a magazine, think about the advertisements. Are the advertisements arguments? Do some of them present a claim and data? Do they employ fallacies? How do they compare to the arguments you find in speeches and essays?
5. As you listen to a public lecture on campus, think about the argument made by the speaker. Can you identify the speaker's thesis? What sort of data and evidence does the speaker use? Does the speaker create a sound argument based on the criteria discussed in this chapter?

CHAPTER 14

Designing Visual Aids
to Reach an Audience

When Tim Russert—host of the NBC News program *Meet the Press* and the Washington bureau chief of NBC News—collapsed from a massive heart attack in 2008, the news of his death dominated American media coverage. Though it may seem hard to believe in this era of divisive politics, Russert was admired by journalists *and politicians* for many things: his hard work and meticulous interview preparation; his commitment to asking politicians pointed questions; his good humor; his generous mentorship of young journalists; and his outspoken love for his family, especially his father and his son. Russert was a remarkably successful political journalist, in part because of the dual role he played as a Washington insider and a regular citizen. He was a graduate of the law school at Cleveland State University, though he moved in circles dominated by Ivy League graduates. He came from working-class roots (his father was once a trash collector in Buffalo, New York), and he loved Bruce Springsteen and the Buffalo Bills. At the same time, as Howard Kurtz wrote in 2004, Russert was "a man with tentacles deep into the political and media worlds, one of the few journalists in a puffed up, preening profession, who really matter."[1] Then President George W. Bush said, upon Russert's death, "America lost a really fine citizen

NBC News political journalist Tim Russert, holding his now-famous, remarkably simple visual aid on election night 2000.

yesterday when Tim Russert passed away. I've had the privilege of being interviewed by Tim Russert. I found him to be a hardworking, thorough, decent man. And Tim Russert loved his country, he loved his family, and he loved his job a lot."[2]

As journalists, politicians, and American citizens mourned Russert's untimely death, many recalled one particular moment of television footage involving Russert's use of a visual aid. It was during the 2000 presidential election night coverage. Russert, as NBC's top Washington journalist, was on-air much of the evening. As election results poured in, it's not an exaggeration to say there was widespread confusion, even mayhem, because the race was too close to call. Based on polling station exit surveys, the major television networks first called the state of Florida for Al Gore, then retracted and called Florida for George W. Bush. Al Gore even phoned George W. Bush to concede the race, and then phoned him back to retract his concession. As television hosts, campaign managers, and pollsters scrambled to determine whether either candidate could win the race without Florida, Russert grabbed a small rectangular white board to do the math on electoral votes. The television networks then reversed their projected Florida winner *a second time* and stated, with some embarrassment, that the race was "too close to call." *NBC Nightly News* Anchor Tom Brokaw, on air with Russert, wondered aloud whether Gore could win the election with either Oregon or Wisconsin—whose projected electoral votes were not yet determined. Russert grabbed his red dry-erase pen and scribbled emphatically, "Florida Florida Florida." Either candidate would have to win Florida to win the election, he explained. Later in the evening, as a Florida recount was triggered and Americans realized they would go to bed not knowing who the new president was, Brokaw regretted that the major news networks had had to retract their projected election winner not once, but twice. Russert, sensing the opportunity for humor, held up his white board again, still showing the red "Florida Florida Florida" and chided his friend Brokaw, "If you just stayed with these simple boards, you wouldn't have those problems. Those highfalutin computers, Tom. *This* is the answer. Get it right!"[3]

Beyond the unprecedented vote recounting in Florida still to come, part of what made Russert's election night visual aid so memorable was its shocking simplicity in an age of sophisticated, digitized visual aids. The white board seemed out of place amid election-night logos and animated network graphics. But for many, the white board and its emphatic "Florida Florida Florida" also captured much of what made Tim Russert a great journalist: he avoided complicated when plain and simple would do. He understood that a journalist's job is to reach the American citizens through direct language, and, like much of his news coverage and interviews, Russert's visual aid cut to the heart of the matter in just three words.

In this chapter, we discuss the use of visual aids in public speaking. While we assume many oral presentations in this day and age of widely available presentation technology will incorporate visual aids, we *do not think visual aids are always necessary*, and, like Tim Russert, we believe that visual aids are most effective when they are elegantly simple.

This chapter proceeds by first talking about why you should consider the use of visual aids in public speaking. We then introduce you to the rhetorical elements of visual communication, and discuss how visual communication can promote or hinder civic engagement. Next, we briefly outline the types of visual aids available to speakers, paying particular attention to popular presentation software like PowerPoint, Keynote, Prezi, and Google Presentation. We will help you wade through the many types of visual aids available, as well as discuss the advantages and disadvantages of the different types. Finally, the chapter ends with a discussion of design principles that will help your visual aids stand out. We give specific guidelines for preparing and delivering your speech with visual aids.

VISUAL AIDS CAN BENEFIT SPEAKERS

In today's world—whether in business, school, or community politics—it is increasingly hard to imagine giving a presentation without visual aids. Professor of communication Elizabeth Daley writes that the "multimedia language of the screen has become the current vernacular," and she argues that "those who are truly literate in the twenty-first century will be those who learn to both read and write the multimedia language of the screen."[4] In fact, she argues that we need to expand our concept of literacy (the ability to read and write) to include the language of the screen. **Multimedia literacy** includes the ability to construct and decode complex meanings on the screen and to engage in modes of thought and to communicate via screen-based technology.[5] Given the growing multimedia literacy of international audiences, we imagine most of the speeches you will be asked to give will be **multimodal presentations**, or presentations that integrate oral, written, and visual modes. But our goal in this chapter is to help you think carefully about face-to-face oral presentations that might include visual aids. We'll help you consider what visual aids to use, why to use them, when to use them, and even whether to use them.

In short, the goal of a visual aid is not to replace your carefully crafted speech. Visual aids should complement your speech, not vice versa. Ideally, the speech would not be as clear or as memorable without the images, but at the same time, the images would not make sense on their own or be nearly as persuasive without the speech.

Visual Aids Can Increase Clarity

Visual aids have the power to make your ideas clearer to your audience. Many audience members are visual learners, and well-designed visual aids help them comprehend what you are saying. Leading presentation design author and consultant Nancy Duarte advises speakers to help audiences "see what you're saying. . . . Think like a designer and guide your audience through ideas in a way that helps, not hinders, their comprehension. Appeal not only to their verbal senses, but to their visual senses as well."[6] A visual aid can help your audience comprehend an abstract concept or complex idea. Think of a well-designed visual aid as a highlighting pen. You make your point orally, and the visual aid makes the point stand out from the others.

Beyond that, it is likely in our increasingly globalized world that members of your audience may have different levels of fluency with the language you speak. Furthermore, depending on the content and your professional specialty, audience members will have different levels of familiarity with the technical knowledge or specialized language of your field. In these cases, visual aids can help define terms and clarify concepts and ideas.

Visual Aids Can Summarize Ideas Quickly

Like Tim Russert's white board with the hastily scrawled "Florida Florida Florida," an image can quickly convey what might take many words to communicate. There are images that become so iconic that they sum up a complex idea or a significant historical event in a photograph. Examples include photographs of the bombing of the World Trade Center on September 11, 2001, or a photograph of Neil Armstrong walking on the moon. You will want to exercise some caution, however, when you draw on well-known images because many feel they are overused. In the right context, however, a visual aid can be a powerful summarizing tool. We remember Russert's visual aid in part for its simplicity, but also because it summarized what many remember about the 2000 presidential election: five weeks of news coverage and questions about Florida's vote recount—and questions about whether the ballots were counted fairly. The image captured a complex historical event in a word.

Visual Aids Can Increase Audience Attention and Recall

Another advantage of visual aids is that they can help hold or increase your audience's attention. If members of the audience find their minds wandering—or if one or two glance down at an incoming text message—the introduction of a new image or the change of a PowerPoint slide can draw that person's attention back to your words and ideas. Well-planned and well-designed images make your speech more interesting. When someone later asks an audience member what your speech was about, a person might recall a visual image from your presentation and then explain the idea you presented with it. In other words, the image assists the audience in remembering your message after the fact.

Visual Aids Have the Power to Affect Your Credibility as a Speaker

Perhaps most importantly, a thoughtfully prepared, effective visual aid increases your credibility as a speaker. This is true for at least two reasons. First, it illustrates to your audience how carefully you prepared your speech. Well-designed and executed visual aids reveal the great amount of forethought and time spent in outlining and planning your delivery. (Remember, however, that the converse is also true: a hastily prepared visual presentation can undercut an otherwise well-prepared oral presentation.)

BOX 14-1

Advantages of Visual Aids

When well-designed and executed, visual aids:

- Heighten your clarity
- Summarize your ideas quickly
- Help the audience recall your message
- Increase your credibility

Second, good visual aids foreground your ideas. An effective visual aid increases your credibility precisely because it helps your audience grasp what you want to communicate. "That person was a great communicator!" someone might say when recalling your speech. "Her points were very clear."

VISUAL RHETORIC AND CIVIC ENGAGEMENT

The previous sections outlined the advantages of visual aids for you as a speaker and—because these elements are always related in rhetorical acts—for your audience and your message. But there are additional elements to consider when you are contemplating whether and how to use visual aids. In this next section, we talk about the rhetoric of images themselves and then turn to how the use of images can aid or hinder civic engagement.

Images Function as Visual Rhetoric

Recall that in chapter 1 we defined rhetoric as "a civic art devoted to the ethical study and use of symbols (verbal and nonverbal) in order to address public issues." While rhetorical studies was for centuries dominated by the art of public speaking, today we recognize that communication and persuasion happen verbally and nonverbally. We have thus broadened our study to include visual rhetoric. **Visual rhetoric** can be defined as any image that functions as symbolic action. Such images may seek to persuade or otherwise work to shape perceptions and actions of an audience. Indeed, in our technology-driven, multimedia-saturated contemporary culture, audiences are inundated with visual images that work to shape their perceptions and actions.

They seek not simply to be admired or contemplated but to evoke response; images themselves persuade. In this textbook, of course, we are specifically interested in how verbal and nonverbal symbols shape audiences' knowledge of and involvement in issues of shared public concern. As you select visual aids for your presentation, be attentive to how images may function persuasively for your audience. Evaluate whether the images you select work to clarify or to manipulate, mislead, or confuse issues.

Rhetorical scholar Sonja K. Foss writes that we can understand and evaluate the nature of an image by paying attention to both the presented elements and suggested visual elements. **Presented visual elements** are the "major physical features of the image." When you examine presented elements, you note size, color, shapes, form, background, and so forth. **Suggested visual elements** are "the concepts, ideas, themes, and allusions that a viewer is likely to infer from presented elements."[7] In other words, suggested elements may help us determine how audiences receive and understand the image.

Let's look at an example to clarify how these two elements work. In the 2000 presidential election, as noted earlier, Americans watched closely as the state of Florida recounted the ballots that were cast on the night of November 7. Florida was too close to call for either Bush or Gore (both of whom needed Florida's electoral votes to win the election). As the recount proceeded, and Americans waited five weeks for the final results of the election, multiple concerns arose over the design of the ballots themselves. Many who worried about disenfranchising voters were concerned that some Floridians' votes would be incorrectly counted or discarded due, in part, to ballots that could not be read either because of voter or machine-reading error. The *New York Times* reported that "more than 29,000 votes in Palm Beach County were thrown out because they included votes for more than one presidential candidate or had no names punched." This prompted lawyers for the Democratic Party to argue "the ballot was too confusing and possibly illegal."[8] An image of the Palm Beach ballot in question was circulated by several news outlets, and it showed how Al Gore and Joe Lieberman were listed as the second option for presidential candidate but—because of the ballot design—a voter would have to punch the third hole on the ballot to vote for these two candidates. The second hole on the ballot corresponded to a vote for the first candidate in the right-hand column, the Reform Party candidate. Indeed, the Reform Party candidate Pat Buchanan, who never campaigned in Palm Beach County, received almost 2,700 more votes in Palm Beach County than in any other Florida county.[9] This large discrepancy in votes for Buchanan prompted some to argue that the votes were clearly intended for Gore, but the ballot itself led voters astray.

When journalists presented and circulated an image of the Palm Beach County ballot (pictured), it became a visual aid, helping to clarify or illustrate the controversy. But it also serves as visual rhetoric. The image itself sought to communicate, was presented as evidence, and was designed to persuade audiences that the ballot was indeed confusing. To understand the nature of this image as a visual aid, let's look at both the presented and the suggested elements.

The *presented visual elements* are rather straightforward. We see a presidential election ballot. Audiences would recognize it as such because of the candidates listed. It is an image in black-and-white block print, and a series of circles to punch out if one wants to vote for that candidate. The ballot is meant to be read and used to cast a vote;

Confusion over Palm Beach Count Ballot

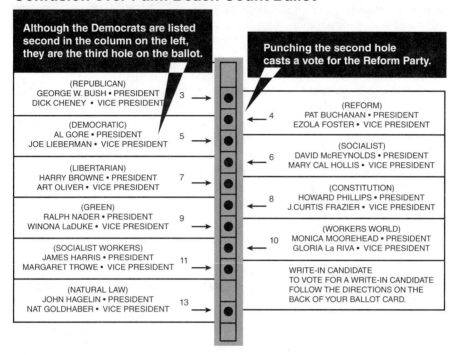

Image of the Palm Beach County ballot in the 2000 presidential election reproduced and circulated by news media outlets. The image includes explanatory bubbles and arrows added by journalists. This ballot prompted many complaints because it was seen as too confusing for voters.

it is not meant to be admired for its aesthetic qualities or innovative design. Notice, too, that in the news coverage, the presented elements of the visual aid include a title, "Confusion over Palm Beach County Ballot," as well as the black explanatory boxes with arrows at the top of the page. The image is also more than a reproduction of a ballot, then. It is an explanatory image.

The *suggested elements* in this visual aid are the ideas the audience is likely to draw from the image—namely, that it is possible that some voters were confused by it. Those who viewed the ballot might more fully understand the complaints about the Palm Beach County ballots. According to Foss, when we look at suggested elements in the image, we study what meaning the audience is likely to infer from the visual image.[10] The audience for this image is not the original Palm Beach voter, but the person turning to the news media to understand why there is so much argument and confusion over the Florida recount.

Of course, once we recognize that images function rhetorically—that they seek to persuade or promote response—we quickly arrive at questions of the ethical and un-ethical use of images. Like any rhetorical act, images can be used to clarify, or they can be used to obscure and mislead. As you consider the visual aids for your presentation, then, it is important to incorporate images in a way that promotes productive discourse and civic engagement.

Visual Aids and Public Discourse

In chapter 2 we outlined qualities of unproductive discourse and of productive discourse, noting that unproductive discourse impedes and discourages civic engagement, while productive discourse can enhance and promote civic engagement. As a speaker, one of your goals is to encourage your audience to participate in public issues, and you can do this by making your message as clear and comprehensive as possible within the allotted time. You can also do this by selecting visual aids that help clarify issues and include a variety of audience members, rather than selecting images that primarily entertain, exclude, mislead, or confuse.

The Pitfalls of Oversimplification, Unnecessary Complexity, and Unproductive Discourse

It is important to stress that images, as well as video and audio clips, have a tremendous power to oversimplify or misrepresent issues. Chances are, you've seen enough presentations in your life to be able to readily name some of the most frequently *mis*-used aspects of presentation software. These misuses not only bore an audience, they can also have more serious implications. In her April 27, 2010, *The New York Times* article, entitled "We Have Met the Enemy and He Is PowerPoint," Elisabeth Bumiller reported on the US military's extensive use of PowerPoint as well as on the military's concern that PowerPoint tends to oversimplify complex issues. Brig. Gen. H. R. McMaster lamented that PowerPoint is "dangerous because it can create the illusion of understanding and the illusion of control. Some problems in the world are not bullet-izable." Bumiller further explained McMaster's worry that "rigid lists of bullet points (in, say, a presentation on a conflict's causes) ... take no account of interconnected political, economic and ethnic forces."[11] Though well-intentioned, visual aids that highlight the main points of a difficult or complex issue (typically by using bullet points on a screen) can inadvertently suggest the issue is simpler than it really is. Here they make the mistake of oversimplification.

On the other hand, when speakers try to solve this problem and use presentation software to convey complexity, the result can be confounding rather than useful. In the same *New York Times* article, Bumiller mentioned a slide used by the military in Kabul. The slide, she wrote, "was meant to portray the complexity of American military strategy, but looked more like a bowl of spaghetti." Some in the audience saw the difficulty of the task, rather than a coherent military strategy in the face of complexity. According to Bumiller, after seeing this slide, Gen. Stanley McChrystal, then leader of American and NATO forces in Afghanistan, quipped, "When we understand that slide, we'll have won the war."[12]

Clearly, then, as you select visual aids, there are two pitfalls to avoid. The first is the pitfall of oversimplifying complex issues and thus leading your audience into thinking that there are simple solutions to problems they have not fully thought through. The second is not taking into account how the audience will perceive the image. In Bumiller's example, the presenter believed the slide would illustrate strategy, even in the face of complexity. Some in the audience, however, looked at the slide and saw only confusion—to the point of humor. By not considering the image or visual aid from the audience's perspective, you risk being misunderstood, or worse, making your visual aid the butt of a joke.

Because images are also symbolic action, they themselves can be forms of unproductive discourse. They may do this by highlighting or encouraging division, dichotomous thinking, combativeness, and certainty (some of the qualities of unproductive discourse outlined in chapter 2). When you present images that simplify a complex issue into two choices, or when your images offer data with several interpretations as decisive and certain, you have made a choice to give your audience a false impression. As a presenter, you have an ethical obligation to select images that treat topics or subjects fairly and that encourage civic engagement through productive discourse.

The Rhetoric of Visual Aids as Productive Discourse

Of the nine qualities of public discourse outlined in chapter 2, three are particularly important to keep in mind as you select visual aids. Productive discourse is characterized by (among other qualities) learning, lateral communication, and imagination. As you select images, choose ones that help your audience learn about the issue at hand but that do not require highly technical knowledge to discern. The image of the Palm Beach County ballot, above, is not particularly beautiful, but it is clear. It helps readers learn about the source of the controversy.

If you are prompting lateral communication, you will design and select images that distill the information so that audience members with different levels of knowledge or background on the topic can converse with one another on a more level playing field once they have heard your presentation.

Finally, your visual aids want to do more than present the facts to the audience. They help audiences *see* the issue by the manner of presentation. Notice that the word "imagination" is related to the word "image." Productive discourse helps audiences visualize new possibilities or creative solutions; it prompts them to build a new vision for solving controversies. When you use visual aids, you should design and select images that help the audience *imag*ine your message or the public issue in a different way.

Now that we have outlined some of the advantages of using visual aids in public speaking, as well as the concept of the visual as rhetoric and its implications for productive discourse and civic engagement, we turn to specific types of visual aids and some of their advantages and disadvantages.

TYPES OF VISUAL AIDS

There are many types of visual aids you can use in public speaking: handouts, props, charts, or Prezi frames, just to name a few. In today's world of omnipresent technology, most people think first of presentation software when they think of visual aids. While it's probably the case that most of your speeches will incorporate visual aids via software like Prezi or PowerPoint, there are other types of visual aids that may be appropriate or even preferred in some contexts. In this section, we will devote the most space to presentation software, but we end with a brief outline of other of visual aids and some factors to consider when you use them (Table 14.1). After this section, we will turn to more general design advice for a range of visual aids.

Presentation Software

Chances are you are familiar with presentation software: your professors use it, you use it for class presentations, and you have encountered it in a number of settings outside school. Programs like PowerPoint or Google Presentation are designed as digital slide shows, and thus presenters refer to their digital visual aids as "my slides." A **slide deck** is your set of digital visual aids, no matter which software you use.

There are several software programs designed to make it easy to create digital slides. Some, like Apple's Keynote and Microsoft's PowerPoint, are desktop based. That is, they are programs housed on your computer and stored on your hard drive. They may be backed up on thumb drives, you may e-mail them as attachments, or you may choose to store them on web-based file sharing sites like DropBox or Google Drive. Other presentation software is based in the cloud. Such programs include Prezi and Google Presentation. These programs are accessible anywhere you access the Internet. As you can imagine, there are advantages and disadvantages to both desktop- and cloud-based software: If your laptop is not compatible with the projector in the presentation room and you forget to backup your slide presentation or misplace your thumb drive, you cannot access your visual aids. On the other hand, if there is a temporary Internet outage and you have a cloud-based presentation, your visual aids are inaccessible. Knowing the advantages and limitations of each type of software, however, will let you anticipate and plan for any possible glitches on presentation day.

Before we go any further, we want to point out that presentation software has become so ubiquitous you may sometimes hear presenters refer to their PowerPoint slides or Prezi frames as "my presentation." While the slides may be a central component of your presentation, they are still just your visual aids. You will be a much better presenter if you think of your slides as an "aid" to communication rather than the entire communication act itself. The lynchpin of your presentation is your speech and the way you use your words to connect with your audience!

PowerPoint

PowerPoint is part of the Microsoft Office Suite, and just as Microsoft Word is the standard software for creating text-based documents, PowerPoint dominates the field of presentation software. People in need of a tissue ask for a Kleenex, those in need of an adhesive bandage ask for a Band-Aid, and speakers around the world tend to refer to their visual aids as "my PowerPoint." Those who invite you to give a presentation may ask if you have "a PowerPoint."

Microsoft provides online tutorials for PowerPoint if you are unfamiliar with the program or would like to explore some of its more advanced features.[13] Like most presentation software, PowerPoint's features allow you to create graphs, import images, and embed audio and video content. PowerPoint was designed as a digital slide show, and its structure is linear. You proceed from one slide to the next, and you cannot return to a previous slide without copying the slide to a later point in the sequence or clicking backward through slides.

Just as there is a plethora of advice online and in print on how to create effective PowerPoint presentations, there are also endless jokes and cartoons about PowerPoint abuses. Audiences dread a bad PowerPoint presentation—and with good reason. Many of these complaints have to do with the way PowerPoint allows (some might say encourages) bad visual design. Designers and presentation consultants warn against standard PowerPoint templates (built in color, font, and design schemes). Audiences have seen many of these several times, and the templates start to look repetitive or uninventive. Also, be cautious about using features like transitions, animations, and builds. These have the tendency to look more amateur than professional.

PowerPoint can be text-heavy; if you are so inclined, you can create a slide that looks like a document in a large font. In the final section of this chapter, we will give more specific design advice for visual aids, but for the time being, if you choose to use PowerPoint, remember to present your slides as *visual* elements rather than as enlarged text-based documents. Among other things, it is PowerPoint's overreliance on text or its document orientation that has led other software designers to develop additional, more visually oriented products.

Keynote

Keynote is Apple's answer to Microsoft's PowerPoint. It is also a desktop-based program that performs similarly to PowerPoint but has more integrated tools and features for advanced slide design. Reviewers note that it pays much more attention to design or will be more satisfying to design-oriented users.[14] Apple has many online tutorials for exploring Keynote's features.[15]

The drawback to Keynote is that it is an Apple-based program in what is still a PC-dominated professional world. Apple computers generally run PC software, but PCs do not run Apple platform programs. Thus, presenters will find that Keynote slide decks do not translate seamlessly into some versions of Windows, and if your presentation space has a projector hooked up to a Windows-based PC, you may need to allow extra time for connecting your own Apple laptop or for working out other technology hiccups before your presentation.

Prezi

Prezi is a cloud-based presentation software that has an updated, more contemporary feel than PowerPoint. The Prezi website has very helpful online tutorials that teach you to build your own presentation if you are unfamiliar with their software.[16]

Unlike the linear slide design of PowerPoint and Keynote, Prezi is a zooming software. Each presentation starts with a title or overview frame that displays the entire map of the presentation. As you click through the presentation, you zoom to a different area of that background frame—sometimes entering a portal and then coming back. But the entire presentation is designed to zoom from one frame of the background or title slide to another and then back again. One of the best advantages of Prezi is that this zooming between sections of the overview frame is ideal for presenting ideas that are highly interrelated. If you want to show the relationships among your ideas—say, for instance, your presentation is about integrative service bureaus in your community—or if there is reason to toggle back and forth between slides, Prezi is a good option. Metaphorically speaking, Prezi allows you to zoom in and out between the "forest" and the "trees"—to show both the big picture and the details that comprise that picture.

Prezi designers often point out that their software is designed to communicate through *visual metaphors* rather than blocks of text. Of course, there is nothing inherent in PowerPoint or other presentation software that forces you to present bullet-pointed lists, but one of Prezi's selling points is the idea that because this software works through visual metaphor, it is ideal for showing connections among ideas in your presentation. Consider, for instance, two slides designed by Scott Hastings which show a text-based slide transformed into a visual metaphor frame using Prezi (pictured).

Because Prezi is stored in the cloud, it can streamline the process of embedding audio or video content into a slide deck. You do not have to worry about downloading or saving files in certain formats; as long as links are available on the Internet and you have Internet access, your embedded content should function without a glitch.

In terms of Prezi's drawbacks, the program can seem, to some audiences, a bit busy or overly animated for a presentation. Consultants and designers frequently warn that Prezi can make audiences "dizzy," especially when a presenter does too much zooming.[17] Prezi can seem like a lot of fancy animation without added benefit. Thus you want to ensure, if you use Prezi, that you have a presentation which tells a clear story and uses the overview frame or visual metaphor in a way that adds clarity.

You should also note that Prezi is public. Unless you pay a subscription fee, your Prezis will be available and searchable. Subscribers purchase additional storage space and have the option of keeping their presentations private.

Google Presentation

Presentation, by Google Docs, is another cloud-based presentation software. The Google Presentation interface will look familiar to PowerPoint and Keynote users, though this program has fewer templates and design elements. One advantage to Google Presentation is that, like Prezi, presenters do not need to own or locate a presentation computer with a certain software platform to run their presentation; as long as they have Internet access, the presentation slides are available and without translation issues. As with the other presentation software, there are many online tutorials for Google Presentation.[18]

The key feature Google Presentation has, compared to other presentation platforms, is built-in collaboration tools. Google Presentation permits you to invite advisors or coworkers to live chat with you as you build the slides. These collaborators can see your in-progress slide deck because it is stored on Google Drive. Without the need to circulate a single copy of your slide deck via e-mail or juggle feedback from several collaborators in separate files, Google Presentation has the potential to streamline group projects and collective work.

Google Presentation generally receives criticism for having fewer and less interesting design elements than the other presentation software platforms. It is, however, a great option for those who prefer cloud-based presentation software and do not have design skills or content that is well-suited for Prezi.

Prezi's presentation software works by visual metaphor. Here you see similar information presented on a traditional slide and a Prezi canvas.

TABLE 14.1 Other Visual Aids: Affordances and Aspects to Consider Regarding Their Use

While presentation software is certainly ubiquitous in contemporary oral presentations, there are other types of visual aids you might turn to for impact, emphasis, or perhaps due to venue constraints.

TYPE OF AID	AFFORDANCES	CONSIDERATIONS
Props *(tangible objects, other than handouts or charts)*	Useful in venues unsuitable for presentation software. Memorable when they contain an element of novelty or surprise. Can be circulated among the audience for added interest and personal involvement. Example: Russert's whiteboard on television	When you circulate it, ensure you leave enough time for each person to see the prop. The passing of the object may distract audience attention for a moment. With rare objects or in large spaces, there is some risk it will not be returned to you.
Handouts	Useful if no projector is available and you want your audience to have a text or an image in front of them. Valuable when you want the audience to take information home or return information to you. Example: Voter registration forms at an event to train volunteers to help people register.	Rustling paper is loud, and therefore distracting when circulated. Circulate at the point you want the audience to read the information; otherwise, you risk losing an audience who begins reading the handout during an unrelated part of your speech. Consider enlisting others to pass them out so you can stay focused on the speech.
Video Content	Tells a story or gives an example in visual and audio modes of communication; grasps and holds audience attention. Offers a nice break from a single-voice presentation. Example: YouTube clip.	Often overused and misused because clips are too long or poorly integrated into the speech. Shorten the clip to include *only* the take-away message or most central part. Consider narrating the video image yourself to keep the focus on your message—as long as the audio component is not important to the clip. May not work well in outdoor venues.
Audio Content	Creates a sense of intimacy among the audience by making them part of the event or the original audience for the audio clip. Offers a break from a single-voice presentation. Musical clips add another mode of communication; can set the tone or mood. Example: Clip from an important political speech that you want your audience to hear or recall.	Keep the clip short—it should not take over your speech. Be sure to integrate the sound clip into your message; tell your audience what it means or how it should be interpreted. Do not expect the clip to speak for itself. May not work well in outdoor venues.

Final Thoughts on Presentation Software

We hope that the previous brief outline gives a good overview of available presentation software. But as you explore different ideas for your visual aids, don't overlook the many resources on social media. Pinterest, for instance, has many pins on Prezi, Keynote, and PowerPoint that include templates, design ideas, and tutorials, as well as many sample slides.

Leading authors on presentation and design Nancy Duarte and Garr Reynolds both write blogs that discuss contemporary issues and sources of inspiration (www .duarte.com/blog and www.garrreynolds.com). Each of their websites has a section on presentation tips. You might also consult Zoom into Prezi, the Prezi company blog (http://blog.prezi.com) which publishes posts ranging from converting PowerPoint slides to Prezi, to new Prezi templates, to how to rethink your charts so that your data has the best visual representation. There is a blogging world beyond these three sites, of course. Many instructors in public speaking and professionals in web design also blog their ideas for teaching and presenting. You may want to take some time to search for your own favorite writers on presentation and design (or start your own blog!). Such blogs are often the places where the freshest ideas appear and circulate, long before they make it into a book, for instance.

Now that we have outlined various types of visual aids available to speakers, we turn to specific advice—dos and don'ts—for visual aids. Much of what follows applies to many forms of visual aids—for instance, handouts and posters—not simply to presentation software slides.

SPOTLIGHT ON SOCIAL MEDIA:
Twitter and Public Activism: TEDTalks:
Aimee Mullins's "My 12 Pairs of Legs"

At the start of Aimee Mullins's TEDTalk "My 12 Pairs of Legs," you see a tall, striking blond woman standing on the middle of a stage. As she begins to speak, a stagehand walks behind her and sets down a pair of prosthetic legs. Suddenly you notice that this pair of legs has joined one that was already there—although you didn't see it—when Aimee began speaking. She tells a story about a presentation she made to 300 children at a children's museum, where she laid out her 12 pairs of prosthetic legs on a table for the kids to touch, try on, and ask about, if they wanted to. She notes that children are naturally curious and inclined to look at things like prosthetic legs, but adults teach them to look away, to "see" disability by not asking questions about prosthetics or pretending to ignore differences.

As visual aids, Mullins's prosthetic legs are highly effective props, inviting us to look even though we have been trained that it is rude to stare at people who are disabled. The props Mullins has chosen are paired with a presentation slide deck that show all the ways Mullins has used her prosthetic legs—all the ways she has donned the various types of legs to illustrate ability and "poetry" (her word) rather than disability.

Mullins, who is an athlete, actor, model, and activist, lost both of her legs at the age of one year due to a birth defect. But she grew up actively participating in athletic activities thanks, in part, to prosthetic legs.[19] As she gives this particular TEDTalk, she wears a pair of prosthetic legs with stiletto heels. She walks the stage where other pairs of prosthetic legs are arranged behind her, and slides of her as a model and athlete (wearing different pairs of legs in each) are displayed on the screen above her head. Mullins's props and slides combine with her words to invite us to rethink *dis*ability.

Mullins says that thanks, in part, to an earlier TEDTalk where she called on innovators and designers outside the field of medical prosthetics to "come bring their talent to the science *and to the art* of building legs," we have made tremendous strides in recent decades. Mullins tells her audience, "It is no longer a conversation about overcoming deficiency. It's a conversation about augmentation. It's a conversation about potential. A prosthetic limb doesn't represent the need to replace loss anymore. It can stand as a symbol that the wearer has the power to create whatever it is that they want to create in that space."

Aimee Mullins's TEDTalk is a powerful example of the use of visual aids to provoke an audience and to promote clarity. It is also a speech deeply invested in the principles of civic engagement, calling on innovators to create prosthetic limbs that change our definitions of what it means to be disabled—and calling on audience members to rethink their assumptions about prosthetic legs and those who wear them.[20]

Discussion Questions

Watch Aimee Mullin's TEDTalk and then answer the following questions:

- What do you notice about Aimee Mullins's use of visual aids? (Consider both her props and slides.)

- What choices does she make as a presenter to keep the focus on visual aids secondary to her words and her connection with her audience?

- Once her talk is complete, what idea most stands out to you? Is she successful in persuading you of anything? If so, what?

VISUAL AIDS AND THE ART OF DESIGN

Garr Reynolds, a leading voice in presentation design, writes, "Design matters, but design is not about decoration or about ornamentation. Design is about making communication as easy and clear for the viewer as possible."[21] When we pay attention to design in visual aids, we are concerned with how clearly ideas are communicated through visual elements.

There are four basic principles of design that will help you design effective visual aids: contrast, repetition, alignment, and proximity. **Contrast** is difference, and the principle here is that you should make elements that are different from each other in kind, *visually* different as well. Contrast can create a visual "pop" and can quickly help the eye determine what is important—because it is different. Lack of contrast, on the other hand, creates confusion. Whether the element is color, size, shape, type, or space, you can help your audience "see" your point though contrast.

Repetition in design is simply reuse. Think of the way a well-known logo or icon prompts you to quickly, almost unconsciously, identify the product as Nike, Apple, or Microsoft. Through repetition, these companies have made themselves known to us. On a smaller scale, the same can be true of your central idea in a visual aid. Repetition can create a sense of unity and consistency. You create repetition by choosing a consistent background color or template, by using a consistent font (though size may vary for contrast), by repeating a photograph if you have used it to illustrate a central concept, or by inserting your employer's logo. But you might also consider how you can

Slides with poor contrast are hard to read and thus distract audiences from the presentation.

enhance design through repetition of other visual elements—a use of color, a photograph, an icon, and so on.

Alignment is concerned with the deliberate placement of the elements in a given slide. Alignment includes how photos, text, and captions are lined up with one another (center them, left-justify them, etc.) You don't want anything (text, image, photo caption, logo, or subtitle) to look randomly placed. When elements on your slide, like main headings or logos, have visual similarity in where they appear on the slide and in relation to each other, your presentation looks more professional. When elements are not aligned, your visual aids can look amateur—more like a middle school science fair poster than a polished presentation.

The **proximity** principle in design says that items that are similar to each other should be placed next to each other. Placing items together creates a visual unit, and the eye readily understands that these elements are part of a group. If you are talking about the advantages or drawbacks of a particular solution, for instance, the proximity principle says the advantages should appear together and the disadvantages should appear together. Mixing or randomly placing these elements leads to confusion rather than clarity. When an audience sees words or images far apart from each other, they do not read these elements as related or members of the same group. The purpose of proximity in design is to help organize the slide or material for the audience.

Additional Considerations in Artistic Design

In addition to these four basic principles of design, there are other design considerations that will make your visual aids stand out. These include your strategic use of white space, font, and color, as well as careful editing of slides for things that may distract, confuse, or tire audience members who are working hard to process your slides.

White Space

Any graphic designer will tell you not to be afraid of white space. Your audience will have a much easier time processing your slide, chart, or graphic if it is not crowded with too much or even superfluous information. Just as silence can be used strategically to emphasize speech, white space can strategically emphasize image. As you put together your visual aid, ask yourself what the central message of your slide or visual aid is. Will a member of your audience find his or her eye drawn to that message? If not, is there a way to remove excess information so that your main point pops out?

Font

Fonts come in serif and sans serif varieties: with or without lines or embellishments on the ends of the letters. Think of serif fonts as fancy calligraphy or the typescript used on formal wedding invitations. They are hard to read—even if they are beautiful. Because your goal is to communicate clearly, you should stick to sans serif fonts in presentation.

Color

As you choose font color and background, remember the design principle of contrast. Colors that are too similar to each other are hard to distinguish and therefore hard to read. A good resource for understanding color and its relationship to both design and audience psychology is color professor Jill Morton's website ColorMatters.com.

Finally, it is important to keep in mind that certain colors have emotional and cultural connotations. We associate red with anger or passion, for example; pink with femininity. In Western cultures white connotes purity (the origin of the traditional white wedding dress), whereas in China, white is associated with death and is the color of mourning. Chinese brides wear red, a color that signifies good fortune. Cultural color contexts may be important to keep in mind as you choose the pallet for your presentation.

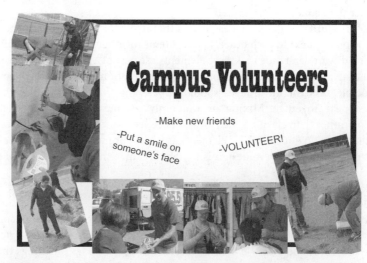

A slide with poor use of white space. Do not be afraid to leave ample white (or blank) space on a slide. Cluttered slides like this one are difficult for audiences to process.

Ease of Processing

You probably know from experience—and most designers will tell you—it is impossible for an audience to listen to your words and read a slide, chart, or handout at the same time. If you have a handout or chart that you need the audience to digest, give them time to do so. The better choice, however, may be to simplify your visual aid to cut down on processing time. Can you deliver the context or background orally and then present a slide with the central idea, most important statistic, or conclusion in large typeface? If not, consider two slides, one that (briefly) gives the context and a second that highlights or otherwise draws attention to the conclusion you want your audience to draw.

Image Quality

Just like a typo is perceived as sloppy or careless by your audience, a low-quality image can hurt your credibility. If you cannot find a high-quality image of the photograph you want to use, find a different photograph. The image needs to be large enough for the people in the back of the room to see, and it should not be blurry when enlarged.

Slide Readability for All Audience Members

Remember that what is clear and visible on your computer screen may not be large enough for the audience members in the back of the room. Remember, too, that audience members may have varying quality of vision. As you choose images and font sizes, go larger than your initial instincts suggest. When you practice with your slide deck (and preferably in your presentation venue or a room of similar size), be certain you check out your slides from the back of the room.

Content Overload

Once you have finished a first draft of your slide deck, chart, or handout, you can almost always reduce your content. The hardest elements to let go of are things you think are really cool or that you spent a long time creating, but, in the final analysis, sometimes these visual aids don't add clarity. Be brave enough to edit them out when you realize their absence may make for a cleaner, more streamlined, more polished speech.

As you design your slides, reduce the number of words on your slide wherever possible. This does not mean you need to simplify your presentation; it only means you need to simplify your slides.

Transition and Animation Overload

One mark of a new PowerPoint user is that he can get very excited by transitions, animations, and builds. Similarly, a new Prezi user zooms too much. If your presentation contains too many of these features, it will look unprofessional. Ask someone you trust to provide an honest critique about whether a piece of animation looks professional or hokey.

The "Oops" Factor

While it may seem wildly unfair, nothing undercuts the impact of a carefully prepared speech like a typo. Audience members read such seemingly small errors as marks of carelessness or lack of preparation, and thus you should read and reread your visual aids for errors before your presentation. Remember that it is hard to catch small errors after you've been looking at the same screen for many hours or days, and this is why it is good to enlist a friend or colleague to read your visual aid before your presentation. If you cannot find someone to proofread it, at the very least, set your slides or handout aside, take a long break, and then come back to them. Our eyes are often better at catching mistakes after a break.

INTEGRATING THE VISUAL
WITH THE ORAL PRESENTATION

While we stress the importance of visual aids throughout this chapter, please remember you're still giving an oral presentation. Do not make the mistake of assembling well-designed slides while failing to craft a compelling speech. No amount of color, no quality of image, no contrast can cover for poor speech content. If there were technical difficulties, and you could not show your visual aids, could you still give a clear, compelling speech?

Your goal is for your audience to leave your presentation talking about your ideas, not your slides or animation features. And your audience is most likely to get excited by your ideas when the ideas are clearly communicated and when they connect with you and what you have to say, rather than with a projection screen.

As you put the final touches on your oral presentation, here is some final advice for giving a speech that artfully integrates the oral and the visual presentation.

Research Venue Constraints

A **venue constraint** is an element of your physical presentation space that will limit how you connect with your audience. Recall that in chapter 5 we discussed the environmental factors that may influence how you plan for delivery and engage your audience. Venue constraints are one aspect of these environmental factors; they should shape your presentation because you must account for them in how you prepare.

Does your presentation space have Internet access? A projector and screen? Are there any posts or pillars in the room that might obstruct the audience's view of the screen? If you can, try to visit the space where you'll be presenting ahead of time to determine the answers to these questions. Even better, try to arrange a practice session—with your visual aids—in the venue prior to the presentation.

If the space does not have a projector and screen, or does not have Internet access, you may decide against visual aids prepared with presentation software. Instead, you might opt for a handout, a large chart to display on an easel, or no visual aids at all. Your speech must be successfully designed for the audience, and part of this means designing it for the venue where you will present.

Practice with Your Aids

Even if you cannot practice your presentation in the venue, it is still important that you practice with your visual aids. In fact, it is one of the best pieces of advice we can offer. There are many times when a presentation could be more powerful if slides or the circulation of handouts was timed better. When you practice your speech, think about *when* you want the audience to read something (for example, a significant quotation), practice prompting them to read the slide, and then pause so they can do so. If you do not coordinate the timing of your visual aids with your oral presentation, you risk losing your audience's attention as they turn away from your words in order to process the information on the visual aid.

Once the lights dim and your slide deck comes onto the screen, it may be tempting for your audience to close their eyes and take a cat nap. If you have chosen a visual aid that requires the lights to be dimmed, you should practice and plan for ways to compensate and maintain your audience's attention. Moving away from the screen or podium and into the audience as the lights go down is one way to let the audience know that you are there to engage them.

Don't Read from Your Slides

When you use presentation software, we emphatically insist: Don't read from your slides! Don't stand to the side of your projection screen and stare at the slides as if looking for answers. Many people can get caught up in the intricacies and special features of visual aids when that time would be better spent honing the content of the speech and practicing its delivery. Practicing your speech with your visual aids will give you a chance to make sure your focus is on your speech and your audience, rather than on your visual aids.

Don't Be Afraid of a Blank Screen

Again and again, skilled presenters and presentation consultants remind PowerPoint users to press "B" (the key stroke to toggle between a blank screen and your last image) or the blank screen button on the presentation remote. You do not need to give your audience an endless series of images while you speak, and shifting to a blank screen at key points in the speech—for instance, when you want to tell a story or prompt discussion—is a great way to refocus attention on you and your ideas.

In conclusion, we remind you that visual aids are powerful—and potentially fun—public speaking tools. As you plan and design your visual aids, keep your focus on the ways visual aids can assist and build civic engagement in a well-crafted speech. You do important civic work when you help your audience visualize a new and creative solution or find language for discussing a problem in a way that minimizes differences. When your words and visual aids combine in a way to make this kind of civic engagement possible, your audience will not soon forget your message.

SUMMARY

Visual aids are rhetorical tools for adding clarity, interest, and recall to an oral presentation. There are many reasons to include visual aids as you plan and practice your speech, but visual aids are frequently used poorly and can be more distracting than beneficial. In order to use them effectively, you need to make several audience and design choices.

- Images are forms of visual rhetoric; that is, they communicate, influence, and persuade audiences. Because of their persuasive power, it is especially important that you use them ethically, in a way that promotes civic engagement.
- Images that oversimplify complex issues or participate in division, combativeness, or certainty can discourage civic engagement.
- There are several platforms for presentation software, and while they have many similar features, they each have some unique features and drawbacks. Be certain you plan for the potential drawbacks of your chosen software.
- In addition to presentation slides, you might consider visual aids like props, handouts, video content, and audio feed. Like presentation software, each of these types of visual aid has its own affordances and limitations.
- There are several basic design principles that will help your visual images—whether slides or physical objects—stand out and be memorable. Follow the guidelines for integrating alignment, contrast, proximity, and repetition to create coherent, visually pleasing visual aids.
- Once you have selected and designed your visual aids, remember that your presentation is, first and foremost, an oral presentation. Practice with your visual aids so that you can keep the connection with your audience and the communication of your ideas central. Do not spend so much time on your visual aids that you forget to prepare a stellar speech.

KEY TERMS

alignment p. 305
contrast p. 304
multimedia literacy p. 291
multimodal presentations
    p. 291

presented visual elements
    p. 294
proximity p. 305
repetition p. 304
slide deck p. 298

suggested visual elements
    p. 294
venue constraint p. 308
visual rhetoric p. 293

REVIEW QUESTIONS

1. What are some good reasons to include visual aids in your presentation?
2. What is visual rhetoric? How do visual aids function as visual rhetoric?
3. What are the advantages and disadvantages of cloud-based versus desktop-based software? How can you compensate for the disadvantages in preparing your visual aids?
4. What are the four basic principles of design? Define them.

DISCUSSION QUESTIONS

1. What types of visual aids do you think are most underused? Explain.
2. How is the use of visual aids connected to civic engagement? Give an example.
3. Find an example of an image or visual aid that you think exhibits excellent design. Bring it to class and discuss how it implements design elements with your classmates.
4. How does the use of visual aids affect the credibility of speakers? When do you think the judgments we make about speakers' visual aids are fair and when are they unfair?

CHAPTER 15

Rhetorical Criticism
as Civic Engagement

Chapter Objectives

Students will:

- Understand the meaning and purpose of rhetorical criticism.
- Identify the qualities of good rhetorical criticism.
- Discover the basic process of analysis undertaken by rhetorical critics and scholars.
- Observe the role rhetorical analysis plays in civic engagement and democratic participation.

What changed? That was the question that business school lecturer Conor Neill sought to answer about two dramatically different listener reactions to two performances by musician Joshua Bell, a virtuoso violinist who has performed in top music halls around the world and produced over 40 albums. On January 9, 2007, Bell performed for over a thousand people at Boston's Symphony Hall. Three days later, he exchanged formal clothes for a T-shirt and a baseball cap and played for commuters as they entered the subway in Washington DC. Few noticed, but Bell played classical music on his multimillion dollar violin for nearly 45 minutes. The video of Bell's performance went viral on YouTube.[1]

In 2013, in an animated TEDTalk considering Bell's performance, speaker Conor Neill asked a fundamental question: Why did the subway travelers react as they did? That is, why did so few stop to listen or even seem to notice him? In determining his answer, Neill turned to Aristotle and his claim that there are three elements that cause rhetoric to be persuasive: logos, ethos, and pathos.[2] Neill identified ethos and pathos as determinative in this instance. The performance in the subway, Neill contended, lacked the credibility and trustworthiness generated by a grand symphony hall.

311

Violinist Joshua Bell playing for morning commuters in one of the entrances to the Washington DC subway.

Violinist Joshua Bell playing at Lincoln Center with Louis Langree conducting.

Similarly, Neill noted that a music hall is designed to foster an emotional bond between the performer and the listeners, but in the hustle and bustle and rushed movements of the travelers in the subway entrance such a bond was highly unlikely. This is a good example of rhetorical criticism because Neill helps us understand the curious reaction this public act generated from its audience.

In the final section of this textbook, we focus on rhetorical analysis in the service of civic engagement and democratic participation. To this point, our focus has been on civic engagement through the creation of discourse in oral and written forms. Now the focus is on analysis, typically referred to as rhetorical criticism. In this chapter we explain the relationship of rhetoric and rhetorical criticism, describe rhetorical criticism as an intellectual discipline, set out the foundational elements of rhetorical criticism, and demonstrate how rhetorical criticism can be employed to evaluate democratic practice. This chapter is followed by a chapter on public communication analysis (chapter 16) and a chapter on ideological criticism (chapter 17).

RHETORIC AND RHETORICAL CRITICISM

In chapter 1 we defined rhetoric as a civic art devoted to the ethical study and use of symbols (verbal and nonverbal) to address public issues. The most common symbol humans use is language, our words, but symbols also include nonverbal forms of communication, visual images, and music. In this chapter we examine the use of symbols more closely to see how they act, what they accomplish, and how symbolic action can best be analyzed and understood. We take as our guiding inspiration the conception of rhetoric as symbolic action which comes from the most influential rhetoric scholar of the twentieth century, Kenneth Burke (1897–1993). Burke contended that we see and understand our world and ourselves through the medium of symbols.

Rhetoric as Symbolic Action
Symbolic action refers to the power of symbols to *do* things and to shape our thoughts and actions. A symbol is something that expresses an idea or refers to something beyond itself. For example, the icons on a computer screen are symbols as are street signs. The words we use are also symbols, and they are ubiquitous and powerful. As Burke explains, our words are simultaneously reflections, selections, and deflections of reality. Words offer a *reflection* of reality, that is, they can be used to describe all aspects of human society, our world, and the universe. Words offer a *selection* of reality because we can never describe everything about something or all the angles or perspectives that can be taken on it. Thus, all descriptions are incomplete selections of reality. That is, they are reductions of the material world. Finally, words provide us with a *deflection* of reality in that all descriptions focus our attention on certain aspects and take our attention away from others.[3] As a college student, for example, you may make plans to hold an event at your parents' house when they are away. When you invite your friends you may choose to describe the event as a party. However, when you describe the event to your parents you may describe it as having a few friends over to hang out. Likewise, we can talk about the act of dying in many different ways: pass away, kick the bucket, move on, go to the great beyond, quick trip home

to glory, check out, and rest in peace, to name a few. We make such language choices because we recognize that our words *do something*. They shape the way others come to understand and interpret what we are describing to them. In each case the words we use function as symbolic action in that they reflect reality (for having a party or dying) but simultaneously select and deflect portions of reality (by emphasizing a more positive or negative portrayal of the party or dying). In so doing, our words create for auditors a way to see and understand the world.

Rhetorical Criticism

Rhetorical criticism (or its synonym, rhetorical analysis) is the description, interpretation, and evaluation of rhetoric in order to form judgments about its meaning, effect, and impact. This process of analysis is not new. It reaches back to the birth of rhetoric as a discipline in Aristotle's *Rhetoric*. Specifically, Aristotle's description of how various types of speeches persuade their audience, his discussion of how arguments work, and his discussion of the function of style and figures are forms of rhetorical analysis. Similarly, we have utilized informal rhetorical criticism earlier in this text in the criticism of public discourse (chapter 2), in the analyses of various perspectives on tough issues (chapter 10), and in considering how best to appeal to an audience in persuasive speeches (chapter 12).

There are many ways to study human society. We can imagine a psychological approach that tries to get inside the head of each person. We can also imagine a biological approach that would inquire into the person at the cellular level or the genetic level. Or we might imagine an approach based on economics and the choices individuals make to maximize the accumulation of wealth or the use of their time. When we take a rhetorical approach to the study of human society the focus is not on the individuals themselves but rather on the symbolic interaction or communication that takes place between them. Another way to make this point is to say that in rhetorical analysis we study messages, whether they are verbal, textual, visual, or material.

The phrase rhetorical criticism does not refer to complaint or fault finding but rather to analysis and study. When a person conducts rhetorical criticism, he or she is examining a rhetorical act or artifact in a thoughtful, serious, systematic, and comprehensive manner. The rhetorical analyst or critic is one who stands, figuratively speaking, outside the rhetorical object of analysis and seeks to understand the functioning of that act or artifact in all its richness. How does the artifact create meaning? How does its framing invite us to view humanity? Is it persuasive—why or why not?

Description and Interpretation

Ultimately, rhetorical criticism shares many similarities with other types of qualitative research in the humanities. Perhaps the most fundamental way it does so is in the three basic steps of humanistic, qualitative analysis: description, interpretation, and evaluation. Each is important to rhetorical criticism, and we engage in these three modes of thought regularly in our interactions with others and as we encounter messages of all types. For example, imagine that you are visiting New York City, and as you walk near Times Square, you come upon the following display:

This billboard-sized display of the national debt was originally designed in 1989 by real estate developer Seymour Durst. It remains active and now resides on Sixth Avenue. As of December 29, 2014, the national debt was over $18 trillion.

If you were on your cell phone with a friend at this moment and wished to describe it to them, you might start by saying something like, "I am looking at a huge sign that has a digital counter on it with fourteen digits that shows how much the national debt is and how much each family in America owes." That is *description* because it explains what you have observed. Fairly quickly in a situation like this we tend to move to *interpretation*. In this case that might be exclaiming, "Wow, the size and height of that huge sign helps convey the enormity of the debt!" or, "The use of the word *our* on that sign drives home the shared burden all Americans have." And from interpretation we move to *evaluation*, such as, "That's a helpful sign because it reminds Americans what is happening every day, which is that each and every one of us is going further and further into debt!" or, "That sign is misleading and will likely be used by a politician or political action committee in order to reduce the size of government and cut funding on social services for the poor."

Evaluation

While we made the point that the *criticism* in rhetorical criticism is not meant in the standard (negative) way the term is employed, that is not to say that rhetorical analysis does not make an evaluation, because it does. Good rhetorical critics are explicit, transparent, and clear both about their evaluation of a rhetorical act and the basis or perspective from which they make that evaluation. And, good rhetorical critics and students of rhetoric recognize that a different person, conducting an analysis of the same object from a different perspective, will probably make a different evaluation.

Often the evaluation generated by rhetorical criticism helps us see an aspect of our culture or society that we had not seen clearly before. For instance, rhetoric scholar Michael Butterworth has described how the continued regular performance of "God Bless America" at sporting events since 9/11 can be understood to promote nationalistic thinking that places sport in the service of US militarism. In doing so, Butterworth has allowed us to see deeper meaning in what many might otherwise consider a harmless and even soothing ritual.[4] Other times the evaluation teaches us something about a particular group or audience we had not known. Examples include criticism that provides insight into the rhetoric of political and social movements ranging from the Tea Party to right-to-die advocates. Here evaluation highlights the implications and ethics of tactics designed to move audiences and generate support for a cause. And sometimes the evaluation teaches us about how a particular type of rhetoric is having an impact on the values, attitudes, and behaviors of those who experience it. This might range from a critic judging what he or she perceives to be the damaging gender stereotypes promoted in some Disney films to valorizing the depiction of superheroes, such as Captain America, as embodying cherished values including freedom, equality, justice, and courage.[5] Evaluation is the most complex and significant component of rhetorical criticism.

Raising the Flag on Iwo Jima was taken by Joe Rosenthal for the Associated Press on February 23, 1945. It became the only photo to win the Pulitzer Prize for Photography in the year it was taken. It may also be the single most reproduced image in history.

If we consider Raising the Flag on Iwo Jima—one of the most iconic and frequently reproduced images in American history—we can see all three stages of qualitative analysis and demonstrate how the work of rhetorical critics can comment on the practice of American democracy.

Even if you can't quite place the photograph or recall its details, chances are good that you've previously seen this image of the US flag being raised in victory on the Island of Iwo Jima during WWII. You may have seen it on a calendar marking great moments in American history; or perhaps you have seen one of the prominent monuments, stationed at various US locations, that memorialize the event; or maybe you have seen it on the cover of a book or DVD commemorating World War II. It is also likely that you have seen more than one reinvention of the photograph—a political cartoon that evokes the image but changes elements of it, the image reproduced on a T-shirt or other item intended to promote patriotism, or even Homer Simpson pausing before consuming a potato chip that bears a striking resemblance to the soldiers raising the flag. In each case, you were presented with an opportunity to consider how the image is a form of symbolic action and to perform rhetorical criticism on the repeated use of the image. Why do you think it is it so widely commemorated and reproduced?

Rhetoric scholars Robert Hariman and John Louis Lucaites explore such questions in a chapter of their book *No Caption Needed*.[6] Their examination of the famous Iwo Jima image begins with an explanation of its context including the publication of the photograph and the responses it generated. The authors provide a rich *description* that makes the image tangible through a discussion of its composition, the terrain and debris captured in the photograph, how the positioning of the soldiers suggests a unity to their movements and efforts, and how they present an anonymous, workman-like appearance. Subsequently, Hariman and Lucaites *interpret* the original image as promoting the best of what it means to be a citizen through its embrace of egalitarianism, its promotion of nationalism, and its embodiment of civic republicanism. Egalitarianism is represented in that all the soldiers are equal in effort and participation while raising the flag. The image promotes nationalism by centering the flag as the revered symbol of the nation, while it is raised in a ritual act of citizenship that is repeated every day in locations ranging from homes to schools.

But there is more to the interpretation as the image has been reappropriated countless times over the decades, often to promote consumption, such as selling war bonds, museum memberships, insurance, and other products. Hariman and Lucaites interpret these appropriations for how they reveal that the visual image retains such broad identification that its repeated use and reinterpretations allow it to represent democratic solidarity, evoke a sense of nostalgia, or be appealed to in a way that reflects growing public cynicism. Their analysis concludes with an *evaluation* that the image, its continued circulation, and its many appropriations "reveal a complex process in which democratic citizenship is continually renegotiated through artistic variation on what has become a conventional model of civic identity."[7] In this way the image is a vehicle for democratic participation that is used to highlight, reinterpret, and reaffirm democratic principles. The point is that the image teaches us something about what it means to be a citizen and how democracy works. In full the analysis provides an excellent example of how rhetorical criticism can deepen our understanding of rhetorical artifacts found and used in public.

In the remainder of this chapter you will be asked to see how the practice of rhetorical criticism can function as a form of civic engagement. As we shall see, the practice of rhetorical criticism is an intellectual activity that engages our minds in thoughtful questions about and reflection on messages. Not all such criticism is a means of civic engagement, but much of it is.

RHETORICAL CRITICISM
AS AN INTELLECTUAL DISCIPLINE

To perform rhetorical criticism is to enact certain qualities of mind, qualities not unlike those necessary for productive civic engagement. Here are five such qualities:

- *Curiosity*—The persistent and consistent desire to understand how discourse functions for audiences. This curiosity drives us to go beyond what one wants to see or simply expects to see to detailed observation and analysis.
- *Imagination*—The ability to break apart and examine rhetorical artifacts from multiple theoretical and practical perspectives and for diverse audiences.
- *Systematic Examination*—The employment of a thorough and orderly approach when analyzing discourse by moving from description to interpretation to evaluation.
- *Discernment*—The ability to see beyond the surface of a text and move from description to interpretation. A critic determines which rhetorical elements to focus on to generate the greatest insight into the functioning of a text or discourse.
- *Reasoned Analysis*—The use of credible evidence, appropriate and representative examples, and an adherence to the standards of valid argumentation.

It is not enough to understand the qualities of rhetorical criticism. It is also important to consider *why* one practices rhetorical criticism. Through rhetorical criticism, we gain a better understanding of human society and our world. We understand messages, arguments, and ideological positions better through this close consideration. Second, we become better, more knowledgeable consumers of public information. We are bombarded with messages, be they political or commercial, and rhetorical analysis helps us see through the appeals, understand meanings and goals, and think more deeply about the implications of public messages. In addition, by learning how to analyze communication about civic affairs, we can move from being passive spectators of a community to being active members within it. Third, such critical inquiry allows individuals to engage in democratic practice in their communities by helping create an informed citizenry, starting with ourselves. This is because through rhetorical criticism we gain understanding of persuasive strategies and tactics. This knowledge can be utilized to educate fellow community members and counter polarizing rhetoric; to weigh policy options and advocate positions; and to lend support for or voice resistance to the policies and ideas of others. Analyzing public communication enables democratic participants to improve the quality of both the discourse around them and the decisions made by their communities. Finally, a reason for rhetorical criticism embraced by rhetoric scholars is to contribute to and advance rhetorical theory. Rhetorical criticism allows scholars to draw connections between rhetorical acts and to understand better how discourse functions in society.

FOUNDATIONAL ELEMENTS
IN RHETORICAL CRITICISM

At its root, rhetorical criticism is about discovering the meaning and functioning of visual and verbal artifacts. It seeks to explain what a text means and how it works, and to evaluate its impact or effect on human society. How rhetorical criticism goes about doing this varies depending on the questions one asks, and on the rhetorical method one uses. In the chapters that conclude this text, we discuss two perspectives or methods for analyzing the meaning of rhetoric for democracy and civic engagement (public communication analysis in chapter 16 and ideological criticism in chapter 17). In this chapter we identify a set of foundational elements at the center of the analytical work of all critical methods. The next section outlines steps to take and elements to consider in getting started: selecting a rhetorical artifact, situating the rhetorical artifact in an appropriate context, reading the rhetorical artifact, and considering audience.

Selecting Rhetorical Artifacts

A **rhetorical artifact** is an object of study in rhetorical criticism. It is the focal point of analysis and what the critic seeks to bring meaning to through the analysis. One of the wonderful characteristics of rhetorical analysis is that the range of potential objects of study is limitless. In the early twentieth century, the modern field of rhetorical studies in the United States was referred to as "speech" and a focus on public, political speeches was the norm. However, since the 1960s the range of rhetorical artifacts studied has been expanding and now includes areas such as literature, art, film, television, social movements, the Internet, and social media. As the examples in this chapter illustrate, a rhetorical artifact can be anything from a violinist's performance to a national debt billboard to a building. For the purposes of this text, which focuses on civic engagement and democratic participation, it is important that a rhetorical artifact be chosen that addresses a substantive public matter.

Situating Rhetorical Acts in Context

A second major aspect of rhetorical analysis is the context in which the rhetorical act takes place. **Context** refers to the conditions or situation within which rhetoric is produced. It addresses the who, what, when, where, and why surrounding the production of the rhetoric. All rhetorical acts take place in a context of some type—be that a particular social context, historical context, financial context, and so forth—and that context helps shape the meaning of the act. And this relationship is reciprocal in that context shapes the formation of artifacts and an artifact can speak to and attempt to influence a context.

An example demonstrating how context is important to rhetoric is found in the relationship of the political cartoon (pictured) to the previously discussed iconic photograph of the flag-raising at Iwo Jima:

Pat Bagley, *Salt Lake Tribune*, March 8, 2009.

In contrast to the original photograph by Rosenthal, consider what this image asks us to think about Wall Street chief executive officers (CEOs) and what sort of response it invites. Further, how does it make or communicate that meaning? The original Iwo Jima image provides a *context* for reading this reappropriation. Moreover, this image takes place in a particular historical context, during the federal bailout of banks and Wall Street during the financial crisis of 2008–2009. There is a third potential context invoked by the bystander uttering, "drill, baby drill!" which is a reference to political debates at the time regarding offshore oil drilling in the United States. Knowledge of these contexts influences our understanding of this cartoon as well as our ability to interpret it. This reappropriation takes the concepts of egalitarianism, nationalism, and civic republicanism identified by Hariman and Lucaites in the original Iwo Jima image and challenges them in ways that comment quite negatively on contemporary democracy. Egalitarianism has been preserved as the suited CEO's work together, but their substitution in place of soldiers creates a sense of irony. This is seen in that American nationalism has shifted from a form of patriotic unity to CEOs unified in their dedication to winning a war that is being waged against common Americans, those who are getting *screwed* by the unified actions of big business. The cartoon might be evaluated further as suggesting that our national virtues and values have undergone a damaging transformation and now rest on greed and self-interest.

This example demonstrates that every rhetorical act and artifact takes place in a context. In order to critique an artifact well, one must understand and explain the layers of context made visible in the artifact. Those who listen to or see the artifact may accept or reject the portrayal of the context, but the context is, nevertheless, important to the meaning of the artifact and is portrayed in a particular way by it. A critic might examine the context of an artifact through research of reliable news sources, both in print and online, in published books, online databases, and other sources. Examining each rhetorical act within its context provides important insights into the working and functioning of the rhetoric.

BOX 15-1

Questioning Contexts

- How would you describe the context of the rhetorical act or artifact you are studying? (You might think about the historical context, political context, and the ideological context as a way to begin).

- What more do you need to learn about the context to better understand the rhetorical act or artifact?

- How does the rhetorical artifact construct, describe, or portray the context?

- What about the context is left out or undervalued?

- What is the relationship between the rhetorical act or text and its context? How do these two elements influence one another?

Reading Rhetorical Artifacts

Once a rhetorical critic has identified a particular object for analysis and examined its context they must determine the most appropriate way to conduct the analysis. Often this means making use of a particular method. A **rhetorical method** is a perspective, approach, or orientation for analyzing an artifact. A method privileges certain questions for analysis and provides a framework for understanding and evaluating the text. Each method focuses our attention on particular elements and aspects of rhetoric and thus *away* from other elements. For example, within rhetoric studies there are methods that focus on metaphors, myths, and narratives among many others. As each name suggests, the method directs our attention to the use and meaning of certain elements in a text.

To illustrate this process recall the lenses that are used when you go to the optometrist. Often in that setting, after the optometrist has checked your eyes and determined the correction you need, he or she will place a series of lenses in front of your eyes as you look at the eye chart. If the optometrist has correctly measured your eyes and selected the right lenses, what was blurry comes into crystal clear focus. The lenses change the way you see and what you are able to see. Rhetorical analysis is like using a powerful lens that focuses our attention and shapes our vision, resulting in new insights about and understandings of the world. Different methods, like different lenses, change what we see and how we see it. When done well this analysis provides profound insights into human communication.

Building from this basic function of analysis we can see that no matter the particular perspective or method, the critic is always seeking to describe, interpret, and evaluate both the *content* and the *form* of the rhetorical artifact. In terms of rhetorical *content* we can examine the message or argument(s) that is advanced, whether it is advanced verbally, visually, or otherwise. We also can seek to understand how the rhetorical act appeals to the emotions of auditors. Our discussion of invention in chapter 12 is important here because when you analyze the rhetoric of another person, you start with their finished product and work your way backward to their work of invention or creation while asking, "Why this and not that?" over and over again.

At the same time, rhetorical analysis investigates the *form* that rhetoric takes, asking both why and to what end the form of the rhetoric functions. For example, it is one thing for an animal rights activist to write an editorial in the paper on the cruel treatment of animals and another for the same activist to throw a cup of blood on a celebrity wearing a fur coat. In both cases the point being made—expressing opposition to animal cruelty—is the same, but the differences in the form of the protests likely create differing interpretations and evaluations. A final question concerning form and content is to inquire how form and content might work together or in opposition to one another.

One of the most ubiquitous forms rhetoric takes is visual. Within rhetorical studies the study of visual rhetoric has developed and deepened dramatically over the last several decades. Today visual images from around the globe are readily available to anyone with a smartphone, tablet, or computer. Extending from their work in *No Caption Needed*, scholars Robert Hariman and John Louis Lucaites maintain a blog featuring rhetorical analyses of visual artifacts. Notice in the Spotlight on Social Media entry how Robert Hariman provides a rhetorical analysis of both the content (what is shown) and the form (the manner in which this content is framed) of a photograph.

SPOTLIGHT ON SOCIAL MEDIA:
Analyzing Visual Images as Rhetorical Artifacts

On January 23, 2013, Robert Hariman posted the following entry on the No Caption Needed *blog in which he analyzed a picture from the destruction in Aleppo, Syria, due to the ongoing civil war there. In his rhetorical analysis, Hariman helps us see more in the artifact than we first realize is there. Notice how he explicitly directs readers to observe things in and through the photograph that they probably had not detected. Also notice how his analysis considers the multiple messages and meanings the photograph conveys.*

One of the basic ideas that I bring to this blog is that a lot can be learned from photographs that are *not* striking, dramatic, or otherwise visually assertive. Of course, most of the time I'm still working with high-grade professional images, but the distinction holds all the more for that.

Few photography instructors would advise their students to take a distant, poorly lit shot of people walking aimlessly across a pile of rubble. But they might need to think otherwise if they were preparing those students for a tour of duty in a war zone. This is an all-too-typical scene from Aleppo. The electronics remaining along the roof line suggest this had been a high-tech building, but now it's been bombed back to the stone age.

Instead of downloading, people are scavenging. Not for food (not here and not yet at least) but more for something to do. And that is what the photo reveals: not just destruction, but how much war is about killing time. Soldiers know all too well how bursts of activity can be separated by long stretches of boredom, but that is nothing compared to what many civilians experience. War imprisons them—whether in their homes or a refugee camp—while destroying virtually all work, schooling, or play. As the built environment around them is degraded more and more every week, their opportunity to do anything productive becomes ever more constricted and difficult. Time looms large as something to be filled—with what?—but in fact that time is being lost. Lost to them and to the rest of society. Time that could be used to do so much: to learn, work, entertain, invent, and not least to actually live and not merely survive. . . .

Look at the photo again and consider how you can see what I'm talking about. Not just the destruction of the building, with all the hardship that will cause, but also how time is actually present in the photograph, expanding to fill the craters and exposed buildings, spreading across the rubble that now blocks any attempt to *do* anything in that place. Look at how helpless those in the picture are to beat back the emptiness. Even the playfulness evident in the figure on the right will soon be exhausted, and more time will be lost to the bewilderment and hopelessness evident in the other boy and the adult to the left. Their time will be like the space in the photo: there is too much of it, now that it can no longer be productively organized by the buildings and routines of ordinary life.[8]

This analysis by Hariman helps us see beyond the surface and expands our understanding of the deep tragedy of war. His analysis helps us to see how the visual image works or could work on those who view it. This blog post is an excellent example of how to read a rhetorical artifact. Notice that he did not take the artifact on face value; he asked questions of it and considered elements beyond what is shown. This is precisely what good rhetorical criticism does.

In addition, this example reveals how social media, like blog posts, enables most every person with a computer, tablet, or cell phone and an Internet connection to publicly comment on events and world affairs. It then enables others to react to those postings, which occurs on the site No Caption Needed.

BOX 15-2

Questions to Ask When Reading Rhetorical Artifacts

- What is the content of the artifact? What seems to be its primary argument, point, or message?
- What is the form of the artifact? How do the medium and selected symbols help it function persuasively? How does it make its argument, point, or message?
- What does the artifact leave out that could have been included?

Considering Audience

A fourth element of rhetorical analysis is audience. In rhetorical criticism **audience** refers to those targeted, reached, influenced, or impacted by the rhetorical act. Rhetoric creates meaning through or in relation to audiences as it is they who respond to, endorse, or reject a message. We can see audience operating in at least two ways. First, there is the audience for which a rhetorical act or text was created and to whom it is presented. In other words, the people who actually watch or listen to the rhetoric. So, in a very simple case, we can imagine a student presentation to a class in which the audience consists of classmates and a professor. This situation is about as straightforward as it gets. As a second example, imagine a state of the union address given by the president. Who is the audience? It is a multifaceted one because it includes the senators and representatives who are present, as well as members of the Supreme Court, the president's cabinet, and special guests. It also includes the American populace, political pundits and news outlets, and the leaders and citizens of all the other countries in the world who listen to or watch the address.

Second, rhetorical artifacts also work to *construct* audiences in particular ways. This idea was first advanced by rhetoric scholar Edwin Black as he described how texts themselves create at least an implied audience that is to one degree or another different from the actual audience.[9] For example, we might imagine a coach giving a pregame pep talk to his or her team in which the coach constructs the players as the dominating force they aspire to be by visualizing victory over an opponent. The players may feel differently, but, through the speech, the players are invited to re-envision themselves in the coach's description of triumph. Such inspirational speeches that construct their audience as successful are common, including film examples of Coach D'Amato (Al Pacino) in *Any Given Sunday*, Coach Dale (Gene Hackman) in *Hoosiers*, and Coach Boone (Denzel Washington) in *Remember the Titans*. Alternatively, think about the rhetorical strategies used by businesses to pitch their various rewards clubs. Promotional materials appeal to our desire to perceive ourselves as special and gain otherwise unavailable perks (e.g., airline miles and upgrades, hotel discounts, etc.) in order to entice us to buy or obtain memberships. As the old American Express ad put it, "membership has its privileges." These messages seek to construct would-be members as part of an elite club that possess advantages that nonmembers do not. An auditor or group of auditors may resist the manner in which an artifact seeks to construct them, but, at the very least, each rhetorical act can be seen as an attempt to construct an audience.

As you might imagine, these two ways of viewing the role of audience can work in tandem. As an example, consider the Crystal Cathedral in Garden Grove, California.

The bell tower of the Crystal Cathedral reaches 236 feet into the sky and for three decades served as a visual marker of the grandiosity of the megachurch movement within evangelical Christianity. It was constructed for a particular audience; at his peak in the 1980s, the founding minister Robert Schuller preached to 10,000 people in the sanctuary of the Crystal Cathedral and to millions more through his *Hour of Power* television broadcast.

In an insightful essay in *The American Scholar*, author Jim Hinch describes how the structure fit the mores and desires of the baby boomers who populated Southern California suburbs in the last half of the twentieth century, particularly those in Orange County. Schuller arrived in Orange County in 1955, the same year that Disneyland opened. As Hinch writes, "Like the much beloved, much pilloried Disneyland three miles to the northwest, the Crystal Cathedral is a monument to Americans' inveterate ability to transform dominant cultural impulses—in this case, Christianity itself—into moneymaking enterprises that conquer the world."[10] Though actual crystal was not used in the structure, an astounding 10,000 panes of glass were. The inside was quite different from the standard church facility, at least at the time, as it included a massive stage with theater-style lighting and sound, theater-style seating, and an indoor reflecting pool that ran the length of the interior between the rows. These features enabled Schuller to construct very different church services than the traditional services of Protestant churches: "The suburban style of evangelicalism Schuller pioneered was showmanlike and inspirational, emphasizing feel-good messages and entertaining worship services rather than liturgical tradition and theological complexity."[11] As many have remarked, the services moved congregants from the role of participants in a liturgy to one of spectators of a performance conducted by professionals.

This example shows the role that audience plays in the creation and interpretation of rhetorical acts and artifacts. As stated earlier, rhetoric is both created for an audience and it works to shape and influence audiences in various ways. The cathedral was designed to appeal to Southern California suburbanites rapidly moving to the area, and, at the same time, the facility shaped and influenced those who attended services in it. Even physical structures, like the Crystal Cathedral, function in both of these ways on those who attended the church during the several decades when Rev. Robert Schuller was the pastor.

BOX 15-3

Questioning Audience

- Who is the intended audience of the discourse? Are there secondary and tertiary audiences?
- How does the rhetorical artifact portray or construct its audience?
- How does the explicit or implicit characterization of the audience shape or influence the rhetorical act itself?
- How would you predict or anticipate the audience would react to the rhetoric under examination?

EVALUATING DEMOCRACTIC PRACTICE
AND CIVIC ENGAGEMENT

The examples used in this chapter were selected to show the varied ways that rhetorical criticism plays an important role in American democracy. The work of Hariman and Lucaites on the Iwo Jima image and its continued reimaginings encourage us to use rhetorical criticism to understand what it means to be a citizen and how democracy works. The example of the Crystal Cathedral demonstrates how physical structures are constructed with particular audiences in mind and how they also shape and form audience expectations and values. In addition, Conor Neill's analysis of Joshua Bell's subway performance helps us understand more fully how context shapes audience reaction to rhetorical acts. These specific examples support several larger points about the power and utility of rhetorical criticism. Such criticism helps inform the public by putting specific rhetorical artifacts in context, connecting them to other rhetorical elements, and explaining how they function to shape our understandings. It also provides a mechanism for holding public officials and public speakers accountable through the investigation and study of their public statements. Moreover, such criticism enriches deliberative discussions by expanding our knowledge base of rhetorical acts and artifacts and their contexts. Finally, it can have the effect of causing publics to pause and reflect on the meaning, significance, and implications of the messages that are exchanged. This sounds very much like what Kenneth Burke describes as the consumer protection function of rhetorical analysis.

More broadly, rhetorical criticism is the examination of the choices made by rhetors and how symbolic inducements function to create meaning and move public audiences. Returning to Kenneth Burke's concept of symbolic action, one of Burke's earliest works of rhetorical analysis was a study of Adolf Hitler's *Mein Kampf* that underscores the powerful contributions rhetorical criticism can make in society. Burke's essay, "The Rhetoric of Hitler's Battle," appeared in the literary journal *The Southern Review* in the summer of 1939, before Hitler ordered the German military to invade Poland. *Mein Kampf* had been published in English earlier that year as a Book-of-the-Month Club selection. Thus the American public had only seen the book in a highly abridged form, some 14 years after it was first published in German in 1925.

In his critique, Burke begins by stressing the importance of analyzing Hitler's book rather than simply dismissing it as fascist propaganda. He calls *Mein Kampf* "a testament of a man who swung a great people into his wake," and Burke seeks, through rhetorical analysis, "to discover what kind of 'medicine' this medicine-man has concocted."[12] What Burke means by this is that Hitler's language—his rhetoric—was a form of symbolic medicine for the German people. Burke's focus is on demonstrating the way the text works to unite the Christian, or at least non-Jewish, German population by blaming German Jews for the ills that had befallen the German state. Burke understood this symbolic and rhetorical process of unification through division to be a common human pattern.

Identification, as noted in chapter 5, is the degree to which individuals or groups find their interests joined or linked. Identification seeks to create a sense of collectivity among audience members by utilizing positive or binding associations. The flipside of identification, division, operates through the construction of separation. **Division** attempts to separate an individual or group from the collective, thereby scapegoating them and creating solidarity through the rejection of that which is different. Burke argues that many will follow this pattern even in the face of less than convincing reasons to do so: "The yearning for unity is so great that people are always willing to meet you halfway if you will give it to them by fiat, by flat statement, regardless of the facts."[13] It may be that this is one reason why our public dialogue is so polarized today, this same human pattern of uniting through dividing. In any case, the essay demonstrates how symbol use shapes and forms both individual and group identity in a powerful way. This can happen in ways that are productive or unproductive for society. It can likewise happen in either ethical or unethical ways. Rhetorical analysis makes this process and its results visible. To the extent that we share this analysis publicly it is a form of civic engagement.

RHETORICAL CRITICISM
AS DEMOCRATIC PARTICIPATION

The practice of rhetorical criticism in the service of democratic participation focuses our attention on how the rhetorical artifact operates within our democracy. We believe rhetoric that addresses the public's business should strengthen democracy. Traditionally, the speakers and speeches Americans have considered great have been those that aided democracy. That was true in 1948 when communication scholar Earnest Brandenburg noted that "every orator of sufficient prominence to be considered in the area of Statecraft has been a champion of democracy and the will of the people. Or, to state it another way, rhetorical critics and historians have seemed to decree that prominence be accorded to those who have championed democracy."[14]

The same holds true today. Look at lists of great speeches, such as Stephen Lucas and Martin Medhurst's list of the top 100 speeches in the twentieth century, and you'll find advocates of democratic ideals, from Martin Luther King Jr.'s "I Have a Dream" speech to John Kerry's 1971 speech against the Vietnam War.[15]

In contrast, notoriety accrues to the speakers and speeches that place their personal gain over that of democracy. Some of these speakers have practiced **demagoguery,** which is a rhetoric that explicitly claims to speak for the public's best interests but implicitly gains more political power for the speaker and exacerbates divisions among the public, thereby weakening democracy. People who employ demagoguery are called demagogues, and their discourse typically overly relies on emotional appeals (especially fear and hatred), exaggeration, and divisiveness to encourage listeners to blame others for their problems and to act before thinking through a matter. Demagoguery, such as in Senator Huey Long's 1934 speech, "Every Man a King," and Senator Joseph McCarthy's 1950 speech, "Enemies from Within," are considered important speeches, but never great because of the ways they undermined and ultimately weakened democracy.

So how do you decide if an artifact strengthened or weakened democracy? You should attend to the principles upon which democracy depends or, as Bitzer states, the "higher principles of art, those that separate genuine public communication from propaganda, deception, power wielding, or self-aggrandizement."[16]

Democratic principles are the behavioral standards necessary for democratic governance to exist and thrive. Such principles include, but are not limited, to:[17]

- Participation of ordinary people in civic affairs.
- Equality of all people. (Giving all people the ability to participate in civic affairs rather than discriminating based on race, religion, sexuality, etc.)
- Tolerance of, and protection for, a variety of voices, including minorities or those with minority opinions.
- Open and thoughtful engagement of public issues, arguments, and positions.
- Unity or shared identity of community members as the public or as "we the people."
- Importance of the common good in balance with personal gain.
- Accountability of officials and public leaders to the will of the people.
- Transparency in civic affairs so the public knows what officials and leaders are discussing or deciding and why.
- Responsible and ethical use of power rather than using power for corrupt ends.
- Respect for, and protection of, the basic human rights of all people, including freedom of speech and the pursuit of life, liberty, and happiness.
- Rule of law. (Everyone, including leaders, is subject to prosecution if they violate the law.)

Artifacts that prioritize, reinforce, and/or practice such principles strengthen democracy. As you decide how a rhetorical artifact strengthens or weakens democratic principles, keep four considerations in mind. First, consider the artifact's context when judging its effects on democratic principles. The artifact was created at a specific moment for a particular audience or set of audiences. So rather than ask if the text strengthens or weakens democracy in a general sense, you need to more specifically ask whether and how it aided or hampered THESE democratic principles for THIS community at THIS place and time in relation to THIS issue.

Second, a rhetorical artifact can aid democratic principles while forwarding an ideology with which you disagree. In fact, the inclusion of diverse perspectives and the tolerance for disagreement are two hallmarks of democracy. Demagoguery can become an overly used accusation to silence those with whom we disagree. Public figures ranging from conservative media host Glenn Beck to liberal Senator Elizabeth Warren have been charged with demagoguery.[18] A person's political stance, background, and vision do not necessarily make their rhetoric demagogic; rather, their expression, proposals, and appeals determine whether their rhetoric harms or aids democratic principles. Thus, we need rhetorical critics who can carefully examine specific examples of rhetoric to determine how they are functioning. If we don't have these critics at work, we risk a cynical public who believes all politicians or public figures receive (and deserve) the same types of disparagement.

Third, the rhetor's conscious motive should not dictate your evaluation of an artifact's impact on democratic principles. Senator Joseph McCarthy may have truly believed he was saving the United States from a communist takeover even as his speeches undermined democratic ideals by silencing dissent, creating division among Americans, and securing greater authority for himself. Alternatively, a rhetor may appear to be aiming to hurt American democracy, perhaps by aggressively critiquing the country, while their rhetoric actually strengthens democratic principles by pointing out violations of those principles.

Fourth, the success of a rhetorical artifact may not necessarily correspond with its impact on democracy. It is possible that a rhetor might fail to accomplish his or her goals but still succeed in promoting public participation in the contemplation of the ideas under discussion and, thus, despite failing to reach the desired objective, still reinforce a fundamental democratic value.

Notice how three of the four warnings we offered for determining whether a rhetorical artifact strengthens or weakens democratic principles—to not base the judgment on the rhetor's ideology, conscious motives, or success—turn the critic's attention to the artifact itself. Rhetorical criticism presumes the critic can make evaluations about the impact of the artifact only after carefully describing and interpreting its rhetorical features. The critic's primary focus is on the public communication artifact itself, though it locates the artifact within its context.

SUMMARY

This chapter introduced you to rhetorical criticism as an intellectual discipline that can be employed in democratic participation, and it has presented you with the tools you need to conduct analysis of public communication. The chapter utilized a range of rhetorical forms including political cartoons, visual images, blog posts, and a musical performance. In particular it has shown how:

- Rhetoric works as symbolic action as symbols have the power to *do* things and to shape thought and action.
- Rhetorical criticism is the description, interpretation, and evaluation of rhetoric in order to form judgments about its meaning, effect, and impact.
- Rhetorical criticism functions as an intellectual discipline including qualities of mind such as curiosity, imagination, discernment, systematic study, and reasoned analysis.
- Rhetorical criticism examines the content, that is the message or argument that is communicated, and the form of that message.
- Context refers to the conditions or situation within which rhetoric is produced. It addresses the who, what, when, where, and why surrounding the production of the rhetoric.
- Audience refers to those targeted, reached, influenced, or impacted by the rhetorical act. Rhetorical criticism also inquires as to how particular rhetorical artifacts and contexts construct audiences.
- Rhetorical criticism is a form of civic engagement, democracy, and public participation.

KEY TERMS

audience p. 324	division p. 324	rhetorical method p. 321
context p. 319	rhetorical artifact p. 319	symbolic action p. 313
demagoguery p. 327		
democratic principles p. 328	rhetorical criticism p. 314	

REVIEW QUESTIONS

1. What does it mean to refer to rhetoric as symbolic action?
2. What is rhetorical criticism?
3. What are the intellectual qualities necessary for rhetorical criticism?
4. What are the three primary elements of rhetorical analysis?
5. What does it mean to evaluate when conducting rhetorical analysis?

DISCUSSION QUESTIONS

1. How might you use tools of rhetorical criticism in your everyday life?
2. How might rhetorical criticism allow you to see more deeply into the rhetoric around you, from a political speech to a popular film to a segment on the Daily Show?
3. What are the ethics of creating identification through division? Is it ever appropriate? When and why?
4. How is the process of rhetorical criticism similar to or different from scientific inquiry?
5. Which of the qualities of mind necessary to conduct rhetorical criticism have you already developed? Which do you need to strengthen?
6. Where can you find examples of rhetorical criticism that address civic issues? How do editorials or cable news shows function in this way?

CHAPTER 16

Public Communication Analysis

Chapter Objectives

Students will:

- Locate an appropriate rhetorical artifact for a public communication analysis.
- Determine the context for the rhetorical artifact.
- Describe and interpret a range of rhetorical features in the artifact.
- Evaluate the artifact's success or failure in achieving the rhetor's goals and in strengthening or weakening democratic principles.

On June 1, 2014, on his HBO show, *Last Week Tonight with John Oliver,* comedian John Oliver delivered a satirical tirade against a proposal then sitting before the Federal Communications Commission (FCC). The proposal recommended allowing Internet providers like Comcast, Time Warner, and Verizon to create a "fast lane" through which well-funded technology companies could send customers their content at faster speeds. In his 13-minute—and quite humorous—diatribe, Oliver argued that the proposal violated "net neutrality" whereby all online data is "treated equally no matter who created it, which is why the Internet is a weirdly level playing field and start-ups can supplant established brands." Oliver comically added, "The point is, the Internet, in its current form, is not broken. And the FCC is taking steps to fix that." Oliver wittily ridiculed the telecommunication companies for, in his estimation, extorting money from technology companies ("This has all the ingredients of a mob shakedown.") and using their influence with politicians to push the proposal forward. After referencing a study that named the amount of money Verizon spent to lobby the government as second only to a major government contractor, Oliver explained, "So just to be clear, the ranking of who buys government influence is, number one, military industrial complex, and number two, the provider of *Lizard Lick Towing.*" Throughout the segment, Oliver interspersed references to several studies to support

331

Comedian John Oliver, host of HBO's show *Last Week Tonight with John Oliver.*

his position, along with brief news clips, pictures, and graphs. Oliver concluded by charging viewers to argue against the proposal on the FCC's website for public comments. He called particularly on Internet "trolls" to direct their "indiscriminant rage" toward the FCC. Comments left on the FCC's website about the proposal totaled 24,550 during the two days following Oliver's plea (June 2 and 3), nearly equaling the number of comments received during the previous 18 days (27,954).[1] By July 28, 2014, the FCC had received over one million comments about the proposal, marking the "biggest response that the commission has ever received for a policy proposal."[2]

Oliver clearly succeeded in entertaining viewers and motivating them to accept his call to action,[3] but *how* did his rhetoric so successfully accomplish his goals? Perhaps more importantly, how did Oliver's HBO show impact democracy? Did it strengthen or weaken the principles on which democracy depends as we introduced and outlined in chapter 15? An advocate can successfully achieve his speaking goals without necessarily strengthening democratic principles.

BOX 16-1

Public Communication Analysis Steps

1. **Locate** an appropriate rhetorical artifact.
2. Determine the artifact's **context.**
3. Describe and interpret the artifact's **rhetorical features.**
4. Evaluate the artifact's effects in terms of achieving the rhetor's goals and strengthening democratic principles.

Public communication analysis is an approach to rhetorical criticism that helps critics ascertain the *effects* of a rhetorical artifact. It focuses on these central questions: Does the rhetorical artifact achieve the rhetor's goal and how or why not? Does the rhetorical artifact strengthen or weaken democratic principles and how? This approach expands and updates the traditional method of criticism known as Neo-Aristotelianism to address this interest in democracy and to include several more contemporary rhetorical concepts. We see this critical approach as an important building block for you as a new rhetorical critic and as a democratic participant. It is an approach that will cultivate your analytical sensibilities and enhance your understanding of public speaking fundamentals as you focus on how other rhetors have employed them. In this chapter, we outline the principles of public communication analysis and give you the tools to conduct your own rhetorical critique, following the approach's four major steps: locating an appropriate rhetorical artifact, determining the artifact's context, describing and interpreting the artifact, and evaluating the artifact.

LOCATING A RHETORICAL ARTIFACT

Recall from chapter 15 that a rhetorical artifact is an object of study in rhetorical criticism. Public communication analysis is particularly well suited to rhetorical artifacts that qualify as public communication. **Public communication** includes any publicly shared message or discourse that addresses significant community concerns or issues.[4] Artifacts can address public concerns in a number of ways, from trying to convince the audience a problem exists, to defining the key points in the debate about an issue, to advocating a particular solution—and many more. Rhetorical practitioners and scholars have often deemed rhetoric that addresses substantive, public issues essential for maintaining a healthy democracy. For instance, in 1919 as the Chautauqua circuits began to wane, Associate Editor of *The Century* Glenn Frank called on traveling lecturers to address the serious problems of the day in contrast to the then-popular lecturers "who tickle the fancy and flatter the prejudice of the crowd." He claimed the best speakers "will be able to introduce the community to the facts and principles of some underlying problem of our national life; and . . . [they] will be able to answer questions from the crowd and to stimulate a genuine community discussion."[5] More recently, communication scholars Ferald Bryan et al. have said the best public speeches are concerned with "worthy ideas to express, ideas that merit the attention and efforts of the speaker and the concern of the audience."[6]

BOX 16-2

Guidelines for Selecting an Artifact

- Addresses a significant public issue
- Attempts to persuade an audience
- Mostly uses verbal symbols
- Offers a single voice

To begin a public communication analysis, we recommend you choose an artifact that addresses a significant public issue; is attempting to persuade an audience (i.e., not a purely informative artifact); is mostly or significantly verbal (i.e., uses more words than images); and offers a single voice, whether written by an individual or a group (i.e., not a group discussion, dialogue, or online exchange). You will also find it easier to conduct a public communication analysis if you have a complete transcript of your artifact and, ideally, access to audio or video. We offer these recommendations because a public communication analysis best illuminates artifacts that meet these criteria. If we think of Oliver's HBO segment against the proposal to end net neutrality as a rhetorical artifact, for instance, we find it meets the guidelines. It attempted to persuade viewers to protest the proposal before the FCC; was largely a verbal argument, though it incorporated many audiovisual clips as support; and was delivered by Oliver in his singular voice. Rhetorical artifacts that more heavily use visual symbols are typically better suited to different rhetorical methods, such as ideological criticism described in chapter 17. Whatever type of verbal, persuasive rhetorical artifact you choose to analyze, it must address the problems, questions, and health of a community—or what rhetoric scholar Lloyd Bitzer calls the public's business.[7] Such artifacts can take many forms, including speeches and public statements by officials, concerned community members, and protesters; editorials and letters to the editor published in newspapers and magazines; and even relevant blog postings and websites.

DETERMINING THE CONTEXT

Once you've identified an appropriate rhetorical artifact, you need to determine its context. We defined context in chapter 15 as the conditions or situation within which rhetoric is produced. In that chapter we said that context "addresses the who, what, when, where, and why surrounding the production of the rhetoric." The answers to these questions help the critic determine how the context prompted and shaped the rhetoric. In this section, we briefly explain how finding answers to these questions can enhance your public communication analysis.

First, find out what the audience might have known about the rhetor (the "who"). In chapter 1, we defined rhetor simply as a person who speaks publicly. We will slightly extend that definition here to include the author or creator of the rhetorical artifact under examination—the "voice" of the artifact, be that an individual or group. The rhetor's public reputation at the time the artifact was produced, the rhetor's position in society, and/or the rhetor's background could have influenced what the audience expected from him or her. Oliver, for instance, became famous in the United States as a British comedian on the *The Daily Show with Jon Stewart* (2006–2013), an actor on the television show *Community* (2009–2011, 2014), and a political satirist on the podcast he coproduces, *The Bugle* (since 2007). So viewers familiar with Oliver probably expected him to offer witty or satirical political commentary on current events.

Second, consider what prompted the artifact (the "why") and the rhetor's goal (the "what"). Oliver's segment, for example, was provoked by the proposal to allow Internet providers to create an Internet "fast lane." He hoped to incite enough negative public reaction to dissuade the FCC from adopting the proposal. Knowing the reason or motivating cause for the rhetoric's production and the speaker's goal can help guide your analysis as you look for strategies the rhetor employed to respond to the provocation and attempt to achieve the goal.

Third, research the audience(s) who heard, read, and/or saw the artifact (the "to whom"). Such information can help you later analyze whether and how the rhetor adapted his or her message adequately to them. We discussed audience analysis and adaptation in chapter 5. Oliver's audience included the New York City residents and tourists in his live studio audience at the CBS Broadcast Center in New York City and viewers who watched the episode on HBO or on YouTube. Oliver had to adapt to their desire to be entertained and their presumed general ignorance regarding the proposal.

Fourth, reflect upon an artifact's location (the "where") to help you later analyze how the rhetor adapted to it. Location can include the specific place the rhetor delivered or disseminated the artifact (e.g., the geographic location and/or actual building or street) and/or the medium by which the rhetor distributed the artifact (e.g., face to face, television, YouTube, newspaper, online blog). All locations pose limitations on, and offer opportunities for, how a rhetor can most effectively present his or her message. In chapter 5, we touched on the environmental factors a physical location may offer a speaker, and we suggested ways a speaker may need to adjust to them. Here we add that the medium a rhetor chooses impacts how a rhetor develops a message and how it may be received. For Oliver, television and YouTube viewers have come to expect visually stimulating imagery and quick editing, which require a sophisticated team to produce.

Finally, consider the timing of an artifact (the "when"). Timing includes both the specific date and time for the artifact as well as the time period in which the rhetoric was situated. The latter is important to consider because communities may think and talk about public issues differently over time as new problems and perspectives emerge. For instance, during the 2008 presidential election, "Drill, baby, drill" became a refrain of several Republican Party nominees and eventually of the Tea Party movement, and offshore oil drilling was widely supported by Americans. After a British Petroleum (BP) deep-sea oil well exploded in the Gulf of Mexico on April 20, 2010, and began leaking thousands of barrels of oil a day, however, President Obama declared a six-month moratorium on such "ultra deep" drilling. Many people who had once declared enthusiasm for such drilling expressed concerns, revoked their support, or simply stopped publicly advocating for it. A critic analyzing an editorial advocating drilling during either of these time periods (2008 or 2010) would need to take into account the generally favorable or unfavorable public climate in which it was delivered because the strategies necessary to adapt to the audience would probably differ considerably. The rhetoric produced about an issue is as much shaped by a particular moment in time as it is an attempt to shape the future direction of that moment.

Reconstructing an artifact's context helps the critic determine whether and how the artifact achieved its goal(s) and strengthened or weakened democracy. The context explains the pressures, influences, and/or problems addressed or negotiated by the artifact, which can enable the critic to understand exactly how the artifact functioned for and in that moment. This is particularly important when considering the artifact's impact on democratic principles. While we can talk about democratic ideals in general or broad terms, a community defines, prioritizes, and enacts those principles in relation to a specific issue at a particular moment in time.

Determining an artifact's context involves identifying the rhetor, what prompted the artifact and the rhetor's goal, the audience, location, and timing. Together, this information informs and guides the critic's analysis of the artifact as he or she interprets how the artifact was shaped by and helped shape its context.

BOX 16-3

Questions to Ask About Context

- What might the audience have known about, or expected from, the rhetor?
- What prompted the rhetor to produce the artifact?
- What was the rhetor's goal(s) for the artifact?
- Who was the audience for the artifact, and how did the rhetor need to adapt to them?
- What was the artifact's location, and what restrictions or opportunities might that have created for the rhetor?
- What was the timing of the artifact?

DESCRIBING AND INTERPRETING THE RHETORICAL FEATURES

With the context firmly in mind, the critic can proceed to analyze the internal rhetorical features of the artifact itself. For public communication analysis, description involves recognizing and accurately identifying the rhetorical features at work in the artifact. The critic finds, labels, and observes each of the rhetorical features—from argumentation to delivery, if possible—with specificity. Interpretation will closely follow description as you ask what each of the rhetorical features is *doing* in terms of symbolic action. In the previous chapter, we defined symbolic action as the power of symbols to *do* things and to shape our thoughts and actions. Critics infer interpretations; you can rarely prove your inferences as definitively as you can describe the artifact. For example, you can name a text's organizational structure ("notice how it moves chronologically from past to present to the future"), but you infer how that structure functioned ("by moving chronologically, the speaker shifted the audience's attention from the past crisis to the more hopeful future, leaving them feeling more optimistic and comforted").

BOX 16-4

Tips for Your Analysis

For each rhetorical feature:
- **Find** the feature in the artifact
- **Describe** the feature with specificity
- **Interpret** how the feature may have influenced the audience's thoughts or actions

---

Not every rhetorical feature you examine will be important or even present in every artifact, but you cannot know that until you closely attend to the text and determine its central features. We recommend you conduct your rhetorical criticism by initially describing and interpreting each element systematically and then decide which elements provide the most important rhetorical insights to share with others. We now turn to specific rhetorical features to describe and interpret for your artifact: argumentation, appeals to emotions and loyalties, rhetor's credibility, construction of the desired audience, construction of the undesired audience, organization, style and framing, and delivery.

Argumentation

Many rhetorical artifacts include argumentation. Recall from chapter 13 that an argument is the advocacy of an idea, position, or course of action that is supported by evidence. Drawing from Stephen Toulmin's model, we identified the three main components of any argument as including a claim, data, and warrant, or justification for using the data to support the claim.[8] In chapter 12 we noted that Aristotle considered argumentation to be a form of proof he called logos.

BOX 16-5

Argumentation Reminders

Patterns of Reasoning

- Deductive reasoning
- Inductive reasoning
- Reasoning from example
- Reasoning from analogy
- Reasoning from cause
- Reasoning from sign
- Reasoning from authority

Reasoning Fallacies

- Hasty generalization
- Faulty analogy
- Faulty cause
- Slippery slope
- Appeal to authority
- Appeal to popularity
- Appeal to common practice
- Begging the question
- Ad hominem
- False dilemma

Analyzing an artifact's argumentation does *not* mean simply restating its main point(s) or message. Rather, it means helping your audience understand *how* its arguments are made by carefully identifying the artifact's claims, data, and warrants to determine the type and validity of the argumentation. A critic may also note the patterns of reasoning utilized as well as the inclusion of fallacies, which we described in chapter 13 as flaws or defects in reasoning that undermine the validity of an argument. A critic may also consider whether and how an artifact includes counter-arguments to its claims or proposals. Rhetorical criticism requires going beyond merely describing these components, however, to interpreting how they may have persuaded (or failed to persuade) an audience to accept the rhetor's position or point of view.

In his HBO segment, Oliver constructed an argument against the FCC proposal using causal reasoning. He claimed that if the proposal passed, then Internet providers would "run hog wild," charging exorbitant prices for the "fast lane" of content delivery that only the biggest technology companies could afford (i.e., net neutrality would end). His data, featured largely through news clips, graphs, and images, included the three common types of evidence explored in chapter 13: example, statistics, and testimony. Oliver, for instance, provided a historical example of Comcast previously slowing down Netflix's delivery speeds until Netflix agreed to pay more. He cited the statistics provided by a federal study that 96% of Americans can only choose from two or fewer cable providers. Oliver also offered testimony through news clips of cable company executives and lawyers attesting to their plans.

By utilizing causal reasoning, Oliver encouraged the audience to accept his prediction of the dark future that would occur if the proposal passed. He made his prediction appear believable by grounding it in multiple types of evidence the audience could see and hear. He frequently utilized news clips of cable company executives and lawyers alongside images of graphs and survey results, often appearing to have been visually lifted right from the pages of the external sources. Seeing and hearing the evidence firsthand suggested the veracity of his claim. Of course, Oliver's use of humor may have encouraged the audience to playfully accept his argument rather than think very hard about it. Also, the brevity of the news clips, graphs, and study results prevented the audience from scrutinizing them or Oliver from fully citing his sources or even providing the context from which he drew the clip or results. Consequently, accepting the evidence as adequate backing for Oliver's causal reasoning required the audience to place a fair amount of trust in Oliver to have ethically researched the topic and presented his findings.

BOX 16-6

Questions to Ask about Argumentation

Description

- What claims, data, and warrants did the artifact provide or not provide?
- Did the artifact use valid and sound arguments? How so or how not?
- What patterns of reasoning did the artifact include?
- How well did the artifact identify and reasonably respond to counter-arguments?

Interpretation

- Why did the artifact include the claims, data, and warrants it did? How might they have resonated with the audience?
- Why might the argument(s) have persuaded, or failed to persuade, the audience of the speaker's viewpoint, given the context?
- What kinds of attitudes, values, conclusions, or actions did the argumentation encourage or discourage?

Appeals to Emotions and Loyalties

Rhetorical artifacts typically appeal to the audience's emotions (e.g., happiness, sadness) and loyalties (e.g., liberty, family), or what Aristotle called pathos. As we explained in chapter 12, pathos is concerned with the psychological state of the audience; it is a measure and reflection of the extent to which we are moved by and feel invested in a topic and a message. A critic analyzing an artifact's appeals to emotions and loyalties must name the *specific* emotions and/or loyalties elicited by the artifact. It is not enough to simply state that the artifact appealed to emotions or that it solicited loyalties (vaguely stated), because such unclear statements fail to tell us much about the text's strategies or symbolic action. Instead, identify the specific emotions and loyalties solicited by the artifact and describe *how* the rhetor appealed to them.

After describing the artifact's pathos appeals, interpret how they functioned persuasively. Infer how soliciting particular emotions and loyalties may have aided (or hurt) the rhetor's goal, such as by relating specific feelings and allegiances with the rhetor's position. Recall from chapter 12 that rhetors typically associate emotions linked with pleasure—such as love, confidence, and joy—as well as loyalties held dear by the audience—such as patriotism, democracy, and freedom—with the proposals or ideas they advocate. In contrast, rhetors typically associate emotions linked with pain—such as fear, shame, and anger—and the disloyalties the audience rejects—such as terrorism, socialism, and tyranny—with counter-proposals, a standing policy, or a problem. You might also pay attention to the balance or imbalance of positive and negative appeals to emotions and loyalties as well as to the balance or imbalance of these appeals with argumentation. Recognizing an artifact's extensive reliance on fear appeals, for example, may indicate that a rhetor attempted to frighten the audience into accepting his or her position.

In his HBO episode, Oliver attempted to overcome public apathy about the proposal before the FCC by developing fear and rage in his audience. He presented net neutrality as something very precious the public was about to lose, using statements such as "if you've turned on the news lately, you may have heard some worrying references to the Internet changing"; "net neutrality is actually hugely important"; and "what's being proposed is so egregious that activists and corporations have been forced onto the same side." Oliver's language—worrying, hugely important, and egregious—attempted to amplify the audience's perception of the proposal's magnitude, causing them to fear its passing. Oliver then shifted the audience's anxiety toward feelings of indignation and rage against the cable companies promoting the proposal by presenting the companies as liars, extortionists, and corruptors of government. By emphasizing negative emotions and shifting from feelings of anxiety to indignation, Oliver motivated his audience to care about the issue and to ultimately accept his charge to do something about it.

BOX 16-7

Questions to Ask about Appeals to Emotions and Loyalties

Description

- Which specific emotions and/or loyalties did the artifact invoke or appeal to? Where? How?

- Which emotions and/or loyalties did the artifact associate with the position advocated, and with which emotions and/or (dis)loyalties did it associate counter-viewpoints?

- To what extent did the artifact balance positive and negative emotions and loyalties?

Interpretation

- How might the artifact's appeals to emotions have made the audience feel moved by and interested in the message—or fail to do so?

- What did the rhetor gain or lose from the emphasis or de-emphasis on appeals to emotion and audience loyalties?

- How did the emotional appeals focus the audience's attention? Toward what? Away from what, given the context?

Rhetor's Credibility

A third feature typically found in rhetorical artifacts is credibility, or what Aristotle called ethos. In chapter 3 you learned that ethos refers to the state of a rhetor's public character or persona. This definition should draw your attention to the rhetor's credibility as a construction or rhetorical creation.[9] Analyzing ethos involves examining how a rhetor presented him or herself as a character that the audience would perceive as credible. As we explained in chapters 3 and 12, credibility exists in the minds of the audience; a rhetor only has credibility to the degree the audience grants it to him or her. A rhetor's previous reputation plays a role in this perception, but the critic is interested in how a rhetor strengthens, modifies, or builds credibility through the public message under examination. Beginning critics can make the mistake of merely explaining a rhetor's prior reputation without examining the artifact itself or of saying the rhetor established credibility without clarifying the type or means.

For example, President Obama addressed the nation on July 19, 2012, a few days after George Zimmerman was found not guilty for murdering Trayvon Martin. Zimmerman, a neighborhood watch coordinator for his Sanford, Florida, community, fatally shot Martin, a 17-year-old African American boy who was walking home through the neighborhood. Saying Obama had credibility when speaking because he was the president would ignore the persona he emphasized in the speech as an African American man: "Trayvon Martin could have been me 35 years ago. . . . There are very few African American men in this country who haven't had the experience of being followed when they were shopping in a department store. That includes me."[10] Looking to the text for ethos reveals that Obama drew upon his personal experience as an African American man and as a member of the African American community to depict himself as an authoritative source on race conflicts.

As this example shows, critics must specify what *kind* of credibility or persona the rhetor attempted to construct *within the artifact being analyzed* and *how that credibility is developed*. In chapters 3 and 12, we suggested rhetors typically try to establish their credibility in terms of one or more qualities: (1) competence (expertise, preparation, intelligence), (2) trustworthiness (moral standing, integrity), (3) goodwill (having the audience's best interests at heart), and (4) dynamism (charisma).[11] Rhetors may use a variety of rhetorical means to establish any of these qualities, including, but not limited to, all the other rhetorical features highlighted in this chapter: argumentation, appeals to emotions and loyalties, construction of the audience and the other, organization, style, and delivery.

In his HBO segment, Oliver developed at least three types of credibility through a variety of rhetorical features. His use of audio-visual evidence to support his claims cultivated the impression that he was well researched on the net neutrality debate (competence). His expression of outrage suggested he wanted what was best for his viewers (goodwill). Lastly, his comedic charm and wit—manifested through his facial expressions, vocal tone, and timing—fostered a personal magnetism and vitality (dynamism). Together, these three qualities—competence, goodwill, and dynamism—presented Oliver as a trustworthy and forceful spokesperson against the FCC proposal, helping cultivate the viewers' trust in his claims and evidence. Of course, just because a rhetor constructs a particular persona does not mean everyone necessarily accepts it. Some analysts and critics of Oliver's segment, for example, later questioned Oliver's competence by attacking the accuracy of his facts.[12]

BOX 16-8

Questions to Ask about the Rhetor's Credibility

Description

- What type(s) of credibility did the rhetor try to cultivate through the artifact? How?
- What type of character did the rhetor present for him- or herself? How?
- What overall impression did the rhetor attempt to create for him- or herself?

Interpretation

- Why might the rhetor have chosen to develop the credibility he or she did, given the context?
- How did the rhetor's credibility appeals leave the rhetor vulnerable to attack or refutation?
- How did the qualities emphasized in the rhetorical artifact relate to the rhetor's reputation at the time?

Construction of the Desired Audience

In addition to analyzing how a rhetor developed his or her own credibility, critics can also examine how the rhetor constructed his or her desired audience. You might think of the desired audience as another character the rhetor constructs in and through their artifact, similar to how they developed their own persona. In chapters 5 and 15, we explained that a rhetor can offer a vision of a desired audience, that is, of an audience that does not yet exist. That vision may emphasize key qualities and attitudes the rhetor wishes from audience members and/or attempt to unite listeners into a mobilized and idealized community for a better future.[13] We briefly gave the example of Martin Luther King Jr., who did not simply target an existing audience but also presented a vision of Americans as people who ensure equality "for all God's children."[14]

As a critic, try to identify the rhetor's desired audience. Consider, for example, whom the rhetor addresses or seems to talk to. Identify the "you" or "us" the rhetor associates with positive qualities, and try to name those qualities, attitudes, and actions. As you do, examine the strategies the rhetor uses to develop his or her construction of the desired audience. Identifying an artifact's desired audience enables the critic to infer what qualities the rhetor invited actual audiences to adopt.

Oliver developed two different desired audiences in his HBO segment. First, he presented a desired audience that included intelligent and reasonable people who, once made aware of the threat posed by the FCC proposal, would join the "hippie protesters" and technology corporations in their righteous fight to protect net neutrality. Oliver referenced this audience in his occasional mentions of "you":

> "You might wonder. . . . "
> "I could show you. . . . "
> "When you look at the companies. . . . "
> "There might be something you can still do."

Oliver constructed an ideal audience that could logically follow his presentation and conclude with him that they must fight the proposal. This desired audience functioned as a smart adaptation to Oliver's actual audience. Viewers of Oliver's politically oriented HBO program were probably already fairly politically informed and active, thus, they were more open to being persuaded by Oliver's message and more likely to leave comments on the FCC's website.

Oliver developed a second desired audience in the last few minutes of his satirical tirade when he decided to "directly address the Internet commenters out there":

> Good evening, monsters. This may be the moment you've spent your whole lives training for. . . . We need you to get out there and, for once in your lives, focus your indiscriminant rage in a useful direction. Seize your moment, my lovely trolls! Turn on caps lock, and fly, my pretties, fly! Fly! Fly! Fly!

Obviously, Oliver delivered a very funny depiction of this audience. Interestingly, it was also quite negative, depicting the audience as subhuman ("trolls," "monsters," and akin to the Wicked Witch's flying monkeys in *The Wizard of Oz*) and as typically leaving useless ("for once in your lives") and exaggerated ("turn on caps lock") online commentary. Yet Oliver encouraged this group to direct their commentary toward the FCC to help prevent the proposal's adoption. In doing so, he provided a picture of the commendable audience he hoped they would become—politically active community members making a meaningful difference for the public good. This second desired audience was a somewhat odd choice, however, since his actual viewing audience probably did not consist of, or see themselves as, Internet trolls. Perhaps Oliver hoped the segment would go viral, as it did, to a broader audience through news coverage and YouTube, both of which tend to draw people who leave online comments.

BOX 16-9

Questions to Ask about the Desired Audience

Description

- What qualities or characteristics did the artifact associate with the desired audience? How? Where?
- Through what strategies did the artifact construct the desired audience?
- What kind of relationship did the artifact create between the rhetor's presentation of him- or herself and his or her desired audience?

Interpretation

- How did the artifact's desired audience attempt to transform an existing group into this desirable group?
- How might the artifact's desired audience have encouraged those who actually heard, viewed, or read the artifact to think or act?

Construction of the Undesired Audience

Yet another rhetorical feature critics can examine is how the rhetor constructed his or her *un*desired audience. This is the audience the rhetorical artifact negates by denying or dismissing their relevance or existence.[15] Artifacts typically construct an undesirable audience in one of two ways. First, they may silence a group by failing to include them in the text although that audience is directly affected or implicated by the artifact. A history textbook that relates the United States' westward expansion without ever referencing the perspectives of Native American peoples, for example, negates these groups' existence and silences their voices, thereby making them an undesired audience.

Second, a rhetorical artifact may construct an undesired audience by characterizing it negatively, typically associating the person or group with the "characteristics, roles, actions, or ways of seeing things to be avoided," making the undesired audience the opposite or flipside of the rhetor's desired audience.[16] If the history textbook referenced earlier included Native Americans in its explanation of the United States' westward expansion, but presented them as blood-thirsty, unreasonable, and uncivilized, then it would negate the Native Americans' human existence by portraying them as animalistic and, thus, undesirable—possibly in contrast to the qualities ascribed to the white settlers. Of course, just like the rhetor's credibility and desired audience, the undesired audience is a rhetorical construction that does not necessarily bear resemblance to the actual existing group it represents.

Critics, then, should identify and describe an artifact's undesired audience(s) by either noticing who is conspicuously absent or missing from the text or, more often, by examining how the artifact depicts a person or group negatively. Identify the "they," "he," or "she" the rhetor associates with negative qualities; name those qualities, attitudes, and actions; and identify the strategies the rhetor uses to construct the undesired audience(s). The critic must next interpret how the artifact uses the undesired audience(s) to accomplish the rhetor's goals, such as by helping rationalize the position or action being advocated, fostering unity among the desired audience by creating a common enemy or discouraging the adoption of particular qualities or perspectives.

In his HBO segment, Oliver constructed cable company executives as an undesired audience by characterizing them very negatively. He compared Tom Wheeler, former cable industry lobbyist, to a dingo (an undomesticated Australian dog) when he said appointing Wheeler the new head of the FCC was like hiring a dingo as a babysitter. A dingo is believed to have dragged a nine-week-old baby from an Australian campsite in 1980.[17] Oliver painted this savage image of Wheeler alongside references to cable executives as mobsters, members of a drug cartel, monopoly game characters, Hitleresque in their "evil," and as liars. In so doing, Oliver presented cable executives as detestable, representing the worst elements of society and driven by widely rejected vices: insatiable greed, unchecked power, and corruption. This portrayal justified their undoing through an overwhelming and outraged public response.

BOX 16-10

Questions to Ask about the Undesired Audience

Description

- Whose perspective or voice, if any, was missing from the artifact that could or should have been included?

- With what negative qualities, actions, or viewpoints did the artifact associate the undesired audience?

- How did the artifact relate the desired and undesired audiences? Typically, they are presented as opposites. How did the artifact offer such a construction, or what other kind of relationship did it build?

Interpretation

- What attitudes and actions might the undesired audience have helped rationalize or encourage (or debunk/discourage)?

- What type of community did the undesired audience help unify or define?

- How did the construction of the undesired audience possibly mobilize the desired audience?

Organization

A text's organization can also be a useful feature to analyze. The ordering of points or arguments—what Aristotle called arrangement—can reveal several things. First, the organization can expose the rhetor's logic or way of thinking. In chapter 6 we described how several patterns of arrangement represent the most common ways people tend to think. A few of the patterns included chronological, spatial, problem-cause-solution, and Monroe's motivated sequence. Identifying the artifact's pattern or structure can illuminate how the rhetor thought through the issue, possibly revealing his or her habits of mind.

Second, an artifact's organization can reveal the rhetor's presumptions about the audience. Rhetors typically structure their artifacts differently for audiences that are knowledgeable or ignorant about the topic or for audiences that are favorable, apathetic, or hostile toward the rhetor's thesis. Again, recall that in chapter 6 we explained how the patterns of arrangement are tailored to different types of audiences. So discerning the pattern can help you reveal the rhetor's expectations about the audience. Finally, examining an artifact's organization can suggest what the rhetor deemed important or unimportant. The amount of time or space the rhetor devotes to each topic, reason, emotion, and so forth may reveal what the rhetor viewed as more or less important and, perhaps, what he or she wanted the audience to perceive as important.

One of the best ways to determine the artifact's organization is to create an outline of the text, noting its main points and sections. Such work should help you determine the text's pattern of arrangement, such as those discussed in chapter 6. By specifying the structure, you will avoid the mistake of simply restating what the rhetor said in the order he or she said it: "She started by saying . . . then she claimed . . . and she ended by concluding that. . . . " Notice that such statements do *not* describe or interpret the artifact; they merely summarize or restate it.

Once you identify an artifact's pattern of arrangement, you can infer how the organization took the audience on a rhetorical journey. Interpret how each part of the artifact, starting with its beginning, may have shaped or influenced how the audience received what came next in the artifact; how that section of the artifact then affected how the audience received what followed; and so on until the text concludes. Such rhetorical movement is similar to what rhetoric scholar Stephen Lucas has called the **textual context**, which is the evolving environment created within an artifact as it interacts with and conditions the audience's responses to the text from its beginning to its ending. Lucas explains that "a text creates its own internal context as it unfolds in time and is processed by the listener or reader."[18] The textual context is quite different from how we used the word "context" earlier in this chapter, for textual context exists entirely within the artifact itself. It forces the critic to infer how the structure may have impacted the audience's reaction to the text *because of* the organization. It prevents organization from being undervalued by suggesting that how a rhetor moves strategically from the beginning to the end of the artifact matters.

Oliver's HBO segment loosely followed a problem-cause-solution structure. He seemed to presume a naive and unmotivated audience, bored into apathy about net neutrality, by taking time to slowly lay out the problem and cause before suggesting a solution. Oliver established the problem as the proposal to "allow big companies to buy their way into the fast lane, leaving everyone else in the slow lane," a proposition he claimed nearly everyone was against. He identified the causes as the tremendous financial benefits cable companies would reap by charging more for the fast lane, enabled by their lack of genuine governmental oversight and their monopolistic existence. He ended by offering the solution of leaving comments on the FCC's website against the proposal. By first establishing the problem and its cause(s), the structure created an appetite in the audience for a solution that would stop the proposal. However, Oliver's solution of attempting to influence the FCC's decision could not fully satisfy that appetite because he already presented the FCC as in league with the cable companies. The solution, then, seemed doomed, possibly reinforcing the picture Oliver created of the cable companies' overwhelming power over ordinary Americans.

BOX 16-11

Questions to Ask about Organization

Description

- What pattern of arrangement did the artifact follow? How would you label the structure employed by the artifact?
- What logic or way of thinking was suggested or encouraged by the artifact's organization?
- What parts of the artifact received the most emphasis or time? The least?
- What presumptions about the audience were revealed by the artifact's organization?

Interpretation

- How did the artifact rhetorically build, flow, or grow from beginning to end (or fail to do so)? How did each part influence the impact or meaning of the part(s) that followed?
- How might the artifact's structure have impacted the audience's impressions of the topic/issue?
- Why did the rhetor choose the structure, given the context?

Style and Framing

We defined style in chapter 8 as language or expression. In some ways, you are already analyzing an artifact's style when you consider the rhetorical features discussed earlier, such as the language a rhetor adopted to make arguments, appeal to emotions, construct him- or herself, create the desired and undesired audiences, and even indicate organizational structure. To enhance your analysis of an artifact's style, however, you can attend to at least three additional aspects of an artifact.

First, examine the level or type of language the rhetor employed. You can approach this in several ways, such as by determining the simplicity or complexity of the language (e.g., folksy versus grandiloquent); the informality or formality of the style (e.g., colloquial versus learned); or even the type of rhetorical "voice" it reflects (e.g., lawyerly, sermonic, motherly, etc.). Then interpret how these choices may have shaped the audience's impression of the rhetor, themselves (how they were addressed), and the topic or issue. For instance, President Ronald Reagan adopted a rather simple and gentle grandfatherly style to address the nation after the space shuttle *Challenger* exploded in

1986.[19] Most of his sentences and words were short, and they relied heavily on inclusive pronouns like "we." He spoke tender words such as those expressed to the astronauts' families: "But we feel the loss, and we're thinking about you so very much" and those delivered to the schoolchildren who watched the explosion on television: "I know it's hard to understand, but sometimes painful things like this happen." By adopting this style, Reagan assumed the authority of a wise elder who could comfort the American audience and declare that space exploration would continue despite the tragic setback.

Second, consider the stylistic devices a rhetor employs. Recall from chapter 8 that such devices are language techniques and literary tools that clarify meaning, express ideas in a compelling manner, and appeal emotionally to an audience. Identifying and describing these devices can aid you in interpreting how the rhetor used them to create a sense of rhythm, encourage visualization, enhance argumentation, or develop a sense of community (for example, Reagan's use of "we").

Finally, analyze the rhetor's framing of the issue addressed. In chapter 8 we defined framing as the use of language to order and make sense of the world. We explained that "framing is how we employ language to help shape perceptions of reality." For any public issue, people will notice and highlight some information as meaningful, and they will overlook, ignore, or downplay other aspects of the issue as less significant. The result of these choices will be the rhetor's preferred framing of the issue, which will include and typically even promote a definition of the *problem*, its *cause* (i.e., who's to blame), and best *solutions*.[20] To analyze framing, then, identify how the rhetor defined each framing component—problem, cause, solution. To do so, you might look to the artifact's use of language (to label or describe aspects of the issue) or other rhetorical features described previously.

Analyzing how the rhetor framed the issue enables the critic to determine how the rhetor's presentation of the problem matched, or failed to match, the actual issue that prompted the artifact (the "why" in the context). Drawing from chapter 12, you can also consider whether the framing appears to be an honest attempt to persuade the audience to adopt the rhetor's solution or a potentially dishonest effort to win supporters by intentionally confusing the audience's understanding of the issue.

As mentioned previously, Oliver's framing of the net neutrality issue was reflected in the problem-cause-solution organizational structure of his HBO segment. His definition of the problem as the proposal before the FCC to end net neutrality matched the issue that motivated the production of his television segment. Yet, he recognized that too few Americans perceived the proposal as a problem, leading him to suggest no longer referring to the proposal as ending "net neutrality" but, rather, as "cable company fuckery." That phrase, he added, "might actually compel people to want to do something." Unfortunately, as argued earlier, Oliver did not provide the audience with a meaningful way to actually improve the problem because he encouraged online commentary on the website of the agency he denigrated as corrupt just minutes earlier in his presentation.

We can add to this consideration of Oliver's framing an analysis of his use of stylistic devices. Stylistic devices helped enhance his argumentation as he repeatedly drew upon satire, irony, and metaphor/similes. The entire discourse was couched as satire as it attacked the FCC, cable companies, Internet commenters, and even the boring talk about net neutrality. Much of the ridicule was delivered in the form of metaphors and similes. He likened cable industry insiders to drug dealers: "It's almost as if [the cable companies] have agreed to stay out of each other's way like drug cartels." He equated Internet commenters with the actor who played the protagonist in *Karate Kid*: "Like Ralph Macchio, you've been honing your skills waxing cars and painting fences. Well, guess what? Now it's time to do some fucking karate." Oliver also employed irony: "The internet, in its current form, is not broken. And the FCC is taking steps to correct that." Together, these stylistic devices strengthened Oliver's argument by startling the audience into reflecting on the information and making the message more understandable and memorable. His comparisons with groups and movies the audience was probably familiar with helped Oliver explain and justify why the audience needed to get involved in stopping telecommunication providers from ending net neutrality.

BOX 16-12

Questions to Ask about Style and Framing

Description

- What level or type of language did the artifact adopt?
- What stylistic devices did the artifact employ?
- How did the artifact frame the issue (define the problem, cause, and solution)?
- How did the artifact's framing relate to the issue that motivated the artifact? How did the framing relate to (or contrast with) alternative framings of the same issue at the time?

Interpretation

- How might the artifact's style have shaped the audience's impressions of the issue? How might those impressions have encouraged the audience to adopt the rhetor's perspective (or not)?
- How did the stylistic devices create a sense of rhythm, encourage visualization, enhance argumentation, or develop a sense of community?
- How did the style and framing complement or contradict the other rhetorical features, such as argumentation, appeals to emotion, and the desired and undesired audiences?

Delivery

To analyze a rhetor's delivery of an artifact, you must have access to an audio or visual recording. In chapter 9, we defined delivery as the actual means of expression: "It is how a speaker physically conveys words and ideas, verbally and nonverbally, to the audience." Critics can analyze a rhetor's vocal delivery (how the voice and mouth is used to deliver words), nonverbal delivery (how the body is used to communicate), and use of memory (how one stores and recalls the information that is shared in a speech).[21] Critics can also consider whether and how the delivery of an artifact may have been hurt by a rhetor's communication apprehension—the heightened fear or sense of anxiety that arises when a person anticipates public speaking and interferes with the ability to do so effectively.

After identifying and describing the specific components of a rhetor's delivery (such as tone, rate, gestures, eye contact, etc.), a critic can interpret why the rhetor delivered the artifact as they did and how well. As explained in chapter 9, delivery is situational; its effectiveness depends on the rhetor's ability to adjust to situational factors (e.g., occasion, purpose, audience composition, and audience size) and conditions and constraints (e.g., distance from the audience, the arrangement of the speaking platform or lectern, and the formality of the occasion). We might add the communication medium as another potentially relevant element of the situation, since speaking in person at a meeting hall requires different delivery skills than talking into a microphone and through a television camera. A critic can identify the delivery choices the rhetor made for their speaking situation and infer how well they met the demands of that situation.

In his HBO segment, Oliver enhanced his credibility and further incited the audience's indignation by modeling this emotion through his delivery. Oliver mostly sat down behind his desk but leaned over it toward the camera while looking directly into the camera lens. He seemed truly angry about the FCC proposal and desperate to awaken viewers to the impending calamity as he moved toward, and made eye contact with, them. The unflinching eye contact also made Oliver appear to speak from the heart, though most television viewers would know he probably read from a teleprompter. Nonetheless, his eye contact and flawless delivery, devoid of vocal fillers or annoying gestures, suggested his confidence in his information and the righteousness of his cause. During the final two minutes of the segment, when Oliver directly addressed Internet commenters, he brought the segment to a climax by standing, walking away from his desk toward another part of the set, pointing directly into the camera, and backing his voice with music. Together, this ending further heightened the sense of crisis and stoked viewers' desire to respond to Oliver's call to action. While many of the artifacts you select for analysis may not be this dramatic or have as much money invested in their production, you can nonetheless analyze the rhetor's delivery for its impact on the audience and the way it complements the persuasive goal.

BOX 16-13

Questions to Ask about Delivery

Description

- How would you characterize the rhetor's vocal delivery in terms of his or her volume, tone, rate, pauses, articulation, pronunciation, and vocal fillers?

- How would you characterize the rhetor's nonverbal delivery in terms of his or her eye contact, facial expressions, gestures and movement, and appearance?

- How did the rhetor adjust his or her delivery to suit the situation, or how did he or she fail to do so?

- What mode of delivery did the rhetor adopt (extemporaneous, memorized, impromptu, manuscript)?

Interpretation

- How might the rhetor's delivery have influenced the audience's impression of the rhetor?

- How might the rhetor's delivery have aided or hurt their attempt to persuade the audience?

- How did the rhetor's delivery complement or distract from the artifact's other rhetorical features?

SPOTLIGHT ON SOCIAL MEDIA:
A Blog Devoted to Rhetorical Criticism of Public Communication

On September 30, 2010, a group of Carnegie Mellon University graduate students studying rhetoric launched *The Silver Tongue,* a blog devoted to sharing rhetorical criticism of public communication. Writers for the blog include the founding members and additional contributors from Carnegie Mellon and several other universities and colleges.[22]

The founders of *The Silver Tongue* present their work as "rhetorical criticism for the engaged citizen." They explain:

> If rhetoric really matters to the public, as rhetoricians often claim, then we have a responsibility to aid the public in making sense of it. We are obligated to make our expertise available to engaged citizens who want "assistance in evaluating an art that plays a direct role in the affairs of the state."[23]

To that end, the writers analyze various examples of public communication, using many of the rhetorical concepts and features discussed in this chapter.

Maggie Goss's November 10, 2014, submission focuses on framing. Goss examined an interview with actress Jennifer Lawrence published in *Vanity Fair* on October 17, 2014, a few weeks after nude pictures of Lawrence were leaked on the Internet. Goss argues that Lawrence reframed the images "not as a scandal or something to be embarrassed about, but rather as a sex crime committed against her." Goss outlines, and supports with evidence, three ways Lawrence accomplished the reframing:

> "**1.** By telling us the images weren't meant for the public to see,
>
> **2.** By calling the publicity surrounding the photo leak a sex crime, and
>
> **3.** By insisting that those who hacked and viewed the photos be ashamed of themselves."

We might add to Goss's analysis that Lawrence's reframing reflects at least two components of most frames: the problem and its cause (i.e., who's to blame). In this case, Lawrence shifted the problem from her decision to pose nude (a sex scandal) to the photos being leaked and publicized (a sex crime). She switched the blame from herself to the hackers and viewers of the photos. Though Goss does not indicate that a solution is stated—the third component of most frames—Goss provides links to two websites that have "information about what is being done to address the issue" of "celebrity photo hacking."[24]

Goss's analysis demonstrates how a critic can employ a rhetorical feature, such as framing, to better understand how a public figure uses rhetoric to shape a current public conversation.

The Silver Tongue welcomes submissions by interested readers so long as the submission is grounded in knowledge such as rhetorical theory.[25] You might consider offering your next public communication analysis to the blog for possible publication!

Discussion Questions

- How might you use public communication analysis to help fellow community members make sense of rhetoric?
- What public issue is currently being discussed, and what specific artifact could you analyze that addresses the topic?
- How might choosing an artifact disseminated through social media influence how you contextualize, describe, interpret, and evaluate it?
- In addition to *The Silver Tongue*, where can you publish your analysis so others benefit from it?

EVALUATING THE RHETORICAL ARTIFACT

Once you have systematically described and interpreted your artifact for features such as the ones listed previously, you can judge the artifact's impacts, both in terms of its success or failure in achieving the rhetor's goals and in strengthening or weakening democratic principles. We will discuss both of these assessments in turn.

Did the Artifact Achieve the Rhetor's Goals? Why or Why Not?

Critics should judge if and why the artifact achieved the rhetor's goals. The critic should use her understanding of the context and interpretations of the rhetorical features to argue how the features helped the rhetor achieve his or her goals or why they fell short. Return to your research about the artifact's context—the answers to who, what, when, where, and why—and consider how each rhetorical feature responded to and attempted to shape that context to accomplish the rhetor's desired outcome(s).

Of course, when we look more closely at achieving goals, we quickly discover how complicated determining success can be. What counts as success, with what audience, and how quickly must that improvement occur? Speech scholar W. Norwood Brigance, for instance, has claimed "the success of any speech is determined, not by whether it carries the day, but by how far it moves toward that goal."[26] As a critic, you must decide, and ultimately argue to your audience, how to define success or failure for the artifact, given its context.

Oliver's HBO segment successfully motivated viewers to leave tens of thousands of comments on the FCC's website about the proposal to end net neutrality. He transitioned the audience's ignorance and apathy into fear and indignation through his appeals to pathos and logos; style; identification and depiction of the problem and cause; and his portrayal of himself, his desired audience, and the undesired audience. These features seem to have overcome the previously argued shortcoming of presenting the FCC's website as a solution. Indeed, after hearing from over 4 million Americans "overwhelmingly in support of a free and fair internet," the FCC retained net neutrality by voting on February 26, 2015 to reclassify Internet service as a public utility.[27] This ruling prohibited Internet providers from charging more money for faster Internet speeds. Consequently, we can label Oliver's segment as a rhetorical success, because he motivated his audience to voice their opposition to the FCC proposal, which helped to pressure the commission to retain net neutrality. However, the finality of the FCC's decision is uncertain. In the months that followed the FCC's decision, multiple telecommunication companies and tradegroups filed lawsuits against the FCC's reclassification.[28] Also, a future president could influence the outcome through new appointments to the FCC (who could then overturn the FCC's ruling) or by encouraging Congress to pass legislation that would overrule the FCC's decision. If the ruling is ultimately overturned, will that mean Oliver's rhetorical effort was, in fact, a failure in the long term?

Did the Artifact Strengthen or Weaken Democratic Principles? How?

In addition to assessing the artifact's ability or failure to achieve the rhetor's goals, a public communication analysis requires the critic to also consider the artifact's impact on democratic principles. We argued in chapter 15 that rhetoric that addresses the people's business should strengthen democracy, and we suggested that critics evaluate an artifact's impact on democracy by determining whether it strengthens or weakens democratic principles. In that chapter, we defined democratic principles as the behavioral standards necessary for democratic governance to exist and thrive, and we gave examples such as the participation of ordinary people in civic affairs; the equality of all people; and the tolerance of, and protection for, a variety of voices. Artifacts that prioritize, reinforce, and/or practice such principles strengthen democracy. To help you assess your artifact's impact on democratic values, we will delve into this idea a bit further by considering, separately, how an artifact might support democratic principles directly *or* indirectly.

How Did the Artifact Directly *Support or Hurt Democratic Principles?*

A rhetorical artifact might *directly* strengthen democracy by advocating for or addressing one or more democratic ideals. For instance, Oliver's HBO segment strengthened democratic principles because it directly argued for the equality of all Internet content, no matter who produced it (versus privileging companies that can pay more for faster speeds). Alternatively, an artifact can directly weaken democratic principles by explicitly calling for their dismissal, subjugation to other values, or inapplicability to particular groups of people. Some gay rights activists, for instance, have critiqued rhetoric opposed to gay marriage as undemocratic on the grounds that it explicitly promotes inequality among Americans regarding marriage.

How Did the Artifact Indirectly *Support or Hurt Democratic Principles?*

An artifact can strengthen democracy *indirectly* by modeling or practicing democratic principles. All the discursive practices of productive public discourse established in chapter 2, for instance, reinforce democratic principles. Those discursive practices include commonality, deliberation, inclusiveness, provisionality, listening, learning, lateral communication, imagination, and empowerment. Any behaviors in addition to these that put democratic principles into practice strengthen democracy. Oliver's segment strengthened democracy indirectly because his explanation and argument made the proposal before the FCC and the surrounding debate more

Mother and daughter in Denver, Colorado join a protest supporting gay marriage before it was granted legal protection by the Supreme Court in 2015.

transparent to the public, and his charge to directly engage the FCC empowered viewers to get involved in civic affairs. Alternatively, artifacts can indirectly weaken democratic principles by modeling or practicing undemocratic behavior.

Remember that an artifact does not necessarily have to adopt the qualities of productive discourse, outlined earlier, to strengthen democratic principles. In chapter 2, we claimed that uncivil discourse can be productive if it prompts public discourse that leads to more inclusivity and the common good (i.e., if it helps achieve democratic principles). Democracy needs harsh critics, too. Aspects of Oliver's HBO segment qualified as uncivil, such as his personal attacks on cable company executives by calling them "evil" and using vulgarity. Such rhetoric emphasized differences between the executives and the rest of Americans rather than attempt to find common ground or even consider the executives' perspective. Oliver certainly used this exaggerated and crude discourse to entertain viewers, but its shocking nature could have also awakened them to the issue, prompting viewers to get involved in the public conversation and protect the common good.

As this example demonstrates, a rhetorical artifact may fall along a sliding scale between strengthening and weakening democratic principles. Most texts probably improve some principles and hurt others. Clearly, the more ways a single artifact strengthens democratic principles, the better. You will need to decide in which direction your text tends by paying close attention to the artifact's rhetorical features and context.

SUMMARY

Public communication analysis is an approach to rhetorical criticism that enables critics to determine whether and how a rhetorical artifact achieves its goals and whether and how it strengthens democratic principles. The approach assumes that rhetoric that addresses public issues should strengthen democracy. This chapter provided the methodological steps necessary to conduct such an analysis.

- A critic begins by locating a suitable rhetorical artifact. For public communication analysis, such an artifact must address a public issue and should be persuasive, verbal, and expressed in a single voice.
- The critic then determines the context for the artifact by discovering what the audience might have known about the rhetor; what prompted the artifact; the rhetor's goal(s); the audience(s) who heard, read, or saw the artifact; and the artifact's location and timing.
- Next the critic describes and interprets several rhetorical features, including argumentation, appeals to emotions and loyalties, the rhetor's credibility, the desired audience, the undesired audience, organization, style and framing, and delivery.
- Finally the critic makes two types of judgments about the artifact, using what he or she learned from the context and rhetorical features. The critic evaluates whether the artifact was successful or failed to achieve the rhetor's goals, recognizing the need to argue for what counts as success or failure. The critic also judges whether the artifact strengthened or weakened democratic principles by considering the principles the artifact attempted to directly reinforce (or violate) and indirectly practiced or modeled (or failed to do so).

KEY TERMS

public communication
p. 333

public communication
analysis p. 333

textual context p. 345

REVIEW QUESTIONS

1. What kinds of rhetorical artifacts are best suited to public communication analysis?
2. Which aspects of an artifact's context should you discover? Why?
3. How do you describe and interpret an artifact's argumentation, appeals to emotions and loyalties, organization, and style and framing? What mistakes should you avoid?
4. What is the difference between the rhetor's construction of him- or herself (credibility), the desired audience, and the undesired audience?
5. By what means might you evaluate an artifact's success in achieving its goals?
6. By what means might you evaluate an artifact's impact on democratic principles?

DISCUSSION QUESTIONS

1. How well could public communication analysis be applied to visual or audio arti-facts or to discursive exchanges or dialogues? How would you need to alter or modify the method?

2. To what degree do you think artifacts develop in response to preexisting issues, and to what degree do skilled rhetors create such issues? Commercials, for exam-ple, want viewers and readers to believe they have a problem that the product or service being marketed can solve. Did that problem preexist *as* a problem? Can you think of an instance of public communication that helped create the percep-tion of an issue that needed to be addressed?

3. Which of the rhetorical features seem most important to analyze? How can a critic decide which to focus on or to include when sharing his or her work?

4. What kinds of evidence best support a critic's interpretations of an artifact's rhe-torical features? How does a critic know when his or her inferences are right? How should we judge the merit of a critic's interpretations, especially when two critics disagree about how a rhetorical feature functioned?

5. How can a critic ever really make judgments about an artifact's success or failure or impact on democratic principles? What kinds of evidence does that require?

CHAPTER 17

Ideological Criticism

Chapter Objectives

Students will:

- Define ideology in its dominant and resistant forms.
- Identify the central aims of ideological criticism.
- Locate a rhetorical artifact suitable for ideological criticism.
- Describe and interpret the function of ideology within the artifact.
- Evaluate the success of a rhetorical artifact in promoting civic participation and democratic principles.

When American singer-songwriter Nina Simone debuted her song "Mississippi Goddam" at Carnegie Hall in 1964, she crossed the line. She crossed the line between entertainment and social critique.

In the early days of her career, Simone was loath to make any political statement in her music that would risk offending her audience and result in the loss of performance gigs. Born in North Carolina in 1933, Simone, who was African American, knew much about segregation and the Jim Crow South, but performing in jazz clubs was a way to make a living, to pay the bills while she had her sights set on more respectable concert venues.[1] On the one hand, she did not want to ruffle feathers. On the other hand, like many African American artists of her era, Simone saw art itself as a means to break down racial barriers and stereotypes.

But when the 16th Street Baptist Church in Birmingham, Alabama, was bombed on a Sunday morning on September 15, 1963—less than a month after the March on Washington where Martin Luther King Jr. gave his "I Have a Dream" speech and just three months after World War II veteran and activist Medgar Evers was shot in the back in his own driveway—Nina Simone was enraged. America,

American musician Nina Simone (born Eunice Kathleen Waymon) was known as "The High Priestess of Soul."

too, was shocked and speechless. The 16th Street Baptist Church had served as a center for civil rights activities, and members of the Ku Klux Klan were responsible for the bombing. Four 14-year-old girls were killed, and many other children were wounded as they entered the basement for a children's service. Simone felt she must do something, and, despite the unspoken code that said musical performances were for entertainment and not for racial protest, she wrote "Mississippi Goddam" in response. She would later say, "I'm not beyond killing. Nobody is. But I wrote 'Mississippi Goddam' instead."[2]

Simone never made a studio recording of the song, but for a rhetorical critic, the live recordings are much richer, for we can hear the audience response to her performance. In one recording, you first hear Simone declare as the song begins, "The name of this tune is Mississippi Goddam! And I mean every word of it." The audience laughs—a sign that they expect entertainment and comedy at a Simone concert. The laughter also seems appropriate given the music Simone and her band are playing as she introduces the song: the music is frantic but playful. It creates a sense of expectation, maybe even of comedy. And then when the lyrics begin, there is rupture between the sound of the music and the meaning of the words:

Alabama's gotten me so upset
Tennessee made me want to lose my rest
And everybody knows about Mississippi Goddamn

After this introduction, Simone can be heard on the live recording telling her audience, "This is a show tune, but the show hasn't been written for it yet." Again they laugh, but the crisis in the lyrics continues:

Hound dogs on my tail
School children sittin' in jail
Black cat across my path
I think everyday's gonna be my last

Lord have mercy on this land of mine
We all gonna get it in due time
I don't belong here, I don't belong there
I've even stopped believing in prayer[3]

Part of what makes Simone's song so provocative—and risky—is that she calls into question a reigning ideology in that era of United States history: the ideology of racial segregation. This ideology placed African Americans outside the category of "American" by devaluing their civic participation and making violence against them common, expected, and normal to much of the white power structure that controlled politics and cultural and economic institutions.

An **ideology** is a set of shared beliefs and values that forms an interpretation of the world and suggests appropriate ways for a group to act in it. One way of understanding ideology is as a set of ideas that tells people how to think. Another way to understand it is as a way of explaining *how* people think in order to evaluate whether that thinking is useful or destructive in a democratic society. Not all ideologies are so clearly violent and destructive as racism; an ideology can be any shared lens through which a group or culture understands and explains the world.

BOX 17-1

Examples of Ideologies

Agricultural sustainability

Atheism

Buddhism

Christianity

Democracy

Environmentalism

Existentialism

Fair trade

Heteronormativity

Hinduism

Humanism

Imperialism

Islam

Judaism

Libertarianism

Locotarianism (food movement)

Marxism

Neoliberalism

Nihilism

Pacifism

Patriarchy

Racism

Social Darwinism

Socialism

Ideologies include political or social philosophies, major religions, scientific models, and economic systems. But ideologies are not simply ideas. Because they shape how people see the world, ideologies inform how people behave, and thus we find that ideologies are expressed in nearly every aspect of human society, including popular music, film, advertisements, and social media. See Box 17-1 for a list of some major ideologies. As a way of trying to understand how ideology works, choose any one of these ideologies and brainstorm a list of the values and beliefs that define them. How do those values and beliefs lead to behaviors that influence knowledge, actions, and social relationships?

"Mississippi Goddam" is a compelling musical recording for many reasons, but chief among these is the way it exposes the values and beliefs of leading segregationists and political leaders, and makes the audience see them as laughable, incredible, and intolerable. The song unmasks an ideology of racism and forces the audience to see it in a new light.

When any critic—be she a songwriter or a student in a public speaking class— invites her audience to see how an ideology is at work in an artifact and how it asks us to accept something as normal or natural that is, in fact, a manufactured reality, this critic is engaged in ideological critique. **Ideological criticism** is a method of reading and interpreting rhetorical artifacts that exposes the expressions of power and control inherent in the artifacts. This type of critique begins by describing the ideas and beliefs communicated by a given artifact, interprets the assumptions and meaning of the ideological message, and then evaluates the effect of this ideology on democratic principles and civic participation.

In this chapter, we first outline the primary goals of ideological criticism within the field of rhetoric, and we foreground its investment in empowering members of the public to enact change. Then we walk you through the four steps of conducting an ideological critique of your own rhetorical artifact: locating an artifact, determining the artifact's context, describing and interpreting the artifact's ideological assumptions, and evaluating how the ideology supported in the artifact elevates or challenges democratic principles.

BOX 17-2

Ideological Criticism Steps

1. **Locate** an appropriate rhetorical artifact.
2. Determine the artifact's **context**.
3. Describe and interpret the artifact's **ideological assumptions**.
4. **Evaluate** how the ideological assumptions in the artifact elevate or challenge democratic principles.

IDEOLOGICAL CRITICISM AND CIVIC PARTICIPATION

This final section of the textbook focuses on rhetorical criticism, and in chapters 15–17 we are particularly interested in how the tools of rhetorical criticism can help promote democratic participation. We believe that the move from public speaking to rhetorical critique can encourage students to recognize, name, and counter unproductive discourse and work for positive social change. In this belief, we are influenced by rhetorical scholars who see ideological criticism as a tool particularly well suited to promoting social change, especially when this form of critique is employed in the service of civic engagement and the promotion of democratic principles.

Ideological critics are most interested in the power of ideological expressions to dictate and control groups through language and other forms of symbolic action. Rhetorical scholar Michael Calvin McGee writes that ideology "is a political language, preserved in rhetorical documents, with the capacity to dictate decision and control public belief and behavior."[1] Ideological critics work to make this political language more obvious or visible to public audiences so that they may have increased capacity to respond to such messages—rather than simply be controlled by them.

Ideological criticism's focus on empowerment of the public and on social change makes it a powerful tool for those who wish to be better, more educated participants in democratic society. Rhetorical scholar Dana L. Cloud notes that the study of "how power, consciousness, and resistance are crafted, articulated, and influenced in and by the act of speaking, is vital to the projects of critique and social change."[5] In other words, for some rhetorical critics, the *whole point* of studying rhetoric is to articulate how power shapes the perceptions and beliefs of audiences precisely because this study provides a gateway to social change.

If ideology has the power to shape consciousness, then it is particularly important to understand *how* individuals may resist its cultural programming. To explain how individuals alter the forces that shape their social, political, and religious realities, ideological critics turn to the concept of agency. **Agency** is an individual's ability to act freely or to independently intervene in a situation, his or her own life, and the world. Philosophers, rhetoricians, and everyday citizens engage in endless debate about the degree to which any one of us has true agency, and there is no doubt we are all constrained by economic situation; gender; and national, religious, social, and political contexts. We agree that agency is always limited in a given situation, but we stress that ideological critics are interested in the *degree* to which rhetors can expand or contract agency through language and symbolic action. Agency is a central concept in ideological criticism because the individual actions that marshal language, sound, and visual symbol do indeed have power—the power to expand or contract the liberty of others.

Ideological criticism can illuminate the parameters and influence of civic participation in a society. This is because those who engage or choose not to engage in civic life often do so at least in part based on a system of values and beliefs they hold collectively. For example, from her social location as an African American woman in the 1960s, Nina Simone was actively discouraged from making political speeches on national television or running for the US Senate. Her choice to write and perform a protest song for a predominantly white audience at Carnegie Hall, then, was a brave and even shocking challenge to the ideology of racism. Though her agency and civic participation were limited by her race and her gender, Simone found a way to participate in a pressing political issue of her day, and—at least for the duration of the song— she asked her audience to do the same. "Mississippi Goddam" is a song, yes, but it is also a searing ideological critique.

As we turn now to the specific steps of ideological critique, keep in mind that the ultimate goal of ideological analysis is to make visible the ways "power, consciousness, and resistance are crafted, articulated, and influenced" in rhetorical artifacts.[6] This goal is important precisely because when we have tools to recognize how these artifacts shape our thinking and culture, we are better able to evaluate which rhetorical acts elevate democratic principles and which, in turn, discourage full democratic participation.

LOCATING A RHETORICAL ARTIFACT

The first step of ideological critique is to locate an appropriate rhetorical artifact. Expressions of ideology pervade nearly every aspect of human society; they are present in our social and religious rituals, our political lives, our intellectual commitments, our economic choices, and our forms of entertainment. This means you might find rich artifacts among television advertisements, popular music, viral YouTube clips, music videos, or political cartoons—just to name a few possibilities.

Artifacts reveal their ideologies and attempt to persuade audiences in two ways. First, they embody or elevate a particular value or belief. Second, they resist a dominant ideology by challenging powerful interests. Sometimes artifacts do both at once. Consider, for instance, the way Nina Simone's song elevates a more tolerant America by criticizing the pervasive violence against African Americans and suggesting the entire country suffers—and may perish—as a result. "Lord have mercy on this land o'mine," she sings. "We all gonna get it in due time."[7] Here she criticizes the current system of racial relations *and* urges her audience to hold and applaud different views.

As you work to locate an artifact for ideological criticism, begin by looking for one that expresses a shared belief, makes a recommendation for collective action, or calls a commonly held value into question. The artifact may make these statements directly or indirectly. Remember, ideologies can be positive, negative, or neutral. You do not have to look for statements about something as insidious as racism, but you do want an artifact that tries to persuade an audience about something related to communal thought or action. Does the artifact advance a perspective on how one should live life or take a stand on a significant social issue? What are those who watch, read, or listen to your artifact being asked to think about, reject, or accept?

You may find it particularly fruitful to look for an artifact that you believe is easily absorbed or taken in by others, but that you feel deserves a closer look because it says something unexpected, positive, or troubling on the issue of social roles, political power, or economic choices. Perhaps the lyrics of your favorite rap musician are violent toward women, yet you see friends rapping along without thinking about what messages they are coming to view as normal. Or perhaps you find the Cheerios commercial featuring an interracial family a positive revision of what counts as normal in American culture. Or maybe you notice friends laughing at a particular Super Bowl commercial that presents a newer, more expansive view of masculinity. You might like them to look past the humor to see what is compelling in the message. Would they be different consumers, or different political participants, if they better understood the message of this artifact? These themes and questions are good places to start when selecting an artifact for ideological analysis.

You will want to steer away from artifacts that are written primarily to entertain or to inform *if* those artifacts do not contain significant statements about power or resistance. It is rather easy to find a song you love or a blog you enthusiastically follow that does not lend itself well to ideological critique. If you happen to choose this type of artifact, you may become more and more frustrated as the assignment progresses because you can find little to critique about ideology in the artifact. This does not mean you've chosen a bad song or an uninteresting blog. It may mean, however, that your artifact does not directly relate to questions of power and social, economic, or political assumptions. Unless the artifact reinforces a widely accepted way of seeing the world—or challenges that widely accepted way of seeing the world—it is not a good choice for ideological criticism.

BOX 17-3

Characteristics of an Artifact Well Suited for Ideological Critique

- Uses **verbal, audio,** or **visual** symbols—or a combination.
- **Elevates** or **challenges** a common way of seeing the world.
- Attempts to **persuade** an audience to live or act in a certain way.
- May be familiar to your audience, but the **audience has not reflected on its ideological assumptions**.

Once you have located a suitable artifact, you have a great opportunity as a critic to help your audience examine *why* they may instinctively like or dislike a particular song, or *how* a video they have seen a few times is communicating something significant about shared beliefs. This is exciting and important work because raising knowledge and awareness among your audience is a crucial element of social change. But before you move to interpretation, the next step in ideological critique is to determine the context of the artifact.

DETERMINING THE CONTEXT
OF THE RHETORICAL ARTIFACT

The context of an artifact helps you analyze why the artifact looks and sounds the way it does. This step is central to interpreting how the artifact challenges or reinforces an ideology. Rhetorical critics are not generally interested in the *timelessness* of artifacts (in the way an art historian or a literary critic might be). Instead, a rhetorical critic seeks to understand how the artifact is a product of the location, time, and rhetor that created it. A rhetorical critic also seeks to understand the artifact not only as a product of its context but also as a *participant* in its time, place, and culture.

To determine the artifact's context, you should consider five related elements: the rhetor, the social or political events that prompted the artifact's creation, its primary audience, its timing, and its form of circulation. As you research each of these elements, ask yourself questions and jot down notes about how each element helps you better understand the artifact. Such questions and notes can point you toward arguments and conclusions you may make in the later interpretation phase of your critique.

The rhetor of your artifact should be the author or creator of the artifact. When we discussed public communication analysis in chapter 16, we focused primarily on single-voiced artifacts and noted that the rhetor was almost always the speaker. With ideological artifacts such as photographs, popular songs, editorials, or television commercials, the rhetor may be harder to pinpoint. Your rhetor may be the photographer, the singer, the songwriter, the author—or it may be the news organization that selected and framed the photograph, or the company that produced the commercial and is using it as a vehicle to sell a product. While the question of "who" your rhetor is can be potentially complicated, it is a very important one. This is the person or entity most responsible for the creation of this artifact as it appears in context and the one that intends to influence others' thinking or behavior through symbolic action. In the case of Nina Simone's song "Mississippi Goddam," Simone is the rhetor. She is the songwriter and the performer who hopes to influence public action about racial discrimination. When *Newsweek* ran a much criticized cover during the 2012 presidential election campaign asking whether Mitt Romney was too much of a wimp to be president, the rhetor was not the photographer or the designer responsible for the layout, but the magazine's editorial staff. They were the ones whose choices and intentions framed the photograph and text in its final form. To determine the rhetor, ask: Who sought to alter a social, economic, or political situation through this act of rhetoric?

Second, look for the specific social, economic, or political events that led to the creation, performance, or circulation of your rhetorical artifact. This is the step where you ask why the artifact makes the arguments it does in the ways that it does, and what the rhetor hoped the artifact would accomplish. You might begin by thinking about or looking for references to the social, economic, or political realities that may have motivated the rhetor and those who participated in the artifact's circulation. For example, the opening of this chapter explains how specific social and political events connected with the bombing of the 16th Street Baptist Church in Birmingham, Alabama, led Nina Simone to write "Mississippi Goddam."

Third, consider who the audience is for the chosen symbolic action. Such information can help you later analyze whether and how the rhetor adequately adapted his or her message to them. Nina Simone's audience—at least in the live performance— was a primarily white, economically comfortable one (in 1964 they could afford tickets and an evening off to attend a concert at Carnegie Hall). At this point, you might jot down a question asking why Simone chose a primarily white, middle- and upper-class audience for her protest song. Such a choice was much riskier for her future as a performer; there was real incentive to keep her audience good-humored and entertained. On the other hand, she may have believed that white audiences— more than African American ones—needed to be convinced that racist actions should no longer be tolerated, and she may have wanted her audience to see her as a member of the group enduring discrimination, rather than a woman whose fame and talent allowed her to exist outside of it.

The next step is to consider the artifact's timing. If possible, find the date the artifact was produced, delivered, or published. Also consider the time period in which the artifact circulated. What was happening politically, socially, economically, and so forth that may have influenced how audiences responded to the artifact? How did the artifact relate to similar types of artifacts that preceded it or to other types of commentary on the issue it addresses? We know, for instance, that Simone performed "Mississippi Goddam" at Carnegie Hall on March 21, 1964 and released a live recording of the concert later that year on her album *Nina Simone—In Concert*.[8] In this way and as established earlier, Simone participated in a national civil rights movement that challenged the racist policies and practices against African Americans. Simone's recording departed from the racist expectation of deference toward white listeners, but joined the increasing number of black voices in protest against such practices and presumptions.

The final element of context to consider is how the artifact was circulated. This helps you determine whether it reached its audience and who its *unintended* audience might have been. Is your artifact a confidential or classified document that was later leaked to the press? If it is a text, document, or film, has it been translated into other languages? Is your artifact a video or Internet meme that went viral? If so, how many views has it received? Thinking about circulation will help you and your audience consider more fully how ideologies infiltrate cultures. You may begin to explain how certain beliefs or values come to be shared and widely held—or how certain forms of resistance gain wide adherents—when you identify how artifacts spread among groups.

As a final illustration of how one establishes the context of a real-world artifact, we turn to an example that emerged in the days and months following the fatal shooting of Michael Brown, an unarmed, 18-year-old African American male, in Ferguson, Missouri, on August 9, 2014. Brown was killed by white police officer Darren Wilson in a confrontation on a residential street that had few witnesses and no video footage.

Our artifact will be a Twitter feed under the hashtag #IfTheyGunnedMeDown that was prompted by the mainstream media coverage of the event. Tweets using this hashtag first appeared on August 10, 2014, the day following Brown's death.

The social and political context for the artifact was established in reaction to Brown's death *and* the media coverage. Brown's death was followed by two weeks of rioting and protests in Ferguson—tensions that many reported had been mounting for years between the predominantly African American Ferguson residents and the predominantly white law enforcement. In the days that followed the fatal shooting, tension also emerged about how Michael Brown was portrayed in the media. His family and friends stressed that he was a recent high school graduate and a good kid who was about to begin college classes. Police spokespersons, however, released video footage that appeared to show Brown stealing cigars from a convenience store on the morning of his death, and they suggested he had physically attacked the police officer who shot him.[9]

Our artifact, the #IfTheyGunnedMeDown Twitter feed, was most immediately a response to a photo of Brown NBC News tweeted the day after his shooting.[10] The photo portrayed Michael Brown without a smile, in front of a brick building, with a hand gesture that some have said was a peace sign, and others interpreted as a gang sign. In other words, in the photograph, Brown could be read as unfriendly and even aggressive.

The photograph did not appear in a historical vacuum, however. Media critics and civil rights activists have long noted that the news media visually portray some minorities—and African American men in particular—with a negative bias. Portrayals of violent or threatening men of color will sell news, this protest contends, and these negative portrayals, in turn, feed cultural perceptions of African American men as dangerous and untrustworthy.[11] As a result, we as media consumers are much more likely to encounter images of African American men as criminals than as teachers, fathers, preachers, or political leaders. Given this long-running critique of media portrayals, some Twitter followers viewed the NBC News-circulated photograph of Michael Brown as yet another occasion where a mainstream news organization chose a threatening-looking photograph of an African American man, when they could easily have chosen a photograph that showed Brown smiling or in his graduation cap and gown. As blogger P. J. Vogt wrote, "A photo can be an argument, and the photo NBC News tweeted made a different argument than a more typical victim photo (at a graduation, or at home) would have."[12]

To protest this media representation of the victim—and to make visible the ideology of racial bias that still circulated in some media portrayals—many Twitter users, particularly young men and women of color, started tweeting photographs of themselves under the hashtag #IfTheyGunnedMeDown. These Twitter users constitute the rhetors of our artifact, while Twitter is the medium of communication and the public postings of the images provide broad circulation of the artifacts. The posted photopairs show one photo where the subject might be partying, smoking, making an offensive hand signal, or looking at the camera in an especially provocative way. In the second photo, the same subject is shown in his military uniform, in her graduation cap and gown, caring for his children, smiling or looking friendly, or perhaps reading a story in an elementary classroom. The visual contrasts are striking, and they make

Kuai Lang (@King_Ghidorah5) is one of many who challenged, with their tweets to #IfTheyGunnedMeDown, the way the media depict people of color who are accused of crime.

powerful statements about the choices news outlets have when they select and publish photographs.

Michael Brown's death and the protests that followed—combined with the photograph NBC News chose to accompany its coverage in the hours after Brown's death—are all important elements of the context for tweets to the #IfTheyGunned-MeDown hashtag. As you analyze the artifact and interpret how your artifact functions in society, your observations should be informed by the artifact's context. The context includes five related elements: the rhetor; the social, economic, or political realities that prompted the creation of the artifact; the audience; the artifact's timing; and its circulation. With the context firmly in mind, you are prepared to move to the next phase of your ideological critique.

BOX 17-4

Questions to Ask about Context

- Who is the rhetor for this artifact—that is, the person or entity most invested in how the artifact looks, sounds, and is received by the audience? Is there anything compelling in the rhetor's biography that led to the creation of this artifact?

- What social, economic, or political realities prompted the creation of this artifact? If there are earlier or historical references in the artifact, what connection does the rhetor hope the audience will see between the past and the artifact's present?

- Who is the audience for this artifact? What can you learn from your research? What visual or textual clues in the artifact hint at the audience? Is there a group intentionally excluded from the audience for the artifact?

- What is the artifact's timing? What date was it delivered, produced, or published? What was occurring politically, socially, or economically that may have influenced the audience's response to the artifact? How did the artifact compare with or differ from similar types of artifacts that preceded it?

- What is notable about this artifact's circulation? Whom did it reach and how? Did it become well known to groups that were not intended to see it?

    Whichever context questions yield the most interesting answers may become part of the features you describe and interpret in the next section.

DESCRIBE AND INTERPRET THE ARTIFACT'S IDEOLOGICAL ASSUMPTIONS

After you have identified and explained the major components of your artifact's context, it is time to describe and interpret your artifact. In the previous section, we said you should note the parts of the context particularly related to statements of power, control, and resistance. You can use this information to help guide and inform your analysis of the artifact as you determine its ideological message. Begin by briefly *describing* the elements in the artifact that expose its values, assumptions, or patterns of belief. Some of the ideological assumptions may not be fully articulated, and thus your job as rhetorical critic is to make them plain for your audience. Focus on the artifact's visual, verbal, and audio elements that are central to its ideological message. If it is a photograph, how is it framed? Is it black and white, or color? What is the eye drawn to first? Is there text within the photograph itself or superimposed on the photograph? If it is a music video, what lyrics accompany what scenes? How are these scenes framed? How is the singer or character in the video dressed? What does the lighting emphasize or place in the shadows? How does the music change in volume and tempo as the video progresses? Look closely at the artifact, and help your audience attend to it more carefully than they ever have before. This means you should use descriptive, specific language and perhaps pair it with well-designed visual aids. What are the parts you particularly want your audience to notice? Show them—don't just tell them—what you want them to see. Perhaps you will include an audio or video clip that focuses attention on some element of the message.

BOX 17-5

Rhetorical Elements to Describe and Interpret in an Ideological Critique

- **Visual elements:** color, lighting, framing, font of text in the image, camera angle, distance, editing or juxtaposition of images, symbols, materials, size.

- **Verbal elements**: word choice, juxtaposition of words with visual or audio elements.

- **Audio elements**: sound quality, tempo, pitch, volume, juxtaposition of sound with visual or verbal elements.

Once you have described aspects of the artifact that you want your audience to notice, interpret how they help communicate an ideological message. Begin by asking, "What is highlighted and what is hidden in these aspects of the artifact?" Every artifact contains a preferred reading—a way that the audience is intended to understand and respond to the artifact. You might interpret how the artifact's key elements communicate particular ideological assumptions—that is, specific values, attitudes, and beliefs—and whether they invite the audience to accept or reject those assumptions.

Both description and interpretation are required to complete an ideological analysis. If you only identify an artifact's key elements but don't interpret how they function persuasively, you will merely have summarized or narrated the artifact. If you jump to your interpretations without pointing out the presence of ideological elements in your artifact, your interpretation will lack validity due to the absence of clear evidence.

As you describe and interpret the key ideological elements of your artifact, you can draw on the concepts of agency, hegemonic ideology, and resistant ideology. These terms help you think about whether the visual, verbal, and audio elements elevate or challenge ideologies, and how they empower or disempower audiences to respond. The concepts also help you with your most important goal: telling your audience why all of this matters.

Ideological Assumptions and Agency

We noted earlier that agency is particularly important in ideological criticism because it helps us articulate how the rhetors who marshal verbal and nonverbal symbols can expand or contract the liberty of others. When you analyze an artifact for agency, you describe and interpret how the artifact depicts an individual or group's freedom to act or intervene in a situation, his or her own life, or the world. In doing so, you help your audience see the role rhetoric plays in communicating ideological messages about our freedom and power relationships. You can also reveal the ways democratic participants can alter such messages.

If we return to "Mississippi Goddam," we can see how Nina Simone asserted her agency and invited her audience to join her in seeking social change. At one point in her song, Simone sings:

> Don't tell me I tell you
> Me and my people just about due
> I've been there so I know
> They keep on saying "Go Slow!"[13]

Here, you might notice Simone distinguishes "I" (the singer) from "you" (the predominantly white audience) by saying, "Don't tell *me*, I tell *you*." She places herself in a position of authority (you don't talk; I'll talk), boldly inverting the normal power structure by asserting her agency over the audience. Simone also identifies a "They." As in, "*They* keep on saying 'Go slow!'" Here she differentiates her audience from southern segregationists and conservative reformers who keep saying that change should happen slowly (individuals and groups that want to limit agency). Thus, the audience ("you") is invited to exercise agency, to be better than "they" are by working quickly for an end to racial violence.

When you examine your artifact closely, ask what assumptions it makes about agency. How much and what type of freedom does the artifact depict people as having or exercising? How do its visual, verbal, and audio elements portray individuals or groups as expanding their actions and intervening in the world? Alternatively, how do its rhetorical elements present the expressions and actions of others as limited? How does the artifact depict an individual or group as lacking freedom or being controlled by, or under the power of, others? Think back to your considerations of the artifact's context, and particularly those whom the artifact includes and whom it excludes. Who is missing from the artifact, and how might their exclusion expand or restrict their and others' agency? Help your audience members see how you have reached these conclusions about your artifact by arguing how specific visual, verbal, and audio elements in the artifact render an individual's or group's agency.

BOX 17-6

Questions to Ask about Agency

Description

- Who is portrayed as "in the know"—and who is "out of it" or ignorant—in the artifact?

- Which groups are portrayed as powerful—and which as powerless—in the artifact? Or who is portrayed as more powerful than whom?

- Are people punished or rewarded for speaking out, or remaining quiet, in the artifact?

Interpretation

- Why might the individuals or groups in the artifact have been portrayed as they are?

- What do the rewards or punishments for speaking out or remaining quiet suggest about a group's ability to enact change?

- How does the artifact's depiction of agency help to justify or challenge a particular ideology?

Ideological Assumptions and Hegemony

When an ideology becomes a dominant way of seeing the world, we say it is hegemonic. **Hegemony** is the influence over social, cultural, political, and economic relations exhibited by the dominant group, and a **hegemonic (or dominant) ideology** is a set of values, beliefs, interpretations, and assumptions that serve the political and economic interests of the majority or of those who hold power. Because this ideology serves powerful interests, it is important to those in power that the public see these values, interpretations, beliefs, and assumptions as natural, given, even (in religious contexts or among groups of religious believers) as ordained by god. If the public believes and participates in the naturalness of the ideological perspective, then they will not question it or attempt to change it. Do you see visual, verbal, or audio elements of your artifact that express a hegemonic ideology? Is the artifact designed to support and uphold that ideology? If so, show your audience how the artifact's elements assert the value of the ideological view.

The reason a particular ideology gains ascendancy is not because we are forced into these views; instead, we are exposed to them repeatedly and come to accept them over time, or we may perceive them as good, neutral, or irrelevant—and thus give assent. Other times, we may dislike an ideology but feel powerless to challenge it. In any case, the more widespread an ideology becomes, the more natural it seems. You might say we are culturally programmed to accept its values as givens. The NBC News-circulated photograph of Michael Brown, and other media coverage of Ferguson that portrayed threatening photos of men of color as natural, reflected and reinforced a hegemonic ideology of race in America. It is to this dominant perspective that those who tweeted photo-pairs of themselves with the #IfTheyGunnedMeDown hashtag responded. In an interview, C. J. Lawrence, who is credited with starting the hashtag, explained his motivation: "With the lack of interaction with one another outside of media, it's easy to craft that narrative when people don't know you, based on a snapshot."[14] His Twitter feed sought to disrupt the hegemonic, racist depiction of African American men by juxtaposing typically circulated images with snapshots that told a different story.

When you examine a hegemonic ideology, consider which groups benefit and which groups do not benefit from a particular ideology. Who may be living under the ideology but may not share its assumptions? Help your audience see how a dominant way of seeing the world is reflected in your artifact's visual, verbal, and audio elements. Ask them to consider how this system of values and beliefs may function as a kind of social programming in the artifact—and may thus exert power over and control in their communities and their lives.

BOX 17-7

Questions to Ask about Hegemonic Ideology

Description

- What way of acting or behaving in the world is highlighted—or even praised—in the artifact?

- How does the artifact depict a dominant group or those who wield economic, social, or political power? How are those who stand outside dominant groups portrayed in the artifact?

- What ideas, beliefs, or values does the artifact obscure or hide—or perhaps overtly discredit?

Interpretation

- How does the artifact's visual, verbal, or audio elements perpetuate a particular belief or participate in cultural programming?

- Does the artifact imply that behaving or acting in an accepted way will give the audience tangible rewards or more access to the current power structure?

- How does the artifact discourage behaviors and values that differ from those it depicts as preferable?
- Which audience members have the ability to respond to the artifact in a desired way, and what does this suggest about the artifact's inclusion or exclusion?

Ideological Assumptions and Resistance

Just as there are hegemonic ideologies, there are also resistant ideologies. A **resistant ideology** is one that seeks to challenge and expose a hegemonic ideology. In 2012, the Pakistani teenager Malala Yousafzai became a household name after she was shot in the head by Taliban militants because she spoke out about girls' right to be educated. Yousafzai was 15 at the time of the incident, and, since recovering from her injuries, she has become an international spokesperson for women's education.[15] Yousafzai's work as a public figure and international spokesperson promotes a resistant ideology that embraces the education of women and calls the Taliban's ideology of gender division into question.

When resistant ideologies begin to circulate, a system of social, political, and economic relations that seemed natural to many members of society becomes exposed as a social construct. A **social construct** is a category, idea, or description that humans have created to explain reality. The important idea here is that a social construct is a product of human language and interactions, rather than something biological, natural, or essential. Social constructs may be taken for granted or believed to reflect nature, but the goal of resistant ideologies is to expose social constructs as human, rather than natural, conceptions. Do women make inferior soldiers, or is that a social construct? Are fathers inherently less nurturing than mothers, or is that an explanation that enabled fathers to spend more time in the workplace and mothers more time at home with children?

When an ideological critic explains how a resistant ideology functions in an artifact, she may start by showing how the artifact's visual, verbal, and audio elements challenge or expose some social constructs. The artifact may have a preferred reading that invites the audience to see a social construct in a new way. The critic may also ask how those who resist a preferred way of seeing the world are portrayed as leaders, heroes, or somehow happier and freer than those who persist under a hegemonic ideology.

BOX 17-8

Gender Critique as a Form of Ideological Criticism

You may note from some of the examples in this section that questions and assumptions about gender are often rooted in ideology. Philosophers and rhetorical critics see many commonly held ideas about appropriate masculine and feminine behavior as social constructs.

If this is a topic that interests you, you might wish to focus your critique on how masculinity or femininity is portrayed and prescribed in your artifact. Do you see your artifact's portrayals of men or women as limiting or policing how men and women should behave? Do you want to argue that your artifact is working to expand what the culture defines as acceptable behavior and gender expression for men and women? If your answer to these (and similar) questions is "yes," then your ideological criticism is performing a gender critique.

Returning to the #IfTheyGunnedMeDown hashtag a final time, we observe how those who tweeted contrasting images of themselves participated in an act of resistance. They asked media outlets to think more carefully about how they portray those involved in altercations with law enforcement, and they challenged all who viewed the Twitter feed to consider how we read and consume media photos. They reminded us that media portrayals often perpetuate an ideology of racial bias. They seemed to be asking, "Would you think of the victim differently if you saw him photographed while caring for children?"

Whether a Twitter feed can change the behavior of million-dollar news corporations remains to be seen, of course, but the feed may have been more immediately successful in changing audience perceptions among those who viewed the photographs and were persuaded by the visual argument. This is one way the Twitter users resisted a dominant ideology and why their rhetoric matters. Those who saw and reflected on their tweets may very well be different news consumers in the future.

BOX 17-9

Questions to Ask about Resistant Ideology

Description

- How does the artifact's visual, verbal, or audio elements challenge a hegemonic ideology?
- Does the artifact highlight a way of acting or behaving in the world that runs counter to the values of a hegemonic ideology?
- What social constructs are challenged or exposed?
- How does the artifact depict a dominant group in an unflattering way and/or present those with less societal power favorably?

Interpretation

- Why might the artifact have framed the issue (or image) the way it did?
- What does the artifact suggest is wrong with our collective way of seeing, and how does it make this argument?
- To what degree do audience members have the agency to respond to the artifact in a desired way?

A final word of caution about description and interpretation in the production of ideological criticism: not everything that is interesting about your artifact and its context may make it into your critique. You are looking, in particular, for one of two things. First, you might highlight those elements in your artifact that reinforce a particular belief or behavior as "natural"—when in fact, this belief or behavior is socially constructed. Second, you may illuminate those elements in the artifact that explicitly challenge a widely held belief. Such elements may suggest that we can and should think differently about the accepted idea—especially for the benefit of those groups that are traditionally silenced, overlooked, or politically and economically oppressed. As you begin your interpretation, it will help to remember that in any given artifact, there is a preferred reading—a way of seeing that the artifact expects the audience to participate in—but there is also a plethora of other readings.

SPOTLIGHT ON SOCIAL MEDIA:
A Mighty Girl Blog and Facebook Posts

One example of a website, blog, and Facebook page that works to challenge confining gender ideology is *A Mighty Girl,* a project started by Carolyn Danckaert and Aaron Smith who were concerned that their four nieces would not find enough positive role models of strong girls and women in popular culture. Danckaert and Smith explain on their website:

> After years of seeking out empowering and inspirational books for our four young nieces, we decided to create A Mighty Girl as a resource site to help others equally interested in supporting and celebrating girls. The site was founded on the belief that all children should have the opportunity to read books, play with toys, listen to music, and watch movies that offer positive messages about girls and honor their diverse capabilities.[16]

A July 2014 post on the *A Mighty Girl* Facebook page celebrated 14-year-old Carleigh O'Connell's decision to speak out against body shaming and the social pressure on

Carleigh O'Connell takes a stand against body shaming.

young women to be uber-thin. The Facebook post reached over four million people, and many comments first thanked Carleigh for her bravery and then went on to share their own stories of body shaming. Carleigh's guest blog on the *Mighty Girl* website tells the story in her own words:

Carleigh O'Connell

How does a 14-year-old girl stand up on a graffiti-covered rock that makes fun of her body, take a picture, and then have the picture go viral on the internet reaching over 4 million people? Well, it happened, and it happened to me. . . .

The way I saw it, I had a choice. I could have just walked away, cried in my room or tried to ignore it altogether, but that wasn't an option for me. I knew the moment I saw the graffiti that I had to respond, and that's exactly what I did. I responded back to someone's hurtful behavior instead of becoming the victim and letting them get away with it.

Some call this bullying; I just call it "mean." Whoever wrote this wanted to bring attention to themselves. I can only assume that they were trying to be funny or cool around their friends at my expense. So, I turned the tables and highlighted the fact that it wasn't about them, it was about me, and I am not okay with being someone's target or springboard for popularity. . . .

It's not an easy thing standing up to bullies or aggressors, but by creating awareness of this issue and actually talking about it will help kids step up in their own way. Whether it's through art, writing, or sports, encouraging kids, teens and adults not to bottle up their emotions, but to talk about them and express their feelings will help immensely. I am lucky enough to have an incredible built-in support system in my family, and amazing friends who have stood by me. I fully recognize that this may not be the case for everyone. However, through websites like www.amightygirl.com or www.reachout.com anyone who is struggling can realize that they're not alone and use these avenues to vent, seek advice, or just get information.

What I now know. . .

I have realized that so many people, kids and adults, have faced and can relate to this type of negativity.

I have realized that sometimes you have to stare cruelty in the face and not drop your head.

I have realized that owning who you are and how you are made is much better than feeling ashamed or bad about yourself.

I have realized that [it] is okay to not have everyone agree with you and your actions, because sometimes negativity can bring bigger and better things.

I am beyond thankful for the positive words of encouragement and love. I still cannot comprehend the amount of support that I have received. I hope my story continues to inspire kids and adults to stand up on their own rock, in their own way, whatever that may mean. I would like to thank A Mighty Girl for having me as their guest!

"Yours Truly",
Carleigh O'Connell[17]

Discussion Questions

- What ideology does Carleigh's post resist?
- How does Carleigh's photograph and post depict her exercising agency? Do you think the photograph and post function as an act of resistance against a powerful ideology?
- How does the photograph function as a rhetorical artifact? How does the blog post add to or change the rhetorical artifact?

EVALUATE HOW THE ARTIFACT'S IDEOLOGICAL ASSUMPTIONS ELEVATE OR CHALLENGE DEMOCRATIC PRINCIPLES

We wrote this chapter and we teach ideological criticism to our students because we are interested in educating civically engaged critics. We believe you are more able to participate in and shape democratic organizations when you can recognize and critique how rhetoric and ideology influence ideas, behaviors, and exert social control. With this in mind, the final step to any rhetorical critique is to help your audience understand how your artifact relates to democratic principles and practices. In chapter 15 we defined democratic principles as the behavioral standards necessary for democratic governance to exist and thrive, and we gave examples such as the rule of law; unity or shared identity of community members; and the open and thoughtful engagement of public issues, arguments, and positions. In your ideological criticism, make certain you not only offer your interpretation, but also show how the artifact elevates or challenges democratic principles, so that your audience members are equipped to be fuller participants in democratic society.

Recall from chapter 2 that productive discourse—the type of communication that enables and encourages civic participation—is characterized by features that include deliberation, inclusiveness, learning, imagination, and empowerment. You might illustrate how your artifact supports democratic principles by showing how it invites audiences to consider another viewpoint; how it expands a group to include new voices; how it is invested in learning from the experiences of others; how it encourages its audience to imagine another solution or way of seeing a current social problem; or how it empowers a group to act.

Artifacts that challenge democratic principles tend *not* to do these things. In chapter 2 we also said unproductive discourse includes features such as division, dichotomous thinking, hierarchical communication, and dogmatism. If you see that your artifact seeks to divide rather than unite people and viewpoints; that it tends to view the world or solutions in only two opposed ways; that it reinforces unequal power relationships; or that its viewpoints are fixed and predetermined, then you likely have an artifact that discourages democratic principles.

The Twitter phenomenon that pairs photos of young people of color supports the democratic principles of free speech and the participation of people in civic affairs by enabling the young people—whose voices had largely been excluded from news coverage—to tell their own stories. It also enables equality by offering images that better match the news media's typical, and more humanizing, photographs of Caucasian individuals. By revealing how the Twitter feed upholds democratic principles, an ideological analysis of the paired images can help viewers better understand the photographs as rhetorical artifacts functioning persuasively in our world. But will such a critique change the way American news outlets select pictures for their publications? Maybe not. Perhaps all an analysis of the Twitter feed will do is plant a seed of awareness that will move some viewers to think differently about the way they receive news and the way members of their community are portrayed in the media. Such seeds of awareness, however, have the power to grow and reshape culture when enough people take notice.

The important point is that ideological criticism is ultimately interested in *social change*. The power of consciousness raising should not be ignored as it encourages the sharing of diverse opinions, talents, and knowledge for the good of the whole. Ultimately, however, ideological critique is most powerful—and most true to its roots—when it opens up avenues for more people to participate in their society, culture, and politics. For the ideological critic, the critique should be designed to move people to respond, and to respond with action. Certainly, those who are aware of how audio and visual messages seek to shape their thinking are more capable of resisting those methods of control, but the original proponents of ideological critique wanted their analyses to lead to the change of social structures and material conditions. Professor of communication James Arnt Aune makes the point this way:

> There remains the risk . . . of the scholastic illusion that "raising consciousness" will create liberation, failing to recognize the inertia which results from the inscription of social structures in bodies.
>
> Radical social change—dare I say "revolution"?—appears to come when bodies learn to move in different ways, when Rosa Parks refuses to move, when drag queens riot at Stonewall, when Egyptians take to the streets against Mubarak, or when workers of all kinds shut down the Wisconsin State Capitol Building.[18]

As you craft your ideological critique then, find ways to share that critique with others. Write an essay. Write a blog post and tweet the link to it. Give a speech and invite your audience to participate in an action or protest to counter the form of ideological control you analyze.

Whatever you do, make your insights available to the public, and invite them to *move* on this evidence. As rhetorical scholar Raymie McKerrow writes, "A critical practice must have consequences."[19] The consequences of your ideological critique should be to move others to act in ways that change the contours of ideology, that force it to adjust and shift because the people refuse to receive its messages without reflection.

SUMMARY

As a method of criticism, ideological analysis seeks to understand how a range of rhetorical artifacts from a variety of media work to shape commonly held beliefs, values, and ideas. But this method is also deeply invested in social change. Ideological criticism's goal is to unveil how these rhetorical artifacts work so that audiences can exercise more agency in response to ideological messages.

- Ideology is a set of beliefs and values that provides a way to view the world and suggests a way to act in it. It is also a way to describe how a social group behaves or what it values.
- When an ideology gains enough adherents that it becomes a dominant viewpoint and is a primary influence in institutions, politics, and religion, we say it is a hegemonic ideology.
- Ideologies can also be resistant. Those that are established to counter or challenge a hegemonic ideology are called resistant ideologies.
- In order to complete his or her own ideological critique, a critic must first locate an artifact that makes a statement about power, control, or resistance.

- The critic studies the context of the artifact to understand the rhetor, what social and political events may have led to its creation, its primary audience, timing, and form of circulation.
- The critic describes the artifact with specificity, noting key verbal, visual, and audio elements in the artifact that expose its values, assumptions, or patterns of belief.
- Next, the critic interprets whether and how the artifact reinforces a hegemonic ideology or offers a resistant ideology.
- Finally, because ideological criticism is deeply invested in social change, it is important that critics evaluate how the artifact's ideological assumptions elevate or challenge democratic principles. These evaluations are often acts of resistance and open up ways for democratic participants to enact social change.

KEY TERMS

agency p. 360

hegemonic (or dominant)
    ideology p. 369

hegemony p. 369

ideological criticism p. 359

ideology p. 358

resistant ideology p. 371

social construct p. 371

REVIEW QUESTIONS

1. What is ideology?
2. What is the ultimate goal of ideological criticism?
3. Describe some of the key characteristics that make a rhetorical artifact a good topic for ideological criticism.
4. Explain the difference between hegemonic ideology and resistant ideology.
5. Why should you share your rhetorical analysis with others?

DISCUSSION QUESTIONS

1. Think of a current television commercial or music video that bothers you for some reason (for example, the way it portrays a group you belong to or a group you don't belong to). Explain to your classmates why you find the commercial problematic. Can you identify an ideology at work in the artifact?
2. What ideologies do you think are good or useful? Explain.
3. Do you agree that prescriptions about ideal masculinity and ideal femininity can be limiting? Discuss a time when you saw these messages work in a way that limited another person.
4. Is resistance truly futile? In other words, can you think of a time when resistance to a shared viewpoint made a marked difference in the lives of others?
5. Describe a time when someone made you see an ideological message—one you hadn't previously noted or fully considered—at work. What was your response, and why?

Glossary

active listening The act of listening closely, critically, and constructively. An active listener concentrates on what the speaker is saying, thinks about and reflects on the meaning of the speaker's content, and focuses on the potential of the message rather than on merely tearing it down.

ad hominem A reasoning fallacy that occurs when a person attacks the speaker making an argument, rather than responding to the argument itself. This fallacy is marked by personal attacks that ignore the substance of an argument.

agency An individual's ability to act freely or to independently intervene in a situation, his or her own life, and the world.

alignment A basic design principle, defined as the deliberate placement of the elements in a given slide so that like elements, such as photos, text, and captions, are lined up with one another and do not appear randomly placed.

analogical reasoning A pattern of reasoning in which one attempts to prove a claim by comparing one situation or case with a similar situation.

appeal to authority A reasoning fallacy that occurs when an argument is based on data offered by a source speaking outside his or her area of expertise.

appeal to common practice A reasoning fallacy that occurs when a claim is justified by appealing to the commonality or tradition of a belief or activity.

appeal to popularity A reasoning fallacy that occurs when a claim is based exclusively on the popularity of an idea, belief, or action.

appreciative listening Enjoying a presentation and its aesthetics. A listener can and should appreciate, even be inspired by, a well-crafted speech when its style and the spirit of its message are pleasant to the ear.

argument The advocacy of an idea, position, or course of action that is supported by evidence.

assertion A claim that lacks an evidentiary basis and is offered without reason, support, or data.

audience Those targeted, reached, influenced, or impacted by the rhetorical act.

audience adaptation How a speaker makes use of audience-analysis cues to explain, frame, and support ideas in order to increase the chances of achieving a desired audience response.

audience analysis The practice of assessing audience factors and characteristics that are likely to influence an audience's reception of a message.

audience demographics Personal characteristics of the audience that are likely to shape their views and perspectives on a topic. Common demographic factors include age, gender, race and ethnicity, socioeconomic status, culture, geography, education, occupation, and group memberships.

balance An outlining principle which dictates that each main idea receives roughly the same amount of time and attention in the speech.

begging the question A reasoning fallacy that occurs when the data for a claim is merely a restatement of the claim itself rather than offering additional data. This is also known as circular reasoning.

bias A predetermined commitment to a particular ideological or political perspective.

Boolean search A method to retrieve relevant research by using specific operating terms, such as OR, AND, and NOT, to improve results when searching an online database and using some search engines.

causal reasoning A pattern of reasoning in which the argument is based on a cause-effect relationship that suggests an event is caused by a particular circumstance or action.

citation The basic identifying information of a source. The information provided depends on the type of source being cited.

civic Those matters that relate to the city or citizens.

civic engagement Participation in organizations, institutions, and societies with the goal of contributing to the public good.

claim The central term in the Toulmin model, the claim of an argument is what a speaker is attempting to prove and wants the audience to accept.

closed question A type of question that prompts a single, one-word answer—usually yes or no—during a deliberative discussion.

common ground The perspectives, interests, values, or concerns shared by some or all members of a deliberative discussion.

communication apprehension A heightened fear or sense of anxiety that arises when anticipating public speaking and interferes with the ability to do so effectively. Also commonly known as speech anxiety.

consciousness-raising speech A speech designed to create audience awareness of a problem or issue.

constraints Part of Lloyd Bitzer's theory of the rhetorical situation, defined as those things that can restrain, influence, or even dictate the decisions and actions needed to improve the exigence of a rhetorical situation.

context The conditions or situation within which rhetoric is produced.

contingency A condition in which events and circumstances are dependent on a number of variables that change in unpredictable ways.

contrast A basic design principle, defined as difference. Elements that are different from each other in kind should be visually different as well. Contrast can help the eye quickly determine what is different—and therefore important.

coordination An outlining principle which dictates that ideas of similar importance should be on the same level of the outline and should be visually represented by the same level of notation and indentation.

counterpublics Gatherings of people excluded from the public sphere who raise and discuss issues that are ignored or trivialized by the broader public. Counterpublics have important political potential because group members can use them to learn and teach methods of challenging their exclusion.

credibility The authority, expertise, or reputation a source has concerning a topic.

data Material and reasons, most often called evidence, that support the acceptance of the claim. Data are essential to forming a valid argument.

database An organized online storehouse of information that can easily be searched to retrieve desired research materials.

deductive reasoning A classic form of argument with reasoning that moves from valid premises to a specific conclusion.

deliberative discussion A group conversation through which a community, guided by one or more moderators, thoughtfully and thoroughly examines a complex public problem and a range of available solutions to ultimately arrive at a choice, decision, or conclusion.

deliberative presentation A speech in which the speaker fairly and even-handedly describes a civic problem and multiple approaches to solving the problem with emphasis on the benefits and drawbacks of each approach.

deliberative process A deliberative presentation and subsequent deliberative discussion.

delivery A speaker's means of expression; how words and ideas are physically conveyed, verbally and nonverbally, to an audience.

demagoguery Rhetoric that explicitly claims to speak for the public's best interests but implicitly gains more political power for the speaker and exacerbates divisions among the public, thereby weakening democracy.

democracy A political system which locates control and power in the people themselves.

democratic participants Those who participate in public conversations about issues that matter to groups, institutions, and organizations in a democratic society.

democratic principles The behavioral standards necessary for democratic governance to exist and thrive.

direct question A type of question that targets one participant in a deliberative discussion and is especially useful for drawing out timid group members.

dissoi logoi Contrasting arguments or twofold arguments. The term also refers to an anonymous text, written circa 400 BCE in Greece, that illustrates the exercise of forming contrasting arguments.

division The separation of an individual or group from the collective, thereby scapegoating them and creating solidarity through the rejection of those who are different.

empathetic listening An approach to listening ideally suited to deliberative practices due to the closeness it fosters between speaker and listener. This type of listening reflects an openness to change, shows respect and value to the speaker, and exhibits a sense of social responsibility that extends beyond self-interest by listening to understand a speaker's perspective.

enthymeme An informal, incomplete syllogism in which a speaker, rather than stating all premises for a conclusion, relies on the audience to use its knowledge and experience to supply missing information or alternative explanations that complete the argument; termed by Aristotle as a rhetorical syllogism.

environmental factors Elements of the speaking situation such as time of day, location, size of audience, and configuration of the speaking venue that can influence how the audience receives a message.

ethical code A set of rules or guidelines agreed to by a culture or group in order to regulate behavior.

ethical listener A listener who demonstrates responsibility to the speaker and to the society in which we live by practicing active listening, listening to improve as a speaker, and embodying the qualities of ethical listening.

ethical listening attitude A positive disposition in which a listener approaches public communication with an open mind and without fixed opinions. Doing so allows the audience to undertake appreciative listening, makes the audience available for empathetic listening, and orients the audience toward listening that is reflective and learning focused.

ethics Generally associated with the field of philosophy, a set of moral principles governing human action or conduct as it pertains to motives, ends, and the quality of one's actions. The ethical quality of an action or conduct is generally evaluated based on how it reflects what is deemed "good" or "bad," or "right" or "wrong," in a culture.

ethos One of the three modes of proof, used in the service of invention, identified by Aristotle. Ethos refers to one's public character or persona. In public speaking, ethos involves a listening audience's perceptions of a speaker's goodwill, trustworthiness, competence, and dynamism.

evaluative listening Thinking critically about a speech's content and testing its arguments in order to form judgments about the merits of its ideas.

evidence Data and backing in the form of examples, statistics, and testimony that are used to support a claim. It is a necessary component of a valid argument.

example Evidence that supports a claim by providing a concrete instance in the form of a fact or occurrence. An example seeks to make a claim tangible or verifiable to the audience by pointing to something that has actually happened (specific example) or is plausible but does not represent an actual event (hypothetical example).

extemporaneous delivery Mode of delivery in which the speaker devotes significant time to preparing and practicing a polished speech but uses limited notes during presentation. The speaker commits key ideas, important examples, and structure to memory, but rather than memorizing the speech relies on key words in order to maintain a conversational tone.

fallacy A flaw or defect in reasoning that undermines the validity of an argument. A fallacy occurs due to the use of poor evidence to support an argument or a faulty warrant that does not reasonably connect data with a claim.

false dilemma A reasoning fallacy that presents only two possibilities or outcomes for an issue.

faulty analogy A reasoning fallacy that occurs when a speaker attempts to compare two situations that possess more differences than similarities and thus cannot be reasonably compared. Also known as a faulty comparison.

faulty cause A reasoning fallacy in which a cause-effect relationship is misattributed to two items that are not actually directly connected. When this fallacy is based on claiming a relationship after the fact or in hindsight the fallacy is known as post hoc.

field search A way to find search terms within a specific section, or field, of the documents within an online database of research. Sample fields include the author's name, publication title, article title, publication date, abstract, and keywords.

framing The use of language to order and make sense of the world; that is, framing is how we employ language to help shape perceptions of reality.

groan zone A stage of confusion and frustration that results from the broad representation of viewpoints, opinions, and ideas shared during a deliberative discussion. This term was coined by Sam Kaner and associates.

groupthink A phenomenon that occurs when group members' desire for harmony outweighs their willingness to critically examine alternative perspectives.

hasty generalization A reasoning fallacy that occurs when one attempts to reason from an insufficient number of examples or the example provided isn't representative of the larger situation.

hegemonic (or dominant) ideology A set of values, beliefs, interpretations, and assumptions that serve the political and economic interests of the majority or of those who hold power. It is important to those in power that the public see these values, interpretations, beliefs, and assumptions as natural, given, or even ordained by god because the public will be less likely to question or attempt to change them.

hegemony The influence over social, cultural, political, and economic relations exhibited by the dominant group.

heuristics Linguistic strategies for generating new ideas when inventing the content of a speech.

identification The degree to which individuals or groups find their interests joined or linked. For Kenneth Burke identification is the primary means of persuasion as an audience will be persuaded by a speaker only to the degree that they feel a connection with him or her.

ideological criticism A method of reading and interpreting rhetorical artifacts that exposes the expressions of power and control inherent in the artifacts.

ideology A set of shared beliefs and values that forms an interpretation of the world and suggests appropriate ways for a group to act in it.

impromptu delivery Mode of delivery in which the speaker must rely on instant recall in presenting ideas without advance preparation or warning.

indirect question A type of question that targets an entire group and tends to stimulate thought during a deliberative discussion.

inductive reasoning A form of reasoning in which a speaker uses a series of examples or instances to support the likelihood or probability of a generalized conclusion. Inductive arguments, less formal than deductive arguments, are judged based on quality more than logical validity through examination of the strength of observational data offered in support of a claim.

informative speaking A form of rhetoric through which the speaker strives to educate an audience about a topic without leading them toward a particular position, conclusion, or outcome.

invention The process of investigation and thought that produces the content of your speech.

key fact A piece of information that can be measured or tested, often by an expert, and is critical to understanding the problem under consideration.

logos The logical or reasoned basis of an appeal.

manuscript delivery Mode of delivery in which the speaker writes the entire address—including prompts for vocal and nonverbal delivery—in advance and utilizes the text in delivering the speech.

memorized delivery Mode of delivery in which the entire speech is memorized word for word with the intent of precisely recalling and delivering its content without the aid of notes or a manuscript.

memory How a speaker stores and recalls information that is shared in a speech.

modes of delivery Methods by which a speaker delivers information. The common modes of delivery are extemporaneous, impromptu, manuscript, and memorized delivery.

multimedia literacy The ability to construct and decode complex meanings on the screen and to engage in modes of thought and communicate via screen-based technology.

multimodal presentation A presentation that integrates oral, written, and visual modes of communication.

nonverbal delivery How the body is used to communicate. Important nonverbal cues include eye contact, facial expressions, gestures and movement, and appearance.

open question A type of question that calls for more than a one-word response, making possible a range of answers during a deliberative discussion.

organization The manner in which a speaker orders the points or arguments in a speech and verbally connects those elements so the audience can follow. In the classical canons of rhetoric, organization is called arrangement.

outline A sketch or condensed version of a speech that includes its arguments, supports, transitions, and references.

parallelism An outlining principle which dictates that subpoints need at least two elements or points in order to justify the subdivision and to be in balance. When it comes to outlining, "every little one has a little two."

pathos One of the three modes of proof, used in the service of invention, identified by Aristotle. Pathos refers to the psychological state of the audience and rests upon a speaker's effective, ethical appeals to their emotions and motivations.

pattern of arrangement A specific guide, or template, for choosing and organizing the main points of a speech. The arrangement helps determine both the content of the main points and their order.

patterns of reasoning Forms of reasoning derived from what kind of data or evidence is used to support an argument and how that data or evidence is used to support a claim. The primary patterns of reasoning are reasoning from example, reasoning from analogy, reasoning from sign, reasoning from cause, and reasoning from authority.

persuasion The strategic use of verbal and nonverbal symbols in an attempt to influence the beliefs, values, and/or actions of an audience.

plagiarism The unacknowledged use of another's words and ideas as one's own. In a public speaking context, it is plagiarism to present someone else's ideas or speech as one's own, including the use of language and ideas developed by another source without appropriate citation.

policing discourse Discourse that aims to censor the speech or actions of others. It frequently censors by calling another's words "inappropriate" because they are misinformed, too angry, poorly timed, or aimed at the wrong audience.

preparation (or key word) outline A brief sketch of a speech designed to help a speaker deliver a speech as free from notes as possible, so he or she can make maximum interpersonal connection with the audience while speaking.

presentation outline The sketch of a speech that a speaker writes as he or she plans and organizes. It is much more detailed than a presentation outline, and each element is written in complete sentences.

presented visual elements What a viewer literally sees in an image; that is, its physical elements, such as size, color, shape, form, and background.

preview statement A sentence or sentences that announce the main points of a speech. It is a clear indication of how the speech will proceed, and it tells the audience what to listen for.

productive discourse Public communication that is responsible to one's community and manages differences constructively. It requires active engagement in civic life by talking *and* listening; it reflects sound reasoning; it pursues multilateral problem-solving; and it relies on ethical standards of inclusivity, communication, and interaction. It is focused on ideas, not personalities, and it is respectful but not compliant, meaning that it has learning and the public good among its highest ideals.

proximity A basic principle in design which says that elements that are similar to each other in kind should be placed next to each other. Placing similar items together creates a visual unit, so that the eye readily understands that these elements are part of a group.

psychological factors Audience predispositions related to their mental state, attitude, interest in and experience with the topic, occasion, and speaker that may influence their reception of a message.

public A collection or group of people who are joined together in a cause of common concern.

public communication Any publicly shared message or discourse that addresses significant community concerns or issues.

public communication analysis An approach to rhetorical criticism that helps critics ascertain the effects of a rhetorical artifact.

public controversy A matter that concerns the community and is difficult to resolve as it involves diverse perspectives and more than one possible option or answer.

public discourse Rhetoric that is publicly offered to address an issue, problem, or question of common concern.

public judgment Community wisdom about a problem and possible solutions, accrued through a deliberative discussion, that aids a group's ability to make a thoughtful choice and take collective responsibility for the outcome.

public knowledge The shared and improved understanding of a problem and possible solutions that develops as deliberative discussion participants offer and hear multiple points of view.

public speaking The process of forming and delivering rhetorical content to an audience in the hopes of persuading, influencing, informing, or entertaining that audience.

public sphere The gathering of community members to discuss matters of common concern—including, but not limited to, public controversies. Conceived by sociologist Jürgen Habermas, it is a space where the public talks, argues, and reasons together as equals, disregarding social and economic inequalities among participants, ideally arriving at a more fulsome understanding of the issues.

reasoning from authority A pattern of reasoning in which a claim is supported with the testimony or credibility of a qualified source.

reasoning from sign A pattern of reasoning that relies on circumstantial evidence—or signs—to demonstrate a claim.

recency The timeliness of a speaker's sources.

relay question A type of question that encourages group members to share their experiences during a deliberative discussion.

relevance The degree of association between the source, a speaker's topic, and his or her audience.

repetition The basic design principle of reuse. In visual aids, repetition can create a sense of unity and consistency through the reuse of color, font, logo, image, size, or template.

research The process of learning about a topic by discovering what credible sources have said or written about it.

research as inquiry The process of studying a topic with the desire to learn.

research as strategy The process of studying a topic only to find sources and evidence that support your preferred solution.

resistant ideology A set of values, beliefs, interpretations, and assumptions that seeks to challenge and expose a hegemonic (or dominant) ideology.

reverse question A type of question that reflects a question originally directed at the leader of a deliberative discussion back to the group.

rhetor One who speaks publicly.

rhetoric A civic art devoted to the ethical study and use of symbols (verbal and nonverbal) in order to address public issues.

rhetorical artifact An object of study in rhetorical criticism. It is the focal point of analysis and what the critic seeks to bring meaning to through the analysis.

rhetorical audience Individuals who experience a communication act (i.e., hear or watch it), are open to being influenced by it, and are capable of facilitating the change(s) called for by the rhetor to improve the rhetorical exigence.

rhetorical criticism (or its synonym, rhetorical analysis) The description, interpretation, and evaluation of rhetoric in order to form judgments about its meaning, effect, and impact.

rhetorical ethics The behavioral expectations for communication exchanges that bond speaker and audience in the shared consideration of a topic that affects the public good. Rhetorical ethics involve the preparation of public speakers, the actions of speakers in presenting information, and the listening behaviors of audiences.

rhetorical exigence Part of Lloyd Bitzer's theory of the rhetorical situation, defined as a pressing public problem or urgent need that can be improved or changed through rhetoric.

rhetorical method A perspective, approach, or orientation for analyzing an artifact. A method privileges certain questions for analysis and provides a framework for understanding and evaluating the text.

rhetorical situation Developed by rhetorical scholar Lloyd Bitzer, an occasion or situation in which speech, while taking into account the constraints of the immediate context, can be used to call an audience of listeners and decision-makers into action in order to address a rhetorical exigence.

rhythm A stylistic device in which one creates a sense of familiarity with the audience, a pattern or a cadence that keeps the audience engaged while also heightening emotion.

signpost A verbal hint or signal in a speech that new information is coming. It indicates the beginning of a new element in a speech.

slide deck A set of digital visual aids, prepared using any presentation software program.

slippery slope A reasoning fallacy in which a speaker claims that a single event or action will lead to a chain reaction of cause-and-effect events, typically ending with a catastrophic final effect. The fallacy occurs when the argument is offered without evidence to show the relationship between the many steps suggested in the argument.

social construct A category, idea, or description that humans have created to explain reality. A social construct is a product of human language and interactions, rather than something biological, natural, or essential.

speeches that offer means to action Presentations that offer listeners a specific way to proceed. The rhetor does more than encourage agreement on an issue—he or she actually requests that the audience act on the issue.

speeches to convince A speech that aims to influence an audience's values or beliefs.

statistics A common form of evidence that represents information in numeric form according to the size, quantity, or frequency of an idea, outcome, or occurrence. Common forms of statistics include averages, raw numbers, trends, and polls.

stereotype Generic categorization of individuals and groups based on the inaccurate conclusion that all people sharing a particular characteristic will automatically possess like qualities and beliefs.

straw man A reasoning fallacy in which a speaker inaccurately presents his or her opponent as holding to a set of extreme beliefs.

style The language or expression a speaker uses—the words he or she chooses. It refers to all those aspects of speech that constitute the manner or way in which ideas are verbally expressed or stated.

style guide Instructions for writing, formatting, and referencing sources. Style guide authors include, but are not limited to, the Modern Language Association (MLA) and the American Psychological Association (APA).

stylistic devices Language techniques and literary tools that clarify meaning, express ideas in a compelling manner, and appeal emotionally to an audience.

subordination An outlining principle which dictates that material that is less important or primarily supportive should be secondary to more central material. Supporting ideas or evidence should be listed under main points.

suggested visual elements What a viewer may infer from an image; the elements that help a rhetor or critic determine how an audience may receive and understand an image—beyond its physical composition of size, shape, color, or form.

syllogism A classic form of argument consisting of two premises and a conclusion. If the premises are valid, then the conclusion must also be true. Also a form of deductive reasoning.

symbolic action The power of symbols (images and words that express ideas or refer to something beyond themselves) to do things and to shape our thoughts and actions.

testimony A form of evidence that consists of facts or opinions derived from the words, experiences, and expertise of another individual.

textual context The evolving environment created within a rhetorical artifact as it interacts with and conditions the audience's responses to the artifact from its beginning to its ending.

thesis statement The central statement of the speech for which the speaker seeks adherence or acceptance from the audience. It is the focal point of the entire presentation.

Toulmin model A seven-part model that provides a way to conceptualize, verify, and critique arguments. Developed by British philosopher Stephen Toulmin, the model provides an alternative approach to the syllogism in an effort to better reflect everyday interactions.

trade-off The relative advantages and disadvantages that accompany every solution to a public controversy.

transition A sentence that connects ideas in a speech and moves from one point to the next.

unproductive discourse Public communication that is purposefully sensational, designed to promote division and misrepresent the complexities of public issues. It features poor arguments that appeal to the least common denominator, name-calling that substitutes for nuanced analysis, and an emphasis on points of division rather than points of agreement.

value A principle or quality that human beings are committed to and upon which they base their thinking and decisions for important issues.

value dilemma A difficult choice among competing values, especially those associated with policy options.

value hierarchy A list of values ranked from the most to the least important.

venue constraint An element of a speaker's physical presentation space that limits how he or she connects with the audience.

visual rhetoric Image(s) that function as symbolic action. Such images may seek to persuade or otherwise work to shape perceptions and actions of an audience.

vocal delivery How the voice and mouth are used to deliver words. Key elements of vocal delivery include volume, tone, rate, pauses, articulation, pronunciation, and avoidance of vocal fillers.

warrant A bridge-like statement, often expressed in the form of a value, that connects data with a claim in an argument; provides justification for using a piece of data to support the claim.

Notes

Preface

1. This is one of many reports included in the following source: Harvard University Faculty of Arts and Sciences, *Curricular Renewal in Harvard College* (Jan. 2006), 123, accessed Jan. 8, 2015, http://isites.harvard.edu/fs/docs/icb.topic830823.files/Curricular%20Renewal %20in%20Harvard%20College.

2. Boyer Commission, *Reinventing Undergraduate Education: A Blueprint for America's Research Universities* (Stony Brook: State University of New York Press, 1998), 12, accessed Jan. 8, 2015, http://www.reinventioncenter.miami.edu/boyer.pdf.

3. AAC&U, *College Learning for the New Global Society* (Washington, DC: 2007), 12, accessed Jan. 8, 2015, http://www.aacu.org/sites/default/files/files/LEAP/GlobalCentury_ final.pdf.

4. Hart Research Associates, A Survey Among Employers Conducted on Behalf of the Association of American Colleges and Universities, *Raising the Bar: Employers' Views on College Learning in the Wake of the Economic Downturn* (Washington, DC: Jan. 20, 2010), 2, accessed Jan. 8, 2015, http://www.aacu.org/leap/documents/2009_Employer Survey.pdf.

Chapter 1

1. The event was called "Congress on Your Corner" and took place on Jan. 8, 2011.

2. This idea is drawn from W. Norwood Brigance W. N. B., "Editorial," *Quarterly Journal of Speech* 28 (1942): 240.

3. Drawn from material written by two of the authors David M. Timmerman and Todd F. McDorman, "Rhetoric and Democracy," in *Rhetoric and Democracy: Pedagogical and Political Practices*, ed. Todd F. McDorman and David M. Timmerman (East Lansing: Michigan State University Press, 2008), xiii.

4. Harvey Yunis, *Taming Democracy: Models of Political Rhetoric in Classical Athens* (Ithaca, NY: Cornell University Press, 1996), 4.

5. An exception was Pericles who won reelection as a *strategos*, one of 10 military and political leaders, 15 years in a row. See David Timmerman, "Pericles," in *Classical Rhetorics and Rhetoricians: Critical Studies and Sources*, ed. Michelle Ballif and Michael G. Moran (Westport, CT: Praeger, 2005), 255; Chris Cillizza, "People Hate Congress. But

Most Incumbents Get Re-elected. What Gives?" *Washington Post*, May 9, 2013, accessed Jan. 10, 2015, http://www.washingtonpost.com/blogs/the-fix/wp/2013/05/09/people-hate-congress-but-most-incumbents-get-re-elected-what-gives/.

6. Josiah Ober, *Athenian Legacies: Essays on the Politics of Going On Together* (Princeton, NJ: Princeton University Press, 2005), 130.

7. The sophists were teachers of rhetoric, philosophy, and other subjects in ancient Greece who prepared their students for participation in the democracy. These teachers were first identified or named "sophists" or "wisdom bearers" in the sixth century BCE. See Edward Schiappa, *"Rhêtorikê*: What's in a Name? Toward a Revised History of Early Greek Rhetorical Theory," *Quarterly Journal of Speech* 78 (1992): 1–15; and David M. Timmerman, "Isocrates' Competing Conceptualization of Philosophy," *Philosophy and Rhetoric* 31 (1998): 145–159.

8. See, for example, *Phaedrus 237b*; *Republic 492b, 493d*; *Theaetetus 172b* in *The Collected Dialogues of Plato,* ed. Edith Hamilton and Huntington Cairns (Princeton, NJ: Princeton University Press, 1961); *Nicocles 19* in *Isocrates I,* trans. David Mirhady and Yun Lee Too (Austin: University of Texas Press, 2000); *On the Peace 52* in *Isocrates II,* trans. Terry Papillon (Austin: University of Texas Press, 2004); and *History of the Peloponnesian War 3.38, 42* in *The Landmark Thucydides,* ed. Robert B. Strasser (New York: Touchstone, 1996).

9. Timmerman and McDorman, "Rhetoric and Democracy," xv–xvi.

10. Robert H. McKenzie, *Public Politics* (Dubuque, IA: Kendall/Hunt, 1994), 3.

11. W. Norwood Brigance, "1946: Year of Decision," *Quarterly Journal of Speech* 33 (1947): 133.

12. Ober, *Athenian Legacies,* 132.

13. Timmerman and McDorman, "Rhetoric and Democracy," xvi–xvii.

14. Steve Charles, "I See Myself at Their Age," *Wabash College* (blog), Mar. 23, 2008, http://blogs.wabash.edu/fyi/2008/03/23/i-see-myself-at-their-age/.

15. Andy Bruner, "Skate Park Gets Funding Boost," *Paper of Montgomery County* (IN), June 4, 2008, accessed Jan. 10, 2015, http://thepaper24-7.com/main.asp?Search=1&ArticleID=16146&SectionID=23&SubsectionID=22&S=1; Frank Phillips, "Skate Park Dream Soon Will Be a Reality," *Paper of Montgomery County,* June 9, 2010, accessed Jan. 10, 2015, http://thepaper24-7.com/main.asp?Search=1&ArticleID=26426&SectionID=23&SubsectionID=22&S=1.

16. Kristin Campbell, "Victory in Philly: How Grassroots Organizing Saved the Libraries," *The End of Capitalism,* Mar. 26, 2010, accessed Aug. 3, 2011, http://endofcapitalism.com/2010/03/26/victory-in-philly-how-grassroots-organizing-saved-the-libraries/.

17. The information utilized in the example of the use of social media related to the Trayvon Martin case was gathered from the following sources: Genie Lauren, "Sharlene Martin: Drop Juror B37 from Martin Literary Management," *Change.org,* accessed Jan. 10, 2015, http://www.change.org/petitions/sharlene-martin-drop-juror-b37-from-martin-literary-management; Terrell Jermaine Starr, "Twitter User Who Helped Stop Juror B37's Book Deal Speaks to NewsOne," *NewsOne: For Black America,* July 16, 2013, accessed Jan. 10, 2015, http://newsone.com/2634913/moreandagain-twitter-zimmerman-juror-b37-book-deal/#.UeXmTJoQ18k.twitter; Heather Kelly, "Zimmerman Book Dies after Twitter Campaign," *CNN,* July 17, 2013, accessed Jan. 10, 2015, http://www.cnn.com/2013/07/17/tech/social-media/twitter-zimmerman-book/index.html.

18. "Young, Educated, and Underemployed: The Face of the Arab World's Protesters," *CNN,* Jan. 28, 2011, accessed July 25, 2011, http://news.blogs.cnn.com/2011/01/28/young-educated-and-underemployed-the-face-of-the-arab-worlds-protesters/?iref=allsearch.

19. Vivian Walt, "Tunisia's Nervous Neighbors Watch the Jasmine Revolution," *Time,* Jan. 31, 2011, accessed July 27, 2011, http://www.time.com/time/magazine/article/0,9171, 2043433,00.html.

20. For a greater understanding of the rhetorical implications of the act of self-immolation see Michelle Murray Yang, "Still Burning: Self-Immolation as Photographic Protest," *Quarterly Journal of Speech* 97 (2011): 1–25.

21. "Times Topics: Occupy Movement (Occupy Wall Street)," *New York Times,* May 2, 2012, accessed Jan. 10, 2015, http://topics.nytimes.com/top/reference/timestopics/organizations/ o/occupy_wall_street/index.html?8qa.

22. This phrase is derived from the work of Rosa Eberly, *Citizen Critics: Literary Public Spheres* (Urbana: University of Illinois Press, 2000).

Chapter 2

1. Rachel Weiner, "Palin: Obama's 'Death Panels' Could Kill My Down Syndrome Baby," *Huffington Post,* Sept. 7, 2009, updated May 25, 2011, accessed Jan. 11, 2015, http://www .huffingtonpost.com/2009/08/07/palin-obamas-death-panel_n_254399.html; Steve Benen, "Conservatives Slam Palin Attack as 'Crazy,'" *Washington Monthly,* Aug. 9, 2009, accessed Jan. 11, 2015, http://www.washingtonmonthly.com/archives/individual/2009_ 08/019420.php; Brian Montopli, "Alan Grayson 'Die Quickly' Comment Prompts Uproar," *CBS News,* Sept. 30, 2009, accessed Jan. 11, 2015, http://www.cbsnews.com/ news/alan-grayson-die-quickly-comment-prompts-uproar/; Jayson Rodriguez, "Kanye West Crashes VMA Stage During Taylor Swift Award Speech," *MTV.com,* Sept. 13, 2009, accessed Jan. 11, 2015, http://www.mtv.com/news/1621389/kanye-west-crashes-vma-stage-during-taylor-swifts-award-speech/; David Gardner, "'If I could, I'd take this ******* ball and shove it down your ******* throat': What Serena Williams REALLY Told Line Judge,'" *DailyMail.com* Sept. 14, 2009, accessed Jan. 11, 2015, http://www.dailymail .co.uk/news/worldnews/article-1213164/Furious-Serena-Williams-dumped-U-S-Open-told-official-If-I-Id-ball-shove-hroat.html.

2. Jürgen Habermas, *The Structural Transformation of the Public Sphere: An Inquiry into a Category of Bourgeois Society* (Cambridge: MIT Press, 1996).

3. John Dewey, *The Public and Its Problems* (Athens: Swallow, 1927), 208; Deborah Tannen, *The Argument Culture: Moving from Debate to Dialogue* (Random House: New York, 1998), 3; W. Barnett Pearce and Stephen W. Littlejohn, *Moral Conflict: When Social Worlds Collide* (Thousand Oaks, CA: Sage, 1997), 95; Benjamin R. Barber, *A Place for Us: How to Make Society Civil and Democracy Strong* (New York: Hill and Wang, 1998), 115.

4. "Jon Stewart on *Crossfire* 'Stop, Stop, Stop, Stop Hurting America,'" *Media Matters for America,* Oct. 15, 2004, accessed Jan. 11, 2015, http://mediamatters.org/research/ 200410160003; Frank L. Cioffi, "Argumentation in a Culture of Discord," *Chronicle Review* 51, no. 37 (May 20, 2005): B6, accessed Jan. 11, 2015, http://chronicle.com/weekly/ v51/i37/37b00601.htm.

5. Bill Carter, "CNN will Cancel 'Crossfire' and Cut Ties to Commentator," *New York Times,* Jan. 6, 2005, accessed Jan. 11, 2015, http://www.nytimes.com/2005/01/06/business/ media/06crossfire.html; Brian Steinberg, "CNN to Force 'Crossfire' Hosts to Find Common Ground." *Variety* Sept. 6, 2013, accessed Nov. 30, 2014, http://variety .com/2013/tv/news/cnn-to-force-crossfire-hosts-to-find-common-ground-1200601762/.

6. Sheryl Gay Stolberg, "Where Have You Gone, Joe the Citizen?" *New York Times,* Aug. 8, 2009, accessed Jan. 11, 2015, http://www.nytimes.com/2009/08/09/weekinreview/ 09stolberg.html?emc=eta1; Ian Urbina, "Beyond the Beltway, Health Debate Turns Hostile,"

New York Times, Aug. 7, 2009, accessed Jan. 11, 2015, http://www.nytimes.com/2009/08/08/us/politics/08townhall.html?ref=weekinreview; Bob MacGuffie, "Rocking the Town Halls—Best Practices," A Political Action Memo, May 2009, accessed Jan. 11, 2015, http://www.sourcewatch.org/images/e/e5/Townhallactionmemo.pdf; "Specter Faces Hostile Audience at Health Care Forum," *CNN,* Aug. 11, 2009, accessed Jan. 11, 2015, http://www.cnn.com/2009/POLITICS/08/11/specter.town.hall/index.html; Monica Van Dobeneck, "Lebanon Man Who Confronted Arlen Specter is Getting National Exposure," *Pennlive.com,* Aug. 12, 2009, accessed Jan. 11, 2015, http://www.pennlive.com/midstate/index.ssf/2009/08/lebanon_man_who_confronted_arl.html.

7. We derived these qualities in part by considering the inverse or opposite of the qualities of "civil talk" proposed by Benjamin Barber in *A Place for Us: How to Make Society Civil and Democracy Strong* (New York: Hill and Wang, 1998). We return to Barber's qualities of civil talk later in the chapter.

8. J. Michael Hogan, "Rhetorical Pedagogy and Democratic Citizenship: Reviving the Traditions of Civic Engagement and Public Deliberation," in *Rhetoric and Democracy: Political and Pedagogical Practices,* ed. Todd F. McDorman and David M. Timmerman (East Lansing: Michigan State University Press, 2008), 75–97; Robert Putnam, *Bowling Alone: The Collapse and Revival of American Community* (New York: Simon & Schuster, 2000).

9. Pearce and Littlejohn, *Moral Conflict,* 96.

10. Susan Herbst, "Change Through Debate," *Inside HigherEd,* Oct. 5, 2009, accessed Jan. 12, 2015, https://www.insidehighered.com/views/2009/10/05/herbst.

11. Al Kamen, "The Miami 'Riot' Squad: Where Are They Now?" *Washington Post,* Jan. 24, 2005, accessed Nov. 30, 2014, http://www.washingtonpost.com/wp-dyn/articles/A31074-2005Jan23.html.

12. Pearce and Littlejohn, *Moral Conflict,* 96.

13. Ibid., 97.

14. Tannen, *Argument Culture,* 4.

15. Takis Poulakos, *Speaking for the Polis: Isocrates' Rhetorical Education* (Columbia: University of South Carolina Press, 1997), 1, 5, quoted in Martín Carcasson, "Beyond Adversarial Communication: Public Speaking and Deliberative Democracy" (paper presented at the Brigance Colloquy, Center of Inquiry in the Liberal Arts at Wabash College, Crawfordsville, IN, Feb. 2009), http://www.liberalarts.wabash.edu/storage/brigance-colloquy/Carcasson_paper.pdf.

16. Sonja K. Foss and Cindy L. Griffin, "Beyond Persuasion: A Proposal for an Invitational Rhetoric," *Communication Monographs* 62 (1995): 1–18.

17. Barber, *A Place for Us,* 122 (emphasis added).

18. Rex W. Huppke, "Unfriending over Politics on Facebook: When Election Season and Social Media Collide," *Chicago Tribune,* Oct., 24, 2012, accessed Jan. 12, 2015, http://articles.chicagotribune.com/2012-10-24/news/ct-met-facebook-politics-friendship-20121024_1_social-media-facebook-page-friendship.

19. Matthew D. Lieberman, PhD, "Thank You for Not Unfriending Me: People Voting for the 'Other' Guy Don't Like Your Facebook Posts Either," *Social Brain, Social Mind* (blog) at *PsychologyToday.com,* Oct. 8, 2012, accessed Jan. 12, 2015, http://www.psychologytoday.com/blog/social-brain-social-mind/201210/thank-you-not-unfriending-me.

20. Nancy Fraser, "Rethinking the Public Sphere: A Contribution to the Critique of Actually Existing Democracy," *Social Text* 25 (1990): 56–80.

21. Anna M. Young, Adria Battaglia, and Dana L. Cloud: "(Un)Disciplining the Scholar Activist: Policing the Boundaries of Political Engagement," *Quarterly Journal of Speech* 96, no. 4 (2010): 431.

22. Audre Lorde, "The Uses of Anger: Women Responding to Racism" in *Sister Outsider: Essays and Speeches by Audre Lorde* (New York: Crossing Press, 2007), 131.

23. Martin Luther King Jr., "Letter from Birmingham Jail," in *The Best American Essays of the Century,* ed. Joyce Carol Oates (Boston: Houghton Mifflin, 2000), 266.

24. Nina M. Lozano-Reich and Dana L. Cloud, "The Uncivil Tongue: Invitational Rhetoric and the Problem of Inequality," *Western Journal of Communication* 73, no. 2 (2009): 221–222.

Chapter 3

1. "MVP Admits Mistake in Speech, Offers to Retire from Ateneo," *ABS-CBNnews.com,* Apr. 6, 2010, accessed Jan. 10, 2015, http://www.abs-cbnnews.com/lifestyle/04/03/10/mvp-admits-mistake-speech-offers-retire-ateneo; Carlos H. Conde, "Filipinos Criticize Eminent Imitator," *New York Times,* Apr. 4, 2010, accessed Jan. 10, 2015, http://www.nytimes.com/2010/04/05/business/global/05speech.html; Jing Castañeda, "Ateneo Official: Our Students Didn't Write MVP's 'Plagiarized' Speech," *ABS-CBNnews.com,* Apr. 15, 2010, accessed Jan. 10, 2015, http://www.abs-cbnnews.com/lifestyle/04/05/10/admu-official-our-students-didnt-write-mvps-plagiarized-speech; "More Plagiarized Speeches from MVP," *ABS-CBNnews.com,* Apr. 14, 2010, accessed Jan. 10, 2015, http://www.abs-cbnnews.com/lifestyle/04/14/10/more-plagiarized-speeches-mvp.

2. Jane Stancill, "NCCU Law Graduate Accused of Commencement Speech Plagiarism," *News & Observer,* May 16, 2011, accessed Jan. 10, 2015, http://www.newsobserver.com/2011/05/16/1202595/nccu-law-graduate-accused-of-commencement.html.

3. Allison Salz, "Dean's Grad Speech Sounded Familiar," *Toronto Sun,* June 13, 2011, accessed Jan. 10, 2015, http://www.torontosun.com/2011/06/13/deans-grad-speech-sounded-familiar; Sarah Boesveld, "University of Alberta Dean of Medicine in Midst of Plagiarism Scandal," *National Post,* Aug. 25, 2011, accessed Jan. 10, 2015, http://news.nationalpost.com/2011/06/13/university-of-alberta-dean-of-medicine-in-midst-of-plagarism-scandal/; "Philip Baker, University of Alberta Dean, Resigns Over Plagiarism Charges," *Huffington Post Canada,* Aug. 17, 2011, accessed Jan. 10, 2015, http://www.huffingtonpost.ca/2011/06/17/philip-baker-dean-alberta_n_879230.html.

4. Richard Johannesen, "Ethics," in *The Encyclopedia of Rhetoric and Composition,* ed. Theresa Enos (New York: Garland, 1996), 235.

5. American Medical Association, "Code of Medical Ethics," accessed Nov. 27, 2014, http://www.ama-assn.org/ama/pub/physician-resources/medical-ethics/code-medical-ethics.shtml.

6. "Honor System," Virginia Military Institute, accessed May 3, 2013, http://www.vmi.edu/content.aspx?id=1330.

7. "About the Leadership Conference," Virginia Military Institute, accessed Nov. 27, 2014, http://www.vmi.edu/Conferences/Leadership/2015/About/.

8. James A. Herrick, "Rhetoric, Ethics, and Virtue," *Communication Studies* 43 (1992): 139, 144, 145.

9. Kurt W. Ritter, "Ronald Reagan and 'The Speech': The Rhetoric of Public Relations Politics," *Western Journal of Speech Communication* 32 (1968): 50–58.

10. "Apple Special Event September 2009," YouTube, 74:18, Sept. 2009, https://www.youtube.com/watch?v=rW5Amx3_L9E.

11. Mike Evangelist, "Behind the Magic Curtain," *The Guardian*, Jan. 5, 2006, accessed Jan. 11, 2015, www.theguardian.com/technology/2006/jan/05/newmedia.medial.

12. William Norwood Brigance, *Speech: Its Techniques and Disciplines in a Free Society* (New York: Appleton-Century-Crofts, Inc., 1952), 16–24.

13. Ibid., 16.

14. Ibid., 16, 18.

15. Ibid., 18.

16. Ibid., 23 (italics in original).

17. Richard D. Rieke, Malcolm O. Sillars, and Tarla Rai Peterson, *Argumentation and Critical Decision Making*, 7th ed. (New York: Pearson, 2009), 155.

18. Jonathan Martin, "Senator's Thesis Turns Out to Be Remix of Others' Works, Uncited," *New York Times*, July 23, 2014, accessed Jan. 11, 2015, http://www.nytimes.com/2014/07/24/us/politics/montana-senator-john-walsh-plagiarized-thesis.html; Jonathan Martin, "Senator Quits Montana Race After Charge of Plagiarism," *New York Times*, Aug. 7, 2014, accessed Jan. 11, 2015, http://www.nytimes.com/2014/08/08/us/politics/john-walsh-drops-campaign-under-pressure-from-democrats.html; Jonathan Martin, "Plagiarism Costs Degree for Senator John Walsh," *New York Times*, Oct. 10, 2014, accessed Jan. 11, 2015, www.nytimes.com/2014/10/11/us/politics/plagiarism-costs-degree-for-senator-john-walsh.html.

19. Christine Haughney, "A Media Personality, Suffering a Blow to His Image, Ponders a Lesson," *New York Times*, Aug. 19, 2012, accessed Jan. 11, 2015, http://www.nytimes.com/2012/08/20/business/media/scandal-threatens-fareed-zakarias-image-as-media-star.html?pagewanted=all; Christine Haughney, "CNN and Time Suspend Journalist After Admission of Plagiarism," *New York Times*, Aug. 10, 2012, accessed Jan. 11, 2015, http://mediadecoder.blogs.nytimes.com/2012/08/10/time-magazine-to-examine-plagiarism-accusation-against-zakaria/.

20. Joshua Compton, "Responsive Audience, Responsive Speakers" (paper presented at the Brigance Colloquy, Center of Inquiry in the Liberal Arts at Wabash College, Crawfordsville, IN, Feb. 2009), http://www.liberalarts.wabash.edu/storage/brigance-colloquy/Compton_Paper.pdf.

21. Michael Osborne and Suzanne Osborne, *The Communication Discipline and the National Issues Forums: Alliance for a Better Public Voice* (Dayton, OH: National Issues Forums Institute, 1991), 20.

22. Brigance, *Speech: Its Techniques and Disciplines*, 89.

23. Ibid., 86–96.

24. Osborne and Osborne, *Communication Discipline,* 25.

25. Ibid., 26.

26. Ibid., 28–29, 35.

27. Elise Hu, "In First Public Comments Since Plagiarism Scandal, Jonah Lehrer Blames 'Arrogance, Need for Attention' for Lies," *Knight Blog*, Feb. 12, 2013, http://www.knightfoundation.org/blogs/knightblog/2013/2/12/first-public-comments-since-plagiarism-scandal-jonah-lehrer-blames-arrogance-need-for-attention/; "Jonah Lehrer Speaks," Knight Foundation, video, 109:31, Feb. 12, 2013, http://www.livestream.com/knightfoundation/video?clipId=pla_df812e9c-fd3b-442d-8bec-5cb78f23192e; Jonah Leher, "My Apology," *Jonah Lehrer.com* (blog), Feb. 13, 2013, http://www.jonahlehrer.com/2013/02/my-apology/; "About the Foundation," Knight Foundation, accessed May 7, 2013, http://www.knightfoundation.org/about/.

28. Charles Seife, "Jonah Lehrer's Journalistic Misdeeds at Wired.com," *Slate*, Aug. 31, 2012, accessed Jan. 11, 2015, http://www.slate.com/articles/health_and_science/science/2012/08/jonah_lehrer_plagiarism_in_wired_com_an_investigation_into_plagiarism_quotes_and_factual_inaccuracies_.html.

29. Most tweets located in J. K. Trotter, "Jonah Lehrer Apologizes, Surrounded by Tweets Still Calling Him a Plagiarist," *The Wire*, Feb. 12, 2013, accessed May 7, 2013, http://www.thewire.com/national/2013/02/jonah-lehrer-apologizes-surrounded-tweets-still-calling-him-plagiarist/62055/.

Chapter 4

1. The distinction between researching as inquiry versus strategy is suggested by Martín Caracasson, "Beyond Adversarial Communication: Public Speaking and Deliberative Democracy" (paper presented at the Brigance Colloquy, Center of Inquiry in the Liberal Arts at Wabash College, Crawfordsville, IN, Feb. 2009), http://www.liberalarts.wabash.edu/storage/brigance-colloquy/Carcasson_paper.pdf.

2. Jane Sasseen, Kenny Olmstead, and Amy Mitchell, "Digital: As Mobile Grows Rapidly, the Pressures on News Intensify," *The State of the News Media 2013*, Pew Research Center, http://stateofthemedia.org/2013/digital-as-mobile-grows-rapidly-the-pressures-on-news-intensify/#fnref-12962-20.

3. Megan Garber, "Survey: Majority of Journalists Now Depend on Social Media for Story Research," *Columbia Journalism Review*, Jan. 25, 2010, accessed Jan. 7, 2015, http://www.cjr.org/the_kicker/survey_majority_of_journalists.php.

4. Ekaterina Stepanova to PONARS Eurasia, May 2011, "The Role of Information Communication Technologies in the 'Arab Spring: Implications Beyond the Region,'" Policy Memorandum No. 159, http://ponarseurasia.com/sites/default/files/policy-memos-pdf/pepm_159.pdf.

5. Laura Petrecca, "After Bombings, Social Media Informs (and Misinforms)," *USA Today*, Apr. 23, 2013, accessed Jan. 7, 2015, http://www.usatoday.com/story/news/2013/04/23/social-media-boston-marathon-bombings/2106701/.

6. Alex Dingman, "Use of Social Media Leads to News Outlets Providing False Information," *WIBS News Now.com*, Apr. 22, 2013, accessed Jan. 7, 2015, http://www.wibwnewsnow.com/use-of-social-media-leads-to-news-outlets-providing-false-information/.

7. Chris Gayomali, "Connecticut Massacre Suspect: How the Media IDed the Wrong Guy," *The Week*, Dec. 14, 2012, accessed Jan. 7, 2015, http://theweek.com/article/index/237888/connecticut-massacre-suspect-how-the-medianbspided-the-wrong-guy.

8. Jon Terbush, "Student Wrongly Tied to Boston Bombings Found Dead," *The Week*, Apr. 25, 2013, accessed Jan. 7, 2015, http://theweek.com/article/index/243339/student-wrongly-tied-to-boston-bombings-found-dead#.

9. "Using EDGAR—Researching Public Companies," Investor.gov, US Securities and Exchange Commission, accessed Jan. 7, 2015, http://investor.gov/researching-managing-investments/researching-investments/using-edgar-researching-public-companies.

10. Todd Wasserman, "Twitter Says It Has 140 Million Users," *Mashable*, Mar. 21, 2012, accessed Jan. 7, 2015, http://mashable.com/2012/03/21/twitter-has-140-million-users/.

11. "Buzz in the Blogosphere: Millions More Bloggers and Blog Readers," Nielson, Mar. 8, 2012, accessed Jan. 7, 2015, http://www.nielsen.com/us/cn/newswire/2012/buzz-in-the-blogosphere-millions-more-bloggers-and-blog-readers.html.

12. The idea of seeking different types of information during an interview was inspired by "Conducting Interviews," University Writing Center at Northern Illinois University, accessed May 29, 2013, Internet archive, http://web.archive.org/web/20121323525900/http://www.engl.niu.edu/wac/interview.html.

13. For more on the "politics" of web searching and how we are directed to some sites and away from others, as well as the "democratic" features of the World Wide Web see Matthew Hindman, *The Myth of Digital Democracy* (Princeton, NJ: Princeton University Press, 2009).

14. Amy Gesenhues, "Study: Delaware Least Likely State to Use Google, While Yahoo is More Popular in Southern & Midwest States," *Search Engine Land,* May 16, 2013, accessed Jan. 7, 2015, http://searchengineland.com/delaware-only-state-with-less-than-70-google-marketshare-in-study-of-search-engine-usage-across-us-159811.

15. Jimmy Wales, quoted in Jeff Young, "Wikipedia Founder Discourages Academic Use of His Creation," *The Chronicle of Higher Education,* June 12, 2006, accessed Jan. 7, 2015, http://chronicle.com/blogPost/Wikipedia-Founder-Discourages/2305.

Chapter 5

1. Jules Witcover, *85 Days: The Last Campaign of Robert Kennedy* (New York: G.P. Putnam's Sons, 1969), 142.

2. Arthur M. Schlesinger Jr., *Robert Kennedy and His Times* (Boston: Houghton Mifflin, 1978), 873–875; Edwin O. Guthman and C. Richard Allen, eds., *RFK: Collected Speeches* (New York: Viking, 1993), 355–358; Witcover, *85 Days,* 139–142; Stuart Gerry Brown, *The Presidency on Trial: Robert Kennedy's 1968 Campaign and Afterwards* (Honolulu: University Press of Hawaii, 1972), 61–62.

3. Lloyd Bitzer, "The Rhetorical Situation," *Philosophy & Rhetoric* 1 (1968): 1–14.

4. "Why This Ad?," Yahoo!, accessed Jan. 11, 2015, https://info.yahoo.com/privacy/us/yahoo/relevantads.html.

5. David F. Gallagher, "Google Floods My Calendar with 'Star Trek' Geekery," *New York Times,* May 8, 2009, accessed Jan. 11, 2015, http://bits.blogs.nytimes.com/2009/05/08/google-floods-my-calendar-with-star-trek-geekery/.

6. "Consumers Say They Prefer Targeted to Random Online Ads," *Marketing Charts,* Apr. 19, 2013, accessed Jan. 11, 2015, http://www.marketingcharts.com/online/consumers-say-they-prefer-targeted-to-random-online-ads-28825/.

7. Plato, *Phaedrus,* in *The Collected Dialogues of Plato,* ed. Edith Hamilton and Huntington Cairns, trans. R. Hackforth (Princeton, NJ: Princeton University Press, 1973), 271d.

8. Ibid., 259e–260a.

9. "VIDEO: Red Sox's David Ortiz Delivers Emotional Pregame Speech after Boston Marathon 2013," *3 News,* Apr. 21, 2013, accessed Jan. 11, 2015, http://www.3news.co.nz/VIDEO-Red-Soxs-David-Ortiz-delivers-emotional-pregame-speech-after-Boston-Marathon-2013/tabid/317/articleID/295028/Default.aspx.

10. Gabe Lacques, "Bud Selig Approves of David Ortiz's Profane Message," *USA Today,* Apr. 25, 2013, accessed Jan. 11, 2015, http://www.usatoday.com/story/sports/mlb/2013/04/25/david-ortiz-expletive-fenway-park-boston-marathon-bombings-bud-selig/2113513/.

11. Kenneth Burke, *A Rhetoric of Motives* (Berkeley: University of California Press, 1950/1969), 55 (italics in original).

12. "Coca-Cola Vows to Reduce Advertising to Kids: Beverage Giant Goes on Offensive with Critics Holding Soda Responsible for Obesity Epidemic," *Advertising Age,* May 8, 2013,

accessed Jan. 11, 2015, http://adage.com/article/news/coca-cola-vows-reduce-advertising-kids/241359/.

13. Federal Trade Commission, "Marketing Violent Entertainment to Children: A Sixth Follow-Up Review of Industry Practices in the Motion Picture, Music Recording & Electronic Game Industries—A Report to Congress," Dec. 2009, http://www.ftc.gov/sites/default/files/documents/reports/marketing-violent-entertainment-children-sixth-follow-review-industry-practices-motion-picture-music/p994511violententertainment.pdf.

14. David Corn, "SECRET VIDEO: Romney Tells Millionaire Donors What He REALLY Thinks of Obama Voters," *Mother Jones*, Sept. 17, 2012, accessed Jan. 11, 2015, http://www.motherjones.com/politics/2012/09/secret-video-romney-private-fundraiser.

15. Ibid.

16. Marty Kaplan, "The Bartender Who Rescued America," *Huffington Post*, May 18, 2013, accessed Jan. 11, 2015, http://www.huffingtonpost.com/marty-kaplan/the-bartender-who-rescued_b_2897436.html.

17. Catalina Camia, "Romney on 47% Comments: 'That didn't come out right,'" *USA Today*, June 6, 2013, accessed Jan. 11, 2015, http://www.usatoday.com/story/onpolitics/2013/06/06/mitt-romney-47-percent-regrets/2397567/.

18. Michael Calvin McGee, "In Search of 'the People': A Rhetorical Alternative," *Quarterly Journal of Speech* 61 (1976): 235–249.

19. Ibid., 242.

Chapter 6

1. Gorgias, "Encomium of Helen," in Aristotle, *On Rhetoric: A Theory of Civil Discourse*, trans. George A. Kennedy (New York: Oxford University Press, 1991), 284–288, sec. 2.

2. Ibid., sec. 6.

3. Ibid., sec. 20.

4. Ibid., sec. 1–6.

5. Ibid., sec. 2.

6. Ryan Trauman, "Twitter as Digital Scholarship: Why You Might Want to Sign Up," *New Media Scholar* (blog), May 28, 2011, Creative Commons Attribution 4.0 International License, http://www.newmediascholar.net/twitter-as-digital-scholarship-why-you-might-want-to-sign-up.

7. Cesear Chavez, Untitled Address at Pacific Lutheran University, Mar. 1989, Tacoma, WA, full text available at UnitedFarmWorkers.org, accessed Jan. 12, 2015, http://www.ufw.org/_page.php?menu=research&inc=history/10.html.

8. Barack Obama, "Address on Comprehensive Immigration Reform," Jan. 29, 2013, Las Vegas, NV, full text available at *AmericanRhetoric.com*, accessed Jan. 12, 2015, http://www.americanrhetoric.com/speeches/barackobama/barackobamaimmagrationreform.htm.

Chapter 7

1. Eli Saslow, "Helping to Write History," *Washington Post*, Dec. 18, 2008, accessed Jan. 12, 2015, http://www.washingtonpost.com/wp-dyn/content/article/2008/12/17/AR2008121703903_pf.html.

2. Ibid.

3. Peggy Noonan, *Simply Speaking: How to Communicate Your Ideas with Style, Substance, and Clarity* (New York: Regan Books, 1988), 24.

Chapter 8

1. Karlyn Kohrs Campbell, "The Discursive Performance of Femininity: Hating Hillary," *Rhetoric & Public Affairs* 1 (1998): 6.

2. Video is available at "Hillary Tears Up in New Hampshire Primary 2008," YouTube, 1:51, Jan. 9, 2008, http://www.youtube.com/watch?v=dqGl-pDnYMQ.

3. Hillary Clinton, quoted in "Newsweek Cover: Hillary Clinton: 'I Found My Own Voice,'" *Newsweek.com,* Jan. 13, 2008, accessed Jan. 10, 2015, http://www.prnewswire.com/news-releases/newsweek-cover-hillary-clinton-i-found-my-own-voice-56889642.html.

4. Aristotle, *On Rhetoric: A Theory of Civic Discourse,* trans. George A. Kennedy (Oxford: Oxford University Press, 1991), sec. 1404b.

5. The film, "The Man from Hope," aired in 1992 during the Democratic National Convention. clintonlibrary42, "The Man From Hope," YouTube, 17:05, Mar. 5, 2013, https://www.youtube.com/watch?v=7LntAEHG5vA.

6. Ronald Reagan, "Address at Pointe-du-Hoc, Normandy, June 6, 1984," in *American Speeches: Political Oratory from Abraham Lincoln to Bill Clinton*, ed. Ted Widmer (New York: Library of America, 2006), 736–740.

7. George W. Bush, "Address to a Joint Session of Congress," *Washington Post*, Sept. 20, 2001, accessed Jan. 10, 2015, http://www.washingtonpost.com/wp-srv/nation/specials/attacked/transcripts/bushaddress_092001.html.

8. John F. Kennedy, "Inaugural Address, January 20, 1961," in Widmer, *American Speeches,* 538.

9. Malcolm X, "The Ballot or the Bullet," in Widmer, *American Speeches,* 576.

10. Martin Luther King Jr., "Address to the March on Washington, August 28, 1963," in Widmer, *American Speeches,* 556, 559.

11. Reagan, "Address at Pointe-du-Hoc," 736.

12. Bush, "Address to a Joint Session of Congress."

13. Matthew 13:31, 44, 45 (New Revised Standard Version).

14. Frederick Douglass, "What to a Slave is the 4th of July?" in Widmer, *American Speeches*, 530.

15. Bush, "Address to a Joint Session of Congress."

16. Douglass, "What to a Slave is the 4th of July?," 538, 534–535.

17. Malcolm X, "The Ballot or the Bullet."

18. Ibid., 586.

19. Reagan, "Address at Pointe-du-Hoc," 740.

20. Ibid., 738.

21. Michael Calvin McGee, "The 'Ideograph': A Link Between Rhetoric and Ideology," *Quarterly Journal of Speech* 66 (1980): 1–16.

22. King Jr., "Address to the March on Washington," 560.

23. Scholars in multiple disciplines, ranging from sociology to cognitive science, have defined framing in slightly different ways. Our definition represents our understanding as rhetorical scholars.

24. Jake Tapper, "New Name for Iraq Mission Meets with Criticism from Left," ABC News (blog), Feb. 22, 2010, http://blogs.abcnews.com/politicalpunch/2010/02/new-name-for-iraq-mission-meets-with-criticism-from-left.html; Arianna Huffington, "Sunday Roundup," *Huffington Post*, Feb. 20, 2010, accessed Aug. 15, 2011, http://www.huffingtonpost.com/arianna-huffington/sunday-roundup_b_470252.html; Jessica Wood, "Operation Iraqi Freedom by Any Other Name Would Smell as Foul," *Daily 49er*, Apr. 28, 2010, accessed Aug. 15, 2011, http://www.daily49er.com/opinion/operation-iraqi-freedom-by-any-other-name-would-smell-as-foul-1.2245147.

25. George Lakoff, *Thinking Points: Communicating Our American Values and Vision* (New York: Farrar, Straus and Giroux, 2006), 38, 40.

26. Charlotte Ryan, *Prime Time Activism: Media Strategies for Grassroots Organizing* (Boston: South End Press, 1991), 56; Lakoff, *Thinking Points,* 31.

27. Lakoff, *Thinking Points,* 38.

28. Will Friedman, "Reframing 'Framing,'" Center for Advances in Public Engagement, Occasional Paper, no. 1, accessed Jan. 8, 2015, http://www.publicagenda.org/files/Reframing%20Framing.pdf.

29. George Lakoff, *Don't Think of an Elephant! Know Your Values and Frame the Debate* (White River Junction, VT: Chelsea Green, 2004), 21–22.

30. See Andy Barr, "Rep. Alan Grayson's 'Taliban' Ad Backfires," *Politico,* Sept. 28, 2010, accessed Jun. 1, 2015, http://www.politico.com/news/stories/0910/42818.html.

Chapter 9

1. Katherine Q. Seelye, "Senate Nominee Speaks of Encompassing Unity," *New York Times,* July 28, 2004, accessed Jan. 12, 2015, http://www.nytimes.com/2004/07/28/us/the-constituencies-african-americans-senate-nominee-speaks-of-encompassing-unity.html.

2. Mark Bowden, "The Power of Oratory," *Statesman,* Jan. 28, 2010, accessed Jan. 11, 2015, http://www.statesman.com/news/news/opinion/bowden-the-power-of-oratory/nRhf2/; Ben Yagoda, "The Comic Stylings of POTUS," *Chronicle of Higher Education,* May 6, 2013, accessed Jan. 11, 2015, http://chronicle.com/blogs/linguafranca/2013/05/06/the-comic-stylings-of-potus/.

3. Father Raymond J. de Souza, "Obama the Orator," *National Post,* Jan. 28, 2010, A16, LexisNexis; See also "Obama's Reliance on Teleprompters (Editorial)," *Washington Times,* Mar. 10, 2009, accessed Jan. 11, 2015, http://www.washingtontimes.com/news/2009/mar/10/obamas-reliance-on-teleprompters/; Michael Gerson, "What the Teleprompter Teaches," *Washington Post,* Mar. 27, 2009, A17, LexisNexis; "Cain Calls out Teleprompter President: Candidate Attacks Obama's Lack of Substance (Editorial)," *The Washington Times,* July 19, 2011, accessed Jan. 11, 2015, http://www.washingtontimes.com/news/2011/jul/19/cain-calls-out-teleprompter-president/.

4. MJ Lee, "The Obama Teleprompter: 10 Best Jokes," *Politico,* Mar. 14, 2012, accessed Jan. 11, 2015, http://www.politico.com/news/stories/0312/74027.html; Gerson, "What the Teleprompter Teaches"; Nick Wing, "Obama Teleprompter Getting Less Use on Campaign Trail," *Huffington Post,* July 17, 2012, accessed Jan. 11, 2015, http://www.huffingtonpost.com/2012/07/17/obama-teleprompter-campaign_n_1679288.html.

5. Aristotle, *On Rhetoric: A Theory of Civic Discourse,* trans. George A. Kennedy (Oxford: Oxford University Press, 1991), sec. 1404a.

6. Karen Kangas Dwyer and Marlina M. Davidson, "Is Public Speaking Really More Feared than Death?" *Communication Research Reports* 29 (2012): 99–107. This study partly replicated the classic 1973 Bruskin Associates survey of common fears, a survey that is often cited as supporting the idea that people are more fearful of public speaking than death.

7. Jerry Seinfeld, *SeinLanguage* (New York: Bantam Books, 1993), 120.

8. Charles Moore, "The Invincible Mrs. Thatcher," *Vanity Fair,* Dec. 2011, accessed Jan. 11, 2015, http://www.vanityfair.com/politics/features/2011/12/margaret-thatcher-201112#; Polly Dunbar, "How Laurence Olivier Gave Margaret Thatcher the Voice That Went Down in History," *Daily Mail* (London), Oct. 29, 2011, accessed Jan. 11, 2015, http://www.dailymail.co.uk/news/article-2055214/How-Laurence-Olivier-gave-Margaret-Thatcher-voice-went-history.html; Patrick Sawer, "How Maggie Thatcher Was Remade,"

The Telegraph (London), Jan. 8, 2012, accessed Jan. 11, 2015, http://www.telegraph.co.uk/news/politics/margaret-thatcher/8999746/How-Maggie-Thatcher-was-remade.html.

9. When speaking on camera, it is generally best to focus your gaze toward the camera or cameras. In such instances, distributing your eye contact across the room will make it appear to a viewing audience as if you are avoiding eye contact.

10. *Saturday Night Live*, "Cold Opening: Gore/Bush First Debate," Yahoo! Screen video 10:03, Oct. 7, 2000, https://screen.yahoo.com/gore-bush-first-debate-000000075.html; Richard L. Berke and Kevin Sack, "THE 2000 CAMPAIGN: THE DEBATES; In Debate 2, Microscope Focuses on Gore," *New York Times*, Oct. 11, 2000, accessed Jan. 11, 2015, http://www.nytimes.com/2000/10/11/us/the-2000-campaign-the-debates-in-debate-2-microscope-focuses-on-gore.html.

11. "Republican Convention Evening Session [Elizabeth Dole 1996 Convention Speech]," C-SPAN Video Library, 6:03:41, Aug. 14, 1996, http://www.c-span.org/video/?74343-1/republican-convention-evening-session. Dole's speech runs from 1:26 to 1:48. "Elizabeth Dole Speaking Before the Republican National Convention [Transcript]," *PBS News Hour*, Aug. 14, 1996, accessed Jan. 11, 2015, http://www.pbs.org/newshour/bb/politics/july-dec96/elizabeth_dole_08-14.html. While detailing the positive response elicited by the speech, Karrin Anderson contends that Dole's speech also promoted her femininity and reinforced traditional gender roles, problematizing some of the implications of the speech for Elizabeth Dole's later presidential campaign. Karrin Vasby Anderson, "From Spouses to Candidates: Hillary Rodham Clinton, Elizabeth Dole, and the Gendered Office of U.S. President," *Rhetoric & Public Affairs* 5 (2002): 105–132.

12. Alcidamas, "Concerning Those Who Write Written Speeches, or Concerning Sophists," in *Readings from Classical Rhetoric*, ed. Patricia P. Matsen, Phillip Rollinson, and Marion Sousa, trans. Patricia P. Matsen (Carbondale: Southern Illinois University Press, 1990), sec. 20–28.

13. Martin Olson, "Phil Davison, GOP Candidate, FREAKS OUT Trying to Sell Candidacy (Video)," *Huffington Post*, Sept. 9, 2010, accessed Jan. 11, 2015. Davison's speech is no longer available on the *Huffington Post* but can be located at Stephen Gebhardt, "Phil Davison, GOP Candidate [Original, Full Video]," YouTube, 5:51, Sept. 10, 2010, https://www.youtube.com/watch?v=djfDZrm9KZs.

14. Sal Gentile, "Interview with Phil Davison, the Man Behind One of the Most Intense Stump Speeches Ever," The Daily Need, *PBS.Org*, Sept. 9, 2010, accessed Jan. 11, 2015, http://www.pbs.org/wnet/need-to-know/the-daily-need/anatomy-of-a-political-freak out-interview-with-phil-davidson/3433/; Nick Wing, "Phil Davison Interview: Political Beserker Answers Questions About YouTube, Political Vision," *Huffington Post*, May 25, 2011, accessed Jan. 11, 2015, http://www.huffingtonpost.com/2010/09/10/phil-davison-interview-po_n_711941.html?.

Chapter 10

1. Cyndy Cole, "Snowbowl Ends Busier Season," *Arizona Daily Sun* (Flagstaff), Apr. 21, 2013, accessed Jan. 7, 2015, http://azdailysun.com/business/local/snowbowl-ends-busier-season/article_c5d4eba9-a017-5233-bcdc-5fcadb3d3a23.html.

2. J. R. Murray, quoted in Leslie Macmillan, "Resort's Snow Won't Be Pure This Year; It'll Be Sewage," *New York Times*, Sept. 26, 2012, accessed Jan. 7, 2015, http://www.nytimes.com/2012/09/27/us/arizona-ski-resorts-sewage-plan-creates-uproar.html?_r=0.

3. The study is referenced in MacMillan, "Resort's Snow Won't Be Pure This Year."

4. "355: The Giant Pool of Money," *This American Life,* Chicago Public Media (Chicago: May 9, 2008).

5. "375: Bad Bank," *This American Life,* Chicago Public Media (Chicago: Feb. 27, 2009).

6. "505: Use Only As Directed," *This American Life,* Chicago Public Media (Chicago: Sept. 20, 2013).

7. "About," The Commons, Kettering Foundation, accessed Jan. 7, 2015, http://the-commons.kettering.org/about/.

8. Carolyn Danckaert and Aaron Smith, "About Us," *AMightyGirl.com,* accessed May 27, 2015, http://www.amightygirl.com/about. A Mighty Girl's *Facebook* page, accessed May 27, 2015, https://www.facebook.com/amightygirl. A Mighty Girl's *Pinterest* page, accessed May 27, 2015, http://www.pinterest.com/amightygirl/. A Mighty Girl's *Twitter* page, accessed May 27, 2015, https://twitter.com/amightygirl.

9. "Crowdsourcing," *Merriam-Webster Online,* accessed Jan. 7, 2015.

10. Aristotle, *On Rhetoric: A Theory of Civic Discourse* (New York: Oxford University Press, 1991), sec. 1357a11–13.

11. Bryan Fisher, "Public Speaking Pedagogy for a Diverse Democratic Society" (paper presented at the Brigance Colloquy, Center of Inquiry in the Liberal Arts at Wabash College, Crawfordsville, IN, Feb. 2009), http://www.liberalarts.wabash.edu/storage/brigance-colloquy/Fisher_Paper.pdf; Chantal Mouffe, *Agonistics: Thinking the World Politically* (London: Verso, 2013).

12. The instruction to anticipate and learn key facts for a deliberative discussion is stressed in Colorado State University Center for Public Deliberation, *CSU Center for Public Deliberation: Student Associate Training Workbook* (Fall 2011), 69, accessed Jan. 8, 2015, http://www.casb.org/_literature_97551/PR_Academy_-_Student_Workbook.

13. Deborah Tannen, *The Argument Culture: Moving from Debate to Dialogue* (New York: Random House, 1998), 10.

14. Translators define *dissoi logoi* differently. T. M. Robinson uses "contrasting arguments." See T. M. Robinson, *Contrasting Arguments: An Edition of the Dissoi Logoi* (New York: Arno Press, 1979). Rosamond Kent Sprague uses "two-fold arguments." See Rosamond Kent Sprague, "Dissoi Logoi or Dialexeis," *Mind* 77 (1968), 155–167.

15. David Roochnik, "Teaching Virtue: The Contrasting Arguments (*Dissoi Logoi*) of Antiquity," *Journal of Education* 179 (1997): 3.

16. Stephen Gencarella Olbrys, "*Dissoi Logoi,* Civic Friendship, and the Politics of Education," *Communication Education* 55 (2006): 355.

17. Ibid., 362.

18. Ibid., 362.

19. Ibid., 354–366.

20. Will Friedman, "Reframing 'Framing,'" Center for Advances in Public Engagement, Occasional Paper, no. 1, p. 2, accessed Jan. 8, 2015, http://www.publicagenda.org/files/Reframing%20Framing.pdf.

21. Ibid., 2.

22. David Matthews, *For Communities to Work* (Dayton, OH: Kettering Foundation, 2002), 22.

23. Ibid., 22.

24. The term "trade-off" (or its synonyms "tension" and "dilemma") can be found in many sources in relation to deliberation, including Elizabeth M. Smith and National Issues Forum Institute, *National Issues Forums in the Classroom: A High School Program on*

Deliberative Democracy (Dayton, OH: Kettering Foundation, 2001) as well as Martín Carcasson, "Tackling Wicked Problems Through Deliberative Engagement," *Colorado Municipalities* (Oct. 2013), 11, accessed Jan. 3, 2014, http://www.cpd.colostate.edu/ carcasson-tackling-wicked-problems.pdf.

25. This open question is offered by both of the following sources as a way of recognizing and/or asking about a trade-off: Colorado State University Center for Public Deliberation, 75; Smith and National Issues Forum Institute, 3.45.

26. Robert H. McKenzie, *Public Politics* (Dubuque, IA: Kendall/Hunt, 1994), 67.

27. Colorado State University Center for Public Deliberation, 14.

28. George Lakoff, *Thinking Points: Communicating Our American Values and Vision* (New York: Farrar, Straus and Giroux, 2006), 82.

29. The phrase "value hierarchy" can be found in several sources, including Chaim Perelman and L. Obrechts-Tyteca, *The New Rhetoric: A Treatise on Argumentation* (South Bend: University of Notre Dame Press, 1969), as well as Harold D. Lasswell and Myres S. McDougal, *Jursiprudence for a Free Society: Studies in Law, Science and Policy* (Hingham, MA: Martinus Nifhoff/Kluwer Academic Publishers, 1992). This textbook's authors, however, first encountered the phrase in Colorado State University Center for Public Deliberation, 15.

30. The phrase "value dilemma" can be found in many different sources. This textbook's authors first encountered the phrase in Colorado State University Center for Public Deliberation, 15.

31. Kenneth Janda, Jeffrey M. Berry, Jerry Goldman, and Kevin Hula, *The Challenge of Democracy: American Government in Global Politics*, 8th ed. (Boston: Wadsworth, Cengage Learning, 2012), 15, 22.

32. Ibid., 24, 123–127.

33. McKenzie, *Public Politics*, 91.

34. Ibid., 140.

35. Colorado State University Center for Public Deliberation, 16.

36. Barnett Pearce and Stephen W. Littlejohn, *Moral Conflict: When Social Worlds Collide* (Thousand Oaks, CA: Sage, 1997), 153.

37. Jurgen Habermas, *The Structural Transformation of the Public Sphere: An Inquiry into a Category of Bourgeois Society* (Cambridge: MIT Press, 1996); Nancy Fraser, "Rethinking the Public Sphere: A Contribution to the Critique of Actually Existing Democracy," *Social Text* 25 (1990): 56–80.

38. Benjamin R. Barber, *A Place for Us: How to Make Society Civil and Democracy Strong* (New York: Hill and Wang, 1998), 116–122. See chapter 2 for a more extended discussion of Barber's principles of civil discourse.

Chapter 11

1. Indiana State Epidemiology and Outcomes Workgroup, *The Consumption and Consequences of Alcohol, Tobacco, and Drugs in Indiana: A State Epidemiological Profile 2012* (Center for Health Policy at Indiana University-Purdue University Indiana, 2012), accessed Jan. 8, 2015, http://www.purdue.edu/swo/aod/KnowItAll/alcoholpoisoning/ AlcoholDrugFactSheets.pdf.

2. For instance, in 2012 Indiana had the 17th highest drug overdose mortality rate in the country. See Trust for America's Health, *Prescription Drug Abuse: Strategies to Stop the Epidemic* (Oct. 2013), 12, accessed Jan. 8, 2015, http://healthyamericans.org/assets/files/ TFAH2013RxDrugAbuseRptFINAL.pdf; in 2011–2012. Indiana was one of the top eight

states for the rate of past-month use of illicit drugs other than marijuana among persons aged twelve or older. See Substance Abuse and Mental Health Services Administration, *2011–2012 National Survey on Drug Use and Health National Maps of Prevalence Estimates, by State* (2013), 12, accessed Jan. 8, 2015, http://www.samhsa.gov/data/NSDUH/2k12State/Maps/NSDUHsaeMaps2012.pdf. In 2012, Indiana had the third highest rate of methamphetamine laboratory incidents. See "The Methiest States in the U.S. (Infographic)," *Huffington Post* (Oct. 7, 2013), accessed Jan. 8, 2015, http://www.huffingtonpost.com/2013/10/07/meth-states_n_4057372.html?view.

3. All materials associated with the Montgomery County, Indiana, public deliberation are available at "Substance Abuse Fall 2013," Wabash College Rhetoric Department, accessed May 27, 2014, https://sites.google.com/site/mccommunityconversations/pastconversations/substanceabusefall2013.

4. William Keith, *Democracy as Discussion: The American Forum Movement and Civic Education* (Lanham, MD: Lexington Books, 2004), 4.

5. The term "public knowledge" can be found in several sources in relation to deliberation, including Robert H. McKenzie, *Public Politics* (Dubuque, IA: Kendall/Hunt, 1994), 40–44.

6. The term "public judgment" can be found in several sources in relation to deliberation and group decision-making, including Daniel Yankelovich, *Coming to Public Judgment: Making Democracy Work in a Complex World* (New York: Syracuse University Press, 1991).

7. McKenzie, *Public Politics,* 85.

8. Irving L. Janis, *Victims of Groupthink: A Psychological Study of Foreign-Policy Decisions and Fiascos* (Boston: Houghton Mifflin, 1971); Irving L. Janis, *Groupthink: Psychological Studies of Policy Decisions and Fiascos* (Boston: Houghton, Mifflin, 1972); James K. Esser, "Alive and Well After 25 Years: A Review of Groupthink Research," *Organizational Behavior and Human Decision Processes* 73 (1998), 116–141.

9. Aristotle, *Politics,* in *The Basic Works of Aristotle,* ed. Richard McKeon, trans. Benjamin Jowett (New York: Random House, 1941), sec. 1281b2, 1281b38.

10. David Matthews, *For Communities to Work* (Dayton, OH: Kettering Foundation, 2002), 23.

11. Information about the Montgomery County, Indiana, educational meetings is available at "Substance Abuse Fall 2013" under the sub-heading "*Continuing* the Conversation on Substance Abuse in Montgomery County."

12. We are heavily indebted to the work done by Keith in *Democracy as Discussion.*

13. "Committees of Correspondence," Boston Tea Party Ships and Museum, accessed Sept. 5, 2013, http://www.bostonteapartyship.com/committees-of-correspondence.

14. Malcolm S. Knolwes, *The Adult Education Movement in the United States* (New York: Holt, Rinehart and Winston, 1962), quoted in Keith, *Democracy as Discussion,* 214.

15. Josiah Holbrook, *American Lyceum* (Boston: Perkins and Marvin, 1829), 3.

16. Glenn Frank, "The Parliament of the People," *Century Magazine* 98 (1919): 407; Keith, *Democracy as Discussion,* 217, 222.

17. Frank, "The Parliament of the People," 407. See also "Our History," Chautauqua Institution, accessed May 27, 2014, http://www.ciweb.org/our-history-about-us.

18. "Our History."

19. Keith, *Democracy as Discussion,* 218.

20. "Navigating the Trail," Chautauqua Trail: A North American Cultural Renaissance, accessed Jan. 8, 2015, http://www.chautauquatrail.com/.

21. Keith, *Democracy as Discussion,* 144, 152, 157.

22. J. Jeffery Auer, "Tools of Social Inquiry: Argumentation, Discussion and Debate," *Quarterly Journal of Speech* 25 (1939): 533, 534.

23. Keith, *Democracy as Discussion*, 158, 193.

24. Frank, "The Parliament of the People," 404; Keith, *Democracy as Discussion*, 237, 223.

25. Frank, "The Parliament of the People," 405.

26. Ibid., 404; Keith, *Democracy as Discussion*, 223–224.

27. Keith, *Democracy as Discussion*, 213, 296–297.

28. Ibid., 113.

29. One measure of the growing interest in deliberative discussions among universities and colleges is the addition of a Public Dialogue and Deliberation division within the National Communication Association in 2014. "Interest Group Descriptions," National Communication Association, accessed Jan. 8, 2015, http://www.natcom.org/interestgroups/.

30. John Gastil, David Brinker, and Robert Richards, *Evaluation and Analysis of Public Discussion and Deliberation in the AmericaSpeaks & Face the Facts USA Joint Civic Engagement Program for the 2012 Presidential Campaign* (Oct. 31, 2013), accessed Jan. 8, 2015, http://www.democracyfund.org/media/uploaded/Evaluation_Report_-_Oct_2013.pdf.

31. Craig Paterson, "Experimenting in Deliberative Conversations," *Deliberative IDEAS* (blog), Oct. 22, 2010, http://delibcaideas.org/?p=200.

32. "Successful Virtual Deliberation Part of June 26 America Speaks OBOE Events," Public-Decisions, accessed Jan. 9, 2015, http://p2tools.blogspot.com/2010/06/successful-virtual-deliberation-part-of.html. See also "AmericaSpeaks . . . in Second Life," Center for Voter Deliberation of Northern Virginia, June 10, 2010, accessed Jan. 9, 2015, http://www.cvdnva.org/2010/06/americaspeaksin-second-life.html.

33. Tim Bonnemann, "Creating Community Solutions: Zilino Cross-Campus Online Dialogue," Intellitics, accessed Jan. 9, 2015, http://www.intellitics.com/blog/2014/05/19/creating-community-solutions-zilino-cross-campus-online-dialogue/.

34. Engagement Game Lab, *Engagement Games: A Case for Designing Games to Facilitate Real-World Action* (Boston: Emerson College), accessed Jan. 9, 2015, http://engagementgamelab.org/resources/.

35. Laura W. Black, "The Promise and Problems of Online Deliberation," Kettering Foundation Working Paper (Dayton, OH: Kettering Foundation, 2011), accessed Jan. 9, 2015, https://www.kettering.org/catalog/product/promise-and-problems-online-deliberation.

36. See, for example, J. Dan Rothwell, *In Mixed Company: Communicating in Small Groups and Teams,* 7th ed. (Boston: Wadsworth, 2010), 62. Rothwell specifies a small group size of seven to ten for groups that prioritize the quality of their decision over the speed in making the decision, such as we find with deliberative discussion groups.

37. For more on National Issues Forums, go to http://www.nifi.org. You can find the deliberative discussion structure specified in NIF's moderator guides, which accompany the issue books they produce, though NIF sometimes uses different words to label the stages. For instance, see the section on "Stages of a Forum" of the following moderator guide: National Issues Forums, "Shaping Our Future: How Should Higher Education Help Us Create the Society We Want?" (Dayton, OH: National Issues Forums Institute, 2012), 3, accessed Jan. 9, 2015, https://www.nifi.org/sites/default/files/product-downloads/shaping_our_future_g_0.pdf. Notice the guide suggests moving from "Getting started" (personal stakes) to "Deliberation" (during which each approach is discussed) to "Ending the forum" (reflection period).

38. McKenzie, *Public Politics,* 79.

39. The phrase "working through" in relation to group discussions and decision-making is associated with Daniel Yankelovich in a series of books, including *Coming to Public Judgment: Making Democracy Work in a Complex World* and *New Rules: Searching for Self-Fulfillment in a World Turned Upside-Down* (New York: Random House, 1981). A helpful discussion of "working through" can also be found in McKenzie, *Public Politics,* 75–82.

40. Sam Kaner, with Lenny Lind, Catherine Toldi, Sarah Fisk, and Duane Berger, *Facilitator's Guide to Participatory Decision Making,* 2nd ed. (San Francisco: Jossey-Bass, 2007), 18, 223.

41. Martín Carcasson, "Tackling Wicked Problems Through Deliberative Engagement," *Colorado Municipalities* (Oct. 2013), 11, accessed Jan. 3, 2014, http://www.cpd.colostate.edu/carcasson-tackling-wicked-problems.pdf.

42. McKenzie discusses the importance of participants answering why they hold particular positions, in *Public Politics,* 77, and the meaning of "talking through," 78.

43. Carcasson, "Tackling Wicked Problems," 11.

44. Ibid.

45. The phrase "common ground" or "common ground for action" can be found in several sources in relation to deliberation, including McKenzie, *Public Politics,* 92; and Colorado State University Center for Public Deliberation, *CSU Center for Public Deliberation: Student Associate Training Workbook* (Fall 2011), 32, 37, accessed Jan. 8, 2015, http://www.casb.org/_literature_97551/PR_Academy_-_Student_Workbook

46. Carcasson, "Tackling Wicked Problems," 10.

47. McKenzie, *Public Politics,* 77.

48. CSU Center for Public Deliberation, *Student Associate Training Workbook,* 75.

49. McKenzie, *Public Politics,* 125.

Chapter 12

1. Sy Stokes, "The Black Bruins [Spoken Word]," *YouTube* video, 5:12, Nov. 5, 2013, https://www.youtube.com/watch?v=BEO3H5BOlFk. As of Jan. 10, 2015 it had been viewed 2,218,155 times.

2. Kendal Mitchell, "Student Posts Video to Spark Discussion about Lack of Diversity at UCLA," *Daily Bruin,* Nov. 8, 2013, accessed Jan. 10, 2015, http://dailybruin.com/2013/11/08/student-posts-video-to-spark-discussion-about-lack-of-diversity-at-ucla/.

3. *Gorgias,* in *The Collected Dialogues of Plato,* ed. Edith Hamilton and Huntington Cairns, (Princeton: Princeton University Press, 1961), 462b–c.

4. Aristotle, *Rhetoric,* in *Aristotle: A Theory of Civic Discourse,* trans. George A. Kennedy (New York: Oxford University Press, 1991), 1355a.

5. Ibid., 1356a.

6. Richard D. Rieke, Malcolm O. Sillars, and Tarla Rae Peterson, *Argumentation and Critical Decision Making,* 7th ed. (New York: Pearson, 2009), 155–156.

7. Aristotle, *Rhetoric* 1356a.

8. George W. Bush, "Address to the Nation," *The New York Times,* Sept. 12, 2002, Accessed Jul. 14, 2015, http://www.nytimes.com/2002/09/12/us/vigilance-memory-transcript-president-bush-s-address-nation-sept-11-anniversary.html.

9. The grounds for this shaky claim rested mainly on the imam's reference to the 2006 Danish cartoon crisis during his September 8, 2010, interview on CNN. Jim Hoft, "Ground Zero Victory Mosque Imam Issues Threat: If You Don't Build It 'They Will Attack,'" *The Gateway Pundit* video, 6:45, Sept. 9, 2010, http://www.thegatewaypundit.com/2010/09/ground-zero-victory-mosque-imam-issues-threat-if-you-dont-build-it-they-will-attack-video/.

10. Gerard A. Hauser, "Rethinking Deliberative Democracy: Rhetoric, Power, and Civil Society," in *Rhetoric and Democracy: Pedagogical and Political Practices*, ed. Todd F. McDorman and David M. Timmerman (East Lansing: Michigan State University Press, 2008), 225–264; Danielle S. Allen, *Talking to Strangers: Anxieties of Citizenship since Brown v. Board of Education* (Chicago: University of Chicago Press, 2004); Sharon R. Krause, *Civil Passions: Moral Sentiment and Democratic Deliberation* (Princeton, NJ: Princeton University Press, 2008).

11. Anita Hill, "Opening Statement to the Senate Judiciary Committee," *American Rhetoric*, Oct. 11, 1991, accessed Jul. 14, 2015, http://www.americanrhetoric.com/speeches/anitahillsenatejudiciarystatement.htm.

12. Will Friedman, "Reframing 'Framing,'" Center for Advances in Public Engagement, Occasional Paper, no. 1, accessed Jan. 8, 2015, http://www.publicagenda.org/files/Reframing%20Framing.pdf.

13. This example is based in part on a deliberative project on this topic completed for a fall 2011 course on citizenship by four then-seniors at Monmouth College: Samantha Hendrix, Mandy Evenson, Gabi Schaerli, and Jessica Lindley.

14. Matthew Yglesias, "Teach for America Teachers Outperform their Peers," *Slate*, Sept. 10, 2013, accessed Jan. 10, 2015, http://www.slate.com/blogs/moneybox/2013/09/10/mathematica_study_of_tfa_and_teaching_fellows.html.

Chapter 13

1. All quotes from "Ruth Bader Ginsburg U.S. Supreme Court Justice Nomination Acceptance Address," *American Rhetoric.com*, accessed Jan. 2, 2014, http://www.americanrhetoric.com/speeches/ruthbaderginsburgussnominationspeech.htm.

2. Robert M. Gaines, "Syllogism," in *Encyclopedia of Rhetoric and Composition: Communication from Ancient Times to the Information Age*, ed. Theresa Enos (New York: Garland, 1996), 710–711.

3. Stephen Toulmin, *The Uses of Argument* (Oxford: Cambridge University Press, 1958), 122.

4. J. K. Rowling, *Harry Potter and the Order of the Phoenix* (New York: Scholastic Press, 2003), 147.

5. "Surveillance: A Threat to Democracy" (Editorial Board), *New York Times*, June 11, 2013, accessed Jan. 11, 2015, http://www.nytimes.com/2013/06/12/opinion/surveillance-a-threat-to-democracy.html.

6. John T. Gage, "Enthymeme," in *Encyclopedia of Rhetoric and Composition: Communication from Ancient Times to the Information Age*, ed. Theresa Enos (New York: Garland, 1996), 223–225.

7. Toulmin, *The Uses of Argument*.

8. William Grimes, "Stephen Toulmin, a Philosopher and Educator, Dies at 87," *New York Times*, Dec. 11, 2009, accessed Jan. 11, 2015, http://www.nytimes.com/2009/12/11/education/11toulmin.html; Toulmin, *The Uses of Argument*, in particular chapter 3 "The Layout of Argument," 94–145; and Richard D. Rieke, Malcolm O. Sillars, and Tarla Rai Peterson, *Argumentation and Critical Decision Making* 7th ed. (New York: Pearson, 2009), 91–97. We relied upon Rieke, Sillars, and Peterson's explanation of the Toulmin model because it seems to best align with Toulmin's later views. See Gary A. Olson, "Literary Theory, Philosophy of Science, and Persuasive Discourse: Thoughts from a Neo-premodernist," *Journal of Advanced Composition* 13 (1993): 291, http://www.jaconlinejournal.com/archives/vol13.2/olson-literary.pdf.

9. "Smoking and Cancer," Centers for Disease Control and Prevention, Apr. 11, 2014, accessed Jan. 11, 2015, http://www.cdc.gov/tobacco/campaign/tips/diseases/cancer.html; "Health Hazards Studies," Americans for Nonsmokers' Rights, accessed Jan. 5, 2014, http://www.no-smoke.org/getthefacts.php?id=19.

10. "How Many People Use Tobacco?" American Cancer Society, Feb. 13, 2014, accessed Jan. 11, 2015, http://www.cancer.org/cancer/cancercauses/%20tobaccocancer/questionsab outsmokingtobaccoandhealth/questions-about-smoking-tobacco-and-health-how-many-use.

11. Wayne LaPierre, "National Rifle Association Press Conference Announcing 'National School Shield' Program Following the Newtown, Connecticut Shootings," *American Rhetoric.com*, accessed Jan. 11, 2015, http://www.americanrhetoric.com/speeches/ waynelapierrenraschoolshieldpresser.htm.

12. "Remarks of President Barack Obama—As Prepared for Delivery. Signing of Stem Cell Executive Order and Scientific Integrity Presidential Memorandum," Whitehouse.gov, Mar. 9, 2009, accessed Jan. 11, 2015, http://www.whitehouse.gov/the_press_office/ Remarks-of-the-President-As-Prepared-for-Delivery-Signing-of-Stem-Cell-Executive-Order-and-Scientific-Integrity-Presidential-Memorandum.

13. "Transcript: Mitt Romney's Acceptance Speech," NPR, Aug. 30, 2012, accessed Jan. 11, 2015, http://www.npr.org/2012/08/30/160357612/transcript-mitt-romneys-acceptance-speech.

14. "Postal Facts 2013," United States Postal Service.com, accessed Jan. 5, 2014, http://about .usps.com/who-we-are/postal-facts/postalfacts2013.pdf; Emily Swanson, "Alien Poll Finds Half of Americans Think Extraterrestrial Life Exists," *Huffington Post*, July 29, 2013, accessed Jan. 11, 2015, http://www.huffingtonpost.com/2013/06/21/alien-poll_n_ 3473852.html; "National Sleep Foundation 2013 International Bedroom Poll First to Explore Sleep Differences among Six Countries," National Sleep Foundation, Sept. 3, 2013, accessed Jan. 11, 2015, http://sleepfoundation.org/media-center/press-release/ national-sleep-foundation-2013-international-bedroom-poll.

15. Ben Shalom Bernanke, "Statement on the Economic Outlook and Monetary Policy to USHOR Committee on Financial Services," *American Rhetoric.com*, accessed Jan. 11, 2015, http://www.americanrhetoric.com/speeches/benbernankeushorfinancialservicescmt .htm.

16. When the "outlier" student who made $40,000 is removed from consideration, the other 24 students earned, on average, $3,333, a number that is considerably different than the mean. This suggests that in this instance the mean actually provides a misleading average. As a result you might benefit from considering the median income, in this case the 13th highest earnings among the 25 students. This method of computing the "average" corrects for outliers by looking at the middle of middle of summer earnings. Alternatively, if you found that six students reported the same summer earnings, say $3,600, you might also consider the mode as it is the data point that occurs most frequently. Thus in this example we can see how the use of a mean, a median, or a mode can result in different perceptions even when dealing with the same data set.

17. Tony Capaccio, "Defense Spending Bill Will Win Acceptance, Moran Says," *Bloomberg News*, Jan. 3, 2014, accessed Jan. 11, 2015, http://www.bloomberg.com/news/2014-01-03/ defense-spending-bill-will-win-acceptance-moran-says.html; Brad Plumer, "America's Staggering Defense Budget, in Charts," *Washington Post*, Jan. 7, 2013, accessed Jan. 11, 2015, http://www.washingtonpost.com/blogs/wonkblog/wp/2013/01/07/everything-chuck-hagel-needs-to-know-about-the-defense-budget-in-charts/.

18. "About Gallup," *Gallup.com*, accessed Jan. 11, 2015, http://www.gallup.com/corporate/177680/gallup.aspx.

19. Jeffrey P. Mehltretter Drury, *Speaking with the People's Voice: How Presidents Invoke Public Opinion* (College Station: Texas A&M University Press, 2014).

20. "SportsNation," *ESPN.com*, accessed Jan. 6, 2014, http://espn.go.com/sportsnation/.

21. All quotes from Eric Holder, "Address at the LBJ Library on Voter Registration and Rights," *AmericanRhetoric.com*, accessed Jan. 11, 2015, http://www.americanrhetoric.com/speeches/ericholderlbjlibraryvoterrights.htm.

22. Peter Grier, "Millions Losing Health Plans Under Obamacare. Did President Mislead?" *Christian Science Monitor*, Oct. 29, 2013, accessed Jan. 11, 2015, http://www.csmonitor.com/USA/DC-Decoder/Decoder-Buzz/2013/1029/Millions-losing-health-plans-under-Obamacare.-Did-president-mislead-video; Mark Robison, "Did Obama Mislead about Keeping Health Plans?" *RGJ.com*, Nov. 9, 2013, accessed Jan. 11, 2015, http://blogs.rgj.com/factchecker/2013/11/09/did-obama-mislead-about-keeping-health-plans/.

23. George McGovern, "George McGovern—With Obama's Strategy, Afghanistan Looks Like Another Vietnam," *Washington Post*, Dec. 13, 2009, accessed Jan. 11, 2015, http://www.washingtonpost.com/wp-dyn/content/article/2009/12/11/AR2009121102596.html.

24. Patricia R. Freeman and Jeffery Talbert, "Impact of State Laws Regulating Pseudoephedrine on Methamphetamine Trafficking and Abuse," National Association of State Controlled Substances Authorities, Apr. 2012, p. 19, http://www.nascsa.org/pdf/NASCSApseudoephedrineWhitePaper4.12.pdf; Nick Hytrek, "Iowa Meth Law Decreases Manufacturing but not use of Drug," *Sioux City Journal.com*, Apr. 6, 2013, accessed Jan. 11, 2015, http://siouxcityjournal.com/news/local/crime-and-courts/iowa-meth-law-decreases-manufacturing-but-not-use-of-drug/article_7fd50c3c-f1da-5b56-b517-554b52b39dd6.html.

25. Geoffrey Pullum, "Being an Apostrophe," *Chronicle of Higher Education*, Mar. 22, 2013, accessed Jan. 11, 2015, http://chronicle.com/blogs/linguafranca/2013/03/22/being-an-apostrophe/. Pullum points out that less than a week after the media outcry over the action by Mid Devon, the council reconsidered its decision.

26. Colleen Curry, "Smithsonian Eyes Trayvon Martin Hoodie for Museum Exhibit," *ABC News*, Aug. 1, 2013, accessed Jan. 11, 205, http://abcnews.go.com/US/smithsonian-eyes-trayvon-martin-hoodie-museum-exhibit/story?id=19836962. Others debated if the sign *caused* George Zimmerman's actions, transforming the sign into evidence in a causal argument. For instance, Geraldo Rivera stated on Fox News: "I think the hoodie is as much responsible for Trayvon Martin's death as George Zimmerman was." Further, in an interview Fox News host Bill O'Reilly said: "The reason Trayvon Martin died was because he looked a certain way and it wasn't based on skin color. If Trayvon Martin had been wearing a jacket . . . and a tie. . . I don't think George Zimmerman would have any problem. But he was wearing a hoodie and he looked a certain way. And that way is how 'gangstas' look." Erik Wemple, "Fox News's Bill O'Reilly Blames Trayvon Martin's Death on Hoodie," *Washington Post*, Sept. 16, 2013, accessed Jan. 11, 2015, http://www.washingtonpost.com/blogs/erik-wemple/wp/2013/09/16/fox-newss-bill-oreilly-blames-trayvon-martins-death-on-hoodie/.

27. "Overview," Congressional Budget Office, accessed Feb. 23, 2014, http://www.cbo.gov/about/overview; "The Effects of a Minimum-Wage Increase on Employment and Family Income," Congressional Budget Office, Feb. 18, 2014, accessed Jan. 11, 2015, http://www

.cbo.gov/publication/44995; Annie Lowrey, "Minimum Wage Increase Would Have Mixed Effects, C.B.O. Report Says," *New York Times*, Feb. 18, 2014, accessed Jan. 11, 2015, http://www.nytimes.com/2014/02/19/business/mixed-results-in-us-study-of-increasing-minimum-wage.html.

28. Stephanie Saul, "Drug Ads Raise Questions for Heart Pioneer," *New York Times* Feb. 7, 2008, accessed Jan. 11, 2015, http://www.nytimes.com/2008/02/07/business/media/07jarvik.html?pagewanted=all; Alice Park, "The Problem with Jarvik's Prescription," *Time*, Feb. 26, 2008, accessed Jan. 11, 2015, http://content.time.com/time/health/article/0,8599,1717350,00.html.

29. Scholar Douglas Walton, in particular, is known for his work on argument fallacies. His books on the subject include *Ad Hominem Arguments* (Tuscaloosa: University of Alabama Press, 1998); *Argument from Ignorance* (University Park: Pennsylvania State University Press, 1995); *Slippery Slope Arguments* (Oxford: Clarendon Press, 1992); *Appeal to Popular Opinion* (University Park: Pennsylvania State University, 1999); and *Begging the Question: Circular Reasoning as a Tactic of Argumentation* (New York: Greenwood Press, 1991).

30. James Hibberd, "'The Walking Dead': How to Comprehend its Massive Ratings," *Entertainment Weekly*, Nov. 11, 2013, accessed Jan. 11, 2015, insidetv.ew.com/2013/11/11/the-walking-dead-ratings/.

31. The form of this example is inspired by an appeal to common practice example found at the *Nizkor Project*. "Fallacy: Appeal to Common Practice," *Nizkor Project*, accessed Aug. 17, 2010, http://www.nizkor.org/features/fallacies/appeal-to-common-practice.html.

32. Jason Whitlock, "More than Sticks and Stones," *ESPN.com*, Nov. 15, 2013, accessed Jan. 11, 2015, http://espn.go.com/espn/story/_/id/9980883/whitlock-using-n-word; Howard Bryant, "Identity Crisis: There's a Code of Black Masculinity That Governs Every NFL Locker Room," *ESPN The Magazine*, Dec. 5, 2013, http://espn.go.com/nfl/story/_/id/10034902/jonathan-martin-failed-follow-locker-room-code-espn-magazine.

33. Norman Byrd, "Ted Nugent Calls President Obama a 'Subhuman Mongrel,'" *Examiner.com*, Jan. 24, 2014, accessed Jan. 11, 2015, http://www.examiner.com/article/ted-nugent-calls-president-obama-a-subhuman-mongrel-video; "What If Ted Nugent Were President? The Nuge Explains," YouTube, 8:36, Jan. 18, 2014, http://www.youtube.com/watch?feature=player_embedded&v=p-KkcIHwaf0, quotation at 6:50–7:20.

34. Manny Fernandez, "Ted Nugent Apologizes for Obama Insult," *New York Times*, Feb. 21, 2014, accessed Jan. 11, 2015, http://www.nytimes.com/2014/02/22/us/ted-nugent-apologizes-for-obama-insult.html.

35. Alexander Marquardt, "Clinton to Congress: You're Either with Us or Against Us," *CNN Political Ticker*, May 1, 2008, accessed Jan. 11, 2015, http://politicalticker.blogs.cnn.com/2008/05/01/clinton-to-congress-you%E2%80%99re-either-with-us-or-against-us/.

36. "Binghamton Speech & Debate: Compete Online," Binghamton University, accessed Feb. 24, 2014, http://speechdebate.binghamton.edu/Compete-Online/.

37. J. L. Schatz, e-mail message to author, Jan. 6, 2014.

Chapter 14

1. Howard Kurtz, "In the Hot Seat: Tim Russert on His Ego, His Bias, His Father Worship and What He Really Thinks about Tax Cuts," *Washington Post,* May 23, 2004, accessed Jul. 29, 2014, http://www.washingtonpost.com/wp-dyn/articles/A37798-2004May18.html.

2. Jacques Steinberg, "Tim Russert, 58, NBC's Face of Politics, Dies." *New York Times,* Jun. 14, 2008, accessed Jan. 7, 2015, http://www.nytimes.com/2008/06/14/business/media/14russert.html?_r=0.

3. "Decision 2000," *NBC News,* Nov. 7, 2000.

4. Elizabeth Daley, "Expanding the Concept of Literacy," *EDUCAUSE Review* (March/April 2003): 33–34.

5. This definition draws on Daley, "Expanding the Concept of Literacy," 33–34.

6. Nancy Duarte, *Slide:ology: The Art and Science of Creating Great Presentations* (Sebastopol, CA: O'Reilly Media, 2008), 257.

7. Sonja K. Foss, "Theory of Visual Rhetoric," in *Handbook of Visual Communication: Theory, Methods, Media,* ed. Ken Smith et al. (Mahwah, NJ: Lawrence Erlbaum Associates, 2005), 146.

8. Don Van Natta, Jr. and Dana Canedy, "The 2000 Elections: The Palm Beach Ballot; Florida Democrats Say Ballot's Design Hurt Gore," *New York Times,* Nov. 9, 2000, accessed Sept. 2, 2014, http://www.nytimes.com/2000/11/09/us/2000-elections-palm-beach-ballot-florida-democrats-say-ballot-s-design-hurt-gore.html?src=pm&pagewanted=2.

9. Ibid.

10. Foss, "Theory of Visual Rhetoric," 146.

11. Elisabeth Bumiller, "We Have Met the Enemy and He Is PowerPoint," *New York Times,* Apr. 27, 2010, accessed Jan. 7, 2015, http://www.nytimes.com/2010/04/27/world/27powerpoint.html.

12. Ibid.

13. Start at "PowerPoint 2013 training courses, videos, and tutorials," Office Online, Microsoft Corporation, accessed Jan. 7, 2014, https://support.office.com/en-us/article/PowerPoint-2013-training-courses-videos-and-tutorials-bd93efc0-3582-49d1-b952-3871cde07d8a?ui=en-US&rs=en-US&ad=US.

14. For example, see Rachel Arandilla, "Presentation Design: Keynote vs. Powerpoint" *1stwebdesginer.com,* Mar. 26, 2011, accessed Sept. 16, 2014, http://www.1stwebdesigncr.com/design/keynote-vs-powerpoint/; and Paul Maidment, "Keynote vs. PowerPoint." *Forbes.com* Jan. 30, 2003, accessed Sept. 3, 2014, http://www.forbes.com/2003/01/30/cx_pm_0130tentech.html.

15. Start at "Keynote," Mac Apps Support, Apple, Inc., accessed Jan. 8, 2014, https://www.apple.com/support/mac-apps/keynote/.

16. Start at "Learn & Support: Get Started With Prezi," Prezi, Inc., accessed Jan. 7, 2015, https://prezi.com/support/.

17. For example, see Adam Noar, "PowerPoint vs. Prezi: What's the Difference?" *PresentationPanda* (blog), Feb. 21, 2014, http://presentationpanda.com/uncategorized/powerpoint-vs-prezi-whats-the-difference/; and Cam Barber, "Prezi vs. PowerPoint for Presentation Visuals," *Cam Barber the Message Man* (blog), Mar. 26, 2013, http://vividmethod.com/prezi-versus-powerpoint-for-presentation-visuals/.

18. For example, see "How to Create a Presentation Using Google Drive," *WikiHow,* accessed Jan. 7, 2015, http://www.wikihow.com/Create-a-Presentation-Using-Google-Drive.

19. "Biography," *AimeeMullins.com,* accessed Feb. 12, 2015, http://www.aimeemullins.com/about.php.

20. Aimee Mullins, "My 12 Pairs of Legs," *Ted2009* video, 9:58, Feb. 2009, http://www.ted.com/talks/aimee_mullins_prosthetic_aesthetics?language=en.

21. Garr Reynolds, *Presentation Zen: Simple Ideas on Presentation Design and Delivery* (Berkeley: New Riders, 2012), 185.

Chapter 15

1. Gene Weingarten, "Pearls Before Breakfast," *Washington Post*, Apr. 8, 2007, accessed Jan. 10, 2015, http://www.washingtonpost.com/lifestyle/magazine/pearls-before-break-fast-can-one-of-the-nations-great-musicians-cut-through-the-fog-of-a-dc-rush-hour-lets-find-out/2014/09/23/8a6d46da-4331-11e4-b47c-f5889e061e5f_story.html. The video can be found at: "Stop and Hear the Music," YouTube, 2:36, Apr. 10, 2007, http://www.youtube.com/watch?v=hnOPu0_YWhw.

2. Conor Neill, "What Aristotle and Joshua Bell Can Teach Us about Persuasion," *Ted2013* video, 4:40, Jan. 2013, http://ed.ted.com/lessons/what-aristotle-and-joshua-bell-can-teach-us-about-persuasion-conor-neill.

3. Kenneth Burke, *A Grammar of Motives* (Berkeley: University of California Press, 1945/1969), 59.

4. Michael L. Butterworth, *Baseball and Rhetorics of Purity: The National Pastime and American Identity During the War on Terror* (Tuscaloosa: University of Alabama Press, 2010).

5. Mark D. White, "Captain America Reminds Nation of Shared Values," *San Diego-Union Tribune*, July 21, 2011, B7.

6. Robert Hariman and John Louis Lucaites, *No Caption Needed: Iconic Photographs, Public Culture, and Liberal Democracy* (Chicago: University of Chicago Press, 2007), 93–136.

7. Ibid., 94–95.

8. Robert Hariman, "Time Lost to Violence in Syria and Texas," *No Caption Needed: Iconic Photographs, Public Culture, and Liberal Democracy* (blog), Jan. 23, 2013, http://www.nocaptionneeded.com/2013/01/time-lost-to-violence-in-syria-and-texas.

9. Edwin Black, "The Second Persona," *Quarterly Journal of Speech* 56 (1970): 109–119.

10. Jim Hinch, "Where Are the People?" *American Scholar* (Winter 2014), 20.

11. Ibid., 25.

12. Kenneth Burke, "The Rhetoric of Hitler's Battle," *Southern Review* 5 (1939), 1.

13. Ibid., 11.

14. Earnest Brandenburg, "Quintilian and the Good Orator," *Quarterly Journal of Speech* 34 (1948): 28.

15. Stephen E. Lucas and Martin J. Medhurst, *Words of a Century: The Top American Speeches, 1900–1999* (New York: Oxford University Press, 2009), xi–xiii.

16. Lloyd F. Bitzer, "Rhetorical Public Communication," *Critical Studies in Mass Communications* (1987): 426.

17. These principles are drawn from the following: "Principles of Democracy," Street Law, Inc., accessed Jan. 10, 2015, http://www.lawanddemocracy.org/pdffiles/amazing.prin.pdf; "Principles of Democracy," Deliberating in a Democracy in the Americas, accessed Jan. 10, 2015, http://www.dda.deliberating.org/images/pdf/principlesofdemocracyhandout.pdf.

18. John Avlon, "America's 9 Worst Demagogues," *DailyBeast.com*, Sept. 2, 2010, accessed Jan. 10, 2015, http://www.thedailybeast.com/articles/2010/09/02/glenn-beck-and-the-history-of-americas-worst-demagogues.html; Ian Tuttle, "Warren's Student-Loan Demagoguery," *National Review*, May 28, 2013, accessed June 11, 2014, http://www.nationalreview.com/article/349420/warren-s-student-loan-demagoguery.

Chapter 16

1. These numbers are based on searching two FCC websites. The first is a search page we used to find comments received regarding proceeding #14-28, "Protecting and

Promoting the Open Internet." See "Send Us Your Comments," FCC, accessed Jan. 10, 2015, http://www.fcc.gov/comments. We searched for the comments "received" on specific dates (May 15–30, June 3). We began with May 15 because that is the day the FCC "launched a rulemaking seeking public comment on how best to protect and promote an open Internet." See FCC, "FCC Launches Broad Rulemaking on How Best to Protect and Promote the Open Internet" (press release), May 15, 2014, accessed Jan. 10, 2015, http://www.fcc.gov/document/fcc-launches-broad-rulemaking-protect-and-promote-open-internet. This search page, however, added the comments received over a weekend to the proceeding Monday. Consequently, the second source we used to obtain the number of comments received regarding proceeding #14-28 on May 31 (Saturday), June 1 (Sunday), and June 2 (Monday) was the "Comma Separated Values (CSV) text file" provided by the FCC of all "open internet comments" received daily and hourly between May 14, 2014 and July 10, 2014, made available at David A. Bray, "Keeping Track of the Open Internet Comments Submitted to the FCC," *Official FCC Blog*, July 14, 2014, http://www.fcc.gov/blog/keeping-track-open-internet-comments-submitted-fcc. Observations and quotations taken from "Last Week Tonight With John Oliver: Net Neutrality," YouTube, June 1, 2014, 13:17, https://www.youtube.com/watch?v=fpbOEoRrHyU.

2. Jessica Van Sack, "Comments on FCC's Net-Neutrality Rules Set Record," *Boston Herald*, July 28, 2014, accessed Jan. 10, 2015, http://bostonherald.com/business/business_markets/2014/07/comments_on_fccs_net_neutrality_rules_set_record.

3. Because we have not closely examined the comments, we cannot be sure they all argued against the proposal, though all of those we randomly read did oppose it, and Van Sack reported that she "couldn't find one comment on the FCC's website supporting a non-neutral Net." Soon after Oliver's charge to comment on the FCC website, hackers shut down the public commenting section of that website. It's hard to know or understand the hackers' intentions; they could have wanted to communicate displeasure with the FCC's consideration of the proposal *or* prevent people from commenting against the proposal, for instance. Van Sack, "Comments on FCC's Net-Neutrality Rules Set Record." Sam Gustin, "The FCC Was Hacked after John Oliver Called for Net Neutrality Trolls," *Motherboard*, June 10, 2014. accessed Jan. 10, 2015, http://motherboard.vice.com/read/the-fcc-was-hacked-after-john-olivers-call-for-net-neutrality-trolls.

4. We adopted the phrase "public communication" and its definition from Lloyd Bitzer, "Rhetorical Public Communication," *Critical Studies in Media Communication* 4 (1987): 425–428.

5. Glenn Frank, "The Parliament of the People," *The Century* 98 (1919), 416.

6. Ferald J. Bryan, R. R. Allen, Richard L. Johannesen, and Wil A. Linkugel, *Contemporary American Speeches,* 10th ed. (Dubuque, IA: Kendall Hunt, 2010), 4, 2.

7. Bitzer, "Rhetorical Public Communication," 425.

8. Stephen Toulmin, *The Uses of Argument* (Oxford: Cambridge University Press, 1958), 94–145.

9. Edwin Black notably referred to a rhetor's appeals to ethos as the "first persona" in his publication, "The Second Persona," *Quarterly Journal of Speech* 56 (1970): 111.

10. President Obama, "Remarks by the President on Trayvon Martin," *White House.gov*, July 19, 2013, accessed Jan. 10, 2015, http://www.whitehouse.gov/the-press-office/2013/07/19/remarks-president-trayvon-martin.

11. See Richard D. Rieke, Malcolm O. Sillars, and Tarla Rai Peterson, *Argumentation and Critical Decision Making*, 7th ed. (New York: Pearson, 2009), 155–156.

12. See Jon Healey, "John Oliver Finds Humor in Net Neutrality, but Loses the Facts," *Los Angeles Times,* June 5, 2014, accessed Jan. 10, 2015, http://www.latimes.com/opinion/opinion-la/la-ol-john-oliver-gets-net-neutrality-wrong-20140604-story.html. Also see Seton Motley, "HBO Pseudo-News Anchor John Oliver Gets Net Neutrality Fundamentally Wrong," *Newsbusters* (blog), June 16, 2014, http://newsbusters.org/blogs/seton-motley/2014/06/16/hbo-pseudo-news-anchor-john-oliver-gets-net-neutrality-fundamentally-w.

13. This rhetorical feature is based on the "second persona" developed by Edwin Black and "the people" developed by Michael McGee. Edwin Black, "The Second Persona," *Quarterly Journal of Speech* 56 (1970): 109–119; Michael Calvin McGee, "In Search of 'the People,'" *Quarterly Journal of Speech* 61 (1976): 235–249.

14. This quote is from Martin Luther King Jr., "I Have a Dream" (speech, March on Washington, Washington, DC, Aug. 28, 1963), accessed Aug. 19, 2014, http://www.archives.gov/press/exhibits/dream-speech.pdf.

15. This rhetorical feature is based on the concept and theory of the "third persona" as developed by Phillip Wander, "The Third Persona: An Ideological Turn in Rhetorical Theory," *Central States Speech Journal* 35 (1984): 210.

16. Ibid.

17. James Gorman, "After 32 Years, Coroner Confirms Dingo Killed Australian Baby," *New York Times,* June 11, 2012, accessed Jan. 10, 2015, http://www.nytimes.com/2012/06/12/world/asia/after-32-years-coroner-confirms-dingo-killed-australian-baby.html?_r=2&.

18. Stephen E. Lucas, "The Renaissance of American Public Address: Text and Context in Rhetorical Criticism," *Quarterly Journal of Speech* 74 (1988): 249.

19. Ronald Reagan, "The Space Shuttle 'Challenger' Disaster Address" (speech, Washington, DC, Jan. 28, 1986), *AmericanRhetoric.com*, accessed Jan. 10, 2015, http://www.americanrhetoric.com/speeches/ronaldreaganchallenger.htm.

20. Charlotte Ryan, *Prime Time Activism: Media Strategies for Grassroots Organizing* (Boston: South End Press, 1991), 56; George Lakoff, *Thinking Points: Communicating Our American Values and Vision* (New York: Farrar, Straus and Giroux, 2006), 31.

21. Of course, Aristotle differentiated between the canons of delivery and memory, but we combine them here for convenience.

22. "About the Authors." *The Silver Tongue* (blog), http://silvertonguetimes.com/about-the-authors/.

23. The quote is from Kathleen Hall Jamieson, *Eloquence in an Electronic Age: The Transformation of Political Speechmaking* (New York: Oxford University Press, 1990), quoted in "About the Blog," *The Silver Tongue* (blog), accessed Jan. 10, 2015, http://silvertonguetimes.com/about/.

24. Maggie Goss, "Scandal or Sex Crime? A Naked Approach to Jennifer Lawrence's Nude Photo Hack Framing," *The Silver Tongue* (blog), Nov. 10, 2014, http://silvertonguetimes.com/2014/11/10/scandal-or-sex-crime-a-naked-approach-to-jennifer-lawrences-nude-photo-hack-framing/#more-2278.

25. "Call for Submissions," *The Silver Tongue* (blog), http://silvertonguetimes.com/write-for-the-silver-tongue/.

26. William Norwood Brigance, "What Is a Successful Speech?" *Quarterly Journal of Speech Education* 11 (1925): 376.

27. President Barack Obama quoted in "Net Neutrality: President Obama's Plan for a Free and Open Internet," *White House.gov*, Feb. 26, 2015, accessed May 28, 2015,

https://www.whitehouse.gov/net-neutrality. See also John Ribeiro, "FCC's Net Neutrality Rules Published in Federal Register," *PCWorld,* Apr. 13, 2015, accessed on May 28, 2015, http://www.pcworld.com/article/2909132/fcc-net-neutrality-rules-published-to-federal-register.html.

28. Brooks Boliek, "FCC Net Neutrality Rules Hit with New Telecom Lawsuits," *Politico,* Apr. 14, 2015, accessed May 28, 2015, http://www.politico.com/story/2015/04/net-neutrality-lawsuit-ctia-116957.html.

Chapter 17

1. Dorian Lynskey, *33 Revolutions Per Minute: A History of Protest Songs from Billie Holiday to Green Day* (New York: Ecco, 2011), 73.

2. Quoted in ibid., 70, from Michael Smith, "The Other (More Serious) Side of Nina . . .," *Melody Maker,* Dec. 7, 1968.

3. Nina Simone, vocal performance of "Mississippi Goddam," by Nina Simone, recorded 1964, Philips PHS 600-135 (LP).

4. Michael Calvin McGee, "'The Ideograph': A Link Between Rhetoric and Ideology," *Quarterly Journal of Speech* 66, no. 1 (1980): 5.

5. Dana L. Cloud, "The Materiality of Discourse as Oxymoron: A Challenge to Critical Rhetoric," *Western Journal of Communication* 58 (1994): 141.

6. Ibid.

7. Simone, "Mississippi Goddam."

8. See Claudia Roth Pierpont, "A Raised Voice: How Nina Simone Turned the Movement into Music," *The New Yorker,* Aug. 11, 2014, accessed June 1, 2015, http://www.newyorker.com/magazine/2014/08/11/raised-voice. "Nina Simone–In Concert," *Discogs,* n.d., accessed June 1, 2015, http://www.discogs.com/Nina-Simone-In-Concert/release/641791.

9. See, for example, Mark Berman and Wesley Lowery, "Police Say Michael Brown Was a Robbery Suspect, Identify Darren Wilson as Officer Who Shot Him," *Washington Post,* Aug. 15, 2014, accessed Jan. 11, 2015, http://www.washingtonpost.com/news/post-nation/wp/2014/08/15/ferguson-police-releasing-name-of-officer-who-shot-michael-brown/.

10. NBC News, Twitter Post, Aug. 10, 2015, 2:50 p.m., https://twitter.com/NBCNews/.

11. For example, see Ronald L. Jackson, *Scripting the Black Masculine Body: Identity, Discourse, and Racial Politics in Popular Media* (Albany: SUNY Press, 2006), Kirk A. Johnson and Travis L. Dixon, "Change and the Illusion of Change: Evolving Portrayals of Crime News and Blacks in a Major Market," *Howard Journal of Communications* 19, no. 2 (2008); and Linda Williams, *Playing the Race Card: Melodramas of Black and White from Uncle Tom to O. J. Simpson* (Princeton, NJ: Princeton University Press, 2001).

12. P. J. Vogt, "If They Gunned Me Down," *TDLR the internet, shorter* (blog), Aug. 11, 2014, http://www.onthemedia.org/story/if-they-gunned-me-down/.

13. Simone, "Mississippi Goddam."

14. C. J. Lawrence, quoted in Layla A. Jones, "#Iftheygunnedmedown: How the Media Killed Michael Brown," *Philly.com,* Aug. 21, 2014, accessed Aug. 22, 2014, http://www.philly.com/philly/blogs/lifestyle/Iftheygunnedmedown-How-media-the-killed-Michael-Brown.html.

15. Nathan Hodge and Jenny Gross, "Pakistani Girls' Education Activist Malala Yousafzai Rose to Global Prominence After Taliban Shooting," *Wall Street Journal*, Oct. 10, 2014, accessed June 1, 2015, http://www.wsj.com/articles/pakistani-girls-education-activist-malala-yousafzai-rose-to-global-prominence-after-taliban-shooting-1412942763; Sara Malm, "The 17-year-old who was pulled out of her Chemistry class to be told 'you've won

the Nobel Peace Prize!' Malala, the girls' education campaigner the Taliban couldn't kill is youngest ever winner," *Daily Mail* (London), Oct. 10, 2014, accessed June 1, 2015, http://www.dailymail.co.uk/news/article-2787773/Nobel-Peace-Prize-Malala-Teenager-shot-Taliban-campaigning-girls-education-honoured-work.html.

16. Carolyn Danckaert and Aaron Smith, "About Us," *AMightyGirl.com,* accessed Dec. 26, 2014, http://www.amightygirl.com/about.

17. Carleigh O'Connell, "Putting the Words 'Behind' Me: A 14-Year-Old Mighty Girl Takes a Stand Against Body Shaming," guest post to *A Mighty Girl* (blog), July 23, 2014, accessed Dec. 26, 2014, http://www.amightygirl.com/blog?p=7083.

18. James Arnt Aune, "The Scholastic Fallacy, Habitus, and Symbolic Violence: Pierre Bourdieu and the Prospects of Ideology Criticism," *Western Journal of Communication* 75, no. 4 (2011): 432.

19. Raymie E. McKerrow, "Critical Rhetoric: Theory and Praxis," *Communication Monographs* 56 (1989): 92.

Credits

Photographs

Page 2, © iStock.com/SteveChristensen; **6**, Image courtesy of Christopher L. Johnstone; **15**, © epa european pressphoto agency b.v./Alamy; **19**, C-SPAN; **23**, © iStock.com/EdStock; **32**, Photo by Jean Weisinger; **41**, © Bettmann/Corbis/AP Images; **58**, Image courtesy of Wabash College; **63**, Photo by Jennifer Y. Abbott; **83**, AP Photo; **93**, Kyodo via AP Images; **99**, Associated Press/LM Otero; **105**, Photo by Uwe Hermann; **127**, AP Photo/The White House, Pete Souza; **154**, AP Photo/Elise Amendola, File; **168**, Arctic-Images/Getty Images; **174**, © epa european pressphoto agency b.v./Alamy; **187**, AP Photo/Bob Galbraith; **196**, AP Photo/*The Daily Courier*, Les Stukenberg; **211**, AP Photo/Manuel Balce Ceneta; **211**, Photo by Target Presse Agentur Gmbh/Getty Images; **219**, Image courtesy of Wabash College; **223**, AP Photo/Winslow Townson; **225**, Photo by Amy Lenzo: www.wedialogue.com; **242**, Sy Stokes: http://dailybruin.com/2013/11/08/student-posts-video-tospark-discussion-about-lack-of-diversity-at-ucla/ **245**, Image courtesy of Jeffrey D. Rankin; **251**, © SCPhotos/Alamy; **262**, AP Photo/J. Scott Applewhite; **271**, © AP Photo/J. Scott Applewhite; **301**, Slide design by Scott Hastings; **301**, Slide design by Scott Hastings; **305**, Slide design by Scott Hastings; **306**, Slide design by Scott Hastings; **312**, Michael Williamson/*The Washington Post* via Getty Images; **313**, Ruby Washington/*The New York Times*/Redux; **315**, © Richard Levine /Alamy; **316**, AP Photo/Joe Rosenthal; **320**, © Pat Bagley; **323**, Reuters/Muzaffar Salman; **332**, AP Photo/HBO; **353**, AP Photo/David Zalubowski; **357**, JazzSign/Lebrecht Music & Arts; **373**, Image courtesy of Daryl O'Connell.

Text and Figures

Page 7, **10**, Josiah Ober, *Athenian Legacies: Essays on the Politics of Going On Together* (Princeton, NJ: Princeton University Press, 2005), 130, 132; **14**, Information submitted by Matthew Timmerman, Masters Student, American University Cairo; **30**, Matthew Lieberman, "Thank You for Not 'Unfriending': People voting for the 'other' guy don't like your Facebook posts either," *Psychology Today*, Social Brain, Social Mind Blog, 8 October 2012; **34**, Reprinted by arrangement with The Heirs to the Estate of Martin Luther King Kr., c/o Writers House as agent for the proprietor New York, NY. © 1963 Dr. Martin Luther King Jr. © Renewed 1991 Coretta Scott King; **39**, VMI "Honor System," Virginia Military Institute, accessed May 3, 2013, http://www.vmi.edu/content.aspx?id=1330; **44**, Reprinted with permission from the

Index